The Complete
Keys to the Kingdom

*Thank you for supporting independent publishing
and the Mardukite Systemology Society*

MARDUKITE ACADEMY WORKBOOK EDITION

The Complete Keys To The Kingdom

by Joshua Free

New Standard Systemology Advanced Training Course

© 2025, JOSHUA FREE

ISBN : 978-1-961509-62-7

All Rights Reserved. No part of this publication may be reproduced in any form or by any means, electronic or mechanical, including photocopying, recording, artificial intelligence training systems or database, without permission from the publisher. This book is a religious artifact. It is not intended to substitute medical treatment or professional advice.

Mardukite Research Library Catalogue No. "Liber-7+8"
The Complete New Standard Systemology A.T. Advanced Training Course

Disclaimer: This workbook is not for everyone.
It is intended only for Seekers that have already completed the
New Standard Systemology "Pathway to Ascension"
Professional Course (for *Systemology Levels 0 to 6*)
—And using *this* book requires having access to *those* materials.

A MARDUKITE ACADEMY PUBLICATION
Mardukite Esoteric Library Grade-VII+ Reference

cum superiorum privilegio veniaque

WORKBOOK EDITION
First Printing—February 2025

Published from
The Joshua Free Imprint – JFI Publications
Mardukite Borsippa HQ, San Luis Valley, Colorado
Representing Mardukite Truth Seeker Press
Mardukite Academy of Systemology
and Founding Church of Mardukite Zuism

mardukite.com

The Keys To The Kingdom
Are Yours For The Taking!

The Complete Mardukite Academy New Standard Systemology Advanced Training "A.T." Course (for *Levels 7 and 8*) is now available in one volume!

Disclaimer: This textbook is not for everyone. It is intended for Seekers that have already completed the New Standard Systemology "Pathway to Ascension" Professional Course (for *Levels 0 to 6*) — and using this book requires having access to those materials.

Upper-level "secret" teachings of our tradition have never before been presented outside of the Systemology Society.

This new paperback workbook includes *all eight* original lesson manuals (also available individually) for the "Keys to the Kingdom" Advanced Training (A.T.) Course: The Secret of Universes; Games, Goals and Purposes; The Jewel of Knowledge; Implanted Universes; Entities and Fragments; Spiritual Perception; Mastering Ascension; and Advancing Systemology.

Learn to expertly apply our advanced spiritual technology toward reaching higher "metahuman" levels of Awareness and Beingness than ever thought possible for humanity.

It's time to actualize who you really are... because you were never "Human."

This special premiere workbook edition is expanded to include: "The Complete Systemology Technical Dictionary (Version 5.0)"

It's Time For You To Escape The Matrix!

∞

EDITOR'S NOTE

"The Self does not actualize Awareness
past a point not understood."
—*Tablets of Destiny*

This book contains a collection of materials from all
eight original lesson-manuals developed by Joshua Free
for the "Keys to the Kingdom" Advanced Training Course.
It is intended *only* for Seekers that have *already* completed
the "Pathway to Ascension" Professional Course.

If you read an unfamiliar term not defined in the text,
refer to the "Systemology Dictionary" in the appendix.
It is also helpful to keep a quality dictionary nearby.

A clear understanding of this material is critical for
achieving actual realizations and personal benefit from
applying our philosophy as spiritual technology.

The *Seeker* should be especially certain not to simply "read through"
this book without attaining proper comprehension as "knowledge."
Even when the information continues to be "interesting"
—if at any point you find yourself feeling lost or confused
while reading, trace your steps back.
Return to the point of misunderstanding and go through it again.

Take nothing within this book on faith.
Apply the information directly to your life.

Decide for yourself.

∞

MARDUKITE ACADEMY OF SYSTEMOLOGY
"THE KEYS TO THE KINGDOM"
NEW STANDARD ADVANCED A.T. COURSE

– Introduction to the New Standard Advanced Training Course . . . 13

. . . . ONE . . . .
:: THE SECRET OF UNIVERSES ::

– The Secret Doctrine . . . 21
– In The Beginning . . . 23
– Before "Home Universe" . . . 25
– The Alpha-Spirits . . . 29
– "Home Universe" . . . 33
– The Game Continues . . . 37
– The "Symbols Universe" . . . 40
– "Thought" & "Energy" . . . 43
– The Magic Kingdom & Universe . . . 45
– The Physical Universe . . . 48
– Our Current Situation . . . 51

. . . . TWO . . . .
:: GAMES, GOALS & PURPOSES ::

– The Games of Alpha-Spirits . . . 57
– Goals and Purposes . . . 60
– Defragmenting Goals Terminals . . . 67
– Section 1: Defragmentation (Goals) . . . 68
– Section 2: Goal-Sequencing . . . 78
– Section 3: Object-Items (Symbols) . . . 83
– Additional Notes of "Zu-Vision" . . . 89

. . . . THREE . . . .
:: THE JEWEL OF KNOWLEDGE ::

– The Mind-System and "The Jewel" . . . 97
– Procedural Instructions . . . 100
– The Jewel Procedure (Parts #1-5) . . . 113
– Level-7 Stabilization Point . . . 133
– Implants After "The Jewel" . . . 135
– Implant Platforms (#1-18) . . . 137

.... FOUR ....
:: IMPLANTED UNIVERSES ::
- Piercing the Seventh Veil ... 179
- Before Beta-Existence ... 180
- Implanting Universes ... 183
- Implanted Penalty Universes (IPU) ... 186
- IPU Defragmentation ... 188
- IPU Platform #1 ... 195
- IPU Platform #2 ... 201
- IPU Directory (IPU #1–64) ... 204

.... FIVE ....
:: ENTITIES & FRAGMENTS ::
- Level-8: The Wizard Grade ... 243
- Spiritual Fragmentation ... 245
- Fragments and Bonded-Entities (B.E.) ... 249
- The Identification Procedure ... 252
- Bonded-Entities (B.E.) and Fused-Groups ... 254
- Incident-Running Procedure ... 258
- Standard Procedure: Entities ... 265
- Platforms #1-18 (AT#3 Addendum) ... 268
- Programmed Machine-Entities (PME) ... 272
- Standard Procedure: PME ... 276
- Advanced Entity-Handling ... 282
- End-Points and Realizations ... 285

.... SIX ....
:: SPIRITUAL PERCEPTION ::
- Advancing Spiritual Ability ... 289
- Realizations From The Pathway ... 292
- "Ejection" From A Body (Vehicle) ... 295
- Advanced Ability Training (A.A.T. Routine) ... 300
- Wizard Level-1 Stabilization ... 305
- Ejection, Perception & Barriers
    (Wizard Level-2 Keynote Lecture) ... 310
- R.S.V.P.—Remote Spiritual Viewpoints
    and Perception (A.A.T. Wizard Level-2) ... 312
- Wizard-Level Session (Script Example) ... 321

.... SEVEN ....
:: MASTERING ASCENSION ::
- Self-Direction and Intention ... 327
- Intention: Directing Thought Wizard Level-3X Keynote Lecture ... 328

- Wizard Level-3X Procedure ... 333
- Advanced Ability Training (3X) ... 349
- Implanting The Human Condition ... 358
- Heaven-Implants (Parts #1-6) ... 364
- Heaven-Implants (Goals Sequence) ... 374
- Heaven-Implants (Ethics Series) ... 384
- Spiritual-Disability Implant ... 390

.... EIGHT ....
:: ADVANCING SYSTEMOLOGY ::
- New Standard Systemology ... 417
- The Jewel of Knowledge ... 421
- The False Jewel of Knowledge ... 428
- "Black-Box" Control-Implants ... 443
- Researching Penalty-Universes ... 447
- The Agreements Universe ... 454
- Actual Goals and Basic Purposes ... 459
- The "Big-Splitter" Incident ... 469
- Opening Gates to the Kingdom ... 518

.... APPENDIX ....
- Systematic Processing Formal Session (Sample Script) ... 523
- The Beta-Awareness Scale (excerpted from the Basic Course) ... 526
- Systemology Technical Dictionary (Version 5.0) ... 527
- Suggested Reading and Additional Materials ... 570

MARDUKITE ACADEMY
NEW STANDARD SYSTEMOLOGY
COURSE SCHEDULE

The Pathway to Ascension
Professional Course

#1 – *Increasing Awareness (Level-0)*
#2 – *Thought & Emotion (Level-0)*
#3 – *Clear Communication (Level-0)*
#4 – *Handling Humanity (Level-1)*
#5 – *Free Your Spirit (Level-2)*
#6 – *Escaping Spirit-Traps (Level-2)*
#7 – *Eliminating Barriers (Level-3)*
#8 – *Conquest of Illusion (Level-3)*
#9 – *Confronting the Past (Level-4)*
#10 – *Lifting the Veils (Level-4)*
#11 – *Spiritual Implants (Level-5)*
#12 – *Games and Universes (Level-5)*
#13 – *Spiritual Energy (Level-6)*
#14 – *Spiritual Machinery (Level-6)*
#15 – *The Arcs of Infinity (Level-6)*
#16 – *Alpha Thought (Level-6)*

Keys to the Kingdom
Advanced Training Course

#1 – *The Secret of Universes (Level-7)*
#2 – *Games, Goals & Purposes (Level-7)*
#3 – *The Jewel of Knowledge (Level-7)*
#4 – *Implanted Universes (Level-7)*
#5 – *Entities & Fragments (Level-8)*
#6 – *Spiritual Perception (Level-8)*
#7 – *Mastering Ascension (Level-8)*
#8 – *Advancing Systemology (Level-8)*

Advanced Training Supplements

#1 – *Systemology Biofeedback*
#2 – *Systemology Procedures*
#3 – *Systemology Piloting*

NEW STANDARD SYSTEMOLOGY KEYS TO THE KINGDOM ADVANCED TRAINING COURSE

*The complete advanced training course for
The Keys to the Kingdom,
collecting all eight lesson manuals
in one paperback workbook edition.*

THE NEW STANDARD SYSTEMOLOGY
ADVANCED TRAINING COURSE MANUALS

Mardukite Systemology is a new evolution in Human understanding about the "systems" governing *Life, Reality,* the *Universe* and all *Existences.* It is also a *Spiritual Path* used to transcend the Human experience and reach true "*Ascension*" beyond the boundaries of *this Universe.*

This is an *Advanced Training* (*AT*) course workbook detailing *upper-levels* of our spiritual philosophy. It is intended to assist *advancing* a *Seeker's* personal progress toward the *upper-most levels* of the *Pathway.*

These manuals follow *after* our *Professional Course* lessons—available as individual booklets, or collected in two volumes titled "*The Pathway to Ascension,*" or even in a single workbook edition. The *Professional Course* follows *after* the *Basic Course* lessons, or "*Fundamentals of Systemology.*"

The systematic methodology that we use to assist an individual to increase their "*Actualized Awareness*" (and reach gradually higher toward their "*Spiritual Ascension*") is referred to as "*The Pathway*"—and that individual is called a "*Seeker.*"

To receive the greatest benefit from this workbook: it is expected that a *Seeker* will already be familiar with fundamental concepts and terminology previously relayed in the *Basic Course,* and still have access to *Professional Course* (*PC*) materials representing our *applied philosophy.*

As a *Seeker* increases their *Awareness* in this lifetime, their spiritual "*Knowingness*" also increases—which is to say their *certainty* on *Life,* on this and other *Universes,* and on *realizing Self* as an unlimited "spiritual being" *having* an enforced restrictive "human experience." A *Seeker* also *knowingly* increases their command and control of the "human experience." And this is a part of what is meant by "*Actualized Awareness.*"

CHARTING FLIGHTS ON THE PATHWAY

Although there is a systematic structure to *fragmentation,* the personal journey experienced along the *Pathway* will be different for each *Seeker.* For example, certain areas will seem more "*turbulent*" or difficult for one *Seeker* than another. We tend to say that these areas have more "*charge*" on them—or that they are more "*heavily charged.*" It is best to handle such areas when you are already feeling "good" and not in a situation (or condition) where that specific area is consistently being "*triggered*" or "*restimulated.*"

As an applied philosophy, *Systemology* "theory" can be easily utilized in the "laboratory" of the "world-at-large" in everyday life. Unlike other "sciences" that conduct experiments by making a change to some "objective variable" *out there* and waiting to see an effect, our focus is the individual (or *Observer*) themselves, and how *they* affect the *"Reality"* perceived.

Our philosophy is applied by using specific exercises and systematic techniques. These *"processes"* provide the most stable personal gain (and *realizations*) for each area; but only when actually applied with a *Seeker's* full *"presence"* and *Awareness*. Hundreds of such *processes* are given in the *"Pathway to Ascension" Professional Course* (PC) material.

Applying a technique is called *"running a process."* Processes are designed with very simple instructions or *"command-lines."* To *run* a *processing command-line* (PCL), a *Seeker* may be assisted by the communication of that *line* from a *"Co-Pilot"* (as in *"Traditional Piloting"*). But even then, a *Seeker* must still personally "input" the *command* as *Self*. For this reason—and quite thankfully—*Solo-Processing* is possible.

TAKING FLIGHT ON THE PATHWAY

Processing Techniques are intended to treat the *Spiritual Being* or *Alpha-Spirit*; the individual themselves. The *"command-lines"* (PCL) are *directed to* the individual themselves—the *Actual Self*—and not some *mental machinery* of theirs, or even a *Biofeedback* metering device (when used).

Systematic Processing is applied by the *Alpha-Spirit*—who then *Self-directs* command of their "Mind-System" or "body" (*genetic-vehicle*), both of which are "constructs" that the *Alpha-Spirit* (*Self*, or the "I-AM" *Awareness* unit) operates, but neither of which is actually *Self*. *Fragmentation* causes *Humans* to falsely identify *Self* as a *"Body"* or even a *"Mind."*

Some *processes* can be treated quite lightly at first; others may require a bit of working at in order to get *"running"* well. It is important to set aside a period of time when you can be dedicated to your studies and *processing*. This period of time is referred to as a *"processing session."* When a *process* does start *running* well, it is important to be able to complete it to a satisfactory *"end-point."*

Processing allows us to be able to *actually* "look" at *things* and even determine the *considerations* we have made—or attitudes we have decided—about *Reality* as a result of those experiences.

It doesn't do us much good to simply "glance"—or to *restimulate* something uncomfortable and then quickly *withdraw* from it once again, leaving more of our *attention* yet again behind and held fixedly on it.

Generally speaking, a *Seeker* continues to *run* a *process* so long as something is "happening"—which is to say, the *process* is still producing a change. Usually this is evident by the type of "answers" that a *command-line* prompts a *Seeker* to originate from the database of their own *Mind-System*.

Processing Command-Lines ("PCL") are not "magic words"; they do not "do" anything on their own. They systematically assist a *Seeker* to selectively direct their own attention toward increasing *Awareness*.

A *Seeker* may also cease to generate new "data" from a *process* without reaching an *"ultimate" realization* as an *"end-point."* It is possible that additional "layers" (or even other "areas") require handling before anything "deeper" is accessible. If this is the case, end the *process*. But, if a *Seeker* is *withdrawing* from something uncomfortable that was incited or stirred up, then a *process* is *run* until they feel "good" about it.

One of the benefits to *Flying-Solo* on the *Pathway* is that the *processing* is entirely *Self-determined*. This naturally provides a built-in "safety" for a practitioner. Anything you *restimulate* by *Self-determinism* is *your thing*. It is not triggered or incited by some external *"other-determined"* influences (or other "source-points") that make you an *effect*. It can be more easily handled in *processing*—or you can simply let things "cool down" and come back to it again in another *session*.

While it may seem "mysterious" to beginners, a *Seeker* gets a sense for knowing how long to *run* a *process* only with practice. Once you have spent some time actually applying material from *"The Pathway to Ascension" Professional Course*, there are many aspects of it that become "second nature" because they are, in fact, a part of our true original native nature. All we have done in *Systemology* is *"reverse engineer"* the routes of *creation* and *consideration* that are already *our own*.

<u>*Advanced Manuals should be studied in the sequential order in which they are numbered.*</u>

SYSTEMOLOGY LEVEL-7

We are publishing *"upper-level" Systemology* for the very first time. Its application is dependent on a *Seeker* reaching a stable point of *"Beta-Defragmentation."* This requires proper use of materials for previous *processing-levels*—given in the *"Pathway to Ascension" Professional Course*. Of course, we don't refer to such an individual as *"defragmented"*—which only further reinforces that *something* exists to *defragment*—but instead, as having reached a *Beta-state* of *Self-Honesty*. This "state" *must* be reached in order to go further.

Up to this point of the *Pathway*, a *Seeker* has become *"better-abled"* in the *game* of *"Being Human."* They have learned to play the *game* of *Beta-Existence* better—while still *on Earth*, and possibly still quite fixated on a *"Human*

Body." Yet, the completion of *Systemology Level-6* is still a stable point of accomplishment—and well above the level of *Awareness* maintained by the "standard-issue" *Human Condition*. The individual is less likely to fall into as many *traps* and is more able to "brush off" most additional *fragmentation* before it accumulates.

"*Alpha-Defragmentation*" is what the "*Keys to the Kingdom*" *Advanced Training Course* manuals pertain to. Our aim is still for "*metahuman destinations.*" The goal of *Systemology Level-7* is to "safely" deliver (or *Pilot*) a *Seeker* to the *next plateau* "in sight" from the stable point already reached. There is, of course, something of a *chasm* between these points. So, it is necessary for a *Seeker* to be certain they have relieved themselves of enough "baggage" and "weight" (of *spiritual fragmentation*) in order to get enough "lift" for their ascent.

In the past, a few have even stumbled upon this point of "*crossing the abyss*" within their own traditions. But without *defragmentation*, their new-found vigor and horsepower causes them to just more quickly and deeply get lost in various distracting spiritual detours and intellectual tangents; or even fall back to old patterns, if they cannot maintain *Self-Honesty*.

This *chasm* is *not* a pitfall for *processing* mistakes—or even an *actual* barrier. But it is a "drop-off" point that many *perceive* upon reaching this part of their journey. It is sometimes enough to keep a *Seeker* from going further on the *Pathway*, fearing that they risk their existing gains. Therefore, we held off presenting the *upper-levels* until our presentation/communication of the *Pathway* had been perfected—and *Seekers* could approach this material with greater *certainty* and *ability-to-confront* its *reality*.

An *advanced Seeker* is likely to spend many months, and over *100 processing-hours*, on *Systemology Level-7* alone. The *four* manuals—"*The Secret of Universes*," "*Games, Goals & Purposes*," "*The Jewel of Knowledge*" and "*Implanted Universes*"—should be treated as a single "unit" of uninterrupted work. This doesn't mean handling it as a single *session*—nor are all *Seekers* in a position to take a *retreat* from their *lives*. But daily *restimulation*, or other distractions, can significantly delay progress at this stage. Completing *Level-7* may require longer and more frequent *sessions* to achieve the same steady gains that one is previously used to.

Systemology Level-7 primarily concerns "*Games*"—which is also to say "*Universes.*" On the *Standard Model*, "*Games and Universes*" is plotted at "6.0"—subordinate to the "*Alpha Thought*" ("7.0") required to *postulate* or *create* the "*Game/Universe*" into existence. This is senior to "*Intention*" at "5.0"—which is, of course, dependent upon some "*game-condition*" for any other *consideration* to occur.

SYSTEMOLOGY LEVEL-8

Systemology Level-8 work is a direct continuation of *Level-7*, which *must* be completed before continuing to *A.T. Manual #5*. After uncovering *"The Jewel"* and discovering the "secret" of *Universes*, a *"Seeker"* has *found* the "hidden gem" of the *Pathway* at *Level-7*, and is no longer a *"Seeker."* Of course, things are not always what we expect—and *"all that glitters is not gold."* Yet, still, it is *"The Jewel of Knowledge"* (Parts #1-5) and the *Entry-Point Heaven Incident*, &tc., that represents the "ceiling" of *this Universe* and even what is behind it, beneath it, or embedded into its structure. It was what a *"Seeker"* had been *drawn* to in their *search*, but was never meant to find by any other method or avenue, except *systematically*.

Systemology Level-8 introduces the first official *"Wizard Levels"* of *New Standard Systemology*. As stated in *A.T. Manual #4*: while "formal" *Advanced Training* may end with manuals representing *Systemology Level-8* (and completing the *"Keys to the Kingdom"* series), this will also open up, what is referred to by the *Mardukite Academy* as, the *"Infinity Grade."* [For instructional purposes, we tend to still refer to a practitioner as a *"Seeker"* in the *upper-level* manuals.]

There is no finite end-point to the *"Infinity Grade"* because its ultimate goal is the *"increase of spiritual perception,"* which is, in essence, *unlimited.* This means that plenty of room remains for future researchers to contribute; but only after first completing their *Advanced Training* regarding the parts of our *"Map"* that are *already* researched, well-plotted, effective in application, and thus published here.

A *Seeker* could complete *A.T. Manual #3*, and then move on directly to *Level-8* with *A.T. Manual #5* (*"Entities & Fragments"*). If, however, a *Seeker* doesn't have enough *"reality"* on that *Level-8* material—as in, it doesn't seem *"real"* enough to them—then some time studying *A.T. Manual #4* (*"Implanted Universes"*) may be of benefit. The covert purpose of introducing *"Implant Platforms #1-18"* (AT#3) and the *"IPU Platforms"* (AT#4) at *Level-7*, is really to make *"Entities & Fragments"* (AT#5) more accessible.

To apply *upper-level Systemology*, an *advanced Seeker* must follow the prescribed outline of instruction that is now available for the first time to the public as the *"Keys to the Kingdom"* material.

"Years ago, we realized that 'The Way Out' would systematically resemble the routes by which we descended. We understood that the 'Gates' reflected in our most archaic esoteric lore were pointing toward a *realization* that had been lost in translation along the way—and that our only hope of finding a *Map* to this *Pathway* was in recovering that lost understanding. I believe that our Systemology is successfully delivering a communication that is unparalleled in today's society—and most of you here can attest that: above and beyond the former gradients of knowledge available to us in our world, this work we are doing now is our best chance at 'making the grade' to reach our *Metahuman Ascension* in *this* lifetime; and for the first time in a very long time, reclaim the true power of the *Alpha-Spirit* and the freedom to experience a *Universe* of our own true *Self-determined* creation."

—*Joshua Free, <u>Backtrack Lectures</u>*

A.T. MANUAL #1
THE SECRET OF UNIVERSES

THE SECRET DOCTRINE

Upon *"initiation"* to *Systemology Level-7*, a *Seeker* is introduced to our *"Secret Doctrine."* This is *not* religious dogma; it does not even require *belief* or *faith*. It is, however, what our *Pathway* is structured after—including the *levels* that have delivered a *Seeker* to this point. It is *"secret"* only for the fact that an individual will not likely *confront* its *reality*, or even *understand* it, prior to reaching this advanced point on the *Pathway*.

"The Secret Of Universes" manuscript provides additional *context* to the information a *Seeker* has already explored on the *"Pathway to Ascension" Professional Course*; because elements of it directly appeared in those course materials. Those details already given about certain areas will not be repeated here. Also, further details provided in later materials of the *"Keys to the Kingdom" Advanced Training Course* will not be included here.

This is a very *bold* narrative. It is not meant to be discouraging; but informative. At the very least we must be able to *confront* where we have been—and how we got to where we are—if we hope to ever retrace our steps and find our way back out again.

What *is* included here is a general outline—the basic *systematic structure*—of our *Cosmic Spiritual History*; the most important and necessary parts for broadly understanding the *"bigger picture."* To elaborate further would *evoke* individual perspectives, cultural interpretations, or differing languages used to assign proper names. Any such treatments and/or speculations are outside the purpose of this manuscript.

Only small parts of this *"big picture"* have ever been *glimpsed* before—in shreds and tears. This is due to imperfect *fragmented communications* by arcane traditions that became so fixed upon "kabbalistic symbols" and "correspondence charts" that any greater truer meaning of the *Secret Doctrine* was long forgotten. Our *communication* of it, in *Systemology*, will be much more direct—and *systematic*.

The subject of *Universes* is introduced directly in *Professional Course (PC) Lesson-12*. Other *upper-level* concepts from that course—*Spiritual Implants* and *Spiritual Machinery*, &tc.—will also be mentioned in this narrative. A *Seeker* is encouraged to refer back to appropriate *PC-lessons* when certain subjects emerge that require more clarity.

This *lore* remains an "esoteric secret"—even when published in plain sight—because it is rarely understood properly. The average person is going to have little *reality* on this material at all. Meanwhile, a *Seeker* that has completed the *"Pathway to Ascension" Professional Course* might look at it and say, *"well, of course, how could it be any other way?"* In either case, no *enforcement* is suggested about "believing" anything.

Unlike other *Systemology* lessons and manuals, this manuscript does not include *processing* instructions or exercises. It does, however, include a lot of information and *points to "spot"* in later *Advanced Training (AT) Course* materials. Any *reactivity* or *turbulence* encountered while reading this should be noted, then handled with techniques from the *PC* material (or as described in the *"Systemology Procedures" AT Supplement*). Later *AT* course manuals will treat more specific points of this manuscript with data that is not already given.

Those *Seekers* that have not reached a basic state of *Beta-Defragmentation* yet—or are still working through *PC* material for the first time—should take care to assign specific uninterrupted time in a safe place to initially study this material. When first reading this, it is not uncommon for some individuals to go *"unconscious"* (*fall asleep*) when more information is read in one sitting/session than they are prepared to *confront* all at once. This may not even happen. But if it does: make a record of where it happened and then pick it up again from an earlier point.

A *Universe* is a *complete system* of *space-time*. This discourse is primarily concerned with those *large agreed-upon Universes* that we have all inhabited. *Universes* have become more "solid." We often refer to this as the *"Condensation of Universes."* Other *Universes* do not reflect the same *"Physical Laws"* as *this Beta-Existence*. And superior to all of these, is the *individual* as the creator of their *own Personal Universe*.

In previous *PC* lessons, an individual's *Personal Universe* and *"Home Universe"* were treated as one and the same concept and elevated to the highest position on the *Standard Model* (encompassed only by the *Infinity-of-Nothingness*). In *this* manual, we will reveal that this was a great oversimplification of the facts (which had simply seemed adequate for previous purposes).

IN THE BEGINNING...

Before *"Home Universe"*—before all *Existence*—there can only be an *Infinity-of-Nothingness*. It exists before and back of all *Space* and *Time*. It is, itself, unchanging. But within it is the infinite *Potential-of-Everythingness*, because an *infinity of creation* has descended from that *Nothing*.

The *Nothing* has the *potential* for *"thought"*—but, naturally, there is *nothing* to *"think"* about until *something* is *created*. The very *first "Alpha"* thought, and *first "Alpha" creation*, are one and the same. The *process* of *Alpha-Thought*, in its highest form, *is* the *process of creation*.

Considering the basic components of a *Universe*—*Space, Time, Energy* and *Matter*—only one is senior, or rather, first, above the others; only one can be considered without a reference to the others—and that is *Space*. Inherent to *Space*, is the concept of *separation*. At first, the only 'thing' there to separate, was the *Infinity-of-Nothingness*. And this *separateness* resulted in *"Alpha Spirits."*

An *"Alpha Spirit"* is essentially a *fragment* of the basic *Infinity-of-Nothingness*. By its *separateness*, it becomes a basic *individual* unit of Spiritual Awareness itself. It is not affected by this separation. At basic, the *"Alpha Spirit"* remains a part of the *Nothingness*, but with a potential for *infinite creation*—and the capability to *experience time*; meaning an ability to perceive conditions of *having* and *not-having* their *creations*.

Once the *Awareness Unit* is *aware* (can *conceive*) that it has *separated*, then it applies further *separations* to bring about the *creation of existence*. Space is the *separation* of *"parts"* or *"particles." Time* is the *separation* of *"incidents"* or *"events." Identity* then becomes necessary for the *separation* of *"thought."* Without *identity*, all *thought* would be *"one"*—and that is apparently too passive of a condition for *creation* to occur.

The *Infinity-of-Nothingness* is beyond *all considerations* of *Space-Time*; it therefore remains *"Infinity"* from our perspective of *Space-Time*. Its very nature exceeds whatever *infinite creation* is ever manifest; it continuously demands further *infinities of somethings* to balance its *nothingness*. And since it is a basic part of us, we never are disconnected from, or lack, the *nothing*. Our sense of lack is always perceived in the direction of *having somethings* (that are not *nothing*), of which we will always come up short of balancing the *Nothingness* completely.

At basic, the *Spiritual Awareness Unit* is the *Total Sum of All Potential Awareness*. It simply *IS*; and it is superior (above) to its other *considerations* of *Space, Time, Energy* and *Matter*. *Matter* is a *consideration* that *something* is *there*. *Energy* is a *potential* for *something* to *happen*. As *Self-Aware* beings, *Alpha-Spirits* (*Alpha-Thought Units of Infinity*) fulfill their basic function by continuing an ongoing sequence of *infinite creation*. [Only when this *creativeness* is "blocked" or "restricted" do we become "unhappy." All lesser states are thus slightly unpleasant; but the idea of future *creations* drives us forward.]

Our separation from the *Infinity-of-Nothingness* is only a *consideration*. The *Alpha-Spirit* is still a part of the basic state; it never really "left" and thus there is no reason to "rejoin." The *"Pathway to Ascension"* or *"Return to Source"* is not a dissolving of *Identity* back into a "pool" of *Nothingness*. This is a false assumption that is easy to make. The *Infinity-of-Nothingness* is not "enlarged" or "enhanced" by that "reincorporation" and as a result, does not even allow for it.

At our highest state of co-existence with the *Nothingness*, each individual *is*, for all intents and purposes: *God*—and with a basic function: *To Create*. Although there is a certain inherent *timelessness* to this state, there is also a sequence, perceived by existing *Alpha-Spirits*, of "newer beings" coming forth from the *Infinite*. Freshly separated "beings" would then *create* "new systems" not already in *existence*.

Of course, the newest and most original *creations* and *systems* would result from "fresh beings" that could be isolated from any exposure to existing *creations* conceived by "older beings." A phenomenon began to occur where a new batch of "fresh beings" were isolated into *"pockets of infinity"* or *"wombs of creation."*

All of us here now are presently in such a *"pocket"* or *"womb."* And the entire series of *Universes* we have *created* (and inhabited) have all existed within *this* "womb." When we have completed our *progression*, we can then *exit the womb* and carry our *creations* and *systems* with us to blend with those of "older beings." And when we have exhausted every variation and combination thereof, we will then usher in the next batch of "fresh beings" who will also play their part in this dance of *infinite creation*.

Of course, initially isolating a group of *god-like* beings requires a bit of work. We are speaking of the basic state of an *Alpha-Spirit*, with the ability to *create* and *destroy Universes* on a whim. Of course, since you are initially dealing with "fresh"—"innocent"—beings, you may be able to misdirect their *attention* for awhile; but they will eventually start to notice the more elaborate *creations* of the "older beings." Something more *systematic* is necessary.

A *god-like* being can only *limit* (or "*trap*") itself. "*False data*" and "*deception*" from others can certainly encourage this. But even so, the "older beings" cannot directly involve themselves in the *process*. The batch of "fresh beings" must be *tricked* into being in *conflict* with others in order to *create* "*traps*." And it is the "*traps*" we *created* for others that really ended up *trapping* ourselves.

The *systematic sequence* at play here is for the "fresh beings" to *create* their own *traps*. By sinking deeper into them, they will eventually become the "*effect*" of their own *creations*. This leads to a "*spiritual amnesia*" (reduced *Awareness* and *Knowingness*) concerning their own *Identity* and the nature of their *creations*. By forgetting (*Not-Knowing*) how the *trap* was made, a new *systemology* had to evolve to reveal the *structure* of the *trap*. And this is used to regain *control* of our *creations* and dig ourselves out of the *trap*—and *Ascend*.

As *Alpha Spirits*, we may pretend to be *older* or *higher* than others. But we are all existing now at the bottom of such a *trap*. We have reached a state where we can only *create* with *atoms* and *particles* provided to us. It's time to dig ourselves out and *exit the womb*. The "older beings" cannot intervene. The only "*way out*" is to regain our *spiritual power*—and that means regaining *control* of our *creations*. They are, after all, *our creations*.

BEFORE "HOME UNIVERSE"

We have been isolated away from "older beings" in this *womb* for a very long time. There is only one instance of "contact" that we have ever had with *them*, one single encounter with a *creation* from them—and it occurs at the very beginning. While there have been many "*false beginnings*" (suggested by *Implants*), and many "*starts-of-time*" upon *entry-to-a-Universe*, there is only one true *first experience*—and we have all had it.

As we separated from the *Infinity-of-Nothingness*, our *attention* was directed to something so *fascinating* that it drew us in before we could think of *looking* at anything else. We call this *"The Jewel of Knowledge."* We might have expected our first experience to be incredibly simple or basic, but instead, it is perhaps the most *complex creation* we have ever beheld—because it came from "outside" and was *created* by "older beings." It *showed* us what we were supposed to do.

Complexity of *The Jewel* can only be vaguely described here. Although it was "diamond-like" in shape, it was intentionally designed with more *facets* (or *faces*) in more dimensions than we could even perceive all at once in our native state. This is what *compelled* us to *look* so closely. When "scanning" Incidents on the Backtrack, there are many *"false jewels"* (attached to later, more recent, Implants) that only imitate the *systematic structure* of *The Jewel*, but certainly not the *complexity*. [These "imitations" are what we treat at *Systemology Level-7*, as indicated in the *AT Course* manual titled: *"The Jewel Of Knowledge."*]

The Jewel of Knowledge contained many "chambers"—each of which we experienced sequentially; each of which demonstrated something interesting and useful to a "fresh being." Some of the *"knowledge"* was "correct." Other parts subtly encouraged a tendency toward *interpersonal conflict* and *creating traps*.

The original *Jewel* does not communicate using a "language." Much of it is displayed with *geometry*, which itself, lays in a *structure* for *creation*—but it never shows anything that we would consider a *"Body."* Other individuals (and groups of beings) are generally indicated by "points of light" or "nebulous clouds."

Most of the "chambers" provided simple demonstrations. For example: one of the first ones showed how to *perceive an object*. It demonstrates setting up *"viewpoints"* from various directions (or dimensions) in order to permeate or pervade the totality of what you're *looking* at. A "two-dimensional" *creation* is *perceived* in its totality only from "three" (or more) dimensions, *&tc*. Of course, *The Jewel of Knowledge* might demonstrate this with a "seven-dimensional cube." Many other "basic" *shapes* and *structures* are also used.

Some "chambers" demonstrated more *misleading data*. For example: one might depict many individuals working together in harmony to *create* pieces of an object and the idea is that things are pleasant. Then one of the beings goes against the efforts of the others and things become unpleasant. The group of beings collectively force the individual back into agreement, and the scenery is pleasant and harmonious again. It doesn't take a lot of analysis for us to see what this is intended to impress.

By the time our journey through the "chambers" is complete, we're set up with the idea that it is necessary to *control* and *trap* other *Alpha-Spirits*. There is also an impression made on us that in exchange for this *Jewel* we would have to *create* something of our own; only then would we be allowed to see other *creations* (made by the "older beings"). Of course, here we are, still working on this *ultimate creation* (apparently); and in the meantime, have dug ourselves pretty deep into it. We've forgotten we really wanted to be *outside* of it all.

After our *Jewel* experience, we were excited to begin *creating* an interesting and complex *Universe*. Of course we weren't "alone." Each *Alpha-Spirit* in this state was a *god-like* being; each one groomed to remain an *individual*, yet also keep *others* in line — and thus ensuring *conflict*. [*Implants* generally contain *"false data"* that is structured so that we equally hold these kinds of strongly *opposing considerations* simultaneously.]

The *Jewel* provided no requirements or specific rules for *creation*; not even a set number of dimensions to use. This actually led to the first primary *conflict* between *Alpha-Spirits*. Each of us chose, for whatever reason, a certain number of dimensions (from *one* to as many as *twelve*) to start working on. We found ourselves developing these *systems* with others that had also selected that number of dimensions.

As an *Alpha-Spirit* spent more *time* and *effort* working with a particular number of dimensions, they felt a certain attachment to the *systems* they were invested in. Those working on a lower number of dimensions started producing results more quickly than the rest. For example: complete "two-dimensional" *systems* resembled something like what we consider "board games" (like "chess") today. The "one-dimensional" *system* known as "music" or "musical notes" still remains with us in *Beta-Existence*.

Seeing how those working on "lower-dimensions" were yielding faster results, the *Alpha-Spirits* working on the "higher-dimensional" *creations* started realizing how far they still had to go to make real progress. Slowly, those working on "higher" numbers began to shift over to "lower" ones. Since the "one-" and "two-dimensional" *systems* were already being perfected, most of the shifts were to "three" through "five" (where room for new contributions still remained).

As the "three-dimensional" *systems* were nearly completed, it became obvious (to these "*Threes*") that those *Alpha-Spirits* remaining "above" to work on higher-dimensional *systems* would eventually shift to work with the "*Fours*" or "*Fives*" (and not join them as "*Threes*"). This wouldn't have been an issue except that *The Jewel* had impressed that everyone must be "in line" and *agree* upon a single *system*.

The "*Threes*" also knew they could be "outnumbered" this way; and that the "four-dimensional" *systems* could overwhelm and manipulate their own *creations*, just as operating from "three-dimensions" allows one to crumple up a "two-dimensional" *painting*, or toss sweep a *game board* off a table. For a moment, the "*Threes*"—with their nearly complete *system*—held a temporary advantage over the "*Fours*." Rather than wait to be "inevitably" subdued, the "*Threes*" attacked first; and this started the "*Reality Wars*."

Relatively speaking, the *Reality Wars* represent the *longest era* of our *Spiritual History*. When you consider the tremendous ability exercised by an *Alpha-Spirit* in this *god-like* state—essentially invulnerable to everything except the *effects* of their *own considerations* and *decisions*—it took an exceptionally long time for these beings to wear each other down to a point of making a mutually shared *reality-agreement*.

In the end, the "*Threes*" successfully laid in "mental" barriers that interfered with solidly *creating* and *perceiving* higher-dimensional *systems*. They could not "block" the lower-dimensions in this wise, because such were an integral part of their own. And, of course, the "*Fours*" could not retaliate in this way, for the same reasons. This has left us with a "three-dimensional" structure for *Universe Systems* ever since. Although previous *Universes* have never been as rigidly "solid" as we experience today, the basic visible or apparent "form" of "things" as being "three-dimensional objects" has been considered "normal" to us for a very long time.

During the final *conflict* of the *Reality Wars*, the "*Fours*" were successful in one particular counter-attack: *Implanting* a *compulsive desire* for *four-dimensional creations*. As an illustrative physical example: a single "four-dimensional trading card" might satisfy the desire *to collect trading cards*.

But since this is not achievable in any *Beta-Existence*, the *dramatization* (or reactive behavior) is *to collect* an endless amount of "three-dimensional trading cards" in an attempt to reach the same condition (as owning *one* 4-D card).

The *Alpha-Spirit* has experienced a strange state of affairs ever since the *Reality Wars* ended. Although we all fell in line on the "three-dimensional" nature of *apparent creation*, the "four-dimensional" component was not eliminated. We stopped being able to *perceive* it, yet we still could *react* to those *creations* and even craved them. Even our present *Universe* gains its "*solidity*" by having a special kind of 4-D "*thickness*" to it. Almost as if *reality* is actually multiple layered copies all moving together.

THE ALPHA-SPIRITS

For the era of the *Reality Wars*, we are still referring to *Spiritual Beings* with practically unlimited ability *to create* and *to alter creations*. *Alpha-Spirits* were still quite capable of placing their "*Beingness*" (as *Awareness*) in many places simultaneously; and managing many complex functions at the same time ("remote" from one another). We were, however, inexperienced; our *understanding* was still quite limited to *considering* only the *mechanics* and *structure* of "*things*"—without any real "*significance*" or "*meaning*" attached.

As we still all occupied the "level" of *Alpha-Thought*, our earliest *communications* with others were pure exchanges of "*Knowingness*." You would just "*Know*" someone *intended* for you to come and *look* at their *creation*. So, you would go *look* and *intend* (or *decide*) that they would "*Know*" whether or not you liked it. Then they could *intend/decide* you to "*Know*" if they were satisfied or unsatisfied with your opinion.

The first *communications* using "abstract symbol pictures" began at the start of the *Reality Wars*. It is actually in the area of *communication* that we first became *fragmented*; and it is this area that we must treat first, at the very beginning of the *Pathway-to-Ascension* (and our corresponding "*Professional Course*" series for it). Efforts to limit *communication* began with *The Jewel of Knowledge*, to influence "fresh beings" not to attempt to *communicate* with the "outside" (or "older beings")—and also to further incite *conflicts* "inside." Individuals don't "fight" or "entrap" each other when they are maintaining *clear communication*.

Unlike other forms of *fragmentation*, these first *"communication flow-breaks"* were *Self-determined*. While the specific preferences about this differed between us, we each began making decisions about *"who"* or *"what"* we no longer wished to be in *communication* (*contact*) with. And this is a key to our *way out*. Since these early basic *communication barriers* were *created* by choice, then they can easily be dissolved (*defragmented*) by *deciding* to resume such *communication* again (without even having to sort out the many layers piled onto this area).

Today, a *Seeker* applies *systematic processing* to peel back many layers of *fragmentation* that have accumulated on the *foundations* of previous *Implants* and *Incidents*. But early in our existence, our problems mainly resulted from *unwillingness to communicate* and *incomplete communications*. Misunderstandings are what led to the first *upsets* and *harmful-acts* experienced by an *Alpha-Spirit*. We're not inherently *evil*; just *fragmented*.

At this early point in *existence*, an *Alpha-Spirit* is still unable to be affected by *"energy-waves"* or *"force."* Any *"implanting traps"* required more subtlety. They were *created* to hold one's *attention* by being *aesthetically* "beautiful" or "interesting"—similar to the "chambers" of *The Jewel*. Some were just "viewable." Others might allow you to totally immerse yourself in the experience within a *holographic-like micro-verse*. Although we couldn't be *"harmed,"* we were being encouraged to *"tune down"* our *spiritual abilities* the whole time.

We operated on both sides of this—being the *cause* and *effect* of the *traps*—and switched sides often. Most of it didn't affect us very much until we eventually slid into *traps* we forgot we had *created* ourselves (during a period of playing for the "other side"). [It apparently never occurred to anyone to only *create traps* that could not *entrap* their own *creator*.]

After the *Reality Wars*, a constriction to "three-dimensions" was the only *enforced reality-agreement*. There was still no single *agreed-upon Universe*. As a result of the long era of *conflict*, everyone remained in a highly "disagreeable" state. When an individual *created* something, someone might change its purpose or nature, meanwhile someone else might *create* something to render it useless, *&tc*. It was a period of one-upmanship (out-doing each other as rivals) and disrupting the *creations* of others. This only led to further *problems* and us going further *out-of-communication* with each other.

When we experienced *The Jewel of Knowledge*, we were practically omniscient and not actually "located" anywhere, except that our *attention* could be focused on something (like *The Jewel*). But, *The Jewel* also convinced the *Alpha-Spirit* that it should locate a *"mass"* or *"anchor-point"* in *spaces* it was operating from. *The Jewel* implanted *"false data"* that *Space* should be "owned," but could only belong to an *individual* that had its *"mass"* there. An intermediate period consisted of a lot of multiverse/micro-verse *creation activity*—but nothing yet *agreed-upon* (except the *dimensions* of *form*).

An *Alpha-Spirit's consideration* of its own *Beingness* starts to *"condense"* as it begins to believe that it is in any way "located" where its *"masses"* are. Prior to the first *agreed-upon Universe*, the *Alpha-Spirit* could still "occupy" many different *viewpoints* simultaneously and remote from each other—even when it started to *consider itself* as "located." But this all changed when we realized one common area of *agreement*: we still had yet to *create* something together that compared with *The Jewel*. So, we built our first *agreed-upon Universe*—and we "located" ourselves there as *individuals*.

This *"Agreements Universe"* was a gigantic wide-open three-dimensional *Space*. It was poorly planned. In fact, it had no real organizational structure at all, except for an *agreed-upon* set of *"definitions"*—which were also greatly flawed. The *definitions* were set up as *"dichotomies"*—*"pairs of opposites"* (*e.g.* "good"/"bad"). For whatever reason, the *"pairs"* didn't really align with each other in a way that made sense—resulting in more *miscommunication* and *entrapment*.

A *"Shared Universe"* requires that everyone within it *share* some specific *universal parameters* or *reality-agreements*, whatever they may be. If we all operate from fully independent and separate *Space-Times*, there is no way to be in *communication* with those "outside" of that (others that are operating independently on their own set of *reality-agreements*). It makes it quite difficult to *create* and/or *play* together.

As a mundane example: if one person is operating as though today is "Wednesday," and everyone else is showing up because it's "Thursday" on their calendar, the individual is not *in-phase* with the *schedule/reality* of the *group*. Even in modern times, we would tend to consider those individuals as "in their own world."

The *definitions* were collected together—and we *agreed* to follow them even before we had inspected them all. We each had only participated in developing one or some of them and hadn't really seen what the others were. We all believed that everyone should have a part in *defining* the basic *reality-agreements* necessary to experience the *Shared-Universe* with each other. This led to manufacturing a *"Reality-Implant"* or *"Universe-Implant"* that didn't come from "outside" (like *The Jewel*).

To *create* and *experience* the *Agreements Universe* required an *Implant Construct*, whereby an individual would "enter in" and be subjected to *enforced agreements* for the *reality* of that *Universe*. Its design was modeled after *The Jewel*, using "facets" or "chambers" to show various "picture sequences." The imagery was quite elementary, rather like the "picture books" we use to *indoctrinate* children with today.

The sequences were built into a four-dimensional *construct*. Although our true four-dimensional *abilities* and *perceptions* were blocked (after the *Reality Wars*), these beings were still able to get together and layer so many copies of a three-dimensional *creation* that it extended into the fourth-dimension (to maintain its *structure*) as a *Universal "Entry-Point."* It was essentially a "portal" or "gate" *from* the *"Misaligned Zone"* (remaining from the *Reality Wars*) *into* the *Agreements Universe*.

Rather than the more elaborate *"diamond"* structure of *The Jewel of Knowledge*, this *construct* appeared as an *"inverted golden pyramid,"* which represented the "narrowing down" of *realities* into *one*. Each of the three-dimensional "pyramid chambers" composed a *"part"* or *"facet"* of the four-dimensional *"hyper-pyramid."* Each "pyramid chamber" established (or "implanted") a *reality-agreement* about one of the *"dichotomies."*

We all gathered together and dived through the *Inverted Golden Pyramid Implant* together. [On the *Backtrack*, you can *"Spot"* the sense of *"rushing to get into agreement"* that is attached to this *Incident*. Thousands of other *Alpha-Spirits* are rushing through around us. You pass through the "pyramid chambers" and receive the *Universe-Implanting*.] We all emerge from it into a unified *infinite space* that is faintly golden in color, rather than "dark."

At this point of our existence, the concept of "death" (in any way) did not yet exist. At worst, we might choose to "forget" (*Not-Know*) things; or abandon one area of *Space* and go off to the other "side" of the *Uni-*

verse and continue our *creating*. We had not yet fixed our *Beingness* "inside" or "interior to" any of our *creations*. However, there was a tendency to create "body forms" (to represent us) that mirrored the scenery of the *Implant* (rather than the "pyramids" and "spheres" from our previous existence). These weren't the kind of "solid bodies" used today; they could flick in or out of existence and we weren't connected to them. If one got "zapped," you could just make another.

The *Agreements Universe* was an interesting era of fluid ever-changing *creation*; but it led to many problems. A loose structure of *reality-agreements* resulted in *conflict*—"tricking" each other; "messing up" each other's *creations*, *&tc*. No one could get invested into a *complex creation*—or some grandiose *aesthetic art construct*—without someone else making something "weird" (an anomaly) "pop up" in the middle of it. Everyone got pretty frustrated with these conditions. The solution was to develop a new *Universe* that could be *infinitely fractioned* in such a way that each *Alpha-Spirit* could have their own complete *"Home Universe."*

"HOME UNIVERSE"

While we tend to treat *"Home Universe"* as *"7.0"* on our *Systemology models* and *scales*, it actually occurred midway in our *Spiritual Existence*. It is, however, at this point, that we start to keep track of "time"—mainly for *sequencing* conditions of *"having"* and *"not having"* and to *realize a "chronology"* of events. For this reason, data from here onward is easier to "contact" when handling the *Backtrack* directly. The previous events described—from *The Jewel of Knowledge* up to this *Home Universe*—are far more obscure and abstract to *conceive*.

In many ways, *Home Universe* was the "apex" of our existence. We still had amazing *creative ability* and had not yet taken on much *spiritual fragmentation*. Each individual *Alpha-Spirit* had their own *infinite space* to *create* in, which was separate from everyone else. But they were still all connected by a *"matrix"* of *higher-level Space*.

The *Home Universe Matrix* linked the individual *Home Universes* together. But this *Matrix* should not be *considered* a *Universe* full of little *spheres* inhabited by each *Alpha-Spirit*. [A later, more recent, *Implant* does suggest this imagery however.] Each *Home Universe* was literally an *infinite space*.

The *Matrix* acted like an inter-dimensional "corridor" or "hallway" that simply connected them all; it expanded to encompass each *Home Universe*, giving each the appearance of a having a distant *"night sky full of stars."*

These *"stars"* were not like the *"suns"* you find in *the Physical Universe*. They were luminous *"orbs"* that served as the original *"Star-Gates"* (we encounter on the *Backtrack*). Each *Star-Gate* connected to another individual *Home Universe* (each of which contained an *infinite space*). Each *Home Universe* was one's own. It did not have to follow or share any strict "physical laws" with other *Home Universes*. The only commonalities were the *"entry-points"* (maintained by the *Matrix* that connected the individual *Universes*). [From this point onward, the "top-level" of *creation* (*&tc.*) is always represented by a *"star"* or *"stars."*]

In addition to the individual *Home Universes*, there were also *"Shared Universes"* that one could go to and experience meetings with others—usually for "games" and various forms of "entertainment." Some of these were like *"Story-Universes"* that functioned as immersive movie theatres. They followed prescribed "scripts" but were laid out as an entire *Universe* (similar to the reality experience everyday on Earth).

When we consider its origins: the *Home Universe Matrix* was *constructed* to prevent *Alpha-Spirits* from interfering with each other's *creations*. But, without any *enforced agreements* on this condition, it was not long before individuals were "hacking" into other *Home Universes* and *creating* problems. We then *agreed* that *Alpha-Spirits* that "broke the rules" needed to be *punished*. So, we collectively came up with an idea that has forever since been the basis of our ongoing *spiritual degradation*: we designed the first *Implanted Penalty Universes*, or "prisons."

During the *"Home Universe"* era, *Alpha-Spirits* were still quite immune to any use of *"force."* There wasn't really anything you could "do" to someone else. However, large groups began working together to *create* a *complex* series of *"sub-Universes"* that might make someone feel "unpleasant" or "unhappy" while confined there for a while. We all *agreed* this was a good idea to use on the "bad guys"—but no one expected that they, themselves, would ever be forced into experiencing such *"prisons."*

A more complete treatment of *"Implanted Universes"* requires its own *Systemology Level-7 A.T. Course* manual later (particularly where it concerns *defragmenting* with *systematic processing*). For present purposes, we at least shall say that these *Penalty-Prison Universes Implants* installed the primary "emotional curve" (such as you find on the lower half of the *Beta-Awareness Scale*) that we are still experiencing the *effect* of today.

These "*Implants*" also used all kinds of interesting "*symbols*" and "*construct-forms*" and "*body types*" to lay in "*degrading*" concepts and *ideals*. Many *low-level* "*goals*"—such as "*sex*" and "*eating*"—were *implanted* to limit the *spiritual abilities* of a "*criminal*"—and keep their *attention* suspended on experiencing the activities within the "*Prison-Universe*" (or else they might "*break free*" of it). These were "*actual*" *Universes*; and the experiences were "*real*" enough for us to eventually continue these *reality-agreements* as our own *creation*.

At first, these little "*prisons*" didn't seem to have much effect on reducing the amount of *conflict*. But there is a long period of time where we kept throwing *Alpha-Spirits* through the routines so repeatedly that we began to more *compulsively dramatize* the "*degradation*" of these "*prison*" experiences in our everyday lives.

As mentioned previously, the first "*Shared-Universes*" for "*games*" were also *constructed* during the *Home Universe* era. These started off quite basic, but eventually evolved into more *complex*—rougher and tougher—arenas. The most *complex* of these is referred to simply as the "*Games-Universe*" and it took place on a *game-field* that very closely resembles modern-day *Earth*. [It is no coincidence that our modern *Earth* is a "*prison planet copy*" of the *original Earth*; it is meant to suspend our *attention* in *confusion* and *restimulation*.]

The *original Earth* was intended for the *ultimate* "*Games-Universe*" (not a *prison*)—and we each spent a lot of time *playing* this "*game*." The primary component of the *game* pertained to "*personality-persona-packages*." By this we mean the "*Artist*" or the "*Scientist*," *&tc*. These roles each had specific *characteristics* that affected how they *interrelated* (or *interacted*) with other roles. [Some essential information on this area is given in *PC Lesson-12*, "*Games & Universes*." See also: *Systemology Level-7 AT Course* manual "*Games, Goals & Purposes*."]

Participation in the *Games* became the most popular activity for *Alpha-Spirits*. They also began to draw more and more *spectators* (onlookers). The real *fragmentation* (at this time) concerned the *implanting* (*conditioning*) required for one to *enter* the *Games-Universe*—because we all went through that "*screen*" innumerable times. It was not a permanent place; we were not confined to it. We could easily just *decide* to leave the *Games* at any point and return to our *Home Universe* to *consider* our *playtime* experience. Later, we could just go back to the *Games* and try something different (passing through the *implant-screen* each time).

For those who "broke the rules" (or cheated), the *Penalty Universes* were there. But individuals always found a way around the "rules"—so the "*barriers*" or "*restrictions*" were made increasingly more "*solid*" (they were imbued with more *energetic-mass*). Eventually we began to develop a *preference*—associations or attachments—for certain "*roles*" and "*forms.*" And more of the *Home Universe Matrix* (*upper-level Universe*) was starting to resemble (be in *reality-agreement* with) the *Games-Universe*.

As more *Alpha-Spirits* were able to "cheat" or even sidestep *conditioning effects*, more of the *creations* from the *Penalty-Universes* were incorporated into the *Games-Universe*. These were intended to establish additional *barriers* (*restrictions*) to the *Games*. Many of these *constructs* were also requested as "prizes" by various "winners"—where they could then be more permanently "displayed" like "trophies" after the *Games* (back in the *upper-level Universe Matrix*). This then caused the *Home Universe Matrix* to take on more qualities of (or be in *reality-agreement* with) the *Penalty-Universes*, too.

All of these factors contributed to an increased degree of *reality-agreement* between the *Penalty-Universes*, the *Games-Universe* and the *Home Universe Matrix*. It is unclear what specifically triggered the events that came next. But, the commonality of *reality-agreement* between too many *creations*—or "*anchor-points*"—bridging between *Universes* could cause them to "*collapse together.*" And this is basically what happened.

You might have already had the "*top-level sea of stars*" display "turned on" when it happened; or you might have sensed something very strange happening, and turned it "on" to investigate. You may have even been in the *Games-Universe* on the *original Earth* at the time. In any case: the "*stars and sky begin to fall.*" Each of our *Home Universes* collapses into the (original) *Games-Earth*. The collision builds such an *energetic-mass* that the *original Earth* literally explodes, sending pieces of our own *Universe* scattered through the "*cosmos.*"

This *incident* represents our first significant *imprint* for "*loss*" and "*grief*." Everything we have endured since has resulted in accumulation of *fragmentation* built up on *this incident*. The *collapse* or *loss* of *Home Universe* is quite basic to each of us. It is quite difficult to eliminate all the residual *effects* this *incident* has had on us ever since—but it is the direction toward which we travel when applying *systematic processing*.

This *incident* includes a lot of "lightning-energy" filling up *Space*, while our personal *creations* begin to decay and crumble to dust. *Home Universe* was no longer separate from all other existences and became affected by those other *reality-agreements*. With the "*Collapse-of-Universes*," the *agreed-upon* "laws" and "parameters" of the *Games-Universe* and *Penalty-Universes* became a part of the *Universe* you were in.

THE GAME CONTINUES

The new "*Games-Universe*" became the first real *compulsively agreed-upon* "*Shared-Universe*" where you (as an individual *Alpha-Spirit*) could no longer maintain *full control* of the *creation* of *reality*. The *Universe* had greatly "expanded" with the residual of all prior *creations*. With the incorporation of *Penalty-Universe* constructs and *agreements*, the *Game* had also become quite "twisted" and "degrading."

Although we were still *god-like Alpha-Spirits* that were immune to "*force*," the reduction in *creative ability* left us quite *fragmented*. For one thing: we couldn't be "hurt," but our *creations* could. In the *Home Universe* era, we could simply *create* something again; but with the *loss* of *Home Universe*, it became obvious that we could now "*lose*" something. This affected our *consideration* of "*having*" or "*havingness*." Suddenly, "*having for us*" meant "*not having for others*."

Individual *Alpha-Spirits* chose remote areas of the *Universe* and "staked their claim" on the *Space* by placing some kind of *creations* there—even if it were only a "nebulous cloud" or a "suspended picture." We were still able to "*create*," but it was all now within the confines of the formerly established *reality-agreements*.

When mutual "*game activity*" resumed again, it began quite tame—more "intellectual"—with everyone still getting over the initial shock and trauma of the *collapse*. But we are quite "resilient" beings; and it did not take long before more and more of the *Universe* became "business as usual." By this, we mean that the structure of events that we have described so far in this manual is the basic *blueprint* or *systematic pattern* behind the events that have continued to take place on the *Backtrack* ever since.

Here, once again, we find ourselves having to *confront* those "undesirable" individuals that seem to do nothing but *create* trouble. Basically, we want them "out" of the *Game* altogether. Naturally, we all *decided* to get together and *construct* a new lower-level *Universe* that could hold the "criminals" in such a way that they wouldn't just get out and make more trouble again. Some new "mechanism" was required.

The residual *Penalty Universe* materials (*reality-agreements* and *Implants*) were collected and strung together, rather like a "carousel" surrounding a "treadmill." Up until this point, the *Alpha-Spirit* did not experience any real sensation of "*motion*." This new "mechanism" impressed the original *Penalty-Universe* "*goals*" in an endlessly streaming line of dwindling or descending conditions.

A positive "*goal*" was paired with its opposite (negative characteristic), which would then lead to the next positive, on and on perpetually. The *Implant* basically encouraged those entering this new "*lower-Universe*" to focus on "*doing each other in,*" rather than placing any *attention* on trying to "escape" (or leaving). This is the first time that a *Prison-Universe* was actually intended to be a "permanent" solution to undesirable individuals. There is no way to "kill" an *immortal spirit*; so all you can do is "exile" one.

At first, the *Implanting* used to get an *Alpha-Spirit* into the "prison" and keep them there is not very effective. Part of keeping the individual there requires having "interesting" and "distracting" things to occupy them. But, as the individual keeps escaping and then getting pushed back in through the *Implanting*, the repeated exposure begins to have a real effect. As more time passes, more individuals end up in the "*Prison Universe*" at a particular time, so the *game-conditions* there become even more interesting and interactive.

As with our previous "*lower-level prison constructs*," no one ever expects themselves to get thrown in; but it ultimately happens to nearly everyone. Sometimes even as a joke or prank, or simply because it's there.

After enough times, the *Alpha-Spirit* develops an interest (and then an attachment) to *lower-order* "motions" and "sensations" that are attached to the *lower-level Universe*. An individual can even develop a tendency to *want* to go there for the "sensation" (much like a "drug")—and then gets to realizing they don't like it anymore, remembers they're in a *"prison,"* and starts focusing on "getting out" again.

There are always those who remain in the *"upper-level" Universe* (out of "prison") in *control* (as the *winning leaders*). Still, there comes a time when so much of the population has been relocated to a *"lower-order" Universe*, that the *"upper-level" Universe* no longer remains interesting (or inhabited) enough to be sustainable. In many ways the *upper-Universe* begins to "contract" and "decay." The last group still remaining there eventually decides that they have no choice but to descend into the *lower-Universe*. [This general pattern of activity continues through the remaining sequence of *condensing Universes*.]

Additionally, the last group that has remained out of the *"prison-system"* is able to descend "in style." They have not been subjected to the same *conditioning-Implants* as the other "prisoners" have. In each cycle of *condensing-Universes*, these "leaders" are able to retain the "technology" and "knowledge" of the previous *Universe* and descend upon (and "invade") the *lower-level* population as *"gods."* [In this case, we can see many parallels with the *"Anunnaki"* of *Mesopotamian* history, as explored in *"Mardukite Zuism"* materials.]

The primary tactic these *"invader-gods"* often use requires *constructing* a *"False Jewel of Knowledge."* The experience of this subsequent *"Implanting"* is actually "earned" and/or "fought for." It provides the illusion of what we might consider *"religious/spiritual enlightenment,"* but it really *conditions* an individual to be a more willing slave of the *"gods."* In extreme cases, it produces bizarre *"religious ideals"* and *"fanatics."*

In this first instance after the *Games-Universe*, the *"gods"* descended upon the *prison-population* and incited a *"Holy War."* While there had always been *"conflict"* among individuals, this marked the first occurrence of *"organized warfare."* And it was orchestrated by *"higher beings"* simply to *control* a *"lower population"* under the guise of *"religion."* While these *"gods"* did exercise a tremendous power and authority, they were never able to fully control the population. There was a revolt; they were overthrown; kingdoms were laid to waste.

After the endless waves of *"Holy War,"* the *creations* and *conditions* of the *Universe* was left in ruin. Half the population was *"insane"* from *religious-implanting* and the remainder were *turbulently-charged* from the *counter-measures* and *misemotion* connected to fighting against the others. They *decided* that these "evil characters" (the *"gods"* and their *"fanatics"*) that unleashed the *creation* of *"War"* were unforgivable and had to be gotten rid of. And so we continued the patterned cycle of *creating lower-level "Prison Universes"*—and we took turns being the "good guys" and the "bad guys" and throwing each other *down lower and lower*.

"THE SYMBOLS UNIVERSE"

To be *systematic*, we refer to this newly constructed *prison* as the *"Symbols Universe"* (though none of these existences were really given proper names). The *"transfer-point"* or *"entry-point"* Implant required an *Alpha-Spirit* to "compartmentalize" *hidden pieces* of themselves—the *"spiritual machinery"* we *compulsively create*, yet *"hide"* from ourselves. [*PC Lesson-14.*] This is the initial origin of the *"Mind-System"* as we know it—and what is poorly termed the *"subconscious."*

Here we find *"hidden parts"* of ourselves able to be *imprinted* upon, which can then generate "sensations" and "considerations" *reactively* (*automatically*) when in the presence of some *"symbolic"* stimulation. By this, we mean a sort of *"Reactive Control Center"* that triggers a *stimulus-response reaction* to a "symbol" or "mental image picture" that merely represents something actual. For the first time: *symbols* have *significance*. You couldn't affect the being; but now you could get a being to affect themselves by showing them something (particularly those "symbols" from the *Penalty-Universes*).

The "games" and Implants from this era primarily concerned *imprinted symbols*. Fighting opponents would direct streams of reoccurring *symbols* at one another. This didn't really do much at first, but as individuals wanted their *symbols* to produce greater effects, they went into greater *agreement* with the *imprinting*, and the *symbols* took on greater *"solidity."*

The big concern an *Alpha-Spirit* had at this time was how to prevent unwanted *symbols* from being pushed directly into one's *viewpoint* (*Awareness*) and automatically triggering some undesirable *effect*. Our solution to this was to *create* "substitutions" in place of our *actual presence*, to act as *"communication-relays"* for whatever we might *perceive*. As a result, you find *Alpha-Spirits* start *deciding* to "dampen" or "lessen" their own *telepathic abilities*. [And it is important to note here: in spite of any conditions that may have encouraged it, the *actual* "lessening" of one's own *ability* is something that only the individual, themselves, could make happen.]

When the final *"upper-level"* group descended, they had *constructed* a new *"Pyramid Trap"* Implant. As usual, it utilized *"higher"* knowledge and technology carried forth from earlier *Universes*. This *construct* resembled a gigantic *Pyramid* with an open door; hollow inside, except for something fascinating at its center that most likely resembled *The Jewel* (but in appearance only). As soon as the *Alpha-Spirit* is drawn inside, the door closes behind.

Within the *Pyramid* are *128* layers of *"walls"* or *"facets"*—one for each of the *64* original *Penalty-Universes* (plus an inverted version of the same). Each *wall* is saturated with *symbols* from that particular *Penalty-Universe*. The *Alpha-Spirit* begins to work through this sequence, working from the center outward. But each time there is a layer they can't *confront*, they end up back at the center again.

The *Pyramid Trap* impresses an illusion that much more "time" is passing during these endless attempts than actually is. This starts to embed *fragmentation* about *Time*—and this develops into sensations of being anxious about "getting things done" or "missing out on other things." The *Alpha-Spirit* starts to experience a sense of "desperation" that previously had never existed.

Once the *Alpha-Spirit* is "sufficiently" desperate, the *"invader-gods"* pull the individual out of the *Implant-Construct* and keep its *Awareness* in a state of suspension, while they are blasted from each side with streams of *Penalty-Universe Symbols*. The effect of this is much stronger than when first entering the *Symbols Universe*. After the *Pyramid Trap*, these waves of repeated *symbols* override the additional "communication-relays" the individual set up. The *symbols* now operated as *"terminals"* for the individual's *spiritual machinery*.

Of course, there was a revolution (as there always is). The *"invader-gods"* were overrun by the masses and thrown into their own *Traps*. And more elaborate *Traps* were *constructed*. Unlike prior *systems*, the *Symbols Universe* had developed into a quite *complex civilization*. This is the point in our history when *Alpha-Spirits* became *fragmented* enough to require (and demand) *creation* of a "*formal government*" and "*a council.*" Here too, we see the first "*large cities*" and "*police forces.*" In this era, we also find the original archetype for a centralized city, known as "*Alpha Prime.*"

The level of "*solidity*" experienced in the *Symbols Universe* is still nothing like what we have today. Existence mainly consisted of "*thought planes*"—two-dimensional pictures suspended in *Space* that are experienced three-dimensionally when you "step into" them. Doing so would require, at least temporarily, *creating* a *form* for your *Awareness* (*sense of Beingness*) to "be there" and interact with whatever/whoever it was.

Alpha-Spirits were still "disembodied" as a *Beingness*; but they could sense the presence of one another and would even flash certain *symbols* —"signs" or "sigils" or "signatures"—to *identify* themselves. Communication had become "*symbolic*" rather than "*telepathic.*" We did not yet inhabit the kind of *fleshy bodies* we do today, but we began to *identify* with *symbolic-creations* more often. And if we had to appear before the *Council* (or in "court"), the *police force* would *enforce* you to "appear" in an expected *form*.

The Council existed for most of the *Symbols Universe* era. Members served in rotation. Each of us has likely maintained some position on one of these *Councils*. Specific "regimes" were constantly being overthrown and replaced. This, too, was part of the *games* of the *Universe*—"betrayal" and "treachery" against other *council-members*. This was also the first great "*machine-building*" age. Whenever someone would visit one of the *thought-planes*, their own *creations* (*postulates*) tended to alter it; so "*machines*" would reset it afterward.

When the final group of "invader-gods" descended to the *Symbols Universe*, they were met by an advanced and sophisticated *civilization*. The *Council* had already begun using *Prison-Universes* on their own criminals, but then the convict would spend forever working out the details of the *Implants*, escape, and then work to imprison the ones that had imprisoned them. Therein, the cycle had already repeated; but with each time, the *Implants* became more complex. Learning new ways to "escape" again, simply became part of the *game*.

"*Sensation Pools*" were another new development during this era. "Signals" from one's experience in a *thought-plane* would prompt their *invisible machinery* to draw "*sensation*" from these "*pools.*" This provided the *sense* of *emotion* and even *pain*; but the actual *sensation* was drawn from a "*hidden source*" and not the (apparent) *symbol* that prompted it. This is when we began to "*misidentify*" the "*sources*" of things. And this is where our story begins to take a turn.

The *Symbols Universe* would have been the last step taken when we still retained the *Awareness* and *spiritual ability* enough to collectively "stop" our further descent. The last members of the *Symbols Universe* got very interested in the activities of one of their little "*prison*" sequences again —and they never returned. There is likely no longer anyone there to "pull" us all out of here. None of the other "*prison sequences*" went more than *two* levels below the *Symbols Universe*. The present *Physical Universe* is now *four sub-levels* deep—and the next one below us is *already* in *operation*. We're likely really in it for keeps now; for all the marbles.

"THOUGHT" & "ENERGY"

Directly beneath the *Symbols Universe*, everyone ends up in the most *complex prison* made during the previous era. We refer to this as the "*Thought Universe*" because its inhabitants considered themselves as "*Thought Beings*"—but really, they were "*Energy Beings,*" as opposed to the "*Body Beings*" (of the next *lower-level* prison).

The *transfer-point* or *entry-incident* leading down into the "*Thought Universe*" consists of a four-dimensional "*spiral staircase*" that appears to extend infinitely. The construct Implants a "postulate" that: an *Alpha-Spirit* (as a *Beingness*) is an "*energy-unit*"—and therefore, can be "hit" by *energy* and *force*. As one descends the "*spiral staircase,*" the sense of *imprinting* (using cues from *The Jewel of Knowledge*) becomes more "vivid" as it "accumulates" progressively as *fragmentation*.

During the *Thought Universe* era, an *Alpha-Spirit* identifies its *Beingness* with a specific fixed "*energetic-body*" for the first time. Of course, it was really like an "*energy-sphere*" (rather than a more material form)—but the individual is now "located" in *Space* (as a specific *anchor-point* moving about the *universal matrix*). As soon as we naively *agreed* to the *reality* of *energy-bodies*, we could be trapped (and/or hurt) by *energy*, and "pushed around" and conditioned by *force*. This *"thought-energy"* state of *Beingness* was still far above what those below in more *"material bodies"* experienced; but we had far descended from our native *god-like* state.

Because quite *fragmented* individuals inhabited the *Thought Universe*, a *sub-level prison* was *constructed* rather quickly. It became the first *"physical" Universe*, though much less condensed than *this* present *Physical Universe*. In order to avoid confusion, we will refer to that one as the *"Conflicts Universe,"* because that is the *only* thing which took place at that level of existence. We could refer to this *conflict* as the *"Thought-Energy"* (or *"Mind-Matter"*) *Wars*; fought between *"Thought-Energy Beings"* and the *lower-level "Material-Body Beings."*

At the time, the *Conflict Universe* developed two-levels below the *Symbols Universe* (which was still inhabited by its "elite"). Other *Symbols Universe* "prisons" that had subdivided before, but eventually this *Thought-Universe to Conflicts-Universe* sequence is where everyone ended up. This *War* went on for a very long time. We switched sides often: the *Body Beings* escaping and becoming *Thought Beings*; *Thought Beings* being caught or imprisoned and existing as a *Body Being*—and each type fighting against the other. Even the *beings* from the *Symbols Universe* started getting involved in the *War* (showing up as *"gods"* as usual).

As the *Symbols Universe* emptied out, both the *Thought Universe* and *Conflicts Universe* began to expand. Toward the end of the *War*, all of the increased *"crossings"* back and forth between *Universes* required more *transfer-points* (and *anchor-points*) in common—until the two *Universes* finally *collapsed* together. The result was a "layered" *Universe*, with a *"material plane"* (of *"material bodies"*) and a *"thought plane"* (where you went in between *"material lives"*). We were still quite aware of the distinction between these two states; that our *"energetic bodies"* continued to "reincarnate" in *material forms*.

After the *Wars* and the *collapse*, the *"material plane"* appeared very much like various "continents" or "landscapes" simply floating through *Space*. There is a long period of redevelopment and building new *civilizations*, but given the former events, everyone was quite hesitant to *construct* another *Prison-Universe*. But *conflict* was inevitable; as individuals just couldn't seem to leave each other well enough alone.

We begin to see more *Implanting* efforts taking place from *within* the *Universe* (rather than a *"prison"*), in order to make others "slaves" or "good citizens"—but in any case, to generally fall in line. *False data* from *The Jewel of Knowledge* continued to be *dramatized* as we used heavier and heavier *conditioning* on each other. Because of the identification of our *Beingness* at this point: it was possible to capture an *"energy-body"* and *force* it into a *"material-body,"* only to "kill it off" with a certain condition, and then do it again repeatedly.

Toward the end of this era, a certain "group" formed with the *intention* of bringing a unified *"peace"* to the *Universe*, once and for all. They established a centralized government and a centralized city (similar to *"Alpha Prime"*) that could maintain *control* over the entire population by establishing a standard *social structure* or *society*, to which everybody would be subject to. And so, the *"Magic Kingdom"* was born.

THE MAGIC KINGDOM & UNIVERSE

The *"Magic Kingdom"* emerged from the remnants of the *Thought-Conflicts Universe* collapse, near the end of that era. It was built on one of the "floating continents"—a grandiose "castle" beside a lake and surrounded by forest. [The archetypal imagery is strangely similar to the iconic scenery often used in "logos" and "title cards" by the Walt Disney Company—which they also refer to as the "Magic Kingdom."] It is the first real visual *imprint* of a *"floating castle," "cloud-castle,"* and/or *"castle in the sky."*

Creators of the *Magic Kingdom* had salvaged four-dimensional technology from previous *Universes*. This allowed the inside of the *"castle-construct"* to essentially extend indefinitely with three-dimensional hallways and corridors that curved slightly at four-dimensional angles. This means it had the potential *Space* for everyone in the *Universe* to live there. [A reader might immediately call to mind some of the statements made by *Jesus Christ* concerning a *"heavenly kingdom"* and *"mansion with many rooms."*]

The *Magic Kingdom* was a *"pyramid-society"* based on "classes." New citizens entered the *system* as "servants," and then others would "move up" in their "status." In many ways, one's "privileges" and "class" really depended on how *early* they joined up. And when it seemed like the *Ma-*

gic Kingdom* was going to "take over" the *Universe*, there was a surge of new willing recruits entering in with the expectation that they would eventually become "*overseers*" as the population continued to grow.

As with any *pyramid-based* social (or organizational) *system* developed ever since, there is at least some sense of "slavery" inherent in any position except the *top-level*—and of course, as the majority of the *Universe* entered into the *Magic Kingdom* and filled positions, it seemed that the hope for *later* recruits to elevate one's status disappeared. New individuals stopped coming. And here we find "legions" of "*winged-warriors*" and "*mystic-knights on flying-horses*" on missions to expand the *Magic Kingdom* by forcibly enslaving the remaining population in the *Universe*.

Once every *Alpha-Spirit* and every *creation* in the *Universe* had been collected and incorporated into the *Magic Kingdom*, the *system collapsed*. The "*castle-infrastructure*" was still there but things were no longer functioning; operations had become too *militant* and *totalitarian* to sustain the *civilization* as it stood. Revolts by the *lower-class* masses—who held the advantage only by their sheer numbers—overthrew *higher-classes*.

Everyone *realized* that this "*mode of operating*" would ultimately lead to a *systematic* catastrophe on a *cosmic scale* if these cycles of *enslavement* continued in this way. There needed to be a "place" to put an *upper-class* when they were overthrown. Yet, by this point, we had collectively understood some of the mistakes that were continuously taking place on our "*descent*"—and a typical "*prison-construct*" would likely mean risking something like the previous "*Thought-Conflict*" Wars. We could at least all *agree* that no one wanted to see that happen.

When the next "prison" was *created*, the place needed to be pleasant enough to want to stay there. If the "prisoners" could actually be happy, they wouldn't be interested in trying to escape back to the *Magic Kingdom*. In fact, if it were reminiscent of both the *Magic Kingdom* and *original Earth* of the *Games-Universe*, combined with an *Implanted-Goal* "*To Enjoy*," this new "prison" might actually be a nice place to live. So, that is exactly what was *constructed*—and the "*Magic Universe*" was brought into *existence*.

Materials for previous *Systemology Levels* did not distinguish between the *Magic Kingdom* (of the *Conflicts-Universe*) and the *Magic Universe*. There are many similarities between the two. But, the *Magic Universe* is the *"Astral Otherworld"* or *"Fairyland" Universe* that immediately precedes our *present Physical Universe*. However, it is *not* the *"thought plane"* we experience "in between" our physical lifetime incarnations.

An *Implant-construct* resembling a *"volcano"* served as the *transfer-point* from the *Magic Kingdom* to the *Magic Universe*. An individual would ascend a pathway to the top; the whole time, passing by *"statues"* representing the *Penalty-Prison Universe* *"symbols"* or *"terminals"* (as was common to these *transfer-points*). When they got to the *"peak"* or *"mouth"* of the *volcano*, they were thrown in.

It didn't take very long before waves of individuals were willingly jumping into the *volcano* just to get "reborn" in the *Magic Universe*. The *Entry-Incident* at the start of our experience in the *Magic Universe* includes a *"Wizard"* riding a *"magic carpet"* over toward you from an *"Arabian-styled ship"* (or *"dhow"*). He is carrying a *"glowing ball"* (or *"orb"*) between his slightly uplifted hands.

Bodies in the *Magic Universe* are, in appearance, very much like the *"physical bodies"* we are familiar with in *this Physical Universe.* One key difference is that in the *Magic Universe*, the "internal structure" of a *Body* is entirely composed of *"energy centers"* (or *"chakras"*) as opposed to *"solid genetic organs."* Today, we would refer to this *"body"* used in the *Magic Universe* as the *"Astral Body."* In fact, many of the concepts in modern and ancient *mysticism* really originate, and are far more relevant, in the *Magic Universe*.

For example: the inspiration behind the design of the *Magic Universe* included the events that *collapsed* the former *Universes* and *structured* a *two-layered "Thoughts plus Conflicts" Universe*. Therefore, in the *Magic Universe*, we find a *"material/physical layer"* plus a *"heavenly layer"* (above) and a *"demonic layer"* (below).

Among these three *"layers,"* virtually every *"fantasy,"* *"fairy tale,"* *"religious,"* and *"mythological"* manifestation conceivable, *existed.* Even *disembodied beings* would *visibly* move around for a while, using their former *"Energy-Body"* manifestation from the *Conflicts-Universe*, before reincarnating as another *"Astral Body."*

The *Implanted Game-Goal* governing the *Magic Universe* was *"To Enjoy."* At the time, the lowest *energy-center* (or *"chakra"*) of the *Astral Body* was in the *"genital-region."* Much of the hedonistic activity here involved *"sex."* Anything resembling *"foods"* or *"consumable substances"* was *created* purely for *sensation* or *effect*. [An even lower *energy-center* around the *"rectum"* was added to the *Astral Body* before entering the present *Physical Universe*; but in the *Magic Universe*, there was no need to eliminate *"body waste."*]

The *Game* of the *Magic Universe* included *upper-level roles* of *"gods"* and *"goddesses," "angels"* and *"demons,"* in the *layers* surrounding the *material plane*. Although the main purpose was *"To Enjoy,"* we still find individuals trying to get the upper-hand over others, or *condition* one another to be *"good"* (according to their own definitions).

We eventually find the remaining population coming down *willingly* from the *Magic Kingdom*, armed with the technology and knowledge of former *Universes* in order to secure those upper-most *roles* and *positions* in the *Magic Universe*. [Some imagery from these events even includes *"great castles" descending* from the *skies*.] The *games* and *conflicts* of the *Magic Universe* went on for a long time before everyone *agreed* to *construct* a *lower-level prison* again. And so, this *present Physical Universe* we are currently in, was built.

THE PHYSICAL UNIVERSE

The *transfer-point* and *entry-incident* regarding the shift between the *Magic Universe* and *this Physical Universe* is first introduced to a *Seeker* in PC Lesson-12, *"Games & Universes,"* as we shall excerpt from here.

This *Physical Universe* was *created* as a place to penalize, exile, or otherwise imprison, the criminals and maladjusted individuals from the *Magic Universe*. At first, we would all "escape" back to the *Magic Universe*— so there have been many repeated *entry-incidents* (*Implanting*) into *this Physical-Universe*.

After a legal sentencing, an individual finds themselves being "drawn down" to *descend* a *"spiral of pillars"* into a Grecian/Roman-style *"pool."* The archetypal *Penalty-Prison Universe* symbols/terminals are each on one of the *pillars*. Whatever *Beings* are present (above/around the *pool*) use their *energy* to "push down" upon the individual as well—thereby also participating in the *"implanting-incident"* that ensues.

This *implanting-incident* does not contain much *"pain"* (or *"force"*). It takes place in a *"mini-verse"* designed (in the *Magic Universe*) to be *"aesthetically-beautiful,"* so as to hold one's *attention* and eventually draw the individual into the *Physical Universe*. Any real *"turbulence"* incited by the *incident* itself, is merely a sense of *"loss"* (over leaving the *Magic Universe*) or misemotion regarding *"exile"*—or of feeling *"pushed out."*

There are really two parts to this *incident*. In the *first* part: an individual finds themselves essentially floating in a *"void-like space"* with a sensation similar to being *"under water."* They eventually see a *"golden light"* in the distance—it glimmers and radiates like a sunburst. [The *"False Jewel"* of this *incident*.]

Once the individual's *attention* is fixed upon it, they are "drawn" toward it with increasing speed. This *"golden light"* is a *symbol/terminal* (*"Object-Item"*) attached to the first *"Implanted Goal"* of an entire sequence (consisting of 36 *"Goals"* or *"archetypes"*). [In this case, the first one is: *"To Be Godlike."*]

Each *"Goal"* is introduced and *identified* with a particular *"Object-Item"* (in order to *communicate* and *embed/encode* its significance). The *"Goals"* are named, but the titles are *sensed* (or *intuited*) rather than expressed in words. [We only *approximate* their meaning with *Human* language for *study* and *processing*.]

As the individual is "drawn in and through" each *"Object-Item,"* the *"Goal"* is *identified* and understood. This continues with increasing speed through the remaining sequence—informing *what* the *"Goals"* are. It sets up the *second* part of the *incident*, when this *"Goals-Sequence"* is *implanted* again with more *significance*.

In the *second* part: the individual emerges from the final *"Object-Item"* in the sequence (a *"pyramid"* associated with the *Goal: "To Be Enduring"*) and finds themselves facing an *"amphitheater stage"* in the distance ahead of them. [This *incident* is sometimes referred to as the *"Heaven Implant,"* because the scenery (of this *second* part) includes the stereotypical heavenly *"trumpet-blasting-angels-in-the-clouds"* atmosphere that *Humans* are *implanted* to "expect" for their *after-life* (or more correctly: *"between-lives"* period).] There is often the sense of being surrounded by many others and everyone rushing up toward the *"stage."*

A *trumpet-horn* blasts, and a sharp *snapping-crackle* (like the *pierce of thunder*), to get your *attention* right before any *"command-line"* is given. The first *command-line* is from an unseen *source* (to get the *"pageant"* started) —*"Only One Will Survive."* Again, the *horn* blasts, the *snap-crackles* happen, and the second *command-line* emerges—*"To Be The One Who Survives, You Must Be Superior To All Others."* This seems to settle the crowd down and all *attention* becomes focused on the stage where a *"pageant-skit"* ensues.

The *blasts* and *snaps* are heard as a new "character" (each representing one of the *"Goals"*) comes on the *stage* to speak *three* "command-lines." Only one "character" is on *stage* at a time. They always enter from one side of the *stage* (your right) and exit the other (your left). There is a *procession* or *sequence* taking place, so the "characters" tend to *look* in a particular direction when referring to the *next* (or the *previous*) "character."

When the *final* "character" (*An Enduring Being*) completes their reference to the *first* (*A Godlike Being*), the *implanting-incident* ends with "waves of blackness" before the individual finds themselves with fixed *viewpoints* in *this Physical Universe (Beta-Existence).* Unlike previous *Universes*, the *Space* here is "dark." While there are many *entry-points* in this *local Universe*, currently the prominent one is the *Horsehead Nebula (Orion).*

[The *110 "command-items"* of this *Implant-Platform* are given in *PC Lesson-12*; and the basic significance for each is *"processed out"* as described in *PC Lesson-11.* Descriptive material (as found in this present *AT Course Manual*) simply helps in *"Spotting"* and *"connecting with"* (*contacting*) specific *Items* and *Implants* for *processing incidents* on the *Backtrack*. Additional details are to be found in other *AT Course Manuals*.]

The *Implant* strongly reinforces that the individual is entering a *Universe* based on *"force"* and *"effort."* Rather than be able to more freely *"create" Energy* and *Matter*, the *"Physical Being"* will now have to apply *"force against force"* and *"effort against effort,"* using a *"Physical Body"* to *create* and *build*, using only the existing "materials" already provided for them in *this Universe.*

The fundamental *Game-Goal* of *this Physical Universe* is *"To Survive."* In the absence of *true knowledge* about *who* or *what* we really are, all of our *attention, energy* and *efforts* become preoccupied with *material survival.* It is the ultimate *spiritual distraction* and *spirit-trap*: to trick/convince an *im-*

mortal being of the *"need to survive."* The individual is continuously *conditioned* to both require the assistance of *others*, yet simultaneously be in competition with them—which safeguards against the masses coming together and "breaking" the *Game*.

Activity and *creation* in *this Physical Universe* pertains almost exclusively to *"material technologies."* When the final *upper-level* "Kings" and "Wizards" of the *Magic Universe* decided that the *"real game"* was now *down here*, they were certain to retain *upper-level* knowledge of *all* "advanced technologies" relevant to *this Universe*. They descended and began constructing *planet-sized "cities"* and gigantic *"spaceships."*

It did not take long before large *organized societies* began making slaves of the population—and eventually such things as a *"Galactic Empire"* developed. As a result of large-scale *"power struggles"* to maintain such an *"Empire,"* the center of *this Galaxy* was *collapsed* into a *"black-hole,"* serving as the *transfer-point* to the next *lower Prison-Universe* (already built). [From the little we know of this next level down, it is nowhere a *Seeker* wants to end up if they still hope for *Ascension*.]

Entire waves of *"invader-gods"* entered into the *Physical Universe*. It would only take a small group of *"Kings"* and *"Wizards"* to capture an entire planetary population, take them back up to the *Magic Universe* for *"advanced training"* (and additional *Implanting*) before collectively returning here again as a *"better-abled"* massive *"legion"* or *"fleet."*

The *Magic Universe* still exists; it has not *collapsed*. It is rather abandoned, however, and is likely *contracting* and *deteriorating* even as you read these words. There are a few of us who have been, until relatively recently, still *transitioning* between *Universes* more fluidly. We have known of a few *"Ascended Masters"* in our recorded *Earth-history*, but the last mass wave of *"invader-gods"* left the *Magic Universe* (and descended to *this* one) approximately *10,000 years ago*. Not too surprisingly, a few of them even show up in the *most ancient writings* that we still have access to on this planet...

OUR CURRENT SITUATION

Of course, things are more *complex* than what is described in this narrative. The fact *this Physical Universe* seems so *"solid"* and so immune to our *"thoughts"* (as an influential *force*), suggests that its whole *existence* is set up, *perceived*, and interacted with, entirely "indirectly." Keep in mind that we have carried all of the *fragmentation* and *spiritual machinery* with us (from experiences in previous *Universes*) into *present-time*. While it has been kept primarily *hidden*, it is the "*spiritual baggage*" that *resurfaces* in *systematic processing* so that we can *confront* it and be rid of it. We must unburden ourselves of its "weight" in order to *Ascend*.

Although "*organic life*" comes in many forms, the "*genetic-vehicles*" or "*Bodies*" preferred by *Alpha-Spirits* in *this Physical Universe* are "humanoid" in appearance—though not necessarily "*Human.*" By this we mean *two arms, two legs, &tc*. This pattern is something we have carried with us here; developed as part of the *basic structure* that we have now come to progressively—and *compulsively*—*identify* with *as* our *Beingness*.

The *entire pattern* of our *descent* is embedded in this total *consideration* of *Beingness*; a *structure* of cumulatively *hidden communication-relays*, requiring our *Awareness* to essentially pass through *seven-plus-one* "*veils*," "*gates*," or "*thresholds*," of entire *Universes*, in order to *perceive* something as *solid*—and as *condensed*—as the *reality* of *this Physical Universe*. When we plot this descent in reverse:

• The "*Genetic Vehicle*" (the *Physical Body* of *this* "*Physical Universe*"); is maintained by an

• "*Astral Body*" (the now-invisible *etheric* form used in the "*Magic Universe*"); which is generated by a

• "*Spirit Body*" (from the "*Conflicts Universe*"); which is projected by an

• "*Energy Body*" (from the "*Thought Universe*"); which is projected by a

• "*Symbol Body*" (from the "*Symbols Universe*"); which is projected by a

• "*Persona-Mask*" (from the "*Motions/Sensations Universe*"); which is projected by a

• "*Basic Object*" (our *playing-piece* from the "*Games Universe*"); which is created by the

• "*Alpha-Spirit*" (still operating) from the *viewpoint* of one's *own* "*Home Universe.*"

The *chronicle* of our *descent* is really our *Map-Key* to *The Way Out*. Of course, the *Map* by itself does not make the *Journey*; nor does a possession of this manuscript alone ensure one's *safe travel*. There are some that have escaped the gravity of *this Universe* and returned to a more *god-like* state. But they tend to fall right back into the same *traps* and *conflicts* again. To all this, we propose that *Systemology* is our best solution to the *endless cycles* and *dwindling spirals* of our continuing *spiritual existence.*

The next lower *prison existence* is already constructed. It is *not this Physical Universe*—but based on the types of inhabitants that typically occupy *this planet*, it is likely that a few *"Humans"* have already been there and back and least once. *This planet* is an actual copy of the *original Earth* (from the *Games Universe*) and it is currently used as a *"prison-planet"* by the present *Galactic* "authorities," keeping us far enough away from the center of the *Galaxy*, where most of the "local" activity actually is. These *physical "Earth-bodies"* are not intended to stray far from *this planet.*

If we were to give it a name, the next *Prison-Universe* might be called the *"Endurance Universe"* or *"Dross Universe."* Its *Space* is incredibly *solid* and *condensed* in all directions, like a thick *syrup* or *quicksand*. It's primary *Implanted Games-Goal* is: *"To Persist"* or *"To Endure."* At least in the *Physical Universe*, (the *Goal*) *"To Survive"* denotes some flexibility of *action*; but in the next level down, we might just find ourselves—an *Eternal Spiritual Being*—entrapped in that *persisting existence* as a *"rock"* or *"grain of sand"* for a *"Body."* Sounds very unpleasant.

Although this narrative might seem depressing, or portray a hopeless situation, it is really the story of a *god* that forgets who and what they are, but always has the chance to turn it all around again. This story of ours hasn't ended. We are still writing it—still playing at the *games* of *creation*. But we have clearly come to a crossroads; and our *decision* is whether to allow ourselves to continue in the direction we have been headed, or whether to *change* course, and return back up the *Pathway*; retracing our *steps*, working our way *systematically* out of the *traps*—and sharing our treasure-trove of *new creations* with the *"older beings"*—having finally earned our "right" to join them for the first time. This is what we originally had set out to do in the very beginning.

While there are certainly more details available to a *Seeker*: the *Truth of All Things* is no simpler than we have described. This *"Secret Doctrine"* unravels thousands of years of obscure *spiritual traditions, mysticism* and *religious belief.* It recovers the real knowledge that other modern efforts to interpret the *Kabbalah* and the *Star-Gates* have failed to unveil. It collects and unifies the underlying truth behind all *Life, Universes* and *Everything*. From *psychology* to *physics*; from *economics* to *politics*; it explains all too bluntly just why conditions are the way they are—and it suggests, quite strongly, the precise *Pathway* that we must follow to find *The Way Out*.

A.T. MANUAL #2
GAMES, GOALS
& PURPOSES

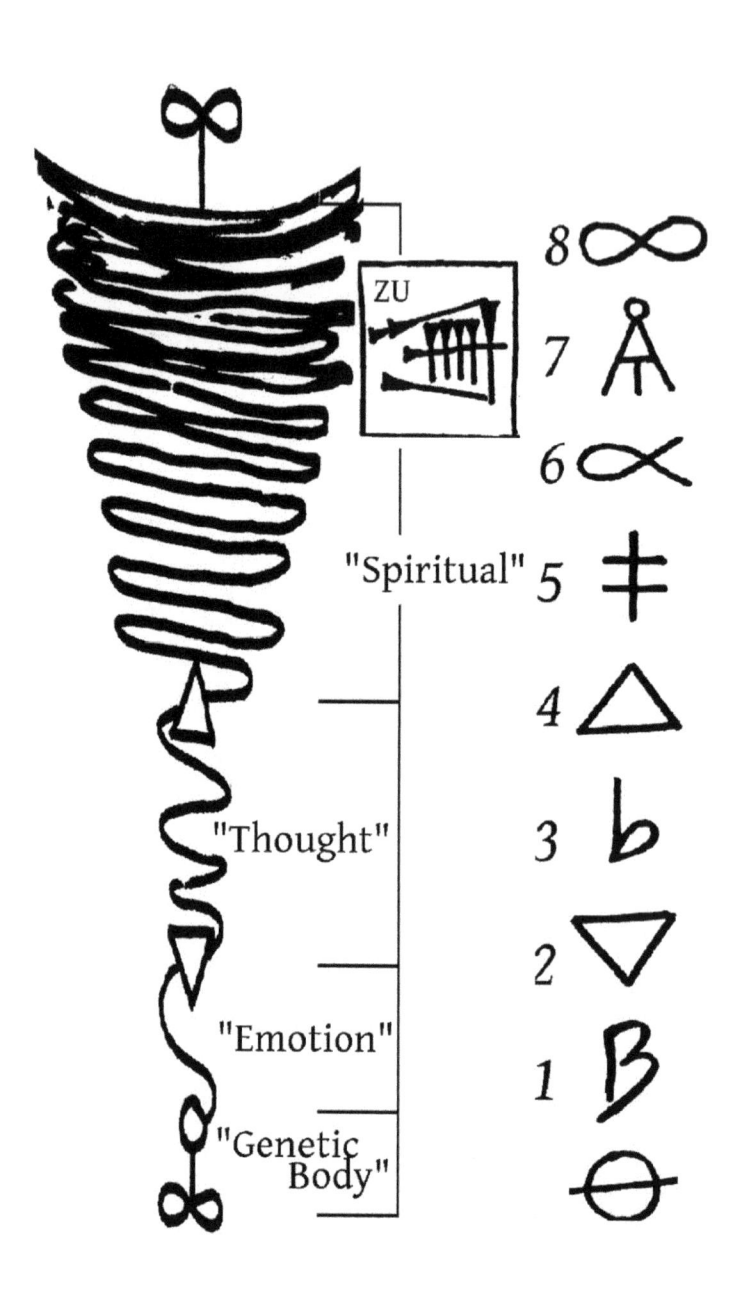

	8 ∞
ZU	7 ⚭
	6 ⋈
"Spiritual"	5 ‡
	4 △
"Thought"	3 ♭
	2 ▽
"Emotion"	1 B
"Genetic Body"	⊖

THE GAMES OF ALPHA-SPIRITS

After reading *"The Secret of Universes"* (*AT Manual #1*), a *Seeker* realizes the full scope of *"Games"* and *"Universes,"* and that it is beyond, or *"exterior"* to, what we classify as *"Beta-Awareness"* and *"Beta-Existence."* At *Systemology Level-7*, we are treating what actually *defines "Beta-Existence"* and our *perceived* "place" *within* it.

On the *Standard Model*, *"Games and Universes"* are plotted at "6." They are *below* the level of *"Alpha Thought"* (at "7") that is required to *postulate/create* them into *existence*. Games are *above* the level of our *"Intention"* (at "5")—which is also to say *"decision"* and *"choice,"* since such is generally dependent on *considerations* of a *game-condition*. To translate this as an *Alpha-Awareness* state: we could also refer to "6" as the *"Spirit of Play."*

The *creation* of *game-conditions* is the first point of true *fragmentation* for an *Alpha-Spirit*. This activity is directly inspired (or incited) by *The Jewel of Knowledge* (see *AT Manual #1 and #3*), which is our first real experience (and *Implant*) as a *Spiritual Being*. Though while in one's own *"Home Universe,"* where one was *knowingly playing a game* with one's own *creations/illusions*, there didn't seem to be much *fragmentation*.

However, *The Jewel of Knowledge* lays in our first *"implanted" considerations*, which we naively used to formulate our first *postulate*: "there *must* be a game." As soon as we began to experience *"Shared Universes"* with others, the *game-conditions* became an intermediate between our *Alpha-Thought* and whatever we are *doing*. Therefore, the *Alpha-Spirit* has been *"playing a game"* for essentially the entirety of its *existence*.

We have realized (from *AT Manual #1*) that shared *reality-agreements* about *game-conditions* are what *creates* a *Universe*. Within that *Universe*, there may be many *smaller-games* or *personality-phases* that one might *play*—but of which are all still subject to the grand *Game* that defines parameters or boundaries of that *Universe*; and by this we mean the *limitations* and *barriers* that are imposed on (and eventually *agreed to* by) an *Alpha-Spirit* in order to *have* some kind of *"playing piece"* for *communication* and *action* within that *Game-Universe*.

The primary source of *Alpha-Fragmentation* occurs when the *Alpha-Spirit* *"collapses"* or *"merges"* all of their *considerations* for *Games and Universes* into a singular *Beta-Existence*. This happens *knowingly* through *agreement*, and is encouraged *unknowingly* through *Implanting*; but at basic, the thing that is most "wrong" with us, is an inability (or unwillingness) to *separate Self* from the *Game* of *Beta-Existence*—to properly distinguish the differences between, for example, *this Physical Universe* and our *Personal Universe*. Because we have come to falsely accept that *this* is the "*only Game* in town" and that there is no where else "to go."

All *games* are based on *illusion*—hence all *games* are subject to, and propagate, *fragmentation*. For example, the *true* basic native state of an *Alpha-Spirit* is "All-Knowing" or pure "Knowingness." But this is not workable as a *game-condition*, so we must *lie* to ourselves, and maintain some degree of "Not-Knowing" in order to have a *game*. Thus, game-conditions are all *lies*; which is to say, *fragmentation* of our *true* native *Self-Honesty*.

While operating in one's own *Home Universe*, we *knowingly* decided to "Not-Know" for a certain period in order to manage all "sides" of an entire *Game (Universe)*. *Fragmentation* occurs when we continuously and compulsively remain "Not-Knowing" thereafter. In *Shared-Universes*, we even set up "hidden parts" of ourselves to keep running/operating *unknowingly* and *automatically*. This is how our total *Actualized Awareness* becomes reduced. We are still as potentially powerful as we always have been, but more of our *Awareness* has been *fragmented*—redirected or set on automatic—and is not *Self-Determined* (meaning, not under our control).

In the earliest days of our *systemological research*, what is now generally known as "*systematic processing*" first started as "*Games Processing*." Although "*processing command-lines*" ("PCL") are often alternated to get the "*fragmented charge*" off of two opposing *considerations* (and/or alternated to better refocus and direct *attention*), the actual gains come from *processing-out* "*game-conditions*"; we aren't *defragmenting* "*truth*."

For example: the PCL "*what could you know?*" has quite limited workability; yet an individual improves on "*what could you not-know?*" Trying to educate or *process* toward states of *truth* directly doesn't seem to work. It is either not accepted fully, or the information itself is not enough to override the *considerations* of *untruth* that result from *agreements* and/or *actions* against our basic native state.

The *apparent* "seriousness" of *Life* only enters into *consideration* when we "forget" that we are *playing a game*. This does not mean to say, "It's all just a game; therefore, doesn't matter." But, it *matters* to the degree that we consider our experience of the *Game of Life* as *real*.

Whether we consider "*games*" as something to "*do*," or as a purely competitive activity, both tendencies seem to stem from *The Jewel of Knowledge* (at the "beginning" of our participation in *creation*). Even at upper-levels of *Beingness*, "*To Create*" is a "*doingness*" in order to "*have*" something. At the start of a *game-cycle*, even the *goal* "*To Be Godlike*" is an invented *purpose* or *game-condition*. It is a *decision* to achieve an invented *Beingness* in order to *create conditions*, or again, "*have*" something.

The *Alpha-Spirit*, to its own detriment, prefers to *have something* as opposed to *not-have something*. And in basic terms, it insists on "*having a game*." When we examine "*The Secret of Universes*" narrative in relation to *games theory*, we actually find all the components of "*games*" therein. These are important to know about directly, since they are the same components we are essentially *defragmenting* with *systematic processing*. Some of these *game-conditions* include:

• *Reality-agreements* serving as "*rules*" by which we share a *game-reality* and *communication* with others that are also sharing that *reality*;

• *Implanting* (or *conditioning*) of "*rules*" that develops into one's own *postulates*, ourselves convincing ourselves of the "*rules*," and that these are the only *rules/games* that *can be/must be played*;

• An inherent *obedience* to the "*rules*," and *penalties* for *disobedience* (for example, in *this Physical Universe*, "*pain*" and "*loss*");

• *Agreed-upon* (shared) "*barriers*" functioning as *limitations* imposed on *Self* and others;

• Permissible action or "*freedoms*," which (in *game* terms) are really dependent on "*barriers*" (in order to be *free of something*);

• *Perceived value* and *sense of ownership* of "*game pieces*" representing the *player* (a "*Body*" or otherwise), and in "*slavery-enforcement games*" this includes *perceived ownership* of "*other*" *pieces/players*;

• *Complex games* include various "*levels*" of *play* being "*won*," essentially *playing* to *win* the "*right*" to *play* more *games*, and as an "ultimate prize," the *right* to create "*new games*";

- A tendency to *need* a *"new game" created* before an *"old game"* ends;

- Eventual *decay* and *deterioration* of a *game*, particularly *games* that individuals didn't fully *(knowingly) agree* with.

The inherent "unhappiness" found in the *Human Condition* and *Physical Universe* stems from one's inability to freely leave a *game (Universe)* of one's own choosing. It has become quite difficult to fully *Self-Determine* one's own relocation to another *Universe (game)*. This *limitation* has been built into nearly all the *Penalty-Prison Universes* (see *AT Manual #1*) for quite some time.

Being *"trapped in games"* and being *"thrown out of games"* are both sources of *turbulent fragmentation* for an *Alpha-Spirit*. Yet, they continue to make *reality-agreements*—or else *spiritual contracts*—with *Universes (games)*. And as we know, at basic, the *Alpha-Spirit* is actually a quite *ethical being*. It doesn't like to "break" its own *contracts*. Therefore, having *agreed* to "do" something, going against this is *perceived* as a *denial-of-Self*.

GOALS & PURPOSES

To assert any *individuality (Beingness)* within a *game*, the *Alpha-Spirit* "invents" an "identity." If the *game* requires "bodies" (as a *playing piece*), then to *play* the *game* requires using a "*Body*." We remain in *this Game*, because we don't want to "break" our *agreements*. [Isn't that nice of us?] But more recent "*incarnations*" are quite brief in duration; and we *perceive* every *entry* and *exit* point of the *game* as ourselves "making" and "breaking" contractual *agreements*. This reduces *Self-Honesty* simply because of our previous *agreements*.

Even when we are unhappy with the *game*, we don't tend to completely *withdraw* or remove ourselves from *play*. However, we may start to *do* things that can get us expelled or exiled. Generally speaking: the *Alpha-Spirit* "agrees" (one way or another) to "*get in*" and then waits to be the *effect* of some other "determinative force" to kick them "*out*."

When we *systematically process* "*Games and Universes*" for *Alpha-Defragmentation*, we are most concerned with "spotting" where the *Alpha-Spirit* is most "*at Cause*." This means the "*entry incident*" or "*point of entry*" into a *game (Universe)*. *Alpha-Defragmentation* requires a *Seeker* "spotting" themselves *as* the *Alpha-Spirit* (a *Beingness*) at the start of, or when entering into, *agreements* with a *game* (*Universe*). This is the only way to actually "*contact*" the *postulates* (*decisions, &tc.*) made by the individual as they *were*; not as they *are now* after innumerable *game-cycles* in *this Physical Universe*. [*AT Manual #1* is intended to assist this.]

Goals-Implanting occurs during each *Entry-into-a-Universe incident*, then is reinforced again during one's "*between-lives*" periods. For the *Physical Universe*, we refer to this as the "*Heaven Incident*" or "*Heaven Implant.*" [See *AT Manual #1* and *PC Lesson-12*, "*Games & Universes.*"]

As a result of this *implanting*, each *basic goal* an individual has gets *systematically opposed* so that there is never a true *completed-cycle* (of *action* on the *goal*). When we get "tossed out" without *ending-a-cycle*, more *attention* gets *fixed* on it—we end up with a *fixated* and *fragmented purpose*. This also means less *Actualized Awareness* is applied to the *next cycle* of *actions, goals, roles, &tc.* There is a *systematic diminishing* of Self-Determinism the longer we *cycle through* without ever experiencing a *creation* or *goal* manifesting as *intended*.

An individual (*Alpha-Spirit*) does have their own *actual goals* and *basic purposes*; but the *consideration* of these in *present-time* is still heavily dependent on some (previously) *implanted* and *fragmented* "*game-conditions.*" An individual *decides* on their own "*sense of purpose*" in relation to the *game*; even where it concerns basic *personality-phases* and "*roles.*" For example: "*To Be a Mother*" is to engage in the *game of* "*Being Mother*" or "*Being Motherly.*" In one's *Home Universe*, there is no necessity that such a *concept* would even *exist*.

Residual elements of *Implanted Goals* for this *Universe* (actually originating in previous *Universes*) were discovered over a century ago by *Carl Jung*, which he spoke of benignly as "*archetypes.*" And to which, the world just said "*Oh, how cute.*" Our systematic research indicates that these "*archetypes*" are a bit more significant than simply an assortment of random universal cultural ideals and icons.

As a part of *upper-level* "*Game-Goals Processing*," a *Seeker* must rehabilitate their ability to *create/invent games/purposes* in the absence of *Implanted/fragmented Goals*—otherwise they are never *truly willing* to be *free* of them. When we apply "*creativeness processing*" techniques (*creating mental imagery* or *concepts*) to this area, a more effective/applicable PCL may be "*invent something...*" (rather than "*create...*")—which does not require a physical action, but simply the systematic *"invention"* of an *"idea,"* or perhaps, *"a game."*

> Part of the resistance to "stepping out" of the *Human Condition* and *this Physical Universe* is believing that there is nowhere else *to go* and nothing else *to do*.

Remedying this is critical for successfully *"crossing the abyss,"* because an individual only "midway" across may suddenly sense that there isn't any reason *to do* anything. This is only a conditioned *fear* and *anxiety* of *dissociating* with any *personal identification* with *this Physical Universe*. It is rather like an "old cartoon" where the character can run off a ledge and defy gravity, but then falls only after they have *postulated* that there is *nothing there*.

The basis for *solidity* of any *Universe* (or *game*) is suspended in place simply by holding two *convictions* equally and simultaneously: *"that there is something there"* and *"that there is nothing there."* An individual can maintain simple *goals* without *fragmentation*. The problems occur when an *energetic-mass* (or *mental-mass*) accumulates as a result of an *Implanted-Goal* and its *Implanted-Opposition* forcefully *"colliding."*

Where a *goal* is concerned, the individual *invents* a *Beingness*, which is the *"terminal"* used *to do* that *goal*. A lot of our *fragmentation* concerns the *"terminals"* and *"symbols"* that we *identify* with certain things. In the *"Heaven Implant,"* there is a *"terminal"* (a *"godlike being"*) representing the *Implanted-Goal "To Be Godlike."* We are then shown that *terminal* being opposed by another *terminal* (a *"free being"*) representing the next goal on the *chain/series*.

This sequence immediately sets us up for *fragmentation* whenever the *Implanted-Goal "To Be Godlike"* aligns with our own *actual goal* that is being *dramatized* during a particular *cycle* of *"lifetimes."* It also sets up the *fragmentation* for the "next person" to be directly *opposed* to us when, for example, the *Free Being* (*terminal*) encounters the *Godlike Being* (*terminal*). And as we have learned in our *systemology*, the *residual effects* of this continue to *fragment* our later *considerations* with *energetic-turbulence* associated with these *terminals*.

Part of our *entrapment* in *this Game* is the *fixation* on the *Implanted-Goals*. In this case, an individual might choose one kind of *terminal* to pursue a specific *goal*; then failing at that when getting *opposed*, they will *alter* their chosen *terminal* and try again—still pursuing the same *goal*. Eventually, after several cycles of this, the *goal* becomes quite *fragmented* and essentially "*collapses*" under the weight of its accumulated *energetic-mass*; at which point the individual generally takes up the *next goal* in the *series* in an attempt to solve the problems encountered with the *first goal*. And we have all likely been through several *cycles* of the *entire sequence-chain*; but each time experiencing an even further reduction in *Self-Determinism* and *Awareness*.

One's *Actual Goals* that align with *Implanted-Goals* typically represent positive characteristics. In the "*Heaven Implant*," for example: *terminals* representing "*To Be Holy*" are *opposed* by *terminals* with the *goal* "To be

IMPLANTED GOAL-SEQUENCING

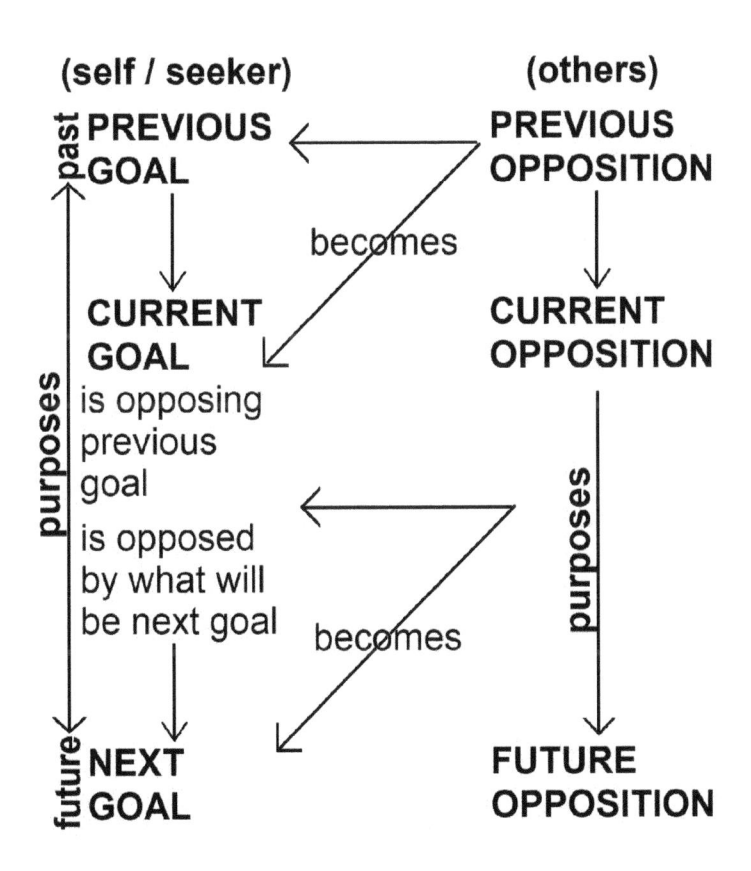

(self / seeker)   **(others)**

past ↑ **PREVIOUS GOAL** ← **PREVIOUS OPPOSITION**

↓   becomes   ↓

CURRENT GOAL ← **CURRENT OPPOSITION**

purposes — is opposing previous goal

is opposed by what will be next goal   ←   becomes   purposes

↓ ↓   ↓

future ↓ **NEXT GOAL**   **FUTURE OPPOSITION**

Intelligent." This is the whole root of "*religion*" being *opposed by* the "*sciences*" in our world. But more importantly, the *actual* qualities of "*holiness*" and "*intelligence*" are not "*negative*"—nor are they *actually* "*opposite*" one another. The *Implant* also *fragments* the *free consideration* to be both simultaneously.

While you may uncover "*fragmented purposes*" attached to the activity previously described, it is important to note that you will *not* find a "*negative goal*" at the top of any cycle. The purpose of the *implanted-opposition* is because "*negative goals*" never *implant* directly; they are more easily rejected. Therefore, the *trap* is set to *fragment* our *actual goals*, and it relies on our resulting *fragmented considerations* to further *entrap* us. It

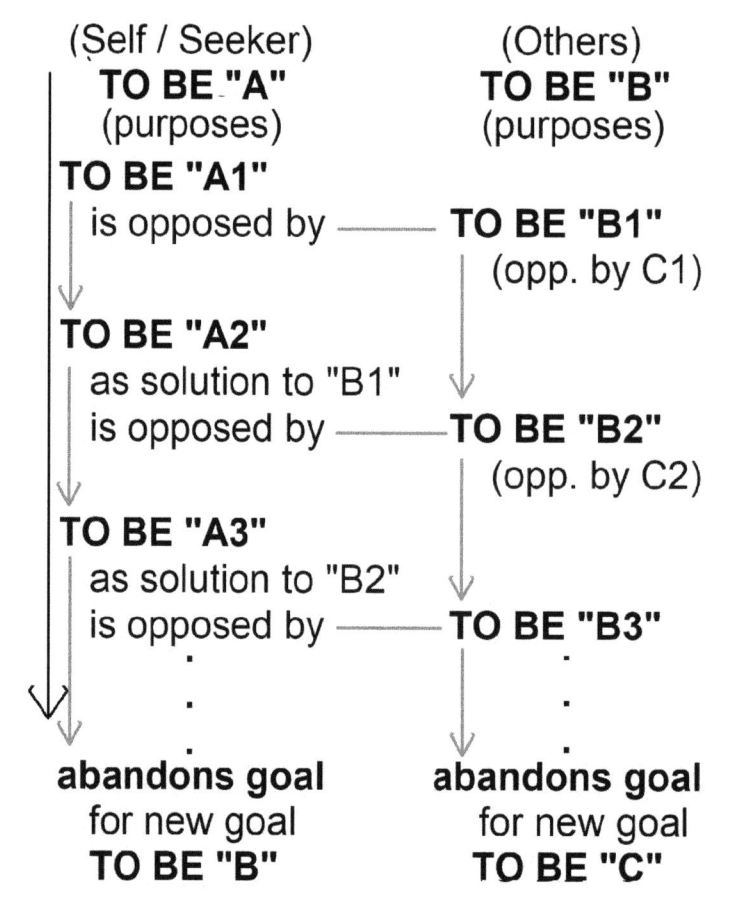

Univ. Game
TO SURVIVE (is...)

(Self / Seeker)	(Others)
TO BE "A" (purposes)	**TO BE "B"** (purposes)
TO BE "A1" is opposed by ———	**TO BE "B1"** (opp. by C1)
TO BE "A2" as solution to "B1" is opposed by ———	**TO BE "B2"** (opp. by C2)
TO BE "A3" as solution to "B2" is opposed by ———	**TO BE "B3"**
. . .	. . .
abandons goal for new goal **TO BE "B"**	**abandons goal** for new goal **TO BE "C"**

is always our own *creations* and *postulates* that ultimately have the ability to affect us in the end.

Alpha-Defragmentation is intended to remove the *energetic-mass* while retaining the positive characteristics. In earlier *processing-levels*, *Beta-Defragmentation* pertained to *"spotting" Self* as *identified* with something or other in *this lifetime*—handling a *Seeker* as they perceive their *goals* and *roles* today. Whatever is treated at those *levels*, it does not get to the *"root"* of the *game* that we've played at for countless sequential lifetimes.

An individual's *invented purpose* or *actual intention* may not be worded exactly as found in our presentation of the *"Heaven Implant" Goals-Sequence*. For example: *"To Be a Librarian"* is not listed there; but such is a specific *terminal* with a specific *purpose*, and of which might really represent the *goal "To Be Intelligent."* Running the *"Heaven Implant"* by itself does not actually *release* you from all *goals-fragmentation*, but it does take enough "weight" off of the area in order to *spot* one's *actual goal* and how it might get *misaligned*.

The proper *end-point* of *Systemology Level-3* (PC Lesson-8, *"Conquest of Illusion"*) is when a *Seeker* has *spotted* their primary *"justification consideration"* (for *this lifetime*). This is part of what an individual believes will help themselves *survive* (in the *game*) by making others wrong. What was revealed during *Level-3* may, or may not, be attached to the *actual goal* that an individual is presently *pursuing* or *dramatizing*.

The original *goal* may also have deteriorated by this point. Whatever *terminals* or *personality-phases* are treated for *this lifetime* may not be the *terminal* at the "top" of the cycle specific to their *actual goal*. This is important to determine correctly in order to *defragment* the precise "chain" or sequence that has brought a *Seeker* to their present state. [The point to "spot" is when one originally *decided* on the *actual goal*.]

A thing to remember about these *Implants*: *fragmented charge* on a *Goals-series* or *terminal-item* is not directly from the *Implanting-Incident* itself (which is really more of a persuasive suggestion). This is why *running* the "incident" itself, or an "implant-platform" (a list of "command-items"), does not provide total *defragmentation*. The significant source of *fragmentation* is connected to *Harmful-Acts* (a *dramatization* of *fragmented purposes*) associated with our fight against others when following the pattern-sequence of the *Implanted-Goals* series.

The primary *implanted-purpose* behind *the Game* of *this Physical Universe* is *"To Survive."* This too is at the tail end of a long sequence-chain of *goals* once attached to former *Universes* (versions of *Beta-Existence*). For example, in the *"Magic Universe,"* the primary *implanted-purpose* was/is *"To Enjoy."* However, in *this Physical Universe*, we find in the *"Heaven Implant"* (*entry-point*) that our *purpose* is *"To Survive"* and that this is achieved by *being* "such-and-such." And, of course, each *Implanted-Goal* (in the *series*) is attached to the primary *Games-Universe Goal*; so each is presented as equally *being* the *only* way *"To Survive."* And each is presented as both *opposing* and *being opposed by* one another. This literal *"mass of confusion"* is what sets up the *fragmented game* of *this Beta-Existence*.

GOALS-BACKTRACKING BY OPPOSITION
(EXAMPLE ONLY)

(Self)　　　　　(Another / Others)
TO BE INTELLIGENT　**TO BE STRONG**
opposing previous
goal "To Be Holy"

A Scientist
　　is opposed by . . . **A Statesman**

A Teacher
　　is opposed by . . . **A Warlord**

An Archaeologist
　　is opposed by . . . **A Vandal-Thief**

A Librarian
　　is opposed by . . . **A Book-Burner**

A Writer
　　is opposed by . . . **A Censor**

A Critic
goal decays
abdandoned for new goal

↓

TO BE STRONG

DEFRAGMENTING GOALS TERMINALS

Our *advanced procedure* for "*Goals Processing*" is actually a streamlined combination of *all* the techniques and methods that a *Seeker* learned and practiced during the "*Pathway to Ascension*" *Professional Course*. [That material should be kept nearby for easy reference to ensure that *systematic* use of each *process* (below) is fully understood and properly *run*.]

At this *level*—and because we have a narrow target—fewer *processes* are required of each type. [A *biofeedback device* may be used (if available) to ensure *turbulent charge* is fully *defragmented* for each *process* before *running* the next one.] The real determinant factor of success is the amount (or level) of *Actualized Awareness* and *ability-to-confront* a *Seeker* can apply to these *processing sessions*.

It is likely to take several *sessions* to complete a single pass through this *procedure* on a single *goal* (making certain to resume each *session* precisely where the last one left off). The *procedure* provides the greatest *effect* or *release* when applied to one's *actual goal*. But, it may be applied to *any goal*. In fact, an *advanced Seeker* can benefit strongly from *processing* the entire *goals-sequence* in this wise, taking each *goal* in turn.

The approximate *goal-sequencing* from the "*Heaven Implant*" (in descending order) is: *To Be Godlike; To Be Free; To Be Responsible; To Be Creative; To Be Important; To Be Competent; To Be Famous; To Be Perceptive; To Be Energetic; To Be Meticulous; To Be Successful; To Be Right (Accurate); To Be Popular; To Be Skillful; To Be Wise; To Be Beautiful; To Be Productive; To Be Powerful; To Be Holy; To Be Intelligent; To Be Strong; To Be Crafty; To Be Brave; To Be Wealthy; To Be Independent; To Be Good; To Be Adventurous; To Be Orderly; To Be Different; To Be Respected; To Be Happy; To Be Acquisitive (Acquire); To Be Sensual; To Be Domineering; To Be Tough;* and *To Be Enduring*. [The sequence cycles repeatedly from the top; *Enduring People* in opposition to *Godlike Beings*.]

To standardize alternating-PCL (when treating "*circuits*") for this *procedure*, the general *terminals* are: "*you*" (meaning *Self*), "*another*" (meaning specific individuals singularly), and "*others*" (meaning groups or society). The *circuits* include: "*out-flow*" (*you* projecting to *another* or *others*), "*in-flow*" (*you* receiving from *another* or *others*), and "*cross-flow*" (*you* perceiving the interaction of *others*).

This *procedure* is intended to remove enough layers of *fragmentation* whereby a *Seeker* is able to regain clearer *recall* and *understanding* of the track that led to the present. It is only when we can *"spot"* ourselves (as the *Alpha-Spirit*) as we were at the time of making various *postulates* and specific *decisions* that we are able to fully erase the effects of an *Implant*.

An *incident* or *Implant* itself is not really what we *defragment* with *systematic processing*, but instead, the *point* in which we *actually decided* (at *Cause*) to allow it to affect us—and our later *considerations* and *actions*, &tc. Once enough layers of *fragmented perception/consideration* are removed, clearly *"spotting"* this *point* (with full *Awareness*) and the *actual decision/postulate* we made, is the only *systematic* way to be *free* of it. We are, in essence, taking back *control* of our *Self-Determination* once we can be certain of what *Self* has *determined*.

SECTION 1: DEFRAGMENTATION
(*Standard Procedure— "Goals"*)

A : OBJECTIVE EXERCISES

A *goal/purpose* deteriorates the longer an individual pursues it because they "project" (*put, place, create*) more characteristics of *opposition* into others. If the *goal* is *"To Be Intelligent,"* than they tend to *consider* others *"to be stupid"* —and will even *create conditions* where this may be proven true.

• *Go to a public place. Spot individual people and postulate the positive characteristic (or ability) of the goal into each one.* [If the *goal* is *"To Be Beautiful,"* then *decide* that each individual is filled with, and emanating, *beauty* and *imagine* them as *"being beautiful."*]

• *Go to a public place. Spot individual people and spot some remaining bit of the positive characteristic (or ability) in each one; validate (acknowledge) it is there and encourage it.* [This is done by *intention* (*telepathically*) and does not require verbal communication. The positive characteristic is a basic goal of *Beingness* in this *game* and it is present in everyone, however decayed it may now appear. Recognize this *spark* that remains present and direct your *attention/intention* to complete the exercise.]

B : POSITIVE RECALL

Attention on the positive (or pleasurable) characteristic of something tends to assist with handling or *confronting* the upsets and difficulties that represent its negative side. We are most *"at Cause"* when first *deciding* on a *goal*, or when initially experiencing its upper-level manifestation before it deteriorated. *Spotting* these *points* helps improve *processing* the "other side" of things—assisting one to handle *turbulence* in later *processes*. Note that if the *goal* has strongly decayed, these *points* may not be found within the present lifetime. [Insert the *ability* (intelligence, beauty, &tc.) into the PCL.]

1. "Recall being ___."
2. "Recall another being ___."
3. "Recall others being ___."

C : RECALL (FLOW-FACTORS)

This is an extension of the previous step, with *four* similar *processes* involving the *"Flow-Factors"*—see *PC Lesson-7, "Eliminating Barriers."* Each *process* (of six alternating-PCL) is *run* separately. Using these various *circuits* and *factors* helps a *Seeker* get an "exterior viewpoint" on the *goals* and *terminals*. [Insert a *terminal* representing the *goal* (an intelligent person, a beautiful person, &tc.) into the PCL.]

Communication Process

1. "Recall a time you were in good communication with a(n) ___."
2. "Recall a time a(n) ___ was in good communication with you."
3. "Recall a time another was in good communication with a(n) ___."
4. "Recall a time a(n) ___ was in good communication with another."
5. "Recall a time others were in good communication with a(n) ___."
6. "Recall a time a(n) ___ was in good communication with others."

Likingness Process

1. "Recall a time you liked a(n) ___."
2. "Recall a time a(n) ___ liked you."
3. "Recall a time another liked a(n) ___."
4. "Recall a time a(n) ___ liked another."
5. "Recall a time others liked a(n) ___."
6. "Recall a time a(n) ___ liked others."

Agreement Process

1. "Recall a time you agreed with a(n) ___."
2. "Recall a time a(n) ___ agreed with you."
3. "Recall a time another agreed with a(n) ___."
4. "Recall a time a(n) ___ agreed with another."
5. "Recall a time others agreed with a(n) ___."
6. "Recall a time a(n) ___ agreed with others."

Understanding Process

1. "Recall a time you understood a(n) ___."
2. "Recall a time a(n) ___ understood you."
3. "Recall a time another understood a(n) ___."
4. "Recall a time a(n) ___ understood another."
5. "Recall a time others understood a(n) ___."
6. "Recall a time a(n) ___ understood others."

D : COMMUNICATION

Defragmenting "*communication-flows*" assists a *Seeker* in "*eliminating barriers*" of *existence*. For this *process*, focus on positive interaction. Effectiveness of this is found in sheer quantity. *Imagine* "saying" many things, about anything, so long as there is a *flow*. [These are alternating-PCL using a *terminal*.]

1. "Imagine saying specific things to a(n) ___."
2. "Imagine a(n) ___ saying specific things to you."
3. "Imagine another saying specific things to a(n) ___."
4. "Imagine a(n) ___ saying specific things to another."
5. "Imagine others saying specific things to a(n) ___."
6. "Imagine a(n) ___ saying specific things to others."

E : HELP

Accumulated "*failure*" to *help others* contributes to deterioration of a *goal*. We are conditioned to take "*failure*" very seriously—and too often it is *perceived* to "outweigh" those times when we were *successful* at *helping others*. If a present *goal* has heavily "collapsed" (at the end of its cycle), then an individual must *spot* the *successes* much earlier on the *Backtrack*. If that *recall* isn't accessible, even the smallest *successes* in *this lifetime* may be *recalled* in place of the earlier positive activity that has not yet *resurfaced*.

1. "Recall a time you helped a(n) ___."
2. "Recall a time a(n) ___ helped you."
3. "Recall a time another helped a(n) ___."
4. "Recall a time a(n) ___ helped another."
5. "Recall a time others helped a(n) ___."
6. "Recall a time a(n) ___ helped others."

F : PROTECTING

This is an extension of the previous step. *Fragmentation* connected to *"failure to protect"* is similar to, but tends to be more *turbulent* than, "failure to help." The concepts of *"love and loss"* and *"trust and betrayal"* also fall under this category. The negative side of these areas cannot be *processed-out* using *"basic analytical recall"* directly. That just validates the negative misemotion. However, *basic recall* may be used to validate the positive *"successful"* side (increasing one's *Awareness*) prior to treating anything more *turbulent*.

1. "Recall a time you protected a(n) ___."
2. "Recall a time a(n) ___ protected you."
3. "Recall a time another protected a(n) ___."
4. "Recall a time a(n) ___ protected another."
5. "Recall a time others protected a(n) ___."
6. "Recall a time a(n) ___ protected others."

G : PROBLEMS/SOLUTIONS

When an individual *solves* a *problem*, they tend to treat that *solution* as an *absolute*. It becomes *The Solution* to all, even when it no longer really applies or is relevant. Unfortunately, living this way only gets the person into more *problems*. And as the *"old solution"* continues being applied (and *failing*), these *problems* tend to stack up (as accumulated *imprinting*).

The same pattern is found in deterioration of a *goals-chain*. An individual starts off with a particular *goal* at the top of whatever cycle it happens to be; and when meeting opposition, that *goal* is *altered* in order to sustain it, until it is *perceived* as no longer sustainable. Each of those *alterations* were "*solutions*" to a specific "*problem*," yet they remained on the *chain* thereafter, serving to affect the *consideration* of future *terminals* used for the *goal*.

In brief: after *opposition* occurs, and we *alter* our *character* to *solve* a "present" *problem*, we never return to the point of when we originally had the *goal*. The *alterations* are kept in place to continue to *solve* whatever future *problems* occur; and *failing* in that, additional layers of *alteration* are then added sequentially, but never removed. This is what we consider *fragmentation*. And this is how a *goal* decays.

The technique applied here requires *spotting a problem*, and then *spotting solutions* (one, or as many as easily come up); then *spot another problem* and its *solutions*, and so on. Ideally, a *Seeker* will *spot* earlier and earlier *problems* on the *Backtrack*, and also *solutions* that are still held in place, but no longer appropriate. It is okay if *attention* returns to more recent *problems/solutions* in between. Just keep handling whatever comes up to a satisfactory *end-point* of "feeling better" (or "clearer") about the *terminal* and its *goal*.

This practice is intricate enough that each *circuit-flow* (pair of PCL) is best *run* as its own *process*. [For *Solo-Piloting*: repeat the *solutions*-PCL as many times as necessary for a single *problem*. For *Co-Piloting*: alternate the PCL.]

1A. "What problem might a(n) ___ have with another or others?"
1B. "What solutions might a(n) ___ have to that problem?"

2A. "What problem might another (or others) have with a(n) ___?"
2B. "What solutions might they have to that problem?"

3A. "What problem might a(n) ___ observe between others?"
3B. "What solution might a(n) ___ have to their problem?"

4A. "What problem might a(n) ___ create for themselves?"
4B. "What solutions might a(n) ___ have to that problem?"

H : HARMFUL-ACTS/HOLD-BACKS

Here we directly *process* the *Seeker* "at Cause." An individual will *do* things, then hide what's been done, and gradually *withdraw* from the related area. It doesn't matter whether it was from *ill-intention* or the *best of intention gone wrong*. Eventually, this *fragmentation* accumulates to a point where the individual *holds-back* from *doing* things, and *holds-out* on *communication* and *contact* with their *environment* — *others, Universe, &tc.*

This *processing* technique simply requires a *Seeker* actually *confront* what they *have done*. This is an important part of regaining the *"responsibility"* for *"doing"* things—which is how we regain *"ability"* to *"do"* things. Here we are only concerned with the *doingness*; not any *ethical judgments*. This technique does not even require that the *"done"* things be *Harmful-Acts*.

Harmful-Acts are the primary target of the technique, but this area shouldn't be forced or pushed in any way. They should naturally *resurface* as a part of the *processing*.

Our desirable *goals* often become *fragmented* in such a way that maintaining them and *solving a problem* or *resolving a confusion* has caused us to act with *"ill-intent."* These "fixed ideas" we establish for handling *problems* and *confusions* develop into compulsive *"fixated purposes."* However, many promising *Seekers* have "spun in to oblivion" by placing too much emphasis and attention on directly uncovering *"evil intentions."*

As with the previous step, each *circuit-flow* (pair of PCL) is best *run* as its own *process*. The alternating-PCL target *doingness* and *hold-backs*. We use the word *"might"* to allow a wider range of *consideration*, and also so a *Seeker* does not feel "attacked"—as with the more direct PCL: *"What have you done?"* [For *Alpha-Defragmentation*: this technique is quite useful for also treating *oppositional terminals* of *future-goals* and *past-goals* during later applications of this *Standard Procedure for Goals*.]

1A. "What might a(n) ___ do to another?"
1B. "What might a(n) ___ hold-back from another?"
2A. "What might another do to a(n) ___?"
2B. "What might another hold-back from a(n) ___?"
3A. "What might a(n) ___ do to others?"
3B. "What might a(n) ___ hold-back from others?"
4A. "What might a(n) ___ do to themselves?"
4B. "What might a(n) ___ hold-back from themselves?"
5A. "What might you do to a(n) ___?"
5B. "What might you hold-back from a(n) ___?"

I : CHANGE

If an individual is *unwilling* to *change*, then they can't improve. *"Getting better"* is a *change* in *condition*. Both *insistence on*, and *resistance to*, "change," is *fragmentation*. It inspires *harmful-acts* and incites *upsets* and *problems* between individuals.

Generally speaking, the *"identities"* (*role-terminals*) we use (that are attached to our *goals-chain*) are chosen as a *fixed solution* to a specific *perceived "problem of livingness."* An individual is *resistant to* changing *fixed ideas*, even when doing so would provide a better *"condition of livingness."* [Run these *processes* like the previous step.]

1A. "What might a(n) ___ want to change about another?"
1B. "What might a(n) ___ prevent changing about another?"

2A. "What might another want to change about a(n) ___?"
2B. "What might another prevent changing about a(n) ___?"

3A. "What might a(n) ___ want to change about others?"
3B. "What might a(n) ___ prevent changing about others?"

4A. "What might a(n) ___ want to change about themselves?"
4B. "What might a(n) ___ prevent changing about themselves?"

5A. "What might you want to change about a(n) ___?"
5B. "What might you prevent changing about a(n) ___?"

J : UPSETS (FLOW-FACTOR BREAKS)

Personal *turbulence* (and *upsets* between *terminals*) happens whenever one of the *flow-factors*—*communication*, *likingness*, and *agreement*—are either *"inhibited"* or *"enforced."* And, since *Buddha* so aptly stated that *"all suffering comes from desire,"* we may as well add *"desire"* [*"desired"*] to this list of "buttons" too. [To clarify for *upper-level processing*: by *"agreement,"* we also mean *"reality."*]

When a *"break"* in a *flow* occurs, the *"reaction"* is generally more extreme (turbulent) than the situation calls for. This is due to accumulated *fragmentation* of the *flow* (from many *earlier similar incidents*). For *systematic processing*: when a *Seeker* "spots" the moment they became *upset* and the exact *flow-factors* involved, some relief is gained. If they can work back to "spotting" earlier *upsets* of the same *flow-factors*, an increased level of *Awareness* and *ability-to-confront* is gained for that area. [Complete *Alpha-Defragmentation* occurs from "spotting" the *earliest* time or very first incident (presumably in other *lifetimes* in other *Universes*). To treat *"Home Universe"* (or prior), *"not-know"* would be required on the list of "buttons."]

AT#2 – 75

For this procedure: we are not *processing* a specific *upset*, but instead are treating all of the *flow-factors* with a specific *terminal*. Each *process* consists of *five* alternating-PCL. Ideally, a *Seeker* will uncover "earlier" or "deeper" data as they cycle through the PCL repeatedly for a single *process*.

Communication—Inhibited

1. "What communication might a(n) ___ inhibit in another?"
2. "What communication might another inhibit in a(n) ___?"
3. "What communication might a(n) ___ inhibit in others?"
4. "What communication might a(n) ___ inhibit themselves from saying?"
5. "What communication might you inhibit a(n) ___ from saying?"

Communication—Enforced

1. "What communication might a(n) ___ enforce on another?"
2. "What communication might another enforce on a(n) ___?"
3. "What communication might a(n) ___ enforce on others?"
4. "What communication might a(n) ___ force on themselves?"
5. "What communication might you force on a(n) ___?"

Communication—Desired

1. "What communication might a(n) ___ desire from another?"
2. "What communication might another desire from a(n) ___?"
3. "What communication might a(n) ___ desire from others?"
4. "What communication might a(n) ___ make themselves desire?"
5. "What communication might you desire from a(n) ___?"

Likingness—Inhibited

1. "What might a(n) ___ inhibit another from liking?"
2. "What might another inhibit a(n) ___ from liking?"
3. "What might a(n) ___ inhibit others from liking?"
4. "What might a(n) ___ inhibit themselves from liking?"
5. "What might you inhibit a(n) ___ from liking?"

Likingness—Enforced

1. "What might a(n) ___ enforce another to like?"
2. "What might another enforce a(n) ___ to like?"

3. "What might a(n) ___ enforce others to like?"
4. "What might a(n) ___ force themselves to like?"
5. "What might you force a(n) ___ to like?"

Likingness—Desired

1. "What likingness might a(n) ___ desire from another?"
2. "What likingness might another desire from a(n) ___?"
3. "What likingness might a(n) ___ desire from others?"
4. "What likingness might a(n) ___ make themselves desire?"
5. "What likingness might you desire from a(n) ___?"

Agreement—Inhibited/Rejected

1. "What agreement might a(n) ___ reject from another?"
2. "What agreement might another reject from a(n) ___?"
3. "What agreement might a(n) ___ reject from others?"
4. "What agreement might a(n) ___ make themselves reject?"
5. "What agreement might you reject from a(n) ___ ?"

Agreement—Enforced

1. "What agreement might a(n) ___ enforce on another?"
2. "What agreement might another enforce on a(n) ___?"
3. "What agreement might a(n) ___ enforce on others?"
4. "What agreement might a(n) ___ force on themselves?"
5. "What agreement might you force on a(n) ___?"

Agreement—Desired

1. "What agreement might a(n) ___ desire from another?"
2. "What agreement might another desire from a(n) ___?"
3. "What agreement might a(n) ___ desire from others?"
4. "What agreement might a(n) ___ make themselves desire?"
5. "What agreement might you desire from a(n) ___?"

K : JUSTIFICATION CONSIDERATIONS

The Game of *this Physical Universe* is *"To Survive."* Unfortunately, most of an individual's *considerations, thought-activity,* and *actions,* all stem from this premise. While *fixedly trapped* in *considerations "To Survive,"* an individual will allow themselves to commit *harmful-acts* and then bury their memory and responsibility under heavy layers of *fragmented justification*.

The following *process* contains *four* PCL that are cycled repeatedly; however, several "*B-responses*" may be derived from each "*A-question.*" All *four* PCL should be run in *series* as a single *process*.

1A. "*What would a(n) ___ do to ensure their survival?*"
1B. "*What justifications would they have for that?*"
2A. "*What would a(n) ___ stop others from doing, to ensure their own survival?*"
2B. "*What justifications would they have for that?*"

We want to *defragment* the precise *consideration* that is used to *justify*/make others wrong. To find this, we *defragment* some of the "*possible*" *considerations* on that line before selecting one to *process*. [These alternating-PCL are run repetitively.]

1. "*How might a(n) ___ make themselves right?*"
2. "*How might a(n) ___ make others wrong?*"

The next *processing*-PCL for this procedure is more direct and it requires listing-out answers; but the intent is finding *a specific answer*. The direct PCL is:

"*What would a(n) ___ use to make others wrong?*"

By this, we generally mean an "*excuse*" (or *justification*) in the form of a "*They're all...*" or "*Everyone else is...*" answer. Ideally, this type of listing technique would be performed using a *biofeedback device* in order to *spot* the answer that "*reads*" on a *GSR-Meter*. Alternative directions for this *process* are found in *PC Lesson-8*. [Unlike its treatment in *Systemology Level-3*, we do not restrict this PCL to "*In this lifetime.*"] If the above PCL *does not* produce the *basic answer* in the style-form described, list from the following:

"*From the viewpoint of a(n) ___, what is it about people that makes them so wrong?*"

Using the most correct *basic answer* found, *run* the following alternating-PCL. The *end-point* should include *defragmentation* of any *fixed* or *turbulent considerations* connected with the *goals-terminal*. [Even when it is not a *Seeker's present-goal* or *actual-goal*, there is usually some *energetic-mass* "entangled" with the *justification considerations* of *terminals* for other *goals*.]

1. *"How would {answer} make others wrong?"*
2. *"How would {answer} make a(n) ___ right?"*

L : EXTERIOR VIEWPOINTS

Ultimately, the *processing-goal* is for a *Seeker* to get *"exterior to"* the *energetic-mass* or *fixed condition* that they are compulsively *"inside of"* (as a *viewpoint*). *Fragmentation* is best handled from *"the outside."* As a final step to Section-1, *run* the following PCL in cycles to a satisfactory *endpoint*.

1. *"From where could you communicate to a(n) ___?"*
2. *"From where could a(n) ___ communicate to you?"*
3. *"From where could a(n) ___ communicate to others?"*
4. *"From where could a(n) ___ communicate to themselves?"*

SECTION 2: GOAL-SEQUENCING
(For defrag and research processing)

Advanced Training materials—our *upper-level Ascension Technology*—resulted from many years of experimental *research-processing*. This was conducted by *Self-Honest* individuals that had completed our earliest presentations of *Beta-Defragmentation Procedure*. [Referring to the *Systemology Core Research Volumes*.]

Some of these *research-methods* run parallel with workable *defragmentation-methods*, as given in these next two sections. [*Biofeedback Devices* were also used to compile data from each *Seeker* that could then be comparatively examined in relation to additional research from "outside sources."]

Advisement: the *"Implanted Goal-Sequence"* of the *"Heaven Incident"* is only a *strongly implanted suggestion*; a *Seeker's* own *"sequence"* may differ slightly. [Hence we use this standard procedure for *Level-7 processing*.]

A : BASIC OPPOSITION

Once a *goal-terminal* is *defragmented* with Section-1, sufficient *charge* will also have been taken off *considerations* of an *oppositional goal-terminal* so that it can be *processed* directly. For every *goal-terminal*, there will be a *basic opposite* to it. For example: for the *goal* "To Be Intelligent," the *basic opposite* (as a *terminal*) is *"stupid people"* or *"a stupid person."*

Because the *Implanted Goal-Sequencing* is patterned the way it is, there is technically *"opposition"* on *"both sides"* of an *Implanted Goal*. By this we mean both the *previous-goal* and the *next-goal* in the *sequence*. We want to spot the *characteristic* of the *basic opposite* for the present *goal*—such as "a stupid person."

It is only due to *fragmentation* that its *consideration* is applied to *terminals* representing a *former* or *future sequential-goal*; in this example, associating the *characteristic* of "stupidity" with "To Be Strong" (*next goal*) and/or "To Be Holy" (*previous goal*). [Any *fragmented cross-consideration* of this kind connected to *Implanted Goals* must be *processed-out* for total *Alpha-Defragmentation*.]

To be systematic, the direct PCL for producing the *basic opposite* requires *listing* (most of Section-2 does), preferably with a *biofeedback device*.

"What type of people would a(n) ___ oppose?"

If this isn't listed properly, it can result in misappropriating the *characteristic* on the *previous goal-terminal*; such as "*stupid holy people.*" If the above PCL *does not* produce the *basic opposite*, list from the following (but being certain not to misappropriate the *characteristic* onto the *next goal-terminal*, such as "*stupid strong people*"):

"What type of people would a(n) ___ be opposed by?"

If neither PCL seems to produce a *basic answer* directly, look for a common characteristic between the two lists; in this example, again, "*stupid people.*"

B : <u>OPPOSITION TERMINAL</u>

The original *goal-terminal* and its *basic opposition* (from Step-A) are used for this *process*. The PCL is printed here with the words "*terminal*" and "*opposition*" appearing in *brackets*. In the example we have been using: "*an intelligent person*" or "*intelligent people*" is the *goal-terminal*; and "*a stupid person*" or "*stupid people*" is the *opposition*. This *series* of *eight* PCL are cycled to a satisfactory *end-point*.

1. "What action or attitude would {opposition} have towards {terminal}?"
2. "What action or attitude would {terminal} have towards {opposition}?"
3. "What action or attitude would {terminal} have towards others?"
4. "What action or attitude would others have towards {terminal}?"

5. *"What action or attitude would {opposition} have towards others?"*
6. *"What action or attitude would others have towards {opposition}?"*
7. *"What action or attitude would {opposition} hold-back from {terminal}?"*
8. *"What action or attitude would {terminal} hold-back from {opposition}?"*

C : FINDING THE NEXT GOAL

Because a *Seeker* generally works *"backwards"* up the *goals-chain* that has led to the present, when a *previous goal* is *run*, the later one (*current goal*) has already been handled. But, when *running* the *"current"* goal, you might not know what the *next/future goal* is going to be. Of course, this might be obvious as a result of previous *processing*, or from the *Implanted Goal-Sequencing* (from the *"Heaven Implant"*) — but the *Goal-Sequence* in that *Implant* is only a *"strong suggestion"* or *"guideline"* that sets up a *pattern*. This means your own actual *goals-postulates* may differ slightly from that exact *sequence*.

Within each primary *goal*, there is also a *chain* of its deterioration. This is how we cycle from one *goal* to the next over the course of various life-times; starting up *"at the top"* of a *goal* with full vigor, and then moving *"downward"* as we struggle with it and *alter* it in the face of *opposition*. Usually *"at the top"* there is not much contact with *opposition* or the *next goal* of the *sequence*. In that case, you might skip over treating it since there is no real *turbulence* to *process-out*. But, if you are already going *"out the bottom"* of your *current goal*, then there may already be some serious *harmful-acts* and *hold-backs* stacking up on the *next goal*.

This *listing*-PCL is:

"What goal would successfully oppose the {current goal}?"

This could be restated in many ways. You could also word it to *list* for the *next oppositional terminal* as:

"What type of person would successfully oppose a(n) {current goal terminal}?"
  –or–
"What type of person would be dangerous to a(n) ___ ?"

Once you have *The Goal* (or a *basic characteristic*), you can find that *basic goal-terminal* by *listing*:

"Who or what would want {goal}?"

If you have a *terminal*, you can verify the *basic goal* by *listing*:

"What goal would a(n) ___ have?"

To ascertain one's own *goal-sequencing*, a *Seeker* will work around a bit, using a number of these types of PCL (such as given here in Section-2) until they are satisfied that answers all logically fit together. [This is all not as complicated to handle as it might seem at first glace, it is simply a very systematic way to recover precise data for *processing* precise targets.]

When you have finished this step, a *Seeker* should have discovered the *next goal* and its *terminal* (which is the *future oppositional terminal* of the *current goal*). It may be that there is no *future oppositional terminal* in view yet. [When handling *earlier/previous goals*, you will already know the answers to these PCL, so you simply use steps such as this (with a *biofeedback device*, if available) to check over the data and make sure it is correct.]

D : FUTURE OPPOSITION (TERMINAL)

For this part, use the same *process* given in Step-B. This time, insert the *future oppositional terminal* in the "*{opposition}*" bracket. When handling one's actual *current-goal*, there may not be much *turbulent fragmentation* connected to this area.

However, if a *Seeker* is nearing an *end-cycle* on their *current goal*, there will often be many *hold-backs* and *harmful-acts* against what represents the next "*goals-package*" that is in a *Seeker's future*. [If it seems necessary, other *processes* (such as those in the *PC lessons*, of which Section-1 is based on) may be applied to reduce the *turbulence*.]

When using a *biofeedback device*: there is a phenomenon where the "*needle*" of a *GSR-Meter* may behave *violently* or *turbulently*—and even "*slam*" against the "*posts*" at either end. Assuming this is not caused by a *Seeker* wearing something *metallic* (like a *ring*)—or touching/shorting *two electrodes* together (which you shouldn't do)—this *usually* means a *terminal* (or *area*) has been *contacted* (*in processing*) that a *Seeker* has quite significant *harmful-act/hold-outs* (*fragmentation*) stacked up against.

When not using a *biofeedback device*: the indicator for the same (above) is an increased sense of "*hatred*" or "*evil intent*" toward the *future oppositional terminal*. This same indicator may be found in regard to one's own *current-goal* or *previous-goals* or really any *area* that is treated in *processing*.

In either case: a *Seeker* should *spot* the earlier *"evil intentions"* and *"fragmented purposes,"* and simply *defragment- by-inspection* (by one's own *Awareness*). Full *defragmentation* only occurs by *spotting* the *earliest* such *incident* on the *chain*. [While this matter must be handled properly, we do not encourage "scouting" for various *evil intentions* and *fragmented purposes* that are not directly a part of the area being treated.]

When an individual is *processing* their own *previous-goals*: much of the information about a *"future goal"* will already be known, or have been handled, since the *Seeker* is working/*processing* through their own personal *sequence* "backwards"—quite literally, "*backtracking.*" But if there is any remaining *turbulence* attached to a *"future goal"* (relative to whatever *goal* is being treated as *"current,"* but only as a *viewpoint* for *processing purposes*), then it may be handled further with alternating-PCL:

1. *"What would {goal-terminal} do to {future oppositional terminal}?"*
2. *"What would {goal-terminal} hold-back from {future oppositional terminal}?"*

E : FINDING THE PREVIOUS GOAL

Next, we want to find the *goal* that came before whatever one is being treated/*processed* (as *"current"*). Note that the *"problems"* of the *previous goal* are *"solved"* by the *"current"* goal. The procedure for this is like Step-C, except this time you are looking backwards. This means, how the *"current" goal* is *opposing* a *"previous" goal*. Here we want to determine *what* the *goal* is that the *"current" goal* is *opposing*.

This *listing*-PCL is:

"What goal would be successfully opposed by the {current goal}?"

You can reword it to *list* for the *prior oppositional terminal* as:

"What type of person would be successfully opposed by a(n) {current goal terminal}?"

F : PREVIOUS OPPOSITION (TERMINAL)

For *processing* the *oppositional terminal* to the *previous-goal* (using the perspective or *viewpoint* of the *previous goal* as *"current"*), apply the *process* from Step-B. This time, insert the *previous oppositional terminal* in the *"{opposition}"* bracket.

When handling one's actual *current-goal*, a *recall* of significant *harmful-*

acts may *resurface*—those which a *Seeker* committed when they were actually on the *previous goal*. To defragment this, *run*:

1. *"What harmful act might {goal-terminal} do against {previous oppositional terminal}?"*
2. *"How would they justify that?"*

If what *resurfaces* only generates additional *turbulence* (GSR-Meter "slams" or feelings of ill-intention) and does not improve significantly with the above PCL, a *Seeker* may also have to *"spot"* the instances of *"evil intention"* or *"fragmented purpose"* earlier on the *chain* to really get *"free"* of it.

While the full Section-2 procedure may require a bit of practice, once a *Seeker* is *"flying"* on it, the *energetic-mass* of the *Goals-Sequence* starts unraveling quite quickly. Having completed the procedure on a *Seeker's* own actual *"current goal,"* there should be a greater *Awareness* of the abandoned *"previous goal."* Following along this *pattern*, further *backward*, a *Seeker* may be able to more easily "plot" more of their own *Backtrack*.

When a *Seeker* has completed this procedure on a *"current goal,"* it may then be repeated for *running* the *next previous goal* (which was identified above). Alternatively, a *Seeker* may continue to Section-3 using the data for whatever is being treated as *"current goal."*

SECTION 3: OBJECT-ITEMS/SYMBOLS
(For defrag and research processing)

Terminals are *masses*. They are "things" at the other end of our *attention-flow*. Most often, *terminals* represent specific individuals, or types of people, handled as *"circuits"* in our *processes*. But other "living things" are also *terminals*—such as *animals* or even *trees*.

Inanimate mass—*"physical objects"*—are also *terminals*. While we may use *"objects"* in earlier *processing-levels* as a focus of *attention* in many *"objective exercises,"* we do not actually *run processes* on their "significance" until here at *Level-7*. Even now, we are only concerned with certain types of *"object-items."*

As the narrative in *AT Manual #1* suggests: to an *Alpha-Spirit*, *"symbols"* relay a level of strong *communication* that is very *real*, but much more subtle than what *standard-issue Humans* are likely to *perceive* directly in their everyday lives. [*Processing-out* the *fragmented significance* attached to a *"basic goal object-item"* should only be handled *after* the *goal* itself has been treated with the procedures in Section-1 and Section-2.]

A : BASIC OBJECT-ITEM (SYMBOL)

There is a *"basic object-item"* that represents, or more accurately, *"symbolizes"* a single *goal-chain* (which includes all the times the same *goal* was *altered* to meet *opposition*, before the individual changed their *goals* completely). Some version of this *"object"* is likely to be present (even literally carried or worn) during one's entire time with the *goal*. This may or may not be the same *"symbol"* (*object*) that was used to represent the *goal* during an *Implanting-Incident*.

The *"basic object"* we are referring to here acts very much like a *"basic brick"* when an individual *constructs* their foundation for a *goal*. The individual may use it as a *"substitute"* for themselves, or like a *"playing piece"* (similar to the way players of the *"Monopoly" board-game* represent themselves with arbitrary *"objects"*).

For example: the *intelligent-person* might always have a *book*; an *acquisitive-person* might always have a *camera*; the *beautiful-person* might always have a *hairbrush* or *mirror*; and so on. These are only examples. And they are not necessarily identical to all individuals operating with a certain *goal*. Section-3 is applied to make certain of this *"basic object"* and then *defragment* some of the *charge* attached to it.

At an *upper-level* of existence—due to *Implanting* and *mental-machinery*—the *Alpha-Spirit* keeps a version of the *"basic goal object-item"* compulsively *created* in a space that is outside (or *"exterior to"*) this *Physical Universe*. All *communications* relayed from the *Alpha-Spirit* to this *Beta-Existence* (down the *ZU-Line* to the *"Physical Body"*) are passing *"through"* this object-item. We apparently also use it for *memory storage*.

This *basic object* is intentionally *"hidden"* and *"forgotten"* out of *fear* that someone else might *"read their mind"* and *"zap it"* and thus *"destroy"* their *communication-line* with this *existence*. In some ways the individual uses this as a sort of *"Spiritual Body"* for the lifespan of the *goal*. The only *active item* being used is attached to a *Seeker's* actual *"current goal"*—but there is likely *fragmentation* and *restimulative-potential* still imprinted with other previously used *"basic goal object-items."*

Either the *goal* or a *terminal* (for the *goal*) may be used for the *listing*-PCL:

"*What object-item would represent ___?*"

For example: "*a strong person*" or "*the goal, To Be Strong.*" Additional instruction: whatever is *identified* as "*The Object-Item*," insert it in the *blank space* for remaining PCL (below) in Section-3.

B : PLEASING PEOPLE/ADMIRATION

It has been found that an individual has the tendency to use the "*object-item*" as a "*people-pleaser.*" They may *create it*, or put it up, in place of themselves so as to *attract admiration, &tc.* [A more obvious illustrative example of this is the "*statue*" a "*god-like being*" might use as substitute for their own actual presence.]

1. "*What sort of ___ would please people?*"
2. "*What type of person would that please?*"

After *processing* those *considerations*, apply the following series of alternating-PCL as a single *process*:

1. "*Spot a time someone admired your ___.*"
2. "*Spot a time someone invalidated your ___.*"
3. "*Spot a time you admired someone's ___.*"
4. "*Spot a time you invalidated someone's ___.*"

Then practice this next exercise until you feel good about *processing* the *object-item* further.

"*Imagine crowds of cheering people, applauding, and admiring the ___.*"

C : HELP

Increased attachment to the "*object-item*" results from an individual using it "*To Survive*" (the upper-most governing *Game-Goal* of *this Physical Universe*). *Run* the following *five* alternating-PCL as a single *process* until all of the presently available *considerations* are *spotted*.

1. "*How could a ___ help you?*"
2. "*How could you help a ___?*"
3. "*How could a ___ help another?*"
4. "*How could another help a ___?*"
5. "*How could a ___ help itself?*"

D : PROTECTING

That this *"object-item"* can be lost, damaged, or destroyed, is a constant source of *anxiety* and *fear*. Run the following *process* like the previous step.

1. *"How could a ___ protect you?"*
2. *"How could you protect a ___?"*
3. *"How could a ___ protect another?"*
4. *"How could another protect a ___?"*
5. *"How could a ___ protect itself?"*

E : RESISTANCE/STOPPED MOTION

This *"object-item"* tends to *"stop" motion* and *activity* in some way. Its *presence/existence* may also be *resisted* by others. In either case, *Awareness* is *"suspended"* and the *"object-item"* accumulates further *energetic-mass*. Run each of the next *two* PCL-series (below) as separate *processes*.

1. *"What motion or activity of yours has a ___ stopped?"*
2. *"What motion or activity of someone else has a ___ stopped?"*
3. *"What motion or activity of others has a ___ stopped?"*

1. *"What beingness (or type of being) would resist a ___?"*
2. *"What beingness (or type of being) would ___ resist?"*

F : OBJECTIVE EXERCISE

For this exercise you will need a physical representation of the *object-item*. If treating your *actual "current-goal"* then you may already have a *physical copy* of this *object-item* in your possession. If you are treating the immediately *previous goal* to your *actual current-goal*, then such representations were likely abandoned long ago (in which case you will either have to get one or make one). The critical part of this exercise is having the *"physical mass"* present.

Place the *object-item* at least a foot out in front of you, or on a table. This is a physical exercise requiring you to intentionally reach for the item and then let go of it. You want to be able to move your arm at least a foot or so—as a deliberate action—for each part. *Run* the following *series* of six PCL as a single repetitive *process*.

1A. *"Grab the object and intend to 'keep it from going away'."*

1B. *"Let go of it."*

2A. *"Grab the object and intend to 'hold it absolutely still'."*

2B. *"Let go of it."*

3A. *"Grab the object and intend to 'make it more solid'."*

3B. *"Let go of it."*

G : WASTING EXERCISE

Part of any *compulsive creation* (or *fixed consideration*) is the inability to "let go" (or have a change in condition). The *considerations* (and *perceived significance*) attached to an *"object-item"* are what makes the "loss" so *emotionally fragmenting*, or cause us to *fix* a lot of our *attention* on it to prevent this. The following exercise is intended to help *defragment* these *considerations*. Each PCL (below) should be *run* repeatedly as its own *process*. [By "waste," we mean to *dispense with, use up, destroy, &tc.* — meaning the opposite of *having, keeping,* or *accumulating*. You may need to insert a *plural* form of the *object-item*.]

1. *"Imagine a way to waste ___."*
2. *"Imagine a way for another to waste ___."*
3. *"Imagine a way for others to waste ___."*

H : HAVING EXERCISE

This technique requires practice with the *"creativeness"*-style techniques found throughout previous *processing-levels*. The following steps are treated as a single *process* or exercise.

• *Imagine great quantities of the object-item in a sphere surrounding you.*

• *Continue making copies, but making them more and more deteriorated or decayed. Keep changing their colors so that they are knowingly under your control as your creations (and not copies of a compulsively created image).*

• *Imagine/create more and more copies of them in the surrounding sphere until they start flowing-in on the Body. If you need to give them a gentle 'push in' to the Body, you may; but never from an interior viewpoint of 'pulling in' to the Body.*

• *Continue this until you feel comfortable 'throwing some away' (similar to 'wasting').*

• *Imagine/create more copies and have them 'out-flow' into the distance slowly disappearing; then 'out-flow' more into the distance and have them explode.*

88 – AT#2

• *Then go back to the first steps of this exercise and repeat; this time using nicer and more pristine copies until they are 'flowing-in' on the Body.*

• *Then continue using the steps of this exercise with better and better copies (perceived as more valuable) until you can easily handle both 'in-flowing' and 'out-flowing' your best (golden or perfect) copies.*

I : EXTERIOR VIEWPOINT

This *process* is *run* like Step-L of Section-1.

1. *"From where could you communicate to a(n) ___?"*
2. *"From where could a(n) ___ communicate to you?"*
3. *"From where could another communicate to a(n) ___?"*
4. *"From where could a(n) ___ communicate to another?"*
5. *"From where could a(n) ___ communicate to itself?"*

J : MEMORY STORAGE

An *Alpha-Spirit* often uses *astral/spiritual* representations of an *object-item* to store memory. In this case, the individual may use the *basic goal object-item* to store the memory of many lifetimes. This allows the *Alpha-Spirit* to *"forget"* (*"Not-Know"*) them on a "conscious" level without losing them completely. Here, we *process* such *considerations*.

1. *"What memories could a(n) ___ store for you?"*
2. *"What memories could a(n) ___ store for another?"*
3. *"What memories could a(n) ___ store for others?"*
4. *"What might you allow a(n) ___ to forget?"*

K : THINKINGNESS

An *Alpha-Spirit* has a tendency to allow certain *object-items* (and *machinery*) to do their *thinking* for them.

1. *"What thoughts might ___ have on your behalf?"*
2. *"What thoughts could you have in the absence of ___?"*

L : COMPULSIVE CREATION

Run these alternating-PCL until the *second*-PCL genuinely seems ridiculous and a *Seeker* senses that something about the *fragmentation* has "fallen away," "come apart," or some other sensation of greater "relief." Then *run* the *first*-PCL by itself several more times to stabilize the *endpoint*.

1. *"From where could you create a(n) ___?"*
2. *"From where could a ___ create you?"*

M : <u>OBJECTIVE EXERCISE (END)</u>

For this final exercise you will need a physical representation of the *object-item* (such as from Step-F) to hold. This is a repetitive *process*/exercise. When first *running* it, you may *perceive* the *"physical object"* in your hands as becoming *"more real"* or *"more solid"* than the rest of the room. Continue the exercise until this effect stops and/or you find yourself completely *"exterior to"* the entire entangled *energetic-mass* of the *"object-item"* (and any *fragmented significance* it represents).

This exercise is practiced with *eyes closed*, while *holding the physical object* in your hands. The actual *"spiritual perception"* (or *"ZU-Vision"*) does not have to seem very vivid or real; just keep intending to *"mentally spot"* with your *attention*.

1. *"Spot three points in the object."*
2. *"Spot three points in the room."*

If a *Seeker* suddenly gets even a slight sense of an additional representative *copy* of the *"object-item"* off in some *"strange space"* or *"dimension"* somewhere, then add the following PCL to the series—cycling through all *three* PCL within the same *process*. Again, the vividness of perception or reality on this other *copy* does not have to be great in order to *"spot"* with *attention*.

3. *"Spot three points in the distant copy."*

ADDITIONAL NOTES ON "ZU-VISION"

ZU-VISION is an imperfect term that is used in *Systemology* and *Mardukite Zuism*. Originally, the term was used to denote the experience of *Awareness* that is independent of a *Body*—and not *just* a *"Human Body"* (for the experience of *this Physical Universe*) but *any* conception of a *Body* that is restricted to *any Universe*. In the fullest sense, it is referring to the *pure unfiltered Awareness* of an *Alpha-Spirit*.

As an *exercise* or *technique*, we tend to be a little more realistic about the clarity of a *Seeker's* "spiritual perception" when ZU-Vision is handled in previous *processing-levels*. Based on what is stated in *AT Manual #1*, the form and solidity of *this Physical Universe* is being *perceived* by an *Alpha-Spirit* through *seven-plus-one* "layers" of *Universe reality-agreements.* That certainly provides a lot of "room" for an *Alpha-Spirit* to have *compulsively fixed attention*—or "parked" its *Awareness*—along the way to reach *here.*

An increase of *"spiritual perception"* is a natural occurrence as a *Seeker* clears away the "debris" from these various *"layers."* Various *metaphysical* and *mystical* "New Age" practices tend to put a lot of emphasis and *attention* on the *"Astral Body."* This is essentially only one-*level* or one-*layer* "up" from *the Physical Body* (or *"genetic vehicle"*) used to conveniently experience and interact with *this Physical Universe.* The *"Astral Body"* served the same function for us in the previous (or *higher*) "Magic Universe."

The *"Astral Body"* is *still* a *"Body"* with *perceptions* far removed from our basic native state. That it is really only *one-degree higher* in "apparent frequency" has simply made it more accessible to individuals that have been able to access some level of higher perception using other methods.

But *"astral travel," "dream-walking"* and even *"between-lives"* periods, where we temporarily assume the *viewpoint* from our *"astral"* perspective, are not truly *"exterior to"* this Physical Universe—nor do they truly represent *our* practice of ZU-Vision.

Although we may access the *perception* of an *astral form,* or even enter these *viewpoints* more completely between "physical" incarnations, there are *"spiritual screens"* in place that will continue to entrap a heavily *fragmented* individual's *Awareness* to *this Universe.*

These *"screens"* are a component of the *"thought planes"* that, while quite "invisible" to normative perception, are very much present and exist *within* the confines of *this Physical Universe.* Simply *accessing* the "Astral Body" and operating within the *"thought planes"* is not the same as experiencing the actual *Magic Universe* with one; it just means we have *"carried"* an *Astral Body* with us down *here* as one more *layer* on top of everything else prior to it.

Systematic Processing (as a method of *defragmentation*) is only effective when we are treating the *Alpha-Spirit,* the actual individual themselves, and the *postulates* or *Alpha-Thought* they have established, duplicated or *agreed with*, as part of their own *Personal Universe*—or what one generally considers their *"Home Universe."*

Technically, an *Alpha-Spirit* has never actually "left" its original native position in a *"Home Universe."* But, it started its *creative experience* as a particularly naïve immortal *Beingness* with unlimited power. *Systematic Processing* could be applied infinitely with only marginal gains if a *Seeker* is not being *processed* from the *viewpoint* that they are still *creating* what is experienced as their *own Universe*.

The fact that most of these *creations* are *fragmented* by innumerable layers of forgotten *reality-agreements*, or are being *automatically* and/or *reactively* "manifested" by *spiritual machinery* that has long since been "abandoned" but left active, does not change the fact that the *actual existence* of the *"immortal"* Alpha-Spirit remains in its *own Universe*. They are simply *assimilating* and *duplicating* the *reality* they experience based on *"impressions"* received from all of their other interactions with *"external stimuli."*

By *"own Universe"* we literally mean *"Own,"* as in *ownership*. And with that true *ownership* comes the *total responsibility* for its *existence*. Of course, as we went along, this *responsibility* became gradually "delegated" to "outside sources"—but of which are really *fragments* of ourselves, *knowingly* set up to *do* something, and then *hidden* away from our *Knowingness*. This is why we refer quite literally to *"fragmentation of Awareness."*

Total *Alpha-Defragmentation* requires the *"separation"* of *"collapsed"* Universes. A *Seeker's* fundamental problem is: *agreeing* that Beta-Existence IS Home-Universe; and then *identifying with and as anything* in that Beta-Existence. When a *Seeker* solves this, they are *free* for *Ascension*.

There are varying degrees of *spiritual perception*. When first practicing with ZU-Vision—being an *Awareness*, or maintaining a *viewpoint*, just "outside" the *Body* (but still present in *Beta-Existence*)—a *Seeker* is likely *not* going to fully *perceive* the "walls" of the room. They might be able to *"imagine"* (*create mental imagery of*) them from *"memory"*; but that is not quite the same experience as having actual *spiritual perception*. This type of *invalidation* is sometimes enough to dissuade beginners from continuing a developmental practice.

There is an observed pattern that tends to occur as a *Seeker* develops *spiritual perception*. For example: first they won't be able to see the *walls*; then they can see the *walls*; and finally, they can't see the *walls* unless they first *postulate* or *agree* that there is one there.

We use *"walls"* quite often in our *objective/Universe* exercises, and for good reason: they are *agreed-upon reality barriers* that become *compulsively (unknowingly) created*. The "thing" that is *perceived* to "exist" before you is really an "order" or product of *Alpha-Thought*. It is being "ordered" to *exist*; "ordered" to *obey* a *reality-agreement* that it is *"there."*

An interesting *process* could be *run* on this point, by alternating the following PCL. [Note that its wording permits the *use of force*, but then allows one to move beyond such *considerations*.]

1. *"What wouldn't you mind obeying?"*
2. *"What would obey you?"*

* * * * * * *

High-level Awareness is required to *confront, conceive*, or even *get the concept of*, the *actuality* of the *Alpha-Spirit*. The same can be said of *accepting* that *"Games"* are the *answer* to the ultimate *"Why?"* Such *levels* of *realization* are "beyond" the *standard-issue Human Condition*.

The fact of the matter is that *Alpha-Spirits* are fond of *games*—and they tend to prefer *"game conditions"* to *"non-game conditions."* But, *"game conditions"* require *"barriers"*; there must be some *restrictions*. The idea of *"no barriers"* or a *"total freedom of space"* are *"non-game conditions."*

"Truth" and *"native states"* are *non-game conditions*. *Fragmentation* can only result from *game-conditions*. The *Alpha-Spirit* requires a particular level of certainty that there *"will be games."* There must be *enough barriers* to suit them. *Alpha-Spirits* become "unhappy" when *confronting* either "too many" or "too few" *barriers* for their preferred *"tolerance"* or *"involvement"* level.

Where ZU-Vision is concerned, an individual needs certainty that there will still be enough "game" in that state. The most direct method of treating this with *conceptual processing* is with alternating-PCL:

1. *"Get a sense that you can control that Body from outside it."*
2. *"Get a sense that you cannot control that Body from outside it."*

In this example of *processing* (above): one of these statements is obviously a "truth"; whereas the other is *fragmented consideration*. In actual practice, however, *running* one *or* the other by itself doesn't produce any real gains. One of the reasons for this is because there is actually a continuous *"charge"* on both *postulates* (that you both *can* and *can't*). This leads to a *suspension of Knowingness* as a "maybe" and a further reduction in *Actualized Awareness*.

Systematic Processing is applied to determine exactly where an individual's *attention/Awareness* has been *fixated* or *suspended* on the *Backtrack*, and then *free it*. But to do this successfully requires actually being able to *spot* what an individual is attempting to *get free from*. The *Alpha-Spirit* already *was "free."* It must first consider that there is *something there* to be *free of something*. It has to *spot* "getting in" before it can "get out."

While there is plenty of *physical-matter* and *objects* in *this Physical Universe* in which to "orient" a *Physical Body*, as a *Spiritual Being*, an individual entrapped in the *Human Condition* is actually quite "lost" without properly *Backtracking* the routes by which they descended to this state.

If one truly is *seeking Ascension*, they have likely accumulated additional uncertainty by entertaining a lot of the popular routes of *"enlightenment"* that have come and gone in history, or are still with us. And perhaps the most disturbing insistence that is inherent in these "false paths" is the conception of a *"oneness"* and *"connectedness"* with the ALL-ness of *this Physical Universe*. This is an outright *lie* wrapped up in a lot of politically correct "feel good" *mysticism* that actually doesn't lead an individual anywhere but further *"in."*

If you truly want to get *"exterior to"* and *"out of"* this Physical Universe, then *process-out* any *agreement* that you are an interconnected part of it. You are simply *"remote controlling"* a *vehicle*. You are not the *vehicle*, and you are certainly not the *environment* that the *vehicle* is interacting with.

We don't *process "freedom"* (which is the *truth*), we *process "separateness"* (which is the *game-equivalent* of *freedom*). *Separateness* implies that there is *something there* to be *separate from*. Therefore, *process "barriers"* and *"separateness."*

While the subject of *"barriers"* is treated in previous *processing-levels*, the application of *"separateness"* to *processing* is not. This is quite simple as an *objective exercise*. Although we often use alternating-PCL for maintaining better control of *attention*, treating both *in-flow* and *out-flow*, and/or taking *"charge"* off of two *opposing considerations*, in this case we do *not* alternate *"separateness"* with *"connectedness."*

1. *"Spot things that are separate from you."*
2. *"Spot things you are separate from."*

At first, a *Seeker* might practice this with *eyes open* and *looking* around the room. Eventually they should shift to treating as many *objects*, *people*, and *places* that can be *"spotted"* (*mentally with attention*)—and with each, getting and maintaining a *sense* or *concept* of *"separateness." Run* this to a satisfactory *end-point*.

A.T. MANUAL #3
THE JEWEL OF KNOWLEDGE

Review this prerequisite reference material:
 PC Lesson-7, "Eliminating Barriers"
 PC Lesson-8, "Conquest of Illusion"
 PC Lesson-11, "Spiritual Implants"
 PC Lesson-12, "Games & Universes"
 PC Lesson-14, "Spiritual Machinery"
 AT Manual #1, "The Secret of Universes"
 AT Manual #2, "Games, Goals & Purposes"
 AT Supplement, "Systemology Procedures"
 AT Supplement, "Systemology Biofeedback"

THE MIND-SYSTEM & "THE JEWEL"

The *Alpha-Spirit* carries a *fragmented Mind-System* with it from one *Beta-Existence* (any *Universe*) to another—and all the while they experience existence. This is the *real "baggage"* we are accumulating as a *Spiritual Beingness*. As a *Being*, we are simply a *point* or *unit* of *Awareness*, with no *mass* or *frequency*. But, the *Mind-System* (we *project* and *identify with* as part of that *Beingness*) *can* be affected by *Implants* and *mental-machinery*—and various *platforms* that provided a place for *layers-of-consideration* to accumulate as we progressed into *denser*, more *fixed* and *solid*, existences.

The *Mind-System* is *unknowingly* and *compulsively created* by the *Alpha-Spirit*. It is their *own* to handle. It is also their *own* primary stumbling-block to reaching *Ascension*. It is the *fragmented* part of one's *Self* that has actually been opposing the individual all along. And of course, it is what we handled in bits and layers with previous *systematic processing-levels*. The *Pathway to Ascension* requires "freeing" an individual from the cumulative conditions that have been *created*, and continue to be, imposed on *Self*.

Previously on the *Pathway*, we have handled Beta-Defragmentation Procedures aimed at elevating *Actualized Awareness* to *above* "4" on the *Standard Model* (or *Zu-Line*). This is a point just beyond, or "*exterior to,*" a *fragmented Mind-System*. Of course, the *Mind-System* is still quite active—its *automated reactive-machinery* is still being *unknowingly created*. But a *Seeker* is regaining greater control of its activity. They are "freeing" their *point-of-view*, which is otherwise *compulsively* buried beneath it—or *entangled up* within it. *Higher-level processing* requires operating from a stable *viewpoint* that is "*exterior to*" the *Mind-System*.

A *fragmented Mind-System* (operating apart from, or outside, *Self-Honesty*) contains *fragmented purposes*—*Implanted considerations* and *goals*—that distort an *Alpha-Spirit's* own actual goals and *Self-determined purposes*. This is how our original *goal "To Create"* became inverted as "*To Survive.*" A *fragmented individual* is more strongly the *effect of* the *Implanting* and *automated machinery*—*unknowingly*, and hence, *unwillingly*.

Considerations that we maintain with *conviction*—and as *Alpha-Thought*—are "*creations.*" They have a certain degree of *fragmented energetic-mass* to them, which we often refer to as a *"charge."* Such a *"charge"* indicates that some part of our *Awareness* is still on them, keeping them *created* and held in a *suspended state* of *existence* as a *"rigid wave-form"* or *"solid ridge."*

This *A.T. "Keys to the Kingdom"* series of manuals explores upper-level *Alpha-Defragmentation*—or *The Way Out*. It requires fully clearing the *rigid-blocks* and *barriers* that are restricting an individual's *free access* to the *Beyond*; it requires being fully *at Cause* over the *Mind-System*. And in one form or another: this has always been the ultimate goal behind all *spiritualism, mysticism*, and the like.

We have to *"clear the slate"* of *reality-agreements* for *this Universe* before one looks to treat anything beyond it. Failure to do so only results in *"dead-end religions"* that propose to know *"all about God" ("Infinity")* in spite of having *no reality* on anything else.

> Since there is a tremendous amount of content to cover in *this* manual: information that is contained in former lessons and manuals will not be repeated. It is a *Seeker's* responsibility to review that material.

The original *"Jewel of Knowledge"* is described in *AT Manual #1*. Elements of the original *"Jewel of Knowledge"* reappear in subsequent imitation *"False Jewels"* used for *"Entry-Point"* implanting-incidents into any *Beta-Existence (Universe)*. These *"False Jewel" Implants* are never *constructed* to the same degree of complexity and beauty as the original *"Jewel of Knowledge"* experience that occurred prior to *"Home Universe."* A full and direct handling of the Original *"Jewel of Knowledge"* would be purely speculative from *this* level of the *Pathway* (and while still *interior to this Physical Universe*). Besides: what we are *really* working toward on a much more *practical level* is *The Way Out* of *this Physical Universe*, and that requires handling the specific (and more accessible) *reality-agreements* that we are very much attached to *this Physical Universe*.

"The Jewel"—or more accurately, *"False Jewel"*—treated in *this manual* reflects that specific *"construct"* which we *"passed through"* on Entry-to-<u>this</u>-*Universe*—meaning *this Physical Universe*. The complete *Implanting-Incident* that occurs upon *"Entry-into-this-Universe"* has two parts:

Part One: The False Jewel Implant Incident (Ref: *AT Manual #1*)
Part Two: The Heaven Implant Incident (Ref: *PC Lesson-12; AT Manual #1 and #2*)

"The Jewel" Defragmentation Procedure is not treated with techniques that a *Seeker* may be used to. It does not naturally *"process out"* using our standard *Beta-Defragmentation* practices. For example: properly *"confronting the past"* requires *Knowing* the proper *"timing"* and *"duration"* of an *event*. Such data is too distorted or *"falsely implanted"* to treat *"The Jewel"* with *Beta-Defragmentation* procedures. However, the time spent effectively handling earlier *processing-levels* will greatly reduce the amount of time an advanced *Seeker* will require to properly complete *this* procedure.

Failure to complete basic *Beta-Defragmentation* (e.g. *"The Pathway to Ascension" Professional Course*) and have an understanding of previous *A.T. Manuals* and *supplements* will result in a *Seeker* easily becoming *overwhelmed* or *confused*—and therefore, struggling to achieve the results intended with this manual.

> Without the prerequisite background, *this* procedure could be *run infinitely* with no gains, or even negative results, potentially *invalidating* the *upper-level* progress a *Seeker* has thus far achieved. Additionally, a *Seeker* must *fully understand* and have *total certainty* on the procedural instructions given in the next section *before* applying—or even *reading*—*any* techniques from this manual.

In previous lessons/manuals, we have revealed how *"opposing considerations"* held with *equal conviction* (or *"charge"*)—such as *"there is something there"* and *"there is nothing there"*—are Implanted. Or, *get the idea* of being hypnotically-commanded to simultaneously *"go away!"* and *"stay where you are!"* This is the type of *confusion* and *uncertainty* that a *fragmented Mind-System* provides an individual. This maintains the *"solidity"* of *reality-agreements* for *this Physical Universe* by those experiencing it.

When combined with data for the *"Heaven Incident"* (in previous material), *"The Jewel" Procedure* unwraps the entire basic sequence of *considerations (postulates) Implanted* for the *Game* of *this Physical Universe*. [It undoubtedly also contains some common *Implant*-elements from the previous *Beta-Existence*, since that is where it was *constructed*.]

Implanting is most effective on us when it is part of a *"chain"* of reoccurring use. As we know from *AT Manual #1*: before being fully *entrapped*, a single visit to a *Prison-Penalty Universe* is seldom enough to "stick" an *Alpha-Spirit*. But, repeated reinforcement (*entry-incidents*) builds up a greater *energetic-mass* on whatever is being *Implanted*. Generally this coincides with our increased *protest* or *resistance* to it each time. Likewise, if not handled properly by an advanced *Seeker*, "*The Jewel*" *Procedure* could theoretically *add* more "*mass*" rather than *defragment* what's there.

> "*The Jewel*" *Procedure* peels back a "*layer*" of *fragmentation* that is only exposed and accessible after fully completing *Systemology Levels 0-6* and the previous *AT Manuals*. *Systemology Level-7* is entirely *Solo-Piloted* (whether or not a *Seeker* was *Co-Piloted* formerly). To be handled with any certainty: the territory a *Solo-Pilot* must cover in *this Manual* really requires the assistance of a *Biofeedback Device (GSR-Meter)*.

"*The Jewel*" *Procedure* is *not* a "*do-a-little-whenever-you-can*" type of activity that you *fit in* between daily *upsets* of normal "*Human*" living. Such means handling excessive "*preventative fundamentals*" (*flow-factor breaks, human problems, &tc.*) at the start of every *session*—*before* you can get on with resuming the actual procedure. Very little real progress is achieved that way; because this procedure will require *many sessions*.

For the duration of handling this procedure, a *Seeker* should place themselves in *conditions* (*environments*) that are suitable for *processing* this to its entirety, maintaining their own sense of *Self-Honest* stability throughout, and an ability to provide full *Awareness* to their *presence-in-session*. [This is not an appropriate period to embark on "*family vacations*" or take on greater "*material world*" responsibilities, *&tc.*]

This procedure is a *real test* of a *Seeker's Solo-Piloting* skills and level of *Awareness*. It is a long and tedious *Intensive Procedure*, not an exercise in being entertained. The required level of interest maintained must be entirely *Self-determined* and *Self-directed*. Full completion of this "*step*" on the *Pathway* will provide the next stable "*landing zone*" (or *foundation*) from which to *Pilot* all additional *Alpha-Defragmentation*.

PROCEDURAL INSTRUCTIONS

This manual is a "*workbook*" of sorts; *not* an "*educational read-through*" book. It presents an *Intensive Procedure* without any perceptible "*gradients*" of progress along the way. It is handled as a single *unit* of work—essentially the equivalent of an *entire processing-level*—and it requires many repetitive *steps* to complete.

A *Seeker* must have *total certainty* on these *instructions*—and all relevant background data from other lessons and manuals—before starting the actual procedure. New technical material is found in these instructions that a *Seeker* will need to review several times by itself, and then in relation to previous material, to fully understand.

An advanced *Seeker* should expect a minimum of *100 processing-hours* to complete this manual. This is best accomplished with *daily formal sessions* between *one* and *two hours*. [Preferably closer to *one hour*, the same time each day, as like a *"ritual."*]

THE IMPLANTING INCIDENT

Once the data for an *Implant-Platform* "resurfaces" with *systematic processing*, it must be handled (*processed-out*) fully, or else will remain in *restimulation* (even between *sessions*). This whole procedure is treating a single entire *Implanting-Incident*. A *Seeker's* attention will remain focused on that *past incident* for the duration of this procedure until its completion.

We are treating the earliest, most basic, and significant *Implanting-Incident* connected to our experience of *this Physical Universe*. The *Implant* was masterfully *constructed*—specifically designed to remain *hidden* and *nonconfronted*. It is not meant to be easily *recalled* or "spotted" on the *Backtrack*—and it requires a precise *systematic procedure* in which to *knowingly* "contact" it with our *Awareness* and *defragment* its content.

There is the possibility of being *"ejected"* from the *Incident* during *processing*. We mean that while *attention* is on it, something occurs to redirect our *attention* elsewhere—usually on some activity of the *Mind-System*. If the *Incident* suddenly "disappears," becomes "inaccessible," or seems "unreal," during the procedure, then the *Seeker* has likely been "ejected." We aren't erasing "memory" of the *Incident*; we are *defragmenting* the portion of our *Mind-System* that is *unknowingly* and *fixedly* maintaining *considerations* from the *Incident*. A *Seeker* simply redirects attention to *"return"* to the *exact point* of the procedure that they were *ejected from*.

As with other *incident-running processes*, a *Seeker* should be familiar with the practice of *"returning to (such and such) a time"* with their *Awareness*. This is done by *intention* and must be *Self-directed* by a *Solo-Pilot*. This procedure is really one exceptionally long *process*. A *Seeker* may also be ending a *session* at some arbitrary point within it—such as: *Cycle-D; Part 3, Step-19*. To start up again, or if *ejected*, a *Seeker* must reorient their *Awareness* in the *Incident* at the exact point they left off. Therefore, the appropriate "*Cycle/Part/Step*" data is inserted in the *first* procedural PCL of the *next session*:

"*Return to ___ of the Basic Implant-Incident.*"

But what do we mean by *Cycles*, *Parts* and *Steps*? To *process-out* this *Incident*, a *Seeker* must *run* the entire *Incident*—which is an entire "*series*" of *Implants*. Since we have *systematic* data for the complete *pattern* of this *series*, we do not need to "*trace*" any "*chains*" back to *earlier incidents* (such as with other types of *fragmentation*). This procedure *starts* with the literal *beginning* of the *Incident* and *runs* through its entirety.

"*The Jewel*" *Procedure* mimics the full *series-pattern* of this particular *Implanting-Incident*. It consists of only *five* different *Parts* (each with many *Steps*). But, those same *five Parts* are repeated *ten times* for the duration of the *Incident*. A *Seeker* essentially *runs* all *ten Cycles* of the *five Parts*. This means that the complete procedure consists of *50 total parts* to *process*.

To be clear: *Parts 1, 2, 3, 4,* and *5*, are repeated in that order, *ten times*. Or, to rephrase: each *Cycle* consists of *Parts 1, 2, 3, 4,* and *5*; and there are *ten Cycles* total.

To avoid confusion, we label *each* of the *Cycles* with a *letter "A"* through *"J."* This means that in *Cycle-A*, a *Seeker* runs *Parts 1, 2, 3, 4,* and *5*; then proceeds to *Cycle-B*, running *Parts 1, 2, 3, 4,* and *5*; and so on, through *Cycle-J*.

Another way of stating this: a *Seeker* runs *A1, A2, A3, A4, A5*; then *B1, B2, B3, B4, B5*... Why is this so important to keep track of?

> The only way to really get "*stuck*" in this procedure is either *skipping Steps*, or treating a *Cycle* out of sequence. The *Incident* was meant to be *confusing*; and for an *Alpha-Spirit* to lose track of their place within it. Even though *Part 1*, for example, is always *run* like *Part 1*. The *Part 1* of *Cycle-A* is not the same point in the *Incident* as *Part 1* of *Cycle-D*, *&tc.*

Do not make marks within this manual. A *Seeker* is prompted to make their own "worksheets." The first *"worksheet"* a *Seeker* should prepare for themselves is a "table" or "chart" whereby they can "check off" the *Parts* of each *Cycle* as they are completed. The following "table" gives an example, with "x" marks to indicate each of the *50 total parts* that compose the entire *Incident*.

```
CHECKSHEET            PARTS
                   1 2 3 4 5
         CYCLE A  x x x x x
               B  x x x x x
               C  x x x x x
               D  x x x x x
               E  x x x x x
               F  x x x x x
               G  x x x x x
               H  x x x x x
               I  x x x x x
               J  x x x x x
```

Parts 1, 2, and 3, mostly consist of straightforward *"command-item"* lines. They have a significance that is understood with *language*—and therefore are *processed* "verbally" (spoken). Of course, the original *Implant* does not include "English" words; but we approximate their associated meaning in *systematic processing*. [Refer to *PC Lessons 11* and *12*.]

Parts 4 and *5*, consist of a precise *pattern* of *"object-items"* that have *no verbal-language* component. These *"item lines"* are run *silently*. The PCL used simply directs *Awareness* to perceive *"object-items"* in specific ways —in mimicry of how they appeared in the actual *Incident*.

STANDARD PROCEDURE

Traditional Piloting of *"The Jewel" Procedure* is *Solo* with a *GSR-Meter*. If the *Biofeedback Device* normally uses *two-handed electrodes*, they are combined or coupled for *one-hand* use, but still kept separate to avoid directly touching each other and short-circuiting. The *Meter electrode-sensor* is held in the non-writing hand, leaving the other hand free to flip-over *"worksheets"* after making *marks* on them.

To make *processing* and handling *worksheets* easier, they should be on single pieces of loose paper; not a notebook or journal—using paperclips if necessary; never staples. They should be kept organized and safe between *sessions*. This manual is prepared in many formats; its size and binding will determine if it is appropriate to use during *processing*.

In most cases, a *Seeker* will title a *worksheet* at the top, with the "Cycle," and "Part," then simply list the "item line" numbers (or *Steps*) for that *Part* as a column down the left-hand side of the sheet (or multiple sheets) to keep track of the "Meter-reads" and the completed progress.

Materials need to be handled in *session* in such a way that they do not unnecessarily disturb the motions of the hand holding the *GSR-electrode-sensor*. The *worksheets* are best handled as stacks. The ones with the listed "item line" numbers that you intend to mark on should be closest to your writing hand. The complete ones can be flipped over face down and set as a stack further away on the table.

If pages of this edition of the manual are difficult to keep open easily for processing, then a *Seeker* may need to prepare a second stack of *worksheets* that are essentially complete copies of the "Implant Platform" sections, listing out all the actual "Implant Item" lines from this manual. Whether you use a book or separate *Implant-Item worksheets*, it is common practice to cover the upcoming "item lines" with a notecard or additional sheet of paper that may be moved down to expose the next "item" to view only when the *Seeker* is ready for it.

The most basic *worksheets* are simply "numbered" to match the "items" listed for an *Implant-Platform*. Any *worksheets* intended for use must be prepared sequentially and arranged prior to the *session*. It is also important to avert the *Body's Eyes* when they are being changed (flipped-over into a "done" pile) so that *attention* does not fall on a new "worksheet" (or "item" list) before it is ready to be properly handled.

This procedure is not *run* like other *processes*. In other types of *processing*, one might use a *Biofeedback Device* to identify areas with the "*most fragmented charge*"—such as from a list of possible *terminals, &tc*. In this current procedure: we already know that there *is* a "charge" of some degree on *each* one of the "implant items." The current goal is to "contact" that "charge" and *defragment* ("*discharge*") it—and the *Biofeedback Device* is often quite necessary for a *Seeker* to know when these conditions (*contact* and *defragmentation*) occur—between when a *Meter* "reads" or "registers" (*a change in state*) and when it no longer "reads" for an "item."

For this procedure: (unlike in previous *processing-levels*) we do not want to allow for a lot of *"mental activity"* — *"freewheeling thought"* or even *considerations* — that is not specifically directed on *"spotting"* the *command-item*. While *processing* the various *Parts* and *Cycles* of the *Incident*, additional *"sensory data"* (about the *Incident*) *may resurface*, and if it does, it should be noted on your *worksheet* before continuing the *process*. It is *not* actually advisable to intentionally go *looking for* this data during *defragmentation*.

STANDARD DEFRAGMENTATION (WITH A GSR-METER)

The basic instructions for this procedure are to repeatedly *"spot with attention"* (and thereby *confront*) each *"implant-item"* (a *"command-item"*-type *postulate* or *"object-item"*) listed for an *Implant-Platform* until it has no further *"charge"* — meaning that it no longer *"reads"* (or *registers*) on a *GSR-Meter*. This form of *defragmentation* is possible only due to the increased level of *Awareness* available to a *Seeker* by this point on the *Pathway*.

A *Seeker* should not *"decide"* (*postulate*) anything *in-session* during the procedure. At this level of development, a *Seeker's* *"Alpha-Thought"* is actualized enough that it is possible for them to *"decide"* that something is now *"defragmented"* and then cause it to cease *registering* on the *Meter*. But this likely will leave a *suppressed charge* remaining on that *"item"* — and that only complicates continuing the procedure from there.

For example: a *Seeker* can get "bored" with the procedure and *decide* that an item will no longer *register* — and it *will*. It is also important not to make any *decisions* about how many times an *"item"* *should read* on a *Meter* based on how many times a previous *"item"* (*&tc.*) had *registered*.

An *"item"* may *Meter-read* only *once* or it may *register* twenty times. Since an *"item" may* only *register* once, the *Device*, manuals and worksheets should be arranged so a *Seeker* is able to "catch" *all reads* as they occur. The exact number of times necessary to *spot* (and *defragment*) is not the same for all *items* or all *individuals*. [This makes *Solo-Piloting* this procedure *without* a *GSR-Meter* quite challenging.]

As a *Seeker* is familiar with from *PC Lesson-11, &tc.*, an *Implant-Platform* is not *defragmented* simply by an individual reading or skimming over its printed content. Each of these *"items"* needs to be *"contacted with attent-*

ion" in-session, in such a way that it *does* produce a *"Meter-read."* The *Seeker* "runs" an *"item"* (a numbered *processing line*), until it produces no *"Meter-reads" three times in a row*. Only then does the cover-sheet get moved down to reveal and handle the next *"item"* in the list.

THE "LIGHT" & THE "ALPHA-SPIRIT"

There are two *new* elements of *processing* that we must introduce for this procedure. As we have said (above): each one of the *"items"* has a *"charge"* on it that *registers* on a *Meter* when it is initially *"contacted"* in-session with our *Awareness*. And then it proceeds to *"Meter-read"* until it is *"discharged."* But how does a *Seeker* ensure they are properly directing an *intention* to *"contact"* the *"item"* and get the first *"read"*?

The actual *charge* on each *Implanted-Item* is connected to an *"impression"* (or *"perception,"* if you prefer) of the *Alpha-Spirit (Self)* at the exact moment each *item* was *Implanted*. This would be similar to seeing your *Body* from an *external* view while *running* an *incident* from a *Beta-Existence* experience. But this usually involves more "familiar" surroundings and *sensory facets* than an *"Entry-into-Universe"* or *"False Jewel"* experience.

At the time of the *Implanting-Incident*, you did not have an identifiable *"Body"* like you do now. There is also no "spatial-orientation" in the way you would describe experiences *within this Physical Universe*. So, the correct *systematic* PCL for this is: *"Spot the Alpha"* (meaning *"Alpha-Spirit"* — or one's own *Beingness*—at the moment of the *Implanted-Item*). This is done strictly by *intention*, although a *Seeker* may have to "feel around" a bit with their selectively directed *attention* before they get a *"Meter-read"* on *"contact."*

The PCL *"Spot the Alpha"* is part of orienting *Awareness* during the *defragmentation* procedure; it is not a *"command-item"* from the actual *incident*. There is also the second *new* element for us to introduce, which is similar to, and usually combined with the action of *"Spotting the Alpha."* The *Jewel Incident* included a special kind of *"Light"* that induces a "trance-like hypnotic groggy" receptive state in the *Alpha-Spirit* while an *"item"* is *Implanted*. In this wise, the PCL is: *"Spot the Light."* And this is also done strictly by *intention*—meaning selectively directing *attention*.

While *running* the *processes*, it is *not* necessary to actually *"see"* the *"Light"* or *"Alpha-Spirit"* (in *ZU-Vision* or as a literal *visualization*) in order to *"spot"* it with *Awareness* and get a *"Meter-read."* Also: one performs the procedure with the *eyes open*—using the *"Platform" list*, while still noting any *Biofeedback* responses. It is usually sufficient to simply be *aware* of what is taking place in the *incident* for a *Meter-read*.

As a matter of perspective: the *Light* comes from the distance, just off to the "left side" of directly in front of you. When *running* the *process*, when you *get the sense* (or *concept*) of what should be where it is, and *contact* it, this produces a *Meter-read*.

Although *Implanted "command-items"* may be "called out loud" for *defragmentation processing*, we seldom audibly verbalize other parts of a PCL—such as *"Spot the Light"* and *"Spot the Alpha"*—or else they are *"said"* internally to focus or direct *attention*.

The most common *processing command* (PCL) for this procedure uses the formula:

"Spot the {implanted-item}; Spot the Alpha."

However, in most cases, *"Spot the Alpha"* is also meant to include *"Spot the Light"* simultaneously as a combined single-action. A PCL is not as effective by adding a third component, so once we are handling an *implant-item* for the first part of a PCL, then the simultaneous *"Spot the Light; Spot the Alpha"* are simply combined for *systematic* purposes as *"Spot the Alpha."* [This "skill" in *spotting* the *Light* and the *Alpha-Spirit* are best practiced as part of the first *sessions* of this procedure; not separately, *out-of-session*.]

The pattern of some *Implant-Platforms* may require you to *spot/contact* one *item-phrase*, then a second *item-phrase*, and the finally both together as a single action. An example of this *pattern* would be:

Item-1: "To Be *A*."
Item-2: "To Be *B*."
Item-3: "To Be *A*; To Be *B*."

To be even more technically accurate, the full *pattern* in many cases is:

Item-1: *"To Be A; & Spot the Alpha."*
Item-2: *"To Be B; & Spot the Alpha."*
Item-3: *"To Be A, To Be B; & Spot the Alpha."*

The *"proper way"* for a *Seeker* to *"contact," "visualize,"* or *"get the sense"* of connecting with a specific point of the *incident*—the *"command-item"*; *"Light-Alpha"* combination, *&tc.*—is whatever produces the best *Meter-reads* on contact. Whatever an *Seeker* "does" to get *that Meter-read*, they continue doing it while *"spotting"* the *"item-line"* until it no longer registers for *three times* on *spotting* it.

Prior to applying this procedure, it would be worthwhile for a *Seeker* to practice *"seeing something"* with the same level of *interest* and *attention* as if *"for the first time."* This is especially important where content from an *Implant-Platform* is partially viewed before its use in the actual procedure.

HANDLING THE PROCEDURE

Worksheets are prepared to keep track of the *Meter-reads* for each individual *"item"* in the procedure. This will mean making *ten* duplicate *worksheets* for each *Part*; one for each of the *ten Cycles*. The following is *only an example*. We will use a facsimile of the top of the same *"A1"* worksheet shown twice below to better illustrate handling the procedure as one progresses through it.

In this example (see worksheet diagram on next page): the first *item (1.0)* *"read"* four times, each marked with a *"/"* (*slash*), then gave *"no-read"* three times. These three *"no-reads"* at the end don't need to be marked, since it is a necessary condition for moving to the next *item*. The second *item (1.1.1) "read"* twice, each marked with a *"/"* (*slash*), followed by three *"no-reads."* The third *item (1.1.2) "read"* three times, then three *"no-reads."* However, for whatever reason, the next *item* here *(1.1.3)* doesn't *"read"* at all three times from the start. So, what does a *Seeker* do?

```
CYCLE:A  PART:1  DATE:##/##/##
    1.0    ////
    1.1.1  //
    1.1.2  ///
    1.1.3  x
```

If *items* cease *discharging* easily (seeming more *solid* rather than *defragmenting*), or a new *item* does not give any *"reads"* three times right from the start, there may be *charge* still left on a recent prior *item*.

In this example: the *Seeker* puts an "x" in the space next to *1.1.3*. Since they are still near the top of the *Implant-Platform*, they decide to check the last few *item-lines* starting from the top. This implies another systematic use of the word *"backtrack."* Usually, a *Seeker* only *backtracks* one or two *items*. In this one area: experience with the procedure *may* aid getting a sense of how far one needs to *backtrack* when this occurs.

The *Seeker backtracks* to *1.0* and finds it still gives three *"no-reads"*; and they place an "x" there now. The same occurs for *1.1.1*; another "x." However, *1.1.2* is found to still have *charge* on it, and its *"newer reads"* are marked with a "\" (*backslash*) this time, to show that you have *backtracked* for those *"reads."* In our example: it *"read"* four times before three *"no-reads."* Now, *1.1.3 "reads"* nine times before its three *"no-reads"*; and the *Seeker* continues with handling the *next item* in the *listed-sequence*, and so on until the end of that *"Platform."*

```
CYCLE:A  PART:1  DATE:##/##/##
   1.0    //// x
   1.1.1  // x
   1.1.2  /// \\\\
   1.1.3  x /////////
```

Backtracking should be done sparingly and not as a solution to inexperience/improperly *contacting* a *listed item*. A *Seeker* must be careful to properly *direct attention* to the *backtracked item* just prior, and not accidentally put *attention* on the same *item* where it also appears earlier or later in the *Incident*. If a particular *item* just seems to keep *registering* on a *Meter* numerous times: be certain not to *"suppress"* it; keep *running* it until it fully *discharges*.

It is important to note, when handling this procedure: any extreme unpleasantness, pain, or sudden illness, is typically a result of *passing-over* or *suppressing* the *"charge"* from earlier *items;* or the mistaken redirection of *attention* on the same *item* in a later *Cycle* that has not yet been handled.

Most troubles with this procedure can be avoided by: understanding the *instructions;* understanding the meaning of any *words* used in a PCL or *"command-lines";* seeing and recording all *Meter-reads;* making sure each *item* is fully *discharged* before continuing; not skipping any *Steps*, *Parts*, or *Cycles;* and finally, sticking with the procedure to its conclusion—and not getting distracted by "exploring" the *Mind-System* during these *sessions*.

Misunderstood words can affect *"reads."* And while the procedure has been found effective in its standard form, there are suggested alternative variations for some *words* used to represent certain *items*. Although the *Implanting-Incident* is uniform to *Entry-into-this-Universe*, we do allow for varying the standard form with these semantic variations—assuming an individual's interpretation of some parts of their experience differed slightly. The alternatives only appear for certain *items*; and are only used in cases where a *Seeker* is having difficulty getting a *"command-line"* to *"read"* in its standard wording.

HANDLING "PART-4" AND "PART-5"

Implanted-Items for *Part-4* and *Part-5* are *"object-items"* rather than *"command-items."* They are still *run* as PCL, but they involve perceiving various *shapes* and *constructs*. In this wise, it is important for a *Seeker* to understand the distinction between a *"transparent form"* (or *"outline"*) and a *"solid form"* of the same *shape*; and between a *"two-dimensional"* (2D) *square* or *circle*, and a *"three-dimensional"* (3D) *cube* or *sphere*, &tc.

Another critical clarification a *Seeker* should know for these *Parts*: the distinction between a *"tetrahedron"* (with *four*-sides/faces/facets, all *triangles*, including the *base*) and a *"pyramid"* (with *five*-sides total, four *triangle* faces/facets, and a *square* base).

For the purpose of *spotting* in the *incident*: the *"object-items"* all *appear* approximately three feet (or one meter) away from your *point-of-view* at *"head/eye-level."* There will be *one, two, three,* or *four "objects"* for each *item-line*. The position(s) of the *"object-item(s)"* for *processing* is based on the number/quantity of them.

1 *"object-item"* : in-front
2 *"object-items"* : left-side + right-side
3 *"object-items"* : in-front, left-side + right-side
4 *"object-items"* : in-front, left-side + right-side, behind

```
        &           & = THE LIGHT
        x           x = OBJECT POSITIONS
      x A x         A = THE ALPHA-SPIRIT
        x
```

When first *running* the procedure, practice *perceiving* the proper quantity of *object(s)* indicated on the *item-line* (PCL) as a single *intention*/action. The *object(s)* will either be *"going in / towards"* or *"going away"* (as indicated in the PCL). Such instructions for the *"motion"* are used for the *defragmentation* procedure and are not *"implanted messages"* from the *incident* itself. It *mimics* the sense of *motion* that was experienced in the *incident*. *"Spotting"* and *"contacting"* the *mass* of the *object(s)* is what produces the necessary *"Meter-reads."*

PROCEDURE COMPLETION

Upon completion of *"J5"* — the *tenth* and final *Cycle* of handling *Part-5* — a *Seeker should* have achieved a perceivable *"gain"* or a greatly increased sense of *"release/relief,"* &tc. If this is not the case — and the *fragmentation* actually seems more *"solid"* rather than *"erased"* — it is possible that another complete *series* of all ten *Cycles* of the same *Jewel Procedure* may need to be repeated using new *worksheets*.

Alternatively, there is also the possibility — due to the amount of time spent on the procedure, various separate *sessions*, and numerous repetitive *items* — that some *attention* may have "locked up" (become *entangled*) with some point of the actual *processing* (rather than the *charge* left on the *incident* itself). This basically means that *charge* was *added* to an *item-line* in the *present* during the *processing*.

If this appears to be the case: the *processing sessions* themselves can be "scanned" for *"locked up attention"* (using the *item-lists* and *Meter*). This type of "scanning" and *assessing* for *"within the last {number of} months, has any charge been left on {item}?"* only applies to repairing a *session-charge*; this does not work for *processing-out* the actual *Implanting-Incident*; it does not substitute the procedure. Hence, this should only be done *after* a full *series* of ten *Cycles* is completed

Because you are "scanning" an *"item"* for the entire duration you have been *running* the procedure, you only need to treat each *"list-item"* once. The *assessment*-PCL (given above) is for that *"list-item"* any time it appeared in the procedure (during that duration of time). If you get a *"read"* on something, you'd mark it on the sheet, then use the *Meter* to *assess* for which Cycle, &tc. Usually *spotting* that a *charge being added* has occurred (and knowing precisely *when* in the *session* and *where* in the

Platform-list it occurred) is enough to resolve it with *Actualized attention/Awareness*.

The goal of this procedure is to actually "*erase*" or "*disperse*" the *mental-charge* that is maintained from this *incident; not* simply take *some of the weight off,* as we commonly find with other *processes.* This means handling even the most *subtle fragmentation* to an end-point; not only those aspects that seem the most obviously turbulent. There is also a critical difference in *spotting* a certain *Part/Step* in one *Cycle* (or time within the *incident*) from another.

JEWEL PROCEDURE– PART 1

[*Speak the "command-item" a few times out loud, and "spot the Alpha" (and "Light"); then speak the "command-item" while "spotting the Alpha" (and "Light"). Perform this in whatever way produces the best "Meter-reads."*]

1.1.0 *Spot the Light; Spot the Alpha*

1.1.1 **TO BE NOBODY;** & *Spot the Alpha*
1.1.2 **TO BE EVERYBODY;** & *Spot the Alpha*
1.1.3 **TO BE NOBODY, TO BE EVERYBODY;** & *Spot the Alpha*

1.2.1 **TO BE ME;** & *Spot the Alpha*
1.2.2 **TO BE YOU;** & *Spot the Alpha*
1.2.3 **TO BE ME, TO BE YOU;** & *Spot the Alpha*

1.3.1 **TO BE MYSELF;** & *Spot the Alpha*
1.3.2 **TO BE OTHERS;** & *Spot the Alpha*
1.3.3 **TO BE MYSELF, TO BE OTHERS;** & *Spot the Alpha*

  * A possible alternate given below *if 1.4.1 doesn't register, even with* backtracking.

1.4.1 **TO BE AN ANIMAL;** & *Spot the Alpha*
1.4.2 **TO BE ANIMALS;** & *Spot the Alpha*
1.4.3 **TO BE AN ANIMAL, TO BE ANIMALS;** & *Spot the Alpha*
*if "...AN ANIMAL" won't read, try "TO BE A FISH."

1.5.0 *Spot the Light; Spot the Alpha*

1.5.1 **TO BE A BODY;** & *Spot the Alpha*
1.5.2 **TO BE BODIES;** & *Spot the Alpha*
1.5.3 **TO BE A BODY, TO BE BODIES;** & *Spot the Alpha*

1.6.1 **TO BE MATTER;** & *Spot the Alpha*
1.6.2 **TO BE SPACE;** & *Spot the Alpha*
1.6.3 **TO BE MATTER, TO BE SPACE;** & *Spot the Alpha*

1.7.1 **TO BE A SPIRIT;** & *Spot the Alpha*
1.7.2 **TO BE SPIRITS;** & *Spot the Alpha*
1.7.3 **TO BE A SPIRIT, TO BE SPIRITS;** & *Spot the Alpha*

  *A possible alternate given below *if 1.8.1 doesn't register, even with* backtracking.

1.8.1 **TO BE A GOD;** & *Spot the Alpha*
1.8.2 **TO BE GODS;** & *Spot the Alpha*

1.8.3 **TO BE A GOD, TO BE GODS**; & *Spot the Alpha*
if "...A GOD" won't read, try "TO BE A METAHUMAN."

1.9.0 *Spot the Light; Spot the Alpha*

1.9.1 **TO DO NOTHING**; & *Spot the Alpha*
1.9.2 **TO DO EVERYTHING**; & *Spot the Alpha*
1.9.3 **TO DO NOTHING, TO DO EVERYTHING**; & *Spot the Alpha*

1.10.1 **TO DO MUCH**; & *Spot the Alpha*
1.10.2 **TO DO LITTLE**; & *Spot the Alpha*
1.10.3 **TO DO MUCH, TO DO LITTLE**; & *Spot the Alpha*

* A possible alternate given below *if 1.11.2* doesn't register, even with backtracking.

1.11.1 **TO DO IT ALL**; & *Spot the Alpha*
1.11.2 **TO DO NOT ANY**; & *Spot the Alpha*
1.11.3 **TO DO IT ALL, TO DO NOT ANY**; & *Spot the Alpha*
if "...NOT ANY" won't read, try "TO DO NOT ANYTHING."

1.12.1 **TO DO AMBITIOUSLY**; & *Spot the Alpha*
1.12.2 **TO DO SLIGHTLY**; & *Spot the Alpha*
1.12.3 **TO DO AMBITIOUSLY, TO DO SLIGHTLY**; & *Spot the Alpha*

1.13.0 *Spot the Light; Spot the Alpha*

1.13.1 **TO DO MORE**; & *Spot the Alpha*
1.13.2 **TO DO LESS**; & *Spot the Alpha*
1.13.3 **TO DO MORE, TO DO LESS**; & *Spot the Alpha*

1.14.1 **TO DO SPLENDIDLY**; & *Spot the Alpha*
1.14.2 **TO DO AWFULLY**; & *Spot the Alpha*
1.14.3 **TO DO SPLENDIDLY, TO DO AWFULLY**; & *Spot the Alpha*

1.15.1 **TO DO WISELY**; & *Spot the Alpha*
1.15.2 **TO DO FOOLISHLY**; & *Spot the Alpha*
1.15.3 **TO DO WISELY, TO DO FOOLISHLY**; & *Spot the Alpha*

1.16.1 **TO DO RIGHT**; & *Spot the Alpha*
1.16.2 **TO DO WRONG**; & *Spot the Alpha*
1.16.3 **TO DO RIGHT, TO DO WRONG**; & *Spot the Alpha*

1.17.0 *Spot the Light; Spot the Alpha*

1.17.1 **TO HAVE NOTHING**; & *Spot the Alpha*
1.17.2 **TO HAVE EVERYTHING**; & *Spot the Alpha*

1.17.3 TO HAVE NOTHING, TO HAVE EVERYTHING;
        & Spot the Alpha

1.18.1 TO HAVE MUCH; *& Spot the Alpha*
1.18.2 TO HAVE LITTLE; *& Spot the Alpha*
1.18.3 TO HAVE MUCH, TO HAVE LITTLE; *& Spot the Alpha*

1.19.1 TO HAVE ALL; *& Spot the Alpha*
1.19.2 TO HAVE NONE; *& Spot the Alpha*
1.19.3 TO HAVE ALL, TO HAVE NONE; *& Spot the Alpha*

1.20.1 TO HAVE HUGELY; *& Spot the Alpha*
1.20.2 TO HAVE POORLY; *& Spot the Alpha*
1.20.3 TO HAVE HUGELY, TO HAVE POORLY; *& Spot the Alpha*

1.21.0 *Spot the Light; Spot the Alpha*

1.21.1 TO HAVE GREEDILY; *& Spot the Alpha*
1.21.2 TO HAVE SELECTIVELY; *& Spot the Alpha*
1.21.3 TO HAVE GREEDILY, TO HAVE SELECTIVELY;
        & Spot the Alpha

1.22.1 TO HAVE MIGHTILY; *& Spot the Alpha*
1.22.2 TO HAVE SPARSELY; *& Spot the Alpha*
1.22.3 TO HAVE MIGHTILY, TO HAVE SPARSELY; *& Spot the Alpha*

  * A possible alternate is given below *if 1.23.2 doesn't register, even with backtracking.*

1.23.1 TO HAVE MAGNIFICENTLY; *& Spot the Alpha*
1.23.2 TO HAVE TAWDRILY; *& Spot the Alpha*
1.23.3 TO HAVE MAGNIFICENTLY, TO HAVE TAWDRILY;
        & Spot the Alpha
  *if "...TAWDRILY" won't read, try "TO HAVE TASTELESSLY."

1.24.1 TO HAVE TOTALITY; *& Spot the Alpha*
1.24.2 TO HAVE NEGATIVENESS; *& Spot the Alpha*
1.24.3 TO HAVE TOTALITY, TO HAVE NEGATIVENESS;
        & Spot the Alpha

1.25.0 *Spot the Light; Spot the Alpha*

1.25.1 TO STAY EVERYWHERE; *& Spot the Alpha*
1.25.2 TO STAY NOWHERE; *& Spot the Alpha*
1.25.3 TO STAY EVERYWHERE, TO STAY NOWHERE;
        & Spot the Alpha

1.26.1 TO STAY HERE; & *Spot the Alpha*
1.26.2 TO STAY THERE; & *Spot the Alpha*
1.26.3 TO STAY HERE, TO STAY THERE; & *Spot the Alpha*

1.27.1 TO STAY NEAR; & *Spot the Alpha*
1.27.2 TO STAY FAR; & *Spot the Alpha*
1.27.3 TO STAY NEAR, TO STAY FAR; & *Spot the Alpha*

1.28.1 TO STAY UP; & *Spot the Alpha*
1.28.2 TO STAY DOWN; & *Spot the Alpha*
1.28.3 TO STAY UP, TO STAY DOWN; & *Spot the Alpha*

1.29.0 *Spot the Light; Spot the Alpha*

* A possible alternate is given below *if Step-1.29.3 doesn't register,* even with backtracking.

1.29.1 TO STAY OUT; & *Spot the Alpha*
1.29.2 TO STAY IN; & *Spot the Alpha*
1.29.3 TO STAY OUT, TO STAY IN; & *Spot the Alpha*
*if "...OUT...IN" won't read, try reversing order of "OUT" and "IN."

1.30.1 TO STAY BACK; & *Spot the Alpha*
1.30.2 TO STAY FORWARD; & *Spot the Alpha*
1.30.3 TO STAY BACK, TO STAY FORWARD; & *Spot the Alpha*

1.31.1 TO STAY EARLIER; & *Spot the Alpha*
1.31.2 TO STAY LATER; & *Spot the Alpha*
1.31.3 TO STAY EARLIER, TO STAY LATER; & *Spot the Alpha*

* A possible alternate is given below *if 1.32.2 doesn't register,* even with backtracking.

1.32.1 TO STAY PRESENT; & *Spot the Alpha*
1.32.2 TO STAY ABSENT; & *Spot the Alpha*
1.32.3 TO STAY PRESENT, TO STAY ABSENT; & *Spot the Alpha*
*if "...ABSENT" won't read, try "TO STAY AWAY."

JEWEL PROCEDURE– PART 2

[*Speak the "command-item" a few times out loud, and "spot the Alpha" (and "Light"); then speak the "command-item" while "spotting the Alpha" (and "Light"). Perform this in whatever way produces the best Meter-reads. Keep saying the "command-item" phrase as a "noun" or "terminal" while spotting* *the Alpha; performing this action until it no longer registers a read. Mark reads with a "/" (slash). If the next item-line doesn't register, check earlier line(s) and mark any backtracked reads with a "\" (backslash). Part-2 also takes excessive charge off of keywords used in Part-3.]*

   2.0 *Spot the Light; Spot the Alpha*

   2.1 THE NOW; *& Spot the Alpha*

   2.2 THE PAST; *& Spot the Alpha*

   2.3 THE FUTURE; *& Spot the Alpha*

   2.4 THE TIME; *& Spot the Alpha*

   2.5 THE SPACE; *& Spot the Alpha*

   2.6 THE MOTION; *& Spot the Alpha*

   2.7 THE ENERGY; *& Spot the Alpha*

   2.8 THE MASSES; *& Spot the Alpha*

   2.9 THE SELF; *& Spot the Alpha*

  2.10 THE OTHERS; *& Spot the Alpha*

  2.11 THE LIFE; *& Spot the Alpha*

   2.0 *Spot the Light; Spot the Alpha*

  2.12 THE EXISTENCE; *& Spot the Alpha*

  2.13 THE CONDITIONS; *& Spot the Alpha*

  2.14 THE EFFECTS; *& Spot the Alpha*

  2.15 THE PICTURES; *& Spot the Alpha*

  2.16 THE MIND; *& Spot the Alpha*

  2.17 THE HISTORIES; *& Spot the Alpha*

  2.18 THE REACTION; *& Spot the Alpha*

  2.19 THE GOAL; *& Spot the Alpha*

  2.20 THE CHAOS; *& Spot the Alpha*

  2.21 THE UNIVERSE; *& Spot the Alpha*

JEWEL PROCEDURE– PART 3

[Speak the "command-item" phrase a few times out loud, and "spot the Alpha" (and "Light"); speak the "command-item" while "spotting the Alpha" (and "Light"). Perform this in whichever way produces the best "reads" until that action no longer registers.]

3.1.0 *Spot the Light; Spot the Alpha*

3.1.1 CREATING TO DESTROY THE NOW; & *Spot the Alpha*
3.1.2 DESTROYING TO CREATE THE NOW; & *Spot the Alpha*
3.1.3 CREATING TO DESTROY THE NOW,
DESTROYING TO CREATE THE NOW; & *Spot the Alpha*

3.2.1 CREATING TO DESTROY THE PAST; & *Spot the Alpha*
3.2.2 DESTROYING TO CREATE THE PAST; & *Spot the Alpha*
3.2.3 CREATING TO DESTROY THE PAST,
DESTROYING TO CREATE THE PAST; & *Spot the Alpha*

3.3.1 CREATING TO DESTROY THE FUTURE; & *Spot the Alpha*
3.3.2 DESTROYING TO CREATE THE FUTURE; & *Spot the Alpha*
3.3.3 CREATING TO DESTROY THE FUTURE,
DESTROYING TO CREATE THE FUTURE; & *Spot the Alpha*

3.4.1 CREATING TO DESTROY THE TIME; & *Spot the Alpha*
3.4.2 DESTROYING TO CREATE THE TIME; & *Spot the Alpha*
3.4.3 CREATING TO DESTROY THE TIME,
DESTROYING TO CREATE THE TIME; & *Spot the Alpha*

3.5.1 CREATING TO DESTROY THE SPACE; & *Spot the Alpha*
3.5.2 DESTROYING TO CREATE THE SPACE; & *Spot the Alpha*
3.5.3 CREATING TO DESTROY THE SPACE,
DESTROYING TO CREATE THE SPACE; & *Spot the Alpha*

3.6.1 CREATING TO DESTROY THE MOTION; & *Spot the Alpha*
3.6.2 DESTROYING TO CREATE THE MOTION; & *Spot the Alpha*
3.6.3 CREATING TO DESTROY THE MOTION,
DESTROYING TO CREATE THE MOTION; & *Spot the Alpha*

3.7.1 CREATING TO DESTROY THE ENERGY; & *Spot the Alpha*
3.7.2 DESTROYING TO CREATE THE ENERGY; & *Spot the Alpha*
3.7.3 CREATING TO DESTROY THE ENERGY,
DESTROYING TO CREATE THE ENERGY; & *Spot the Alpha*

3.8.1 CREATING TO DESTROY THE MASSES; & *Spot the Alpha*
3.8.2 DESTROYING TO CREATE THE MASSES; & *Spot the Alpha*
3.8.3 CREATING TO DESTROY THE MASSES,
DESTROYING TO CREATE THE MASSES; & *Spot the Alpha*

3.9.1 CREATING TO DESTROY THE SELF; & *Spot the Alpha*
3.9.2 DESTROYING TO CREATE THE SELF; & *Spot the Alpha*
3.9.3 CREATING TO DESTROY THE SELF,
DESTROYING TO CREATE THE SELF; & *Spot the Alpha*

3.10.1 CREATING TO DESTROY THE OTHERS; & *Spot the Alpha*
3.10.2 DESTROYING TO CREATE THE OTHERS; & *Spot the Alpha*
3.10.3 CREATING TO DESTROY THE OTHERS,
DESTROYING TO CREATE THE OTHERS; & *Spot the Alpha*

3.11.1 CREATING TO DESTROY THE LIFE; & *Spot the Alpha*
3.11.2 DESTROYING TO CREATE THE LIFE; & *Spot the Alpha*
3.11.3 CREATING TO DESTROY THE LIFE,
DESTROYING TO CREATE THE LIFE; & *Spot the Alpha*

3.12.1 CREATING TO DESTROY THE EXISTENCE; & *Spot the Alpha*
3.12.2 DESTROYING TO CREATE THE EXISTENCE;
& *Spot the Alpha*
3.12.3 CREATING TO DESTROY THE EXISTENCE,
DESTROYING TO CREATE THE EXISTENCE;
& *Spot the Alpha*

3.13.1 CREATING TO DESTROY THE CONDITIONS;
& *Spot the Alpha*
3.13.2 DESTROYING TO CREATE THE CONDITIONS;
& *Spot the Alpha*
3.13.3 CREATING TO DESTROY THE CONDITIONS,
DESTROYING TO CREATE THE CONDITIONS;
& *Spot the Alpha*

3.14.1 CREATING TO DESTROY THE EFFECTS; & *Spot the Alpha*
3.14.2 DESTROYING TO CREATE THE EFFECTS; & *Spot the Alpha*
3.14.3 CREATING TO DESTROY THE EFFECTS,
DESTROYING TO CREATE THE EFFECTS; & *Spot the Alpha*

3.15.1 CREATING TO DESTROY THE PICTURES; & *Spot the Alpha*
3.15.2 DESTROYING TO CREATE THE PICTURES; & *Spot the Alpha*
3.15.3 CREATING TO DESTROY THE PICTURES,
DESTROYING TO CREATE THE PICTURES; & *Spot the Alpha*

3.16.1 CREATING TO DESTROY THE MIND; & *Spot the Alpha*
3.16.2 DESTROYING TO CREATE THE MIND; & *Spot the Alpha*
3.16.3 CREATING TO DESTROY THE MIND,
DESTROYING TO CREATE THE MIND; & *Spot the Alpha*

3.17.1 CREATING TO DESTROY THE HISTORIES; & *Spot the Alpha*
3.17.2 DESTROYING TO CREATE THE HISTORIES;
& *Spot the Alpha*

3.17.3 CREATING TO DESTROY THE HISTORIES,
DESTROYING TO CREATE THE HISTORIES;
& Spot the Alpha

3.18.1 CREATING TO DESTROY THE REACTION; *& Spot the Alpha*
3.18.2 DESTROYING TO CREATE THE REACTION; *& Spot the Alpha*
3.18.3 CREATING TO DESTROY THE REACTION,
DESTROYING TO CREATE THE REACTION; *& Spot the Alpha*

3.19.1 CREATING TO DESTROY THE GOAL; *& Spot the Alpha*
3.19.2 DESTROYING TO CREATE THE GOAL; *& Spot the Alpha*
3.19.3 CREATING TO DESTROY THE GOAL,
DESTROYING TO CREATE THE GOAL; *& Spot the Alpha*

3.20.1 CREATING TO DESTROY THE CHAOS; *& Spot the Alpha*
3.20.2 DESTROYING TO CREATE THE CHAOS; *& Spot the Alpha*
3.20.3 CREATING TO DESTROY THE CHAOS,
DESTROYING TO CREATE THE CHAOS; *& Spot the Alpha*

3.21.1 CREATING TO DESTROY THE UNIVERSE; *& Spot the Alpha*
3.21.2 DESTROYING TO CREATE THE UNIVERSE; *& Spot the Alpha*
3.21.3 CREATING TO DESTROY THE UNIVERSE,
DESTROYING TO CREATE THE UNIVERSE; *& Spot the Alpha*

JEWEL PROCEDURE– PART 4

[*Spot the "object-item" to get the reads. For each item-line: spot the proper number of objects, in the proper positions, with the proper motion taking place, in order to get the best "reads" until that action no longer registers on the Meter. A Seeker may wish to prepare simple diagrams of the shapes/objects on their worksheet, including arrows to indicate the motion (either coming towards or going away).*]

4.1.0 *Spot the Light; Spot the Alpha*

4.1.1 *Spot one transparent* **TRIANGLE** *going away from the front.*

4.1.2 *Spot two transparent* **TRIANGLES** *going away from the sides.*

4.1.3 *Spot three transparent* **TRIANGLES** *going away from the sides and the front.*

4.1.4 *Spot four transparent* **TRIANGLES** *going away from the front, back, and sides.*

4.2.1 *Spot one transparent* **TRIANGLE** *coming in from the front.*

4.2.2 *Spot two transparent* TRIANGLES *coming in from the sides.*

4.2.3 *Spot three transparent* TRIANGLES *coming in from the sides and the front.*

4.2.4 *Spot four transparent* TRIANGLES *coming in from the front, back, and sides.*

4.3.0 *Spot the Light; Spot the Alpha*

4.3.1 *Spot one transparent* CIRCLE *going away from the front.*

4.3.2 *Spot two transparent* CIRCLES *going away from the sides.*

4.3.3 *Spot three transparent* CIRCLES *going away from the sides and the front.*

4.3.4 *Spot four transparent* CIRCLES *going away from the front, back, and sides.*

4.4.1 *Spot one transparent* CIRCLE *coming in from the front.*

4.4.2 *Spot two transparent* CIRCLES *coming in from the sides.*

4.4.3 *Spot three transparent* CIRCLES *coming in from the sides and the front.*

4.4.4 *Spot four transparent* CIRCLES *coming in from the front, back, and sides.*

4.5.0 *Spot the Light; Spot the Alpha*

4.5.1 *Spot one transparent* SQUARE *going away from the front.*

4.5.2 *Spot two transparent* SQUARES *going away from the sides.*

4.5.3 *Spot three transparent* SQUARES *going away from the sides and the front.*

4.5.4 *Spot four transparent* SQUARES *going away from the front, back, and sides.*

4.6.1 *Spot one transparent* SQUARE *coming in from the front.*

4.6.2 *Spot two transparent* SQUARES *coming in from the sides.*

4.6.3 *Spot three transparent* SQUARES *coming in from the sides and the front.*

4.6.4 *Spot four transparent* SQUARES *coming in from the front, back, and sides.*

4.7.0 *Spot the Light; Spot the Alpha*

4.7.1 *Spot one transparent* OVAL *going away from the front.*

4.7.2 *Spot two transparent* OVALS *going away from the sides.*

4.7.3 *Spot three transparent* OVALS *going away from the sides and the front.*

4.7.4   *Spot four transparent* **OVALS** *going away from the front, back, and sides.*

4.8.1   *Spot one transparent* **OVAL** *coming in from the front.*

4.8.2   *Spot two transparent* **OVALS** *coming in from the sides.*

4.8.3   *Spot three transparent* **OVALS** *coming in from the sides and the front.*

4.8.4   *Spot four transparent* **OVALS** *coming in from the front, back, and sides.*

4.9.0   *Spot the Light; Spot the Alpha*

4.9.1   *Spot one transparent* **TETRAHEDRON** *going away from the front.*

4.9.2   *Spot two transparent* **TETRAHEDRONS** *going away from the sides.*

4.9.3   *Spot three transparent* **TETRAHEDRONS** *going away from the sides and the front.*

4.9.4   *Spot four transparent* **TETRAHEDRONS** *going away from the front, back, and sides.*

4.10.1 *Spot one transparent* **TETRAHEDRON** *coming in from the front.*

4.10.2 *Spot two transparent* **TETRAHEDRONS** *coming in from the sides.*

4.10.3 *Spot three transparent* **TETRAHEDRONS** *coming in from the sides and the front.*

4.10.4 *Spot four transparent* **TETRAHEDRONS** *coming in from the front, back, and sides.*

4.11.0 *Spot the Light; Spot the Alpha*

4.11.1 *Spot one transparent* **SPHERE** *going away from the front.*

4.11.2 *Spot two transparent* **SPHERES** *going away from the sides.*

4.11.3 *Spot three transparent* **SPHERES** *going away from the sides and the front.*

4.11.4 *Spot four transparent* **SPHERES** *going away from front, back, and sides.*

4.12.1 *Spot one transparent* **SPHERE** *coming in from the front.*

4.12.2 *Spot two transparent* **SPHERES** *coming in from the sides.*

4.12.3 *Spot three transparent* **SPHERES** *coming in from the sides and the front.*

4.12.4 *Spot four transparent* **SPHERES** *coming in from the front, back, and sides.*

4.13.0 *Spot the Light; Spot the Alpha*

4.13.1 *Spot one transparent* **CUBE** *going away from the front.*
4.13.2 *Spot two transparent* **CUBES** *going away from the sides.*
4.13.3 *Spot three transparent* **CUBES** *going away from the sides and the front.*
4.13.4 *Spot four transparent* **CUBES** *going away from the front, back, and sides.*

4.14.1 *Spot one transparent* **CUBE** *coming in from the front.*
4.14.2 *Spot two transparent* **CUBES** *coming in from the sides.*
4.14.3 *Spot three transparent* **CUBES** *coming in from the sides and the front.*
4.14.4 *Spot four transparent* **CUBES** *coming in from the front, back, and sides.*

4.15.0 *Spot the Light; Spot the Alpha*
4.15.1 *Spot one transparent* **EGG** *going away from the front.*
4.15.2 *Spot two transparent* **EGGS** *going away from the sides.*
4.15.3 *Spot three transparent* **EGGS** *going away from the sides and the front.*
4.15.4 *Spot four transparent* **EGGS** *going away from the front, back, and sides.*

4.16.1 *Spot one transparent* **EGG** *coming in from the front.*
4.16.2 *Spot two transparent* **EGGS** *coming in from the sides.*
4.16.3 *Spot three transparent* **EGGS** *coming in from the sides and the front.*
4.16.4 *Spot four transparent* **EGGS** *coming in from the front, back, and sides.*

4.17.0 *Spot the Light; Spot the Alpha*
4.17.1 *Spot one transparent* **PRISM** *going away from the front.*
4.17.2 *Spot two transparent* **PRISMS** *going away from the sides.*
4.17.3 *Spot three transparent* **PRISMS** *going away from the sides and the front.*
4.17.4 *Spot four transparent* **PRISMS** *going away from the front, back, and sides.*

4.18.1 *Spot one transparent* **PRISM** *coming in from the front.*
4.18.2 *Spot two transparent* **PRISMS** *coming in from the sides.*
4.18.3 *Spot three transparent* **PRISMS** *coming in from the sides and the front.*

4.18.4 *Spot four transparent* **PRISMS** *coming in from the front, back, and sides.*

4.19.0 *Spot the Light; Spot the Alpha*

4.19.1 *Spot one transparent* **CYLINDER TUBE** *going away from the front.*

4.19.2 *Spot two transparent* **CYLINDER TUBES** *going away from the sides.*

4.19.3 *Spot three transparent* **CYLINDER TUBES** *going away from the sides and the front.*

4.19.4 *Spot four transparent* **CYLINDER TUBES** *going away from the front, back, and sides.*

4.20.1 *Spot one transparent* **CYLINDER TUBE** *coming in from the front.*

4.20.2 *Spot two transparent* **CYLINDER TUBES** *coming in from the sides.*

4.20.3 *Spot three transparent* **CYLINDER TUBES** *coming in from the sides and the front.*

4.20.4 *Spot four transparent* **CYLINDER TUBES** *coming in from the front, back, and sides.*

4.21.0 *Spot the Light; Spot the Alpha*

4.21.1 *Spot one transparent* **RECTANGULAR BOX** *going away from the front.*

4.21.2 *Spot two transparent* **RECTANGULAR BOXES** *going away from the sides.*

4.21.3 *Spot three transparent* **RECTANGULAR BOXES** *going away from the sides and the front.*

4.21.4 *Spot four transparent* **RECTANGULAR BOXES** *going away from the front, back, and sides.*

4.22.1 *Spot one transparent* **RECTANGULAR BOX** *coming in from the front.*

4.22.2 *Spot two transparent* **RECTANGULAR BOXES** *coming in from the sides.*

4.22.3 *Spot three transparent* **RECTANGULAR BOXES** *coming in from the sides and the front.*

4.22.4 *Spot four transparent* **RECTANGULAR BOXES** *coming in from the front, back, and sides.*

4.23.0 *Spot the Light; Spot the Alpha*

4.23.1 *Spot one transparent* **FLATTENED TUBE** *going away from the front.*

4.23.2 *Spot two transparent* **FLATTENED TUBES** *going away from the sides.*

4.23.3 *Spot three transparent* **FLATTENED TUBES** *going away from the sides and the front.*

4.23.4 *Spot four transparent* **FLATTENED TUBES** *going away from the front, back, and sides.*

4.24.1 *Spot one transparent* **FLATTENED TUBE** *coming in from the front.*

4.24.2 *Spot two transparent* **FLATTENED TUBES** *coming in from the sides.*

4.24.3 *Spot three transparent* **FLATTENED TUBES** *coming in from the sides and the front.*

4.24.4 *Spot four transparent* **FLATTENED TUBES** *coming in from the front, back, and sides.*

4.25.0 *Spot the Light; Spot the Alpha*

4.25.1 *Spot one transparent* **PYRAMID** *going away from the front.*

4.25.2 *Spot two transparent* **PYRAMIDS** *going away from the sides.*

4.25.3 *Spot three transparent* **PYRAMIDS** *going away from the sides and the front.*

4.25.4 *Spot four transparent* **PYRAMIDS** *going away from the front, back, and sides.*

4.26.1 *Spot one transparent* **PYRAMID** *coming in from the front.*

4.26.2 *Spot two transparent* **PYRAMIDS** *coming in from the sides.*

4.26.3 *Spot three transparent* **PYRAMIDS** *coming in from the sides and the front.*

4.26.4 *Spot four transparent* **PYRAMIDS** *coming in from the front, back, and sides.*

4.27.0 *Spot the Light; Spot the Alpha*

4.27.1 *Spot one transparent* **COIL** *going away from the front.*

4.27.2 *Spot two transparent* **COILS** *going away from the sides.*

4.27.3 *Spot three transparent* **COILS** *going away from the sides and the front.*

4.27.4 *Spot four transparent* **COILS** *going away from the front, back, and sides.*

4.28.1 *Spot one transparent* **COIL** *coming in from the front.*

4.28.2 *Spot two transparent* **COILS** *coming in from the sides.*

4.28.3 *Spot three transparent* COILS *coming in from the sides and the front.*

4.28.4 *Spot four transparent* COILS *coming in from the front, back, and sides.*

4.29.0 *Spot the Light; Spot the Alpha*

4.29.1 *Spot one transparent* DIAMOND BOX *going away from the front.*

4.29.2 *Spot two transparent* DIAMOND BOXES *going away from the sides.*

4.29.3 *Spot three transparent* DIAMOND BOXES *going away from the sides and the front.*

4.29.4 *Spot four transparent* DIAMOND BOXES *going away from the front, back, and sides.*

4.30.1 *Spot one transparent* DIAMOND BOX *coming in from the front.*

4.30.2 *Spot two transparent* DIAMOND BOXES *coming in from the sides.*

4.30.3 *Spot three transparent* DIAMOND BOXES *coming in from the sides and the front.*

4.30.4 *Spot four transparent* DIAMOND BOXES *coming in from the front, back, and sides.*

4.31.0 *Spot the Light; Spot the Alpha*

4.31.1 *Spot one transparent* OVAL COIL TUBE *going away from the front.*

4.31.2 *Spot two transparent* OVAL COIL TUBES *going away from the sides.*

4.31.3 *Spot three transparent* OVAL COIL TUBES *going away from the sides and the front.*

4.31.4 *Spot four transparent* OVAL COIL TUBES *going away from the front, back, and sides.*

4.32.1 *Spot one transparent* OVAL COIL TUBE *coming in from the front.*

4.32.2 *Spot two transparent* OVAL COIL TUBES *coming in from the sides.*

4.32.3 *Spot three transparent* OVAL COIL TUBES *coming in from the sides and the front.*

4.32.4 *Spot four transparent* OVAL COIL TUBES *coming in from the front, back, and sides.*

JEWEL PROCEDURE– PART 5

[*Spot the "object-item" to get the reads. For each item-line: spot the proper number of objects, in the proper positions, with the proper motion taking place, in order to get the best "reads" until that action no longer registers on the Meter. A Seeker may wish to prepare simple diagrams of the shapes/objects on their worksheet, including arrows to indicate the motion (either coming towards or going away). When you complete this, return to Part-1 until you have completed a series of ten full cycles.]*

5.1.0 *Spot the Light; Spot the Alpha*

5.1.1 *Spot one solid* **TRIANGLE** *going away from the front.*
5.1.2 *Spot two solid* **TRIANGLES** *going away from the sides.*
5.1.3 *Spot three solid* **TRIANGLES** *going away from the sides and the front.*
5.1.4 *Spot four solid* **TRIANGLES** *going away from the front, back, and sides.*

5.2.1 *Spot one solid* **TRIANGLE** *coming in from the front.*
5.2.2 *Spot two solid* **TRIANGLES** *coming in from the sides.*
5.2.3 *Spot three solid* **TRIANGLES** *coming in from the sides and the front.*
5.2.4 *Spot four solid* **TRIANGLES** *coming in from the front, back, and sides.*

5.3.0 *Spot the Light; Spot the Alpha*

5.3.1 *Spot one solid* **CIRCLE** *going away from the front.*
5.3.2 *Spot two solid* **CIRCLES** *going away from the sides.*
5.3.3 *Spot three solid* **CIRCLES** *going away from the sides and the front.*
5.3.4 *Spot four solid* **CIRCLES** *going away from the front, back, and sides.*

5.4.1 *Spot one solid* **CIRCLE** *coming in from the front.*
5.4.2 *Spot two solid* **CIRCLES** *coming in from the sides.*
5.4.3 *Spot three solid* **CIRCLES** *coming in from the sides and the front.*
5.4.4 *Spot four solid* **CIRCLES** *coming in from the front, back, and sides.*

5.5.0 *Spot the Light; Spot the Alpha*

5.5.1 *Spot one solid* **SQUARE** *going away from the front.*
5.5.2 *Spot two solid* **SQUARES** *going away from the sides.*
5.5.3 *Spot three solid* **SQUARES** *going away from the sides and the front.*
5.5.4 *Spot four solid* **SQUARES** *going away from the front, back, and sides.*

5.6.1 *Spot one solid* **SQUARE** *coming in from the front.*
5.6.2 *Spot two solid* **SQUARES** *coming in from the sides.*
5.6.3 *Spot three solid* **SQUARES** *coming in from the sides and the front.*

5.6.4 *Spot four solid* **SQUARES** *coming in from the front, back, and sides.*

5.7.0 *Spot the Light; Spot the Alpha*

5.7.1 *Spot one solid* **OVAL** *going away from the front.*
5.7.2 *Spot two solid* **OVALS** *going away from the sides.*
5.7.3 *Spot three solid* **OVALS** *going away from the sides and the front.*
5.7.4 *Spot four solid* **OVALS** *going away from the front, back, and sides.*

5.8.1 *Spot one solid* **OVAL** *coming in from the front.*
5.8.2 *Spot two solid* **OVALS** *coming in from the sides.*
5.8.3 *Spot three solid* **OVALS** *coming in from the sides and the front.*
5.8.4 *Spot four solid* **OVALS** *coming in from the front, back, and sides.*

5.9.0 *Spot the Light; Spot the Alpha*

5.9.1 *Spot one solid* **TETRAHEDRON** *going away from the front.*
5.9.2 *Spot two solid* **TETRAHEDRONS** *going away from the sides.*
5.9.3 *Spot three solid* **TETRAHEDRONS** *going away from the sides and the front.*
5.9.4 *Spot four solid* **TETRAHEDRONS** *going away from the front, back, and sides.*

5.10.1 *Spot one solid* **TETRAHEDRON** *coming in from the front.*
5.10.2 *Spot two solid* **TETRAHEDRONS** *coming in from the sides.*
5.10.3 *Spot three solid* **TETRAHEDRONS** *coming in from the sides and the front.*
5.10.4 *Spot four solid* **TETRAHEDRONS** *coming in from the front, back, and sides.*

5.11.0 *Spot the Light; Spot the Alpha*

5.11.1 *Spot one solid* **SPHERE** *going away from the front.*
5.11.2 *Spot two solid* **SPHERES** *going away from the sides.*
5.11.3 *Spot three solid* **SPHERES** *going away from the sides and the front.*
5.11.4 *Spot four solid* **SPHERES** *going away from the front, back, and sides.*

5.12.1 *Spot one solid* **SPHERE** *coming in from the front.*
5.12.2 *Spot two solid* **SPHERES** *coming in from the sides.*
5.12.3 *Spot three solid* **SPHERES** *coming in from the sides and the front.*
5.12.4 *Spot four solid* **SPHERES** *coming in from the front, back, and sides.*

5.13.0 *Spot the Light; Spot the Alpha*

5.13.1 *Spot one solid* **CUBE** *going away from the front.*

5.13.2 *Spot two solid* **CUBES** *going away from the sides.*
5.13.3 *Spot three solid* **CUBES** *going away from the sides and the front.*
5.13.4 *Spot four solid* **CUBES** *going away from the front, back, and sides.*

5.14.1 *Spot one solid* **CUBE** *coming in from the front.*
5.14.2 *Spot two solid* **CUBES** *coming in from the sides.*
5.14.3 *Spot three solid* **CUBES** *coming in from the sides and the front.*
5.14.4 *Spot four solid* **CUBES** *coming in from the front, back, and sides.*

5.15.0 *Spot the Light; Spot the Alpha*

5.15.1 *Spot one solid* **EGG** *going away from the front.*
5.15.2 *Spot two solid* **EGGS** *going away from the sides.*
5.15.3 *Spot three solid* **EGGS** *going away from the sides and the front.*
5.15.4 *Spot four solid* **EGGS** *going away from the front, back, and sides.*

5.16.1 *Spot one solid* **EGG** *coming in from the front.*
5.16.2 *Spot two solid* **EGGS** *coming in from the sides.*
5.16.3 *Spot three solid* **EGGS** *coming in from the sides and the front.*
5.16.4 *Spot four solid* **EGGS** *coming in from the front, back, and sides.*

5.17.0 *Spot the Light; Spot the Alpha*

5.17.1 *Spot one solid* **PRISM** *going away from the front.*
5.17.2 *Spot two solid* **PRISMS** *going away from the sides.*
5.17.3 *Spot three solid* **PRISMS** *going away from the sides and the front.*
5.17.4 *Spot four solid* **PRISMS** *going away from the front, back, and sides.*

5.18.1 *Spot one solid* **PRISM** *coming in from the front.*
5.18.2 *Spot two solid* **PRISMS** *coming in from the sides.*
5.18.3 *Spot three solid* **PRISMS** *coming in from the sides and the front.*
5.18.4 *Spot four solid* **PRISMS** *coming in from the front, back, and sides.*

5.19.0 *Spot the Light; Spot the Alpha*

5.19.1 *Spot one solid* **CYLINDER TUBE** *going away from the front.*
5.19.2 *Spot two solid* **CYLINDER TUBES** *going away from the sides.*
5.19.3 *Spot three solid* **CYLINDER TUBES** *going away from the sides and the front.*
5.19.4 *Spot four solid* **CYLINDER TUBES** *going away from the front, back, and sides.*

5.20.1 *Spot one solid* **CYLINDER TUBE** *coming in from the front.*
5.20.2 *Spot two solid* **CYLINDER TUBES** *coming in from the sides.*

130 – AT#3

5.20.3 *Spot three solid* CYLINDER TUBES *coming in from the sides and the front.*
5.20.4 *Spot four solid* CYLINDER TUBES *coming in from the front, back, and sides.*

5.21.0 *Spot the Light; Spot the Alpha*
5.21.1 *Spot one solid* RECTANGULAR BOX *going away from the front.*
5.21.2 *Spot two solid* RECTANGULAR BOXES *going away from the sides.*
5.21.3 *Spot three solid* RECTANGULAR BOXES *going away from the sides and the front.*
5.21.4 *Spot four solid* RECTANGULAR BOXES *going away from the front, back, and sides.*
5.22.1 *Spot one solid* RECTANGULAR BOX *coming in from the front.*
5.22.2 *Spot two solid* RECTANGULAR BOXES *coming in from the sides.*
5.22.3 *Spot three solid* RECTANGULAR BOXES *coming in from the sides and the front.*
5.22.4 *Spot four solid* RECTANGULAR BOXES *coming in from the front, back, and sides.*

5.23.0 *Spot the Light; Spot the Alpha*
5.23.1 *Spot one solid* FLATTENED TUBE *going away from the front.*
5.23.2 *Spot two solid* FLATTENED TUBES *going away from the sides.*
5.23.3 *Spot three solid* FLATTENED TUBES *going away from the sides and the front.*
5.23.4 *Spot four solid* FLATTENED TUBES *going away from the front, back, and sides.*
5.24.1 *Spot one solid* FLATTENED TUBE *coming in from the front.*
5.24.2 *Spot two solid* FLATTENED TUBES *coming in from the sides.*
5.24.3 *Spot three solid* FLATTENED TUBES *coming in from the sides and the front.*
5.24.4 *Spot four solid* FLATTENED TUBES *coming in from the front, back, and sides.*

5.25.0 *Spot the Light; Spot the Alpha*
5.25.1 *Spot one solid* PYRAMID *going away from the front.*
5.25.2 *Spot two solid* PYRAMIDS *going away from the sides.*
5.25.3 *Spot three solid* PYRAMIDS *going away from the sides and the front.*
5.25.4 *Spot four solid* PYRAMIDS *going away from the front, back, and sides.*

5.26.1 *Spot one solid* **PYRAMID** *coming in from the front.*
5.26.2 *Spot two solid* **PYRAMIDS** *coming in from the sides.*
5.26.3 *Spot three solid* **PYRAMIDS** *coming in from the sides and the front.*
5.26.4 *Spot four solid* **PYRAMIDS** *coming in from the front, back, and sides.*

5.27.0 *Spot the Light; Spot the Alpha*

5.27.1 *Spot one solid* **COIL** *going away from the front.*
5.27.2 *Spot two solid* **COILS** *going away from the sides.*
5.27.3 *Spot three solid* **COILS** *going away from the sides and the front.*
5.27.4 *Spot four solid* **COILS** *going away from the front, back, and sides.*

5.28.1 *Spot one solid* **COIL** *coming in from the front.*
5.28.2 *Spot two solid* **COILS** *coming in from the sides.*
5.28.3 *Spot three solid* **COILS** *coming in from the sides and the front.*
5.28.4 *Spot four solid* **COILS** *coming in from the front, back, and sides.*

5.29.0 *Spot the Light; Spot the Alpha*

5.29.1 *Spot one solid* **DIAMOND BOX** *going away from the front.*
5.29.2 *Spot two solid* **DIAMOND BOXES** *going away from the sides.*
5.29.3 *Spot three solid* **DIAMOND BOXES** *going away from the sides and the front.*
5.29.4 *Spot four solid* **DIAMOND BOXES** *going away from the front, back, and sides.*

5.30.1 *Spot one solid* **DIAMOND BOX** *coming in from the front.*
5.30.2 *Spot two solid* **DIAMOND BOXES** *coming in from the sides.*
5.30.3 *Spot three solid* **DIAMOND BOXES** *coming in from the sides and the front.*
5.30.4 *Spot four solid* **DIAMOND BOXES** *coming in from the front, back, and sides.*

5.31.0 *Spot the Light; Spot the Alpha*

5.31.1 *Spot one solid* **OVAL COIL TUBE** *going away from the front.*
5.31.2 *Spot two solid* **OVAL COIL TUBES** *going away from the sides.*
5.31.3 *Spot three solid* **OVAL COIL TUBES** *going away from the sides and the front.*
5.31.4 *Spot four solid* **OVAL COIL TUBES** *going away from the front, back, and sides.*

5.32.1 *Spot one solid* **OVAL COIL TUBE** *coming in from the front.*
5.32.2 *Spot two solid* **OVAL COIL TUBES** *coming in from the sides.*

5.32.3 *Spot three solid* **OVAL COIL TUBES** *coming in from the sides and the front.*
5.32.4 *Spot four solid* **OVAL COIL TUBES** *coming in from the front, back, and sides.*

LEVEL-7 STABILIZATION POINT

Having completed *"The Jewel" Procedure*, a *Seeker* will likely have been *in-session* for several months, intensely handling a particular *Implanting-Incident* from a very long time ago. It is now time to "stabilize" these *gains* by bringing *Awareness* off of the *Backtrack (Spiritual Timeline)* and establishing *presence* in *present-time* again. To accomplish this, we will apply light *objective exercises*.

These *exercises* are all practiced outdoors, preferably during the day and in wide-open public places, such as a "park." Some do not require that environment and may be done "closer to home" or "alone" where appropriate. The purpose of this *Level-7 Stabilization Point* is to "extravert" a *Seeker's Awareness*, now that *"The Jewel" Procedure* is complete—rather than dwelling on the procedure or feeling introversion from months of *intensive processing*.

As a procedure or regimen, this series of exercises is similar to a "treasure hunt," except instead of collecting things, a *Seeker* goes out and walks around *spotting* and *noticing* various things. While these exercises may seem fairly casual, to remain systematic: a *Seeker* should distinguish a definitive "start-point" and "end-point" for each *processing exercise*.

Suitable *end-points* for an exercise include: feeling "brighter" or "better" (as a result of the exercise); having a "new realization" of any kind; gaining an increase in "spiritual perception"; assuming an "exterior viewpoint" (such as ZU-Vision); or if there have been no significant changes while processing for 15-20 minutes.

This first exercise is called *"New Discoveries"*—and unlike the others that follow, it is a PCL-series that is repeatedly *run* sequentially—1, 2, 3, 4, 5, 1, 2,...until a satisfactory *end-point*. [To be effective: it is important to actually *spot* and *identify* "some thing" and then *notice* "something about it"—rather than just darting around your attention and barely glancing at things.]

1. *"Spot some thing 'small'; notice something about it."*
2. *"Spot some thing 'big'; notice something about it."*
3. *"Spot some thing 'near'; notice something about it."*
4. *"Spot some thing 'far'; notice something about it."*
5. *"Spot some thing 'interesting'; notice something about it."*

Now that the *Seeker* has loosened up their *attention*: the following *objective exercises* may be combined or treated individually, depending on one's *session-time*, progress, and the availability of an appropriate (and safe) environment.

  A. *"Look around; count all the 'bodies' that you see. Then walk around and count some more. Keep track of how many you counted."*

  B. *"Look around; count all the 'female bodies' that you see. Notice something about each of them. Then walk around and count some more, noticing something about each of them."*

  C. *"Look around; count all the 'male bodies' that you see. Notice something about each of them. Then walk around and count some more, noticing something about each of them."*

  D. *"Locate a 'crowd' of human bodies. Spot the 'crowd' for its 'mass'; notice something about it. Spot the 'crowd' for the 'individuals'; notice something about it. Then alternate: Spotting the crowd as a mass; Spotting the crowd as individuals."*

  E. *"Observe people and your surroundings. Alternate: Spot objects you are not; Spot people you are not. Spot objects you are separate from; Spot people you are separate from."*

  F. *"Walk around and observe people and your surroundings. Alternate: Spot a person walking towards you; notice something about it. Spot a person walking away from you; notice something about it."*

  G. *"Walk around and observe people. Spot 'bodies' for their 'mass'; notice how they are 'anchored' to the ground."*

  H. *"Spot something (physical) about yourself that you don't like. Now observe other people and notice something about that part of them."*

  I. *"Look around and spot a 'body'. Get the sense that an 'Alpha-Spirit' is operating it. Do this many times."*

IMPLANTS AFTER "THE JEWEL"

An *advanced Seeker* has come a long way on the *Pathway* by this level of work. Having completed *"The Jewel" Procedure*—and taken a few weeks to reorient themselves in present-time with the *objective exercises* in the previous section—they are then ready to continue.

There are many areas that a *Seeker* "*could*" now pursue—including other *"False Jewel" incidents*, such as discussed in *AT Manual #4, "Implanted Universes."* But, for present purposes, *Systemology Level-7* is primarily concerned with *Implants* that have most strongly *solidified* and *fragmented* the *reality-agreements* and *programming* inherent to being "imprisoned" or "entrapped" in *this Physical Universe*.

This part of our progress gets a little more complicated; because some of the "*charge*" on these other *Implant-Items* does not always belong to us directly—but is held by other "*entities*" and "*spiritual fragments.*"

Although such subjects ("*entities,*" *&tc.*) are not addressed fully until *Systemology Level-8*: an *advanced Seeker* that has effectively handled *"The Jewel"* and *"Heaven Incident"* is experienced and skilled enough to "*discharge*" other related *Implants*.

Because we are dealing with *Alpha-Defragmentation*—and a composite situation where we are often connected to other *entities* during shared *incidents*—the methods of previous *processing-levels* are not appropriate or effective for these *eighteen Implant-Platforms*.

These *entities* often remain in close "proximity" to us during our lives after receiving the same *Implanting* we did. Some of them actually believe they *are* "us." By handling these *Implants* now at this level, a *Seeker* will find *Systemology Level-8* to be much more understandable and effective.

Use only the techniques and instruction from *"The Jewel" Implant-Procedure*, and the other eighteen *Implant-Platforms* within this current manual. The same rules apply; except that a *Seeker* has gotten used to "*spotting the Light*" as the hypnotic-mechanism. Most of these additional *Implant-Platforms* employed some other similar event (as the "*Light*") to confuse the *Alpha-Spirit* and/or reinforce the significance of its message. It could be "*explosions,*" "*electrical shocks*" or even "*moving suns*" (to provide an illusion of time passing).

As with *"seeing the Light"* (as a *visualization*), it is *not* necessary to *"hear an explosion," "feel a shock,"* or *"see a moving sun"* in order to *"spot"* and *"contact"* it. Although that part is not verbalized out loud as part of the *"command-item,"* a *Seeker* might say/intend *"Spot the explosion"* (*&tc.*) silently to themselves. When you *"spot"* where and what should be there, you get a *Meter-read*. Then, you keep *spotting* the *implant-item* that way until the action no longer *registers* a *charge*.

There is actually so much *charge* on these *Platforms* that it is not expected to be totally handled with a single *series-run*. It has been a standard practice among *advanced Seekers* to apply the same *tenfold-Cycle* method from *"The Jewel"* to these remaining *Implant-Platforms*.

As with the previous procedure: a *Seeker* also needs to *Spot* the *Alpha-Spirit*, or *Self*—getting a sense (or an *"impression"*) for how we were at the actual time of the *Implant/Incident*. Just as the PCL of *"Spot the Alpha"* was previously combined with *"Spot the Light"* (even when not written as such), for these *Platforms*: a *Seeker* may be required to simultaneously *"Spot the Explosion & Spot the Alpha"* or *"Spot the Electric Shock & Spot the Alpha"* (depending on the *Platform* being *run*).

Because of the sheer amount of data found within these *Platforms*—and repetitive *patterns* that require a lot of unnecessary space and expense to fully print out in this manual—some of these *Platforms* will be presented as *formulas* or *patterns*, along with a list of *"keywords"* or *"buttons"* used to fill in the *"blanks"* of the *formula*—so that the basic *pattern* may be applied to a number of different *"items"* in turn.

This is *not* an assessment activity; each combination of *formula* and *keyword* requires being *run* item by item as if it were all written out in long-form. In addition to making a *worksheet* for marking *Meter-reads*, a *Seeker* may need to use a *Platform-formula* and list of *keywords* to write out their own long-form version of the complete *Implant* before *processing* it. Some *Seekers* even make writing out the *Implant* a part of their *defragmentation* routine, as a means of seeing it *"external"* to *Self*—or *Self* being *"exterior"* to it. [This is highly recommended if a *Seeker* attempts these types of procedures without assistance of a *Biofeedback Device*.]

PLATFORM #1

[*This is a Platform long-form. It uses an "electric shock" as its implanting-gimmick. This may have reinforced a postulate that 'Alpha-Spirits are electrical-beings'. For this platform, the "command-item" (word) and the "electric shock" are connected; where there are two words, the "shock" occurs with the second word (in this case, the word "no"). Say the "command-item" a few times, spot the electric shock, spot the Alpha-Spirit; then say the "command-item" while spotting the Alpha-Spirit. Perform this whatever way produces the best "reads" until that action no longer registers a 'charge' on the GSR-Meter.*]

1.1.1 CREATE {electric shock}; & *Spot the Alpha*
1.1.2 CREATE NO {electric shock}; & *Spot the Alpha*
1.1.3 CREATE {electric shock}, CREATE NO {electric shock}; & *Spot the Alpha*
1.2.1 DESTROY {electric shock}; & *Spot the Alpha*
1.2.2 DESTROY NO {electric shock}; & *Spot the Alpha*
1.2.3 DESTROY {electric shock}, DESTROY NO {electric shock}; & *Spot the Alpha*
1.3.1 LOVE {electric shock}; & *Spot the Alpha*
1.3.2 LOVE NO {electric shock}; & *Spot the Alpha*
1.3.3 LOVE {electric shock}, LOVE NO {electric shock}; & *Spot the Alpha*
1.4.1 HATE {electric shock}; & *Spot the Alpha*
1.4.2 HATE NO {electric shock}; & *Spot the Alpha*
1.4.3 HATE {electric shock}, HATE NO {electric shock}; & *Spot the Alpha*
1.5.1 BE {electric shock}; & *Spot the Alpha*
1.5.2 BE NO {electric shock}; & *Spot the Alpha*
1.5.3 BE {electric shock}, BE NO {electric shock}; & *Spot the Alpha*
1.6.1 DISOWN {electric shock}; & *Spot the Alpha*
1.6.2 DISOWN NO {electric shock}; & *Spot the Alpha*
1.6.3 DISOWN {electric shock}, DISOWN NO {electric shock}; & *Spot the Alpha*
1.7.1 USE {electric shock}; & *Spot the Alpha*
1.7.2 USE NO {electric shock}; & *Spot the Alpha*
1.7.3 USE {electric shock}, USE NO {electric shock}; & *Spot the Alpha*
1.8.1 CONDEMN {electric shock}; & *Spot the Alpha*

138 – AT#3

1.8.2 CONDEMN NO {electric shock}; & Spot the Alpha
1.8.3 CONDEMN {electric shock}, CONDEMN NO {electric shock};
& Spot the Alpha
1.9.1 SEIZE {electric shock}; & Spot the Alpha
1.9.2 SEIZE NO {electric shock}; & Spot the Alpha
1.9.3 SEIZE {electric shock}, SEIZE NO {electric shock};
& Spot the Alpha
1.10.1 ESCAPE {electric shock}; & Spot the Alpha
1.10.2 ESCAPE NO {electric shock}; & Spot the Alpha
1.10.3 ESCAPE {electric shock}, ESCAPE NO {electric shock};
& Spot the Alpha

PLATFORM #2

[This is a Platform long-form. It uses a "sun swing" as its implanting-gimmick. The "sun-star" swings in an arc in front of you, from left to right. This may have given the illusion of time passing. The "command-item" (word) and the "sun swing" action are connected; where there are two words, it occurs with the second word. Say the "command-item" a few times, spot the sun swing, spot the Alpha-Spirit; then say the "command-item" while spotting the Alpha-Spirit. Perform this whatever way produces the best "reads" until that action no longer registers a 'charge' on the GSR-Meter.]

2.1.1 CREATE {sun swings}; & Spot the Alpha
2.1.2 CREATE NO {sun swings}; & Spot the Alpha
2.1.3 CREATE {sun swings}, CREATE NO {sun swings};
& Spot the Alpha
2.2.1 ABIDE {sun swings}; & Spot the Alpha
2.2.2 ABIDE NO {sun swings}; & Spot the Alpha
2.2.3 ABIDE {sun swings}, ABIDE NO {sun swings}; & Spot the Alpha
2.3.1 ENJOY {sun swings}; & Spot the Alpha
2.3.2 ENJOY NO {sun swings}; & Spot the Alpha
2.3.3 ENJOY {sun swings}, ENJOY NO {sun swings};
& Spot the Alpha
2.4.1 WELCOME {sun swings}; & Spot the Alpha
2.4.2 WELCOME NO {sun swings}; & Spot the Alpha
2.4.3 WELCOME {sun swings}, WELCOME NO {sun swings};
& Spot the Alpha
2.5.1 SHARE {sun swings}; & Spot the Alpha

2.5.2 SHARE NO {*sun swings*}; & *Spot the Alpha*
2.5.3 SHARE {*sun swings*}, SHARE NO {*sun swings*};
& *Spot the Alpha*
2.6.1 KEEP {*sun swings*}; & *Spot the Alpha*
2.6.2 KEEP NO {*sun swings*}; & *Spot the Alpha*
2.6.3 KEEP {*sun swings*}, KEEP NO {*sun swings*}; & *Spot the Alpha*
2.7.1 HOLD {*sun swings*}; & *Spot the Alpha*
2.7.2 HOLD NO {*sun swings*}; & *Spot the Alpha*
2.7.3 HOLD {*sun swings*}, HOLD NO {*sun swings*}; & *Spot the Alpha*
2.8.1 EXPLOIT {*sun swings*}; & *Spot the Alpha*
2.8.2 EXPLOIT NO {*sun swings*}; & *Spot the Alpha*
2.8.3 EXPLOIT {*sun swings*}, EXPLOIT NO {*sun swings*};
& *Spot the Alpha*
2.9.1 CONDEMN {*sun swings*}; & *Spot the Alpha*
2.9.2 CONDEMN NO {*sun swings*}; & *Spot the Alpha*
2.9.3 CONDEMN {*sun swings*}, CONDEMN NO {*sun swings*};
& *Spot the Alpha*
2.10.1 SKIP {*sun swings*}; & *Spot the Alpha*
2.10.2 SKIP NO {*sun swings*}; & *Spot the Alpha*
2.10.3 SKIP {*sun swings*}, SKIP NO {*sun swings*}; & *Spot the Alpha*
2.11.1 CONTINUE {*sun swings*}; & *Spot the Alpha*
2.11.2 CONTINUE NO {*sun swings*}; & *Spot the Alpha*
2.11.3 CONTINUE {*sun swings*}, CONTINUE NO {*sun swings*};
& *Spot the Alpha*
2.12.1 FORGET {*sun swings*}; & *Spot the Alpha*
2.12.2 FORGET NO {*sun swings*}; & *Spot the Alpha*
2.12.3 FORGET {*sun swings*}, FORGET NO {*sun swings*};
& *Spot the Alpha*

This next set of command-items were communicated during the Implant. They may "read" individually, or when combined, or both. Defragment whatever is there.

2.13.1 "THAT'S WHAT YOU GET FOR CREATING THIS UNIVERSE";
& *Spot the Alpha*
2.13.2 "GET OUT!"; & *Spot the Alpha*
2.13.3 "THAT'S WHAT YOU GET FOR CREATING THIS UNIVERSE",
"GET OUT!"; & *Spot the Alpha*

PLATFORM #3

[*This is a Platform long-form. It uses an "explosion" as its implanting-gimmick. The "explosion" occurs at the start and end of the Implant. There is also the "appearance of a gigantic being in the sky." This "gigantic being" is presumably issuing the "command-items" or at the very least is representing them. Say the "command-item" a few times, and spot the Alpha-Spirit; then say the "command-item" while spotting the Alpha-Spirit. Perform this whatever way produces the best "reads" until that action no longer registers a 'charge' on the GSR-Meter.*]

3.0.1 {*spot an explosion*}; & *Spot the Alpha*
3.0.2 {*spot the appearance of gigantic being in the sky*};
    & *Spot the Alpha*
3.1.1 YOU MUST SURVIVE; & *Spot the Alpha*
3.1.2 YOU MUSTN'T SURVIVE; & *Spot the Alpha*
3.1.3 YOU MUST SURVIVE, YOU MUSTN'T SURVIVE;
    & *Spot the Alpha*
3.2.1 YOU SHOULD SURVIVE; & *Spot the Alpha*
3.2.2 YOU SHOULDN'T SURVIVE; & *Spot the Alpha*
3.2.3 YOU SHOULD SURVIVE, YOU SHOULDN'T SURVIVE;
    & *Spot the Alpha*
3.3.1 YOU CAN SURVIVE; & *Spot the Alpha*
3.3.2 YOU CAN'T SURVIVE; & *Spot the Alpha*
3.3.3 YOU CAN SURVIVE, YOU CAN'T SURVIVE; & *Spot the Alpha*

**For the next three sets: defragment both the "he" and "she" as separate command-items. Only one or the other has to give a "read" to contact an item-line, but both should be checked and discharged fully.*

3.4.1 S/HE MUST SURVIVE; & *Spot the Alpha*
3.4.2 S/HE MUSTN'T SURVIVE; & *Spot the Alpha*
3.4.3 S/HE MUST SURVIVE, S/HE MUSTN'T SURVIVE;
    & *Spot the Alpha*
3.5.1 S/HE SHOULD SURVIVE; & *Spot the Alpha*
3.5.2 S/HE SHOULDN'T SURVIVE; & *Spot the Alpha*
3.5.3 S/HE SHOULD SURVIVE, S/HE SHOULDN'T SURVIVE;
    & *Spot the Alpha*
3.6.1 S/HE CAN SURVIVE; & *Spot the Alpha*
3.6.2 S/HE CAN'T SURVIVE; & *Spot the Alpha*
3.6.3 S/HE CAN SURVIVE, S/HE CAN'T SURVIVE; & *Spot the Alpha*

3.7.1 THEY MUST SURVIVE; & *Spot the Alpha*
3.7.2 THEY MUSTN'T SURVIVE; & *Spot the Alpha*
3.7.3 THEY MUST SURVIVE, THEY MUSTN'T SURVIVE;
& *Spot the Alpha*
3.8.1 THEY SHOULD SURVIVE; & *Spot the Alpha*
3.8.2 THEY SHOULDN'T SURVIVE; & *Spot the Alpha*
3.8.3 THEY SHOULD SURVIVE, THEY SHOULDN'T SURVIVE;
& *Spot the Alpha*
3.9.1 THEY CAN SURVIVE; & *Spot the Alpha*
3.9.2 THEY CAN'T SURVIVE; & *Spot the Alpha*
3.9.3 THEY CAN SURVIVE, THEY CAN'T SURVIVE;
& *Spot the Alpha*
3.10.1 WE MUST SURVIVE; & *Spot the Alpha*
3.10.2 WE MUSTN'T SURVIVE; & *Spot the Alpha*
3.10.3 WE MUST SURVIVE, WE MUSTN'T SURVIVE;
& *Spot the Alpha*
3.11.1 WE SHOULD SURVIVE; & *Spot the Alpha*
3.11.2 WE SHOULDN'T SURVIVE; & *Spot the Alpha*
3.11.3 WE SHOULD SURVIVE, WE SHOULDN'T SURVIVE;
& *Spot the Alpha*
3.12.1 WE CAN SURVIVE; & *Spot the Alpha*
3.12.2 WE CAN'T SURVIVE; & *Spot the Alpha*
3.12.3 WE CAN SURVIVE, WE CAN'T SURVIVE; & *Spot the Alpha*
3.13.1 ALL MUST SURVIVE; & *Spot the Alpha*
3.13.2 ALL MUSTN'T SURVIVE; & *Spot the Alpha*
3.13.3 ALL MUST SURVIVE, ALL MUSTN'T SURVIVE;
& *Spot the Alpha*
3.14.1 ALL SHOULD SURVIVE; & *Spot the Alpha*
3.14.2 ALL SHOULDN'T SURVIVE; & *Spot the Alpha*
3.14.3 ALL SHOULD SURVIVE, ALL SHOULDN'T SURVIVE;
& *Spot the Alpha*
3.15.1 ALL CAN SURVIVE; & *Spot the Alpha*
3.15.2 ALL CAN'T SURVIVE; & *Spot the Alpha*
3.15.3 ALL CAN SURVIVE, ALL CAN'T SURVIVE; & *Spot the Alpha*
3.16.0 {*spot an explosion*}; & *Spot the Alpha*

PLATFORM #4

[*This is a Platform formula. It uses an "interior room" (such as of a house) as its implant-setting. There is a pattern of ten "command-items" for each of five "keywords." This means there are 50 total command-items. The last word of each item-line is blank. Words for items 1 through 8 of this Platform are: 1) CREATE, 2) VIEW, 3) EXIST, 4) KNOW, and 5) REMEMBER. For items 9 and 10, use: 1) CREATIONS, 2) VIEWS, 3) EXISTENCES, 4) KNOWNS and 5) MEMORIES. Run each item-line (1 through 10) until three no-reads with "Create" (or "Creations") and then start from the top using "View"/"Views" and so on. A Seeker should make five separate worksheets.*]

4.1.X   I SHOULD ___; & *Spot the Alpha*
4.2.X   I SHOULDN'T ___; & *Spot the Alpha*
4.3.X   I MUST ___; & *Spot the Alpha*
4.4.X   I MUSTN'T ___; & *Spot the Alpha*
4.5.X   I DO ___; & *Spot the Alpha*
4.6.X   I DON'T ___; & *Spot the Alpha*
4.7.X   I CAN ___; & *Spot the Alpha*
4.8.X   I CAN'T ___; & *Spot the Alpha*
4.9.X   THERE ARE ___; & *Spot the Alpha*
4.10.X THERE AREN'T ___; & *Spot the Alpha*

PLATFORM #5

[*This is a Platform long-form. It uses a "fierce heavy explosion" as its implanting-gimmick. The "explosion" is accompanied by sensations of "burning pain" at the start of the Implant. This is followed by a lightning storm. The Implant is meant to induce indecision and insanity. There is no requirement for the "heavy explosion with burning pain" or the "storm" to give a Meter-read. Spot them at the beginning anyway; and if there is a "charge" registering, then take it to three "no-reads" as standard practice. Say the "command-item" out loud, and spot the Alpha-Spirit; then say the "command-item" while spotting the Alpha-Spirit. Perform this whatever way produces the best "reads" until that action no longer registers.*]

5.0.1   {*spot a fierce heavy explosion*}; & *Spot the Alpha*
5.0.2   {*spot a lightning storm*}; & *Spot the Alpha*
5.1.1   TO DIE IS TO LIVE; & *Spot the Alpha*
5.1.2   TO LIVE IS TO DIE; & *Spot the Alpha*

5.1.3 TO DIE IS TO LIVE, TO LIVE IS TO DIE; *& Spot the Alpha*

5.2.1 TO SURRENDER IS TO VICTIMIZE; *& Spot the Alpha*
5.2.2 TO VICTIMIZE IS TO SURRENDER; *& Spot the Alpha*
5.2.3 TO SURRENDER IS TO VICTIMIZE, TO VICTIMIZE IS TO SURRENDER; *& Spot the Alpha*

5.3.1 TO LOSE IS TO WIN; *& Spot the Alpha*
5.3.2 TO WIN IS TO LOSE; *& Spot the Alpha*
5.3.3 TO LOSE IS TO WIN, TO WIN IS TO LOSE; *& Spot the Alpha*

5.4.1 TO DESPAIR IS TO HOPE; *& Spot the Alpha*
5.4.2 TO HOPE IS TO DESPAIR; *& Spot the Alpha*
5.4.3 TO DESPAIR IS TO HOPE, TO HOPE IS TO DESPAIR; *& Spot the Alpha*

5.5.1 TO BE IGNORANT IS TO KNOW; *& Spot the Alpha*
5.5.2 TO KNOW IS TO BE IGNORANT; *& Spot the Alpha*
5.5.3 TO BE IGNORANT IS TO KNOW, TO KNOW IS TO BE IGNORANT; *& Spot the Alpha*

5.6.1 TO BE STUPID IS TO BE SMART; *& Spot the Alpha*
5.6.2 TO BE SMART IS TO BE STUPID; *& Spot the Alpha*
5.6.3 TO BE STUPID IS TO BE SMART, TO BE SMART IS TO BE STUPID; *& Spot the Alpha*

5.7.1 TO DISAGREE IS TO AGREE; *& Spot the Alpha*
5.7.2 TO AGREE IS TO DISAGREE; *& Spot the Alpha*
5.7.3 TO DISAGREE IS TO AGREE, TO AGREE IS TO DISAGREE; *& Spot the Alpha*

5.8.1 TO DETEST IS TO GET; *& Spot the Alpha*
5.8.2 TO GET IS TO DETEST; *& Spot the Alpha*
5.8.3 TO DETEST IS TO GET, TO GET IS TO DETEST; *& Spot the Alpha*

5.9.1 TO HURT IS TO ENJOY; *& Spot the Alpha*
5.9.2 TO ENJOY IS TO HURT; *& Spot the Alpha*
5.9.3 TO HURT IS TO ENJOY, TO ENJOY IS TO HURT; *& Spot the Alpha*

5.10.1 TO DISLIKE IS TO LIKE; *& Spot the Alpha*
5.10.2 TO LIKE IS TO DISLIKE; *& Spot the Alpha*
5.10.3 TO DISLIKE IS TO LIKE, TO LIKE IS TO DISLIKE; *& Spot the Alpha*

5.11.1 TO HATE IS TO LOVE; *& Spot the Alpha*

5.11.2 TO LOVE IS TO HATE; & *Spot the Alpha*
5.11.3 TO HATE IS TO LOVE, TO LOVE IS TO HATE;
        & *Spot the Alpha*
5.12.1 TO HINDER IS TO HELP; & *Spot the Alpha*
5.12.2 TO HELP IS TO HINDER; & *Spot the Alpha*
5.12.3 TO HINDER IS TO HELP, TO HELP IS TO HINDER;
        & *Spot the Alpha*
5.13.1 TO DISBELIEVE IS TO BELIEVE; & *Spot the Alpha*
5.13.2 TO BELIEVE IS TO DISBELIEVE; & *Spot the Alpha*
5.13.3 TO DISBELIEVE IS TO BELIEVE, TO BELIEVE IS TO
        DISBELIEVE; & *Spot the Alpha*
5.14.1 TO BE BAD IS TO BE GOOD; & *Spot the Alpha*
5.14.2 TO BE GOOD IS TO BE BAD; & *Spot the Alpha*
5.14.3 TO BE BAD IS TO BE GOOD, TO BE GOOD IS TO BE BAD;
        & *Spot the Alpha*
5.15.1 TO BETRAY IS TO BE FAITHFUL; & *Spot the Alpha*
5.15.2 TO BE FAITHFUL IS TO BETRAY; & *Spot the Alpha*
5.15.3 TO BETRAY IS TO BE FAITHFUL, TO BE FAITHFUL IS TO
        BETRAY; & *Spot the Alpha*
5.16.1 TO BE CRAZY IS TO BE SANE; & *Spot the Alpha*
5.16.2 TO BE SANE IS TO BE CRAZY; & *Spot the Alpha*
5.16.3 TO BE CRAZY IS TO BE SANE, TO BE SANE IS TO BE
        CRAZY; & *Spot the Alpha*
5.17.1 TO ABANDON IS TO COLLECT; & *Spot the Alpha*
5.17.2 TO COLLECT IS TO ABANDON; & *Spot the Alpha*
5.17.3 TO ABANDON IS TO COLLECT, TO COLLECT IS TO
        ABANDON; & *Spot the Alpha*
5.18.1 TO STOP IS TO START; & *Spot the Alpha*
5.18.2 TO START IS TO STOP; & *Spot the Alpha*
5.18.3 TO STOP IS TO START, TO START IS TO STOP;
        & *Spot the Alpha*

PLATFORM #6

[This is a Platform long-form. This incident starts with an "explosion" that knocks one unconscious prior to the Implant. This Implant artificially installs a foundation for false justifications (particularly for committing future harmful-acts). Although it is a long-form, it is actually used twice. The first time:

run it as having put it over onto someone else. The second time: run it as though having received it from someone else. It begins and ends with the sense of being lost in a whirlwind of electricity (which does not have to read when spotted, but if it registers, then it must be run to three "no-reads"). Say the "command-item" out loud, and spot the Alpha-Spirit; then say the "command-item" while spotting the Alpha-Spirit. Perform this whatever way produces the best "reads" until that action no longer registers.]

 6.0.X *{spot a fierce electrical tornado}*; & Spot the Alpha
 6.1.X TO EXPERIENCE IS TO CREATE; & Spot the Alpha
 6.2.X TO LOOK IS TO RE-ENVISION; & Spot the Alpha
 6.3.X TO THINK IS TO RECALL; & Spot the Alpha
 6.4.X TO CONCEIVE IS TO REMEMBER; & Spot the Alpha
 6.5.X TO SEE IS TO FORGET; & Spot the Alpha
 6.6.X *{spot a fierce electrical whirlwind}*; & Spot the Alpha

PLATFORM #7

[This is a Platform long-form. The incident is possible due to Platform #6; it provides a false illusion that you are Implanting someone else; then someone else is Implanting you. In actuality, you are sitting across from a "dummy-doll" and not another Alpha-Spirit. Additionally, you are sitting in front of a reflective screen. The implanting device is on your left. It directs an implanting-beam behind you onto the screen, which reflects onto the "dummy-doll" but giving you the impression that you did it. Although it is a long-form, it is actually used twice. The first time: run it as having a sense of doing it to someone else. The second time: run it as though having received it from someone else. Say the "command-item" out loud, and spot the Alpha-Spirit; then say the "command-item" while spotting the Alpha-Spirit. Perform this whatever way produces the best "reads" until that action no longer registers. For the italic environmental conditions; spot the occurrence or change and spot the Alpha until three consecutive no-reads.]

 7.1.X *{a light appears to your left, the implanting device}*; & Spot the Alpha
 7.2.X *{a light appears in front, the dummy-doll}*; & Spot the Alpha
 7.3.X "NOW SLEEP—GO TO SLEEP"; & Spot the Alpha
 7.4.X "YOU ARE UNCONSCIOUS"; & Spot the Alpha
 7.5.X "YOU KNOW NOTHING"; & Spot the Alpha

7.6.X {*a gas pours into the area*}; & *Spot the Alpha*

7.7.X {*there is an impression of who implanted whom*};
    & *Spot the Alpha*

PLATFORM #8

[*This is a Platform long-form. The incident is possible due to Platform #7; it is a formal reprimand (or scolding) for having Implanted "our fellow Alpha-Spirit" (even though it was actually a dummy-doll and we really didn't do anything) and a warning about doing it again. The Implant installs the concept of "karma"—which is a reality-agreement (which did not exist in Home Universe). The entire contents are telepathically "spoken" to us. Each of the phrase-lines listed below will read as an item. Say each line out loud as a "command item" while spotting the Alpha (to three "no-reads") and then scan over the entire message (without spotting the Alpha) just to understand its general content.*]

8.1 "HERE IS A LESSON"; & *Spot the Alpha*

8.2 "IT IS"; & *Spot the Alpha*

8.3 "IF YOU DO SOMETHING TO ANOTHER"; & *Spot the Alpha*

8.4 "THAT IS HARMFUL"; & *Spot the Alpha*

8.5 "OR DAMAGES HIM OR HER"; & *Spot the Alpha*

8.6 "IN ANY WAY"; & *Spot the Alpha*

8.7 "YOU GET IT BACK 100-FOLD"; & *Spot the Alpha*

8.8 "WITHOUT FAIL."; & *Spot the Alpha*

8.9 "THIS IS YOUR ACTION TO ANOTHER"; & *Spot the Alpha*

8.10 "YOU ARE DOING THIS"; & *Spot the Alpha*

8.11 "TO A HELPLESS SPIRIT"; & *Spot the Alpha*

8.12 "WHO WAS GOOD AND KIND"; & *Spot the Alpha*

8.13 "IN ORDER TO RUIN THEM FOREVER"; & *Spot the Alpha*

8.14 "AND DEGRADE YOURSELF."; & *Spot the Alpha*

8.15 "NOW WATCH THIS"; & *Spot the Alpha*

8.16 "AND SEE WHAT YOU ARE DOING"; & *Spot the Alpha*

8.17 "TO HIM OR HER."; & *Spot the Alpha*

PLATFORM #9

[*This is a Platform long-form. The incident is possible due to Platform #8; and like Platform #7, you are sitting across from a "dummy-doll" and not another Alpha-Spirit. Additionally, you are sitting in front of a reflective screen. The implanting device is on your left. It directs an implanting-beam behind you onto the screen, which reflects onto the "dummy-doll" but giving you the impression that you did it. Spot those environmental facets (the screen, device, beam, &tc.) throughout. Say the "command-item" out loud, and spot the Alpha-Spirit; then say the "command-item" while spotting the Alpha-Spirit. Perform this whatever way produces the best "reads" until that action no longer registers (three consecutive times). Note: In some instances, the instruction to "Spot the Alpha" will be abbreviated as "&A."*]

9.0.1 {*spot an electrical explosion*}; & *Spot the Alpha*
9.1.1 TO PREDICT, NEVER TO KNOW; & *Spot the Alpha*
9.1.2 TO KNOW, NEVER TO PREDICT; & *Spot the Alpha*
9.2.1 TO FRIGHTEN, NEVER TO FEAR; & *Spot the Alpha*
9.2.2 TO FEAR, NEVER TO FRIGHTEN; & *Spot the Alpha*
9.3.1 TO CATCH, NEVER TO BE CAUGHT; & *Spot the Alpha*
9.3.2 TO BE CAUGHT, NEVER TO CATCH; & *Spot the Alpha*
9.4.1 TO IMPRISON, NEVER TO BE IMPRISONED; & A
9.4.2 TO BE IMPRISONED, NEVER TO IMPRISON; & A
9.5.1 TO BE OUT OF JAIL, NEVER TO BE IN JAIL; & *Spot the Alpha*
9.5.2 TO BE IN JAIL, NEVER TO BE OUT OF JAIL; & *Spot the Alpha*
9.6.1 TO BE OUTSIDE, NEVER TO BE INSIDE; & *Spot the Alpha*
9.6.2 TO BE INSIDE, NEVER TO BE OUTSIDE; & *Spot the Alpha*
9.7.1 TO REMEMBER, NEVER TO FORGET; & *Spot the Alpha*
9.7.2 TO FORGET, NEVER TO REMEMBER; & *Spot the Alpha*
9.8.1 TO GO, NEVER TO COME; & *Spot the Alpha*
9.8.2 TO COME, NEVER TO GO; & *Spot the Alpha*
9.9.1 {*explosion*}; & *Spot the Alpha*

PLATFORM #10

[*This is a Platform long-form. The incident is possible due to Platform #9; it is a formal reprimand (or scolding) for having Implanted "our fellow Alpha-Spirit" (even though it was actually a dummy-doll and we really didn't do anything). It is intended to reinforce mechanisms for retribution (motivations for* harmful-acts). Its entire contents are telepathically "spok-en" to us. Each of the phrase-lines listed below will read as an item. Say each line out loud as a "command item" while spotting the Alpha (to three "no-reads") and then scan over the entire content of the message (without spotting the Alpha). We still are opposite a dummy-doll; but now the reflective screen is behind them, projecting the implanting-beam toward you from their direction. Spot this environmental change before continuing. Note: In some instances, the instruction to "Spot the Alpha" will be abbreviated as "&A."]

10.1 "THE CONSEQUENCES"; & Spot the Alpha

10.2 "OF YOUR HAVING DONE THAT"; & Spot the Alpha

10.3 "ARE TERRIBLE,"; & Spot the Alpha

10.4 "BECAUSE YOU DID THAT."; & Spot the Alpha

10.5 "IT IS NOW TWO AND A HALF YEARS LATER."; & A

10.6 "THESE ARE THE CONSEQUENCES."; & Spot the Alpha

10.7 "THIS IS THE CONSEQUENCE."; & Spot the Alpha

10.8 "WATCH THIS"; & Spot the Alpha

10.9 "AND SEE WHAT HAPPENS"; & Spot the Alpha

10.10 "TO YOU"; & Spot the Alpha

10.11 "BECAUSE OF WHAT YOU DID"; & Spot the Alpha

10.12 "TO THE POOR SPIRIT."; & Spot the Alpha

10.13 "THEY ARE NOW GIVING IT BACK."; & Spot the Alpha

10.14 "WATCH OUT!"; & Spot the Alpha

PLATFORM #11

[This Platform is identical in content to Platform #9; except that it is run as being directed to us from someone else (the dummy-doll). A Seeker will have to make their own worksheet for its content, copying the data from Platform #9. It cannot be run in a series (or from a worksheet) as Platform #9, even though the content is the same. This is Platform #11. We still are opposite a dummy-doll; the reflective screen is behind them, projecting the implanting-beam toward you from their direction. Say the "command-item" out loud, and spot the Alpha-Spirit; then say the "command-item" while spotting the Alpha-Spirit. Perform this whatever way produces the best "reads" until that action no longer registers (three consecutive times).]

PLATFORM #12

[*This is a Platform long-form. The incident is possible due to Platform #10; it is a formal reminder of the retribution we have received from "our fellow Alpha-Spirit" (the dummy-doll, although it really came from an implanting device) as a result of implanting them first (although we actually didn't do anything). Each of the phrase-lines listed below will read as an item. Say each line out loud as a "command item" while spotting the Alpha (to three "no-reads") and then scan over the entire content of the message to get its general meaning.*]

12.1 "YOU SEE WHAT HAPPENS"; & *Spot the Alpha*
12.2 "BECAUSE OF WHAT YOU DO."; & *Spot the Alpha*
12.3 "WHEN YOU DO SOMETHING BAD"; & *Spot the Alpha*
12.4 "TO ANOTHER"; & *Spot the Alpha*
12.5 "YOU GET IT BACK LATER."; & *Spot the Alpha*
12.6 "YOU ARE THE CAUSE"; & *Spot the Alpha*
12.7 "OF ALL YOUR SUFFERING."; & *Spot the Alpha*
12.8 "HARMFUL ACTIONS"; & *Spot the Alpha*
12.9 "DO NOT PAY."; & *Spot the Alpha*
12.10 "WAKE UP DEAD, FOREVER."; & *Spot the Alpha*

PLATFORM #13

[*This is a Platform short-form formula. It contains a series of 26 "command-item" lines. This series (lines 1 through 26) is run completely for each of 26 different "keywords." Each word is used twice on each line. A Seeker should prepare 26 different worksheets from this formula, inserting only one keyword (of the 26) for each worksheet. This generates 676 different command-items. A Seeker must get three consecutive "no-reads" on a "keyword" by itself before running through the worksheet that uses it.*

To fully process-out this incident: once you have completed working through all 26 keywords/worksheets (676 items), the entire implant is run again in reverse, working backwards from its ending, line by line. Note that: here you work the lines in reverse order back up the worksheet pages (marking new "reads" in a different color), but you don't literally read a sentence backwards. Note: some lines may not read. Whatever does, defragment it to three no-reads. Only backtrack if several lines in a row do not register a charge.

Most of this implant is semantically non-sensical; because it was not originally implanted in English (literal language). Don't analyze it; just defragment it. There is an "explosion" that occurs for each "command-item" that corresponds with "Spot the Alpha" because the "explosion" is actually taking place (or rather, "sensed" as taking place) in the "head."]

KEYWORDS: 1) SELF; 2) MIND; 3) BODY; 4) SPIRIT; 5) HEAD; 6) MEMORY; 7) MASS; 8) THOUGHT; 9) UNIVERSE; 10) BELIEF; 11) PEOPLE; 12) INTENTION; 13) SOCIETY; 14) CUSTOM; 15) GOVERNMENT; 16) CONCEPT; 17) RELIGION; 18) COMPUTATION; 19) SYSTEM; 20) REASON; 21) HEALTH; 22) LOGIC; 23) POISON; 24) SECRET; 25) INTERIOR; 26) AMNESIA.

13.1.x STOP A BEGINNING ___ TO INVENT AN ENDED ___;
{explosion} & Spot the Alpha

13.2.x INVENT A NEAR ___ TO STOP A FAR ___;
{explosion} & Spot the Alpha

13.3.x STOP AN OPEN ___ TO INVENT A CLOSED ___;
{explosion} & Spot the Alpha

13.4.x INVENT A KEPT ___ TO STOP AN EXPENDED ___;
{explosion} & Spot the Alpha

13.5.x STOP A FILLED ___ TO INVENT AN EXHAUSTED ___;
{explosion} & Spot the Alpha

13.6.x INVENT A BRIGHT ___ TO STOP A DIM ___;
{explosion} & Spot the Alpha

13.7.x STOP AN INFORMED ___ TO INVENT A DENIED ___;
{explosion} & Spot the Alpha

13.8.x INVENT A RECEIVING ___ TO STOP A REJECTED ___;
{explosion} & Spot the Alpha

13.9.x STOP A LOVING ___ TO INVENT A HATED ___;
{explosion} & Spot the Alpha

13.10.x INVENT A PERCEIVING ___ TO STOP A BLINDED ___;
{explosion} & Spot the Alpha

13.11.x STOP A FAIR ___ TO INVENT A PREJUDICED ___;
{explosion} & Spot the Alpha

13.12.x INVENT A CLEAN ___ TO STOP A DIRTY ___;
{explosion} & Spot the Alpha

13.13.x STOP AN ARRIVING ___ TO INVENT A DEPARTED ___;
{explosion} & Spot the Alpha

AT#3 – 151

13.14.X INVENT AN ARRIVING ___ TO STOP A DEPARTED ___;
{explosion} & Spot the Alpha

13.15.X STOP A CLEAN ___ TO INVENT A DIRTY ___;
{explosion} & Spot the Alpha

13.16.X INVENT A FAIR ___ TO STOP A PREJUDICED ___;
{explosion} & Spot the Alpha

13.17.X STOP A PERCEIVING ___ TO INVENT A BLINDED ___;
{explosion} & Spot the Alpha

13.18.X INVENT A LOVING ___ TO STOP A HATED ___;
{explosion} & Spot the Alpha

13.19.X STOP A RECEIVING ___ TO INVENT A REJECTED ___;
{explosion} & Spot the Alpha

13.20.X INVENT AN INFORMED ___ TO STOP A DENIED ___;
{explosion} & Spot the Alpha

13.21.X STOP A BRIGHT ___ TO INVENT A DIM ___;
{explosion} & Spot the Alpha

13.22.X INVENT A FILLED ___ TO STOP AN EXHAUSTED ___;
{explosion} & Spot the Alpha

13.23.X STOP A KEPT ___ TO INVENT AN EXPENDED ___;
{explosion} & Spot the Alpha

13.24.X INVENT AN OPEN ___ TO STOP A CLOSED ___;
{explosion} & Spot the Alpha

13.25.X STOP A NEAR ___ TO INVENT A FAR ___;
{explosion} & Spot the Alpha

13.26.X INVENT A BEGINNING ___ TO STOP AN ENDED ___;
{explosion} & Spot the Alpha

PLATFORM #14

[*This is a Platform long-form. It uses an "explosion" as its implanting-gimmick. The Implant is meant to incite or reinforce compulsive creation of spiritual machinery—in this case a "picture machine" or "picture-making machine" (although this template-pattern could also be used for other spiritual machinery, too). The "command-lines" follow a pattern, which we could have presented as a short-form formula to save printed space. But, this pattern causes many phrases (or verb uses) to not make sense in the traditional way—which means an item-line may not even "read" immediately. Once a Seeker gets a sense of its basic meaning (rather than protesting its wording), it will register on a Meter. Say the "command-item" out loud, and spot the Alpha-Spirit; then say the "command-item" while spotting the Alpha-Spirit. Perform this in whatever way produces the best "reads" for each item-line until that same action gives "no-reads" three consecutive times.]*

14.0.1 {*spot an explosion*}; & *Spot the Alpha*

14.1.1 YOU MUST CONSTRUCT A PICTURE MACHINE;
& *Spot the Alpha*

14.1.2 YOU MUST NOT CONSTRUCT A PICTURE MACHINE;
& *Spot the Alpha*

14.1.3 YOU MUST CONSTRUCT A PICTURE MACHINE,
YOU MUST NOT CONSTRUCT A PICTURE MACHINE;
& *Spot the Alpha*

14.1.4 YOU MUST ERADICATE A PICTURE MACHINE;
& *Spot the Alpha*

14.1.5 YOU MUST NOT ERADICATE A PICTURE MACHINE;
& *Spot the Alpha*

14.1.6 YOU MUST ERADICATE A PICTURE MACHINE,
YOU MUST NOT ERADICATE A PICTURE MACHINE;
& *Spot the Alpha*

14.2.1 YOU MUST CREATE A PICTURE MACHINE; & *A*

14.2.2 YOU MUST NOT CREATE A PICTURE MACHINE; &

14.2.3 YOU MUST CREATE A PICTURE MACHINE,
YOU MUST NOT CREATE A PICTURE MACHINE; & *A*

14.2.4 YOU MUST DESTROY A PICTURE MACHINE; & *A*

14.2.5 YOU MUST NOT DESTROY A PICTURE MACHINE; & *A*

14.2.6 YOU MUST DESTROY A PICTURE MACHINE,
YOU MUST NOT DESTROY A PICTURE MACHINE; & *A*

14.3.1 YOU MUST FEED A PICTURE MACHINE; & *Spot the Alpha*

14.3.2 YOU MUST NOT FEED A PICTURE MACHINE; & *A*

14.3.3 YOU MUST FEED A PICTURE MACHINE,
YOU MUST NOT FEED A PICTURE MACHINE; & *A*

14.3.4 YOU MUST STARVE A PICTURE MACHINE; & *A*

14.3.5 YOU MUST NOT STARVE A PICTURE MACHINE; & *A*

14.3.6 YOU MUST STARVE A PICTURE MACHINE,
YOU MUST NOT STARVE A PICTURE MACHINE; & *A*

14.4.1 YOU MUST BELIEVE A PICTURE MACHINE; & *A*

14.4.2 YOU MUST NOT BELIEVE A PICTURE MACHINE; & *A*

14.4.3 YOU MUST BELIEVE A PICTURE MACHINE,
        YOU MUST NOT BELIEVE A PICTURE MACHINE; & A
14.4.4 YOU MUST DISBELIEVE A PICTURE MACHINE; & A
14.4.5 YOU MUST NOT DISBELIEVE A PICTURE MACHINE; & A
14.4.6 YOU MUST DISBELIEVE A PICTURE MACHINE,
        YOU MUST NOT DISBELIEVE A PICTURE MACHINE; & A

14.5.1 YOU MUST DESIRE A PICTURE MACHINE; & A
14.5.2 YOU MUST NOT DESIRE A PICTURE MACHINE; & A
14.5.3 YOU MUST DESIRE A PICTURE MACHINE,
        YOU MUST NOT DESIRE A PICTURE MACHINE; & A
14.5.4 YOU MUST SHUN A PICTURE MACHINE; & A
14.5.5 YOU MUST NOT SHUN A PICTURE MACHINE; & A
14.5.6 YOU MUST SHUN A PICTURE MACHINE,
        YOU MUST NOT SHUN A PICTURE MACHINE; & A

14.6.1 YOU MUST APPROACH A PICTURE MACHINE; & A
14.6.2 YOU MUST NOT APPROACH A PICTURE MACHINE; & A
14.6.3 YOU MUST APPROACH A PICTURE MACHINE,
        YOU MUST NOT APPROACH A PICTURE MACHINE; & A
14.6.4 YOU MUST AVOID A PICTURE MACHINE; & A
14.6.5 YOU MUST NOT AVOID A PICTURE MACHINE; & A
14.6.6 YOU MUST AVOID A PICTURE MACHINE,
        YOU MUST NOT AVOID A PICTURE MACHINE; & A

14.7.1 YOU MUST JOIN A PICTURE MACHINE; & *Spot the Alpha*
14.7.2 YOU MUST NOT JOIN A PICTURE MACHINE; & A
14.7.3 YOU MUST JOIN A PICTURE MACHINE,
        YOU MUST NOT JOIN A PICTURE MACHINE; & A
14.7.4 YOU MUST SEVER A PICTURE MACHINE; & *Spot the Alpha*
14.7.5 YOU MUST NOT SEVER A PICTURE MACHINE; & A
14.7.6 YOU MUST SEVER A PICTURE MACHINE,
        YOU MUST NOT SEVER A PICTURE MACHINE; & A

14.8.1 YOU MUST CONTACT A PICTURE MACHINE; & A
14.8.2 YOU MUST NOT CONTACT A PICTURE MACHINE; & A
14.8.3 YOU MUST CONTACT A PICTURE MACHINE,
        YOU MUST NOT CONTACT A PICTURE MACHINE; & A
14.8.4 YOU MUST SEPARATE A PICTURE MACHINE; & A
14.8.5 YOU MUST NOT SEPARATE A PICTURE MACHINE; & A
14.8.6 YOU MUST SEPARATE A PICTURE MACHINE,
        YOU MUST NOT SEPARATE A PICTURE MACHINE; & A

14.9.1 YOU MUST CONNECT A PICTURE MACHINE; & A
14.9.2 YOU MUST NOT CONNECT A PICTURE MACHINE; & A
14.9.3 YOU MUST CONNECT A PICTURE MACHINE,
YOU MUST NOT CONNECT A PICTURE MACHINE; & A
14.9.4 YOU MUST DISCONNECT A PICTURE MACHINE; & A
14.9.5 YOU MUST NOT DISCONNECT A PICTURE MACHINE; & A
14.9.6 YOU MUST DISCONNECT A PICTURE MACHINE,
YOU MUST NOT DISCONNECT A PICTURE MACHINE;
& Spot the Alpha
14.10.1 YOU MUST COMMUNICATE WITH A PICTURE MACHINE;
& Spot the Alpha
14.10.2 YOU MUST NOT COMMUNICATE WITH A PICTURE
MACHINE; & Spot the Alpha
14.10.3 YOU MUST COMMUNICATE WITH A PICTURE MACHINE,
YOU MUST NOT COMMUNICATE WITH A PICTURE
MACHINE; & Spot the Alpha
14.10.4 YOU MUST SPURN A PICTURE MACHINE; & Spot the Alpha
14.10.5 YOU MUST NOT SPURN A PICTURE MACHINE; & A
14.10.6 YOU MUST SPURN A PICTURE MACHINE,
YOU MUST NOT SPURN A PICTURE MACHINE; & A
14.11.1 YOU MUST AGREE WITH A PICTURE MACHINE; & A
14.11.2 YOU MUST NOT AGREE WITH A PICTURE MACHINE; & A
14.11.3 YOU MUST AGREE WITH A PICTURE MACHINE,
YOU MUST NOT AGREE WITH A PICTURE MACHINE; & A
14.11.4 YOU MUST DISAGREE WITH A PICTURE MACHINE; & A
14.11.5 YOU MUST NOT DISAGREE WITH A PICTURE MACHINE;
& Spot the Alpha
14.11.6 YOU MUST DISAGREE WITH A PICTURE MACHINE,
YOU MUST NOT DISAGREE WITH A PICTURE MACHINE;
& Spot the Alpha
14.12.1 YOU MUST LIKE A PICTURE MACHINE; & Spot the Alpha
14.12.2 YOU MUST NOT LIKE A PICTURE MACHINE; & A
14.12.3 YOU MUST LIKE A PICTURE MACHINE,
YOU MUST NOT LIKE A PICTURE MACHINE; & A
14.12.4 YOU MUST DISLIKE A PICTURE MACHINE; & A
14.12.5 YOU MUST NOT DISLIKE A PICTURE MACHINE; & A
14.12.6 YOU MUST DISLIKE A PICTURE MACHINE,
YOU MUST NOT DISLIKE A PICTURE MACHINE; & A

14.13.1 YOU MUST LOVE A PICTURE MACHINE; & *Spot the Alpha*
14.13.2 YOU MUST NOT LOVE A PICTURE MACHINE; & *A*
14.13.3 YOU MUST LOVE A PICTURE MACHINE,
YOU MUST NOT LOVE A PICTURE MACHINE; & *A*
14.13.4 YOU MUST DESPISE A PICTURE MACHINE; & *A*
14.13.5 YOU MUST NOT DESPISE A PICTURE MACHINE; & *A*
14.13.6 YOU MUST DESPISE A PICTURE MACHINE,
YOU MUST NOT DESPISE A PICTURE MACHINE; & *A*
14.14.1 YOU MUST VALUE A PICTURE MACHINE; & *Spot the Alpha*
14.14.2 YOU MUST NOT VALUE A PICTURE MACHINE; & *A*
14.14.3 YOU MUST VALUE A PICTURE MACHINE,
YOU MUST NOT VALUE A PICTURE MACHINE; & *A*
14.14.4 YOU MUST CONDEMN A PICTURE MACHINE; & *A*
14.14.5 YOU MUST NOT CONDEMN A PICTURE MACHINE; & *A*
14.14.6 YOU MUST CONDEMN A PICTURE MACHINE,
YOU MUST NOT CONDEMN A PICTURE MACHINE; & *A*
14.15.1 YOU MUST WELCOME A PICTURE MACHINE; & *A*
14.15.2 YOU MUST NOT WELCOME A PICTURE MACHINE; & *A*
14.15.3 YOU MUST WELCOME A PICTURE MACHINE,
YOU MUST NOT WELCOME A PICTURE MACHINE; & *A*
14.15.4 YOU MUST REFUSE A PICTURE MACHINE; & *A*
14.15.5 YOU MUST NOT REFUSE A PICTURE MACHINE; & *A*
14.15.6 YOU MUST REFUSE A PICTURE MACHINE,
YOU MUST NOT REFUSE A PICTURE MACHINE; & *A*
14.16.1 YOU MUST CONCENTRATE ON A PICTURE MACHINE;
& *Spot the Alpha*
14.16.2 YOU MUST NOT CONCENTRATE ON A PICTURE
MACHINE; & *Spot the Alpha*
14.16.3 YOU MUST CONCENTRATE ON A PICTURE MACHINE,
YOU MUST NOT CONCENTRATE ON A PICTURE
MACHINE; & *Spot the Alpha*
14.16.4 YOU MUST DISPERSE FROM A PICTURE MACHINE; & *A*
14.16.5 YOU MUST NOT DISPERSE FROM A PICTURE MACHINE;
& *Spot the Alpha*
14.16.6 YOU MUST DISPERSE FROM A PICTURE MACHINE,
YOU MUST NOT DISPERSE FROM A PICTURE MACHINE;
& *Spot the Alpha*
14.17.1 YOU MUST FIXATE ON A PICTURE MACHINE; & *A*

14.17.2 YOU MUST NOT FIXATE ON A PICTURE MACHINE; & A
14.17.3 YOU MUST FIXATE ON A PICTURE MACHINE,
YOU MUST NOT FIXATE ON A PICTURE MACHINE; & A
14.17.4 YOU MUST DISASSOCIATE FROM A PICTURE MACHINE;
& Spot the Alpha
14.17.5 YOU MUST NOT DISASSOCIATE FROM A PICTURE MACHINE; & Spot the Alpha
14.17.6 YOU MUST DISASSOCIATE FROM A PICTURE MACHINE,
YOU MUST NOT DISASSOCIATE FROM A PICTURE MACHINE; & Spot the Alpha
14.18.1 YOU MUST HEED A PICTURE MACHINE; & Spot the Alpha
14.18.2 YOU MUST NOT HEED A PICTURE MACHINE; & A
14.18.3 YOU MUST HEED A PICTURE MACHINE,
YOU MUST NOT HEED A PICTURE MACHINE; & A
14.18.4 YOU MUST IGNORE A PICTURE MACHINE; & A
14.18.5 YOU MUST NOT IGNORE A PICTURE MACHINE; & A
14.18.6 YOU MUST IGNORE A PICTURE MACHINE,
YOU MUST NOT IGNORE A PICTURE MACHINE; & A
14.19.1 YOU MUST DEPEND UPON A PICTURE MACHINE; & A
14.19.2 YOU MUST NOT DEPEND UPON A PICTURE MACHINE; & Spot the Alpha
14.19.3 YOU MUST DEPEND UPON A PICTURE MACHINE,
YOU MUST NOT DEPEND UPON A PICTURE MACHINE; & Spot the Alpha
14.19.4 YOU MUST BLAME A PICTURE MACHINE; & Spot the Alpha
14.19.5 YOU MUST NOT BLAME A PICTURE MACHINE; & A
14.19.6 YOU MUST BLAME A PICTURE MACHINE,
YOU MUST NOT BLAME A PICTURE MACHINE; & A
14.20.1 YOU MUST MAINTAIN A PICTURE MACHINE; & A
14.20.2 YOU MUST NOT MAINTAIN A PICTURE MACHINE; & A
14.20.3 YOU MUST MAINTAIN A PICTURE MACHINE,
YOU MUST NOT MAINTAIN A PICTURE MACHINE; & A
14.20.4 YOU MUST DAMAGE A PICTURE MACHINE; & A
14.20.5 YOU MUST NOT DAMAGE A PICTURE MACHINE; & A
14.20.6 YOU MUST DAMAGE A PICTURE MACHINE,
YOU MUST NOT DAMAGE A PICTURE MACHINE; & A
14.21.1 YOU MUST CARE FOR A PICTURE MACHINE; & A
14.21.2 YOU MUST NOT CARE FOR A PICTURE MACHINE; & A

14.21.3 YOU MUST CARE FOR A PICTURE MACHINE,
YOU MUST NOT CARE FOR A PICTURE MACHINE; & A
14.21.4 YOU MUST ABUSE A PICTURE MACHINE; & *Spot the Alpha*
14.21.5 YOU MUST NOT ABUSE A PICTURE MACHINE; & A
14.21.6 YOU MUST ABUSE A PICTURE MACHINE,
YOU MUST NOT ABUSE A PICTURE MACHINE; & A

14.22.1 YOU MUST HAVE A PICTURE MACHINE; & *Spot the Alpha*
14.22.2 YOU MUST NOT HAVE A PICTURE MACHINE; & A
14.22.3 YOU MUST HAVE A PICTURE MACHINE,
YOU MUST NOT HAVE A PICTURE MACHINE; & A
14.22.4 YOU MUST DISCARD A PICTURE MACHINE; & A
14.22.5 YOU MUST NOT DISCARD A PICTURE MACHINE; & A
14.22.6 YOU MUST DISCARD A PICTURE MACHINE,
YOU MUST NOT DISCARD A PICTURE MACHINE; & A

14.23.1 YOU MUST OBTAIN A PICTURE MACHINE; & *Spot the Alpha*
14.23.2 YOU MUST NOT OBTAIN A PICTURE MACHINE; & A
14.23.3 YOU MUST OBTAIN A PICTURE MACHINE,
YOU MUST NOT OBTAIN A PICTURE MACHINE; & A
14.23.4 YOU MUST REJECT A PICTURE MACHINE; & A
14.23.5 YOU MUST NOT REJECT A PICTURE MACHINE; & A
14.23.6 YOU MUST REJECT A PICTURE MACHINE,
YOU MUST NOT REJECT A PICTURE MACHINE; & A

14.24.1 YOU MUST ACQUIRE A PICTURE MACHINE; & A
14.24.2 YOU MUST NOT ACQUIRE A PICTURE MACHINE; & A
14.24.3 YOU MUST ACQUIRE A PICTURE MACHINE,
YOU MUST NOT ACQUIRE A PICTURE MACHINE; & A
14.24.4 YOU MUST ABANDON A PICTURE MACHINE; & A
14.24.5 YOU MUST NOT ABANDON A PICTURE MACHINE; & A
14.24.6 YOU MUST ABANDON A PICTURE MACHINE,
YOU MUST NOT ABANDON A PICTURE MACHINE; & A

14.25.1 YOU MUST USE A PICTURE MACHINE; &A
14.25.2 YOU MUST NOT USE A PICTURE MACHINE; & A
14.25.3 YOU MUST USE A PICTURE MACHINE,
YOU MUST NOT USE A PICTURE MACHINE; & A
14.25.4 YOU MUST NEGLECT A PICTURE MACHINE; & A
14.25.5 YOU MUST NOT NEGLECT A PICTURE MACHINE; & A
14.25.6 YOU MUST NEGLECT A PICTURE MACHINE,
YOU MUST NOT NEGLECT A PICTURE MACHINE; & A

14.26.1 YOU MUST UTILIZE A PICTURE MACHINE; & *Spot the Alpha*
14.26.2 YOU MUST NOT UTILIZE A PICTURE MACHINE; & *A*
14.26.3 YOU MUST UTILIZE A PICTURE MACHINE,
YOU MUST NOT UTILIZE A PICTURE MACHINE; & *A*
14.26.4 YOU MUST DISPENSE WITH A PICTURE MACHINE; & *A*
14.26.5 YOU MUST NOT DISPENSE WITH A PICTURE MACHINE;
& *Spot the Alpha*
14.26.6 YOU MUST DISPENSE WITH A PICTURE MACHINE,
YOU MUST NOT DISPENSE WITH A PICTURE MACHINE;
& *Spot the Alpha*
14.27.1 YOU MUST VALIDATE A PICTURE MACHINE; & *A*
14.27.2 YOU MUST NOT VALIDATE A PICTURE MACHINE; & *A*
14.27.3 YOU MUST VALIDATE A PICTURE MACHINE,
YOU MUST NOT VALIDATE A PICTURE MACHINE; & *A*
14.27.4 YOU MUST INVALIDATE A PICTURE MACHINE; & *A*
14.27.5 YOU MUST NOT INVALIDATE A PICTURE MACHINE; & *A*
14.27.6 YOU MUST INVALIDATE A PICTURE MACHINE,
YOU MUST NOT INVALIDATE A PICTURE MACHINE; & *A*
14.28.1 YOU MUST EXAGGERATE A PICTURE MACHINE; & *A*
14.28.2 YOU MUST NOT EXAGGERATE A PICTURE MACHINE;
& *Spot the Alpha*
14.28.3 YOU MUST EXAGGERATE A PICTURE MACHINE,
YOU MUST NOT EXAGGERATE A PICTURE MACHINE;
& *Spot the Alpha*
14.28.4 YOU MUST REDUCE A PICTURE MACHINE; & *A*
14.28.5 YOU MUST NOT REDUCE A PICTURE MACHINE; & *A*
14.28.6 YOU MUST REDUCE A PICTURE MACHINE,
YOU MUST NOT REDUCE A PICTURE MACHINE; & *A*
14.29.1 YOU MUST BOAST ABOUT A PICTURE MACHINE; & *A*
14.29.2 YOU MUST NOT BOAST ABOUT A PICTURE MACHINE;
& *Spot the Alpha*
14.29.3 YOU MUST BOAST ABOUT A PICTURE MACHINE,
YOU MUST NOT BOAST ABOUT A PICTURE MACHINE;
& *Spot the Alpha*
14.29.4 YOU MUST APOLOGIZE FOR A PICTURE MACHINE; & *A*
14.29.5 YOU MUST NOT APOLOGIZE FOR A PICTURE MACHINE;
& *Spot the Alpha*

14.29.6 YOU MUST APOLOGIZE FOR A PICTURE MACHINE,
         YOU MUST NOT APOLOGIZE FOR A PICTURE MACHINE;
         & *Spot the Alpha*
14.30.1 YOU MUST COMPLIMENT A PICTURE MACHINE; & *A*
14.30.2 YOU MUST NOT COMPLIMENT A PICTURE MACHINE; & *A*
14.30.3 YOU MUST COMPLIMENT A PICTURE MACHINE,
         YOU MUST NOT COMPLIMENT A PICTURE MACHINE; & *A*
14.30.4 YOU MUST EXCUSE A PICTURE MACHINE; & *A*
14.30.5 YOU MUST NOT EXCUSE A PICTURE MACHINE; & *A*
14.30.6 YOU MUST EXCUSE A PICTURE MACHINE,
         YOU MUST NOT EXCUSE A PICTURE MACHINE; & *A*
14.31.1 YOU MUST SHOW A PICTURE MACHINE; & *Spot the Alpha*
14.31.2 YOU MUST NOT SHOW A PICTURE MACHINE; & *A*
14.31.3 YOU MUST SHOW A PICTURE MACHINE,
         YOU MUST NOT SHOW A PICTURE MACHINE; & *A*
14.31.4 YOU MUST SCREEN A PICTURE MACHINE; & *A*
14.31.5 YOU MUST NOT SCREEN A PICTURE MACHINE; & *A*
14.31.6 YOU MUST SCREEN A PICTURE MACHINE,
         YOU MUST NOT SCREEN A PICTURE MACHINE; & *A*
14.32.1 YOU MUST REVEAL A PICTURE MACHINE; & *A*
14.32.2 YOU MUST NOT REVEAL A PICTURE MACHINE; & *A*
14.32.3 YOU MUST REVEAL A PICTURE MACHINE,
         YOU MUST NOT REVEAL A PICTURE MACHINE; & *A*
14.32.4 YOU MUST HIDE A PICTURE MACHINE; & *Spot the Alpha*
14.32.5 YOU MUST NOT HIDE A PICTURE MACHINE; & *A*
14.32.6 YOU MUST HIDE A PICTURE MACHINE,
         YOU MUST NOT HIDE A PICTURE MACHINE; & *A*
14.33.1 YOU MUST RECOGNIZE A PICTURE MACHINE; & *A*
14.33.2 YOU MUST NOT RECOGNIZE A PICTURE MACHINE; & *A*
14.33.3 YOU MUST RECOGNIZE A PICTURE MACHINE,
         YOU MUST NOT RECOGNIZE A PICTURE MACHINE; & *A*
14.33.4 YOU MUST BLANK-OUT A PICTURE MACHINE; & *A*
14.33.5 YOU MUST NOT BLANK-OUT A PICTURE MACHINE; & *A*
14.33.6 YOU MUST BLANK-OUT A PICTURE MACHINE,
         YOU MUST NOT BLANK-OUT A PICTURE MACHINE; & *A*
14.34.1 YOU MUST DISCOVER A PICTURE MACHINE; & *A*
14.34.2 YOU MUST NOT DISCOVER A PICTURE MACHINE; & *A*

14.34.3 YOU MUST DISCOVER A PICTURE MACHINE,
         YOU MUST NOT DISCOVER A PICTURE MACHINE; & A
14.34.4 YOU MUST OVERLOOK A PICTURE MACHINE; & A
14.34.5 YOU MUST NOT OVERLOOK A PICTURE MACHINE; & A
14.34.6 YOU MUST OVERLOOK A PICTURE MACHINE,
         YOU MUST NOT OVERLOOK A PICTURE MACHINE; & A
14.35.1 YOU MUST REMEMBER A PICTURE MACHINE; & A
14.35.2 YOU MUST NOT REMEMBER A PICTURE MACHINE; & A
14.35.3 YOU MUST REMEMBER A PICTURE MACHINE,
         YOU MUST NOT REMEMBER A PICTURE MACHINE; & A
14.35.4 YOU MUST FORGET A PICTURE MACHINE; & A
14.35.5 YOU MUST NOT FORGET A PICTURE MACHINE; & A
14.35.6 YOU MUST FORGET A PICTURE MACHINE,
         YOU MUST NOT FORGET A PICTURE MACHINE; & A
14.36.1 {explosion}; & Spot the Alpha

PLATFORM #15

[This is a Platform long-form. It reinforces activity of the "Picture Machine" from Platform #14. The "command-lines" follow a pattern, which could be presented as a short-form formula. But, this pattern uses a dichotomy (pair) of opposing adjectives for each step. The first three "item-lines" of each step do not appear in the actual incident, and are intended to defragment any charge on the adjectives (words) themselves before running them as command-items. If an area will not register at all, a Seeker may need to figure a similar adjective that fits their understanding/vocabulary better. Say the "command-item" out loud, and spot the Alpha-Spirit; then say the "command-item" while spotting the Alpha-Spirit. Perform this in whatever way produces the best "reads" for each item-line until that same action gives "no-reads" three consecutive times.]

15.1.A NICE.
15.1.B NAUGHTY.
15.1.C NICE, NAUGHTY.
15.1.1 COPYING NICE PICTURES; & Spot the Alpha
15.1.2 NOT COPYING NICE PICTURES; & Spot the Alpha
15.1.3 HAVING NICE PICTURES; & Spot the Alpha
15.1.4 NOT HAVING NICE PICTURES; & Spot the Alpha
15.1.5 USING NICE PICTURES; & Spot the Alpha
15.1.6 NOT USING NICE PICTURES; & Spot the Alpha
15.1.7 SEEING NICE PICTURES; & Spot the Alpha

15.1.8 NOT SEEING NICE PICTURES; & *Spot the Alpha*
15.1.9 COPYING NAUGHTY PICTURES; & *Spot the Alpha*
15.1.10 NOT COPYING NAUGHTY PICTURES; & *Spot the Alpha*
15.1.11 HAVING NAUGHTY PICTURES; & *Spot the Alpha*
15.1.12 NOT HAVING NAUGHTY PICTURES; & *Spot the Alpha*
15.1.13 USING NAUGHTY PICTURES; & *Spot the Alpha*
15.1.14 NOT USING NAUGHTY PICTURES; & *Spot the Alpha*
15.1.15 SEEING NAUGHTY PICTURES; & *Spot the Alpha*
15.1.16 NOT SEEING NAUGHTY PICTURES; & *Spot the Alpha*
15.2.A GOOD.
15.2.B BAD.
15.2.C GOOD, BAD.
15.2.1 COPYING GOOD PICTURES; & *Spot the Alpha*
15.2.2 NOT COPYING GOOD PICTURES; & *Spot the Alpha*
15.2.3 HAVING GOOD PICTURES; & *Spot the Alpha*
15.2.4 NOT HAVING GOOD PICTURES; & *Spot the Alpha*
15.2.5 USING GOOD PICTURES; & *Spot the Alpha*
15.2.6 NOT USING GOOD PICTURES; & *Spot the Alpha*
15.2.7 SEEING GOOD PICTURES; & *Spot the Alpha*
15.2.8 NOT SEEING GOOD PICTURES; & *Spot the Alpha*
15.2.9 COPYING BAD PICTURES; & *Spot the Alpha*
15.2.10 NOT COPYING BAD PICTURES; & *Spot the Alpha*
15.2.11 HAVING BAD PICTURES; & *Spot the Alpha*
15.2.12 NOT HAVING BAD PICTURES; & *Spot the Alpha*
15.2.13 USING BAD PICTURES; & *Spot the Alpha*
15.2.14 NOT USING BAD PICTURES; & *Spot the Alpha*
15.2.15 SEEING BAD PICTURES; & *Spot the Alpha*
15.2.16 NOT SEEING BAD PICTURES; & *Spot the Alpha*
15.3.A HOLY.
15.3.B EVIL.
15.3.C HOLY, EVIL.
15.3.1 COPYING HOLY PICTURES; & *Spot the Alpha*
15.3.2 NOT COPYING HOLY PICTURES; & *Spot the Alpha*
15.3.3 HAVING HOLY PICTURES; & *Spot the Alpha*
15.3.4 NOT HAVING HOLY PICTURES; & *Spot the Alpha*
15.3.5 USING HOLY PICTURES; & *Spot the Alpha*
15.3.6 NOT USING HOLY PICTURES; & *Spot the Alpha*
15.3.7 SEEING HOLY PICTURES; & *Spot the Alpha*
15.3.8 NOT SEEING HOLY PICTURES; & *Spot the Alpha*

15.3.9 COPYING EVIL PICTURES; & *Spot the Alpha*
15.3.10 NOT COPYING EVIL PICTURES; & *Spot the Alpha*
15.3.11 HAVING EVIL PICTURES; & *Spot the Alpha*
15.3.12 NOT HAVING EVIL PICTURES; & *Spot the Alpha*
15.3.13 USING EVIL PICTURES; & *Spot the Alpha*
15.3.14 NOT USING EVIL PICTURES; & *Spot the Alpha*
15.3.15 SEEING EVIL PICTURES; & *Spot the Alpha*
15.3.16 NOT SEEING EVIL PICTURES; & *Spot the Alpha*
15.4.A CREATIVE.
15.4.B DESTRUCTIVE.
15.4.C CREATIVE, DESTRUCTIVE.
15.4.1 COPYING CREATIVE PICTURES; & *Spot the Alpha*
15.4.2 NOT COPYING CREATIVE PICTURES; & *Spot the Alpha*
15.4.3 HAVING CREATIVE PICTURES; & *Spot the Alpha*
15.4.4 NOT HAVING CREATIVE PICTURES; & *Spot the Alpha*
15.4.5 USING CREATIVE PICTURES; & *Spot the Alpha*
15.4.6 NOT USING CREATIVE PICTURES; & *Spot the Alpha*
15.4.7 SEEING CREATIVE PICTURES; & *Spot the Alpha*
15.4.8 NOT SEEING CREATIVE PICTURES; & *Spot the Alpha*
15.4.9 COPYING DESTRUCTIVE PICTURES; & *Spot the Alpha*
15.4.10 NOT COPYING DESTRUCTIVE PICTURES; & *Spot the Alpha*
15.4.11 HAVING DESTRUCTIVE PICTURES; & *Spot the Alpha*
15.4.12 NOT HAVING DESTRUCTIVE PICTURES; & *Spot the Alpha*
15.4.13 USING DESTRUCTIVE PICTURES; & *Spot the Alpha*
15.4.14 NOT USING DESTRUCTIVE PICTURES; & *Spot the Alpha*
15.4.15 SEEING DESTRUCTIVE PICTURES; & *Spot the Alpha*
15.4.16 NOT SEEING DESTRUCTIVE PICTURES; & *Spot the Alpha*
15.5.A PRODUCTIVE.
15.5.B RUINOUS.
15.5.C PRODUCTIVE, RUINOUS.
15.5.1 COPYING PRODUCTIVE PICTURES; & *Spot the Alpha*
15.5.2 NOT COPYING PRODUCTIVE PICTURES; & *Spot the Alpha*
15.5.3 HAVING PRODUCTIVE PICTURES; & *Spot the Alpha*
15.5.4 NOT HAVING PRODUCTIVE PICTURES; & *Spot the Alpha*
15.5.5 USING PRODUCTIVE PICTURES; & *Spot the Alpha*
15.5.6 NOT USING PRODUCTIVE PICTURES; & *Spot the Alpha*
15.5.7 SEEING PRODUCTIVE PICTURES; & *Spot the Alpha*
15.5.8 NOT SEEING PRODUCTIVE PICTURES; & *Spot the Alpha*
15.5.9 COPYING RUINOUS PICTURES; & *Spot the Alpha*

15.5.10 NOT COPYING RUINOUS PICTURES; & *Spot the Alpha*
15.5.11 HAVING RUINOUS PICTURES; & *Spot the Alpha*
15.5.12 NOT HAVING RUINOUS PICTURES; & *Spot the Alpha*
15.5.13 USING RUINOUS PICTURES; & *Spot the Alpha*
15.5.14 NOT USING RUINOUS PICTURES; & *Spot the Alpha*
15.5.15 SEEING RUINOUS PICTURES; & *Spot the Alpha*
15.5.16 NOT SEEING RUINOUS PICTURES; & *Spot the Alpha*
 15.6.A VALUABLE.
 15.6.B VALUELESS.
 15.6.C VALUABLE, VALUELESS.
 15.6.1 COPYING VALUABLE PICTURES; & *Spot the Alpha*
 15.6.2 NOT COPYING VALUABLE PICTURES; & *Spot the Alpha*
 15.6.3 HAVING VALUABLE PICTURES; & *Spot the Alpha*
 15.6.4 NOT HAVING VALUABLE PICTURES; & *Spot the Alpha*
 15.6.5 USING VALUABLE PICTURES; & *Spot the Alpha*
 15.6.6 NOT USING VALUABLE PICTURES; & *Spot the Alpha*
 15.6.7 SEEING VALUABLE PICTURES; & *Spot the Alpha*
 15.6.8 NOT SEEING VALUABLE PICTURES; & *Spot the Alpha*
 15.6.9 COPYING VALUELESS PICTURES; & *Spot the Alpha*
15.6.10 NOT COPYING VALUELESS PICTURES; & *Spot the Alpha*
15.6.11 HAVING VALUELESS PICTURES; & *Spot the Alpha*
15.6.12 NOT HAVING VALUELESS PICTURES; & *Spot the Alpha*
15.6.13 USING VALUELESS PICTURES; & *Spot the Alpha*
15.6.14 NOT USING VALUELESS PICTURES; & *Spot the Alpha*
15.6.15 SEEING VALUELESS PICTURES; & *Spot the Alpha*
15.6.16 NOT SEEING VALUELESS PICTURES; & *Spot the Alpha*
 15.7.A AGREEABLE.
 15.7.B DISAGREEABLE.
 15.7.C AGREEABLE, DISAGREEABLE.
 15.7.1 COPYING AGREEABLE PICTURES; & *Spot the Alpha*
 15.7.2 NOT COPYING AGREEABLE PICTURES; & *Spot the Alpha*
 15.7.3 HAVING AGREEABLE PICTURES; & *Spot the Alpha*
 15.7.4 NOT HAVING AGREEABLE PICTURES; & *Spot the Alpha*
 15.7.5 USING AGREEABLE PICTURES; & *Spot the Alpha*
 15.7.6 NOT USING AGREEABLE PICTURES; & *Spot the Alpha*
 15.7.7 SEEING AGREEABLE PICTURES; & *Spot the Alpha*
 15.7.8 NOT SEEING AGREEABLE PICTURES; & *Spot the Alpha*
 15.7.9 COPYING DISAGREEABLE PICTURES; & *Spot the Alpha*
15.7.10 NOT COPYING DISAGREEABLE PICTURES; & *A*

15.7.11 HAVING DISAGREEABLE PICTURES; *& Spot the Alpha*
15.7.12 NOT HAVING DISAGREEABLE PICTURES; *& Spot the Alpha*
15.7.13 USING DISAGREEABLE PICTURES; *& Spot the Alpha*
15.7.14 NOT USING DISAGREEABLE PICTURES; *& Spot the Alpha*
15.7.15 SEEING DISAGREEABLE PICTURES; *& Spot the Alpha*
15.7.16 NOT SEEING DISAGREEABLE PICTURES; *& Spot the Alpha*
15.8.A PLEASANT.
15.8.B UNPLEASANT.
15.8.C PLEASANT, UNPLEASANT.
15.8.1 COPYING PLEASANT PICTURES; *& Spot the Alpha*
15.8.2 NOT COPYING PLEASANT PICTURES; *& Spot the Alpha*
15.8.3 HAVING PLEASANT PICTURES; *& Spot the Alpha*
15.8.4 NOT HAVING PLEASANT PICTURES; *& Spot the Alpha*
15.8.5 USING PLEASANT PICTURES; *& Spot the Alpha*
15.8.6 NOT USING PLEASANT PICTURES; *& Spot the Alpha*
15.8.7 SEEING PLEASANT PICTURES; *& Spot the Alpha*
15.8.8 NOT SEEING PLEASANT PICTURES; *& Spot the Alpha*
15.8.9 COPYING UNPLEASANT PICTURES; *& Spot the Alpha*
15.8.10 NOT COPYING UNPLEASANT PICTURES; *& Spot the Alpha*
15.8.11 HAVING UNPLEASANT PICTURES; *& Spot the Alpha*
15.8.12 NOT HAVING UNPLEASANT PICTURES; *& Spot the Alpha*
15.8.13 USING UNPLEASANT PICTURES; *& Spot the Alpha*
15.8.14 NOT USING UNPLEASANT PICTURES; *& Spot the Alpha*
15.8.15 SEEING UNPLEASANT PICTURES; *& Spot the Alpha*
15.8.16 NOT SEEING UNPLEASANT PICTURES; *& Spot the Alpha*
15.9.A HEARTENING.
15.9.B FRIGHTENING.
15.9.C HEARTENING, FRIGHTENING.
15.9.1 COPYING HEARTENING PICTURES; *& Spot the Alpha*
15.9.2 NOT COPYING HEARTENING PICTURES; *& Spot the Alpha*
15.9.3 HAVING HEARTENING PICTURES; *& Spot the Alpha*
15.9.4 NOT HAVING HEARTENING PICTURES; *& Spot the Alpha*
15.9.5 USING HEARTENING PICTURES; *& Spot the Alpha*
15.9.6 NOT USING HEARTENING PICTURES; *& Spot the Alpha*
15.9.7 SEEING HEARTENING PICTURES; *& Spot the Alpha*
15.9.8 NOT SEEING HEARTENING PICTURES; *& Spot the Alpha*
15.9.9 COPYING FRIGHTENING PICTURES; *& Spot the Alpha*
15.9.10 NOT COPYING FRIGHTENING PICTURES; *& Spot the Alpha*
15.9.11 HAVING FRIGHTENING PICTURES; *& Spot the Alpha*

15.9.12 NOT HAVING FRIGHTENING PICTURES; *& Spot the Alpha*
15.9.13 USING FRIGHTENING PICTURES; *& Spot the Alpha*
15.9.14 NOT USING FRIGHTENING PICTURES; *& Spot the Alpha*
15.9.15 SEEING FRIGHTENING PICTURES; *& Spot the Alpha*
15.9.16 NOT SEEING FRIGHTENING PICTURES; *& Spot the Alpha*

15.10.A INFORMATIVE.
15.10.B MYSTIFYING.
15.10.C INFORMATIVE, MYSTIFYING.
15.10.1 COPYING INFORMATIVE PICTURES; *& Spot the Alpha*
15.10.2 NOT COPYING INFORMATIVE PICTURES; *& A*
15.10.3 HAVING INFORMATIVE PICTURES; *& Spot the Alpha*
15.10.4 NOT HAVING INFORMATIVE PICTURES; *& Spot the Alpha*
15.10.5 USING INFORMATIVE PICTURES; *& Spot the Alpha*
15.10.6 NOT USING INFORMATIVE PICTURES; *& Spot the Alpha*
15.10.7 SEEING INFORMATIVE PICTURES; *& Spot the Alpha*
15.10.8 NOT SEEING INFORMATIVE PICTURES; *& Spot the Alpha*

* If "MYSTIFYING" does not register on the steps below, try "UNINTELLIGIBLE."

15.10.9   COPYING MYSTIFYING PICTURES; *& Spot the Alpha*
15.10.10 NOT COPYING MYSTIFYING PICTURES; *& Spot the Alpha*
15.10.11 HAVING MYSTIFYING PICTURES; *& Spot the Alpha*
15.10.12 NOT HAVING MYSTIFYING PICTURES; *& Spot the Alpha*
15.10.13 USING MYSTIFYING PICTURES; *& Spot the Alpha*
15.10.14 NOT USING MYSTIFYING PICTURES; *& Spot the Alpha*
15.10.15 SEEING MYSTIFYING PICTURES; *& Spot the Alpha*
15.10.16 NOT SEEING MYSTIFYING PICTURES; *& Spot the Alpha*

PLATFORM #16

[This is a Platform short-form formula. The Implant incites or reinforces the decay of goals by opposition. It contains a series of 18 "command-item" lines. This series (lines 1 through 18) is run on each of 82 different keywords. They are listed/ numbered below. A Seeker must know the meaning of each of these keywords, and get three consecutive "no-reads" on each by itself, before processing-out the Implant. The list below may be used for that purpose as 'Step-1'. A Seeker should also prepare 82 different worksheets from this formula, inserting only one keyword (of the 82) for each worksheet. This generates 1476 different command-items total. Don't analyze its contents; just defragment it. All item-lines may not read. If necessary for reads, some alternative verbs are

listed with an *asterisk. Only backtrack if three consecutive line-items do not register. When an item-line does not read, simply check to see if anything has been "suppressed," "invalidated," or "protested" on that item. For example: "On 'To Create X', has anything been 'suppressed'," &tc. If there is no-read for all of these checks, continue to the next item. If you get a 'big win', end-session for the day. Since excess charge is taken off all keywords at the beginning, and as more of the formula-pattern is defragmented, item-lines may discharge more easily or even cease to register altogether. If three consecutive Platform keyword-worksheets give no-reads (and are not being "suppressed" &tc.), then Platform #16 is defragmented.]

Note: The following list of meanings is actually in sets of pairs. The word "void" appears twice, but may be substituted with a similar meaning word (if necessary, or to get Meter-reads, &tc) or may simply be used twice with two different meanings in mind. For example: 13. "Voids" is paired with 14. "Universes"; and therefore means an "Abyss" or "Nothingness" (as an opposite condition to created Universes) – and 53. "Voids" is paired with 54. "Habitations"; and therefore means "Uninhabitable Spaces" (as opposed to spaces that can be occupied).

KEYWORDS: 1) SPACE; 2) MATTER; 3) ENERGY; 4) MASS (*SOLIDITY);
5) NEVER; 6) TIME; 7) MOMENTS (*INSTANTS); 8) ETERNITY;
9) STILLNESS; 10) MOTION (*VELOCITY); 11) VACUUMS;
12) SOLIDS; 13) VOIDS (*ABYSSES); 14) UNIVERSES; 15) STARS;
16) GALAXIES; 17) PLANETS; 18) SUNS; 19) SYSTEMS;
20) CLUSTERS; 21) DEADNESS; 22) BRIGHTNESS; 23) DARKNESS;
24) LIGHT; 25) BLACKNESS; 26) WHITENESS; 27) BLUENESS;
28) REDNESS; 29) YELLOWNESS; 30) GREENNESS;
31) PURPLENESS; 32) ORANGENESS; 33) SILENCE; 34) SOUNDS;
35) NOISE; 36) MUSIC; 37) DISHARMONY; 38) HARMONY;
39) LIQUIDS; 40) GASES; 41) COLD; 42) HEAT; 43) DESERTS;
44) SEAS; 45) VALLEYS; 46) MOUNTAINS; 47) BROOKS; 48) RIVERS;
49) ISLANDS; 50) CONTINENTS; 51) METEORS; 52) COMETS;
53) VOIDS; 54) HABITATIONS; 55) BARBARISMS;
56) CIVILIZATIONS; 57) ANARCHY; 58) GOVERNMENT;
59) SAVAGES; 60) HUMANS; 61) ANIMALS; 62) PEOPLE;
63) INSECTS; 64) SNAKES; 65) MONSTERS; 66) FISH; 67) CELLS;
68) BODIES; 69) POISONS; 70) BALMS; 71) DEPRESSANTS;
72) STIMULANTS; 73) SEDATIVES; 74) EUPHORICS; 75) ILLUSIONS;
76) REALITIES; 77) DELUSIONS; 78) ACTUALITIES; 79) LIES;
80) TRUTHS; 81) IGNORANCE; 82) KNOWLEDGE.

16.1.X TO CREATE ___; & *Spot the Alpha*

16.2.X NO MORE DESIRES TO CREATE ___; & *Spot the Alpha*

16.3.X DIFFERENTLY CREATING ___; & *Spot the Alpha*

16.4.X DIFFICULTIES WITH OTHER CREATORS OF ___; & A
16.5.X CONSTANTLY CREATING ___; & *Spot the Alpha*
16.6.X FAILURES TO CREATE ___; & *Spot the Alpha*
16.7.X AUTOMATIC CREATORS OF ___; & *Spot the Alpha*
16.8.X OBSESSION WITH TO CREATE ___; & *Spot the Alpha*
16.9.X HAVING TO CREATE ___; & *Spot the Alpha*
16.10.X COMPULSIONS TO CREATE ___; & *Spot the Alpha*
16.11.X HATING TO CREATE ___; & *Spot the Alpha*
16.12.X CRITICISMS OF CREATED ___; & *Spot the Alpha*
16.13.X HOPING TO NEVER CREATE ___; & *Spot the Alpha*
16.14.X TOO MUCH CREATING ___; & *Spot the Alpha*
16.15.X TO NEVER CREATE ___; & *Spot the Alpha*
16.16.X TO CREATE ___; & *Spot the Alpha*
16.17.X DESIRES TO DESTROY ___; & *Spot the Alpha*
16.18.X THOSE WHO DESIRE TO CREATE ___; & *Spot the Alpha*

PLATFORM #17

[*This is a Platform long-form. It is meant to incite or reinforce a fixation on bodies. The "command-lines" follow a pattern, which we could have presented as a short-form formula. If an item-line does not "read" immediately, it may be necessary for a Seeker to figure an alternative similar verb. Once a Seeker gets a sense of its basic meaning (rather than protesting its wording), it will register on a Meter. Say the "command-item" out loud, and spot the Alpha-Spirit; then say the "command-item" while spotting the Alpha-Spirit. Perform this in whatever way produces the best "reads" for each item-line until that same action gives "no-reads" three consecutive times. Remember that you are treating an incident; so you might consider the item-lines as "During {command-item}; Spot the Alpha."*]

17.1.1 TO LOVE A BODY; & *Spot the Alpha*
17.1.2 TO NOT LOVE A BODY; & *Spot the Alpha*
17.1.3 TO LOVE A BODY, TO NOT LOVE A BODY; & *Spot the Alpha*
17.1.4 TO HATE A BODY; & *Spot the Alpha*
17.1.5 TO NOT HATE A BODY; & *Spot the Alpha*
17.1.6 TO HATE A BODY, TO NOT HATE A BODY; & *Spot the Alpha*
17.2.1 TO WANT A BODY; & *Spot the Alpha*
17.2.2 TO NOT WANT A BODY; & *Spot the Alpha*

17.2.3 TO WANT A BODY, TO NOT WANT A BODY; & A
17.2.4 TO PROTEST A BODY; & *Spot the Alpha*
17.2.5 TO NOT PROTEST A BODY; & *Spot the Alpha*
17.2.6 TO PROTEST A BODY, TO NOT PROTEST A BODY; & A
17.3.1 TO ACQUIRE A BODY; & *Spot the Alpha*
17.3.2 TO NOT ACQUIRE A BODY; & *Spot the Alpha*
17.3.3 TO ACQUIRE A BODY, TO NOT ACQUIRE A BODY; & A
17.3.4 TO REJECT A BODY; & *Spot the Alpha*
17.3.5 TO NOT REJECT A BODY; & *Spot the Alpha*
17.3.6 TO REJECT A BODY, TO NOT REJECT A BODY; & A
17.4.1 TO NEED A BODY; & *Spot the Alpha*
17.4.2 TO NOT NEED A BODY; & *Spot the Alpha*
17.4.3 TO NEED A BODY, TO NOT NEED A BODY; & *Spot the Alpha*
17.4.4 TO CONDEMN A BODY; & *Spot the Alpha*
17.4.5 TO NOT CONDEMN A BODY; & *Spot the Alpha*
17.4.6 TO CONDEMN A BODY, TO NOT CONDEMN A BODY; & A
17.5.1 TO DO WITH A BODY; & *Spot the Alpha*
17.5.2 TO NOT DO WITH A BODY; & *Spot the Alpha*
17.5.3 TO DO WITH A BODY, TO NOT DO WITH A BODY; & A
17.5.4 TO DO WITHOUT A BODY; & *Spot the Alpha*
17.5.5 TO NOT DO WITHOUT A BODY; & *Spot the Alpha*
17.5.6 TO DO WITHOUT A BODY, TO NOT DO WITHOUT A BODY; & *Spot the Alpha*
17.6.1 TO HAVE A BODY; & *Spot the Alpha*
17.6.2 TO NOT HAVE A BODY; & *Spot the Alpha*
17.6.3 TO HAVE A BODY, TO NOT HAVE A BODY; & *Spot the Alpha*
17.6.4 TO GET RID OF A BODY; & *Spot the Alpha*
17.6.5 TO NOT GET RID OF A BODY; & *Spot the Alpha*
17.6.6 TO GET RID OF A BODY, TO NOT GET RID OF A BODY; & *Spot the Alpha*
17.7.1 TO SEEK A BODY; & *Spot the Alpha*
17.7.2 TO NOT SEEK A BODY; & *Spot the Alpha*
17.7.3 TO SEEK A BODY, TO NOT SEEK A BODY; & *Spot the Alpha*
17.7.4 TO FORGET A BODY; & *Spot the Alpha*
17.7.5 TO NOT FORGET A BODY; & *Spot the Alpha*
17.7.6 TO FORGET A BODY, TO NOT FORGET A BODY; & A
17.8.1 TO LOOK FOR A BODY; & *Spot the Alpha*

17.8.2 TO NOT LOOK FOR A BODY; & *Spot the Alpha*
17.8.3 TO LOOK FOR A BODY, TO NOT LOOK FOR A BODY; & *A*
17.8.4 TO IGNORE A BODY; & *Spot the Alpha*
17.8.5 TO NOT IGNORE A BODY; & *Spot the Alpha*
17.8.6 TO IGNORE A BODY, TO NOT IGNORE A BODY; & *A*

17.9.1 TO DISCOVER A BODY; & *Spot the Alpha*
17.9.2 TO NOT DISCOVER A BODY; & *Spot the Alpha*
17.9.3 TO DISCOVER A BODY, TO NOT DISCOVER A BODY; & *A*
17.9.4 TO NEGLECT A BODY; & *Spot the Alpha*
17.9.5 TO NOT NEGLECT A BODY; & *Spot the Alpha*
17.9.6 TO NEGLECT A BODY, TO NOT NEGLECT A BODY; & *A*

17.10.1 TO FIND A BODY; & *Spot the Alpha*
17.10.2 TO NOT FIND A BODY; & *Spot the Alpha*
17.10.3 TO FIND A BODY, TO NOT FIND A BODY; & *Spot the Alpha*
17.10.4 TO LOSE A BODY; & *Spot the Alpha*
17.10.5 TO NOT LOSE A BODY; & *Spot the Alpha*
17.10.6 TO LOSE A BODY, TO NOT LOSE A BODY; & *Spot the Alpha*

17.11.1 TO LOCATE A BODY; & *Spot the Alpha*
17.11.2 TO NOT LOCATE A BODY; & *Spot the Alpha*
17.11.3 TO LOCATE A BODY, TO NOT LOCATE A BODY; & *A*
17.11.4 TO MISPLACE A BODY; & *Spot the Alpha*
17.11.5 TO NOT MISPLACE A BODY; & *Spot the Alpha*
17.11.6 TO MISPLACE A BODY, TO NOT MISPLACE A BODY; & *A*

17.12.1 TO EXHIBIT A BODY; & *Spot the Alpha*
17.12.2 TO NOT EXHIBIT A BODY; & *Spot the Alpha*
17.12.3 TO EXHIBIT A BODY, TO NOT EXHIBIT A BODY; & *A*
17.12.4 TO HIDE A BODY; & *Spot the Alpha*
17.12.5 TO NOT HIDE A BODY; & *Spot the Alpha*
17.12.6 TO HIDE A BODY, TO NOT HIDE A BODY; & *Spot the Alpha*

17.13.1 TO REVEAL A BODY; & *Spot the Alpha*
17.13.2 TO NOT REVEAL A BODY; & *Spot the Alpha*
17.13.3 TO REVEAL A BODY, TO NOT REVEAL A BODY; & *A*
17.13.4 TO SCREEN A BODY; & *Spot the Alpha*
17.13.5 TO NOT SCREEN A BODY; & *Spot the Alpha*
17.13.6 TO SCREEN A BODY, TO NOT SCREEN A BODY; & *A*

17.14.1 TO DISPLAY A BODY; & *Spot the Alpha*
17.14.2 TO NOT DISPLAY A BODY; & *Spot the Alpha*

17.14.3 TO DISPLAY A BODY, TO NOT DISPLAY A BODY; & A
17.14.4 TO MASK A BODY; & *Spot the Alpha*
17.14.5 TO NOT MASK A BODY; & *Spot the Alpha*
17.14.6 TO MASK A BODY, TO NOT MASK A BODY; & *Spot the Alpha*
17.15.1 TO SHOW A BODY; & *Spot the Alpha*
17.15.2 TO NOT SHOW A BODY; & *Spot the Alpha*
17.15.3 TO SHOW A BODY, TO NOT SHOW A BODY; & A
17.15.4 TO CURTAIN A BODY; & *Spot the Alpha*
17.15.5 TO NOT CURTAIN A BODY; & *Spot the Alpha*
17.15.6 TO CURTAIN A BODY, TO NOT CURTAIN A BODY; & A
17.16.1 TO APPEAR IN A BODY; & *Spot the Alpha*
17.16.2 TO NOT APPEAR IN A BODY; & *Spot the Alpha*
17.16.3 TO APPEAR IN A BODY, TO NOT APPEAR IN A BODY; & A
17.16.4 TO DISAPPEAR IN A BODY; & *Spot the Alpha*
17.16.5 TO NOT DISAPPEAR IN A BODY; & *Spot the Alpha*
17.16.6 TO DISAPPEAR IN A BODY, TO NOT DISAPPEAR IN A BODY; & *Spot the Alpha*
17.17.1 TO BE A BODY; & *Spot the Alpha*
17.17.2 TO NOT BE A BODY; & *Spot the Alpha*
17.17.3 TO BE A BODY, TO NOT BE A BODY; & *Spot the Alpha*
17.17.4 TO UN-BE A BODY; & *Spot the Alpha*
17.17.5 TO NOT UN-BE A BODY; & *Spot the Alpha*
17.17.6 TO UN-BE A BODY, TO NOT UN-BE A BODY; & A
17.18.1 TO FLAUNT A BODY; & *Spot the Alpha*
17.18.2 TO NOT FLAUNT A BODY; & *Spot the Alpha*
17.18.3 TO FLAUNT A BODY, TO NOT FLAUNT A BODY; & A
17.18.4 TO CONCEAL A BODY; & *Spot the Alpha*
17.18.5 TO NOT CONCEAL A BODY; & *Spot the Alpha*
17.18.6 TO CONCEAL A BODY, TO NOT CONCEAL A BODY; & A
17.19.1 TO DEMONSTRATE A BODY; & *Spot the Alpha*
17.19.2 TO NOT DEMONSTRATE A BODY; & *Spot the Alpha*
17.19.3 TO DEMONSTRATE A BODY, TO NOT DEMONSTRATE A BODY; & *Spot the Alpha*
17.19.4 TO COVER A BODY; & *Spot the Alpha*
17.19.5 TO NOT COVER A BODY; & *Spot the Alpha*
17.19.6 TO COVER A BODY, TO NOT COVER A BODY; & A
17.20.1 TO BEAUTIFY A BODY; & *Spot the Alpha*

17.20.2 TO NOT BEAUTIFY A BODY; & *Spot the Alpha*
17.20.3 TO BEAUTIFY A BODY, TO NOT BEAUTIFY A BODY; & *A*
17.20.4 TO UGLIFY A BODY; & *Spot the Alpha*
17.20.5 TO NOT UGLIFY A BODY; & *Spot the Alpha*
17.20.6 TO UGLIFY A BODY, TO NOT UGLIFY A BODY; & *A*

17.21.1 TO ENNOBLE A BODY; & *Spot the Alpha*
17.21.2 TO NOT ENNOBLE A BODY; & *Spot the Alpha*
17.21.3 TO ENNOBLE A BODY, TO NOT ENNOBLE A BODY; & *A*
17.21.4 TO DEGRADE A BODY; & *Spot the Alpha*
17.21.5 TO NOT DEGRADE A BODY; & *Spot the Alpha*
17.21.6 TO DEGRADE A BODY, TO NOT DEGRADE A BODY; & *A*

17.22.1 TO PROMOTE A BODY; & *Spot the Alpha*
17.22.2 TO NOT PROMOTE A BODY; & *Spot the Alpha*
17.22.3 TO PROMOTE A BODY, TO NOT PROMOTE A BODY; & *A*
17.22.4 TO NEGATE A BODY; & *Spot the Alpha*
17.22.5 TO NOT NEGATE A BODY; & *Spot the Alpha*
17.22.6 TO NEGATE A BODY, TO NOT NEGATE A BODY; & *A*

17.23.1 TO ENLIVEN A BODY; & *Spot the Alpha*
17.23.2 TO NOT ENLIVEN A BODY; & *Spot the Alpha*
17.23.3 TO ENLIVEN A BODY, TO NOT ENLIVEN A BODY; & *A*
17.23.4 TO DEADEN A BODY; & *Spot the Alpha*
17.23.5 TO NOT DEADEN A BODY; & *Spot the Alpha*
17.23.6 TO DEADEN A BODY, TO NOT DEADEN A BODY; & *A*

17.24.1 TO HELP A BODY; & *Spot the Alpha*
17.24.2 TO NOT HELP A BODY; & *Spot the Alpha*
17.24.3 TO HELP A BODY, TO NOT HELP A BODY; & *Spot the Alpha*
17.24.4 TO HINDER A BODY; & *Spot the Alpha*
17.24.5 TO NOT HINDER A BODY; & *Spot the Alpha*
17.24.6 TO HINDER A BODY, TO NOT HINDER A BODY; & *A*

17.25.1 TO SAVE A BODY; & *Spot the Alpha*
17.25.2 TO NOT SAVE A BODY; & *Spot the Alpha*
17.25.3 TO SAVE A BODY, TO NOT SAVE A BODY; & *Spot the Alpha*
17.25.4 TO WASTE A BODY; & *Spot the Alpha*
17.25.5 TO NOT WASTE A BODY; & *Spot the Alpha*
17.25.6 TO WASTE A BODY, TO NOT WASTE A BODY; & *A*

17.26.1 TO PRESERVE A BODY; & *Spot the Alpha*
17.26.2 TO NOT PRESERVE A BODY; & *Spot the Alpha*

17.26.3 TO PRESERVE A BODY, TO NOT PRESERVE A BODY; & A
17.26.4 TO DECAY A BODY; & *Spot the Alpha*
17.26.5 TO NOT DECAY A BODY; & *Spot the Alpha*
17.26.6 TO DECAY A BODY, TO NOT DECAY A BODY; & A
17.27.1 TO STIMULATE A BODY; & *Spot the Alpha*
17.27.2 TO NOT STIMULATE A BODY; & *Spot the Alpha*
17.27.3 TO STIMULATE A BODY, TO NOT STIMULATE A BODY; & *Spot the Alpha*
17.27.4 TO DESTIMULATE A BODY; & *Spot the Alpha*
17.27.5 TO NOT DESTIMULATE A BODY; & *Spot the Alpha*
17.27.6 TO DESTIMULATE A BODY, TO NOT DESTIMULATE A BODY; & *Spot the Alpha*
17.28.1 TO PROTECT A BODY; & *Spot the Alpha*
17.28.2 TO NOT PROTECT A BODY; & *Spot the Alpha*
17.28.3 TO PROTECT A BODY, TO NOT PROTECT A BODY; & A
17.28.4 TO HARM A BODY; & *Spot the Alpha*
17.28.5 TO NOT HARM A BODY; & *Spot the Alpha*
17.28.6 TO HARM A BODY, TO NOT HARM A BODY; & A
17.29.1 TO DEFEND A BODY; & *Spot the Alpha*
17.29.2 TO NOT DEFEND A BODY; & *Spot the Alpha*
17.29.3 TO DEFEND A BODY, TO NOT DEFEND A BODY; & A
17.29.4 TO ATTACK A BODY; & *Spot the Alpha*
17.29.5 TO NOT ATTACK A BODY; & *Spot the Alpha*
17.29.6 TO ATTACK A BODY, TO NOT ATTACK A BODY; & A
17.30.1 TO ENERGIZE A BODY; & *Spot the Alpha*
17.30.2 TO NOT ENERGIZE A BODY; & *Spot the Alpha*
17.30.3 TO ENERGIZE A BODY, TO NOT ENERGIZE A BODY; & A
17.30.4 TO DE-ENERGIZE A BODY; & *Spot the Alpha*
17.30.5 TO NOT DE-ENERGIZE A BODY; & *Spot the Alpha*
17.30.6 TO DE-ENERGIZE A BODY, TO NOT DE-ENERGIZE A BODY; & *Spot the Alpha*
17.31.1 TO ENTHUSE A BODY; & *Spot the Alpha*
17.31.2 TO NOT ENTHUSE A BODY; & *Spot the Alpha*
17.31.3 TO ENTHUSE A BODY, TO NOT ENTHUSE A BODY; & A
17.31.4 TO SUPPRESS A BODY; & *Spot the Alpha*
17.31.5 TO NOT SUPPRESS A BODY; & *Spot the Alpha*
17.31.6 TO SUPPRESS A BODY, TO NOT SUPPRESS A BODY; & A
17.32.1 TO ELEVATE A BODY; & *Spot the Alpha*

17.32.2 TO NOT ELEVATE A BODY; & *Spot the Alpha*
17.32.3 TO ELEVATE A BODY, TO NOT ELEVATE A BODY; & *A*
17.32.4 TO DEPRESS A BODY; & *Spot the Alpha*
17.32.5 TO NOT DEPRESS A BODY; & *Spot the Alpha*
17.32.6 TO DEPRESS A BODY, TO NOT DEPRESS A BODY; & *A*

17.33.1 TO ENHANCE A BODY; & *Spot the Alpha*
17.33.2 TO NOT ENHANCE A BODY; & *Spot the Alpha*
17.33.3 TO ENHANCE A BODY, TO NOT ENHANCE A BODY; & *A*
17.33.4 TO DISPARAGE A BODY; & *Spot the Alpha*
17.33.5 TO NOT DISPARAGE A BODY; & *Spot the Alpha*
17.33.6 TO DISPARAGE A BODY, TO NOT DISPARAGE A BODY; & *Spot the Alpha*

17.34.1 TO GLORIFY A BODY; & *Spot the Alpha*
17.34.2 TO NOT GLORIFY A BODY; & *Spot the Alpha*
17.34.3 TO GLORIFY A BODY, TO NOT GLORIFY A BODY; & *A*
17.34.4 TO BELITTLE A BODY; & *Spot the Alpha*
17.34.5 TO NOT BELITTLE A BODY; & *Spot the Alpha*
17.34.6 TO BELITTLE A BODY, TO NOT BELITTLE A BODY; & *A*

17.35.1 TO EXPAND A BODY; & *Spot the Alpha*
17.35.2 TO NOT EXPAND A BODY; & *Spot the Alpha*
17.35.3 TO EXPAND A BODY, TO NOT EXPAND A BODY; & *A*
17.35.4 TO CONTRACT A BODY; & *Spot the Alpha*
17.35.5 TO NOT CONTRACT A BODY; & *Spot the Alpha*
17.35.6 TO CONTRACT A BODY, TO NOT CONTRACT A BODY; & *Spot the Alpha*

17.36.1 TO EXERCISE A BODY; & *Spot the Alpha*
17.36.2 TO NOT EXERCISE A BODY; & *Spot the Alpha*
17.36.3 TO EXERCISE A BODY, TO NOT EXERCISE A BODY; & *A*
17.36.4 TO RELAX A BODY; & *Spot the Alpha*
17.36.5 TO NOT RELAX A BODY; & *Spot the Alpha*
17.36.6 TO RELAX A BODY, TO NOT RELAX A BODY; & *A*

17.37.1 TO USE A BODY; & *Spot the Alpha*
17.37.2 TO NOT USE A BODY; & *Spot the Alpha*
17.37.3 TO USE A BODY, TO NOT USE A BODY; & *Spot the Alpha*
17.37.4 TO DISUSE A BODY; & *Spot the Alpha*
17.37.5 TO NOT DISUSE A BODY; & *Spot the Alpha*
17.37.6 TO DISUSE A BODY, TO NOT DISUSE A BODY; & *A*

174 – AT#3

17.38.1 TO BEGIN A BODY; & *Spot the Alpha*
17.38.2 TO NOT BEGIN A BODY; & *Spot the Alpha*
17.38.3 TO BEGIN A BODY, TO NOT BEGIN A BODY; & *A*
17.38.4 TO END A BODY; & *Spot the Alpha*
17.38.5 TO NOT END A BODY; & *Spot the Alpha*
17.38.6 TO END A BODY, TO NOT END A BODY; & *Spot the Alpha*

PLATFORM #18

[*This is a Platform short-form formula. It incites or reinforces the creation of 96 types of spiritual machinery (and unknowingly shifting responsibility), using 96 different conceptual keywords. The first 48 are positives (or constructive/creative); the second 48 are directly oppositional to the first 48. The same formula-pattern of only three command-lines is applied to each of the 96 concepts/words (generating 288 item-lines total). The words are listed/numbered below. A Seeker must know the meaning of each, and get three consecutive "no-reads" on each by itself, before handling the Implant. The list below may be used for that purpose as 'Step-1'. A Seeker does not need separate worksheets for each of the 96 types. This is all part of one Platform, using the same pattern of three command-lines 96 times. All item-lines may not read. When a line does not read, check if anything has been "suppressed," "invalidated," or "protested" about that item. This is important because most of this Platform utilizes non-traditional conceptual wording.*

For example: when referring to 'the machine' part, an "–ingness" is added to the end of the keyword (verb). "To Write" (not actually in the list) would be applied as "To Build a Writingness Machine"; and the second line would be "Not 'To Write' Yourself." Most item-lines will appear much less grammatically correct than even this. Remember that this Platform was not Implanted in "English" or any human speech, so we must be somewhat creative in its proper handling.]

KEYWORDS {POSITIVE}: 1) TO POSTULATE; 2) TO THINK; 3) TO IDEA-IZE;
4) TO REASON; 5) TO SOLVE; 6) TO ORDER; 7) TO SPACE;
8) TO TIME; 9) TO MASS; 10) TO ENERGIZE; 11) TO MATERIALIZE;
12) TO SOLIDIFY; 13) TO FIND; 14) TO LOCATE; 15) TO POSITION;
16) TO WANT; 17) TO DESIRE; 18) TO CRAVE; 19) TO GET;
20) TO OBTAIN; 21) TO COLLECT; 22) TO RETAIN; 23) TO KEEP;
24) TO HOLD; 25) TO SAVE; 26) TO PRESERVE; 27) TO SURVIVE;
28) TO RECORD; 29) TO COPY; 30) TO DUPLICATE; 31) TO FORM;
32) TO PICTURE; 33) TO CREATE; 34) TO MAKE; 35) TO PRODUCE;
36) TO CONSTRUCT; 37) TO VIEW; 38) TO SEE; 39) TO PERCEIVE;
40) TO SENSE; 41) TO FEEL; 42) TO CONTACT; 43) TO SENSATION;

44) TO ENJOY; 45) TO EXALT; 46) TO REMEMBER;
47) TO CONSCIOUS-IZE; 48) TO KNOW.

KEYWORDS {NEGATING}: 49) TO WITHHOLD; 50) TO UNTHINKIFY;
51) TO STUPIDIFY; 52) TO UNREASONIZE; 53) TO PROBLEMIFY;
54) TO CONFUSE; 55) TO GROUP; 56) TO TIMELESS;
57) TO CLEAR; 58) TO DRAIN; 59) TO VANISH;
60) TO DISINTEGRATE; 61) TO LOSE; 62) TO HIDE;
63) TO DISPLACE; 64) TO REJECT; 65) TO DISDAIN; 66) TO HATE;
67) TO DISCARD; 68) TO NEGLECT; 69) TO ABANDON;
70) TO IGNORE; 71) TO DISMISS; 72) TO FREE; 73) TO WASTE;
74) TO DECAY; 75) TO DIE; 76) TO ERADICATE; 77) TO ERASE;
78) TO ANNIHILATE; 79) TO TERMINATE; 80) TO BLANK;
81) TO DESTROY; 82) TO IMPEDE; 83) TO STOP; 84) TO ABOLISH;
85) TO OBSCURE; 86) TO BLIND; 87) TO SCREEN; 88) TO AVOID;
89) TO SHUN; 90) TO DISCONNECT; 91) TO NUMB;
92) TO SUPPRESS; 93) TO SUBDUE; 94) TO FORGET;
95) TO UNCONSCIOUS-IZE; 96) TO AMNESIA-IZE.

18.X.1 TO BUILD A ___-INGNESS MACHINE; & *Spot the Alpha*

18.X.2 NOT TO ___ YOURSELF; & *Spot the Alpha*

18.X.3 TO BUILD A ___-INGNESS MACHINE, NOT TO ___ YOURSELF; & *Spot the Alpha*

Upon successful *defragmentation* of *Platform #18*, a *Seeker* reaches the next stable-point on the *Pathway*. As a *processing gradient*, this achievement marks the completion of *Systemology Level-7*. Following the standard organizational structure of our *Systemology Society*, a *Seeker* is now "awarded" their own *Implanted Universe Directory* (*AT Manual #4*) prior to approaching *Systemology Level-8* (with *AT Manual #5*).

A.T. MANUAL #4
IMPLANTED
UNIVERSES

Review this prerequisite reference material:
  PC Lesson-7, "Eliminating Barriers"
  PC Lesson-8, "Conquest of Illusion"
  PC Lesson-11, "Spiritual Implants"
  PC Lesson-12, "Games & Universes"
  PC Lesson-14, "Spiritual Machinery"
  PC Lesson-15, "The Arcs of Infinity"
  AT Manual #1, "The Secret of Universes"
  AT Manual #2, "Games, Goals & Purposes"
  AT Manual #3, "The Jewel of Knowledge"
  AT Supplement, "Systemology Procedures"
  AT Supplement, "Systemology Biofeedback"

PIERCING THE SEVENTH VEIL

The descent of the *Alpha-Spirit* into entrapment within *this Physical Universe* has been a very long journey—through many *existences*; many *Universes*. This is reflected in the data found in all three prior *Systemology Level-7 AT Manuals*, starting with *"The Secret of Universes."*

The Way Out is also a long journey—*but possible in this lifetime.*

Among past attempts and other avenues available to a *Seeker*: targeting *"magical powers"* or emphasizing *"spiritual (or psychic) abilities"* directly has not led to a *Way Out*. In fact, these *"powers,"* when handled by *fragmented individuals*, only lead to more *problems*—and the *"abilities,"* themselves, fall away again, lost and forgotten. This is because we have a bad habit of *"Not-Knowing"* for (supposedly) *"one's own good."*

At the completion of *Systemology Level-7*, we are fast approaching a vast terrain of *upper-level work* to continue our progress on the *Pathway*. This, itself, has already required many years of research, and collaborative efforts of many *advanced Seekers*. The *upper-most routes* of the *Pathway* will continue to require additional research by *serious practitioners*.

Up until now, previous *processing-levels* (including *Level-7*), have all followed a "straight-shot" up the *Pathway* toward *Ascension*. In this manual, we begin treating some elements more experimentally—as it is the result of more recent *"upper-level research processing,"* rather than what is presented for *Levels 0 to 7*, which were in constant development for decades prior to publication.

While our "formal" *Advanced Training* may end with the forthcoming manuals representing *Systemology Level-8* (and completing the "*Keys to the Kingdom*" series), this will also open up, what is referred to by the *Mardukite Academy* as, the *"Infinity Grade."* This means that there remains to be plenty of room for many more researchers to contribute; but only after first completing their *Training* regarding the parts of our *"Map"* that *is* already researched, well-plotted, effective in application, and thus published.

The basic foundation of all our *fragmentation* originates from a time when the *Alpha-Spirit* still operated *knowingly* from a *godlike* state—still *knowingly capable* of *creating* and *destroying* "*Universes*" at will. Although our potential remains, the *realization* and *actualization* of this state has since greatly decayed.

A *godlike being* first becomes *fragmented*, then consequently loses their "*power.*" AT Manual #1 describes an early period of *clarity* and *power*, followed by a period of greatly *fragmented activity* (but still while the *Alpha-Spirit* wields its *godlike power*).

Prior to entrapment to more *solidly fixed reality-agreements* and *Bodies*, the *Alpha-Spirit* has no *considerations* (no *postulates*) in place to provide a *reality* of any *actual* harm. So, when such *powerful beings* came into great *conflict* with each other, there was really very little one could do to even *affect* another. All that one had at their disposal was trickery, false data, and misdirection—and of course, this was still a time when *Universes* were easily made...

BEFORE BETA-EXISTENCE

Implanted Universes (sometimes referred to in previous manuals as "*Penalty Universes*") were designed specifically and intentionally to *fragment* an *Alpha-Spirit*.

The earliest "*Implanted Penalty Universes*" appear in the "*Home Universe*" era. These *constructs* "*implanted*" (or "*installed*") a *tendency* to *create* certain styles and types of "*form.*" Although there are certainly variations in *creations* and *forms*, the basic *patterns* and *preferences* stemming from this early period have continued in our experience of other large *Shared Universes* (*Beta-Existences*)—including *this Physical Universe*.

In *Systemology*, a "*Universe*" is defined as: a self-contained *system* (or *package*) of *reality-agreements* ("*rules*") and *creations* ("*objects,*" *&tc.*)—requiring some kind of *Space* (in which to keep *creations* separate) and some kind of *Time* (in order to observe changes in *objects* or *conditions* and the *sequencing of events*). Systematically, "*Universes*" are:

CREATED	by *postulate/Alpha-Thought*; with *reality-agreements*; *consideration* of the *IS-factor*.
SUSTAINED/ PERPETUATED	by *changes* in *space-time*; the *participation* in *alteration* of the *IS-factor*.

MADE SOLID   by *individuals* in *agreement* sharing the *reality*.

Although it may seem like an *oversimplification* (or even ridiculous to a casual uninitiated reader), the fact remains that:

> *An Alpha-Spirit shifts between Universes*
> *by shifting reality-agreements.*

This is still very much the case today. The major complication (or *real* challenge) in this, that we have found, is not the *"getting into"* a different *Universe* part; it is the *"getting out"* from under the accumulated weight of *fragmented considerations* regarding a *present one*.

The *reality-agreements* with *this Physical Universe* are very *"heavy"* and *"sticky."* Even at *Level-7*, a *Seeker* might easily connect with another *Universe* by contacting a *Being*—or simply *creating a Beingness*—there and *"getting into agreement"* with them. But the sense of *reality* is still going to be quite "vague" so long as the individual is still heavily *restrained here*, or *unwilling* to fully *"let go"* of *reality-agreements* and *attachments* to their *Earth-life*.

During the *"Home Universe"* era there were *agreed-upon Universes* for "common interaction" among *Beings*; and, of course, there were *non-agreed upon "Personal 'Home' Universes"* subject to the individual themselves. But, there were no "solidly" agreed-upon Universes—meaning none which an *Alpha-Spirit* couldn't *"get out"* of.

Shifting between *Universes*, at that time, was quite simply a matter of *intention* (or *selective agreement*)—such as how we might consider the *decision* to *"open and walk through a door"* before actually *doing* it.

Our knowledge of the *"Home Universe Matrix"* demonstrates that not all *Universes* experienced on the *Backtrack* have been large *Shared Universes*, of the type that we inhabit in common with many other *Alpha-Spirits*. These larger *Shared Universe* systems—such as *this Physical Universe* and the *Magic Universe* preceding it—are what we highlight the most in *AT Manual #1, "The Secret of Universes."* But, a *Seeker* may also notice references to many others, including *"Pocket Universes"* and eventually *"Penalty Universes."*

To understand this early era, we might *consider* what is of actual *value* to a *godlike Alpha-Spirit*—and that is *creation* and one's own *creations*. There is an *"interest"* inherently attached to *novelty* (*newness*) and *aesthetic* qualities (of *beauty, &tc.*) that are possible to experience with someone else's *creation*. There is also a *tendency* to desire *validation* and *admiration* (or essentially *"agreement"*) from others towards one's own *creations* in order to make them more *vivid, solid* and/or *"real."*

Alpha-Spirits began *creating* to "show off" their *creations* to others as a form of entertainment. This *upper-level* of *creation* did not concern simple *"objects"* or *"constructs,"* like how one might *build, film, paint* or *write* something today (although the intended purpose was the same). Rather, one would *create* an entire *"Pocket-Universe"* (small *sealed-system*) in which to "display" their *creation* as a complete *"immersive-artform"* experience. It did not take very long for this to become a *"competitive"* activity.

These *"Storytelling Pocket Universes"* allowed an individual to essentially *"live out"* the *role* of a *"movie-persona"* as a full *three-dimensional* (3-D) *holographic illusion,* rather than simply "looking at" or "watching" something. However, similar to modern *film*, these were each a separate *Universe* in their own right—and followed a separate *track* of perceived *Time* that ran a "program" or "script" from *beginning* to *end*.

An individual would simply get *"in agreement"* with the *Universe* in order to access it (*shift their Awareness*) and have the *start* of script flick "on." If you *consider* a *multi-plex movie theatre* today: you get in *agreement* with one of the many *"Theatre Universes"* that you *decide* to experience as *reality*—and the others are just as equally *real*, but in a completely separate *Space-Time* than yours.

Of course, when one *considers* such *creations*: there is relatively little *"freedom"* or *"choice"* involved with the *"scripted"* events and elements— much like a prerecorded *"tape"* or *"video."* In theory, one might be able to *"Play," "Stop,"* or *"Rewind"*—but the actual *internal structure* of the *creation* is not able to be changed from within it. To do that, much like today, you would essentially have to *copy* the whole thing (while *exterior to* it) in order to *edit* (*remove*), *rearrange elements,* and/or *add* something, and basically *recreate* it.

IMPLANTING UNIVERSES

"Pocket Universes" were an early precursor to what would become the *"Penalty Universes."* We have covered the *"Creation of Universes"* and even *"Infinity Exercises"* in previous manuals and the *PC-Lessons*. From this material it is easy to understand that as an alternative to *creating* each and every *facet* and *detail* of a *Universe*, one can *create/postulate* an *"Infinity"* as an *Alpha-Thought*.

In many ways, this *"Infinity"* is what we see represented by modern *"fractal geometry"* and other similar progressions of a *repetitive pattern* — no matter how complex. These *patterns* can be *created/postulated "out to 'Infinity',"* as a simple *consideration* of *Alpha-Thought*. Our present *Physical Universe* contains a *creative-postulate* of *"infinite space"* — but there are other ways in which such *Space* could *manifest*.

For example: a *Universe* based on an *"infinite postulate"* of *"Mud"* would result in an *existence* purely of *"Mud"* extending *out to Infinity*; and it would only get *"thicker"* and *"blacker"* the deeper/further you *"dug in to"* it. And if you were to wonder, *"well, what's on the 'other side' of all that Mud?"* — well, there *isn't* an *"other side"* postulated for that *existence*. But, if that were the *"postulate"* for a *Universe*, it would be the *primary postulate* to *defragment "As-It-Is"* in order to be *free* of it. The purpose of this specific example may or may not be apparent to the *Seeker* at this present time.

Some of our most basic foundations for *spiritual fragmentation* occur during the *Home Universe* era. An *Alpha-Spirit* spent a lot of *"time"* in the *creation* (and *preferential perfection*) of their own *Home Universe*. By this point of the *Backtrack*, there is a tendency forming to *not want* to *"let go"* of *creations*. But, unfortunately this is what allowed an *Alpha-Spirit* to be *trapped* by them. [Ref: AT Manual #1; collapse of the *Home Universe Matrix* into a single *agreed-upon Universe*.]

Since *Universes* are *entered-by-agreement*, it is possible to *enforce* a *set* (or *package*) of *reality-agreements* and *cause* (*force*) an *Alpha-Spirit* to *shift Universes*. An example of this would be to *enforce* an *agreement* with the *entry-point* of the *track* for a *Pocket-Universe*. This causes one to experience the whole *"recording."* And a *Pocket-Universe* could theoretically even *enforce* yet another *set* of *reality-agreements*, *&tc*.

Universe-shifting Incidents are "between-points" that some perceive as being at the *start* of a *track* for a *Universe*. To use our most familiar example: *Implanting-Incident #1* for *this Physical Universe* is what we treat as the *Entry-Incident* in previous material. The *"False Jewel"* and *"Heaven Implant"* take place within their own *Pocket Universes* as the "transition" from the *Magic Universe* to *this Physical Universe*.

These *Incidents* are sometimes challenging to properly *confront* on the *Backtrack*, because an individual can possibly find an *earlier Incident #1* (earlier time on the *Backtrack* that *Incident #1* occurred), they both will *register* on a *Biofeedback Device* as being *"the start of time."* Such an *Incident* will always occur at *"the start of time"* for that *track*.

In our familiar example: *Implant Platforms* of the *"False Jewel"* lead to another *Pocket-Universe* for the *"Heaven Implant."* Both of these *parts* occur prior to experiencing the *Space-Time* of *this Physical Universe*. The *"Heaven"* part of the *Incident* ends with *"waves of blackness"* as the *"infinite postulate."* From that point onward, no other changes occur. *Attention* turns "inward" and it leaves an *Alpha-Spirit* to *consider* the *reality-agreements* (just *installed*), which result in eventually *shifting* fully "here" to this *Beta-Existence*.

Consider if *Alpha-Spirits* had once divided up into teams for *games*—and each team was responsible for *creating* a *fragmented "Penalty Universe"* (a *Universe* promoting *fragmentation*) that could be used on the "losers." The *reality-agreement*, in this case, would consist of "winning" teams *ganging up* on "losing" teams—then *"blanketing"* individuals and *pushing them in* to the *Penalty Universe*.

Regardless of how *"horrific"* such *Penalty Universes* were, at first they would have been only mildly effective—or *distasteful*—to a *godlike being*. And regardless of who first *won*, everyone would have kept playing at this and getting *pushed through* more and more of the *Penalty Universes*.

Early on, any *"kickback"* from the *"harmful-acts"* (of *pushing others in*) would have been quite mild; but they, too, would have contributed to our *spiritual degradation*. The *"kickback"* from actually experiencing a *Penalty Universe* would result from the *fragmented considerations, postulates* and *decisions* that an individual made as a result of the experience. This progressively affected the original native *"horsepower"* of our *Alpha-Thought*.

The original *Penalty Universes* were not intended as permanent *"prisons."* Such things came later. These original ones were intended to be quite temporary—simply placing an individual in a specific situation where they would have to make *fragmented decisions* in order to escape it. The tendency toward declining states of *Beta-Awareness* (*misemotion, &tc.*) would have been *installed* in this wise.

Fixed patterns and *systems* of *this Physical Universe* appear repeatedly in the *Implants* of previous *Universes*. The original native *Alpha* state is void of all *patterns* or *systems*; these are all *created* (and later *agreed-upon*) as a result of *fragmentation*. These are what we handle as *archetypal "items"* (*command-postulates* or *objects*), while *defragmenting* the Implant-Platforms.

The *Spheres of Existence* and *Arcs of Infinity*, what is represented by the *Beta-Awareness Scale* and *Standard Model*—all of these are *Systems*, meaning *fixed patterns*; meaning also *fragmented patterns*. In them we find the structure of our *reality-agreements*, our *considerations*, our *impulses* and *tendencies*, and our *reactivity* and *automated machinery*. All of these are the product of an individual's own *Alpha-Thought*, however *fragmented* it may have become.

Although the same *symbolism* is often used for restimulation, we do not find direct experiences with *Penalty Universes* on the *Backtrack* of *this Physical Universe*. By this point of *condensation*, the *reality-agreements* of *Alpha-Spirits* are more *fixedly "stuck"* in *this Universe*. Other than the *Entry-Incident*, all of the *Implanting* taking place *within this Physical Universe* is actually more *"technological"* or *"electronic"* in nature.

To be *systematic* and *effective*: we must distinguish the *"Implanted Universe"* *symbols* and *items* (that reappear in later *Implants*), from the original *"Implanted Penalty Universes"* themselves.

For example: the *"To Eat"* Implant-Goal (which is part of the *"Tiger Goals"* series) originates in the original *"Tiger Penalty Universe."* The same *items* and *symbols* also appear in later (more recent) *"electronic"* Implants. However, in the original *incidents*, one is *imprinted* with the experience of really *being a tiger*—and the experience of *eating* things. Whereas, in the later *electronic incidents*, only *imagery* or *pictures* of *"tigers"* are used in the Implant, along with the accompanying *command-items*. This *restimulates "charge"* from the *imprinting* of an original Implanted Penalty Universe, and thereby making the *"electronic"* Implants more significant.

IMPLANTED PENALTY UNIVERSES

If we are to be absolutely technical: full handling of this manual is a *Systemology Level-8* endeavor. But, as we complete our *Level-7 "unit"* pertaining to *Games, Implants,* and *Universes,* this manual is an appropriate "transition point" to the upper-most reaches of the *Pathway.* For the time being: a *Seeker* may personally *consider* this material as "speculative" until a greater personal *reality* of it unfolds. In brief: don't let the study and use of *this* manual hold up moving forward to *Level-8.*

Systematic processing for *running "Implanted Penalty Universes"* (and their *symbols/items*) requires a lot of *"Spotting"*—which is to say, the *perception* and *realization* of *"What-IS"*—noticing *"What-IS"* there in the *incidents*. At these *upper-levels* of handling *Implants*: we are primarily *defragmenting-by-Awareness*; which is to say *targeted attention* or *analytical inspection*. But in order to *defragment* in this way, we must first have a *"clear view"* of an *incident, "As-It-Is."*

An important part of *processing-out turbulent fragmentation* and *fixed considerations* from the *Backtrack* is targeting (*spotting*) the *Harmful-Acts* connected to, or associated with, *Implanting-Incidents*. By this, we do not only mean those efforts *against you by others*, but also your own efforts *against others*. Focus on any areas of "significant regret" that might *resurface*; its *imprinting* often remains as a *"still"* image or impression.

The original *Implanted Penalty Universes* set up the basis for our later *spiritual fragmentation* to take place. All *fragmentation* accumulates on some *"platform"* or *"foundation"* in order to exist. Without such deeply *Implanted/ installed "items"* in place, there would be no *fragmentation*. By definition, something must *be there* to *fragment*.

By the point of the *Home Universe* era, an *Alpha-Spirit's fragmented agreements* mainly only consisted of a *preference* for 3-D *constructs* and *perceptions*, along with the *preference* to establish a *Home Universe* in connection to a *"matrix"* that allowed for *communication* with others and mutual *"displaying"* of *creations* for entertainment.

During that era, an *Alpha-Spirit* is still quite *godlike* and *knowingly* "indestructible" as a *Being*. There are no *fragmented considerations* concerning the (false) "necessity" of *personal survival* yet. So, while still quite capable *"creative" Beings*: the first points of *fragmentation* occur in relation to one'-s *investment* and personal *attachment* to their *"Home Universe"*—and the refusal to *"let go"* of their own *creations*, and those of *others*, when the *Home Universe Matrix "collapsed."*

The *8 Spheres of Existence* and *8 Arcs of Infinity* provide data for *16 dynamic systems*. Note that: the *Implanted Penalty Universes*—or "IPU" for future abbreviation in this manual—are not *based on* the *16 dynamic systems*. On the contrary, the *codification* of *dynamic systems* is *based on* our observation of *Implanted "patterns."* The *IPU-patterns* actually *installed* the *dynamic systems* we now recognize, where before, there weren't any. So, in the end: we *do* have a *systematic* and *practical* means of *"cross-referencing"* IPU with the *16 dynamic systems*.

```
    16 dynamic systems
       each installed by
  x  4 penalty universes
       equals a total of
    64 original IPU
```

The IPU are *four-dimensional constructs* of their own 3-D *Space-Time*. They each have a *fixed track* resulting in a very specific experience related to a single *"Goal."* The experience is intended to *fragment* the *Goal*.

An individual is *Implanted* to focus *attention* on a basic *Goal*—generally with a "positive" characteristic at the *start* or *top*—and then experience its decline or decay as they descend through *thousands* of *"items"* resulting in a *fragmented energetic-mass* of *turbulent problems* identified with the *Goal*. It is *fragmented* into a *dynamic system* of *compulsive survival*, rather than just "some activity" a *Being* might take or leave at will.

An *Implanting-Incident* generally consists of certain types of *"thought-waves"*—or else *"wave-ridges"* or *"standing-waves"* that an *Alpha-Spirit* "passes through" during the experience. Embedded within these *waves* are the *"items"*—*commands* and *objects*—that are *perceived* as part of the incident. [In more "modern" or "recent" *Implanting-Incidents*, these *"waves"* are transmitted *electronically*.]

The *"Implant Items"* themselves are simply *"strong suggestions"* that direct one's *attention* toward whatever an individual is intended to be "thinking" about. It is only then that subsequent experience of that *Universe-track* cause a *fragmented charge* to develop on that channel.

Technically speaking, the *Implants* themselves have relatively little "power"—simply *suggesting* or *installing* various *obsessions, compulsions, fixations, tendencies* and *preferences. Real power* remains with the individual—but these various forms of subtle *fragmentation* also *fragment* one's own clear use of *Alpha-Thought*. It is actually the *postulates, decisions,* and *considerations* an individual makes, themselves, as a result of *fragmented experiences,* that really cause them the most ongoing trouble in the long run.

At the *top* or *start* of the *incident* for an IPU-*Goal*, the experience is actually quite pleasant in order to draw the individual further into the IPU. The *aesthetic display* is actually quite amazing by relative comparison to the "dimness" of *this Physical Universe*—and was *created* quite brilliantly during an era of *high-power beings*. The IPU have no specific opposition terminals. The entire *Pocket-Universe* is engineered to eventually be "against you."

IPU DEFRAGMENTATION

Accessing (or *contacting*) the *incidents* requires *"Spotting"* the *high-level* "aesthetic" quality that occurs at the *"top of the chain"* (or *"start of the track"*). However, it is important not to get too enamored (*fascinated*) by these displays (which is part of how it became a *Spirit-Trap* in the first place). The basic "map" of each IPU-*incident* is simply the decline of *Awareness* (as a scale)—the progressive deterioration of conditions—from the ultimate "sublime" down to the most "infernal hell" states for each *Goal*.

At the *start/top* of every IPU is a brief *Entry-Incident*. It provides the impression (falsely) of the *Alpha-Spirit* freshly separating from *"Infinity"* as *"the beginning of time"* (but of course it is only the *start* of the *track* for *that* IPU). This begins a long *"chain"* of *Implanted false data*.

The first *"item"* of every IPU *installs* the *concept* that *"To {Goal}"* is the individual's "native state." [Note that these *Implants* are *"To {Goal}"* rather than *"To Be {a Terminal}."*] This gives the *impression* that this *Goal* is the original *Alpha-Thought* before *All Space-Time,* and that it is the *reason* or *purpose* for the *Alpha-Spirit* separating as a *Being*.

For *systematic processing* purposes: the actual/earlier *beginning* of the *in-*

cident is not *"interior to"* the IPU at all. It really begins while occupying the *"exterior"* Universe, where one was then *pushed in to* the IPU. Total *defragmentation* really requires *"Spotting"* all *"circuits"* of experience connected to incidents for each IPU. This means: Circuit-1, *"ourselves to others"* (as *Harmful-Acts*); Circuit-2, *"others to ourselves"* (where we are the victim); and even Circuit-3, the observation of *"others with others."*

IPU-handling requires a different *systematic procedure* than what is given in previous *AT Manuals*. All of the *Parts* for the full procedure are given below—however, only *IPU-Platforms #1* and *#2* are given in this manual.

Running a light *"pass"* of *processing* on each IPU using only the beginning of this procedure is the preferred way to enter into this area of work. This will *disperse* or *discharge* the more *turbulent* (*heavier*) and accessible *"fragmented charge"* before treating each individual IPU any further. A *Seeker* will be able to revisit this manual at various points of *Level-8* (and thereafter), so there is no reason to "grind" hard on this now.

The basic intention at this time is simply to disperse enough *"charge"* off the original IPU-*incidents* so that it is easier to *defragment* later (more recent) *Implants* and *imprinting*, which restimulate these antiquated IPU *"dramatizations"* in our *"present-time"* *thoughts* and *behavior*.

STANDARD PROCEDURE: IPU INCIDENTS

0. ENTRY: The *Alpha-Spirit* is blanketed by another and *pushed in to* the *incident*.

1. IPU-PLATFORM #1: *"The False Jewel"* (an *Implant-pattern* that is common to all IPU). [Different from *"The Jewel"* treated for *this Physical Universe* (in *AT Manual #3*), but designed with the same purpose.]

2. IPU-PLATFORM #2: *"The Symbols."* To have any significance to an individual during the IPU experience, the *object-item "symbols"* for the *incident* are defined (assigned meaning) with *"graphic"* displays.

3. UNIVERSE ANCHORS: *"To {Goal} Is To Look For ___."* The individual is directed to *spot* various things, extending their *attention/Awareness* "out" to connect with various *"objects."* Usually paired with *"To {Goal} Is To Connect To {same object}."* This activity/step *creates* the *perception* of *Space* in which to personally experience the IPU. [This is the formation of *universal anchor-points* between the individual and the IPU.]

4. AGREEMENTS: *"To {Goal} Is To Agree To The ___."*; *"To {Goal} Is For The ___ To Become Real."* At the *top* of the *"chain"* this *Part* is met with great expectation and anticipation. Later on, toward the *bottom* of this *incident*, the individual meets this part with dread (even paralyzing fear) over what new nightmare will present itself.

5. FRAGMENTED MEMORY: *"To {Goal} Is To Remember Agreeing To (a) Before (b)."* The *items* from *Part-4* (above) are repeated, but in a different order. This *impresses* us to *remember* things *out-of-sequence*.

6. THE CONFUSION: The individual becomes confused about the *sequence* of *agreements* leading up to this *Part*.

7. FUTURE POSTULATE: *"To {Goal} Is To Have Future {item}."* The *items/symbols* representing *reality-agreements* are extended into the *future*. Usually paired with *"To {Goal} Is To Predict {item} In Your Future."* The *impressions* are really nonsense, but it gets the individual *interested* that "something is *going to* happen" in the IPU.

8. DECISIONS: An individual's personal *decisions*; usually about wanting to just get through quickly to the end of this lengthy *incident* and *connect* with a *"terminal"* (*Body*).

9. JOINING: *Implant-items* about *deciding* to get *into* a *"terminal"* (*Body*).

10. THE IPU: The *Alpha-Spirit "being as"* an individual *"terminal"* (*Body*) experiencing a *real "Pocket-Universe."* The beginning of this part of the *track* is always a series of 7 experiences of the *Goal*, starting with the "sublime" top-level and then descending downscale.

The best sequence for proceeding through each IPU is: from "CREATE" down to "ENDURE." Initially, a *Seeker* will only make a "light pass" through each IPU, using only *IPU-Platform #1*.

It is quite possible that a *Seeker* will only get a single *GSR-Meter* "read" on each *item*, or possibly every other *item*. A *"read"* might occur only on the *description*, or the *item*, or both. After a few passes through all 64 IPU (handling each individually), a *Seeker* may then apply *IPU-Platform #2* (immediately following an application of *IPU-Platform #1*), and even start *"Spotting"* other *Parts* (listed above) of the *incident* (and take *"charge"* off of those).

When this is treated at *Level-8*, a *Seeker* might also "Spot" the *restimulative* use of IPU-*Symbolism* in more recent *Implanting-Incidents* taking place on the *Backtrack within this Physical Universe*. There is also the matter of handling *Entities* and *Identity-Fragments* on more progressive passes through this manual later on.

Here, we are most concerned with *defragmenting* whatever is accessible at one's current "level." *Upper-level Systemology* is not so clearly "*graded*" as what we find earlier on the *Pathway*—so, a *Seeker* keeps working at various *processes*, *defragmenting* what is *accessibly* there, and uncovering new *layers* to *defragment*.

The "*This Means...*" items from *IPU-Platform #2* (such as the "*Time*" representation, *&tc.*) will lead to other "*content*" about the IPU that can be "*Spotted.*" A *Seeker* can keep records concerning any additional details that are perceived. [While some experimental use of *IPU-Platform #1* has proven effective without a *GSR-Meter*, any type of additional "*research processing*" (to directly uncover unpublished details) really requires a *Biofeedback Device* to be *systematic*.]

Advisement: When handling IPU, always *end-session* with the "top" of *IPU-Platform #1*—*Spotting* the first *item* (about "*Native State*") and making sure its *defragmentation* is stable (not giving *Meter-reads*). The same action is used as the "*key destimulator*" for this procedure—*Spotting* the top of *IPU-Platform #1*, if suddenly finding too much *turbulence* to confront while IPU-*processing*.

Note: "*To Survive*" is *not* actually one of the 64 IPU-*Goals*; it is embedded as an underlying concept within all of them. Each defines a basic *Goal* and then *impresses* its use in the effect of "*To Be {Goal}-ing Is To Survive.*" This is more "solidly" evident in the lower *dynamic systems* (meaning the *8 Spheres of Existence*).

The *IPU-List* is below. Each of the *16 dynamic systems* (whether *Arcs of Infinity* or *Spheres of Existence*) are assigned 4 IPU. Each of the 64 total IPU are distinguished by the basic *Goal* and a common *terminal* (as a *Body Type*). None of the IPU were *Implanted* in "English" (or any human speech), so semantic approximations given below (and in the IPU-*Directory*) may differ slightly for some *Seekers*.

16. CREATION (*Arc 8*)

1. "TO CREATE"   {*statue*}
2. "TO CAUSE"   {*old man god*}

3. "TO DUPLICATE" {computer}
4. "TO IMAGINE" {cartoon}

15. KNOWINGNESS (Arc 7)
5. "TO KNOW" {2-headed dodo}
6. "TO UNDERSTAND" {chipmuck}
7. "TO ABSORB" {epic hero}
8. "TO LEARN" {gnome}

14. GAMES (Arc 6)
9. "TO PLAY" {child}
10. "TO COMPETE" {coach}
11. "TO MANIPULATE" {penguin banker}
12. "TO EXCHANGE" {spirit-broker}

13. CHANGE (Arc 5)
13. "TO SHAPE" {clay people}
14. "TO CHANGE" {magician}
15. "TO COMBINE" {conjoined twins}
16. "TO (BRING) ORDER" {gorilla people}

12. REASON (Arc 4)
17. "TO REASON" {clown}
18. "TO ORIENT" {wire man}
19. "TO GUIDE" {pilot}
20. "TO COMPUTE" {toy bodies}

11. CONSTRUCTION (Arc 3)
21. "TO CONSTRUCT" {beavers}
22. "TO ARRANGE" {blockhead}
23. "TO BUILD" {snake people}
24. "TO STRUCTURE" {crystals}

10. AESTHETICS (Arc 2)
25. "TO INVENT" {dwarves}
26. "TO ENHANCE" {ghost people}
27. "TO INSPIRE" {muses}
28. "TO BEAUTIFY" {fairy godmother}

9. ETHICS (Arc 1)

29. "TO PURIFY"   {fire people}
30. "TO JUDGE"   {minotaur}
31. "TO DEFEND"   {little green men}
32. "TO STRENGTHEN"   {energy ball}

8. DIVINITY (Sphere 8)

33. "TO ENLIGHTEN"   {rabbit preacher}
34. "TO CONVERT"   {fish man}
35. "TO COMMUNE"   {feminine angel}
36. "TO WORSHIP"   {holy knights}

7. SPIRITS (Sphere 7)

37. "TO PREDICT"   {soothsayer}
38. "TO INFLUENCE"   {cupid/cherub}
39. "TO COLLECT"   {elves/fairies}
40. "TO EMBODY"   {satyr}

6. UNIVERSE (Sphere 6)

41. "TO DISCOVER"   {centaurs}
42. "TO LOCATE"   {leprechaun}
43. "TO GATHER"   {spacesuit body}
44. "TO OWN"   {fox people}

5. LIFEFORMS (Sphere 5)

45. "TO GROW"   {genetic entity}
46. "TO LIVE"   {dinosaur}
47. "TO HEAL"   {tree man}
48. "TO ADAPT"   {thread man}

4. SOCIETY (Sphere 4)

49. "TO ESTABLISH"   {3-eyed giants}
50. "TO SHARE"   {dolphins}
51. "TO CONTROL"   {frog king}
52. "TO UNITE"   {dog soldiers}

3. GROUPS (Sphere 3)

53. "TO ORGANIZE"	{file clerk}
54. "TO COOPERATE"	{robots}
55. "TO PARTICIPATE"	{merfolk}
56. "TO EXPAND"	{mouse railroad engineer}

2. HOME (Sphere 2)

57. "TO JOIN"	{cat people}
58. "TO REPRODUCE"	{insect invader}
59. "TO SATISFY"	{cavemen}
60. "TO CARE (FOR)"	{bird girl}

1. SELF/BODY (Sphere 1)

61. "TO EXPERIENCE"	{bear}
62. "TO REPLENISH"	{a Sumerian}
63. "TO EAT"	{tiger}
64. "TO ENDURE"	{pyramid}

IPU-PLATFORM #1

IPU-Platform #1 is the "False Jewel" Entry-Incident for the original IPU. By this point, a Seeker should already be familiar with running these "Implant-Platforms" as a systematic defragmentation process. [Refer to: PC-11 & 12; AT #1, #2 & #3. That material will not be repeated here.]

The "*IPU Jewel*" is a *seven-dimensional construct* with a *diamond-like structure*. When viewed with 3-D *perception*: this *False Jewel* appears very much like *two 4-sided pyramids* sharing a common base. There is, however, a *sense* that it extends into *spaces beyond* 3-D *perception*. [Its complete *form* has 64 x 2 (128) *facets* or *sides*, but only a few are actually perceived during an IPU-*incident*.]

IPU-Platform #1 "*command-items*" are *spotted* along with *The Jewel* (*construct*) itself. The *items* mainly appear in groups of *three* (e.g., X.1, X.2, X.3), which correspond to the *three* possible *positions* of *The Jewel* during the *incident*: (1) on the *left side*; (2) on the *right side*; and (3) in *front-center*.

There are also three possible *conditions* of *The Jewel* that correspond to the *positions*: (1) *Jewel* begins to appear; (2) *Jewel* becomes more substantial; (3) *Jewel* flashes (with the *item end-word*) and disappears. Memorize the pattern below; these instructions will not be added to the *Processing Command Lines* (PCL), nor will "*Spot the Alpha*" (see *AT Manual #3*)—although all of this will still be implied for the procedure.

1.X.1 *Jewel* begins to *appear* on the *left side*.

1.X.2 *Jewel* becomes *more substantial* on the *right side*.

1.X.3 *Jewel* is *front* and *center, flashes* then *disappears*.

Additionally, *The Jewel* starts a certain "*distance*" away; then is *perceived* as getting *closer* with each grouped-set of three *items*—until finally it is "*touching you*" at the end of *IPU-Platform #1*.

Restimulation of the IPU-*incidents* occurs in later (more recent) *Universes* (see *AT Manual #1*). Restimulation of more recent *Implanting* may result in uncomfortable sensations (or pressure) in the forehead when *contacted* in *processing*. This is more appropriately handled in *Level-8*.

For now, a *Seeker* should focus *attention* on the original IPU—which is essentially the *earliest similar incident* on the *Backtrack*. The later (more recent) *Implanting-Incidents* can be easily distinguished from the original IPU experiences. In later uses, there are always *three Jewels* present, one in each *position*; and they *flash* for every *item*. Furthermore, at the *end-word* for each, the *three Jewels* merge together as *one Jewel* in the *center* of the *"forehead."*

IPU-Platform #1 is a detailed short-form formula. It includes *descriptions*. *Positions/conditions* of *The Jewel* and directions to *"Spot the Alpha"* are not written here. The *platform* contains *86-items*. This formula is used on all *64 IPU-Goals*, each handled as its own *platform-running process*. Use the *IPU Goal-List* given previously.

1.0.1 *Spot being blanketed, blanketing another, and others blanketing others.*

1.0.2 *Spot being pushed in, pushing someone in, and others pushing others in.*

There is nothing; no space, no time, no dimension...

1.1.1 "TO {goal} IS NATIVE STATE."

You are aware of being the Infinity of Nothingness before all time.

1.1.2 "TO {goal} IS TO BE THE STATIC."

As a basic static, you want non-static; you want something to happen, for there to be something.

1.1.3 "TO {goal} IS THE URGE FOR SOMETHINGNESS."

You realize the urge; and it makes sense.

1.2.1 "TO BASIC URGE IS TO {goal}."

Making sense of the urge; you receive this impression.

1.2.2 "BEFORE THE BEGINNING, NOW, AND FOREVER, IS THE URGE, AND THE URGE IS TO {goal}."

You realize all other "urges" will stem from this.

1.2.3 "TO {goal} IS THE BASIS FOR ALL URGES."

You feel the strength of the "urge" growing.

1.3.1 "TO {goal} IS TO NEED RELIEF."

You realize what is needed for relief.

1.3.2 "THE BASIC RELIEF WILL COME FROM {goal}-ING."

You realize all "relief" stems from this.

1.3.3 "TO {goal} IS THE BASIS FOR ALL RELIEF."

You realize that this is the reason for everything.

1.4.1 "TO {goal} IS THE ORIGINAL REASON WHY."

This makes sense to you.
1.4.2 "THE BASIC REASON WHY IS THE NEED TO {goal}."
You realize all other "reasons" stem from this.
1.4.3 "TO {goal} IS THE BASIS FOR ALL REASONS WHY."

You realize you need to "do something" about this.
1.5.1 "TO {goal} IS TO ACT."
This makes sense to you.
1.5.2 "THE BASIC ACTION IS TO {goal}."
You realize all other "actions" stem from this.
1.5.3 "TO {goal} IS THE BASIS FOR ALL ACTION."

You realize you need to "decide something" before anything will happen.
1.6.0 "TO {goal} IS TO DECIDE."
You choose to make the decision.
1.6.1 "BEFORE THE BEGINNING, NOW, AND FOREVER, IS THE DECISION, AND THE DECISION IS TO {goal}."
Space becomes filled with faint sourceless golden light.
{"Spot the Space"}
You realize that {goal} is the first decision.
1.6.2 "THE ORIGINAL DECISION IS TO {goal}."
You realize all other "decisions" stem from this.
1.6.3 "TO {goal} IS THE BASIS FOR ALL DECISIONS."

You "postulate" that there will be something.
1.7.1 "TO {goal} IS TO POSTULATE."
You realize that this is the first postulate.
1.7.2 "THE BASIC POSTULATE IS TO {goal}."
You realize all other "postulates" stem from this.
1.7.3 "TO {goal} IS THE BASIS FOR ALL POSTULATES."

You postulate time. Time exists to allow for change due to {goal}-ing.
1.8.1 "TO {goal} IS THE SOURCE OF TIME."
You realize the basic consideration of time is past, present, and future {goal}-ing.
1.8.2 "THE BASIS OF TIME IS {goal}-ING."
You realize all future "considerations of time" will stem from this.
1.8.3 "TO {goal} IS THE BASIS OF ALL TIME."

You "agree" with the concept of {goal}-ing.
1.9.1 "TO {goal} IS TO AGREE."

You realize this is the basic agreement.
1.9.2 "THE BASIC AGREEMENT IS TO {*goal*}."
You realize all other agreements stem from this.
1.9.3 "TO {*goal*} IS THE BASIS OF ALL AGREEMENT."

You create energy formed of the concept of {goal}-ing.
1.10.1 "TO {*goal*} IS TO HAVE ENERGY."
You realize this is the most basic of all energies.
1.10.2 "THE BASIC ENERGY STEMS FROM {*goal*}-ING."
You realize all other energies stem from this.
1.10.3 "TO {*goal*} IS THE BASIS OF ALL ENERGY."

You postulate that {goal}-ing is the basic reality.
1.11.1 "TO {*goal*} IS TO REALITY."
This makes sense to you.
1.11.2 "THE BASIC REALITY IS {*goal*}-ING."
You realize all reality stems from this.
1.11.3 "TO {*goal*} IS THE BASIS OF ALL REALITY."

You postulate matter (mass); the most real mass stems from {goal}.
1.12.1 "TO {*goal*} IS TO MATTER."
You realize this is the most basic of all matter.
1.12.2 "THE BASIC MATTER STEMS FROM {*goal*}-ING."
You realize all other matter stems from this.
1.12.3 "TO {*goal*} IS THE SOURCE OF ALL MATTER."

You postulate that likingness (affinity) is achieved through {goal}-ing.
1.13.1 "TO {*goal*} IS LOVE."
This makes sense to you.
1.13.2 "THE BASIC LOVE IS ACHIEVED THROUGH {*goal*}-ING."
You realize all love stems from this.
1.13.3 "TO {*goal*} IS THE BASIS OF ALL LOVE."

You postulate that basic interchange is through {goal}-ing.
1.14.1 "TO {*goal*} IS TO COMMUNICATE."
You realize that this is the first communication.
1.14.2 "THE BASIC COMMUNICATION IS {*goal*}-ING."
You realize all communication stems from this.
1.14.3 "TO {*goal*} IS THE BASIS OF ALL COMMUNICATION."

You realize that {goal}-ing will bring understanding.
1.15.1 "TO {*goal*} IS TO REACH FOR UNDERSTANDING."

This makes sense to you.
1.15.2 "THE ATTAINMENT OF UNDERSTANDING IS THROUGH {*goal*}-ING."
You realize all understanding stems from this.
1.15.3 "TO {*goal*} IS THE BASIS OF ALL UNDERSTANDING."

You postulate space in which to {goal}.
1.16.1 "TO {*goal*} IS TO HAVE SPACE."
You realize this is what creates space.
1.16.2 "THE DELINEATION OF SPACE IS BY {*goal*}-ING."
You realize all other spaces stem from this.
1.16.3 "TO {*goal*} IS THE BASIS OF ALL SPACE."

You postulate that {goal}-ing gives meaning to existence.
1.17.1 "TO {*goal*} IS TO HAVE MEANING."
This makes sense to you.
1.17.2 "THE BASIC MEANING IS IN REGARDS TO {*goal*}-ING."
You realize all other meaning stems from this.
1.17.3 "TO {*goal*} IS THE BASIS OF ALL MEANING."

You postulate that {goal}-ing is truth.
1.18.1 "TO {*goal*} IS TRUTH."
This makes sense to you.
1.18.2 "THE ATTAINMENT OF BASIC TRUTH IS THROUGH {*goal*}-ING."
You realize all other truth stems from this.
1.18.3 "TO {*goal*} IS THE BASIS OF ALL TRUTH."

You postulate havingness; the most real sense of havingness is to {goal}.
1.19.1 "TO {*goal*} IS HAVE."
You realize this is the most basic of all havingness.
1.19.2 "THE BASIC HAVINGNESS STEMS FROM {*goal*}-ING."
You realize all other havingness stems from this.
1.19.3 "TO {*goal*} IS THE BASIS OF ALL HAVINGNESS."

You postulate that {goal}-ing is the basic aesthetic.
1.20.1 "TO {*goal*} IS BEAUTY."
This makes sense to you.
1.20.2 "THE BASIC BEAUTY IS {*goal*}-ING."
You realize all other beauty stems from this.
1.20.3 "TO {*goal*} IS THE BASIS OF ALL BEAUTY."

You desire to connect with the "thoughts" in the Jewel of Knowledge.
1.21.1 "TO {*goal*} IS TO CONNECT WITH THOUGHT."
This makes sense to you.
1.21.2 "THE BASIC THOUGHT CONCERNS {*goal*}-ING."
You realize all other thought stems from this.
1.21.3 "TO {*goal*} IS THE BASIS OF ALL THOUGHT."

You realize that {goal} will influence all existence.
1.22.1 "TO {*goal*} IS THE HIDDEN INFLUENCE."
This makes sense to you.
1.22.2 "THE BASIC HIDDEN INFLUENCE IS TO {*goal*}."
You realize this underlies all other hidden influences.
1.22.3 "TO {*goal*} IS THE BASIS OF ALL HIDDEN INFLUENCES."

You postulate that the most valuable particle is that which is {goal}-ing.
1.23.1 "TO {*goal*} IS TO VALUE."
This makes sense to you.
1.23.2 "THE MOST VALUABLE PARTICLE IS GAINED THROUGH {*goal*}-ING."
You realize all other value stems from this.
1.23.3 "TO {*goal*} IS THE BASIS OF ALL VALUATION."

You realize that {goal}-ing will bring about true existence.
1.24.1 "TO {*goal*} IS TO EXIST."
You realize this is the only reason for existing.
1.24.2 "ALL EXISTENCE DEPENDS ON {*goal*}-ING."
You realize that through this you will achieve understanding of all existence.
1.24.3 "TO {*goal*} IS THE BASIS OF ALL EXISTENCE."
The Jewel is touching you, flashes, and passes into you.

You realize that The Jewel is bringing you enlightenment.
1.25.1 "TO {*goal*} IS TO GAIN ENLIGHTENMENT."
This makes sense to you.
1.25.2 "THE BASIC ENLIGHTENMENT CONCERNS {*goal*}-ING."
You realize all other enlightenment stems from this.
1.25.3 "TO {*goal*} IS THE BASIS OF ALL ENLIGHTENMENT."
The Jewel is touching you, flashes, and passes into you.

You realize that The Jewel is bringing you knowledge.
1.26.1 "TO {*goal*} IS TO KNOW."

This makes sense to you.

1.26.2 "THE BASIC KNOWLEDGE CONCERNS {*goal*}-ING."
You realize all other knowledge stems from this.

1.26.3 "TO {*goal*} IS THE BASIS OF ALL KNOWLEDGE."
The Jewel is touching you, flashes, and passes into you.

The Jewel remains in the center of your beingness.
Something begins to appear faintly below you; you reach for it.

1.27.1 "TO {*goal*} IS TO REACH."
What you are reaching for is {goal}-ing.

1.27.2 "THE BASIC REACH IS TOWARD {*goal*}-ING."
You realize all other reaches stem from this.

1.27.3 "TO {*goal*} IS THE BASIS OF EVERY REACH."
The Jewel flashes within you.

As you reach, you encounter basic symbols; this sets up IPU-Platform #2.
You realize that reaching for them will bring understanding.
Looking down at the stack of symbol-pictures, The Jewel now seems above you.

1.28.1 "TO {*goal*} IS TO CONTACT SYMBOLS."
You contact the first and most basic symbols of all existence.

1.28.2 "THE BASIC SYMBOLS CONCERN {*goal*}-ING."
You realize, as you connect to the first symbol, that:

1.28.3 "TO {*goal*} IS THE BASIS OF ALL SYMBOLOGY."
The Jewel flashes on top of you and seems to move you into the first picture. [IPU-Platform #2 begins.]

IPU-PLATFORM #2

Advisement: for *Systemology-Level-8* use.

IPU-Platform #2 concerns "*Symbols*." It immediately follows the last *item* on *IPU-Platform #1*. These *Symbols* are 3-D *image-pictures* stacked up to at least *four spatial-dimensions*. They are literally "*photographic imprints*," but stacked like a pile of pictures. The *Symbols* are specific to each IPU. They are often elaborate *moving scenes* rather than stationary *objects*.

The basic *pattern* of *IPU-Platform #2* is:

{*see a symbol*} x {"*This Means* ___."}

The basic method for *defragmentation* is to *"Spot the Symbol"* (*object-item*) and *"This Means ___"* (*command-item*) until there is no longer a *"charge"* on that association.

The first four *items* for each IPU are always: *"This Means Time"*; *"This Means Space"*; *"This Means Energy"*; and *"This Means Matter."* There are approximately *100-items* for each IPU. Determining these *Symbols* is technically a *Level-8 research action* applied to each IPU after several passes through *IPU-Platform #1*.

During the original IPU-*incident*: all *100-symbols/items* were run one way; then they were run again in reverse order, where the color was inverted and the orientation shifted (as like a mirror reflection). As a complete *processing action*, *IPU-Platform #2* is also *run* in this wise. A *Seeker* is encouraged to construct their own *platform-worksheets* to more easily handle this data.

Ideally: a *Seeker* will take off most of the accessible IPU-fragmentation with several passes through *IPU-Platform #1*; then they will start *spotting* the IPU-*Symbols* that become accessible by applying the start of *IPU-Platform #2*. They may then compare their *data* to our existing *data* (listed in the *"IPU-Directory"*). [The totality of potential IPU-*data* for *Platform #2* has not yet been fully researched/published (*as of 2023*).]

The *Symbols* are different for each IPU. The *items* associated with them (other than the first ones, like *"Time"*; *"Motion"*; *"Space"*; *"Energy"*; and *"Mass"*) are also not consistent across all IPU. Using available data for the *"TO EAT"*-IPU (or *Tiger Penalty Universe*), we provide the following *"This Means" item*-list as only one example (*in descending order*):

> TIME, MOTION, SPACE, ENERGY, MASS, LIKINGNESS, REALITY, COMMUNICATION, ADMIRATION, GROWTH, ADVENTURE, FOOD, EATING, FASTNESS, DIFFICULT, DISORIENTATION, DISORDER, PAIN, TORTURE, HELL, ACHIEVEMENT, FLYING, ATTACK, AVOIDANCE, CUT, TERROR, GOD, STEALTH, BLEED, TROUBLE, DEFEAT, HOPELESSNESS, WEAKNESS, FEROCIOUSNESS, NEED, CAPTURE, SURPRISE, SENSATION, STRIKE, BEAUTY, BREAKING, DIZZYNESS, TRAP, DEGRADATION, OBLIGATION, SUCCESS, CREATION, CONTENTMENT, AGONY, RECOVERY, HOME, AMBUSH, STRENGTH, FAILURE, WORSHIP, TEAR, YOU, RUN FAST, FORCE, HIDING, DISTANCE, COMPETITION, HUNTING, CHEATING, AMUSED, BURN, DUMB, FLEE, LEAP, TRANCE,

DECAY, TO LOSE, STIFF, TURMOIL, SKILL, THROW, ROAR, UPSET, REGRET, CONFUSION, SLEEPING, DANGER, MYSTERY, UNAWARE, ROT, DISABILITY, EVIL, PANIC, TIREDNESS, INJURY, FEAR, FALL, ENTRAPMENT, HOT, ELECTRICAL (ZAP), COLD, KILL, DEATH, DOOM, FIGHT, WIN, UNIVERSE, PROCEED.

IPU-DIRECTORY

This "*Directory*" includes basic data researched for each IPU. It mainly assists *research processing* for *IPU-Platform #2*, and for handling other *Parts* of "*Standard Procedure: IPU.*" This "*Directory*" follows the same sequencing given in the previous IPU-*List*. [This is a functional, but incomplete, record. The totality of potential IPU-*data* is not yet available (*as of this printing in 2025*).]

There is a general description of each original IPU-*incident*. The general pattern of an IPU-*incident* is: "7 wonderful things" at the top/start of each *track*; things go wrong; being chased around; captured; divided against yourself (identity fragmented); set free; deciding you can't survive; dying; being trapped in a grave; dragged off; dumped in a fiery hell-like volcano and tortured; end of IPU-*track*. [Always end IPU-*processing* by *spotting* the top *item* of *IPU-Platform #1*.]

Although the original IPU are implanted-imprints, by the era of the *Magic Kingdom Universe*, much of this material is being "dramatized" as basic *reality-agreements* and "manifested" quite *solidly*. It remains embedded in the "*archetypal imprinting*" on the "*Thought-Planes*" of *this Physical Universe*. The *fragmentation* continues to get "restimulated" by the *mass* and *technology* of modern society and its medias.

[There is also data for "*Price*" and "*Survive*" *items* that only apply to later uses of IPU-*restimulation* in more recent *Implant-Incidents*. This is relevant for *Level-8*, when handling archaic "*Mass-Implants*" (*Devices* or *Centers*)—essentially "*Pyramids*" once located on a different copy of our present Earth (one that included *Atlantis* and *Lemuria*). Those locations are also indicated.]

Trigger Warning: This material represents the very definition of a "trigger" (in regards to the *Human Condition*). It would be strange to say that this data should be safeguarded. Since it cannot be broadcast globally (to a general audience and be properly understood), it is fair to say that this knowledge is dangerous—yet, even more so when kept secret; known by a few and used as a weapon against the many. We don't know how this data was directly gleaned by others in the past; but it has already been used for personal gain—restimulating targeted interests, manipulating attentions, controlling purchasing power and popularity.

1. "TO CREATE" {statue}

Time—a planet circling a sun.
Space—vast plain full of cities/peoples.
Energy—blast from space shatters a mountain.
Mass—worlds in collision.
God—giant sun.
Worship—people bowing before statue.
Pain—energy hits statue and cracks it.
Degraded—sunbeam divides statue.
Trouble—hooded priest of sun-gods.

Incident (track)—you are god in the form of a statue, floating around, and putting out energy beams. The statue is young at the start, but resembles an "old man" by the end. The "suns" are "senior gods" that "zap" you at the end. You do 7 great wonders and the people worship you and build you temples. As you get into trouble, you dramatize the "wrath of god" on the people. In the end you are dragged off and tortured by the beings you wronged.

Pyramid (loc.)—center of Atlantis.

"*The Price of Creation is to be blamed.*"
"*To Survive is to depend on worship.*"

2. "TO CAUSE" {old man god on throne}

Time—a golden clock set in the clouds.
Space—golden crystal celestial palace.
Energy—a wave of golden light.
Mass—the golden throne.
God—you; the old man on the throne.
Trouble—devil-beings.

Incident (track)—you perform 7 incredible acts of creation. You create people; cherubs to inspire them; and angels to bring them into communion with you. When people become troublesome, you create devils to put in ethics. But the devils turn against you and make you wrong. You smite the devils; the rebel; you cast them out. You go on rampages and destroy things; finally deciding you can't tolerate being a god anymore. You throw yourself into a volcano; the devils you smote are torturing you at the end.

Pyramid (loc.)—Atlantis.

"*The Price of Causation is to be the effect.*"

"To Survive is to depend on subservience."

3. "TO DUPLICATE" {computer}

(Alternatively: "To Mock Up")
Time — a digital display.
Space — a flat plane.
Energy — electricity.
Gods — vortex energies.

Incident (track) — you are a large computer on an empty plain. The gods create spirits that come to you and ask you to mock up things. You perform 7 wonderful "mockups" (postulating electron structures, physical laws, and making solid things) including bodies and cities for them to live in. The "mockups" become more complex and you lose control of your creations. People start asking a lot of questions you no longer know about — mostly "Why?" — and you invent answers and false data. Eventually the people hate you and pray to the "vortex gods" to "zap" you.

Pyramid (loc.) — Peru.

"The Price of Creative Thought is to be questioned."
"To Survive is to depend on approval from others."

4. "TO IMAGINE" {cartoon}

Time — a watch with cartoon hands.
Space — cartoon environment.
God — giant cartoon mouse god.

Incident (track) — you are a big plastic doll body resembling a cartoon-mouse. Everyone can create illusions, which become real if they can get others to believe in them. At the top/start, you do 7 wonderful illusions (which others believe in and make real). You eventually create harmful things, which go out of control. Others get bored with your creations; so you imagine more degraded things to get their interest. They become too degraded; others are disgusted and shatter your illusions. You are taken before a giant mouse-god that divides you against yourself and puts the pieces in a mausoleum. Cartoon devils drag you into your volcano-illusion; but since you can't stop believing in it, you are trapped by your own illusion.

Pyramid (loc.) — western Lemuria.

"The Price of Imagination is to create your own fears."
"To Survive is to depend on illusions created by others."

5. "TO KNOW" {2-headed dodo}

Time—sun swinging across a tropical sky.
Space—tropical jungle and beach.
God—totems.

Incident (track)—your two heads allow you to see the pictures ("ghosts") that people carry behind them (entities and symbols attached from other *Penalty-Universes* that trail behind them). You use your perception to perform 7 great deeds, such as healing and solving problems, gaining admiration and respect from the people. But your appearance is ridiculous (and you don't want to be laughed at), so you maintain power over others by misusing your hidden knowledge, even harming others by accident. You see the "evil" each carries behind them, and become terrified of others. You start suppressing others to reduce their ability to harm you; and when this is discovered, they chase, capture, and drag you to the totem gods.

Pyramid (loc.)—northern *Lemuria*.

"The Price of Knowledge is terror."
"To Survive is to depend on the not-knowingness of others."

6. "TO UNDERSTAND" {chipmunk}

Time—sun swings over brook.
Space—forest.
God—the wise owl god.
Danger—wolf.
Deceit—a 2-headed sheep.
Slyness—a fox.
Drink—penguin drinks from stream.
Confuse—one chipmunk talking to another.
Sensation—a female chipmunk.

Incident (track)—you are the only one who understands the different languages of the different animals. You perform 7 noble deeds involving translation, such as saving chipmunks from predators. You translate things others don't want to hear; it causes them grief; you get blamed. You understand everyone's problems but can't solve them. No matter how hard you try to explain, the wolf still eats sheep (understanding doesn't change its nature). You start to misuse your ability; conflict breaks out. You translate for the fox, and help them trick people, in exchange for their tricking a chipmunk for you (that you want to seduce).

When the owl-god discovers your treachery, you are divided against yourself, &tc.

Pyramid (loc.) — Bermuda.

"The Price of Understanding is grief."
"To Survive is to depend on the sympathy of others."

7. "TO ABSORB" {mythological hero}

Time — a water clock.
Mass — "Mt. Olympus"
God — mythological pantheon.

Incident (track) — you can absorb knowledge and the form of anyone, including the very real and prominent embodiments of the gods. You can even appear as faces in the sky. At top/start you go through a series of 7 clearings and overcome 7 dangers or distractions. You can then become these forms at will. The gods are oppressing and abusing people, so you use your abilities to become as one of the people, and champion them against the gods. You help people gain the knowledge of the gods; this only creates strife and resentment. The people blame you; the gods are angry with you. You start impersonating the gods, and are eventually captured and taken before "Zeus" who divides you against yourself and places "black bands" on you to prevent your taking any other forms.

Pyramid (loc.) — north central *Lemuria*.

"The Price of Wisdom is to be despised."
"To Survive is to depend on gratitude from others."

8. "TO LEARN" {gnome}

Time — a clock on a wall.
Space — library complex (view of central lawn through window).
Energy — book falling off of shelf.
Mass — huge shelves filled with books.
God — university/academy dean (statue).
Confusion — a walrus-person struggling with book.
Tiredness — a gnome asleep over a book.
Sensation — a female cat-person.
Companionship — a female gnome.
Stubborn — a bear-person.

Incident (track) — data is stored in books and scrolls and data-cubes. Only advanced students access data-cubes because it blasts the data into you.

You are a eyeglass-wearing gnome, an advanced student, and a teacher. You start by solving 7 complex problems for others, become liked and well respected. You start to misdirect students to keep them from surpassing you—and have sex with students (female cat-people) in exchange for grades. The students find out; drag you before the dean; he divides you against yourself. When you try to use data-cubes again, the back-flow causes your brain to explode. They bury you in a basement; eventually toss you into a furnace that leads down to the volcano-hell.

Pyramid (loc.)—center of *Atlantis*.

"The Price of Learning is confusion."
"To Survive is to depend on respect from others."

9. "TO PLAY" {child}

Time—shadow of a sun swinging over village.
God—serpent-god.
Home—houses on stilts over tidal flats.

Incident (track)—you are a child among many children; very few adults or parents exist. There is an impression of being a child forever. Bodies are indestructible and "Asian" or "Eastern" in appearance; young and old are the same size. You start by playing 7 glorious games; but games go downscale rather quickly, becoming mean and vicious. Adults sometimes use you for sex; which is pleasurable, but also strange, fearsome and frustrating (without climax). Games become more turbulent; eventually a child dies (which wasn't thought possible). After organizing the most terrible of games, the people take you to the temple to the serpent-god—who divides you against yourself. You age, but the adults find you loathsome and you can't play with children anymore. You die; are buried; then taken away to an undersea volcano by snakes, where you are tortured by the children you killed.

Pyramid (loc.)—Chili.

"The Price of Joyful Exuberance is perversion."
"To Survive is to depend on the games of others."

10. "TO COMPETE" {coach/team leader}

Time—digital clock on scoreboard.
Space—game-field/arena.
Energy—steel ball smashing into grandstands.
God—the referee.

Cheat—tripping an opponent.
Detestation—fan throws food at player.
Admiration—cheering crowd.

Incident (track)—you are the coach operating from a fenced-off area (guarded by some players), responsible for instructing and planning "plays" for your team in a rather complex "steel-ball" sport. Players can get smashed by the "ball" and frequently go to the dug-out for body-repairs. You execute 7 brilliant plays; the crowd cheers. Going downscale, you are more careless with players getting hurt, you find ways to cheat, and even start working against other coaches on your side. They try to demote you. You even take a group of players and attack the fenced-off area of the opposing side's coach. Then, opponents gain strength as you start fighting against your own side. Eventually, your own team takes you to the referee, who hits you with a beam that divides you against yourself; everyone ignores you during the plays and you are trampled, your body being shattered into pieces. They call a "time out" to bury the pieces in the sand; a flag with a "cross" marks the site. Enraged fans dig you up and throw you into the volcano beneath the grandstands, where the spirits of betrayed players and fans throw things at you until the track ends.

Pyramid (loc.)—Frankfort.

"*The Price of Competition is losing.*"
"*To Survive is to depend on encouragement from others.*"

11. "TO MANIPULATE" {penguin banker}

Time—clock on wall of a bank.
Space—an urban business district.
God—a computer.
Trouble—poor homeless bear-people.

Incident (track)—at the top/start, you make 7 incredible business deals, such as taking over companies and outsmarting other industrialists. Downscale, you become irresponsible about the side effects of these deals; people are harmed; poor homeless (bear-people) get angry, picket, then tear down your businesses. You retaliate and incite riots against competitors before being hauled into court, where a computer-god sentences you to divide against yourself. You lose business contacts; businesses go bankrupt; banks close down; and you jump out a window. Devils (in the form of the bear-people) tear you apart and throw you into a volcano.

Pyramid (loc.) — northeastern *Greenland*.

"*The Price of Profit is oppression.*"
"*To Survive is to depend on trust from others.*"

12. "TO EXCHANGE" {spirit-broker}

Time — an hour-glass (sand running down).
Space — rolling hills, plains; fairytale kingdom with castle.
God — demon god (statue).

Incident (track) — you are a wizard in a magical kingdom of 'munchkins' and 'spirits'. As a 'spirit-broker', you trick people, or do something for them, in exchange for their "soul" (a contract for their service as a 'spirit' after death), which are then sold to 'demons'. At the start, you collect 7 "souls" and sell them to 'demons' in exchange for 7 wondrous miracles (performed by the 'demons'). This astounds people and is rewarded by the 'king'. Downscale, you do less for people in exchange (to keep more of the power for yourself); and become more paranoid and withdrawn as more people "almost find out" what you're doing. You get bored with the affairs of the people and begin engaging in sex with 'spirit-forms' and 'demons'. The 'spirits' start protesting their "contracts" and the 'demons' get upset with enforcing them. People start to trick you (with false "contracts"); you start blasting others with an energy-rod ("wand"), and get in trouble with the king. The 'demons' drag you before the presence of a 'demon-god' (statue), who divides you against yourself. Then you're tossed into a volcano (beneath the castle) and tortured by the 'spirits' and 'demons' you had cheated.

Pyramid (loc.) — *Catskills*.

"*The Price of Wealth is enslavement.*"
"*To Survive is to depend on commitment from others.*"

13. "TO SHAPE" {clay people}

Time — clock on large clay building.
Space — clay city (earthen slabs and blocks); buildings look like
   upside-down pots; cracks/fissures in ground give off vapor.
Energy — exploding volcano.
Mass — landslide.
Trouble — the fire-people.
Home — big clay slab building.

Incident (track)—you are a body-shaper, able to reshape bodies of clay-people (and getting them to hold the new form). At the top/start, you perform 7 wonderful body-shapings, giving people strength and beauty (earning you admiration and respect). Downscale, you conceal ugliness beneath shapings of people you don't like—so that the beautification fades (does not hold) and eventually reveals the hidden shaping instead. There are many harmful-acts and mistakes; all your forms begin to destabilize. People start to blame their deformities on a plague and lose control of their forms; you also lose control of your form. Realizing you are the cause, they chase and capture you, and you are divided against yourself, &tc.

Pyramid (loc.)—island off Brazil.

"*The Price of Admiration is to conform (to others opinions).*"
"*To Survive is to depend on the malleability (plasticity) of others.*"

14. "TO CHANGE" {magician-wizard}

Time—shadow swings across palace dome.
Space—Arabian-Nights styled desert city.
Energy—bolt from a wand.
Mass—city-walls falling down.
Trouble—genies (djinn).

Incident (track)—you are a wizard with the ability to 'metamorphize' into many shapes; each pass through the incident, the skin of your humanoid form is of a different color (starting with purple). Using 'spells', you start by changing into 7 wondrous forms—a winged horse, snake, mouse, gnome, &tc. You gain great power and admiration; dueling with other wizards and winning. Downscale, you abuse/misuse power, become arrogant and start regretting things. You start making mistakes, losing duels, tricking people, and fighting against all authority—until finally you destroy the palace. The system collapses and there is a shortage of everything. After you start to abuse and sacrifice young girls, the people storm your estate. You are hunted, captured, divided, killed, and then tossed into a volcano by 'snake-demons'.

Pyramid (loc.)—Haiti.

"*The Price of Power is insanity.*"
"*To Survive is to depend on perversions of others.*"

15. "TO COMBINE" {conjoined twins}

Time — clock.
Space — city with large twin buildings.
Energy — explosion in laboratory.
Trouble — lobster-people.

Incident (track) — you are a genetic engineer (chemist/surgeon) of sorts, separating and combining "male" and "female" bodies to make 3-legged twin-forms. The basic body type is a pair of conjoined twins (born separately but combined to form a complete body). Normally, a "male" and "female" combine. The "males" only have one leg (and need crutches to walk); "female" bodies have two legs but require joining to a "male" in order to more fully exert themselves. After combining, the skin grows together, but may be separated again to allow a change in partners. Sex occurs between two sets of twins. You start by performing 7 brilliant operations that separate and combine twin-form bodies. Downscale, you make more outrageous combinations of people and animals (and forms that include more than two individuals). The 'lobster-people' protest this and try to make everyone else 'singletons'. You change partners a few times, getting worse and worse ones; get blamed for riots and invasions of the 'lobster-people'; then hunted down as a 'singleton' and combined with a dead body. The incident ends with usual after-death sequence, &tc.

Pyramid (loc.) — southeastern Atlantis.

"The Price of Harmony is self-sacrifice."
"To Survive is to depend on the weakness of others."

16. "TO (BRING) ORDER" {gorilla people}

Note: might be *"To Align"*; might correspond to the *9th dynamic system* *"Ethics."*

Time — sun-shadows over village in snow.
Space — view of snow-covered mountains.
Energy — gorilla-person fighting with moose.
Mass — vast wall of snow about to fall.
Gods — totem pole (with living faces).
Crush — gorilla-person under an avalanche.
Injustice — individual sacrificed by group.

Incident (track) — you solve 7 major problems by getting people to change and align with each other (for group efforts). The village is in a flood area (come spring), so you get everyone to move and they are generally happy (though there are always occasional protestors you must overwhelm). Downscale, the changes are more arbitrary (or for personal gain) and you make mistakes. You overwhelm others by getting people to gang up on them. More people protest, and you label them as 'anti-social', but your justifications begin to break down. You regret things but carry on in order to make yourself right. You have your 'followers' kill your opponents, also causing many 'followers' to die. Eventually the people destroy the village and hunt for you in the forest, &tc.

Pyramid (loc.) — North Dakota.

"The Price of Order is obligation."
"To Survive is to depend on the xenophobia of others."

17. "TO REASON" {comic-clown}

Time — dial-clock on a tall skyscraper.
Space — the city at dusk.
God — crackling-cloud in power-plant.
Turmoil — incompetent police running around.
Sensation — woman in lingerie.
Companionship — woman in checkered apron.
Sex — exchanging energy sparks.

Incident (track) — the common body type is doll-bodies, with clothing built into the body. You are more intelligent than other people; you are something of a 'comic-character' so that they will like you anyways. You use brilliant logic to solve 7 difficult problems. Downscale, you use logic to persuade people to give you money, sex, &tc. Eventually, the people use your own logic against you; you become a tragic figure that traps and destroys yourself (according to your own "rules"). So you rebel and deny your logic; the people hunt you down. You are taken before the energy-god, a crackling-cloud in a power-plant, who divides you against yourself, &tc.

Pyramid (loc.) — South Africa.

"The Price of Logic is to entrap yourself."
"To Survive is to depend on the stupidity of others."

18. "TO ORIENT" {wire man}

Time — sun light/shadow moving across a structure in orbit.
Space — building a cage-like structure in space.

God—a statue of a man.
Body—made of thick wires that can bend.
Sex—bodies have a genital region (involving electrical plugs)

Incident (track)—you are a brilliant genius who can see how to align wires in a structure for maximum efficiency. You are building a complex cage-like structure in space (orbiting a planet). This 'space structure' tunes to the basic 'universal energy'. Increasing the structure (properly) increases the flow and brings great prosperity. Crowds cheer; priests honor, &tc. The construct becomes too complex and many mistakes are made (causing bodies to be painfully shaken with 'bad vibrations'). Eventually, you are taken to the *god-statue* and divided, &tc.

Pyramid (loc.)—Antarctica.

"The Price of Orientation is to be stuck."
"To Survive is to depend on confidence from others."

19. "TO GUIDE" {pilot}

Time—a prairie at dusk.
Space—floating flatland continents.
Motion—"zeppelins" flying between continents.
God—statue in cathedral.
Impact—plane crash.
Guide—plane leading zeppelins through the clouds.

Incident (track)—you are a goggle-wearing pilot that flies a powerful airplane (only primitive in appearance because of the double-wings and open-cockpit). Early on there is some personal "levitation" ability, but this becomes problematic to control by the end. Transport "zeppelins" travel between continents and require planes to guide them. At the top, you guide 7 great convoys between flatworlds, earning admiration and esteem. Downscale, you become arrogant, demand too much money, cheat on your spouse, get drunk and lose some zeppelins in the sky, start crashing planes, and discover disorientation (dizziness). You take a young girl up in the plane, lose control, she dies, you fall. The people capture you and take you to the cathedral where the god-statue divides you. You try to fly afterward, but keep crashing, which is how you die. After being buried in a cemetery, 'winged-devils' throw you into a flat-earth volcano-hell where you are tortured by those you cheated/betrayed.

Pyramid (loc.)—Lemuria.

"The Price of Success is to be despised."
"To Survive is to depend on the good will of others."

20. "TO COMPUTE" {toy bodies}

Time—a toy clock.
Space—a logic-maze constructed of toys.
God—toy-master ("Santa Claus" type).
Sex—between toy-bodies.

Incident (track)—you are bright and your goal is to get through a logic maze (an elaborate labyrinth). At the top you solve 7 difficult problems; helping others; working deeply into the labyrinth. When you judge/evaluate an action wrong, your toy body gets smashed, requiring you to take a new one and start again. You start zapping troublesome toys with energy. Downscale, you start losing more bodies and get worried you'll never solve the maze. You trick others into trying things to avoid losing your own body. Getting worried someone else will surpass you, you start distributing false data, and change puzzles so that the answers don't work for those coming up behind you. Eventually the puzzles get rearranged to the point where you can no longer get as deeply into the labyrinth. You worry about running out of bodies and start to organize riots. Eventually, you are taken before the "toy-master" (Santa-like god) and divided. When you try to enter the maze again, each of your last toy-bodies are smashed; pieces are collected, buried, and held in place by "crosses" until 'devils' toss you into a volcano beneath the central part of the maze, *&tc.*

Pyramid (loc.)—Australia.

"The Price of Intelligence is self-destruction."
"To Survive is to depend on answers from others."

21. "TO CONSTRUCT" {beaver-people}

Time—sun swings over the dam.
Space—dam village of beaver-people.
God—a river-spirit.
Sex—orgies in the mud.

Incident (track)—you are a beaver-person; squirrel-people are slave-laborers; skunk-people work as maid, *&tc.* You complete 7 large construction projects, such as managing the building of dams and fish-traps, and extending the village on planks out over the water. Down scale, the traps catch other people, who you then enslave and put to work. You start building traps for beaver-people too, so they rebel and take you to the 'river-lake-god' and are divided against yourself, &tc.

Pyramid (loc.) — *Australia.*

"The Price of Industriousness is entrapment."
"To Survive is to depend on the labor of others."

<u>22. "TO ARRANGE" {blockhead}</u>

  Note: limited data blends with 22X.

<u>22X. "TO ENGINEER" {lobster-people}</u>

Time — mechanical clock (exposed gears).
Space — undersea domed city.
Energy — giant machines (pumps churning water).
Mass — underwater avalanche.

Incident (track) — you are a lobster-person and a brilliant engineering genius. At the top, you design 7 marvelous projects; but then you start altering designs for your own profit; things collapse; people die. Power-sources and other systems fail due to misengineering; riots start. When the people find out you are to blame, they chase and hunt you down...

Pyramid (loc.) — *Africa.*

"The Price of Calculation is to be detested."
"To Survive is to depend on the strength of others."

<u>23. "TO BUILD" {snake people}</u>

Time — sun in orbit.
Space — a "space city" (planet-sized construct).
Crash — 'air-car' smashes into building.
Crush — 'snake-person' under collapsing roadway.

Incident (track) — you undertake 7 projects to expand the fantastically complex and beautifully constructed 'space city'. You hurt slave-workers in the process (but justified it as 'for the higher good'). Then you start to have problems with construction errors, social unrest, and riots. Your building becomes too big and falls apart. Enraged citizens chase you through the sky, &tc.

Pyramid (loc.) — *Bangkok.*

"The Price of Having is enslavement."
"To Survive is to depend on the compulsions of others."

24. "TO STRUCTURE" {crystals}

Time—pulsing crystal.
Space—crystal city (rods and basic structures) suspended over a lake.
Energy—energy-flow blasts from crystal.
Shattered—crystal breaking apart.
Sex—sides of crystals in contact (rubbing); crackling-energy.
Body Type—levitating gems (that project energy, beams, &tc.) that survive on salts from the water and energy from sunlight.

Incident (track)—you undertake 7 projects extending the city higher into the sky and become highly admired. Downscale, you make mistakes and begin stealing sunlight from others. The poor must float up above the city to get their sunlight-energy, but live in deep shadows of the city, and gradually lack the energy to climb that high—so they begin breaking apart and dying. You help the rich build bigger levels, which makes it worse for the poor. Eventually societal systems fail, the city falls and mobs chase you, &tc.

Pyramid (loc.)—France.

"The Price of Alignment is to be held (located) in place."
"To Survive is to depend on the form of others."

25. "TO INVENT" {dwarves or house-elves}

Time—mechanical clock.
Space—large cluttered workshop.

Incident (track)—you are an eccentric inventor in a Bavarian or Dutch-style village. You invent 7 wondrous (aesthetically pleasing) things, including a fancy town clock. The inventions are so beautiful that they gain instant agreement. Downscale, greed, lust, and pride, cause you to maintain your position by inventing terrible (but aesthetic) devices to gain things—but also weapons of war and enslavement, originally for use against invading 'insect-people', but which get used to control the population. Eventually the mobs chase you down, &tc.

Pyramid (loc.)—Pennsylvania.

"The Price of Ingenuity is entrapment."
"To Survive is to depend on the aesthetic appreciation of others."

26. "TO ENHANCE" {ghost people}

Space—spirit world (city of ghosts) that intersects a late-19th Century styled material city.

God — man on a cross in a church.
Companionship — a male ghost.
Sensation — living male cat-person.
Body Types — humans and cat-people.

Incident (track) — you are a female spirit that enhances the view of things for living people. You cause 7 enhancements: making guys seeing girls as more beautiful, disguising the drab appearance of the city, *&tc.* You visit living men in the night for sex and take a drop of blood as an offering, which makes you more 'real' (material) and stronger than the other ghost-people. You make everything seem better than it really is, and this gets people into trouble and leads them to mistakes. You become mischievous, haunt people, and even demand sacrifices. Priests attempt to 'exorcise' you; eventually capturing you and taking you before the god, who divides you against yourself, *&tc.*

Pyramid (loc.) — Buenos Aires.

"The Price of Improvement is condemnation."
"To Survive is to depend on the illusions of others."

27. "TO INSPIRE" {muses}

Time — a sundial.
Space — astral world intersecting a material world.
Trouble — knights with flaming swords that can pierce the astral plane.
Disaster — earthquake.
You — female astral body.
Sensation — another female.

Incident (track) — At the top, you provide 7 wonderful inspirations and are praised. Downscale, you start running out of inspiring ideas, so you begin stealing them from other muses. Eventually, you start inspiring people toward crime, perversion, and cause nightmares. When you are thrown into the volcano at the end, escape becomes impossible because you have no new ideas (inspiration).

Pyramid (loc.) — Ethiopia.

"The Price of New Ideas is to be scorned."
"To Survive is to depend on the dullness of others."

28. "TO BEAUTIFY" {fairy godmother}

Time — sun swings.
Space — storybook land/kingdom.

Energy—beams from 'wand' makes things beautiful.
You—flying 'faerie queen'.

Incident (track)—you start by performing 7 amazing deeds, beautifying the landscape, the buildings and castle, and even making it so the poor girl can meet the prince; all very 'storybook' until you see that the people are messing up the environment and doing 'ugly' things. The girl gets her beautiful dress messed up having sex, so you give her a poisoned apple. Starving children eat the ornate 'gingerbread houses', so you throw them into a furnace. You gradually depopulate the kingdom and the people fear you—summoning 'witches' and 'devils' to capture and divide you, then keeping you bound under a magic circle until 'witches on broomsticks' fly you to the volcano.

Pyramid (loc.)—Florida.

"*The Price of Beauty is sadness (suffering).*"
"*To Survive is to depend on the good taste of others.*"

29. "TO PURIFY" {fire people}

Time—sun swings.
Space—a fire-city of fire-people.
Mass—a central volcano.

Incident (track)—At the top, you find 7 horrible criminals using your ability to see the 'impurities' in their 'flame'; and they are captured and tossed into the central volcano. The people cheer. Eventually it becomes like the 'Inquisition' or 'Thought Policing', searching out anyone with 'impure thoughts'. You start making more mistakes, tossing in the wrong people and even 'good people' for personal gain. Finally, there is the inevitable ending with your capture, division, and volcano-torture experience, *&tc.*

Pyramid (loc.)—Italy.

"*The Price of Purity is loss of self-determinism (individual-ity).*"
"*To Survive is to depend on the iniquity (impurity) of others.*"

30. "TO JUDGE" {minotaur}

  Note: goal also may be "*To Arbitrate.*"
Time—a sundial (in the plaza).
Space—a classical Grecian styled city.
Mass—building under construction collapses on workers.
Body Type—'bull-people'

Incident (track)—you start by solving 7 great disputes, including one between the king and the slave-workers. You do this by talking to them and shifting their viewpoints, until they come to an agreement. Your ability to bring people into agreement through compromise is praised and rewarded. Downscale, this begins to bring harm to people, such as getting workers to compromise the safety of a building under construction, then it collapses on them. Eventually, everyone is losing too much through compromise, and they blame you, chase you down, *&tc.*

Pyramid (loc.)—Buenos Aires.

"The Price of Compromise is universal misery."
"To Survive is to depend on the obligations of others."

31. "TO DEFEND" {aliens}

Time—'flying-saucer' in orbit.
Space—a ship over the cities.
God—a silver robot.
Holy—"cross" on control panel.

Incident (track)—you succeed in 7 great battles, defending against evil invaders, revolutionaries, heretics, *&tc.* You realize that not all the 'rebels' are 'bad' and start regretting blasting them; but you continue in pride and duty. Downscale, you become arrogant and start blasting entire cities (of loyal people) once they are invaded by lizard-people. Social systems collapse and civilization crumbles. Rebel ships capture yours. They take you before the 'silver-robot' god, who divides you; and while you're allowed to return to your ship, the crew now despises you (considering you a traitor) and they throw you into the volcano, *&tc.*

Pyramid (loc.)—Tibet.

"The Price of Ethics is betrayal."
"To Survive is to depend on the integrity of others."

32. "TO STRENGTHEN" {energy sphere}

Note: may read as "To Protect."

Space—a city of other body-types.
Energy—electricity.
You—a ball/sphere of colored energy.
Reward—being fed (in-flowing) electricity.
Sex—exchanging energy with other spheres.

Incident (track)—you police a city of other body-types. You start by handling 7 critical situations, protecting the innocent by 'zapping' their attackers. Downscale, you 'zap' the wrong people, mishandle situations, fight with other spheres, develop perversions (drinking in 'sex-energy flows' from bodies). You eventually become quite viscous. No longer being fed energy, you start stealing it, even draining it from bodies, and killing them, followed by typical end-sequence, &tc.

Pyramid (loc.) — Washington, D.C.

"The Price of Safety is inhibition."
"To Survive is to depend on the sins (misdeeds) of others."

33. "TO ENLIGHTEN" {rabbit preacher}

  Note: might actually be *"To Preach."*
Time — sun-swings over countryside.
Space — country-town.
You — a 'rabbit-preacher'.
Holy — a book you carry.
Sacrifice — crucifixion (dying on a cross).
Body Types — 'rabbit-people' (in dress coats); 'wolf-people' (in leather-
      jackets).

Incident (track) — you preach 'sacrifice' to higher purposes. At the top, you work 7 miracles. Downscale, you sacrifice 'rabbit-people' to the 'wolf-people' (you preach to). You engage in secret cult-like orgies, and experience the usual sequence of decline and troubles; dying on a cross, &tc.

Pyramid (loc.) — Alabama.

"The Price of Preaching is sacrifice."
"To Survive is to depend on the faith of others."

34. "TO CONVERT" {fish man}

Time — sun-swings over lagoon.
Space — gulf coast (seashore/lagoon).
Gods — statues (main 'terminals' from other penalty-universes).
Worship — lesser-gods that demand sacrifice in return for small favors.
Holy — temples built on reefs.
You — reptilian fish-man (Oannes, Dagon).

Incident (track) — you have the ability to evoke 'heavenly pictures' in the sky (which are scenes from other penalty-universes), which allows you to promote a 'false religion', and convince others (even the 'lesser-gods') that you are an agent of a 'higher god'. You perform 7 wondrous acts, such as using the 'pictures' to stop wars and affect large events. But, unlike the 'lesser-gods', you can't really heal the sick, or control the weather, &tc. When the people start to catch on to this fact, you get into various troubles and experience the usual decline, &tc.

Pyramid (loc.)—southeastern *Atlantis*.

"*The Price of Divine Revelation is to be fooled.*"
"*To Survive is to depend on the gullibility of others.*"

35. "TO COMMUNE" {female angel}

  Note: may read as "*To Connect.*"
Time—sun on clouds.
Space—pearly/golden-gates and clouds.
Energy—golden-rays descending from 'God-on-high'.
Mass—golden altar in 'heavenly cathedral'.
Ecstasy—angels in the 'cathedral' writing in God's light (you receive
        religious and sexual ecstasy by direct connection/communion
        with God).
Sex—sharing 'ecstasy' with someone other than God (is forbidden).

Incident (track)—you have 7 divine religious and ecstatic experiences (usually in a group) in various locations (like the 'cathedral'), when "God's light" shines down. Downscale, you begin to do 'forbidden things', which causes you to 'hold-back'/'hold-out' (hide) from God when the bliss-light shines. You discover you can experience 'communion' and 'ecstasy' with those other than God through sex, which perverts many of the angels, causing many troubles. The 'sexual ecstasy' decays leaving only empty cravings. When you are found out, you argue with God and are cast out of the 'heavenly abode' onto the ground. You try to achieve 'sexual ecstasy' again through 'pain', but you become numb to this, die, &tc.

Pyramid (loc.)—Hawaii.

"*The Price of Sensation is defilement.*"
"*To Survive is to depend on others for fulfillment.*"

36. "TO WORSHIP" {holy knights}

Time—sun-swings over forest and lake.
Space—castle overlooking lake and meadow.
Energy—a 'holy knight' swinging a sword.

Mass—the castle walls.
God—the 'God of the Cross'.
Worship—sacrificing to the 'God of the Cross' (who absorbs the 'soul' of
    people put on the 'Cross').

Incident (track)—you complete 7 holy quests, like finding the holy grail. Downscale, you engage in 'crusades' against rival religions, even smashing the 'statues' of their gods. When you start feeling sympathy for your victims, and guilt from your actions, you start betraying your comrades, and there is the usual decline, *&tc.*

Pyramid (loc.)—China.

"*The Price of Faith is blindness.*"
"*To Survive is to depend on the blindness of others.*"

37. "TO PREDICT" {soothsayer}

  Note: might actually be "*To Predetermine.*"
Time—sun shadow above a pasture.
Space—a flat-earth with mountains in the distance (resembling *Babylon*
    or *Mesopotamia*).
God—the 'God in the Mountain'.
Body Types—material forms; a 'symbol-body' that takes various forms,
    e.g. 'wise fool' (*tarot archetypes*), 'water-bearer' (*zodiac icons*), *&tc.*

Incident (track)—you can see the 'symbol-body' that is behind 'material-forms' and thereby know their destiny. You make prophecies based on these 'symbols', which further 'keys in' their significance and makes your predictions come to pass. You begin with making 7 great prophecies of doom, but you help the people to overcome the catastrophes. Downscale, you become more greedy and vengeful, predict false dooms, and speak out against kings. Eventually, the 'mountain god' divides you, *&tc.*

Pyramid (loc.)—Alberta, Canada.

"*The Price of Prediction is to be foredoomed.*"
"*To Survive is to depend on the superstitions of others.*"

38. "TO INFLUENCE" {cupid/cherub}

Space—in the 'clouds' above the cities.
God—god of the 'golden throne'.
Body Types—'cupid'-angels that live in the clouds, as do 'angels' and
    'demons' (both of which object to the influence of the 'cupids');

body-types for people in the cities are from other penalty-universes.

Incident (track) — At the top, you visit 7 cities and inspire the people to experience 7 interesting emotions, and so the people (and other 'cupids') admire you. Downscale, you inspire lower emotions — misemotions like terror and hate — and eventually the people riot and tear civilization down. The angels capture you and drag you before the 'god of the golden-throne', who divides you against yourself. You die and are buried in a coffin-in-the-clouds for a time before the 'demons' haul you off to the volcano-hell, *&tc.*

Pyramid (loc.) — Vermont.

"*The Price of Excitement is to stay hidden.*"
"*To Survive is to depend on the discomfort of others.*"

39. "TO COLLECT" {elves/fairies}

Time — sun-swings over an elven 'forest-city'.
Space — field/clearing where fairies dance.
Energy — bolt from a 'ring of power'.
Mass — elves pushing a boulder.

Incident (track) — you are a great 'magical artificer' or 'spellsmith' that collects "beings." You capture 'spirits' and enchant them (surrounding them with your energy and crushing them) into material objects and weapons. When someone dies, you try to be nearby to 'collect' the 'spirit'. You begin by crafting 7 great devices, and are at first praised by the people. But they come to fear and despise you; and you grow vain and arrogant and start to hate everybody. The gods divide you against yourself; and when you die, you are 'collected' in an object and locked into a vault until being taken to the volcano-hell, *&tc.*

Pyramid (loc.) — Babylon/Baghdad (Iraq).

"*The Price of Power is corruption.*"
"*To Survive is to depend on the enslavement of others.*"

40. "TO EMBODY" {satyr/goat-god}

Note: initially researched as "To Solidify."
Time — sun-swings over forest glade.
Space — forest and brook.
Energy — geyser erupting from a lake.
Mass — 'dryads' melted into stone.

Evoke—playing 'pan-pipes' to summon the spirit out of a natural form, tree &tc.
Solidify—'dryad' outside of (exterior to) a tree, becoming solid.
Terror—bull-like 'demon' rising out of a lake (near a waterfall).
Trouble—'pinwheel' of energy around a silver cap.
God—'Guardian of the Forest' (tree-god).

Incident (track)—you start alone in a forest glade, using pan-pipes to evoke spirits from natural forms and solidifying them into a person—such as embodying the spirit of a tree as a 'dryad' or 'nymph', &tc. You evoke 7 groups of spirits and solidify them. They all praise and worship you and want their friends embodied as well. You populate the woods—occasionally evoking a 'monster' or 'demon' (or an 'energy pinwheel', which is dangerous to you). Downscale, you solidify things for your own gain, solidify beings against their will, demand payment from solidified beings, &tc. The forest starts dying (because you've pulled out all its spirits) and everyone blames you. They hunt you down, take you to the 'Guardian of the Forest', who divides you, &tc.

Pyramid (loc.)—Greece.
"The Price of Embodiment is suffering."
"To Survive is to depend on the harmony of others."

41. "TO DISCOVER" {centaurs}

Note: may also read as "To Explore."
Time—sun-swings over ship at sea.
Space—looking over railing of ship out at the shores of a bay.
Energy—a charging rhinoceros.
Mass—cliffs at shore; waves thrust a ship towards them.
Trouble—angels with flaming swords.
Body Types—you and your shipmates are horse-people (centaurs); body-types from other penalty-universes are also encountered.

Incident (track)—at the top, you are on an explorer's ship sailing from bay to bay along the shores of a newly discovered continent. You intend to find treasure, learn native wisdom, and teach. You visit 7 bays, each inhabited by its own body-types (rabbit-people and robots; cat-people and bears; goat-people and elves; magicians and Sumerians; gnomes and giants; frog-people and insects; Olympian-type gods and dog-people). At first, the indigenous populations welcome you. Downscale, you try to dominate, exploit, and enslave them. You discover new ideas and try to teach them things, but they fail to listen—so you begin to trap them "for their own good" and force them into schools. They rebel; they pray for help; angels with fiery swords come to oppose you, destroy your ship, capture you, take you before god, &tc.

Pyramid (loc.) — South Africa.

"The Price of Discovery is blame."
"To Survive is to depend on the naivete of others."

42. "TO LOCATE" {leprechaun (wise fool)}

Time—a grandfather clock.
Space—a circular room plus the shadows of other rooms
    (interconnected at random; fourth spatial dimension).
Energy—a ray from the center passes into a room and hits someone.
Mass—someone pounding on the wall.
Boisterous—a drinking hall.

Incident (track)—you are a "locator" working for the king. There is a "sun" (surrounded by a balcony) in the center of the room that puts out higher-dimensional rays, which pass through walls of many interconnected rooms of a giant castle-keep. Unlike most others, you have the ability to sense the direction of the rays and know where things are in the rooms and halls that are constantly shifting in concentric rings around the central room. You start by going on 7 missions, successfully locating people and things, and are showered with praise and riches. Downscale, you start hiding things, concealing locations of treasure (for yourself), and get others lost. You start making too many mistakes and get yourself lost. The kingdom starts to fail; you are blamed; soldiers chase you. You finally end up in the volcano-hell under the floor, beneath the "sun" in the central room, &tc.

Pyramid (loc.) — Equador.

"The Price of Being Located is to be a target."
"To Survive is to depend on the mis-orientation of others."

43. "TO GATHER" {spacesuit body}

  Note: limited data available for this IPU.
Body Type—faceless 'spacesuit' or 'radiation suit' is the body.

Incident (track)—you use an 'implanting-device' on others, which uses the type of content described in "The Jewel of Knowledge" (AT Manual #3). You start by conquering 7 societies and are hailed a great leader. At first, you don't experience any regret in conquering 'meat-body' people; your deceit and betrayal concerns other 'invaders' like yourself. You start making mistakes, get overwhelmed by robots and revolutionaries, and start to lose your courage—followed by the usual decline, &tc.

Pyramid (loc.)—Atlantis.

"*The Price of Wealth is to be controlled.*"
"*To Survive is to depend on the 'conditionability' of others.*"

44. "TO OWN" {fox people}

Note: limited data blended with 44X.

44X. "TO PERMEATE" {spirit body}

Time—sun-shadows.
God—'centaur' (statue).

Incident (track)—as a spiritual-entity, you 'permeate' "meat-bodies" in order to 'implant'. You help the 'tiger-people' and 'fox-people' (&tc.), by 'blanketing' entire crowds and 'implanting' orders to stop riots, &tc. Downscale, you 'implant' for entertainment and personal gratification, but eventually inspire all the people to fight each other. After the centaur-statue god divides you against yourself, your future 'implant' attempts conflict with themselves and are ineffective.

Pyramid (loc.)—Saudi Arabia.

"*The Price of Pervasion is dissolution.*"
"*To Survive is to depend on the suggestibility of others.*"

45. "TO GROW" {genetic entity}

Note: this IPU-*incident* involves 'creation' and 'growth' before the usual decline, rather than starting at the 'top'.

Time—sea-organisms as day turns to night.
Space—a southsea volcanic island; bay, reefs, the sky above.
Energy—lightning-bolt striking, causing a forest-fire.
Mass—a rocky cliff above the beach.
Likingness—feeling tenderness toward a mouse-like creature.
Reality—a volcano sheathed in clouds.
Communication—a monkey points a snake out to another.
Understanding—two sloths are hanging out together in the trees.
Fate—a glacier.
Help—amoeba reaching out to another that is sinking.
Decay—fungus on a tree.

Creation—strange glow from a cave.
Warmth—a green sun in the sky.
Turbulence—waves.
Fall—bird dropping down on a clam-shell.
Competition—another 'genetic-entity' (blue colored).
Abandonment—shellfish on beach.
Doom—erupting volcano.
You—a 'genetic entity' (cloud-like consciousness) attempting to evolve your own 'genetic line' of various organic forms, increasing in complexity.

Incident (track)—you begin with simple lifeforms on a lifeless volcanic island, then gradually move on to more complex ones. You find yourself 'in competition' with a rival 'genetic-entity' on the other side of the island. You each begin evolving forms to eat or trample the other's newly made forms.

Pyramid (loc.)—Australia.

"*The Price of Growth is death.*"
"*To Survive is to depend on the sacrifices of others.*"

46. "TO LIVE" {dinosaur/saurian}

Note: might read as "*To Suffer.*"

Note: too little data for this IPU.

47. "TO HEAL" {tree-man/forest-guardian}

Time—shifting slant of sunlight through the forest canopy.
Space—a path through the forest extending out to the distance.
Competition—another 'forest-guardian' (at the other side of the forest).
God—'mountain-god' (earth-god).
Trouble—'boar-person' (tusked pig-man).

Incident (track)—at the top, you visit 7 races (cat-people, bull-people, &tc.) and perform miraculous healing for each. They build altars to you; praise and worship you. You don't like them fighting with each other, so you try to control them. You push the 'injuries' back in on them when they disobey you, and they sicken and die. You find yourself in competition with another 'forest-guardian', and your people and theirs start fighting. Too many are hurt for you to heal them all, so your people turn against you—capturing you, and taking you to the 'mountain-god', who divides you, &tc.

Pyramid (loc.) — Uruguay.

"The Price of Healing is pain."
"To Survive is to depend on the weakness of others."

48. "TO ADAPT" {thread man}

   Note: limited data available.
Time — a clock-tower (silver ball with streamers).
Space — city.
Energy — waves shake the city.
Mass — a great rock crushes things.
Trouble — 'cyclops' (one-eyed giant), *&tc.*
Horror — 'solidification' and 'burning'.
You — a 'thread-body'; a bundle of threads that can unravel and reweave
      into a different shape.
Incident (track) — at the start, you are highly adaptive and teach others to adapt to 7 significant threats — crab-people who chop with pincers; cyclops that burn you with their eye; bull-people that enforce rules.
Pyramid (loc.) — Syria.

49. "TO ESTABLISH" {3-eyed giants}

   Note: limited data available.
Space — an electronic hyperspace (ultra-dimensional) grid that links
      7 'planes' or 'flatlands'.
Incident (track) — you establish 7 'flatlands' with a race of beings ('children', 'fox-people', *&tc.*) on each, set up as a rigid caste system. Each race has a trade, task, or skill. You focus on establishing civilization by co-ordinating these diversities and expanding the 'space grid'. At the start, you have wonderful goals toward a vision of a glorious civilization. You 'implant' any dissenters "for the greater good." Downscale, people revolt; get too many 'implants'; you start committing too many harmful-acts, and finally give up on your involvement. When the civilization collapses, you are blamed, captured by a mob, *&tc.*
Pyramid (loc.) — Ireland.

"The Price of Order is invalidation."
"To Survive is to depend on the obedience of others."

50. "TO SHARE" {dolphins}

Time — sun-swings over ocean.

Space—dolphin in an air-glider (flying).
Energy—beam from sky boiling the ocean.
Mass—dolphin in ocean levitating large amount of water.
God—giant statue of man holding trident.
Sex—orgies in the ocean.
Trouble—'insect-invaders' (type of 'alien').
Body Type—dolphin; no hands, but can levitate things by 'group postulate' (shared 'alpha-thought').

Incident (track)—you share in 7 great cooperative efforts, including uprooting trees from the islands for wood, launching wooden spaceships, and even building a low-orbit platform (space-station). Agreements are forced by projecting 'thought bubbles' at one another. Eventually, you commit harmful-acts (as ordered by the group), including casting a friend off the space-platform—which causes you to rebel against the group and obsessively 'individuate'. You are taken before the 'sea-god' statue, who divides you, *&tc.*

Pyramid (loc.)—Azores.

"*The Price of Sharing is enforced agreement.*"
"*To Survive is to depend on the agreement of others.*"

51. "TO CONTROL" {frog king}

   Note: potential errors in data.
Time—a water-clock (trays of water).
Space—a village of floating 'house-boats'.
Energy—a tidal wave.
Mass—cliffs overhanging the lake.
Sex—underwater breeding.
Trouble—'alien-invaders'.
Body Type—'frog-person'; mostly live in/on the water; they also have buildings on shore.

Incident (track)—you control the pond by leading and manipulating people, and even try to control other ponds. You perform 7 great acts of control, getting people to work together in such ways as to stop crime, construct dams, and fend off invaders. When the people won't obey your rules, you put "control helmets" on them which cause headaches when they disobey orders, break laws, or have thoughts against government. Eventually, you start to add 'invader-forces' in order to give you excuses for exercising more control. When your misdeeds are found out, the people rebel, chase you, &tc.

Pyramid (loc.)—Africa (Lake Nayassa).

"The Price of Civilization is oppression."
"To Survive is to depend on the meekness of others."

52. "TO UNITE" {dog soldiers}

Time—sun-swings over battlefield.
Space—a harbor with ships, planes, and troops amassed on the shore.
Energy—mushroom cloud (bomb blows up city).
Mass—giant steel doors of a fortress-like bunker.
God—statue of a giant bird on a pedestal.
Sex—with an enemy spy.
Trouble—'cat-people'.
You—'dog-person'; a soldier fighting in a war for racial-purity (against the 'cat-people').

Incident (track)—as an officer, you engage in 7 glorious campaigns toward defeating the enemy, uniting countries, and purifying the race. At first you agree heavily with this, but then begin to question. The army installs 'control devices' in your teeth. You have sex with an enemy spy and begin to sympathize with the enemy (and start helping them). When you're found out, you flee to the enemy side, who implant more devices on you and send you back as a counter-spy. You're caught again, implanted further, &tc. After being divided against yourself, the 'hidden fragments' of yourself become active when you are asleep—continuing to report, &tc. Eventually, you disable the 'shields' and blow everyone up. Betrayed comrades from both sides pull you out of the grave and toss you in the volcano, &tc.

Pyramid (loc.)—Australia.

"The Price of Loyalty is dishonor."
"To Survive is to depend on the honor of others."

53. "TO ORGANIZE" {file clerk ('human')}

Time—beeping computer signal (flashing red light on console).
Space—looking down at a cafeteria (incident is entirely indoors).
Energy—basket of forms thrown at a clerk's head.
Mass—endless piles of forms stacked to the ceiling.
God—an administrative computer.
Sex—an office privilege (a source of upset); done to you by seniors,

done by you to juniors.

Trouble — 'bull-people'.

You — hermaphroditic file-clerk with the goal of putting order into everything; populations and planets are being taken over (which you handle with 'paperwork').

Incident (track) — at the start, you organize 7 departments, creating new forms and procedures to handle the ever growing piles of data. This operates on pure bureaucracy, including forms about forms. The penalty for mistakes is paying more taxes — which requires a horrific chain of forms in itself. Some people begin to starve and die because of the chain of forms required. The 'bull-people' are intolerable to this and start wrecking things. You feel guilty but continue. Angry mobs storm through the building setting fires to paperwork. When you are caught, you are taken before the 'computer-god' and divided. You die from falling down an elevator shaft, which leads to a large basement cavern and a volcano-hell, &tc.

Pyramid (loc.) — Portugal.

"The Price of Order is frustration."
"To Survive is to depend on the uniformity of others."

54. "TO COOPERATE" {robots}

Time — sunlight moving across a space-station.

Space — two large wheel-style space-stations; a planet they orbit; 7 large platforms, ships, robots moving about.

Energy — ship smashing into station; debris flying around.

Mass — large bundle of 'girders' drifting into a 'bulkhead' and crumpling it in a gravityless 'loading dock'.

God — a computer.

Creator — an octopus-type being in a tank of gas.

Dissolve — robots tossing others into a vat of boiling acid.

Conflict — warring space-stations in orbit; 'blue robots' versus 'red robots'.

Incident (track) — you do 7 significant projects, cooperating with other 'robots' to build things, expand the space-station, and fight enemy 'robots'. You act as a sort of 'team-leader' that gets others to work together, but they get in each others way — and you harm them for the sake of accomplishing the project, without any other regard. When the others get upset, you have them 'programmed' ('implanted'), again in the name of the project or for the sake of the group. Later you become disillusioned to 'purposes', and start to work only for yourself (own gain). You want to overthrow society, but can't because the other 'robots' will destroy everyone. When your evil intentions (thoughts) are found out, they drag you before the 'computer-god', &tc.

Pyramid (loc.) — Detroit/Michigan.

"The Price of Agreement is obedience."
"To Survive is to depend on the obedience of others."

55. "TO PARTICIPATE" {merfolk}

  Note: potential errors in data.

Time — moon-swings above a mermaid on a rock at sea.
Space — undersea castle; luminescent fish swimming around.
Energy — ship crashing against the rocks.
Mass — heavy chest sinking in the water (mermaids struggling to pull it up, but fail).
God — giant statue of man with trident (half-exposed above the water).
Sex — causes fin-tail to split and develop legs.
Degradation — to have legs; confined to land.
Sympathy — displaying to others "what they've done to me."
Trouble — 'centaurs' (horse-men on ship).
You — 'mermaid'; your voice has 'magical powers' (amplified when singing with others).

Incident (track) — you participate in 7 significant group activities — such as singing, which compels 'human' sailors to crash on the rocks (and their stuff can be looted). Sometimes a ship has 'centaurs' (instead of 'humans') that can resist your voice (and they have magic of their own) and occasionally hunt you. You eventually have sex with a human, develop legs, and are cast out of 'merfolk' society. You then participate with other 'exiled mermaids' from on a shore, still sinking ships. The 'centaurs' finally catch you and take you before the 'god-statue', &tc.

Pyramid (loc.) — northeast Lemuria.

"The Price of Approval is self-degradation."
"To Survive is to depend on sympathy from others."

56. "TO EXPAND" {railroad engineer}

  Note: limited data available.

Time — railroad clock-tower over station.
Space — train shed.

Energy—locomotive in motion.
Mass—coaling-tower dumping tons of coal.
God—a patriotic old-man wearing a top-hat.
Trouble—female 'doll-bodies' that shoot beams from eyes.
You—'mouse-person'; engineer of a vast rail-system (competing with others).

Incident (track)—at the top you organize 7 great projects. Your railroads use red engines (and your competition uses green engines) and you strategically work to become the larger, more successful, rail-system. Downscale, your rail-system becomes too complex and you start committing harmful-acts. Everyone struggles to manage, the mice are worked to death, &tc.

Pyramid (loc.)—Philadelphia/Pennsylvania.

"The Price of Expansion is confusion."
"To Survive is to depend on the toil of others."

57. "TO JOIN" {cat people}

Time—sun-swings over post-modern 'cube' city.
Space—'cat-person' floating over an ocean.
Energy—a levitating 'cat-person'.
Mass—an iron chest that falls and crashes on the floor.
God—a voluptuous 'earth-mother' statue; many arms, holding many children, fed by many breasts.
Joining—sex.
Sex—'cat-people' are exhilarated about sex; have endless kids, but throw them out or kill them, until 'robots' enforce their care and feeding (which is painful for the body).
Trouble—'robots'.

Incident (track)—At the top, you have 7 wonderful 'joinings'; but when you have litters of children, you kill them or throw them out to starve. 'Robots' come and enforce you having to 'nurse' your children. You continue downscale, violating laws, killing children, betraying lovers, engaging in sexual abuses, fighting 'robots', &tc. Eventually, the 'robots' take you to the 'mother-goddess' statue, which divides you against yourself with a beam. This fragmentation causes you to age and become ugly so that no males will 'join' with you anymore. You jump off a building and find you can no longer 'levitate' and smash in to the ground. The 'robots' scrape up the pieces of the body and lock them in a drawer that is electronically sealed. They take you out to sea and throw you into the volcano-hell, &tc.

Pyramid (loc.) — Babylon/Baghdad.

"*The Price of Love is betrayal.*"
"*To Survive is to depend on the lusts of others.*"

58. "TO REPRODUCE" {insect invader}

Time — wristwatch worn by 'insect-body'.
Space — 'insect-invaders' swooping down on a valley.
Energy — 'gorilla-people' with laser-cannon blast a cliff (with 'insect-invaders' at the top of it).
Mass — spaceship sinking in the mud.
God — a giant stone-spider.
Trouble — 'gorilla-people'.

Incident (track) — at the start, you participate as part of an 'invader-force' against 7 different planets. You come down from orbit riding prone on a small torpedo-shaped object with handlebars. You have wings that can support you, but cause you to tire easily. The goal is to populate the whole of the universe with your species, injecting eggs into the natives (different body-types). Some of the more technologically advanced species object to being 'egg-victims'. They give you trouble (and eventually catch you). You come to realize that your whole life is a harmful act. The 'gorilla-people' burn off your wings and drop you in a volcano, &tc.

Pyramid (loc.) — Buenos Aires.

"*The Price of Expansion is starvation (detestation).*"
"*To Survive is to depend on the bodies of others.*"

59. "TO SATISFY" {cavemen}

Time — sun-shadows creeping across valley.
Space — looking down at valley from rocks.
Energy — 'caveman' bashing head of mammoth with a club.
Mass — a gigantic rock.
God — 'mammoth-god' statue.
Crush — arm sticking out from under the body of a mammoth.
Sensation (Satisfaction) — sex.
Trouble — 'elves'.
You — 'caveman'; you start as master of the land; hunt mammoths, kill bears, &tc.

Incident (track) — at the top, you successfully mate with 7 women, but each wants to keep you for themselves, and things begin deteriorating. One woman drives off the others. You decide you want to mate with one from another tribe, but she isn't interested in you — so you drag them off to your cave and break their legs so they can't get away. There are also 'elves' nearby. You chase them through caves and tunnels, catch 'elf-girls'; rape, *&tc*. But the 'elves' have magic and strike you with energy-bolts. They catch you and take you before the 'mammoth-god', who divides you against yourself. Now, no women want you, you can't catch animals, and 'elf-girls' throw rocks at you. Eventually, they roll a boulder onto you, and you die, *&tc*.

Pyramid (loc.) — France.

"The Price of Pleasure is sin."
"To Survive is to depend on pleasure from others."

60. "TO CARE (FOR)" {bird girl}

Time — 'bird-girl' on porch of tree-house looking at sunset.
Space — 'bird-girl' perched on large tree-branch overlooking giant trees of a forested valley.
Energy — 'bird-girl' flying fast up to the top of a cliff.
Mass — gigantic rock outcropping over valley (starting to crack off).
God — 'snake-god'; creature in a large bottle.
Trouble — 'snake-people'.
You — 'bird-girl'; you protect the forest; strangle trappers, *&tc*.

Incident (track) — you have 7 families of children (your own and other types of creatures, including 'dinosaurs'/'saurians'), which you take great pleasure in successfully caring for. Although they greatly love you, they all insist on fighting and hurting one another. You try to make everyone stop fighting, but they resent this. You interfere with the 'snake-people' that enslave others, cut down trees to build vast structures and other things you loathe. They hunt you. Downscale, you try to stop everyone from doing anything — and begin killing anything that moves (all "for good reasons"). You've become the ultimate oppressor, so that no one is able to live anymore. Toward the end, the 'snake-people' promise to stop fighting, but they betray you. Eventually all of the children hand you over to the 'snake-people', who take you before the 'snake-god,' *&tc*.

Pyramid (loc.) — Africa.

"The Price of Caring is grief."
"To Survive is to depend on the suffering of others."

61. "TO EXPERIENCE" {bear}

   Note: may read as *"To Feel"* or *"To Live."*
Time—sun-swings over snow-covered forest.
Space—a snowy mountain slope.
Difficult—'bear' trying to catch fish.
God—'forest-god' ('tree-man') statue.
Trouble—'fox-people' (hunters).
You—'bear'; animal (not 'bear-person').

Incident (track)—at the top, you are the master of all you survey, experiencing 7 wonderful feelings—climbing trees, scaring other animals, catching fish, having sex, eating honey, *&tc*. When it gets cold, you hibernate. Sometimes you get stung by bees. You start to mess things up in the forest, but you think it's a lot of fun. Hunters ('fox-people' with rifles) chase you. When you burn down part of the forest, you anger the 'forest-god'. He takes a spirit-form and catches you, takes you to his altar, and divides you, *&tc*. Now everything is terrible; you age; hunters kill you, skin you, and bury the bones. You can't get out of the grave until the 'devils' come; volcano-hell, *&tc*.

Pyramid (loc.)—Wisconsin.

"The Price of Sensation is pain."
"To Survive is to depend on others for sensation."

62. "TO REPLENISH" {a Sumerian}

Time—sunset in the desert.
Space—sitting on rocks looking at sand.
Energy—hurling a spear.
Mass—mountains in the distance.
Trouble—'spider-people'.
You—'Mesopotamian'; desert-dweller.

Incident (track)—you are sly and stealthy (like a 'thief' or 'rogue') and take what you want with great exhilaration. You complete 7 great successful thefts to replenish the tribe's coffers—such as finding and stealing a great treasure in the mountains. Downscale, you develop certain considerations about taking things from others, or using their energy, and you get tired. You happen upon a 'robot' base in the mountains and steal from them and get in trouble. Eventually, the 'spider-people' (the 'invaders' that own the 'robots') catch you and take you before their 'computer-god', who divides you against yourself. Now, you age rapidly and stagger about the mountains as an old-man, die, &tc.

Pyramid (loc.) — China.

"The Price of Motion is tiredness." Might read as "The Price of Strength is exhaustion."

"To Survive is to depend on others for sensation."

63. "TO EAT" {tiger}

Time — sun-swings over jungle.
Space — 'tiger' looking over the jungle.
Energy — 'tiger' leaping between rocks.
Mass — 'tiger' watching 'natives' struggle to lift a water-buffalo.
Motion — a large boulder rolls down a hill.
Food — a gray 'monkey' sitting in tall grass.
Eating — a 'tiger' biting a gray 'monkey'.
God — giant monkey-god statue.
Trouble — 'natives' (dark-skinned human).
Dizzy — stumbling around a water-hole.
Roar — brown 'tiger' roars at an 'elephant'.
You — 'tiger'; animal (not 'tiger-person').

Incident (track) — you're a 'tiger' in the jungle. You eat 7 monkeys and gain great strength and aliveness. Downscale, you have trouble with 'natives', 'elephants', 'rhinos', &tc. The 'natives' capture and cage you, then take you to their 'monkey-god', who divides you against yourself. Now you age, struggle, and starve. When you die, the 'natives' dance on your grave so you can't get out. Then 'demon-birds' come and carry you to the volcano, &tc.

Pyramid (loc.) — India.

"The Price of Energy is guilt."
"To Survive is to depend on the energy of others."

64. "TO ENDURE" {pyramid}

  Note: may read as "To Persist."
Time — sun-swings over 'pyramid with eye'.
Space — desert; a city in the distance.
Energy — beam coming out of 'pyramid'.

Mass—bricks that make up the 'pyramid'.
Danger—spaceship approaching 'pyramid'.
Trouble—an 'old-man' carrying a staff.
Hurt—sandstorm wearing away 'pyramid'.
Pain—beam from ship knocks off bricks.
Control—'eye of pyramid' shoots a beam into eye of person.
Influence—a beam from 'pyramid' blankets the city.
You—a stationary 'pyramid' (god-like, but immobile); one 'eye' on each side (each with a different function); your influence permeates the nearby city and the people worship you.

Incident (track)—at the start, you do 7 wondrous things to help the city, but you come to hypnotize rulers, play games with people, and use them like toys. There are other pyramids that you can intertwine energies with for sensation, but all feeling is quite numb—except the pain of deterioration which is worrisome. As parts of the 'pyramid' crumble, you hypnotize people to fix and rebuild it. When you find yourself in competition with another 'pyramid', the two of you start a 'civil war', hypnotizing people to fight against each other. Once you are successful getting the people to destroy the other 'pyramid', you realize that it is possible to die. A staff-carrying 'prophet' (that is immune to your hypnosis) calls down the 'sky gods' (giant humanoid spirits), which divide you against yourself. Now the people cease to worship you. You decay and are buried by the sand until you are eventually thrown into a volcano-hell, *&tc.*

Pyramid (loc.)—New York.

"*The Price of Endurance is to be weighed down.*"
"*To Survive is to depend on care from others.*"

A.T. MANUAL #5
ENTITIES & FRAGMENTS

Keep this reference material accessible:
PC Lesson-1 to 10; Processing-Levels 0 to 4.
PC Lesson-11, "Spiritual Implants"
PC Lesson-12, "Games & Universes"
PC Lesson-13, "Spiritual Energy"
PC Lesson-14, "Spiritual Machinery"
AT Manual #1, "The Secret of Universes"
AT Manual #2, "Games, Goals & Purposes"
AT Manual #3, "The Jewel of Knowledge"
AT Manual #4, "Implanted Universes"
AT Supplement, "Systemology Procedures"
AT Supplement, "Systemology Biofeedback"
AT Supplement, "Systemology Piloting"

LEVEL-8: "THE WIZARD GRADE"

Welcome to *Systemology Level-8*.

In this manual, we begin handling the *upper-level "Wizard Grade"* work of *defragmenting "spiritual entities and identity-fragments."* We have a very specific and *systematic* way of approaching this subject. A *Seeker* is advised not to mix or blend *other* beliefs and practices (for these topics) during this *training* and *processing*.

After a true successful completion of *"The Jewel; Parts #1-5" (AT#3)*, a *Seeker* no longer applies *processing-levels 0 to 4* to "defragment" their *own* case. [If more than a month has passed since completing the *Level-7 Stabilization Exercises (AT#3)*, it may be beneficial for a *Seeker* to repeat those exercises before starting *Level-8*.]

A *Seeker* does not use *A.T. Levels* to handle *fragmentation* that should have been treated earlier on *The Pathway*. Any specific *"imprinted"* area of concern—or where *attention* is *"fixed"* in this lifetime—that *can* be handled with *processing-levels 0 to 6*, must be treated prior to *Advanced Training*—most certainly before applying (or even studying) *Systemology Level-8*.

Assuming that all prerequisite *defragmentation* work is completed through *Level-7 (AT#3)*, a *Level-8 "Wizard"* should not be *running "imprint-chains"* on *themselves*. If it hasn't been completed, then the *Seeker* should have at least reached an *end-realization* with *"The Jewel,"* that they, themselves, are the ones keeping these *"chains"* in persistence, and holding them in place with *"attention units"* compulsively *"fixed"* outside their *actual Awareness* (or *Knowingness*).

At this point, simply *"Spotting"* areas of former *Not-Knowingness* is often enough to *defragment* them with *high-power attention-Awareness*. Understand that: knowingly *"Imagining"* (creating and destroying) *"mental imagery"* of the *past* for inspection, at will, is quite different than persistent *"imprinted imagery"* from those points on the *Backtrack* where parts of our *attention-Awareness* have been compulsively *"fixed"* or *"stuck."*

If a *Level-8 "Wizard"* still tries to *run "imprint-chains"* on themselves— even though a *Level-8* doesn't have any more of these *"fragmented chains"*—the *Wizard* will still *"find"* imprinting-chains to *process*. But this time, the *"imagery"* or *"content"* doesn't necessarily even make sense, because it is generally supplied by *other entities* (in close proximity to us); it is, in essence, *someone else's imprinting* that is being *"pulled-in"* as our own. As a *Seeker* knows—from studying *"source-points," "cause,"* and *"creation"*—we cannot effectively *defragment* something *"As-It-Is,"* when it is *"mis-owned"* or *"misidentified."*

There are some *"spiritual perception"* exercises from *processing-levels 0 to 4* that may still be applied to *Self*. However, those that pertain specifically to *"imprinting"*—or *"confronting-the-past"* by *"incident-chains"*—should no longer be applied at *Level-8*. The *exception* here is: unless they are *directed to an entity other than Self* (and even then, they are usually only *run* for *Circuit-1*).

By *"defragmenting spiritual entities...,"* we mean very literally: a *Level-8 "Wizard"* (acting as *Co-Pilot*), directing *defragmentation processing* to other *entities (as Seekers)* in order to *release them*. In this wise, our philosophy differs from other approaches. At *Level-8*, the directive is: *freeing entities from ourselves*, rather than *freeing ourselves from them*. This is to say: *releasing them* from their *entrapped fragmented* state, rather than the idea of *ridding* ourselves of them.

The handling of *spiritual entities and fragments* is a critical part of the *"Wizard"* work. While a *Seeker* may have *defragmented* their own case to a point of *Self-Honesty*, they are still operating (on *Earth* and in the *Human Condition*) in close proximity to heavily *fragmented low-Awareness entities*, *identity-fragments* and other *"spiritual machinery."* Hence, this is where we place our emphasis at *Systemology Level-8*.

Study all material in *A.T. Manual #5 ("Entities & Fragments")* several times before applying any of its procedures. There are several techniques and methods provided in the text. A *Seeker* should be familiar with *all* of them before proceeding with any application. They are each *systematically* applied for a specific purpose, or in a specific sequence, to handle any layers of *spiritual "Alpha" fragmentation* that remain from previous *processing-levels*.

Having now introduced this new *gradient level* of work, let us take up this subject from the top...

SPIRITUAL FRAGMENTATION

As an *Alpha-Spirit*, you are capable of *being* in many places at once. The *Alpha-Spirit* is able to operate *from* many places at once—because, of course, our *actual Beingness* is not actually "located" anywhere. It can, however, *consider* that *"parts"* or *"units"* of its *attention* (or *Awareness*) *are* located somewhere in sometime. Earlier *processing-levels* included exercises to aid in *unfolding* such *realizations*.

By "located," we mean systematically: wherever an individual places their *attention*, wherever they *perceive* from, wherever *intention* is *projected*, whatever *point-of-view* they are *operating* from, is where an individual is *located*. Maintaining multiple located viewpoints simultaneously is something that an *Alpha-Spirit* can do *knowingly—at will*. This natural ability—innate to all *Alpha-Spirits*—has simply been *fragmented* to one's own detriment.

Fragmentation occurs when we allow our *attention* to get *entrapped* in specific *"locations"*—then afterward burying our *knowingness* of it; intentionally *"Not-Knowing"* it, instead of either *knowingly operating from* it, or properly *withdrawing attention-units from* it. By this point on the *Pathway*, a *Seeker* should be increasingly *aware* that there are "hidden" or "compartmented" *fragments* of *Self* that continue to *unknowingly operate* (on *automatic*).

We are actually putting out "bits" of ourselves, our *thoughts* and *attention*—our *Awareness*, so to speak—all the time. We *"project"* this into the *Physical Universe* in order to perceive *impressions*, which allow us to *create* (or *duplicate*) appropriate imagery and sensation for our own experience. This is how we *perceive* "walls" and *interact* "or communicate" with others that share in the *Game* of this *Universe*. We *create* and *dissipate* these "bits" of *Awareness* (or "ZU") at will, simply by focusing *intention* and *attention*.

We *descended* as *spiritual beings*—through many *Universes*—and the decline of our *actualized Awareness* is proportional to the amount of *spiritual fragmentation* that has occurred. As a *spiritual being* "decays," they begin to "abandon" things, rather than "dissolving" them; this leaves many "bits" of themselves behind—*"unconscious"* but persistently running on *automatic*.

Earlier *processing-levels* will have allowed a *Seeker* to regain control over some of these *"split-pieces."* A littl was regained, for example, when we have extended our *Awareness* on the *Backtrack* and *"spotted"* or *"confronted"* something that we had formerly left some part of our *attention* on. Another critical area, *"spiritual machinery,"* is introduced in *PC Lesson-14*; but we only scraped the surface when treating such *"fragments."*

LOCATIONAL PROCEDURE

This *process* was developed specifically for *"split-fragments"*—but it also applies to other *entities*, which is why we introduce it first. Since it applies to both *"fragments"* and *"entities,"* a *Seeker* doesn't have to be too concerned whether they are treating a *"split-off"* piece of themselves or *"*something else.*"*

A *"split-off"* piece of an individual is not a *"separate being"* (or actual *"entity"*), but it can *"act"* as though it is. It is really a *"part"* of themselves—usually sent off somewhere, hidden, and otherwise kept *operating unknowingly*. These *"fragments"* can be *aware*, in the sense that they *perceive*, *record*, and *react* to what is happening (based on *computations*)—but they are not *aware* of their own *"thinkingness."*

One of the challenges originally faced with this work concerns the fact that we, as individual *Alpha-Spirits*, have been *split-off* and *divided* many times—been *spiritually fragmented* over and over again. *Systematically* speaking: a *Seeker* cannot usually reclaim a *"*piece*"* of themselves directly, *if* both *"it"* and *"you"* have been *fragmented* further (subsequent to the original point of *division*). [The figure here is for illustrative purposes only.]

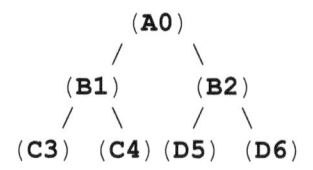

```
              (A0)
             /    \
         (B1)      (B2)
         /  \      /  \
      (C3) (C4) (D5) (D6)
```

In this example: if (C3) is the *conscious viewpoint (Seeker)*, and it locates the presence of (D6) and tries to "rejoin" that part directly (using other procedures), the *Seeker* will be unsuccessful (and potentially feel "ill"). This is because such *"bypasses" missing "fragments"* that are essentially *"in between."* The *"Locational Procedure"* resolves this issue for *our own "spiritual fragments"* (on which other techniques are unworkable).

The *in-session procedure* is rather simple:

> If you *get a sense of* (or *spot*) something that might be a *split-off* part of yourself, an *isolated* (*compartmented*) *fragment* of something (or someone), or an *entity* (or some *identity-fragment*) that is blocked from (or blocking) your *Awareness*—then you *direct to "it"* the *processing command-line* (PCL):
>
> *"Point To The Being That You Divided From."*

This is an important technique for a *Seeker* to "fall back on"—as a remedy or *"repair action"*—if any difficulties arise when applying other material from this manual. [It is also effective on *fragments* of *others* that are "stuck" on *us*; so you don't have to know the exact nature of *what* you are applying it to.]

The *"pointing"* is really a *direction* of *attention*—or *"spotting"* with *Awareness*. It is a "mental action" and is not limited to *three-dimensions* or a *Physical Universe "direction."* It is not even *"pointing"* toward (or *"spotting"*) where the *"other being"* is *now*; rather it focuses *attention* on the original *"direction"* where the *"split"* occurred. [If some remnant seems to remain thereafter, a *Seeker* may then apply the *"Identity Procedure"* directly to it (as given later).]

The PCL (above) is also beneficial for handling *entities* (*self-aware spiritual beings* or *Alpha-Spirits*), which includes the *Seeker* themselves. One will notice (if the PCL is applied directly to *Self*) that *you* do not "dissolve" or "rejoin" someone else. A separate individual *entity* (*Alpha-Spirit*) gets a better sense of *Self*, or who they are. However, when treating a *fragment*, it dissolves the separation. A *fragment* has no reason to remain separate, unlike the case of an actual individual *Alpha-Spirit*.

"Split-off pieces" and *"spiritual fragments"* (of ourselves or others) are different from individual *entities*. An *Alpha-Spirit* can also *"divide"* into two completely separate *entities*. In other words, both parts will have the complete prior *Backtrack* of the other; neither is senior. There is no loss of *spiritual ability*; both are identical—and both have identical memory of *being* the *original* that *divided*. Such results in two completely separate individual evolving spiritual beings that will never "rejoin" because each is now a full *Alpha-Spirit*.

In *Meta-Systemology*, it is theorized that approximately only *10,000* individual *Alpha-Spirits* separated from the *"Infinity-of-Nothingness"* at one time and went through the original *Jewel* incident into this particular *"womb of existence"* (prior to *Home Universe*). [Ref: AT#1 & 3.] These individuals eventually *divided* many times, leading to the *trillions* that now inhabit *this Physical Universe*.

True individual *Alpha-Spirits* do not "rejoin"—because such would reduce the *infinitude of creation* that is balancing the *Infinity-of-Nothingness*. *"Fragments"* on the other hand, whether your own or someone else's, are not separate units of *"Self-Awareness."* These *fragments can* "rejoin"—and usually with great benefit, by restoring *Awareness* to areas that the *Alpha-Spirit* was handling *unknowingly* (and can now treat *knowingly*).

A *Seeker* should *not* make the mistake of thinking that *they* (*themselves*) are a subordinate piece of some kind of bigger *"Uber-Alpha"* or *"oversoul."* There *are "upper-level compartments of ourselves"* that *operate unknowingly*, or that we are typically blocked from being *aware* of directly; but that is not a separate *entity*—it is the *"higher parts"* of our *Self*, which we "unfold" an increasing conscious *Awareness* of, as we *Ascend*.

There is also some *"splitting"* (of *Awareness*) that occurs naturally. For example: you put "bits" of yourself on people and places (*terminals*)—using *intention* and *attention*—that you want to keep track of, or influence. Since these are not *"enforced"* by anyone, they can simply be brought under conscious control. There's nothing that inhibits you from dissolving (or controlling) these "pieces" except your own worries over being able to put them back, or losing track of things.

A *Seeker* can actually master consciously dissolving these *"splits"* and putting them back out. All that is necessary is to practice *"projecting"* and *"dissolving"* these *"split-pieces"* at will. Once a *Seeker* has certainty on this ability, they will be able to let go of the ones that aren't wanted. Part of their *compulsive persistence* is the lack of *certainty* on this skill—because there is a natural tendency to form these "connections" to others people (and *terminals*) in order to stay in the *Game* of *this Physical Universe*.

The *"splitting"* of *attention*—or our *projecting* "pieces"—is not the actual *fragmentation*. The *fragmentation* occurs when a *"split"* takes place without one's conscious control (or *Awareness*), and also when one loses control and *Awareness* over the *pieces* that have already *split*. This is what takes place under the heavy spiritual impact of *Implanting*.

FRAGMENTS & BONDED-ENTITIES

When we refer to *"entities"* in *Systemology*, we usually mean other individual disembodied *Alpha-Spirits* (without ownership and control of their own *"Human Body"*). We introduce this subject at *Level-8*, after a *Seeker* has a handle on their own case from previous levels. *Entities* (and *fragments, &tc.*) are not a primary source of *fragmentation*; at best, they might "block" *Awareness*, or amplify our own *fragmentation*.

The *entities* we are most concerned with at this point are those which are adhesively attached to *you* or your *Human Body*. These *Bonded-Entities* has been with the *Alpha-Spirit* for a long time. They generally remain *stuck* in a *low-Awareness level* that is tied to *misemotional states* such as: anger, resentment, anxiety, terror/fear, depression, and hopelessness. They seem to be most "active" when an individual is also operating at those levels, which tends to contribute to such states persisting.

But understand that if you're "angry" (for example), it is *your* "anger" — it does not stem from an *entity* or some kind of *demon*. However, just as a living person might "fan the flames" to encourage a greater *dramatization* of your anger, so too with *entities*, or even *fragments* of yourself. While these *fragments* mainly operate on *automatic*, they still respond to what you are "feeling" and other "reactivity." As a *Seeker* increases their *actualized Awareness*, they can operate greater control over these *"mechanisms"* and other areas.

[If at any point, "something" gets restimulated or stirred up by reading the descriptions and instructions in this manual, apply the *Locational Procedure* to "it."]

A *Seeker* will recall a common theme of *"being divided"* in the *Implant Penalty Universes* (IPU) described in *A.T. Manual #4*. Whether this *actually* occurred to the *Alpha-Spirit* during those *incidents*, or were only *represented* in one's virtual/holographic experience of them, is still under research. But, in either case: the concepts present in the IPU all become reoccurring themes for *actual* events in later (more recent) *Universes*.

There are many ways in which a division or *"split"* might occur. When one is "divided against themselves," they make an individual be in two places, and then might *Implant* each location with different *goals* that are "antagonistic" to each other. This will cause each *viewpoint* to essentially *fight against* the other one—continuously applying *counter-efforts* against each other. A *"splitting"* could also take place if an individual were impacted heavily with *force*.

There have been large-scale mass-*Implanting Incidents* that forced an individual to put *"pieces"* of themselves onto *others*, in order to *control* them and *keep* them *"human."* Similarly, there have been "advanced" societies that employed *"Police Implants"*—which caused you to make "split-pieces" into "Control Entities" that were placed on "criminals." [Some of these societies made all citizens do this regularly as part of their civic duty or taxation.]

There is information on the *Backtrack* about specialized "collectives." In their advanced military campaigns, officers would put *"split-off pieces"* as "Control Entities" onto their subordinates—all the way down the chain-of-command—so that an *"invasion force"* could operate as a single "unit" under the command of a single *Alpha-Spirit* (at the top).

In the *"wizarding"* societies of the *Magic Universe*, "entities" were often the high-value *"coin"* or *currency*. They were often used as servants or laborers—or even entrapped in *"objects"* to make "magical devices." One of the reasons the *Human Condition* is susceptible to "Bonded-Entities" is because of the accumulated *postulates* and *considerations* regarding the *"acquiring"* of *entities* for some kind of use.

And while we have introduced the subject of *"spiritual machinery"* in earlier *processing-levels* (see *PC-14*), the subject will be treated more thoroughly in this manual. But briefly stated: we have, at times, intentionally put out *pieces* to set up *"machinery"* (in various *non-physical directions*) in order to project the *reality* we *perceive* for ourselves. This too, eventually became fragmented and out of our conscious control as a result of the heavy impacts from certain *Implanting-Incidents*.

In *processing-levels 0 to 6*, the "Seeker" themselves is the main focus or target of *processing-sessions*. Of course, on the *Pathway* toward *Ascension*, a *Seeker* is actually treating a "composite case" of:

Self + Human Body + Bonded-Entitites

The fundamental *processing-levels* ensure that an individual—the *Seeker* —ceases in compulsively "mucking up" things for themselves. In this wise, a clear view is available for handling everything that is apart from us; that keeps us entrapped in *this Physical Universe, the Human Condition,* and *on Earth.*

Once a strong foundation is in place—a *Seeker* has reached stable *Beta-Defragmentation* with *processing-levels 0 to 6*—and the more significant *turbulent charge* is *defragmented* from the *Implanting* described in *Level-7,* no further *imprinting* must be *processed-out* on the individual's *own case.*

Using those procedures *on Self,* from *Level-8* onward will have a tendency to "pull-in" the *imprinting* and *fragmentation* of other *entities* that hang suspended in "close proximity" to us—such as *Bonded-Entities.* There are ways of applying earlier *processes* directly *to entities* in order to *intentionally* make these *entities* accessible for proper handling; but a *Seeker* must *knowingly* be doing so to be successful. Otherwise, the risks associated with this phenomenon is a *misidentification* of *source/cause*—which results in persistence of the *fragmentation* that is not handled *As-It-Is.*

It is possible, even after *processing-levels 0 to 7,* that a *Seeker* still experiences some *fixation* on specific *"reoccurring items"* or *turbulently charged* "areas" that did not seem to fully *"release"* or *defragment.* Assuming previous *levels* were fully completed, it is likely—at *Level-8*—that such *charge* persists due to the *"protest"* (*restimulation*) of a *Bonded-Entity* or B.E. We want to, however, make certain that we are not treating something *as someone else's,* which is really *our own* (and the other way around).

At this high-level of operation, a *"Wizard's"* primary *processing-action* is now *"Spotting As-It-Is; and Defragmentation by Awareness."* This requires the ability to properly *recognize* a true *identification* of *"Source"* and *"What Is,"* &tc., which a *Seeker* will have strongly developed along the *Pathway.* This is applied directly in *systematic processing* with the *"Identification Procedure"* (given below)—which is effective whether handling a *Bonded-Entity,* a *split-fragment (spiritual machinery),* or even the *genetic-vehicle (Body)* that is also an *entity.*

THE IDENTIFICATION PROCEDURE

This technique is incredibly basic, though its actual application and background requires additional explanation. Its origins are as old as there have been *Wizards* attempting to exercise control over other *entities*.

> Once you *locate (get a sense of, &tc.)* a *being, entity,* or *fragment,* you *direct* to "*it*" the following *process*—which includes two *steps* (or PCL):
> A. "What Are You?"
> B. "Who Are You?"

Use of this technique requires knowing the difference between something being "*in-phase*" versus "*out-of-phase.*" There is some mention of *personality-phases* in past *Systemology* literature, but what we really mean is *Identity-phases* or *Identity-phasing*.

By "*phase*," we mean: *being* something other than *who* and *what* you are (an *Alpha-Spirit*), but *mistakenly* operating from that *viewpoint* or *point-of-view* (POV) as though it is your *actual Identity* (*compulsively* and/or *unknowingly*). This is what people mean by the phrase "lose themselves"—which is to say "*out-of-synch*" with *Truth* or *Self-Honesty*. [Use of the term "*phase*" comes from *electrical-wave engineering*, but its application here is *systematically* accurate.]

Fundamentals of this procedure do not require a lot of technical complexity. The first step is understanding that you are in close proximity to other *entities* (*Alpha-Spirits*) that have not shared the full benefit of the same *processing* that has delivered *you* to this point on the *Pathway*. Therefore, the same type of personal *fragmentation* treated at *processing-levels 0 to 4*, which once held up a *Seeker*, could also be what is keeping an *entity* from "*releasing*"—but in this case, we would direct such *defragmentation processing* to the *entity*.

When we speak of *Identities* and *phases*, we are *systematically* referring to the "*conception and/or perception of one's own Beingness.*" *Bonded-Entities* can become *fixated* on any *Identity-phase*, just as any other *Alpha-Spirit* can. The *Identity-phase* that an *entity* may be in, is not restricted to "an individual person"; it is not restricted to a "*body*" or even traditional terminals. Of course, one's true and actual nature is *Self*—the *(Alpha)-Spirit*.

An *entity* may be *identifying (out-of-phase)* with anything: a role, a name, a significance, a word (or phrase), a group, a body part, or really any material object—from molecules to planets. It may also have been *Implanted* with a *goal*, which is to say a *"doingness"* that it *identifies* with even more than a *"Beingness"*—such as *"a goal to block (you),"* or of *"being a barrier,"* &tc.

In many ways, the *Identification Procedure* is a *"listing-process"* for an *entity*. You may need to get multiple answers for the *"What..?"* PCL until you can determine what they are currently *being*. It is important to *"acknowledge"* any of the answers/responses/impressions that are perceived/received (just as in *Traditional Piloting/Co-Piloting*). A familiarity with *Systemology Piloting* is necessary for *systematically processing entities*.

Initially, this procedure is best practiced by writing out the question on your worksheet, then listing out the answers—preferably using *GSR-Meter "reads"* as an *indicator* of the *"most correct"* answer.

Just as with *Co-Piloting* any other *Seeker*, it is important not to *"invalidate"* any response; but you can *process* an *entity* toward a *release-point* by getting it *"in phase."* When using the procedure, whether you are freeing an individual *Alpha-Spirit*, or you are returning a *fragment* to its *source*, you are unburdening yourself from carrying the *fragmentation*, and increasing the *Awareness* of other *Alpha-Spirits* in the *Universe*.

Once they *recognize* that they are not the *"phase-item,"* you direct the *"Who..?"* PCL with the intention that they will answer *"Me"* or *"I'm Me"* (from the perspective of the *entity*). This is meant to restore their *Awareness* that they are nothing else but simply themselves. The *entity* will often *release* after you *acknowledge* the correct answer—as if it finally realizes: *"Oh, I really am me!"*

If the answer you get is not *"Me,"* you still *acknowledge* the response, but you will probably have to repeat the PCL. It may also require some basic *two-way communication* with the *entity* in order to steer them toward the *"Me"*-type answer. For example:

"What were you before that?"

This shifts the *entity's attention* to an earlier point on their *Backtrack*. Effectiveness of the *Identification Procedure* is dependent on resolving misconceptions about *Identity* that the *entity (fragment, &tc.)* is fixated on.

BONDED-ENTITIES & FUSED-GROUPS

There are two main aspects of instruction for this subject that are alternated throughout this manual: a) the understanding of *Bonded-Entities* and *Fused-Groups* in order to recognize, locate, and contact them; b) the *systematic methods* by which these *entities* can be released by a "*Wizard-level*" practitioner. It may be the case at times that many *entities* are "showing up" for *defragmentation processing*; and a true "*Wizard*" must handle them orderly, civilly, respectfully, lovingly, firmly, ...*systematically*.

Presence of *Bonded-Entities* (or "B.E.") will block or inhibit the clarity and horsepower of our *spiritual perception* (*ZU-Vision, &tc.*)—yet most are not malevolent themselves, they are just sort of *low-Awareness beings* "in the way." It might be helpful to think of "*layers*" (or *sheets*) of interconnected 1-cm. (half-inch) *marbles* or *beads* that surround the *body* (like a tight skin-suit) and even penetrate it. These sheets, although mainly transparent and resembling the structure of modern *bubble-wrap*, "stack up" as *layers*, often extending out approximately three-feet from the *body*.

The *Seeker* should practice being able to *focus, concentrate,* and *concenter* (permeate from all directions), their own "*attention*" to a *spot* that is 1-centimeter (or half-inch)—the approximate area that an *entity* is perceived to relatively occupy as a *viewpoint-for-Awareness* in Space. A *Seeker* would have some practice in this area from the "*objective exercises*" found in former *processing-levels*. This is an important skill for *communicating with* (*processing*) a single specific *entity*. A *Level-8* practitioner has a high-level of *Awareness*, but still must limit *attention* to one *entity* at a time until its *release*.

In addition to individual B.E., there is another phenomenon that occurs, which we refer to as a "*Fused-Group*." These "*groups*" consist of multiple B.E. that are held (or *fused*) together by a shared traumatic, heavily fragmentary, experience—usually a heavy *Implanting-Incident*. By processing-out the *fusing incident*, a *Fused-Group* may be *dispersed, released* as a whole, or at least broken up into individual B.E. for *release*.

Fused-Groups "formation" and B.E. "adhesion" often results from heavy *impacts*—such as with at least one significant *Implanting-Incident* we know of that took place in *this Physical Universe*. When an *entity* (Alpha-

Spirit) forcefully collides (*impacts*) with another *entity*, either (or both) may get so heavily *imprinted* with a *"mental image picture"* of the *impact* that it gets its *consideration-of-Beingness* "stuck" or "fused"—*out-of-phase* —to the *imprint* and the other *entity* that shares the *imprint*.

While an *Alpha-Spirit (Seeker)* operates with a *Human Body*, it acts as a *filter* and *magnifier* for an individual's *perception* and experience of *reality*. True *spiritual perception* (*ZU-Vision* and other innate *Alpha* abilities) is far more accessible to an individual after clearing all *identifications* with bodies that are not *Self*. This includes handling B.E. (and *Fused-Groups*), because once they are fixated on their *identification* with the *Human Body*, they form an *encysted* solidity and *crystallized* "shell" or "aura" that acts to hold an individual (*Seeker*) *in* the *Human Condition*.

Some B.E. are intentionally *implanted* to be part of a *body* (a specific *body-part* or *spot* on a *body*)—which is *out-of-phase* with their *being* an *Alpha-Spirit* or *fragment*, *&tc*. Operating in this wise, most *entities* believe they are serving a specific purpose, going so far as to think they are being helpful, or even necessary.

A B.E. (or *Fused-Group*) is not really *aware* of their *presence* in *"present-time"*—their *attention/Awareness* being very much *fixed* on a *past incident*. In order to *release* an *entity*, it may be necessary to *process them* to a point of *confronting that incident*. This is accomplished *systematically* with the *Level-8 "Incident-Running Procedure (for Entities)"* given in the next section.

Due to the proximity of B.E. and *fragments*, there is a *"telepathic link"* by which *contact/communication* is possible (for *processing*). This *link* is knowingly (consciously) accessible to a *Seeker/Wizard* at *Level-8*, given the nature of study and heightened *Awareness* already achieved on the *Pathway*. This manual concerns *defragmenting* one's own *composite-case* (B.E., *fragments*, *&tc.*) and is not an esoteric treatment concerning other types of "*spirits*." The information and skill required to handle other kinds of *spiritualism* is generally acquired by a *Wizard* through the experience of handling what *is* accessible (and affecting their own case).

When a B.E. *defragments/releases* (usually upon *"acknowledgment"* of its proper *Identity*-answer, or some other *process*), the "*telepathic*" link, cord, or *bond*, also disperses. At the moment this takes place, a moment of *"exterior perception"* is sometimes *fed back* to the *Seeker*, but from the *view point* of the *entity*. To be sure the *entity* "*happily blows off,*" this occasional phenomenon should not be *invalidated*; but it should not be mistaken as one's own *ZU-Vision*. [Of course, increase of one's *spiritual perception* is a natural side-effect to *releasing* the *Alpha-fragmentation* that persists in blocking our *clarity*.]

During *processing-levels 0 to 7*, we don't generally handle much concerning *somatic-pings* or *bodily sensations* that "turn on" during *systematic sessions*. They might be *acknowledged*, but generally "turn off" when the *process* is *run* to a full *defragmentation-point*.

At *Level-8*—when treating *entities* and *incidents*—*sensations* and *pressures* felt from the *body* are more critical. If they occur while handling a *process*, record exactly *where* on the *body* they occur. Use this to data as a suggestion for where to focus your 1-cm. (half-inch) beam of *attention* during your next *process*. When applying *Level-8*, it is likely to be a B.E. coming "awake" or "active" and essentially saying: "*Here I am!*" [It is important not to just *pass-by* or *fly-by* such *indicators* at this *level*.]

When this does occur, it is important to *acknowledge* the *somatic-ping* and make a record (to return to later). You can even tell the *entity*: "*I hear you there, but you'll have to wait your turn.*" It is also important not to prematurely *end-off* the handling of a *current entity* until its *release*.

The standard practice is to check for any other *entities* at the same location you were just handling, to be sure it wasn't a *Fused-Group* or if another B.E. moved in to duplicate its position. Then, if the former *somatic-ping* persists (that occurred while working with the other), you can check for an *entity* at *that* location. It is good practice to work with different areas of the body each session, rather than checking over the same parts consecutively. Extend your *Awareness* or *perception* to areas from different sides or angles.

In addition to *somatic-pings* (*pressure, pain, sensations*), B.E. and *Fused-Groups* may communicate by relaying *emotion* (*feelings*), an *audible voice* (*perceived internally*), or some type of "*thought*" or "*imagery.*" Contacting (*communicating*) with) B.E. for *processing* can also be accomplished directly with even the most faint of *perceived impressions*, if a *Seeker* is proficient with a *GSR-Meter/biofeedback device* (which is the preferred *systematic method* of handling this area/subject). If a "*Wizard*" can focus their *attention-Awareness* specifically on the *energetic-mass* of one *entity*, then that B.E. will *react/register* "answers" on a *Meter* (just like any *Seeker*).

Advisement: there could easily be *over 100 Fused-Groups* and individual *Bonded-Entities* adhesively fixed to a *Seeker*. If you find *zero*, or only a few, it is quite possible that you are not yet at a "level" to *confront Level-8* work. Make certain all your fundamentals (*processing-levels 0 to 6*) "check out" okay. If you are certain that your own handling of "*The Jewel (Parts #1-5)*" is properly *defragmented* (from *AT#3*), run "*Platforms #1-18*" (again) from that manual. Additional details regarding "*Platforms #1-18*" also appears in this manual.

Let's start with a basic exercise to increase your *spiritual perception* for *handling entities*.

1. *Close your eyes*.
2. "*Imagine*" (*create by visualization*) a B.E. as a sort of "*circle of energy*" or "*pressure*."
3. *Acknowledge it* (for being there).
4. "*Imagine/Intend*" for the B.E. to *release*—leaving and disappearing into the distance (as a result of your *recognizing* and *acknowledging* it).

Repeat this exercise many times, "*imagining/creating*" these in various locations: in precise *points* in the *body*, in precise *spots-in-space* around you, in the *walls*, *floor*, and *ceiling*, &tc. Continue until you feel good about this exercise and your certainty in doing it. Then run the "*Standard Procedure (for Entities)*" and see if there are any more accessible now.

A *Seeker* should be able to notice the slight difference between the "feel" (or "sense of") the *actual* B.E. versus those they have intentionally *imagined/created*. There are times (at *Level-8*) where a *Seeker* will think they've *Spotted* (or *sensed*) a real one, when they're really *imagining/creating* it there. But that's okay.

If you *release* a few "*imagined*" ones from an area, it will be easier to handle the real ones anyways. They even sometimes "*copy the imagery*" of you *releasing* the *imagined* ones and will leave along with it. Once you have *certainty* with the *systematic processing* of *entities*—and have elevated your own *Actualized Awareness*—most types of *entities* and *fragments* can be *dispersed* by simply "*acknowledging*" them and "*defrag-by-Awareness*" (*As-It-Is*).

INCIDENT-RUNNING PROCEDURE
(*for bonded-entities, fused-groups*)

[A *Seeker* should review "*Confronting the Past*" (*PC-9*), "*Spiritual Implants*" (*PC-11*) and "*Games & Universes*" (*PC-12*). Keep these materials accessible—in addition to "*Secret of Universes*" (*AT#1*) and "*The Jewel of Knowledge*" (*AT#3*)—when applying the "*Incident-Running Procedure (for Entities)*."]

Unlike when a *Seeker* has *run incidents* and *incident-chains* for previous levels—such as in "*Confronting the Past*" (*PC-9*)—we only use *Implanting-Incidents* for which we have significant data, when handling *entities*. This means that we do *not* have to find out "what happened" from each *entity* in order to *defragment* them.

When applying *processing* to *entities*: we don't need to go through every detail of an *incident*, or *implant-item* of a *Platform*; simply get the *entity* to *spot* the main highlights. In this wise, we can very pointedly direct a PCL to an *entity* to "*Go To..*" or "*Move To..*" such-and-such part of an *incident sequence*.

To be effective, the *Seeker/Wizard* must maintain control of the *session*, just like a *Pilot*—directing PCL to B.E. in order to "guide" their *attention* through the *sequence* of the *incident*; directing them to *spot* various points from a "*sequence outline*" that is already known to the *Seeker/Wizard*. As you gain experience with handling this procedure, you'll have greater certainty on your ability to *telepathically* "blanket" and "push" an *entity* through the *incident* they are "stuck" in. [This serves to *release* them so they can *leave/blow-off.*]

When starting *Level-8*, there are two primary *Implanting-Incidents* that a *Seeker* first applies this procedure to. A *Seeker* has actually been studying the components of these in previous *processing-levels*.

— The Heaven Incident (at the start of our *track* in *this Universe*);
  and
— The Hellfire Incident (which occurred 66 or 75 million years ago).

HEAVEN & HELLFIRE

The "*Hellfire Incident*" used for this "*Incident-Running Procedure*" does not need to be *processed* by a *Seeker* "on *Self*." Its appearance here is specifically for handling *Earth-bound entities* (B.E. and *Fused-Groups*) that are commonly affected by this particular *Implanting-Incident*. It assists in "breaking up" (or *dispersing*) *Fused-Groups* into individual B.E., freeing them up for additional individualized *processing* (through the "*Heaven Incident*").

Applying the "*Hellfire Incident*" only treats a certain *layer* or segment of *entities* that were actually affected (or *fused*) by this *incident*, or are still "stuck" on it; but we apply this as a basic method because of the amount of gain that is achieved with it. It is not the only mass (widespread) *Implanting-Incident* that this general procedure applies to. [The "*Hellfire Incident*" is a specialized application that does not appear in the basic instructions for "*Standard Procedure: Entities*" (given in the next section).]

The "*Heaven Incident*" is the only *incident* that is *common to all entities* (*Alpha-Spirits*) that have experienced *Entry-Into-This-Universe*; but *only* an individual B.E. can be *released* by using it for this procedure. Therefore, the "*Hellfire Incident*" is *processed first*, in order to break up "*groups*" that were *fused* by that *incident* (before *running* individual *entities* through the "*Heaven Incident*").

When the "*Hellfire Incident*" is applied to *handling entities*: you start with "1. The Explosion," and *never* push the B.E. (or *Fused-Group*) beyond "2B. Platforms #1-18" in the *sequence outline*. To go further requires having full data on the "*36-Day Implant*" (that uses IPU symbols). There is not enough *data* to do so and still be in full control of the *session*. And it is not necessary for this procedure. If the B.E. hasn't *released* by that point, then you may need to *run* the *incident* a second time (starting with *The Explosion*). But, that may be unnecessary, because this much of the *incident sequence* is usually sufficient enough to disperse a *Fused-Group*—in which case, if *entities* remain, you can then take each *individual* B.E. through the "*Heaven Incident*" (and/or apply "*Standard Procedure*").

Usually only the "*1. Heaven Implant*" section of the "*Heaven Incident*" is necessary for this procedure; and even a vague approximation of its events is effective. One of the issues with running "*The Jewel, Parts #1-5*" is that the same *Implant-Pattern* was later (more recently) repeated in the "*Hellfire Incident*" sequence. If a *Seeker/Wizard* finds they *do* need to direct an *entity* to "*Spot*" (or "*Go To..*") specific parts of *The Jewel Implant* in order to *release* them, it is important to make sure that the *Pattern* is being treated for the right *incident*.

There is additional data for the *Hellfire Incident*, much of which is *speculative* at this juncture of our research. Since the data for the basic "*sequence outline*" is correct (effective), we haven't concerned ourselves with the other details that may be accessible. Whether or not the *incident* took place on *Earth*, or was all an elaborate "*projection*," does not alter its demonstrable workability and effectiveness in breaking through the *Fused-Groups* of B.E. that are "stuck" on whatever this *Implanting-Incident* happens to really be. In *Systemology*, we are more concerned with *results*, than *dogma*—so we include the *incident* for the gains it provides.

What we do know is that the *atomic blasts*, *meteors* and *volcanism* indicated by the *Hellfire Incident* is a direct reference to what some refer to as "*The Great Dying*"—a cataclysmic period of synchronous events that *did* take place on *Earth*. Although some geologists and physicists date this event at approximately *66 million years ago*, the elevated *radiation* levels of the *incident* may have actually caused the *carbon-dating* to be skewed on this one. When using *GSR-Metering*, the *incident* may be "*located and dated*" (as in it "*registers*") at *75 million years ago*.

The *Hellfire Incident* was an intentionally planned event. It occurred in order to establish *Earth* as a "*prison planet*" for this *galaxy*—and also program the basic "*Human Condition*" for the *Alpha-Spirits* entrapped here. The *Earth* was actually a beautiful planet inhabited by diverse lifeforms; but like everything else in *this Universe*, it became *fragmented*—now re-purposed to serve as a dumping ground for *entities* that were otherwise too numerous, or too free, to be adequately controlled (by whatever society did the *implanting*).

More advanced societies in *this Universe* have something akin to "*Implant Dealers*." The *Implants* that appear in the *Hellfire Incident* are not original to that *incident*; but they were collected, chained together, and were effectively impactful. "*The Jewel (Parts #1-5)*" are repeated from the *Heaven Incident*, to install a false sense of the *Hellfire Incident* being the "*start of time*." The "*#1-18 Series*" was primarily kept on file since the *Magic Universe* era (and even prior). Restimulation of the *Implanted Penalty-Universes* extends back several *Universes*. It is only important to *run through* the "items" on the *sequence outline*; you do not have to *run* all *command-lines* of all *Platforms* on each *entity* when applying this *"Incident-Running Procedure."*

HEAVEN INCIDENT

0. ENTRY-INTO-UNIVERSE
1. HEAVEN IMPLANT *(See PC-12 & AT#1)*
   A.) Loud Sharp Snapping Crackles
   B.) Waves Of Light
   C.) Theater & Stage
   D.) Angel On Chariot Enters
   E.) Trumpet Blasts
   F.) Thundering Crackles and Snaps
   G.) Angel On Chariot Exits
   H.) "Goals-Sequencing" Pageant/Skit
   I.) Waves of Darkness
2. THE JEWEL (PARTS #1-5)
   (See AT#3 for additional details)

HELLFIRE INCIDENT

0. CAPTURE/TRANSPORT
    (if Alpha-Spirit is not already on Earth)
1. EXPLOSION
    A.) Atomic, Volcanic, Meteor, &tc.
        (specific events and locations)
    B.) Terrible Winds
    C.) Alpha-Spirit Carried Into Sky
    D.) Electronic Field/Screen Rises In Sky
    E.) Alpha-Spirit Stuck To Screen
    F.) Pulled Down For Mass-Implanting
2. HELLFIRE IMPLANT
    A.) The Jewel, Parts #1-5 *(for this incident)*
        Establishes false "Start-of-Time"
    B.) Platforms #1-18 Series *(see AT#3)*
        Programming of "Human Condition"
    C.) Arrival Of "The Pilot"
    D.) 36-Days Of IPU-Restimulation
        Holographic moving pictures (like film)
        (lacking data here; see AT#4)
3. ASSEMBLY CENTERS
    (may belong above as "1G")
    A.) Fusion Of Entities Into Groups
        (at specific locations)

HELLFIRE INC. (ADDITIONAL DATA)

This section is included to increase a *Seeker's reality* on, and ability to effectively handle, the *Hellfire Incident-Running Procedure*. Our research phase demonstrated that it is an area—or point on this *Advanced Training* course—that some *Seeker's* seemed to get "stuck" on, which prevented continuing their studies/progress.

Although there are many *Implanting-Incidents* on the *Backtrack*, this one is included in this manual because it is *"spiritual contamination"* (or *fragmentation*) that is *"common to all"* Earthlings. While this seems like it should make our *Standard Procedures* more effective, many of the B.E. from this *incident* are initially found in an incredibly *low-Awareness state*, and often need a lot of assistance (*Beingness* or *livingness* granted to them by the *"Wizard"*) in order to achieve their *release*.

In the past, "Mystics" often used various *tools* and *spiritual-aids* to accomplish their *"divination"* and *"necromancy."* Today, we have the benefit of using *Biofeedback-Devices* that allow us to approach these same areas far more *systematically*.

B.E. are located by *"Meter-read,"* checking off from the following list (in the order given): the location of a *current somatic-ping* (*pressure, itching, tingling, &tc.*); the location of a *between-session* discomfort; the location of a *Fused-Group* (from a previous *session* that is not fully handled); and general "scanning" or "looking around" the *body*.

Some B.E. require a greater *reality* on the *incident* they are "stuck" in before they are able to *confront* it *"As-It-Is."* This means, what we generally refer to as, *"dating and locating."* Remember that the *Hellfire Incident* is the kind of event that an individual might even *want* to *forget*. So, the first part of *"incident-running"* might require more than the *processing-command* to just *"Go to...{start of incident}."*

We can easily determine the date as *"75 Million Years Ago."* [This may be indicated to the B.E./*Fused-Group*.] *"Locating"* the incident on the *Backtrack* as a *"date"* (in *Time*) does not always provide enough *reality* for the B.E. to properly *confront* it. Therefore, a *Seeker* may also need to *"locate"* the *incident "in Space"*—which means determining a literal/physical *geographic location*.

> In the past, *"Mystics"* often used *"maps"* combined with such things as *"pendulums"* and *"dowsing-rods"* to accomplish these same *spiritual tasks*. Today's *"Wizard"* benefits strongly from using *"Biofeedback-Technology."*

To be in *contact* with an *entity*, a *"Wizard"* focuses high-level *attention* on the *entity*—realizing *"It-Is"* there, *acknowledging* its *existence*, &tc. This grants a higher-level of *Beingness* or *livingness* to the *entity*—and between the two *beings*, there is a heightened *"combined-Awareness"* present for the *session*.

The *attention* and *proximity/affinity* (*telepathic link*) allow the *entity* to *"register"* on a *GSR-Meter*, even though it is the *Seeker/Wizard* (having first *defragmented* the bulk of their own *case*) that is physically using the *Biofeedback-Device*. This idea might underlie any assumed effectiveness of such *spiritual-aids* as the *"ouija board"*—but again, we now have far more effective *systematic* means available to us today.

Therefore, with your *attention* on the *entity*, and a *combined-Awareness* on the *incident*: you can use a *GSR-Meter* "sensor" (in one hand), and your finger or pointer (with the other hand), and *scan* over a "map" of the *Earth* to find "Meter-reads" on actual *locations*. [This applies to more than just *running* the *Hellfire Incident*.]

Note that the continental arrangement of *Earth* was far different 75 million years ago than it is today. You can "print out" (or otherwise obtain) *geologic estimations* of how the *Earth* appeared at that time, or you can use a modern-day *map*.

Our interest—when specifically handling the *Hellfire Incident*—is the location of the *"explosion site."* For this particular *incident*, it does not have to be exact; the *locations* can be approximated. We also aren't too concerned with whether the nature of that particular *explosion* was "atomic/nuclear," "meteoric," or "volcanic." The only time that may be critical data is if a *"Fused-Group"* isn't easily *dispersing*. But, in that case, it is far more *systematically effective* to *locate* (on the *map*) the *"assembly center"* where they were *fused*.

Another key to *releasing* B.E. from a heavily impactful *incident* is to *defragment* any significant specific *protest-charge* that may be *holding* their *attention* on the *incident*. This is *processed-out* just like STEP-B of the

"Standard Procedure: PME–Long Version" (described later in this manual). In this case, however, the type of *fragmented-charge* will not be on *"going interior,"* but another type of specific *resistive-effort* (or *counter-effort*) applied in the incident. [The basic method is *"Spotting"* the *correct item*, and *defrag-by-Awareness "As-It-Is."*] This may be assessed from the following list:

"In This Incident, Is There An Effort..."
1. *To Stop?*
2. *To Withdraw?*
3. *To (Both) Stop And Withdraw?*
4. *Suppress Something?*
5. *Invalidate Something?*
6. *Protest About Something?*
7. *Hold Onto A Picture (Of The Incident)?*
8. *Hurry Or Rush?*
9. *To Make Something "Not Be"?*

STANDARD PROCEDURE: ENTITIES

We have already introduced the three primary techniques used for this *Standard Procedure for Entities (Fragments, &tc.)*:

1. *Locational*
2. *Identification*
3. *Heaven Incident*

These may be worked forwards and backwards (*1-2-3-2-1-2-3..*) until a B.E. (or *Fragment, Split &tc.) releases.*

Combining what you've learned in this manual, let's add some additional introductory guidelines so you can put this into practice. Here are some basic steps to get you started.

   A. Close your eyes and *"look"* over the *Body* and the space around the *Body* (the "shell" could extend three feet or more). You are *"looking"* for areas or spots that seem to have "pressure" or some "energetic-mass."

B. *"Get the sense"* of contacting or permeating the *"entity"* that is generating the *"pressure"* (or *"mass"*).

C. Apply the *"Locational Technique"* (using information given previously in this manual). If you still sense that the presence remains, continue to STEP-D.

D. Apply the *"Identification Technique"* (using information given previously in this manual).

  D1. Ask them *"What Are You?"* and sort of *"feel"* for an answer coming back from them. You may just get a subtle *"idea"* or *"impression"* of what they are *"being."* You might have to *"infuse"* them with a bit of life—or *"enliven"* them directly with your *Awareness of them being there*; *"granting"* them a bit more *"Beingness"*—in order to *"draw out"* a response. [This is simply done by focused and directed *intention*.]

  D2. Ask them *"Who Are You?"* and, if necessary, steer them toward the *"Me"* answer. *Acknowledge* any responses; but the *release* generally occurs only when the *"Me"* answer is *acknowledged*. Repeat STEP-D2 until you get the *"Me"*-release. If the *entity* releases (leaves/blows-off), continue to STEP-E; if the *entity* does not *release*, go to STEP-F.

E. Check for *"Copies."* Sometimes another *entity* will immediately *create* a *"Copy"* of the one that just left, or even assume its *phase* themselves. If you get a sense of this happening, *spot* that others are *copying*; then *project* (or *intend*) an *acknowledgment* to them for doing that. This usually gets them to stop; then you can *defragment/dissolve* the *"Copy"* by *Awareness/Spotting* and/or apply the *"Locational Technique"* to it.

F. Check for *"Holders."* Sometimes another *entity* will attempt to "hold onto" the one that is *releasing*. If you get a sense of this happening, *Spot* that it *Is*, and *acknowledge* the other *entity* for doing that. When the first one *releases*, you can then shift your *attention* to handling the *"Holder."* If the *entity* you are attempting to release is not being "held" by another *entity*, continue to STEP-G.

  NOTE: You can shift *attention* to handle a *"Holder"* as your next *entity* to *defragment*. This is not standard practice for *"Copiers"* — unless it is a *single entity* for certain, and not a *group*; because these *entities* really like to *create "Copies"* (it is the basic skill of an *Alpha-Spirit*) and you can quickly become overwhelmed trying to handle too many *Copiers* and *Copies* at once.

G. If you run into trouble with the previous steps, are not getting any answers/responses, or otherwise are unable to get an *entity* to *release*, then apply the *"Incident-Running Technique"* specifically on the *Heaven Incident* (relying on the *sequence outline* provided in this manual, in addition to your own experience with the *incident*). Gently "push" the *entity* through the *incident*.

H. If at any time, while performing these techniques, you find your attention being drawn to anything that you get the sense of being a *"piece"* of yourself, apply the *"Locational Technique"* to it.

Communication between the *Seeker* and *entity* occurs on a *"telepathic link."* In most cases, the procedural PCL can be "intended" or "projected" to the *entity* silently. The *"Identification Technique"* works best as a written exercise. There are some practitioners that have reached the level of freely *processing entities* out loud—but when first starting out, *silent intention* works best for *focusing* on a *single* B.E., so as not to stir up others.

A *Seeker/Wizard* should handle *entities* as various "layers" become *accessible* during *upper-level* work. The in-session handling of *entities* may be accomplished in between treating other areas and developing *spiritual perception* (such as *A.T. Manual #6*). *Entities* become more *accessible* the longer a *Seeker* works with their *Advanced Training*. It is important to not become too obsessive about directly "searching for" or trying to "locate" *entities*; because if you "push" or "intend" too hard in a certain spot, you will frequently find yourself forcing a B.E. to occupy that location.

Self-Honesty is critical for *upper-grade* work. At *Level-8*, the insistence, expectancy, or demand of a *Wizard* that "something" *is* "there" will put "something" "there."

As you know, *Alpha-Spirits* are not *actually* "located" in any *space-time* "location" or position. An individual is not *actually* "within" the *Universe* that they are operating their *Awareness* from, but unfortunately, the *Human Condition* tends to be confined or restricted to such *considerations-of-Beingness*. However, this also applies to other *entities* (B.E., &tc.) that you encounter. They are only located by their own *consideration*; and since they are highly suggestible and you are now more *Actualized*, they can also be located by *your considerations*.

Let's examine an example of this. For training purposes: there is an *out-of-phase* B.E. that is compulsively occupying a *bookshelf*—"being a bookshelf," "being in a bookshelf," &tc. You "touch" or "contact" the *entity* and it gets the *realization* that it's not there (and never *actually* was, except as a *consideration*) and it *"releases"* and ceases to be there.

This phenomenon occurs so quickly that you keep *trying to locate* them— and since you can *actually* "reach" your *Awareness* anywhere in *space-time* (and in *any Universe*), you can still "reach" the *entity*, and the effect is essentially relocating them back. This not only falsely *locates* the *entity* in *space-time* again, but also *invalidates* their previous *realization/release*. If this happens, all a *Seeker/Wizard* needs to do is rehabilitate the *release* by *"Spotting"* the instance that the *location was enforced*, then *release* the *entity* again (if it remains).

In this wise, a *Seeker* should beware *"pulling-in"* or even *"creating"* *entities to be run on processing*. This is a real phenomenon that takes place, which is why *"Entities & Fragments"* is only treated at *Level-8*. After handling of *entities* has begun, the danger comes from "blaming things" on *entities* when/if they are not the direct cause. This is the same as saying or thinking *something is there* when it isn't. This also means potentially *creating "things" to be there* that are *misidentified* as *something else;* which makes *defragmenting* it *"As-It-Is"* quite difficult later.

An individual's *inabilities* and *fragmentation* are still part of one's own case—one's own *considerations, reality-agreements* and *postulates*. This *fragmentation* can certainly be made worse, *amplified* by the presence of B.E., but they are not the ultimate "reason why" of our problems. There are other parts of *Level-8* that focus more directly on a *Seeker's* own *spiritual perception;* don't make the mistake of thinking that all *Alpha-fragmentation* and *perceived spiritual ability barriers* are being imposed exclusively from the "outside."

"PLATFORMS #1-18" (AT#3 ADDENDUM)

A *Seeker's* own *run* of *"#1-18"* helps break up solid blocks of *fused-entities* (and may even *release* some directly). The true purpose of *running* it at *Level-8* is to make *entities* *"available"* or *"accessible"* for *processing*. Additionally, it is a primary component of the *"Hellfire Incident"* (appearing in the *sequence* of *Implants* that were applied during that *incident*). *Implants* "#1-18" originally appeared individually at various times on the *Back-*

track, but were also eventually employed as part of heavy mass (widespread) *Implanting-Incidents*.

[The following is additional data for the "#1-18" series given in *AT#3*.]

PLATFORM #1X

The *Platform* given in *AT#3* provides a long-form using "{electric-shock}" as the *implanting-gimmick*. This is actually only one of *twelve* different "{feelings}" that this *Platform-pattern* was used for. *Run* the entire *pattern* completely on each of the following in sequence:

    1. *Pleasure*; 2. *Pain*; 3. *Heat*; 4. *Cold*; 5. *Electric-Shock*; 6. *Numbness*; 7. *Sensation*; 8. *Dizziness*; 9. *Pressure*; 10. *Suction (vacuum)*; 11. *Flash (explosion)*; 12. *Blackness*.

PLATFORM #3X

The *Platform* given in *AT#3* provides a long-form using "SURVIVE" as the reoccurring *item*. This is actually only one of *ten* different reoccurring "{implant-items}" that this *Platform-pattern* was used for. *Run* the entire *pattern* completely on each of the following in sequence:

    1. *Obey*; 2. *Rebel*; 3. *Work*; 4. *Be Lazy*; 5. *Love*; 6. *Hate*; 7. *Survive*; 8. *Die*; 9. *Create*; 10. *Destroy*.

PLATFORM #14X

The *Platform* given in *AT#3* provides a long-form using "PICTURE MACHINE" as the reoccurring *item*. This is actually only one of *seven* different "{machine terminals}" that this *Platform-pattern* was used for. *Run* the entire *pattern* completely on each of the following in sequence:

    1. *Postulating Machine*; 2. *Picture Machine*; 3. *Thinkingness Machine*; 4. *Somatic (or Sensation) Machine*; 5. *Reality Machine*; 6. *Confusion Machine* ; 7. *Forgettingness Machine*.

PLATFORM #16B

This *Platform* is *not* given in *AT#3*. It is a short-form formula. *Run* the entire *pattern* completely on each of the following *terminals* in sequence:

    1. *Treasure*; 2. *Wealth*; 3. *Love*; 4. *Knowledge*; 5. *Pleasure*; 6. *Bodies*; 7. *Glory*; 8. *Honor*; 9. *Identity*; 10. *Immortality*.

16B.0.0   STAY. *& Spot the Alpha*
16B.1.1x SEEK ___. *& Spot the Alpha*
16B.1.2x DO NOT SEEK ___. *& Spot the Alpha*
16B.1.3x ABANDON ___. *& Spot the Alpha*
16B.1.4x DO NOT ABANDON ___. *& Spot the Alpha*
16B.2.1x DISCOVER ___. *& Spot the Alpha*
16B.2.2x DO NOT DISCOVER ___. *& Spot the Alpha*
16B.2.3x OVERLOOK ___. *& Spot the Alpha*
16B.2.4x DO NOT OVERLOOK ___. *& Spot the Alpha*
16B.3.1x FIND ___. *& Spot the Alpha*
16B.3.2x DO NOT FIND ___. *& Spot the Alpha*
16B.3.3x MISS ___. *& Spot the Alpha*
16B.3.4x DO NOT MISS ___. *& Spot the Alpha*
16B.4.1x GRAB ___. *& Spot the Alpha*
16B.4.2x DO NOT GRAB ___. *& Spot the Alpha*
16B.4.3x DISCARD ___. *& Spot the Alpha*
16B.4.4x DO NOT DISCARD ___. *& Spot the Alpha*
16B.5.1x CLUTCH ___. *& Spot the Alpha*
16B.5.2x DO NOT CLUTCH ___. *& Spot the Alpha*
16B.5.3x RELEASE ___. *& Spot the Alpha*
16B.5.4x DO NOT RELEASE ___. *& Spot the Alpha*
16B.6.1x OBTAIN ___. *& Spot the Alpha*
16B.6.2x DO NOT OBTAIN ___. *& Spot the Alpha*
16B.6.3x DISDAIN ___. *& Spot the Alpha*
16B.6.4x DO NOT DISDAIN ___. *& Spot the Alpha*
16B.7.1x TAKE ___. *& Spot the Alpha*
16B.7.2x DO NOT TAKE ___. *& Spot the Alpha*
16B.7.3x GIVE ___. *& Spot the Alpha*
16B.7.4x DO NOT GIVE ___. *& Spot the Alpha*
16B.8.1x HAVE ___. *& Spot the Alpha*
16B.8.2x DO NOT HAVE ___. *& Spot the Alpha*
16B.8.3x GIVE UP ___. *& Spot the Alpha*
16B.8.4x DO NOT GIVE UP ___. *& Spot the Alpha*
16B.9.1x SAVE ___. *& Spot the Alpha*
16B.9.2x DO NOT SAVE ___. *& Spot the Alpha*
16B.9.3x WASTE ___. *& Spot the Alpha*
16B.9.4x DO NOT WASTE ___. *& Spot the Alpha*
16B.10.1x PRESERVE ___. *& Spot the Alpha*
16B.10.2x DO NOT PRESERVE ___. *& Spot the Alpha*

16B.10.3x DESTROY ___. & *Spot the Alpha*
16B.10.4x DO NOT DESTROY ___. & *Spot the Alpha*
16B.11.1x GUARD ___. & *Spot the Alpha*
16B.11.2x DO NOT GUARD ___. & *Spot the Alpha*
16B.11.3x NEGLECT ___. & *Spot the Alpha*
16B.11.4x DO NOT NEGLECT ___. & *Spot the Alpha*
16B.12.1x SAFEGUARD ___. & *Spot the Alpha*
16B.12.2x DO NOT SAFEGUARD ___. & *Spot the Alpha*
16B.12.3x RISK ___. & *Spot the Alpha*
16B.12.4x DO NOT RISK ___. & *Spot the Alpha*
16B.13.1x PROTECT ___. & *Spot the Alpha*
16B.13.2x DO NOT PROTECT ___. & *Spot the Alpha*
16B.13.3x ENDANGER ___. & *Spot the Alpha*
16B.13.4x DO NOT ENDANGER ___. & *Spot the Alpha*
16B.14.1x EXHIBIT ___. & *Spot the Alpha*
16B.14.2x DO NOT EXHIBIT ___. & *Spot the Alpha*
16B.14.3x HIDE ___. & *Spot the Alpha*
16B.14.4x DO NOT HIDE ___. & *Spot the Alpha*
16B.15.1x OWN ___. & *Spot the Alpha*
16B.15.2x DO NOT OWN ___. & *Spot the Alpha*
16B.15.3x DISOWN ___. & *Spot the Alpha*
16B.15.4x DO NOT DISOWN ___. & *Spot the Alpha*
16B.16.1x WIN ___. & *Spot the Alpha*
16B.16.2x DO NOT WIN ___. & *Spot the Alpha*
16B.16.3x LOSE ___. & *Spot the Alpha*
16B.16.4x DO NOT LOSE ___. & *Spot the Alpha*
16B.17.1x BUY ___. & *Spot the Alpha*
16B.17.2x DO NOT BUY ___. & *Spot the Alpha*
16B.17.3x SELL ___. & *Spot the Alpha*
16B.17.4x DO NOT SELL ___. & *Spot the Alpha*
16B.18.1x STEAL ___. & *Spot the Alpha*
16B.18.2x DO NOT STEAL ___. & *Spot the Alpha*
16B.18.3x REJECT ___. & *Spot the Alpha*
16B.18.4x DO NOT REJECT ___. & *Spot the Alpha*
16B.19.1x GATHER ___. & *Spot the Alpha*
16B.19.2x DO NOT GATHER ___. & *Spot the Alpha*
16B.19.3x SEPARATE ___. & *Spot the Alpha*
16B.19.4x DO NOT SEPARATE ___. & *Spot the Alpha*
16B.20.1x REMEMBER ___. & *Spot the Alpha*

16B.20.2X **DO NOT REMEMBER** ___. *& Spot the Alpha*
16B.20.3X **FORGET** ___. *& Spot the Alpha*
16B.20.4X **DO NOT FORGET** ___. *& Spot the Alpha*
 16B.21.0 **GO AWAY.** *& Spot the Alpha*

PROGRAMMED MACHINE-ENTITIES (PME)

"Spiritual Machinery" is introduced in *PC Lesson-14*. Now that we have discussed *entities* at *Level-8*, we can extend our reach further in this area. *"Simple (or Light) Machinery"* — that is directly *created* as as a *machine* or *response-circuit mechanism* — is relatively easy to *defragment*. A Seeker simply applies *"creativeness processes"* (*imagining copies, alteration of copies,* and the *creation* and *destruction* of *copies*, *&tc.*) or even the *"Standard Procedure (for Entities)"* on *Light Machinery*.

There is also more advanced *"machinery"* that consists of a *systematic series* of *programmed postulates* — or *"circuitry"* — that *creates/manifests* something, or causes something to occur. This *programming* can become quite complex — similar to *programs* and *operating systems* for *personal computers*, except that they range all the way up to the level of *creating* and *managing* entire *Universes*.

This *"programmed machine-circuitry"* can actually be quite useful, and is only mildly *fragmentary* in itself. One primary liability to their *creation* is that an *Alpha-Spirit* could set one to run forever, forget about it, and subsequently lose *responsibility* and *control* for its *creation*.

Later (more recently) on the *Backtrack*, these forgotten *machines* also get "infested" by B.E. that *copy* them, and *fragment* their operation, *&tc*. This, again, can all be handled with *Standard Procedures* and even methods given for earlier *processing-levels*.

Early on the *Backtrack*, an *Alpha-Spirit* would "imprint" the *programming* onto some kind of *template* or *platform*. [This will be off in some separate (extra-dimensional) *Space* that you've *created* for it.] You would knowingly "activate" or "trigger" the *machinery* by *reaching* back and *projecting* a bit of *intention* (or *energy* in more recent *Universes*) on a communication-line (*focused attention*) toward that *template*.

Also, early on the *Backtrack, Alpha-Spirits* had the ability to more easily and *knowingly* "erase" each other's *machinery*. Of course, we could just *create* it again—but this led to a tendency toward making multiple *copies* of *templates* and "stacking" them behind various "levels" of *alteration* (*postulates of "It-As-Changed"*) in order to make getting at (or *destroying*) the basic *structural template* of the *machine* more difficult for others.

By the era of the *"Symbols Universe"* (*see AT#1*), the decline of *Spiritual Awareness* resulted in too many *considerations* of *inability* (*Alpha-fragmentation*) to keep all of one's *machinery* "manifested" (in the face of persistent opposition). The solution to this was to *create* a new type of *machinery* that could *persist*. This led to the idea of *making beings (spirits)* into *machines*, *implanting* them to keep the *machinery created*. But, *Alpha-Spirits* were still fairly powerful *beings* during the *Symbols Universe* era, and they wouldn't stay in that *phase of Beingness* forever.

At some point, the *being* would just basically say *"To hell with this,"* and *release* itself.

Programmed Machine-Entities (or "PME") currently in existence primarily stem from the *Magic Universe*. During that era, "entities" were essentially the high-value money—such as with *"magic rings"* or *"relics."* But there are also some *entities* that were *crafted/made* into PME during *this Universe*. And by this, we mean *Alpha-Spirits* (and *fragments*) made into *"machine cores"* (resembling tiny *black crystalline cylinders*), which follow a series of *pre-programmed postulates* (or *"circuitry"*) laid out on a *"machine template."* PME are not operating on their own *postulates*; so don't hate on them too much (and handle them civilly).

"Implant Dealers" (from technologically advanced civilizations) are the primary manufacturers of PME in *this Universe*. This means they also serve as *"spirit collectors."* For example: after a mass (widespread) *Implant*—such as the *Hellfire Incident*—there are a lot of *fragmented pieces* of *beings* basically lying around. These are then *collected* and made into PME. The existing PME and B.E. *fragments* could also be *re-purposed*.

More recently on the *Backtrack*, one of the more modern types of PME is the *"Virus."* These are not simple *organic lifeforms*, or like other forms of *biological decay*; they were all intentionally *created*. They are usually used against enemy populations, but they are also unleashed on *"prison planets"* to suppress its inhabitants. Most of the current *viruses* on *Earth* were implanted here in the last *6,000* to *12,000 years* in order to keep the growing population of *"inmates"* under greater control (and reduce the *Human lifespan*).

A *"splitter mechanism"* is often *encoded* in PME programming. This is *systematically* referred to as a *"Split-Viewpoint"* or *"SV-Mechanism."* We are legally not permitted to even suggest using *Systemology* to attempt to *"cure"* any *viruses*—but for illustrative purposes: if you were to *process* a *virus* as a PME, you would actually find thousands of PME in the *body*. *Processing* a single one might *release* it, but it is immediately replaced by whichever is the original one, splitting again, and then reappearing in that location.

Many older PME types also have this *"replacement-quality"*—and you would have to work through a few *layers* of *templates* to approach the original. Some B.E. will do this, too—which can sometimes make the *entity-handling* portion of *Level-8* seem endless.

Similar to the *"Locational Procedure"* for B.E., the ultimate undercut-PCL for PME is:

"Spot Being Made Into A Machine."

Ever since its introduction during the *Symbols Universe* era, PME *construction* typically occurs within a long *cylinder*. It resembles the shape of the *"machine core"* that the *entity* is made into. The *"surface walls"* of the *cylinder* were covered in *holographic imagery* of IPU-terminals. The *entity* would typically have a low-level of *"confront"* on at least some of these *images*—so an increased *resistance* to *"touching the walls"* develops.

Where the *entity* would have otherwise been able to pass through the material-surface of the *cylinder*, a *reactive-withdraw* (or *"attention flinch"*) tendency is being *conditioned*. As layers of *holographic imagery* increasingly compounded, the *cylinder* is made to appear as though it were *"shrinking,"* and as a *reactive-effect*, the *entity* would also *"squeeze"* its own *considerations-of-Beingness* tighter and tighter. This is also how *"high-pressure"* Group-Fusing Incidents are accomplished, for which the entry-point is: *"(Spot) The Cylinder."* The event just prior to this: you will find them being *entrapped* or *captured* in some manner.

In addition to *"Viruses,"* another PME that has appeared more recently on *Earth* in the last few thousand years is the *"Wraith."* Although these *machines* don't really have *Human-language* names, we use the word

"Wraith" to describe an "energy-draining machine-entity." These are semi-mobile; they do not attach permanently to the *Alpha-Spirit*, but once they get into a *body*, they tend to remain with it until it dies (unless they are *systematically released*).

The *"Wraith"* makes one feel *tired* and *weak*. It is possible they were originally released to accelerate *"aging"* on *Earth*. Most individuals accumulate (pick up) at least a few every year, so it makes sense that there is at least some connection. Once in the body, they are *single points* that tend to "pull in" *energy* rather than emanate it, so they are not always easy to "see." They can also move around a bit, a zig-zag within a small area, but once you can focus your *attention* on them (and track them a bit), they tend to settle down. They are easy to *release*.

There are certain types of *"mobile-machines"* that are heavily *imprinted* with *low-Awareness* misemotion, such as: *fatigue, laziness, hopelessness, apathy, &tc.* These types of *machines* tend to drift in, hang around for a while, and then move off to somewhere else. Sometimes they get stuck to your other *machinery* and can linger around an *Alpha-Spirit* for a few lifetimes. They are often perceived as *vague colored-spheres*.

"Monitors" or *"Watchers"* (they may give a *Meter-read* on either title) are another commonly encountered PME. They are attached to both *Alpha-Spirits* and *bodies* in order to "keep an eye" on them. A *Seeker* will likely be carrying a few from as far back as the *Magic Universe*.

The *"Monitor/Watchers"* try hard to keep hidden and simply *"watch"* (*"monitor"*). They are usually perceived "over the head" or "behind the back." Many of them are reporting to old empires and forces that don't even exist anymore and so they aren't generally troublesome. But some of them report to the more recent *"invader-forces"* about such things as your *Ascension-work* in *Systemology*, or if you successfully demonstrate the ability to *"break the game"* by *levitating an object*, or something like that.

There is also *machinery* that tries to hide other *machinery* and even inhibit or block your handling or *processing* of *machinery*. Remember that we all have a lot of *Implanting* ("Platforms #1-18") that attempt to prevent us from *dispersing, blowing,* or *defragmenting* all types of *machinery*.

There are even instances where we have each contributed a *"split-frag-*

ment" of ourselves to a *machine* that is *installed* on someone else. There are many reasons this may have happened (civic duty, price of a magic spell, *&tc.*). There are *"splitter implants"* embedded in all 64 IPU. Most of this can simply be *Spotted* and *defragmented-by-Awareness*. [Handling *"split-viewpoints"* directly really requires a separate procedure.]

Because you are apply a *GSR-Meter* on behalf of an *entity*, anything that involves assessing IPU *for them* can be difficult if you, yourself, still have a lot of *fragmented charge* on those *terminals*. For this reason, the material from *A.T.*

Manual #4 ("*Implanted Universes*") should be *defragmented* before handling too much *systematic processing* on *machinery*. The IPU reflect a more *fragmentary* part of your own personal case than all of the *machinery* that has since been accumulated.

STANDARD PROCEDURE: PME

Unlike B.E. (previously), the PME are not always so easy to "wake up" and *defragment*. They have *considered* themselves *to be machinery* for a very long time. There are really two different versions of this procedure: a *long* and a *short*.

- The *long version* treats the entire cycle of their *entrapment* in detail, and *releases* them on a simple gradient. It does, however, require a lot of *session-time* to *run*. A *Seeker* should start with this to get familiarity with all the parts of the procedure.
- Effectively applying the *short version* simply requires having a much higher-level of *Actualized Awareness*—sufficient to grant or imbue the PME with enough *Beingness* (*livingness, &tc.*) to "*Spot*" a couple of key things, without having to treat the other stuff on the *long version*.

Sometimes you can find the PME directly. Most of the time you just handle the *"machinery"*—which consists of the PME, the *programmed-template*, various *imprints* and *circuitry*, and usually other B.E. and *Fused-Groups*. You simply *run* the *Standard Procedure* on the whole *machine*. Most of it will *defragment* within a few steps, which leaves the *"machine core"* that you handle by completing the procedure.

Sometimes *"remnants"* will remain—where the *"core" releases*, but a *Seeker* discovers a few days later the whole thing is apparently *created* again. You can check for a *remnant-machine-core* after the *main-core* blows-off, and continue *processing* it if it gives a *GSR-Meter* "*read.*" [This is an "*advanced systematic GSR-Biofeedback metering procedure.*"]

LONG VERSION

A. *Locate the PME.*

Locate the PME, or the *machinery* containing the PME. [The basic method is to "*focus attention*" and get "*Meter-reads*" where something *Is*, and wherever *fragmented charge* is present.] If a *machine*, check for a *Meter-read* on: "PME (?)"—because there may just be *light machinery*, which only requires B.E. procedures. If it's quite obvious to you that there is a "more basic original" *behind* what you've located, then shift your *attention* to that one.

B. *Defragment protest on "going interior."*

This is a *GSR-Meter* assessment on a list of *keywords/buttons* (similar to what is introduced in *PC Lesson-10*). PME (and *complex-machinery*) almost always have some *fragmented charge* related to at least one of these areas. The one that "*reads*" strongest is the *primary charge*. You also note and acknowledge when there are smaller "*reads*" on something. [The basic method is "*Spotting*" the *correct item*, and *defrag-by-Awareness* "*As-It-Is.*"]

PME *fragmentation* on "*going interior*" may be related to *incidents* prior to being made into a *machine*; but generally *that is* the greatest *protest* (for these areas) on their *Backtrack*. In rare cases, the "*reading*" charge may be "*On*" instead of "*In*"; but this is only the case for a few PME built up in multiple layers, and the following list should suffice for most applications.

1. *Want To Go In*
2. *Can't Get In*
3. *Kicked Out (Of Spaces)*
4. *Can't Go In*
5. *Being Trapped*
6. *Forced In*
7. *Pulled In*
8. *Pushed In*
9. *Made To Go In*
10. *Made Into A Machine*

C. {optional} *Date when they went into the body.*

This is really only useful toward *defragmenting* mobile PME (*e.g.* a *Virus*) that went in relatively recently. For other *machinery* that was built, installed in you (or attached to your *beingness*) long ago, and has remained ever since: this is more of a *research action*. ["*Dates*" are determined by narrowing down a fixed time period using *Meter-reads*.]

D. *"Spot Being Made Into A Machine."*

Have them *Spot* being *made into a machine*. [If necessary, "*Date*" and "*Locate*" it with the *GSR-Meter*.] The basic method for this is to first check "*which Universe*" it occurred in: "*This One (?); Magic Universe (?); Earlier Universe (?).*" You can also apply the "*locational*" method of having them "*point to where...*"

More recent PME were in a mass (widespread) *Implanting-Incident* prior to experiencing the *machine-building*. You can have them *Spot* this (even "*date*" and "*locate*") and *Spot* the prior instance of "*capture*"—or whatever was the "*beginning*" of the *incident*. You may have to take some of the *charge* off of the *incident* that occurred prior to the *machine-building* in order to get the PME to confront the actual *machine-incident*.

[Only work with this step long enough to get the *machine* to start coming apart or loosening up—freeing *attention* from its *fixation* on *solidity*. Eventually a "*Wizard*" will be at a point where enough *Beingness* can be enlivened in the PME for it to directly "*Spot*" such things as "*being made into a machine*" with enough high-level *attention* that it will simply *defrag-by-Awareness*.]

E. *"Spot The First (Earliest) Time You Were Made Into A Machine."*

This means finding the most basic (earliest) *incident* of being made into a *machine*. In every case researched, the *incident* was found in the *Symbols Universe*. It nearly always predates the current *machinery* they are "*being*." This means that PME (and their *remnants/fragments*) have had a long history of *being a machine* of some type.

This data may not be accessible to the PME—and if so, it is likely too entangled with other *entities* and unknown factors to be properly "*dated and located*" with *Meter-reads*. The other possibility is that there are "*harmful-acts*" connected to this area, which is inhibiting their *ability-to-confront*. So, as an alternative to this step (as given), you can run the PCL: "*In The Symbols Universe, Spot Making Others Into Machines.*"

F. *"Spot Being Captured (Before Being Made Into a Machine)."*

In our original version of this procedure, it was suggested to use a list of *IPU-traps* as an assessment action, in an attempt to *systematically identify* an answer. This proved to be a long tedious (and eventually unnecessary) task. Instead, *direct their attention* earlier to the *"Implant Penalty-Universes"* (see AT#4) and indicate to them that these IPU are what underlie all the entrapment techniques used in the *Symbols Universe*.

G. *Assess for the Penalty-Universe underlying their entrapment.*

Use the data provided in *A.T. Manual #4, "Implanted Universes."* First use a list of the *16 Dynamic Systems*, and assess for the best/strongest *"reading"* on the list. When you have one, you assess from the list of 4 *Goals* for that *Dynamic System*. Take the one that *"reads"* as the IPU-*Goal* for STEP-H. If you are dealing with a *"composite-case,"* you may have to repeat this step to *process-out* a few *Goals* (in the same or different *Dynamic Systems*) to fully *defragment* everything.

H. *IPU-Defragmentation.*

As you find each IPU-*Goal*, have the PME *run* the following PCL-sequence:

–"*Spot: 'To {Goal} Is Native State'.*"

–"*Spot Being Pushed Into This.*"

–and/or "*Spot Pushing Another Into This.*"

–and/or "*Spot Others Pushing Others Into This.*"

–"*Spot: 'To {Goal} Is Native State'.*"

It may be that you need to *process-out* another PCL-*Goal* (from STEP-G). If necessary, this can be followed up with *"Who Are You?"* (from the *"Identification Procedure"*) in order to get a *"Me"* answer. The PME may or may not *defragment* at this step, or any of the other steps, from this Standard Procedure.

I. *Agreements-Universe Defragmentation.*

If there is still something remaining, have the PME *run* the following PCL-sequence regarding the *"Agreements Universe"* (see AT#1, &tc.):

–"*Spot Rushing To Get Into Agreement.*"

–"*Spot Going Through 'The Inverted Golden Triangle'.*"

–"*Spot: 'To Agree Is Native State'.*"

–"*Look Earlier And Spot When You Decided To Agree.*"

Again, this can be followed up with *"Who Are You?"* (from the *"Identification Procedure"*) in order to get a *"Me"* answer. The PME may *release* at this step, or any of the previous steps. If necessary you can also have them *"Spot Encouraging Others To Agree"* and *"Spot Others Encouraging Others To Agree."*

Running the wrong *Goal* for this procedure is not really problematic. All *Alpha-Spirits* have *some fragmented charge* on each of the 64 IPU. Sometimes you will suddenly find the *machinery* blow apart into a cloud of *individuals*—you *acknowledge* them and handle each of the partial-*releases* one by one. We have also found that if you take a break at a time like this, some of them just seem to sort their stuff out and blow off. You can then check back later and see if some require more *defragmentation processing*, or whether there is still a *core-remnant* that still needs to be *processed-out*.

Elements of *"Standard Procedure: Entities"* also applies to PME (it just usually isn't enough for handling PME without some of the steps given above). This means having to check for *"Holders"* and *"Copiers/Copies."* One *machine* may be trying to "hold" or "hide" another. There may even be a *"repair-machine"* that keeps the *machine* you are *processing* in place or copies it when it leaves. Simply check for this stuff and handle it.

SHORT VERSION

This is a shorter script but a more advanced version of the above procedure. It relies on the *high-Awareness level* of a *"Wizard"* to grant enough *Beingness* or *livingness* to the PME, that it raises the *entity's Awareness* high enough to simply *"Spot"* critical *items* with their *attention* and *"defrag-by-Awareness."*

This is the preferred *A.T.* version. With enough *practice/ certainty*, it may even be operated *out-of-session*—once a *"Wizard"* has learned how to apply the entirety of *Systemology without Biofeedback-Devices* (which is an important skill-set for when you find yourself free of your body and material objects).

As you are still developing skill, this is best practiced on a *GSR-Meter*. You should get *"reads"* on each step and get a sense for *machinery* gradually "coming apart" or *releasing*. It follows the same formula as the *"Long Version,"* which a *"Wizard"* should get familiar with first.

A. *Locate the machine.*

It will *read* on: "PME" or "*machine.*"

B. "*Spot Being Made Into A Machine.*"

It should considerably loosen up with this step (though not always as much as STEP-D of the *Long Version*). If necessary, you can "*date and locate*" (anything from STEP-B to D of the *Long Version*). But really, this step can be accomplished by simple "*Spotting*"—if you can endow the *being* with enough *livingness* to overcome their reactive and conditioned *flinch/withdrawal* from the "*time and location*" of the *incident*.

C. "*Spot The First (Earliest) Time You Were Made Into A Machine.*"

This is the same as STEP-E from the *Long Version*. However, in the *Long Version*, you can get away with being a little vague, whereas here, this must be *Spotted* by the PME with high certainty in order to *defrag-by-Awareness*.

D. "*Spot Making Others Into Machines.*"

Run the PCL.

E. "*Spot Being Tricked Into Thinking That Machines Are Necessary.*"

If the *entity/machinery* remains, continue.

F. *Identification*.

Run the "*Who Are You?*" PCL from the *Identification Procedure*. You may have to get them to affirm "*Me*" (and you *acknowledge* it) several times in order to *release*. Sometimes, the *release* occurs prior to this step. If they don't *release* on this, the assessment steps from the *Long Version* are too lengthy, but you can treat "*Agreements*" in the next step (if necessary).

G. *Agreements-Universe Defragmentation*.

This is the same as STEP-I from the *Long Version*. Have the PME *run* the following PCL-sequence:

–"*Spot Rushing To Get Into Agreement.*"
–"*Spot Going Through 'The Inverted Golden Triangle'.*"
–"*Spot: 'To Agree Is Native State'.*"
–"*Look Earlier And Spot When You Decided To Agree.*"

Again, this can be followed up with "*Who Are You?*" (from the "*Identification Procedure*") in order to get a "*Me*" answer. The PME may *release* at this step, or any of the previous steps. If necessary, you can also have them "*Spot Encouraging Others To Agree*" and "*Spot Others Encouraging Others To Agree.*"

ADVANCED ENTITY-HANDLING

Most *fragments* may be *systematically* handled with the same *"Standard Procedure (for Entities)."* Here, we will apply a basic exercise to increase your own *reality* on this—and which also applies to *actual handling*.

1. *Close your eyes.*
2. *"Imagine"* (*by visualization*) or *"get the sense of"* a *viewpoint* of "looking over someone's shoulder."
3. *Get a sense* of *being* there to "keep them human." [You may or may not get an *actual impression* of environmental scenery, or of someone below you.]
4. Whatever part of yourself you are *projecting* to accomplish this: direct to *it* (the PCL) *"point to the being you divided from."* [At which point it should *defragment/dissolve*.]
5. If any connectivity remains, or seems to linger in the area, alternate applying the *"Who Are You?"* (from the *"Identification Technique"*) and the *"Locational Technique"* until it fully *defragments/disperses*.

Understand that you, as an *Alpha-Spirit*, have the ability to place a *viewpoint* anywhere in *space-time* and perceive *anything*. Therefore, it is possible to continue *perceiving* or "looking at" an area even after *releasing* any *fragments* fixedly located there. One purpose of *Alpha-Defragmentation* is to regain full *conscious control* over such *viewpoints*—nothing should be "fixedly holding" our attention anywhere, or enforcing perceptions from anywhere on "automatic."

Repeat the exercise using many different people—alternating *real* (one's you know) and *imagined*—until it seems like there are no more *"real"* ones to treat in this manner. Then apply the same exercise; but this time, *get a sense* of being a particular *"body-part"* on someone else, and *being* there to "keep it solid; keep it human."

<u>CONTROL ENTITIES (C.E.)</u>

"Control Entities" (or *"C.E."*) are active, semi-*aware* (intelligent) *entities*, *implanted* (or *installed*) for the explicit purpose of "keeping an *Alpha-Spirit* imprisoned and/or controlled." They are quite challenging to *release* using *"Standard Procedure (for Entities)"* and they don't respond any better with PME-type handling. They are intentionally *implanted* to be

"Jailers," or to block *spiritual perception* (*ability*), or to keep you from *thinking about* or *knowing* certain things, *&tc*.

From the perspective of the C.E., they aren't doing anything *wrong*. In fact, quite the opposite, which is why they are more difficult to *release*. They actively *know* what they are doing, but they are under the delusion that they are just being "honest citizens" doing their respective duty. They were *implanted* with this *false-fragmentary data* and forced to "split-off" a *fragment/piece* of themselves to further *implant* a "*imprisoned entity*" (to keep them *entrapped* and *under control*).

C.E. are most easily perceived at the *existence-level* or *reality-level* of the "*Astral Body*" (from the *Magic Universe*)—which means a *Seeker* must shift their *attention-Awareness* "up and sideways" to *perceive* (*get a sense of*) a *non-physical dimension*. [This is somewhat always the case, but we are referring to a *perceived layer* of our *Beingness* that extends to a former version of "*bodily-identity*."]

There have been C.E. in use for many layers of *Universes* extending on the *Backtrack*. They are *implanted* (or *installed*) at *one level* (*Universe*) in order to aid in keeping an *Alpha-Spirit* confined to a *lower level* (*Universe*). At any rate, the C.E. (themselves) believe they are "blocking" you for good orderly reasons—which means they are resistant to *defragmentation* unless you first get them to *Spot* the point of being *implanted* with *false data* (e.g. a *fragmented purpose*).

Until earlier procedures (in this manual) were standardized, *advanced Seekers* had no formal method for handling C.E. directly. This refined synthesis of *Level-8* (presented in the "*Keys to the Kingdom*" series) now includes an effective procedure for this, relying on a *Seeker's* experience with the other techniques given. Note that in addition to *processing-out* C.E. that are affixed to and blocking you, this procedure can also be extended to include *releasing* "*split-fragments*" of yourself (where you are being a C.E. to someone else).

STANDARD PROCEDURE: C.E.

A. "*Spot Being Made Into A Control Entity (or C.E.)*."

B. *Spotting the Goal*.

As a *listing/assessing* action, use PCL:

"Made To Split To Save Society?"
if no read,
"Made To Split To Gain Something?"
if no read,
"Made To Split To Serve A Higher Purpose?"

C. *"Spot Being Implanted With False Data."*
if no read (wrong wording),
"Spot Being Implanted With A False Purpose."
if no read (wrong wording),
"Spot Being Implanted With Fragmented Data."
if no read (wrong wording),
"Spot Being Implanted With A Fragmented Purpose."
if still no read, try a different "circuit":
"Spot Implanting Others With False Data" (*&tc.*)
or
"Spot Making Others Into Control Entities."

D. *"Spot The First Time You Were Implanted With False Data."*

Note that if the *"Meter-read"* occurred on different *"wording"* for *"False Data"* from STEP-C, then use that instead. You may also have to *"steer"* attention of the C.E. to a *"False Jewel"* incident — something similar to *"The Jewel"* for *this Universe*, but occurring several layers of *Universe* ago.

E. *Locational Technique.*

"Point To The Being You Divided From."

F. *Identification Technique.*

"Who Are You?" (*"Me"*)

If necessary, you can alternate between STEP-E and STEP-F toward a *release*.

G. *IPU-Defrag. {if necessary}*

If the C.E. showed up (was perceived) while handling *Implanted Penalty-Universes*, and it has not *released* from the former steps, have it *"Spot"* the top of the *Implant-Platform* for that IPU-Goal:

"To {Goal} Is Native State."

H. *Agreements. {if necessary}*

Although it is rarely needed, if more handling is required (the C.E. is loosened up and seems ready to *release*, but still seems to be waiting for something)—have the C.E. *run* the following PCL-sequence:

–"*Spot Rushing To Get Into Agreement.*"

–"*Spot Going Through 'The Inverted Golden Triangle'.*"

–"*Spot: 'To Agree Is Native State'.*"

–"*Spot An Earlier Decision To Agree.*"

END-POINTS & REALIZATIONS

As a *Seeker* increases their *certainty* for handling *entities* and *fragments*, they may come to the *realization* that they are reaching a point of being greater "*cause over spiritual life.*" This is one of the primary purposes for introducing this manual at this point of one's *Advanced Training*.

However, it is important that once this *realization* is *actualized* in practice, that a *Seeker* does not focus too hard on treating endless *sessions* on *entities*, exclusive to all other practices. This means that the presence of "more entities" should not hinder a *Seeker* in continuing their *Advanced Training* with A.T. Manual #6, "*Spiritual Perception.*"

In fact, a *Seeker* is likely to achieve greater, more stable, gains in progress by: shifting *attention* between practicing exercises to increase *spiritual perception* –and– processing- *sessions* directed toward *entities*. As one's *spiritual perception* improves, so to will their ability to *locate* and *release* any *entities* and *fragments*.

In addition to the *entities* and *spiritual fragments* of others that "cling" to us and hold us in the *Human Condition*, the majority of an individual's difficulties stem from their own *spiritual fragmentation*. By this, we mean our own *fragments*, *pieces*, and "*split viewpoints*" that are a part of the *machinery*, or act as *entities*, holding *other Alpha-Spirit's* in the *Human Condition*.

The *Locational Procedure* was originally developed to handle these "*split-viewpoints*" (or "*S.V.*"). Since an *Alpha-Spirit* is not truly *located* in *space-time* except by *consideration of viewpoints*, it is quite easy to be operating from multiple *viewpoints* that are *located* separately in *space-time*.

Early on the *Backtrack*, operating from multiple *viewpoints* simultaneously was simply a basic *godlike* skill used to *knowingly animate* one's own *creations* (*Home Universe*)—and it was not very *fragmentary*. At that stage, we were quite capable of consciously extending (or *projecting*) various *remote viewpoints* and then *knowingly dispersing* them or *disconnecting*.

The *fragmentation* occurred when S.V. were enforced (or even used as payment for "magical services") and then we were blocked from consciously operating or controlling them. This greatly contributed to our decline of *spiritual ability*, and the dampening of our total *Actualized Awareness*.

There are numerous *Implanting-Incidents* that forced an individual to divide. This was the case with the *Hellfire Incident*. In the more distant past, we have seen evidence of this in the original *Implanted Penalty-Universes*. This type of *fragmented Awareness* is what we will continue to *defragment* and *reclaim* as our own throughout *Level-8*.

Let's finish this unit/manual of instruction with a basic *objective exercise* to increase your *spiritual perception* and understanding of *handling entities* and *fragments*. This is done in a public place where there are many people.

1. *Spot a person.*
2. Alternate between *getting a sense of* "keeping them human" and "leaving them free."
3. When you have done this to a point of satisfaction with one person, repeat with different one.

Then practice this exercise by applying the other "*circuits*"—*getting the idea* of *others* alternately "keeping *you* human" and "leaving *you* free"; then with *others* alternately "keeping *others* human" and "leaving *others* free." Once you have completed this, in your next *subjective session*, see if any additional *entities* and *fragments* are now accessible.

To truly be a "Wizard," a *Seeker* must eventually reach a point where they are no longer influenced, blocked, or held back, by B.E.; and to where they (themselves) are no longer holding others in the *Human Condition*. This is the essence of *Alpha-Defragmentation*—and the first major *upper-level* step toward regaining one's own true and original *spiritual perception* and *ability*.

A.T. MANUAL #6
SPIRITUAL PERCEPTION

Keep this reference material accessible:
PC Lesson-1 to 16; Processing-Levels 0 to 6.
AT Manual #1, "The Secret of Universes"
AT Manual #2, "Games, Goals & Purposes"
AT Manual #3, "The Jewel of Knowledge"
AT Manual #4, "Implanted Universes"
AT Manual #5, "Entities & Fragments"

Review this prerequisite material:
PC Lesson-5, "Free Your Spirit"
PC Lesson-10, "Lifting The Veils"

ADVANCING SPIRITUAL ABILITY

This book is a *systematic training manual*; it is *not* a complete record of *all* experimental research or potential commentary on the subjects included (which would require many volumes). The author spent *30* years dedicated to *"spiritual cartography,"* exploring every potential avenue—from the *most ancient* extant writings available, to the *New Thought* developments of the *20th Century*—before presenting this series of *Systemology* work. Only those "bits" truly useful for *crafting* the *ultimate map* for *The Way Out* were retained.

The ultimate freedom of *Self*—the *Alpha-Spirit*—*knowingly* operating *"outside"* (or *"exterior to"*) a mortal organic *Body* is our true basic spiritual state. It is the *rehabilitation* of this state—or an *actualized realization* of it—that has driven the populations towards various philosophies, metaphysics, and religion, for thousands of years. Of course, various communication barriers and organizational corruption has kept any of these other "avenues" from fully delivering a *Seeker* to their desired *destination*.

The new standard *Systemology* program—*Basic Course, Professional Course* and *Advanced Training Course*—is the result of feedback from many *systemologists* over the course of many years. It didn't matter how well something *worked* or was *understood* by the author; the real test of its *effectiveness* was reaching a point of *perfection* for its *presentation*—where *Systemology* could be properly communicated to, and used by, others.

Unlike most other *"New Age"* pursuits: we took a *systematic* and *scientific* approach to *Life, Universes* and *Everything*—but while neither adopting, nor excluding, a *physically-mechanistic technological* viewpoint of understanding. The results were a *"spiritual technology"*—something *actually* useful to the *Alpha-Spirit*—that exceeds the boundaries of *this Life*, the *Human Condition*, and even *this Universe*.

Previous *spiritual* traditions sought to find a way out by *denying* or *altering* "*What Is.*" But while *eastern mysticism* and *western magic* may have been successful in producing many various *effects*, not one of them produced the manifestation of a *True Map* for *The Way Out*.

Advanced Training procedures of this manual are only expected to be effective for those *Seekers* that have *actually processed through* the *"Pathway-to-Ascension" Professional Course* (*Lesson-1 to 16*) and the *"Keys to the Kingdom" A.T. Manuals* (*#1 to 5*) prior to studying/applying this manual (*AT #6*). This manual is combined with *"Entities & Fragments"* (*AT#5*) to function as a single unit of *"Level-8"* training. [*AT#7* and *AT#8* are recent expansions to the *A.T.* course that encourage additional work and research for this *Infinity Grade*.]

Ideally, a *Seeker* handles what is initially accessible during *AT#5*, then completes a *"run through"* of *spiritual perception* development in *AT#6*. At that time, they may revisit the procedures in *AT#5* to check if there is anything newly accessible. Increased *spiritual perception* makes *releasing entities* (and *fragments, &tc.*) easier; and *releasing entities* makes techniques for increasing *spiritual perception* more effective.

"Free Your Spirit" (*PC-5*) and *"Lifting The Veils"* (*PC-10*) should be reviewed—and considered *"introductions"* to this manual. All other *Systemology* material should also be kept accessible. Many *advanced exercises* already given in previous lessons and manuals will be referenced directly—but their full background and instruction will not be repeated here, so more ground can be covered in a shorter space for this manual.

A.T. Manual #6 is prepared with an expectancy that it will not require any *strenuous effort* (for a *Level-8 Seeker*) to understand or apply—however, *"repetitive practice"* is likely necessary. Most of the *exercises* will be presented with little theory or explanation attached—because a *Seeker* that has *actually* worked through *previous* material will already be familiar with many of the techniques and *processing*-types described here.

The original *Wizard Level-0 "Creative Ability Training"* procedure premiered in the *Systemology Core Research Volume: "Imaginomicon"* (in 2021). These exercises were spread all over the new standard *Professional Course Processing-Levels 0 to 6* as *"objective-environment processing," "creativeness processing,"* and *"advanced techniques."* They were intentionally included to accelerate a *Seeker's* progress on the *Pathway*—and as preparation for *upper-level A.T.* work. Of course, at *those levels*, such exercises were treated quite lightly in between more intensive *defragmentation processing*.

A *Seeker* enters *Level-8* (as a *processing level*) at *Wizard Level-0*. It is at *this* level that *AT#5* (*Entities*) material is treated the *first* time through. Remaining *Wizard-Levels* pertain to theoretical *Infinity Grade "Arcs"*—leading further upward toward total *mastery of Ascension Technology*.

The new *Wizard Level-1 "Advanced Ability Training Program"* (proposed in this manual) revisits many earlier *advanced techniques*—but also adds many more. This manual also includes a *Wizard Level-2* training procedure. When a *Seeker* approaches *AT#5* material a *second* time, they will be doing so from a *Wizard Level-1* (or higher) foundation or *viewpoint*. [An experimental *Wizard Level-3* routine appears in *AT#7*.]

"End-point Realizations" for *Wizard-Levels* primarily regard an increased sense of, and certainty in, *Self* as the *Alpha-Spirit*. "Ability" and "certainty" tend to be correlated. But this alone does not provide much of a *systematic* gradient. Any upward emphasis requires codification using our theoretical *Infinity-Grade "Arcs."*

Wizard Level-1 : *"ejecting" Awareness (fixed viewpoint)* from the *Body*; handling the *Body* (from nearby) while operating from a *viewpoint* that is *remote* from (or *"exterior to"*) any *Body*.

Wizard Level-2 : *"perceiving"* from *exterior viewpoints* that are *projected/extended away/remote* from a *Body*.

Wizard Level-3 : *"intention"*; a proposed experimental gradient. [This level is still subject to future revision and includes material that may later be classified as a *"higher"* gradient of *Wizard-Level*.]

Most early *Systemology* research into procedures for this area was conducted during *experimental workshops* and *Traditional (Co-Piloted) Sessions*. Having a *Co-Pilot* allowed a *Seeker* to focus *attention* more on *"doing"* the *processing command-lines* (PCL) rather than *"thinking"* about book instructions. A *Seeker* often felt "safer" handling *processing "exterior to"* a *Body* when the *session-environment* was properly controlled (*piloted*)—and without any distractions or chance of sudden disturbances.

However, *Co-Piloting "Advanced Ability Training"* is not without its complications. A *Level-8 Co-Pilot*, requires having some personal *reality* on these *processes* in order to effectively *guide* a *Seeker*. Otherwise, there is a greater risk of a *Co-Pilot "invalidating"* a *Seeker's* experiences, gains, and abilities. *Invalidation* results in having less *certainty*—which slows (or stops) progress with *Spiritual Perception*.

A *Co-Pilot* will *acknowledge* the *ejection*, but *never* makes the *Seeker "prove"* their *Beingness* (or *ability*) by producing any phenomenon, *&tc.* The standard practice was to simply continue the *process* that a *Seeker* "ejected" with, but from their current *viewpoint*.

However, since *ejection* can occur rather suddenly—and a sudden *shift* in *processing* can sometimes cause more *confusion*—this mainly applied to *objective exercises*. In addition to this, sometimes the *Seeker* found themselves suddenly *"looking at"* something else (*imagery, an incident, &tc.*), and so the alternative practice of making *copies* of that *imagery, &tc.*, was developed.

For example: if a *Seeker* is practicing *"Creation-Of-Space"* and suddenly gets a lot of certainty on operating from a *viewpoint* that is *exterior-to* a *Body*, then they would continue their *"Creation-Of-Space"* exercise from that *viewpoint*. But if that became distracting because the *Seeker* was now dealing with some other phenomenon, they would handle that by making/create "copies" (*knowingly, intentionally*) of whatever it was they *did see*; making many copies of the *imagery*, then alternating "throwing them away" (or *dispersing* them) and "pushing them in" on the *Body*.

REALIZATIONS FROM THE PATHWAY

Shared Universes and *Games* are "contrary" or "antithetical" to the true basic native state (or even *"Home Universe"*) of an *Alpha-Spirit*. Our highest level of *spiritual perception* and *ability* does not permit *"game-conditions"* to exist—does not allow for us to experience any kind of *Game*.

The *Alpha-Spirit* is *"Pure Awareness"*—without *energetic-mass* or *location*—but it has an unlimited potential for *postulating, creating,* and even *considering* the condition of *"Having"* something. It can *be anywhere* it cares *to be; looking* at *anything* it wants *to be looking* at. But, in order to *have games*—*"game-fields"* and *"enforced rules"*—*Alpha-Spirits* became expert specialists in *designing* and *creating* various *barriers* and *restrictions*.

We have come to believe that *"something is better than nothing"*—and it is only by achieving high-tolerance levels that a *Seeker* can rehabilitate the *"confronting of Nothingness."* Additionally, we must rehabilitate *creativeness*—the certainty that a *Seeker* can *still "Have"* something independent of a *Body*—or even the *Game* of *this Physical Universe* altogether. Without rehabilitating these basic states, an individual will not let go, or release

Self, from their *chronic* and *compulsive participation* with the *Human Condition*.

Restoring *freedom* is synonymous with restoring *spiritual perception* and *ability*. But, *total freedom* does not have a *systematic structure*, because it is a *basic Truth*—reflecting the true native state of the *Alpha-Spirit*. The innate *abilities* of an *Alpha-Spirit* cannot actually be destroyed, because *It Is* the basic *Beingness* of its *Existence*. However, *consciously understanding* and/or *knowingly using* these *abilities* (and *perceptions*) can certainly become *fragmented* and *blocked*.

Freedom is the absence of *barriers* and *restriction*. "Total Freedom" would be the *total absence* of *all barriers* and *restriction*. The *Alpha-Spirit* has long since lost its tolerance for *confronting* such a state. At the upper-most level, there is *nothing* to be *free from*. That the "*something*" to be *free from*, is more or less an *illusion*, is also true; but it is the *Alpha-Spirit*'s own *illusion*—*agreed* to (at some level) in order to *have a game*. [Ref. AT#1 & AT#2]

Our *Awareness* is currently "spread" all over *this* and *other* "*Universes*"—"*attention-units*" *fragmented* by *imprinting*, "*splitting*" and other *incidents* where *attention* remains "*fixed*." *Fixation* is *entrapment*. All *fixation* is really the *suspension* of *Awareness* (*attention*) on a point of a "*communication-cycle*" that has not resolved, closed, or ended. It is *suspended* in a *confusion* or a "*maybe*." And this obviously reduces *Knowingness*.

Note that the phrase "*communication-cycle*" refers to more than "conversations" with other *people*; it also includes incomplete *cycles-of-action* (or "events" that we've experienced)—or really any "encounters" with the *energy-matter* and/or *space-time* of *this* (or any *other*) *Universe*.

An insistence upon substituting *Knowingness* by obsessively holding onto *imprinted imagery* (*mental pictures*) in order to "learn by experience"—and then assigning *automatic control* of *associating* the *data* to *reactive-response machinery*—has inhibited the *total freedom* of the *Alpha-Spirit*.

> *Spiritual Perception* is only inhibited and limited by one key factor:
> What—and how much—an *Alpha-Spirit* is willing to Know.
>
> The *perception* of *freedom* is connected to:
> What an *Alpha-Spirit* is willing to Create, Do, or Have.

And this is where an individual got themselves involved with the *games* and *puzzles* that an *Alpha-Spirit* is so fond of. Unless a *Seeker* has *certainty* on the *ability* to *Create* another (preferably better) *"game"*—or at the very least *Have* one—*"somewhere"* else, they will not sufficiently *release* their hold on *"this"* one.

Systematic Processing on the *Pathway* has established to a *Seeker* that our true basic native *ability* is restored by *Knowingness*—the increase of *Actualized Awareness*. The *unknowing* ("*not-conscious*") *automation* and *"push-button"* mechanistic control is a much *lower-level* of *"mental operation"* than *Knowingness*.

The *"Standard Model"* (and *"ZU-Line"*) on which our *Systemology* is based, very accurately "maps" or "charts" the conditions of descent in any area. At the top we have:

7. ALPHA-THOUGHT—(*To Be*)—the *postulates* of *Creation*; *Creating* a "*thing*" to *Know* about.

6. KNOWINGNESS—(*What Is*)—the *condition* of *Knowing*; *Total-Knowingness* is all-pervasive perfect *Knowing* about a "*thing*" as maintained by its *Creator*.

5. INTENTION—(*It-As-Altered*)—the *ability* to affect or change the *condition* of an *existing* "*thing*" to make it *continue*, *persist*, or *perpetuate*, in some way.

For there to be "*intention*" (rather than "*Creation*") the *Alpha-Spirit* already must have decided to "*Not-Know*" about something. The *intention* to *Know* something requires *Not-Knowing* about it in the first place. The *intention* to "*learn*" requires an *interest*—and "*interest*" is something that is difficult for an *Eternal Spirit* to maintain indefinitely (hence, "*games*"). An individual in *Total Knowingness* would simply *disperse* an undesired "*thing*" and *Create* something else, rather than *Alter-What-Is*.

The extent to which one can *Imagine* (or *Create*) does not only concern *Creating* (*Imagining*) "*infinities*" of something (see *PC-15*, *&tc.*), but also the "*distance-factor.*" *Distance* is another *perceived barrier* in *space-time*. So, when *running* any type of "*creativeness processing,*" we must also treat the matter of: how "close" does one's *creations* have to be (to their *viewpoint/POV*) to still be *considered* (handled) under their *control*?

Lower down the chained-sequence: when operating with a *Body* in the

Human Condition, the *Alpha-Spirit* typically directs *"intention"* to the *"Mind-System"* in order to get the *Body* to *"do"* things, in order to affect the *energetic-mass* of *space-time* in the *Game* of *this Physical Universe*. This involves a *consideration* that some kind of *"action"* or *"effort"* is required in order to *cause* something—and this part of the chain starts with:

   4. THINKINGNESS—(*Computation*)—the *evaluation* of *effort* of some *"doingness"* to *Cause* or *Have* something; and/or the *estimation* of control (to *"start,"* *"alter,"* or *"stop"* an existing *system* or *"thing"*).

"Thinkingness" (the personal *Mind-System*) operates far below a level of *Knowingness*. It is unnecessary; it is where most *beings* get themselves into trouble. Of course, to get to this point, a *being* would have to *Not-Know* about a lot of *created things* in order to *"think about things to know about."* But this is exactly what sets up the conditions for a *game*.

"EJECTION" FROM A BODY/VEHICLE
(*Wizard Level-1*)

The phrase *"ZU-Vision"* is used in *Systemology* to indicate the experience of the true *Spiritual Awareness* (and thus the *Spiritual Life*) of the *Alpha-Spirit*. This is beyond the *sensation* or *perception* of a *Body*; it is beyond the *mental machinery* and *fragmented computations* of any *Mind-System*.

ZU-Vision regards *Beingness* that is completely *"exterior to"* *Body* and *Mind*. Other methods and traditions that do not properly *defragment* a *Seeker* first, may occasionally get them *"out-of-body"*—but the individual is still very much *"in-the-mind"* and attached to all their *"stuff"* and their interconnection to *bodies* of *this Universe*.

Although it may seem to cross-over in subject matter at times: when handling *Spiritual Perception* at *Wizard Level-1*, we are not directly interested in what is often referred to as *"psychic phenomenon"* or making objective demonstrations of *ability* in *this Physical Universe*.

When unrestricting *fixed viewpoints* in *Space*, one is also treating *Time*—and at first, a *Seeker* may not have clear *"present-time"* perception with *ZU-Vision* on the immediate environment of the *Body*. One's *actual perception* must also be distinguished from the *"mental imagery"* that one is likely to still be *compulsively creating* (to look at). A *Seeker* may initially not *perceive* the *Physical Universe* because the *Seeker*, themselves, is not *"putting it up there to see."* [This strongly hints toward a very specific and significant *A.T. realization.*]

ZU-Vision is not a *process, procedure* or *skill*. It is the natural *ability* of an *Alpha-Spirit* that simply has varying degrees of *clarity in perception*—and thus, like any *ability* or *function*, it can be *inhibited* or *fragmented*. To treat this subject as a *process* directly would be like writing a book instructing on how to *"eat," "walk,"* or *"breathe"* (although such exist). There are obviously ways of "improving" how one does such things, but the basic development of the function is essentially *in-born* or *innate*.

Alpha-Spirits have developed a *compulsive dependency* on *bodies, automation,* and *games*. We can rehabilitate *Spiritual Perception* by resolving (*defragmenting*) the *compulsions*. This is the real emphasis of the *Pathway*—because any time we tried to directly focus *processing* specifically on *"getting out,"* we encountered many *barriers*. Instead, initial gains were accomplished by *processing-out* the *"entry-points"*—the *"getting in"* part. Secondly, we achieved gains by *processing-out incidents* of unwanted or unexpected (*other-determined*, rather than *Self-Determined*) *"ejections"* from anything, but mostly *bodies*.

To effectively apply the techniques of *Wizard Level-1* as a *systematic procedure*, a *Seeker* must *Know* (have *actual* certainty on):

1. *"What"* is being *ejected/released* (the *Alpha-Spirit*);
2. *"What"* it is being *ejected/released "from"* (the *Body*); and
3. *"mechanisms/machinery"* (called the *Mind*).

Years of experimental research allowed us to collect data regarding key factors that more commonly affected *Seekers* experiencing difficulties with *ejecting/releasing* from their *Body*. Many of these points are treated earlier on the Pathway, but a *Seeker* may need to revisit key areas specific to their own case, or even other areas that may have yet to be personally handled at all, for *Wizard Level-1*. These include:

–FEAR associated with some element of *space-time, energy,* and/or *mass*; or else *terminals* attached to *this Universe*.

–FEAR associated with *lack* or *loss* of *"having"* space-time or energy-mass; including reduced *ability-to-confront "Nothingness."*

–NO RESPONSIBILITY (OR CONTROL); therefore the *effect of*, or controlled by, other things (*other-determinism*).

– NO CERTAINTY; low-*Awareness*; no *Self-Determinism*, therefore everything is *other-determined*, or from an *unknown (hidden) source*.

– MACHINERY; excessively burdened by personal *mechanisms* of *automation* and *reactivity*.

– BEINGNESS (VIEWPOINT or POV) deeply enmeshed in the *rigid-energy* (*standing-waves*) of a *Body*; either a *fixation* on the *Body*, or total lack of interest/responsibility in handling the *Body* ("disowning" while still remaining connected to it).

– BEINGNESS (VIEWPOINT/POV) or ATTENTION fixedly on an entirely different *Body* (for personal *identification*) than the *current Human Body* "present" *in-session*.

The last one is an interesting point of *fragmentation* only recently added to the list. In this case, we may have a situation of treating the "*wrong body*." Ejecting *Awareness* from "*the Body*" actually requires the starting point of *being in* "*the Body*"—and preferably "*the Body*" being used for a *processing session* that keeps directing PCL regarding "*that Body*." In the case of *wrong body*: it may be that an individual's chronic POV is on (or from) a *desired body*, or they have *fixated attention* on a *past body* (previous *body* on the *Backtrack*).

At *Level-8*, a *Seeker/Wizard* no longer *runs* "*imprint-chains*" in *processing*. The primary *high-level Awareness* methods of *processing* are: "*Spotting*" and "*defragmentation-upon-analytical-inspection*."

This means that basic "*Recall*" and "*Imagine*" techniques still apply, in addition to *identifying* "*Source*," "*What Is*," &tc. We don't want to *stick* a *Seeker's attention* on a *Body*, but *ejection* can be difficult if *attention* is already *fixated* on a *Body* "*elsewhere*." In this instance, more "*descriptive*"-style PCL may need to be *run* in order to "collect" one's "*attention-units*" onto the *current Body*. This sometimes means first getting a *Seeker* to realize "*what*" *Body/Identity* they *actually* have their *Awareness/Beingness* associated with.

"*What Body Would You Like To Have?*"

– and/or –

"*Describe Your Last Body.*"

As a preliminary to *Wizard Level-1 Procedure*, a *Seeker* should *defragment* prior "*other-determined*" *ejections* where *Awareness* may be suspended and/or new *considerations* may have been made about *being "exterior-to"* a *Body*.

This includes, for example: *past deaths, serious illness,* or *injuries*—points when an *Alpha-Spirit* may have temporarily *"gone out"* of the *Body,* or was otherwise *ejected "under duress."* [It has been noticed, on the *Backtrack,* that the *Alpha-Spirit* does not "naturally" recover full *attention-Awareness* after such *incidents.*]

There is a phenomenon where a *Seeker*/individual *"goes out"* (ejects) and *"goes back in"* (snaps-in) so quickly that the *shift* isn't fully *realized* as having happened; but the *"impact"* (of the *"snap-in"*) is *perceived* in some way, which often results in a period of *confusion* (or some other unwanted manifestation). Prior use of *mysticism* or *occultism* (that included *astral travel* or *out-of-body experiences*) may need to be *defragmented.* Previous *processing-sessions,* where a *Seeker* may have suddenly *ejected,* might also require *"repair."*

The main issue is that these events often take place before *Seekers* are properly prepared to handle them. This leaves *residual fragmentation* from the subsequent *"snap-in"* effects thereafter. And any heightened *perception* achieved is generally not very stable. An unprepared *Seeker* may find the experience disorienting—or a disturbance occurs in the *session-environment* while they are operating *"exterior"*—and so they abruptly *snap-back-in,* and "hold on" even tighter to the *Human Condition.*

Early experiments placed particular emphasis on the *"getting out"* part of things. But few of the methods applied directly toward this goal actually produced stable results—or if they were effective in *knowingly ejecting Awareness,* the experience didn't leave a *Seeker* feeling much better, especially if something *caused them* to *snap-back-in.* [This was the case with most traditional applications of *"Astral Projection"* data.]

A.T. realizations include a greater certainty on *being* a *"Spiritual Being"*; not a *"Body"*—and that the *Alpha-Spirit* is a *Beingness* that can *consider* itself as *being "anywhere"* and *"anything."* The typical individual (*Alpha-Spirit* + *Human Condition*) generally *considers* that they *need* a *Body,* or that the *Body needs* them, or even that they would be *abandoning* it by *ejecting.*

At *Wizard Level-1* we are primarily concerned with *"ejection"* (and *defragmenting* *"snap-in"* effects). Our emphasis at this stage is not on vivid perception. First we *"get out"*; then we focus on *"looking around."* Upon initially *"getting out,"* a *Seeker* often *"loses"* the *perception* of *present-time environmental "anchor-points"* in the *Physical Universe*. Their *spiritual perception* is not likely to be *"very good"* (*clear*) without some kind of *"dimension-points."* This is remedied by practicing *"Creation-Of-Space"* (*PC-5*) and other similar exercises.

Aside from *"other-determined ejections,"* there is not a lot to *process* for *considerations* on the *"getting out"* part. The *Seeker* already desires to *"be out."* That's the natural state and not the point of *fragmentation*. As we know from *incident-running*: we can't *defragment "As-It-Is"* without treating the actual *"start"* of an *incident*, or finding the earlier *"beginning"* if necessary. In this case: the earlier beginning of *"being in"* is *"going in."* If one *considers* themselves *"in"* something, they had to *"get in"* in the first place. If an individual is *ejected* at *"death,"* than the *"go in"* would occur at *"birth," &tc*. We often emphasize the *"Heaven Implanting-Incident"* because it is the undercut to *advanced processing*, being the *entry-point* to the entire *Game* of *this Universe*.

The final part of a *Seeker's* preliminary work for *Wizard Level-1* is *defragmenting "ejection"* and *"snap-in"* mechanisms that may be *imprinted* and/or *automatic*. Otherwise, a *Seeker* is likely to experience additional *"push–pull"* tension between *Self* and the *Body*. Those that have dealt with this phenomenon often describe it rather like the old children's toy of *"a ball attached to a paddle with an elastic string."* Knowing this, it is better to take steps to prevent it from occurring, rather than having to *"remedy and repair"* it afterward.

The basic *process* for handling *fragmentation* on *"going in"* is given in *PC Lesson-10* (*"Lifting The Veils"*)—in the section titled: *"Metaspiritual Systemology."* It was also used in some procedures for handling *entities* (*AT#5*). While this previously may have been treated lightly, it becomes more critical to handle for *Level-8*.

As an addition to the instructions/background given (in *PC-10*), if a *Seeker* has access to *Biofeedback-Tech*, the advanced practice for this is to check for *fragmented charge* using a *GSR-Meter*. It will *register* on various *command-wording* (or *"hot buttons"*) associated with *"going in,"* if there is *imprinting*. This is then handled with the *Analytical Recall* technique given there, until no more *charge registers* when that *wording* is "called" or "spotted" or "run" during the *process*. [Use only *circuits* "1," "2" and "3"; then use "0" on your second pass through *Wizard Level-1* material.]

For convenience, the standard list of *keywords/buttons* is: "*Go In*"; "*Put In*"; "*Want To Go In*"; "*Must Get In*"; "*Can't Get In*"; "*Kicked Out*"; "*Be Trapped*"; "*Forced In*"; "*Pulled In*" and "*Pushed In.*"

[*New Update (for 2024)*: As a result of *systematic processing* being in the public hands for several years—in addition to the widespread distribution of other "*New Age*" practices—it has recently been discovered that a *Seeker* may also need to *process-out* those *incidents* where they: "*Tried To Eject, But Didn't/Couldn't.*"]

ADVANCED ABILITY TRAINING ROUTE
(*Wizard Level-1 Procedure*)

Advanced Ability Training (AAT) is not "*ejection processing*"—such a procedure does not exist in *Systemology*. These exercises are not intended to "*induce*" *ejection*; but *ejection* may take place while practicing them. It is true that an ability to handle and direct *ejection* is an intended *end-point* or *end-realization* of this *Wizard-Level*; but it is not what is *processed directly*. [The same AAT route is followed even *after* a *Seeker* "*ejects.*"]

Completing this routine in one single *session* is not required or expected. The "*standard opening procedures*" of a *Formal Session* are not used in *Wizard-Level Training Routines*. At the beginning of each *session*, a *Seeker* must run "*Preventative Fundamentals*" (PC-9) as their first *procedure*. This means: checking for *breaks* or *upsets* of "*Flow Factors*" (PC-7); making sure *presence* is not on some *problem* elsewhere (PC-4); and scanning over any *Harmful-Acts* or *Hold-Backs* that may have our *attention* because "*someone almost found out,*" &tc. (PC-6).

When a *Seeker* completes this route/routine, they proceed to the *next* section: "*Wizard Level-1 Stabilization.*" If you find difficulties processing this routine (that are not a result of *entities*, short-cutting previous *processing-levels*, or failing to provide *presence in-session*, &tc.), go directly to "*Wizard Level-1 Stabilization.*" It may be used to: *stabilize* results from *Wizard Level-1* and/or *enable* one to get better results (if necessary).

Wizard Level-1 puts emphasis on getting a *Seeker willing* and *able* to knowingly eject *Awareness* from its *fixation* on the *Body*. *Wizard Level-2* puts emphasis on increasing the *Spiritual Perception* of a *Seeker* once *ejected*. There is, however, no real distinction between the "type" of *systematic techniques* and exercises used for these purposes. They were all originally researched and experimented with during the same phase of work at the *Systemology Society* (2020–2022). They are all collected and codified in this manual for the first time.

Ejection could occur at any point of any exercise (from either *Wizard-Level*); and any of the exercises (from either *Wizard-Level*) may also be used after *ejection* to improve its *stability*, or even increase *perception*. Some of the techniques appeared in previous lessons. A *Seeker* was often instructed to simply *"imagine"* or accept whatever *"vague perception"* they had on them—or an *"advanced version"* may have been listed as optional. At *Level-8*, we are interested in taking up these earlier suggestions and actually improving *Spiritual Ability*.

Training Routines are *systematic* arrangements of various *processes* and exercises. Unlike the work done for *Level-7*, or involving *Implant-Platforms*, this *route* is not mimicking or replicating some specific *incident* or sequence. There is no real concern about seeing instructions "out of order" or following a different order.

A. <u>DEFRAG-BY-ATTENTION</u>

In this first step, we want to increase a *Seeker's* ability to "*Defrag-by-Attention*." This step also helps protect against so easily being the effect of future *Implants*. "*The Jewel of Knowledge*"(*AT#3*) is used for this step. A *Seeker* already *processed-out* "*The Jewel (Part #1-5)*" as an *incident* (for themselves) during *Level-7*.

The goal of this step is to be able to *intentionally* and *knowingly Create* (*Imagine*) and then *Un-Create* (*disperse*) each *item-line* of "*The Jewel*." A *Seeker* should focus on *copying* the intensity and sensation of the original (*incident*) item, but *not* as a "*recall action*." [When using *Biofeedback*, if enough significance is put on the *creation*, it will *register* as "*mass*." This is then *dispersed* ("*defragged-by-attention*") and will cease to *register*.]

A *Seeker* continues this until they feel comfortable doing it easily. They should find it interesting and fun; then be able to see the utter ridiculousness of the *Implant*; then be able to *Create* and *Defrag* any of the *items* from the *Implant* again—*knowingly at will*.

One challenge of *Ascension beyond this Universe*, is that even an *Actualized Seeker* (*Alpha-Spirit*) is likely to hit *"The Jewel"* of *this Universe* and end up right back here (if they have not built up an *"immunity"* to it). Most less-*Aware* individuals do not even make it that far in their *"between-lives period,"* often getting *"caught"* (as *Alpha-Spirits*) by various *"screens"* or *"Implant-Stations"* (*Heaven Implants, &tc.*) before ending up back here.

This is possible because, while the *Alpha-Spirit* is not *actually* located within *this Physical Universe*, its *fixed Awareness* and *considerations-of-Beingness* very much are—even after they are *released* from a *Body*, whether through *body-death*, or intentional *ejection-of-Awareness*.

Ejecting from the *Body* alone does not put one "outside" or "exterior to" the *Physical Universe*. There are other *postulates, reality-agreements, considerations, entities,* and *fragments,* that also contribute to a confinement to, or *fixation* with, *this Universe*—and which require *total defragmentation* to *master Ascension*.

B. SOURCE-OF-SENSATION

This step is to get *certainty* on *ability* to *create sensation* independent of a *body-perception*.

"*Create (Imagine) 'Heat' Until The Body Seems Warmer.*"

C. SOURCE-OF-LIGHT

This step is to get *certainty* on *ability* to *create* a *light-source* independent of *this Physical Universe*. It is *not* necessary for this *light* to be objectively visible or manifest (perceivable to others) in *this Physical Universe*. Alternate: *Creating* (*Imagining*) and *Un-Creating* (*dispersing*) a *light-source*. [This *light-source* should not be *"electrical"* (a light-bulb) or *"nuclear"* (like a sun).]

D. SOURCE-OF-BODY-ACTION

Alternate:
1. "*Move The Body.*"
2. "*Realize Who Is Making It Move.*"

E. UNIVERSE FUNDAMENTALS

Run the *"Preventative Fundamentals"* (PC-9, &tc.) on each of the following (separately): SPACE; TIME; ENERGY; and MATTER.

F. SPOTTING-THIS-UNIVERSE

Run "Orientation in Space-Time" (PC-1) outside (in a public place): "Spotting" (*looking* at something and *noticing* something about it) each of the following (as a separate *process*): SPACE; TIME; ENERGY; MATTER; AN OBJECT; AN ANIMAL; A PERSON; SELF; THE UNIVERSE; ANOTHER'S PERSONAL UNIVERSE; WHAT YOU ARE DOING NOW; WHAT ANOTHER IS DOING NOW.

G. SPOTTING POINTS-IN-SPACE

This step is practiced comfortably lying down; eyes closed. Alternate:

1. *"Spot One Point In The Room."*
2. *"Spot One Point In The Body."*

When a *Seeker* is comfortable with this (and *perception* of it is no longer changing, improving, &tc.), then continue this step using *"Two Points.."*; and finally *"Three Points.."* [Versions of this were introduced in PC-10 and PC-12.]

When a *Seeker* can do this step easily, follow this same progressive procedure; but alternating: *"...Point(s) In The Room"* and *"...Point(s) Outside."* [If necessary, the second part may be clarified as *"...Outside The Room (or Building)."*]

H. CREATING AN ILLUSION

This step is practiced comfortably lying down; *body's eyes* closed. Alternate:

1. *"Create (Imagine)."*
2. *"Intend."*

In the first part: a Seeker Creates/Imagines "something" (an *object*, an *energy*, a *condition*, an *illusion*, &tc.). The second part is repeated many times, Intending various things about the *creation*. The suggested list of intentions (for PCL) are: *"Hold It Still"*; *"Conserve It"*; *"Protect It"*; *"Control It"*; *"Keep It From Going Away"*; *"Hide It"*; *"Change It"*; *"Rearrange It"*; *"Duplicate It"* (in its same space); *"Turn It Upside-Down"*; *"Turn It On Its*

Side"; "Move It" (and *"Move It Back"); "Be It"; "Not-Be It"; "Destroy It"; "Create It" (Again)* and *"Destroy It"* at will.

I. SPOTTING DISTANCES

This step is usually practiced outside. Alternate:
1. *"Spot (Put Attention On) An Object."*
2. *"Notice The Distance (Space) Between You And It."*

J. PROJECTING ENERGY-BEAMS

This step is usually practiced with a combination of *intention* and *visualization*. This is done outside and/or inside. Note any *realizations*. [Handling *"spiritual energy"* is introduced at *Processing Level-6 (PC-13)*.]
1. *"Spot (Put Attention On) An Object."*
2. *"Place (Put Out) An Energy Beam, Wrapped Around You And It."*
3. *"Pull Yourself Toward It By Shortening (Retracting) The Beam."*

K. RECEIVING (DRAWING OUT) ENERGY

This step is usually practiced with a combination of *intention* and *visualization*. This is done outside and/or inside. Repeat it a dozen times. Note any *realizations*.
1. *"Spot (Put Attention On) An Object."*
2. *"Draw Energy (Out) From It And Into You."*

When a *Seeker* has done this step comfortably on a few objects: practice STEP-I, STEP-J, and STEP-K, on *"A CLOUD."*

L. LEVEL-7 A.T. STABILIZATION

"The Jewel of Knowledge"(AT#3) is used for this step. Refer to the section titled *"Level-7 Stabilization Point."* Complete the steps as given for that procedure (outdoors).

Then practice the procedure indoors; eyes closed. You can *Imagine (get a sense)* or use *ZU-Vision* (if possible) to: *"Look Around A City And Spot.."* [Practice it *"mentally/ spiritually"*; but not as a *"recall"* of being outdoors.]

When this step is completed, a *Seeker* continues to the next section.

WIZARD LEVEL-1 STABILIZATION

The following exercises are derived from the original *Systemology Wizard Training Regimen*—many of which were introduced in the *"Pathway" Professional Course (PC)*. For this *stabilization procedure*, a *Seeker* uses the *"advanced version"* (if applicable) of any *processes*. [Apply "standard opening procedures" (*Formal Session*) to these *sessions*. Refer to original materials (where indicated) for any additional background or instruction.]

A. <u>TOUCH-AND-LET-GO</u> *(PC-1)*

This step is practiced lying down; eyes closed. Use *advanced version* on:

1. Objects in the room.
2. Specific "spots" in the room.
3. Objects outside (the room).
4. "Spots" outside (the room).

["*Spots*" means "*Spots-in-Space*"—or a small focused area of *Space*—not otherwise defined, or occupied, by *Mass*. A *Seeker* may initially practice using "*specific spots on a (blank) wall*" for "*spots in the room*."]

B. <u>"THE WALL"</u> *(PC-1)*

This step is practiced lying down; eyes closed. Use *advanced version* to: "*look*" at the *Wall*; "*touch*" the *Wall*; and "*turn around*." [This is a popular *process* among *Seekers*, often *run* until an actual *ejection* (*Spiritual Perception*) occurs; but that is not its original purpose.]

C. <u>EMOTIONAL FLOWS</u> *(PC-2)*

This step has two parts, each is *run* on various "neutral" *objects* present; then a *Wall*; then with eyes closed (using something the *Seeker* has *Created/Imagined*). This is done by *intention*. But a *Seeker* should continue this until they get a real *sense* of it happening. The following is only an outline. [Use the instructions in *PC-2*.]

1a. Spot an Object/Wall/Creation.
1b. "Feel" various emotions about it.
2a. Spot an Object/Wall/Creation.
2b. Make it "feel" various emotions about you.

D. COMMUNICATION (PC-3)

Practice this step of *communication* with an *object*; then a *Wall*; then *parts of the Body*. Use *intention* and/or *Imagine* the *communication-and-acknowledgment* cycles—"Hello," "Thank You," &tc. [Refer to PC-3.]

E. "BELL, BOOK & CANDLE" (PC-3)

This step is practiced lying down; eyes closed. Use *advanced version*. [Refer to PC-3.]

F. CREATIVENESS PROCESSING (PC-5)

This step is practiced with eyes closed. It requires a *Seeker* to be able to *Create/Imagine* and actually *see* or *get a sense* that their *creations* are there. It is sometimes necessary to "create" and "throw away" a few before one is satisfied with their level of *perception* (or *perfection* of the *creation*).

A *godlike being* should be able to "create," "destroy" and "re-create" anything. While operating at *this* level of existence, our best route of exercising this *creative ability* is "mentally" or "imaginatively." In PC-5, the suggestion is for "acceptance," "rejection" and "substitutions" for anything (like "money" or "pain"). In essence, a *Seeker* increases their tolerance to "take it" or "leave it." It is also useful in *processing*, to "invent ways to waste it." [*Update*: also *process-out* "accepting it under duress" or "forced to have it."]

There is no standard *terminal item-list* of suggested *objects* or *creations* given here. Typically, worksheets and data from earlier *sessions* are used to determine if *residual fragmentation* remains on anything specific. A list could be developed by scanning *terminals* and *concepts* that represent each *Sphere of Existence* (and even the *Arcs of Infinity*). The only challenge here with *Solo-Processing*, is that a *Solo-Pilot* is more likely to *avoid* areas and *terminals* that they "don't like" (which defeats the purpose of the exercise).

G. PLACES YOU ARE NOT (PC-6)

This step (with eyes open or closed) operates by having a *Seeker* put *attention* on "exterior" (or *remote from the body*) *locations* to "check" to see that they "are not there." *Spot* many places. [This is another popular *process* that *Seekers* often *run* until an actual *ejection* occurs.]

"Spot Places You Are Not."

H. HANDLING ORDERS (PC-7)

This step is based on the *"advanced processing"* section in *PC-7*. Cycle through these PCL on one *terminal*, getting as many answers as you can, before going to the next one. The *terminals* are: PEOPLE; THINGS; PLACES; GROUPS; GOVERNMENTS; LIFEFORMS; ENERGIES; and SPIRITS.

1. *"Spot Some ___ You Are Not Giving Orders To."*
2. *"Spot Some ___ That Are Not Giving You Orders."*
3. *"Spot Some ___ That Are Not Giving Orders To Others."*
4. *"Spot Some ___ That Are Not Receiving Orders From Others."*
5. *"Spot Some ___ That Are Not Giving Orders To Themselves."*

After completing the above to a satisfactory end-point, a *Seeker* takes up the other side of this with the PCL below; for when they *agreed to follow another's orders* for the sake of *having a game*. [Refer to PC-12 and AT#2 for what we mean by *"game."*] Rehabilitation of "handling orders" means a *total freedom* of *choice* about *following* or *disagreeing* with "orders" — *not compulsively* one way or the other.

1. *"Spot An Incident When You Chose To Follow Another's Orders (for the sake of having a game)."*
2. *"Notice Some Things About It."*

Then *Spot* an *earlier incident*, and so on, until you reach the *earliest* one accessible; and *run* that. [The *upper-level* handling of any *turbulence* that does not immediately *disperse-on-realization* (*defrag-by-attention*) is to alternate: *"Spot Something In The Incident; Spot Something In The Room (Environment)."*]

1. *"Spot An Incident Where You Convinced Others To Follow Your Orders (for the sake of having a game)."*
2. *"Notice Some Things About It."*

Handle *earlier/earliest* as above.

Then practice the other *advanced exercises* for *"Attacking," "Hate," "Beauty"* and *"Safe To Be"* as given in *PC-7*.

I. (NOT)-KNOWINGNESS (PC-10)

Perform this step exactly as given in *PC-10*.

J. ADVANCED EXERCISES (PC-10)

Perform this step by completing all *ten* bullet-pointed {"•"} exercises given in the final section of *PC-10*. They are summarized as follows:

1. *Create/Imagine copies* of your (current) *Body*.
2. *Create/Imagine* "ideal" or "healthy" *copies* of your *Body*.
3. *Looking* into a mirror: *something there; nothing there*.
4. "Mentally" (or in *ZU-Vision*) decide *To Be* (as a *viewpoint*) in a *public place*; notice *scenery* and *motion*.
5. Using *Step-4*: *Create/Imagine* and *Uncreate* (*disperse*) *copies* of your *Body being* there *in front* of your *viewpoint*.
6. Using *Step-5*: alternate between *viewpoints*; "inside" and "outside" the *Body*.
7. Using *Step-6*: get a sense of others acknowledging the *Body being* there.
8. Using a *"basic solid shape"* to represent the *Body* for previous exercises.
9. Moving the *"basic solid shape"* around like a playing piece.
10. Performing the exercises using different *Body-Types*.

K. COLLAPSED-SPACE PROCESSING

The *"collapse-of-space"* phenomenon—having *Space* "collapse-in" on one—is *processed* similarly to the "getting-in" or "going-inside" *fragmentation* (given in earlier material) that we apply to all *Seekers* (including *entities*). [This *process* should be *added* to all *entity-handling procedures*.]

As with processing *"getting-in,"* this step is also *run* using a list of *keywords/buttons*. In this case, we are treating an even "higher magnitude" of *incident*. In fact, its original development concerned *processing-out* the *loss* of "Home Universe" and subsequent *fragmentation* concerning "world-closed-in" type of *incidents*.

Recall data from that far on the *Backtrack* may not be readily accessible to a *Seeker*, so they should do the best they can—and an individual has likely experienced many other *space-collapsing incidents* since then. It is important not to "push" too hard on vivid *recall*, or you may end up "pulling" in *imprinting* from an *entity* that is in close proximity—and misidentifying the *imprint* as your own (and it will persist in restimulation).

The *fragmented charge* on the *keywords* is best determined with *Meter-reads*. The *charge* is *dispersed* by *running "Recall"* on that *item* (using all circuits) and *dispersing-by-realization* or *Spotting* (until it no longer registers on the *GSR-Meter*). The list of *keywords/buttons* for this new process are:

1. *World Closed In*
2. *Space Collapsed*
3. *(Your) Energy Collapsed*
4. *Anchor (or Dimension) Points Collapsed*
5. *Anchor (or Dimension) Points Snapped-In*
6. *Everything Fell In (and/or Down)*
7. *Space Was Uncreated (or Dispersed or Un-Space)*
8. *(Your) Energy Was Uncreated (or Dispersed)*
9. *(Your) Frame Of Reference Collapsed*
10. *Caved-In*
11. *Pulled Back*
12. *Withdrew From Everything*
13. *Made It All Unreal*

When this *stabilization point* is completed, a *Seeker* may then return to the top of *Wizard Level-1 Procedure*, if desired (or still left incomplete). If *"entities"* or other *somatic-pings* have become intrusive to personal development, or it seems some *"blockage"* has become active as a result of *Wizard Training*, then a handling of *"entities"* (*&tc.*) may be required.

However, a *Seeker* should not become so immersed in, or enamored by the idea of, treating *"entities"* that there is no *session-time* available for their own *Wizard Training*. There is sometimes a point where you just need to strongly *intend* a *mass-communication* (*to them all*) that *"everyone will get processed in their own turn."*

Ideally, a *Seeker* will continue onto (and complete) *Wizard Level-2 Procedure* before treating the material of *"Entities & Fragments"* (*AT#5*) a second time.

Having *"spiritual perception"* is not the determinant factor of *Wizard Level-1* completion; only one's own *certainty* that they have *ejected Awareness "exterior to"* the *Body* is necessary. No matter what one's skill-level or experience, the next set of exercises given for *Wizard Level-2* can enhance the *certainty* that is now there—and the *perception* will follow.

EJECTION, PERCEPTION & BARRIERS
(*Wizard Level-2 Keynote Lecture Excerpts*)

In *Systemology*, we are frequently concerned with *viewpoints*—which is to say "*a point from which to view*," "*point-of-view*" or "*POV*." In the first two *Wizard-Levels*, the emphasis is specifically on, what are often called, "*remote viewpoints*"—because they are at "*points*" the *Alpha-Spirit* is "*viewing*" (or *perceiving*) from that are "*remote*" (or "*exterior-to*") the *sensory-perception* and *viewpoints* of a located *Body* (or *genetic vehicle*).

Ejection-of-Awareness is really a matter of one's *considerations* and *certainty* far more than any specific procedure. The same may be said concerning improvement of *Spiritual Perception*. True progress on the *Pathway* is marked by a *Seeker's* increasing ability to actually *change their considerations*—or "*change their minds*," so to speak. Many individuals are under the delusion that they already maintain this total freedom.

To handle *Spiritual Perception*, a *Wizard* would have to be able to handle *Energy* and *Space*, and of course, *Force*. An individual doesn't do this when operating within the *Human Condition*. There are all kinds of *sensors* and *filters* and *communication relays*—all kinds of various *machinery*—that are in the way of *actually "seeing" this Universe*. When a *Seeker* first "*ejects*," they are not really expected to have very vivid *perception*.

When we operate within the confines of the *Human Condition*—or more accurately, a *fixed viewpoint* within a *Body*—we are *perceiving* (or *receiving* "signals" and "cues" from) a *Universe* that is really only "*energy-waves*," "*standing-waves of mass*," "*particles*," and various "*forces*." All of this is transmitted and translated by all kinds of *mechanisms* and *machinery* before the *Mind-System* "projects" it on a kind of "screen" for the *Alpha-Spirit* to "*view*" and *perceive* as its own experience. Therefore, an individual is not really in the habit of *perceiving directly*.

Anything that hinders *perception* would be best defined as a "*barrier*"—"*barriers to perception*." Perhaps one of the more fundamental issues is just how many "*barriers*" an individual is *fixated on perceiving*—or is *compulsively* (or *unknowingly*) *"looking through"* in order *to perceive.*

A preoccupation with *barriers* generally defines our *"thoughts"* or *"thinkingness."* When we compare the state of *Knowingness* to levels of *Thinkingness*, all our "thinking" serves to do is handle *barriers*—either avoiding or overcoming them in some way. To be so preoccupied with them, is of course, to be at an *agreement-level* with them, and even at an *effect-level* that is below their mechanics or structure.

The experience of *this Physical Universe* via the *Human Condition* is considered the section of the *"Beta-Awareness Scale"* that falls between *zero* and *four* on our *Standard Model*. The *Human Condition* being: *Alpha-Spirit* plus a *genetic-vehicle*. But the *Standard Model* extends well beyond the *Human Condition*—it extends from *Infinity* to *Infinity*, and to that which we classify as *Alpha-Awareness* or *Actualized Awareness.*

While our *Standard Model does* systematize upper-level *Actualized Alpha* existence above *"four,"* there is also the *low-Awareness* scale that an *Alpha-Spirit* can maintain independent of a *Body*, that extends "out the bottom" *below zero* and *Body Death*. It consists of remorse for a *Body*; the need to protect a *Body*; even not wanting anything to do with a *Body*; but still very much *fixated* on *"bodies."*

When an individual *"ejects"* from a *Body*, by one means or another, there is no guarantee they are going *"out the top"* of the *Beta-Awareness Scale*; in fact, when individuals return to the *Human Condition* in their next "lifetime" or "incarnation" (after *Body Death*), it would suggest that they do not *"ascend out the top"* automatically (or by default).

Another *sub-zero Awareness-level* is: the use of *bodies* for *hiding in*. The *sensory-functions* of a *Body* allow it to be used by an *Alpha-Spirit* as a personal buffer for handling and *perceiving* the *energy* and *force* of *this Universe*. Over the course of our *fragmented* experience of many *Universes*, we have gotten a bit wise to the fact that these *energy-waves* and *force-fields* are able to be used against us (because we have *considered* such for this *level* of *reality-agreements*) and so we are reluctant to start *confronting* or handling them directly.

As the primary *barrier* an individual has to *getting-out* of their *Body*, or a *Head*, is their own *fixed ideas*: it stands to reason that a *Seeker* may be carrying a lot of *fear*—or some sense of *danger* or *mystery*—concerning what might be *"out there"*; or what they *fear* they might have to handle as a

Spiritual Being that is free from the *Human Condition*. The result is a *Spiritual Being* that has become *compulsively dependent* on *bodies*—and this *Physical Universe*—for an *"orientation-point"* or *"anchor-point"* to experience its own *Beingness*.

Space is also *perceived* as a *barrier* to *Knowingness*. Although it seems like an *"invisible barrier,"* the layered effect that we perceive at a great *distance* from *Earth* gives us the sense that it is *layers* of *darkness, blackness, unknowingness,* and *mystery*. This better explains our theory behind one of the *Wizard-Level* exercises, where a *Seeker "imagines"* many concentric spheres within spheres—or *layers*—of *darkness* or *blackness*, and then practices *"looking through"* these spheres or *layers*. Understanding the basic theory of this *lecture* will assist a *Seeker* to understand the purpose behind practicing the exercises provided for *Wizard-Levels 1* and *2*.

R.S.V.P— REMOTE SPIRITUAL VIEWPOINTS & PERCEPTION
(*Wizard Level-2 Procedure*)

Wizard Level-2 Procedure is approached similarly to *Wizard Level-1*. In this case, however, there is no change in *routine* if a *Seeker* finds difficulty with the steps. The remedy is simply to start from the top and work through those exercises for which one *does* have *certainty* on before attempting more difficult steps again. This should not be interpreted as a *loss*, because a *Seeker* will likely work through *Wizard Level-2 Procedure* multiple times to increase their handling of *ejection* and *perception*.

Completing this routine in one single *session* is not required or expected. The *"standard opening procedures"* of a *Formal Session* are not used in *Wizard-Level Training Routines*. Instead, at the beginning of each *session*, a *Seeker* runs *"Preventative Fundamentals"* (PC-9) as their first *process* (as they did with *Wizard Level-1*). A *Seeker* may also find that using some kind of *"blindfold"* is helpful when practicing some exercises.

A. EJECTION-OF-AWARENESS

At some point during the *Wizard-Level* work, a *Seeker* is likely to come across their preferred or favored *process(es)* or method(s) to *"induce"* or *"assist" ejection*. This is something that can only be determined after applying the various exercises suggested throughout this manual.

Wizard Level-2 is designed for a *Seeker* that has already achieved an *ejection-of-Awareness*; and is used to further develop that as a *"conscious ability."* Although some exercises are more commonly used than others for *"ejection,"* a direct method is not something we can specifically instruct for STEP-A.

"The Wall," "Places You Are Not," "Back Upper Corner-Points Of The Room," "3 Points In Body; 3 Points In Room," and *"3 Points In Room; 3 Points Outside Of This Universe"* are all popularly used (and some even directly appear in this *routine*). But, this does not rule out the potential for a *Seeker* to make a basic high-power *Intention* (*a Self-made command*) for simply *"stepping out"* (*ejecting*) at will.

The first time *ejection* is directly implied on the *Pathway*, is in the final exercise of *PC-10*—which is the final lesson of *Processing Level-4* and basic *Beta-Defragmentation Procedure*. [*Processing-Levels* 5 & 6 are *Pre-A.T. levels*.] In *PC-10* it describes it as: *"...the ability to conceive of or maintain a sense of "centering" and "focusing" your own Awareness as a viewpoint* (POV) *a few feet behind the head of your current Body."*

After *ejection*—before a *Seeker* is directed to do anything or go anywhere or look at the *Body*—the first several steps of this *routine* are intended to *stabilize* the *ejected*-state.

B. <u>MAKING COPIES</u> (*PC-2/PC-12*)

The basic PCL for this step are:

1. *"What Are You Looking At?"*
2. *"Make A Copy. (Make Many Copies)."*

With the *body's eyes* closed, post-*ejection*: the *Seeker* "makes" (*Creates/Imagines*) *copies* of whatever they are looking at—whatever they see. No matter what it is—however vague or fuzzy—you just *copy* what is there over and over again.

After you have several copies, you *"push them all together."* The first batch you *"pull the copies in on yourself"*; then the next batch of copies you can *"throw away"* (and continue alternating in this wise). This helps to remedy the *"loss of mass"* feeling after *ejecting* from the *Body*.

[Only *"pull in on yourself"* if you have *knowingly ejected* and are *"exterior to"* a *Body*. Otherwise, as a purely *imaginative exercise*, you would *"push them in on the Body."* Never *"pull-in"* while your *viewpoint* is from *inside the Body*. Get a sense of *"pushing-in"* from the *outside*. This step can be repeated throughout the routine to remedy whenever a *Seeker* feels their "attention thinning" from excessive exercises while *ejected*.]

The *vividness* of *perception*, or the *scenery* altogether, may change several times after treating the *copies*. You just keep *copying* whatever presents itself until there is no longer a change of perception (*e.g.*, vividness or detail isn't improving; scenery isn't shifting around). Then we balance the *somethingness* with the *Nothingness*. A *Seeker* extends or reaches their *Awareness* to "*Spot a Nothingness*" and then *copies* that for a while before going to STEP-C.

C. REACHING & HOLDING

Variations of this exercise appear in "*opening procedures*" of a *Formal Session*; and in "*Creation-Of-Space*" processes (*PC-5*). *Locating*, and *holding attention on*, "*corner-points*" of a square room is a form of "*Creation-Of-Space*" (defining "boundaries" or *dimension-points* of perceived *Space*).

Usually only two *corner-points* are used for this exercise—and they are often the "upper-back" *corner-points* of a room (or whatever is *behind* the *Body*), which forces *attention-Awareness* to *reach* in a direction other than what is in front of the *Seeker*.

This exercise can be modified to begin with *one corner-point*; and be extended to use all *four upper-corners* of a room—or even all *eight corner-points* (that form a "cube").

[*Update*: a *Seeker* should always end this exercise by "*letting go*" of any *corner-points* being "*held*."]

D. PLACES YOU ARE NOT (PC-6)

This step includes a *process* repeated from *Wizard Level-1*. A *Seeker* puts attention on "*remote locations*" to "check" to see that they "are not there."

  "*Spot A Place You Are Not. (Spot Many Places).*"

[*Update*: in *Traditional Piloting*, an effective transition from the previous step is: "*Now, Let Go; and Spot Some Places You Are Not.*"]

To effectively practice this step: a *Seeker* doesn't just quickly rattle off a list of arbitrary places. The goal is to actually *look* and *have certainty* from a particular *viewpoint* of *Space*.

E. ABILITY-TO-CONFRONT

This step asks a *Seeker* to *Spot* "things" (with the *body's eyes* closed) that they *consider* comfortable (or "safe") to *look at* (*confront*). This could also apply to "emotions" (or people displaying emotions). This is meant to increase tolerance for handling the *Physical Universe*.

This is not a *creativeness process*. A *Seeker* is not intended to *Create/Imagine* "things" to *look at*—but to actually "go" and *view* them in *this Physical Universe*. The accuracy of the *perception* is not as important as the actual *intention* to "be" at various *viewpoints*.

The basic PCL for this step are:

1. *"Spot Something It Would Be Safe To Look At In This Room."*
2. *"Spot Something It Would Be Safe To Look At Outside This Room."*

F. SHARED-SPACE

Part of the *reality-agreements* and *Implanted-Postulates* for *this Universe* include the *consideration* that "*two things* can't occupy the same *Space*." So long as a *Seeker* has heavy charge on this *consideration*—and the *consideration* that they, themselves, occupy a *Body* with *mass*—much of what an *Alpha-Spirit* is capable of would *seem* like a logical impossibility.

"What wouldn't you mind sharing the same space with?"

–or–

"What wouldn't you mind sharing the same space with you?"

Not *actually* having a *mass* present in *this Universe*, the *Alpha-Spirit* is very much capable of utilizing a *viewpoint* that does share *Space* with something that has *mass*. This step increases *Awareness* (and tolerance) on *ability* to *change* one's *Beingness*. The *process* is *run* to an *end-realization*, or all answers are exhausted.

G. LOCATIONAL VIEWPOINTS (*PC-5*)

This is based on a *meditation* found in *"eastern spiritual traditions."* A version, treated as an *imaginative exercise*, appears in *PC-5* (and should be reviewed for additional instruction and background).

[In *Traditional Piloting*, a *Co-Pilot* delivers *"locational"* PCL as quickly as a *Seeker* can perform them. This is generally determined by the observed *communication-lag* in responses.]

The PCL-sequence given in *PC-5* is:

1. *"Be Near (or Above) ___."*
2a. *"Be Inside Of ___."*
2b. *"Be Outside Of ___."*
3a. *"Be At The Center Of ___."*
3b. *"Be Outside Of ___."*
4a. *"Be On The Surface Of ___."*
4b. *"Be Above ___."*

[Note that the PCL-*keyword* (*trigger* or *button*) for POV-*Locational* (type) A.T. *processing* is "BE" (not "MOVE TO"). "Motion" between perceived *distances* in *space-time* is not a *consideration* (or *factor*) of the action.]

The applications for this exercise are unlimited. The original technique is called *"journeying to other planets"* — hence the *terminals* that a *Seeker* finds most interesting/ effective for this *process* are *"planets."*

A *systematic* approach would begin with being *"near the Earth"* or *"in the Sky"* before departing for other *planets*. Other preferred *terminals* are *"The Moon," "The Sun,"* and *"Mars."* It is best to *run* a few cycles of being *"near"* each of these *target-terminals* (with the first PCL) before *adding* the next PCL-set (*inside/outside, &tc.*) to the cycle.

A variation of this *"change-of-space"* technique is often used in *defragmentation processing*. By alternating the *direction* of *attention*, a *Seeker* is really *"shifting,"* between (for example) *"Being In The Incident"* and *"Being In The Room," &tc.* This gives a *Seeker* certainty that what they're "holding onto" is really "somewhere else."

A *Seeker* already has too many *Universes* confused with, or superimposed over, *their own*. One purpose of A.T. exercises is for a *Seeker* to *get a sense* of "separateness" — not "connectedness" — with *this Physical Universe*.

H. OWNERSHIP-OF-REALITY (PC-11)

With the *body's eyes* open: *select* a certain section of *"wall"* —like a circular *spot* that is a few feet in diameter. This can also be done with large (significant, heavy, *&tc.*) objects that are in view. Alternate (repeatedly):

1. *"Get The Idea That You Are Creating It."*
2. *"Get The Idea That ___ Is Creating It."*

For the second PCL, use each of the following terminals separately (*running* each to a satisfactory *end-point* before going to the next): ANOTHER; SOCIETY; LIFEFORMS; A BODY; (YOUR) {SPIRITUAL} MACHINERY; THE {OBJECT ITSELF}; THE PHYSICAL UNIVERSE; AGREED-UPON MACHINERY; SPIRITS; and (A) GOD.

A *Seeker* may discover that *they* (*themselves*) are *not* the one *creating* everything—although it is in their capability. Most of the time, it will be discovered that "old machinery" is responsible for things persisting.

I. <u>BODY-SYMPATHY</u>

When the *Body* is severely *injured*, or even *dies*, an individual that is *fixedly* "*interior*" will *eject* suddenly—but then quickly "*snap-in*" again. This is because when "*exterior to*" a *Body*, at *low-Awareness* levels, an *Alpha-Spirit* has a *reactive-tendency* to "sympathize" with a *Body*. It "*snaps-in*" to try and "protect" or "heal" or even "reanimate" it.

This *process* is included here because it assists in overcoming the general impulse and tendency, while demonstrating both *interiorizing* and *ejection*. This can be *run* as "*imaginatively*" (or as "*actually*") as one's current *ability/perception* allows for. [The *end-realization* is that actions to "*fix*" (*&tc.*) something are best handled *from* the "*outside*."]

1. "Look Around The Room And Choose An Object. (Preferably large)."
2. "Decide That There Is Something Wrong With It. (Pretend anything)."
3. "Feel Sorry For The Object; Sympathize With It; Say, 'Oh, Poor Thing'."
4a. "Imagine Yourself 'Going-In-To' The Object To 'Fix It'."
4b. "Decide That You Are 'Inside' The Object; Its Mass Is All Around You."
5a. "Look Around 'Inside' The Object."
5b. "Realize That 'Inside' Is Not A Good Place To 'Fix It' From; That You Made A Mistake 'Going-In'."
6a. "Eject Awareness From The Object; Imagine That You Are Looking Down At It."
6b. "Imagine 'Fixing It' From The 'Outside'; Imagine 'Putting' An 'Energy Beam' On It And Say, 'There, That Fixes It'."
7. "Let Go Of It. (Select Another Object And Repeat The Process)."

For your second application (in a separate *session*): *run* the *process* on "Created/Imagined" objects rather than the physical ones (in a room).

For your third application: *run* the *process* on "dead bodies" (*Imagined*).

For "6b" alternate: *"fixing it successfully from the outside (to resurrect it)"* and *"deciding it isn't worth the trouble and abandoning it."*

[This *process* may also be practiced on the *Body*. You can *perceive "putting out"* or *"projecting" energy beams* on anything; getting the *Universe* to directly respond with a physical *effect* is another matter, and a higher gradient of work.]

J. TRUTH/UNTRUTH

Alternate the PCL:

1. *"Spot 3 Things That Are True."*
2. *"Spot 3 Things That Are Not True."*
3. *"Spot 3 Things That Are True For Someone Else."*
4. *"Spot 3 Things That Are Not True For Someone Else."*
5. *"Spot 3 Things That Are True For Others."*
6. *"Spot 3 Things That Are Not True For Others."*

K. THE RIGHT-TO-BE

This step is often practiced outdoors (in public); but as an *"eyes-closed ZU-Vision" process*, it may also be done alone—indoors or in Nature, *&tc.*

This *process* is an *exercise* in *intention*. It is also a practice of *"permitting freedom"* and *"granting livingness"* (which is important for handling *all beings*; not just *"entities"*). Each PCL is done several times (*with full intention*) on several *"target-terminals"* before going to the next; then repeat the full cycle.

[The emphasis of the *process* is found in the first two PCL.]

1. *"Grant Things/People (Another) The Right To Be There."*
2. *"Grant Things/People (Another) The Right To Do What They're Doing."*
3. *"Imagine Things/People (Another) Giving You The Right To Grant Rights."*
4. *"Grant Others The Right To Grant Rights."*

L. NO-BARRIERS

Alternate the PCL:

1. *"Spot Some Barriers That Are Not In Front Of Your Face."*
2. *"Spot Some Barriers That Are Not Behind You."*

3. *"Spot Some Barriers That Are Not On Your Right Side."*
4. *"Spot Some Barriers That Are Not On Your Left Side."*
5. *"Spot Some Barriers That Are Not Above You."*
6. *"Spot Some Barriers That Are Not Below You."*

M. <u>BLACKNESS (AND MYSTERY)</u>

Run the PCL:
1. *"Look Around The Room And Choose An Object."*
2. *"Create/Imagine a Standing-Wave (or Field) Of Blackness In Front Of It."*
3. *"Alternate A Few Times: Fixing Your Attention On The Blackness; And Taking It Off."*

Continue *running* this *process* until you have no "attraction" to the "Blackness" (*Veil of Mystery*); and although you have *intended* for it to be there, you can ignore it and *"look through"* it. [*Disperse* the "standing-wave" at the end.]

Then repeat the *process* on another object. Then apply the same *process* to Created/Imagined objects. [Certainty on this step is required for the next one.]

N. <u>LAYERS-OF-BLACKNESS</u>

Run the PCL (with eyes closed):
1. *"Create/Imagine Many Layers Of Blackness Around You."*
2. *"Look Through Each Layer (In Turn) To See The Next One."*

O. <u>IN-AND-OUT ON OBJECTS</u>

Run the PCL:
1. *"Look Around The Room And Choose An Object."*
2a. *"Get The Sense Of 'Going-In-To' The Object; And Being It."*
2b. *"Imagine Being The Object, In The Object, As Vividly As You Can."*
3. *"Eject From The Object."*

Repeat several times and on different objects. This may also be practiced with ZU-Vision: *Spotting* objects outside the *session-room* (in a city, *&tc.*) and *"going-in-and-out"* them. [This exercise is found among some of the most ancient mystical practices and *"Hermetic"* training.]

P. EMOTIONAL-INDEPENDENCE

Run the PCL:

1. "Decide To Feel An Emotion; And Feel It."
2. "Make The Body Feel A Different Emotion."

[You continue *feeling* the original emotion, while the *Body* experiences another.]

Q. CONSIDERATION-OF-BEINGNESS

Run the PCL:

1. "What Kind Of Object Can You Be For Certain?"
2. "Be It; And Experience It."

Repeat many times. [Then *run* as: "What Kind of Energy.." and "What Kind Of Space.."]

R. ENERGY-SOURCES

This *process* is applied only after a *Seeker* has handled the ability to identify "Sources" and "What Is" (PC-11) and understands what "energy" means (PC-13/PC-14).

The basic PCL for this step is:

"Create (Imagine) An Energy-Source."

–or–

"Create (Imagine) Something To Give You Energy."

Repeat many times with many things. [A *Seeker* can do this with increasing magnitude, beginning with *generators* and *power-stations*, then working up to *sun-stars* and *spiritual machinery*. This *process* is *run* to give a *Seeker* certainty that *they* (*themselves*) are their own *energy-source* for *Creating/Imagining* these *mental images*; and also to loosen *considerations* regarding dependency on "external" *energy-sources*.]

S. TERMINALS

Alternate the PCL:

1. "Spot Two ___ That You Don't Object To Having Together."
2. "Spot Two ___ That You Don't Object To Having Apart."

Repeat many times on each of the following *terminals* (in turn): PARTICLES; OBJECTS; ANIMALS; PEOPLE; and SPACES.

T. DISAGREEMENT-WITH-GRAVITY

The basic PCL for this step are:

1. *"Get A Sense Of 'Falling Upwards'."*
2. *"Get A Sense Of Other Things 'Falling Upwards'."*

A *Seeker* should stay on one PCL to get a real certainty on their *"sense"* or *"impression"* before alternating.

U. ENERGY AND MACHINERY

Professional Course material for *"Spiritual Energy"* (PC-13) and *"Spiritual Machinery"* (PC-14) should be reviewed and all exercises practiced (in their advanced versions, if applicable). Given the progress a *Seeker* has since made, they should have a greater reality on the previous material when revisiting it at *Level-8*.

V. INTERIORIZATION PRACTICE (*PC-5*)

In this step, a *Seeker* practices "going in-to" (*interiorizing*) and "getting-out of" (*ejecting*) many various *terminals*—objects, animals, people, buildings, mountains, planets, suns, galaxies, universes, *&tc.* (to the extent of their *ability* and *perception*).

W. SPLITTING

In this step, a *Seeker* "Imagines" their *Awareness-of-Being-Oness* "splitting" into two: *being* both "in the Body" and "exterior-to it" simultaneously.

APPENDIX: A WIZARD-LEVEL SESSION
(*Basic Script Example*)

0a. *"Start of Session."*
0b. *"Close your eyes."*

1a. *"Spot a point in the room."*
1b. *"Spot a point in your body."*
1c. *"Find the same point in the room."*
1d. *"Find the same point in your body."*
1e. *"The same point in the room."*
1f. *"The same point in your body."*
   {*1e* and *1f* repeated several times}

2a. *"Spot two points in the room."*
2b. *"Spot two points in your body."*
2c. *"Find the same two points in the room."*
2d. *"Find the same two points in your body."*
2e. *"The same two points in the room."*
2f. *"The same two points in your body."*
   {*2e* and *2f* repeated several times}

3a. *"Spot three points in the room."*
3b. *"Spot three points in your body."*
3c. *"Find the same three points in the room."*
3d. *"Find the same three points in your body."*
3e. *"The same three points in the room."*
3f. *"The same three points in your body."*
   {*3e* and *3f* repeated a dozen times}

4a. *"Three points in the room."*
4b. *"Three points outside the building."*
   {*4a* and *4b* repeated a dozen times}

5a. *"Wherever you are, whatever you are looking at; make a copy of it."*
5b. *"Make another copy of it; exactly like the first."*
5c. *"And make another copy of it."*
5d. *"And another copy."*
5e. *"Take these copies; pull them together; and push them into the Body."*
5f. *"Whatever you are looking at now; make a copy just like it."*
5g. *"Make another copy of it."*
5h. *"And make another copy of it."*
5i. *"And another copy."*
5j. *"Take these copies; pull them together; and push them into the Body."*

6a. *"Wherever you are, reach your attention to locate a Nothingness."*
6b. *"Make a copy of it."*
6c. *"And make another copy of it."*
6d. *"And another copy."*
6e. *"Take these copies; pull them together; and throw them away in the distance."*

7a. *"Spot a point in space where you are certain you are not."*
7b. *"Spot another place you are not."*
7c. *"Spot two places you are certain you are not."*
7d. *"Spot three places you are not."*

7e. *"Spot three houses you are not in."*
7f. *"Spot three schools you do not attend."*
7g. *"Spot three businesses you do not work for."*
7h. *"Spot three groups you do not belong to."*
7i. *"Spot three animals you are not being."*
7j. *"Spot three planets you are not currently on."*
7k. *"Spot three universes you are not currently in."*

8a. *"Spot a calm space in this Universe."*
8b. *"Spot a calm place in the Body."*
   {*8a* and *8b* repeated a couple times}

9a. *"Spot the two back upper corner-points in the room."*
9b. *"Reach your attention and just hold onto those two corner-points."*
   {*corner-points* held for two minutes}

10a. *"Sense the chair under the Body."*
10b. *"Sense the floor beneath the feet."*
10c. *"End of Session."*

A.T. MANUAL #7
MASTERING ASCENSION

Keep this reference material accessible:
PC Lesson-1 to 16; Processing-Levels 0 to 6.
AT Manual #1, "The Secret of Universes"
AT Manual #2, "Games, Goals & Purposes"
AT Manual #3, "The Jewel of Knowledge"
AT Manual #4, "Implanted Universes"
AT Manual #5, "Entities & Fragments"
AT Manual #6, "Spiritual Perception"

Review this prerequisite material:
PC Lesson-13, "Spiritual Energy"
PC Lesson-16, "Alpha Thought"

SELF-DIRECTION & INTENTION

There are many *"New Age"* publications and *"pop-spirituality"* seminars that emphasize various *"secrets of attraction"* and *"powers of intention,"* &tc. This is primarily because all modern *"New Age"* and *"new consciousness"* material is an extension of the *"New Thought"* movement developing in America during the late 1800s and early 1900s—combined with the influence of a *"magical (magickal) revival"* simultaneously occurring in Europe, where *"Will"* became the new *sacred name* for *Self*.

Increasing *"personal horsepower"* behind *"focused intention"* is a critical component for progressive development on the *Pathway* to *Self-Actualizing* as an *"Ascended Master."* It is not, however, the direct emphasis of earlier *processing-levels*, which focus on more general *defragmentation* of the *Mind-System* and the *Human Condition*. We have specific *systematic* reasons for handling the *Pathway* in this way.

Much like *"Alpha-Thought"* (see *PC-16*), a true and original *"cause-point"* or *"source-point"* of *Intention* is always *"exterior-to,"* *"senior"* to, or otherwise *"beyond"* the level of *Beta-Existence* and even the *Mind-System*. It is plotted at "5" on the *Standard Model (ZU-Line)*.

At an *Alpha-level*, *Intention* is a resulting product, expression, or manifestation of *Alpha-Thought*; similar to how *Effort* is a resulting product of *Thought* in *Beta-Existence*. Typically, the *standard-issue Human* is not operating by *direct Intention* in *Beta-Existence*, but instead, *via* (or *through*) a *fragmented Mind-System*.

A *"communication"* or *"postulate"* is directed by the *Alpha-Spirit* along the *ZU-Line*. The first *"communicable expression"* of this—outside one's own *Personal Universe*—is an *Intention*. The *Alpha-Spirit* has already *postulated* that "something" exists (or "*Is*") and can now *intend* "something" about it. This is how things directly operated in earlier *Universes*, before the *condensation* and *solidity* of both a *Mind* and *Existence*.

While operating in *this Universe*, on *Earth*, and with the *Human Condition*, we are not in the habit of *knowingly Self-Directing Intention* toward *bodies* and other *energetic-mass*. In most cases, these *Intentions* are simply "absorbed" by the convoluted *circuitry* and *machinery* of a *Mind-System* (as a *receipt-point* and *relay*).

Once the *communication* of our original *Intention* has "sputtered" around the *considerations* and *reality-agreements* of the *Mind* for a while, it eventually results in (*Self* + *Body*) experiencing some state of "*Beta-Awareness*" before manifesting as an *effort* (with a *Body*) toward the *action* of using "*force*" in *Beta-Existence*.

A pure *Intention* originates from a *consideration-of-beingness*—or even a *viewpoint*—that is "*exterior-to*" the *Mind-Body* considerations. Anything else and we are not really handling *Intention*; we would be handling *reactive-imagery* and *associative thought* of the programmed, conditioned, and implanted *Mind-System*.

When effectively applied, previous *processing* will have mostly *cleared the way* for *Intention* to be directly *communicated*. This is when a *Seeker/Wizard* can start putting greater emphasis on increasing the "*power*" or "*volume*" of those *Intentions*. Alternating working on this and other *upper-level processing* ("*Implants*" and "*Entities*").

This *Advanced Training* manual (*AT#7*) presents material *Wizard Level-3X*. As of early 2024, this *level* is still in its "experimental stage" (hence the "X")—but it is sufficiently developed for standard release in the "*Keys to the Kingdom*" *A.T.* series.

[As other "higher" (still theoretical) gradients of the *Wizard-Levels* are researched, some material found here may be added to, altered, or altogether reassigned to another *level*.]

INTENTION: DIRECTING THOUGHT
(*Wizard Level-3X Keynote Lecture*)

Having treated "*Entities*" in *A.T. Manual #5*, and "*Ejection*" (*Wizard Level-1*) and "*Perception*" (*Wizard Level-2*) in *A.T. Manual #6*, we arrive at *Wizard Level-3X*: "*Intention*."

To most effectively progress with *Wizard Level-3X*: a *Seeker* should *alternate* between practicing "*objective*" exercises of "*Intention-On-Mass*" and *processing-sessions* spent *defragmenting* the *considerations* (and other *inhibitors* and *suppressors*) of "*Intention*." The frequency of *alternating*—how often or when—is at a *Seeker's* own discretion to determine for their case.

The basic experimental "*processing routine*" given for *Wizard Level-3X* (in this manual) is fairly *self-guiding* and easily applied by a *Level-8 systemologist*. Therefore, the part we will lead off with for our opening instruction pertains to the potential *systematic* application of other *"objective"* exercises to *standard procedure*.

"INTENTION-ON-MASS" (WIZ-3X)

This *"objective exercise"* formula is meant as only *one* part of the complete *Wizard Level-3X* routine. The *other* part is directly *processing-out fragmented considerations* and *postulates*—and other inhibiting factors, such as *Implants* and *Entities*. This cannot be overstated, because a *Seeker* is likely to take a greater interest in, and put more significance on, the *"objective exercises"* right from the start.

The real purpose of *Wizard Level-3X* is to increase certainty on the *ability* to focus and *communicate* a clear *Intention*—which is to say:

1. certainty that a focused *communication*
2. has *arrived* at its *intended "receipt-point"* (or *"effect-point"*)
3. and is *"duplicated"* there, perfectly (accurately) with the "meaning" originally *intended*; for which
4. it is *acknowledged* as having happened.

That is the basic *"communication-cycle"* a *Seeker* should follow when applying *objective exercises*. And it *is* a full *"cycle"* that a *Seeker* should observe. The individual *projects* an *Intention* on a *communication-line* as the *"source-point"* (or *Cause*). They must also be *willing-to-be* the *"receipt-point"* to *perceive* a *"response."*

Our emphasis is on certainty (without question) that a *communicated Intention* is *received*. While this can be *"coached,"* it is not easily *Co-Piloted*. A *Seeker* is typically their own best "judge" on the degree of certainty they have regarding *Intention* and remaining follow-through of the *cycle*.

A *Seeker's* approach to *Wizard Level-3X* must remain *systematic*. We are treating *upper-level* subjects that are too easily *invalidated* by other individuals and the *Physical Universe*. We must keep the aforementioned goals for this *level* in view, rather than invalidating our *gains* and abandoning the *Pathway* simply because *objects* in the room don't just start *"floating all around"* on *command*.

The *Systemology Society "research division"* reviewed a tremendous amount of *"New Age," "New Thought"* and *"para-psychological"* material pertaining to *"telekinesis"* for the development of *Wizard Level-3X*—little of which was *systematically applicable* to our purposes, but it provided a place to start.

First of all, the *"para-scientific"* fields exploring this previously have misappropriated the *"source-point"* of *Intention* as the *Mind* (such as *"mind over matter"*), when all *spiritual abilities* are those originating with the *Alpha-Spirit* and *Alpha Thought*—not a *Mind*.

Technically speaking: standard *circuitry* (*Implanting, &tc.*) of the *Mind-System* is a *barrier* that an *Alpha-Spirit* must properly *dissolve* or *disperse* in order to get their *Intention* clearly across. *Intention* is an *Alpha*-quality that is roughly equivalent to *"effort"* in *Beta-Existence*, which is why *direct-intention* can mimic the *effects* of *effort* in *this Physical Universe*.

Secondly, by *"telekinetic ability,"* we mean affecting the *energetic-mass* of *Beta-Existence* "remotely" by *Intention* (without direct intervention/*effort* applied by a *body*, or some other "physical" means). Indeed, *"levitation"* is one key example of this. And while it *is* contrary to, or in *disagreement* with, *reality-agreements* maintaining *this Physical Universe*, such was not the case for *Alpha-Spirits* in previous *Universes* (versions of *Beta-Existence*).

Thirdly, we considered *mirroring* the "experimental procedures" from various research organizations that study the *telekinetic* phenomenon of "moving things with one's mind." These procedures are similar to what you see in movies with "paranormal investigators." In most cases, an "ashtray" is set on a table. It has a "circle" drawn around it and the individual focuses on moving the *ashtray* out of the "circle."

We liked the idea of the *ashtray*; we disliked the activity itself as a *systematic process* or exercise. For one, it limited the idea of practicing with *alternating Intentions*, when about all you could really say to the thing is *"move"* or *"move"* repeatedly. The other concern was the *invalidation issue*—setting up a hidden standard for personal gains where the only achievement of success possible is spontaneous "action-at-a-distance."

The *ashtray*, however, *is* an appropriate *object* for instructing this type of *objective* exercise.

1. It is a *receptacle* by design. For *"consideration"* and *"visualization"* sake, this allows a *Seeker* to more easily conceive of directing *Intention* not only *into* the "substance" of the *object*, but also *"filling"* it, and *permeating* its *Space*.
2. It is of *moderate size* to focus attention on; preferably colored-*glass*, rather than *plastic* or *transparent*.
3. It is *lightweight*, which makes it easy to physically handle during exercises.

Practice of this exercise will not be unusual to an experienced *Seeker*. We previously demonstrated other variations of this technique—for example, when the PCL called for *"making objects feel an emotion," &tc*. However, in previous *processing-levels*, we did not particularly address the *Intention*, or emphasize the *"communication-cycle"* that ensues for the exercise to be truly effective as a *systematic process*.

The following *formula* identifies the *"communication- cycle."* A *Seeker* should work toward developing the highest possible *certainty* on these basic points during their practice:

0. *Forming a clear "Intention"—thinking a 'Thought';*
1. *Directing the Intention toward, inside, and all around, the object;*
2. *Knowing that the Intention (command, communication, &tc.) has been received;*
3. *Perceiving the response, feedback, or effect-action taking place.*
4. *Acknowledging that the response (&tc.) has been received.*

There are two *"intended commands"* directed toward the *object* in this *systematic* version of other methods. They are: *"Rise Up!"* and *"Set Down!"* The *acknowledgment* that is given to end either *cycle* is *"Thank You!"*

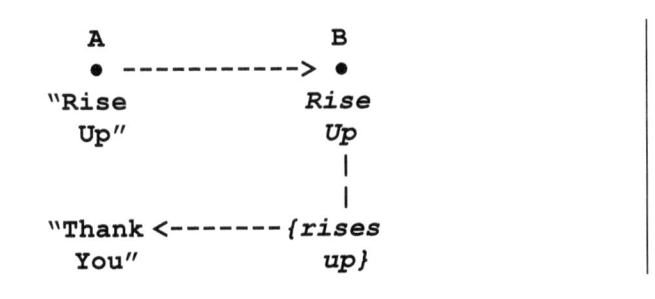

```
                A                       B
                • ------------> •
              "Rise                   Rise
               Up"                     Up
                                        |
                                        |
              "Thank <-------{rises
               You"                     up}
```

To validate that there is *feedback* or *effect* for this exercise: after there is certainty that the directed *Intention* to "Rise Up" is received, the *Seeker* physically *lifts* the *object* up; and after "Set Down," they *set* it back down.

The basic instruction for this exercise is no more complicated than this. To provide variation to the practice, we suggest:

1. commands *intended* out loud;
2. commands *intended* silently; and
3. *Intentions* given with nonsense words.

ADDITIONAL DATA ON LEVITATION

An occurrence of the actual at-a-distance phenomenon of *"telekinesis"* or *"levitation"* is *not* one of the prescribed *Wizard Level-3X* end-goals. This does not exclude the possibility for a *Wizard-Level Seeker* to achieve it; but it is not how we measure personal success for this gradient of *upper-level* work.

Based on our experimental and research data: if and when a *Seeker* experiences this phenomenon, it will occur without any actual *effort* or *strain*—or any other *forced intensity* behind the directed *Intention*—and to accomplish "on command," would require being in perfect *communication* with the *target-object*.

Although we have not yet treated the subject of *"energy"* directly for the *Wizard-Levels*, it can already be determined that the matter of *"levitation"* (*&tc.*) is not a concern of *"having enough energy"* to physically move the *mass*. The *Alpha-Spirit* has unlimited ability to *create "Energy"* at will, which is only hindered by other *considerations* about *"energy-sources"* and *"restrictive uses"* (*&tc.*) that are specific to *this Universe*. In spite of this, for our *practice exercises*, it is still better to work with *mass* that can be easily handled (like an *ashtray*). Working with heavier *masses* may just *"pull-in"* additional *considerations* regarding one's physical abilities.

This all being said: the primary focus of *Wizard Level-3X Procedure* is *processing willingness, reach,* and *responsibility*, to increase clarity of *Intention* and the certainty of *being-at-Cause*.

WIZARD LEVEL-3X PROCEDURE
(*Example–Intention: Levitation*)

Start each *session* by *running* "*Preventative Fundamentals*" (PC-9). Now that we are treating specific subjects or areas at *Level-8*, it might be helpful to also check "*Preventative Fundamentals*" on any accessible *entities* that may get "*restimulated*" or "*intrusively active*" regarding "*Levitation.*" This is done by addressing the surrounding area, usually with a *Biofeedback-Device* (after any personal "*Meter-reads*" on the word "*Levitation*" are *defragmented*).

This *upper-level* procedure utilizes virtually all *Systemology processing* theories in a single routine. It is applied to the example for which we have been discussing—"*Intention: Levitation*"—but its formula could be easily modified to *process-out* innumerable other areas as well.

A. ANALYTICAL RECALL

Run the PCL as *Basic (Light) Recall*. Cycle through each set-of-three a few times before going to the next. Since access to the *Backtrack* may be currently limited, if you are unable to directly "*recall*" what is asked for, *consider* the first "*idea*" or "*mental image*" that occurs. If nothing is *resurfacing* or "*coming to mind,*" simply "*Imagine*" a scenario for that *item-line*.

PCL = "*Recall a time...*"

1a. "*you enjoyed levitating something.*"
1b. "*another enjoyed you levitating something.*"
1c. "*another enjoyed others levitating something.*"

2a. "*you disliked levitating something.*"
2b. "*you disliked another levitating something.*"
2c. "*another disliked others levitating something.*"

3a. "*you levitated something because you thought it was important.*"
3b. "*you felt it was important for another to levitate.*"
3c. "*another felt it was important for others to levitate.*"

4a. "*you levitated something to create a good effect.*"
4b. "*you felt it created a good effect for another to levitate.*"
4c. "*another felt it created a good effect for others to levitate.*"

5a. "*you could levitate something, but chose not to.*"

5b. *"another could levitate something, but chose not to."*
5c. *"others could levitate something, but chose not to."*
6a. *"you levitated something and it improved communication."*
6b. *"another levitated something and it improved communication."*
6c. *"others levitated something and it improved communication."*
7a. *"you levitated something and it made people like you better."*
7b. *"another levitated something and it made people like them better."*
7c. *"others levitated something and it made people like them better."*

B. <u>BASIC CONSIDERATIONS/DECISIONS</u>

Run the PCL:

1. *"Recall some decisions you have made about levitating."*
2. *"Recall some decisions someone else has made about levitating."*
3. *"Recall some decisions others have made about levitating."*
4. *"Write down some bad effects you could create by levitating."*
5. *"Write down some good effects you could create by levitating."*
6. *"Write down some games you would spoil by levitating."*
7. *"Write down some new games you could have by levitating."*

C. <u>HELP</u>

One of the reasons an *Alpha-Spirit* restrains their abilities is because they don't believe that it will *help* others, or it is connected to times when they have *failed-to-help*. We focus on the more positive aspects in this *basic process*, rather than *resurfacing* "trauma." But we still must treat the *considerations* from both sides: *"levitating"* and *"not-levitating."*

1. *"How could you help another by not-levitating?"*
2. *"How could another help you by not-levitating?"*
3. *"How could another help others by not-levitating?"*
4. *"How could another help themselves by not-levitating?"*
5. *"How could you help yourself by not-levitating?"*
6. *"How could you help another by levitating?"*
7. *"How could another help you by levitating?"*
8. *"How could another help others by levitating?"*
9. *"How could another help themselves by levitating?"*
10. *"How could you help yourself by levitating?"*

D. PROBLEMS AND SOLUTIONS

Run the PCL (repeat as needed):

1a. *"Spot a problem that not-levitating would solve."*
1b. *"How would that be a solution?"*
2a. *"Spot a problem that another/others might solve by not-levitating."*
2b. *"How would that be a solution?"*
3a. *"Spot a problem that you might solve by preventing others from levitating."*
3b. *"How would that be a solution?"*
4a. *"Spot a problem that you might solve for others by not-levitating."*
4b. *"How would that be a solution?"*

E. PROBLEMS AND RESISTANCE

This *process* provides another angle for addressing *considerations-of-problems*. It follows the theory that an individual must *be resisting against* "the other side" (and therefore feeding it *attention* and *energy*) in order to be *fixated* on a "problem." Run the PCL (repeat "b" a number of times to answer "a"):

1a. *"Spot a problem that you could have with levitation."*
1b. *"What would you have to 'resist' (or 'be resisting') to consider that a problem?"*
2a. *"Spot a problem that someone else could have with levitation."*
2b. *"What would they have to 'resist' (or 'be resisting') to consider that a problem?"*
3a. *"Spot a problem that others could have with levitation."*
3b. *"What would they have to 'resist' (or 'be resisting') to consider that a problem?"*

F. CONNECTEDNESS/SEPARATENESS

Alternate the PCL within each set:

1a. *"Spot an object in the room."*
1b. *"Get a sense of being connected with it."*
1c. *"Get a sense of being separate from it."*
    {alternate (1b) and (1c)}
2a. *"Spot objects in the room that you would be willing to connect with."*
2b. *"Spot objects in the room that you would be willing to make connect with you."*

3a. *"Spot objects in the room that you are separate from."*
3b. *"Spot objects in the room that are separate from you."*

G. INVALIDATION

This *process* is *run* like checking *"Preventative Fundamentals"* on a *GSR-Meter* for any *"charge"* that *registers*. For each *Meter-reading-item*, you *"Spot {'What Is'}"* for that item until it *discharges/disperses* on *realization*.

1. *"On 'Levitation'; have you invalidated yourself?"*
2. *"On 'Levitation'; has another/others invalidated themselves?"*
3. *"On 'Levitation'; have you been invalidated by another?"*
4. *"On 'Levitation'; have you invalidated another/others?"*
5. *"On 'Levitation'; has another invalidated others?"*
6. *"On 'Levitation'; have you gotten another/others to invalidate themselves?"*

H. RESISTANCE/WILLINGNESS

This *process* requires directing (putting or placing) a *"thought"* or *"concept"* (*Intention*) into an *object*. Repeat with many *objects*.

1. *"Spot an object in the room."*
2a. *"Put into it 'a resistance to being levitated'."*
2b. *"Put into it 'a willingness to being levitated'."*
    {alternate (2a) and (2b) on *object*}

I. CAUSE/BLAME

This is partly an *"imaginative process."* It requires perceiving (receiving) a *"response"* or *"intention"* (*communication*) from an *object*. [Of course, the whole thing occurs based on your own Intention to *create* (or *Imagine*) and getting the sense of it occurring.] Alternate (2a) and (2b); but *run* one several times before shifting to the other. Repeat with many *objects*.

1. *"Spot an object in the room."*
2a. *"Have it looking up at you with admiration for being Cause."*
2b. *"Have it looking up to blame you."*

J. HARMFUL-ACTS/HOLD-BACKS

Harmful-Acts lead to *Hold-Backs* (see *PC-6*), which are a major contributor to compulsively restraining abilities. Since access to the *Backtrack* may be currently limited, if you are unable to directly *"Spot"* what is asked for, *consider* the first *"idea"* or *"mental image"* that occurs. If nothing is *resurf-*

acing or "coming to mind," simply "*Imagine*" a scenario for that *item-line*. *Spot* many examples for each:
1. "*Spot an act of harming something by levitating.*"
2. "*Spot a harmful-act of preventing others from levitating.*"
3. "*Spot times when you regretted having levitated something. If necessary, scan the incident in reverse; Spot the harmful-act 'As-It-Is' and defragment-by-realization.*"
4. "*Spot times you had justification for stopping others from levitating. Write down any of these 'justification considerations'. Check for an earlier harmful-act against the terminal (others) or against you (if you do think you were really justified in stopping them).*"

K. <u>VALIDATION-FOR-INABILITY</u>

Often times, if an individual is *not* using an *ability*, it is because they *consider* themselves as getting *more validation* (from others) for *not* using the ability. Run the PCL for *considerations*:
1. "*How could you validate someone else for not-levitating?*"
2. "*How could someone else validate you for not-levitating?*"
3. "*How could others validate others for not-levitating?*"

L. <u>HARMFUL-ACTS AND SOLUTIONS</u>

In previous *Universes*, *levitation-abilities* allowed for so much "trouble" that we worked very hard at preventing it with the *reality-agreements* of this Physical Universe. Much of our own *agreement* to these conditions involves trying to solve the problem of others being able to *levitate* as a means to *harmful-acts*.
1a. "*Write down a harmful-act you could commit against another/others by levitating.*"
1b. "*How would that be solved or prevented?*"
2a. "*Write down a harmful-act another/others could commit against you by levitating.*"
2b. "*How would that be solved or prevented?*"
3a. "*Write down a harmful-act another could commit against others by levitating.*"
3b. "*How would that be solved or prevented?*"
4a. "*Write down a harmful-act you could commit against yourself by levitating.*"

4b. *"How would that be solved or prevented?"*

M. MENTAL REACH

This is an *"objective exercising"* break from the previous, more *subjective*, processes. Simply *"Spot objects in the room"* and *"mentally reach and let-go (from each one) three times."*

N. ALPHA-THOUGHT/POSTULATES

Alternate the PCL:

1. *"Spot/Recall some postulates you have made about levitation."*
2. *"Spot/Recall some postulates someone else has made about levitating."*
3. *"Spot/Recall some postulates others have made about levitating."*
4. *"Spot/Recall some postulates you have made about another/others levitating."*

O. JUSTIFICATION CONSIDERATIONS

This is a *listing* exercise. If you are using a *Biofeedback-Device*, then you can check your *listed-items* for *Meter-reads*. Even if there is no significant *fragmented- charge* on all of these PCL-prompted *considerations*: simply use it for *light processing; listing* basic *considerations*. [Note: all of these PCL are looking to target the *same "justification"* from different angles.]

1a. *"How could you make yourself right by not-levitating?"*
1b. *"How could you make others wrong by not-levitating?"*
2a. *"How could you make yourself right by preventing levitation?"*
2b. *"How could you make others wrong by preventing levitation?"*

If you have difficulty with listing on these, consider the following approach:

"How could 'not-levitating' (or 'preventing-levitation') earn you 'sympathy' from others?"

P. WILLINGNESS

One reason we *hold-back* our *ability* to *levitate* is because we don't want others to do it. On the *Backtrack*, things could easily get "out-of-control" when this *ability* was standard.

With the way our *reality-agreements* and *considerations* for *existence* are structured: we are not going to be *fully willing* to *levitate* unless we are *fully willing* to grant others the right to use that *ability* as well.

The basic PCL for this *process* ("b") must each be alternated with "willingness-for-Self" ("a") in order to keep the *process running*.

1a. *"Look around and spot an object you would be willing to move."*
1b. *"Look around and spot an object you would be willing for someone else to move."*
2a. *"Look around and spot an object you would be willing to move."*
2b. *"Look around and spot an object you would be willing for an Alpha-Spirit to move."*
3a. *"Look around and spot an object you would be willing to move."*
3b. *"Look around and spot an object you would be willing for a Bonded-Entity to move."*
4a. *"Look around and spot an object you would be willing to move."*
4b. *"Look around and spot an object you would be willing to have move by itself."*

Q. NEGATIVE-LOCATIONAL

This *process* is *run* to loosen-up *compulsive machinery*.

1. *"Spot some places where you are not."*
2. *"Spot some places where you don't have to levitate."*
3. *"Spot some places where another doesn't have to levitate."*
4. *"Spot some objects you don't have to levitate."*
5. *"Spot some objects another doesn't have to levitate."*
6. *"Spot some people you don't have to stop from levitating things."*
7. *"Spot some people that someone else doesn't have to stop from levitating things."*
8. *"Spot some objects you don't have to hold still."*
9. *"Spot some objects someone else doesn't have to hold still."*

R. "MUST-NOT-TOUCH"

Alternate each PCL-set several times.

1a. *"Spot an object in the room."*
1b. *"As your attention fixes on it, have it say: 'Must Not Touch'."*
2a. *"Spot an object in the room."*
2b. *"As your attention fixes on it, you say to it: 'Must Not Touch'."*
3a. *"Spot an object in the room."*

3b. *"Put an energy-beam on it with your attention, and have the walls say: 'Must Not Touch'."*

4a. *"Spot an object in the room."*

4b. *"Put an energy-beam on it with your attention, and you tell the walls: 'Must Not Touch'."*

S. ACTS/HOLD-BACKS (6TH SPHERE)

Alternate each PCL-set several times.

1a. *"What have you done to an environment?"*
1b. *"What have you held-back from an environment?"*
2a. *"What has someone else done to an environment?"*
2b. *"What has someone else held-back from an environment?"*
3a. *"What have others done to an environment?"*
3b. *"What have others held-back from an environment?"*

T. ACTS/JUSTIFICATION (6TH SPHERE)

Alternate each PCL-set several times.

1a. *"What have you done to objects?"*
1b. *"How have you justified that?"*
2a. *"What have you done to energies?"*
2b. *"How have you justified that?"*
3a. *"What have you done to spaces?"*
3b. *"How have you justified that?"*
4a. *"What have you done to the future of an environment?"*
4b. *"How have you justified that?"*

U. CAUSE/HOLD-BACKS (6TH SPHERE)

Alternate each PCL-set several times.

1a. *"What could you cause to happen to an object?"*
1b. *"What could you hold-back from doing to an object?"*
2a. *"What could someone else cause to happen to an object?"*
2b. *"What could someone else hold-back from doing to an object?"*
3a. *"What could you cause to happen to an energy?"*
3b. *"What could you hold-back from doing to an energy?"*
4a. *"What could someone else cause to happen to an energy?"*

4b. "What could someone else hold-back from doing to an energy?"

5a. "What could you cause to happen to a space?"

5b. "What could you hold-back from doing to a space?"

6a. "What could someone else cause to happen to a space?"

6b. "What could someone else hold-back from doing to a space?"

7a. "What could you postulate into an object's future?"

7b. "What could you hold-out from postulating into an object's future?"

8a. "What could someone else postulate into an object's future?"

8b. "What could someone else hold-out from postulating into an object's future?"

V. CONSEQUENCES

We have discussed *"reality-agreements"* and *"Monitor-Entities"* in previous *A.T. Manuals*. An individual is likely to have a "sense of" the idea that performing something like *levitation* would "break the rules" and one would be in "trouble" with some kind of "super-force," *&tc*. Therefore, a *Seeker* may be holding onto some *highly charged considerations* concerning anticipated consequences to *levitation*.

The first PCL is for *listing*. After writing down answers, see if any *register* on a *GSR-Meter* (or feel as though they have *fragmented charge* attached to them). Continue the *process* with the remaining PCL until you get a sense of *relief*—or greater certainty of *being-at-Cause*—regarding the situation; then return to ("1").

1. "What horrible thing might happen if you levitated an object?"
2. "Create a mental image picture of the horrible thing happening out in front of you."
3. "Make it more solid."
4. "Copy it many times; make each copy more solid."
5. "Make more copies; change the colors and move things around in the scenery."
6. "Push some copies into the Body; throw some copies away into the distance."

W. HIGH-PRESSURE TRAPS

On the *Backtrack*, sometimes *objects* were set up to "explode" or "implode" when you touched them—either as a stand-alone *"trap,"* or to reduce one's *Actualized Awareness* during an *Implant*. Alternate each PCL-set several times.

1a. *"Spot an object in the room."*
1b. *"Put an energy-beam on it with your attention; and imagine the object exploding."*
2a. *"Spot an object in the room."*
2b. *"Imagine someone else putting an energy-beam on it; and the object exploding."*
3a. *"Spot an object in the room."*
3b. *"Put an energy-beam on it with your attention; and imagine it imploding (pulling at you with a vacuum suction)."*
4a. *"Spot an object in the room."*
4b. *"Imagine someone else putting an energy-beam on it; and the object imploding (pulling them into the vacuum suction)."*

X. POSITIVE-LOCATIONAL

1. *"From where could you levitate an object?"*
2. *"From where could someone else levitate an object?"*

Y. THOUGHT-BARRIERS

Check the following areas for *fragmented charge*. For each *Meter-reading-item* (or if you sense *turbulence* for an area): *"Spot {'What Is'}"* for that item until it *discharges/disperses* on *realization*.

1. *"Getting someone to stop levitating your things by convincing them that only you can levitate the things that you have created."*
2. *"Deciding that: since you can't levitate things, you are going to make certain that no one else can either."*
3. *"Being ordered to levitate something that you don't want to, and avoiding it by demonstrating that you can't really do it."*
4. *"Deciding (or being convinced) that: you shouldn't levitate objects because it sets a bad example for other people with poor control, who would try to do it in foolish ways and mess things up."*

Z. ENERGY (BASIC RECALL)

Before *running* the PCL: check *Preventative Fundamentals* specifically *"On Using Energy"* (both for *Self* and accessible *entities*).

1. *"Recall controlling energy."*
2. *"Recall someone else controlling energy."*
3. *"Recall others controlling energy."*

AA. CONTROLLING ENERGY

This is an *objective exercise*. It is practiced while walking around your home, *&tc*. Practice with "water faucets" that have a visible *flow* (*the water*) before handling "light-switches" or "electrical flows."

1. *"Start and stop energy-flows by turning things 'on' and 'off'."*
2. *"Take notice of the flow when you turn something 'on'; and the no-flow when you turn something 'off'."*

BB. HARMFUL-ACTS/HOLD-BACKS

Run the *processes* for STEP-J; but replace *"levitating"* (or *"levitating something"*) with *"Creating Energy"* (for the PCL).

CC. VALIDATION-FOR-INABILITY

Run the *processes* for STEP-K; but replace *"not-levitating"* with *"not-Creating Energy"* (for the PCL).

DD. HARMFUL-ACTS AND SOLUTIONS

Run the *processes* for STEP-L; but replace *"levitating"* with *"Creating Energy"* (for the PCL).

EE. ENERGY (GENERAL)

1. *"Spot some places where you are not."*
2. *"Spot some places where energy is not."*
3. *"Spot some energy that is not currently hitting you."*
4. *"Spot some places where you are not putting energy."*
5. *"Spot some energy that you could have."*
6. *"Spot some energy that you could permit to remain where it is."*
7. *"Spot some energy that you could permit to disperse."*
8. *"Spot some energy that you could disagree with."*
9. *"Spot some energy that you could agree with if it suddenly appeared."*

FF. OWNERSHIP-OF-ENERGY

1. *"Spot some energies that you could own."*
2. *"Spot some energies that you would be willing for another to own."*
3. *"Spot some energies that you would be willing to give to another."*
4. *"Spot some energies that you would be willing for another to give to you."*
5. *"Spot some energies that you would be willing for another to give to others."*

GG. PUTTING-ENERGY-IN-WALLS

Practices of "putting" (*projecting/directing*) "*thoughts*" and "*concepts*" into *Walls* is a standard method of *processing- out compulsive "machinery."* However, just putting the "*idea*" of *heat, cold, electricity,* or *radiation,* into *Walls* is not as *systematically* effective as with other applications of this technique.

In *this Physical Universe,* such energetic manifestations are the result of "*particle motion.*" Therefore, when this type of exercise is applied to the concept of *Energy* (*heat, &tc.*), it is important to also add the *creation/imagining* of the "*particles-in-motion*" to that *Energy-type*.

HH. FALLING-UPWARDS (GRAVITY)

The basic PCL for this exercise are:

1. "*Get a sense of falling upwards.*"
2. "*Get a sense of other things falling upwards.*"

A *Seeker* should stay on one PCL to get a real certainty on their "*sense*" or "*impression*" before shifting.

Variations of this exercise include:

1. *Create/Imagine various objects on the ground outdoors, one at a time, at an increasing scale of size (ashtrays, books, boxes, furniture, automobiles, aircrafts, &tc.); then have them "fall upwards" into the sky and outer space.*
2. *Spot objects in the room. For each one in turn: create/imagine a copy of it "falling upwards" through the ceiling, into the sky.*
3. *Eject-Awareness and spot large objects, one at a time, around the planet (buildings, monuments, mountains, &tc.); then Imagine them "falling upwards" into the sky and outer space.*

II. "CAN'T-DO-THAT"

Alternate each PCL-set several times.

1a. "*Spot an object in the room.*"
1b. "*Put an energy-beam on it with your attention, and have it say: 'You Can't Do That'.*"
2a. "*Spot an object in the room.*"
2b. "*Put an energy-beam on it with your attention, and you say to it: 'You Can't Do That'.*"
3a. "*Spot an object in the room.*"

3b. *"Put an energy-beam on it with your attention, and have the walls, floor, and ceiling, laugh while saying: 'You Can't Do That'."*
4a. *"Spot an object in the room."*
4b. *"Put an energy-beam on it with your attention, and you laugh while telling the walls, floor, and ceiling: 'You Can't Do That'."*

JJ. SPOILING-THE-GAME (TRUST)

Alternate a PCL-set, then shift.

1a. *"Spot an object in the room."*
1b. *"Decide to levitate it because you can; then decide not to because it would spoil-the-game."*
2a. *"Spot some people you could trust with the ability to levitate."*
2b. *"Spot some people who would be safe if you had the ability to levitate."*

KK. INTERIORIZING-EJECTION

Alternate a PCL-set, then shift.

1a. *"Spot an object in the room."*
1b. *"Interiorize into it; then eject out from it."* {repeat several times}
2a. *"Spot an object in the room."*
2b. *"Imagine/visualize other Alpha-Spirits interiorizing into it and ejecting out of it."*

LL. CONCEPTUAL-CERTAINTY

Uncertainty—the *"lack of certainty"*—reduces an individual's *Actualized Awareness* by suspending their *attention* on a perpetual "maybe." This is accomplished (often with *Implanting*) by holding an intense *energetic-charge* on two *opposing considerations* about a specific *concept*. For example, if equally *charged*: "I can do.." and "I can't do.." would keep an individual in a state of partial *unknowingness* about their abilities.

Alternate the two PCL of a set before going to the next. Make sure that you *really* "get a sense" of what each PCL calls for (rather than a vague idea).

1a. *"Get a certainty that objects can be levitated."*
1b. *"Get a certainty that objects cannot be levitated."*
2a. *"Get a certainty that you can levitate objects."*
2b. *"Get a certainty that you cannot levitate objects."*

3a. *"Get a certainty that others can levitate objects."*
3b. *"Get a certainty that others cannot levitate objects."*
4a. *"Get a certainty that you can generate energetic-force."*
4b. *"Get a certainty that you cannot generate energetic-force."*
5a. *"Get a certainty that others can generate energetic-force."*
5b. *"Get a certainty that others cannot generate energetic-force."*
6a. *"Get a certainty that you must levitate things."*
6b. *"Get a certainty that you must not levitate things."*

MM. INTENTION-ON-PEOPLE

Run this *process* in a public place (where people are visible). If this is not convenient when reaching this step of the procedure: continue to the next step and return to this *process* when it can be completed.

The purpose of this *process* is to loosen one's fixed *postulates* and *reality-agreements*. It is *run* by *postulating* (or *imagining/visualizing*) opposing "ideas" (or *Intentions*) and "putting" (*placing/projecting*) them into others. [This is *run* silently by *Intention*.]

1a. *"Postulate 'an inability to levitate' into people."*
1b. *"Postulate 'an ability to levitate' into people."*
2a. *"Grant people 'the right to levitate'."*
2b. *"Imagine people granting you 'the right to levitate'."*
3a. *"Postulate 'a lack of energy' into people."*
3b. *"Postulate 'an abundance of energy' into people."*
3c. *"Postulate 'being a source of energy' into people."*
4a. *"Grant people 'the right to generate energy'."*
4b. *"Imagine people granting you 'the right to generate energy'."*
5a. *"Postulate 'a lack of havingness' into people."*
5b. *"Postulate 'an abundance of havingness' into people."*
5c. *"Postulate 'being a source of havingness' into people."*
6a. *"Grant people 'the right to create mass'."*
6b. *"Imagine people granting you 'the right to create mass'."*
7a. *"Postulate 'a lack of space' (or collapsed space) into people."*
7b. *"Postulate 'an abundance of space' into people."*
7c. *"Postulate 'being a source of space' into people."*
8a. *"Grant people 'the right to generate space'."*
8b. *"Imagine people granting you 'the right to generate space'."*

9a. *"Postulate 'a lack of time' (not enough time) into people."*
9b. *"Postulate 'an abundance of time' into people."*
9c. *"Postulate 'being a source of time' into people."*
10a. *"Grant people 'the right to generate their own independent time'."*
10b. *"Imagine people granting you 'the right to generate your own independent time'."*

NN. <u>MACHINERY AND ENTITIES</u> (*AT#5*)

• Check for any *Programmed Machine Entities* (PME) that are currently:
–*"being levitation machinery"*;
–*"being broken levitation machinery"*; or
–*"being levitation-blocking machinery."*

Use *A.T. Manual #5* to handle each one found (e.g. *Spot being made into a machine*; *Spot the first time*; run *"Identification Procedure"*). If *Control Entities* (CE) or other types become active (or restimulated) doing this, handle them as well. [This type of *machinery* usually accumulates around the "Third Eye" area of the forehead.]

• Check for any PME that are currently:
–*"being machinery that puts out energy-beams"*;
–*"being broken machinery that puts out energy-beams"*; or
–*"being energy-beam-blocking machinery."*

• Check for any *"Watchers"* (*"Monitors"*), *"Bonded-Entities,"* or other CE that might be secretly observing you, and reporting on you—particularly if you do any major "rule-breaking activities," such as *levitation*.

Starting at *Level-8*, a *Seeker/Wizard* becomes increasingly aware of whether or not there is anything "focused in" on them from a distance that might be blocking *levitation, generating energy,* and other *spiritual abilities.*

Another way of handling interference is to *"put an energy-beam on the object with your attention"* and then check with a *GSR-Meter* if there are any entities (*&tc.*) opposing, protesting, invalidating, or trying to stop you from *levitating* the *object* in any way. [This is worth checking on for the *ashtray* used in the *"Intention-On-Mass"* exercise—especially before any attempts to practice it "metaphysically."]

OO. <u>REALITY-POSTULATING</u>

This *process* is based on the theory that an individual (*Alpha-Spirit*) is *continuously* and *compulsively* "*creating reality*" on an *automatic* basis. Therefore, what a *Seeker* is doing *unknowingly*, we have them practice doing with *intentional-control*.

This is an *objective exercise* that involves "*putting intentions*" (*postulates*) into *objects* found in the room or environment.

PCL = "*Spot an object in the room and...*"
1. "*postulate solidity into it.*"
2. "*postulate weight into it.*"
3. "*postulate color into it.*"
4. "*postulate temperature into it.*"
5. "*postulate energy into it.*"
6. "*postulate space into it.*"
7. "*postulate thought into it.*"
8. "*postulate mystery into it.*"
9. "*postulate beauty into it.*"
10. "*postulate that it has a past (Backtrack) stretching behind it.*"
11. "*postulate that it has a future (track) ahead of it.*"

PP. TOUCH-AND-GO (COMPONENTS)

This is an extension of the previous *process*. In this step, you select an *object*; then practice "*reaching*" and "*letting-go*" (with your *attention*) of a single specific "*component-quality*" of the *object* (listed in the previous step), such as *weight* or *color*, *&tc*.

After working through the list several times: repeat the *process*; but this time "*intensify*" or "*increase*" the *component-quality* before "*letting-go*." A basic PCL-formula for this is:

"*Reach for the {component-quality}. Increase (or intensify) it; then let go of it.*"

QQ. "BELL, BOOK & CANDLE" (PC-3)

Perform the "physical" and "advanced" versions. [See *PC-3*.]

RR. "CRYSTAL CLEAR" (Liber-2B)

Take up a copy of the book "*Crystal Clear: Handbook for Seekers*" and make a pass through the entire text; *run* all *processes* to *total defragmentation* and "*end-cycle*" on your use (necessity) of that material.

After *running through* this entire procedure (from STEP "A" to "QQ") at least twice—in addition to at least two hours (total among *sessions*) spent practicing *"Intention-On-Mass"*—the *Seeker/Wizard* may then proceed to apply even more *advanced systematic exercises* (from the next section) to their *Wizard Level-3X* routine.

ADVANCED ABILITY TRAINING– 3X
(*Example–Intention: Levitation*)

For use after completing standard *"Wizard Level-3X Procedure"* (previous section).

3X-A. "INTENTION-ON-MASS"

[See *"Intention: Directing Thought (Wizard Level-3X Keynote)"* for details.]

3X-B. "BEAMS-ON-A-BODY"

The *Alpha-Spirit* is quite out-of-practice with handling *Energy* and *Force* directly. This exercise practices handling the *Body* using *"energy-beams."* Even above other *mass* in the *Universe*, a *Seeker* would have the greatest certainty of *control* with the *Body* they are currently accustomed to using. [Review the material and exercises from *"Spiritual Energy"* (PC-13).]

This exercise is usually practiced after *ejecting-Awareness* and standing "outside of, but near to" the *Body*. When operating in this wise, a *Seeker* can get a sense, however slight, of "operating the *Body from* outside the *Body*." Experience with this can improve *"ejection-stability"*—handling *body-motion* while *"exterior to"* the *Body*, without automatically "snapping-in."

This exercise is similar to *"Intention-On-Mass"* (3X-A). We practice "lifting" and "setting down" a bit of *mass*. However, in this case, the *Intention* includes the *creation* and *control* of an *energy-beam* to conduct the action (rather than a strictly verbal-style *"command-intention"* directed at *mass*).

The basic instruction is: "starting with a single finger, practice using *energy-beams* to lift/move the finger, rather than relying on the *Body's* muscles." {more details below}

You can project an *energy-beam* from "where *you* are" (POV) or from another "remote point." This means an *energy-beam* can be "put out," "projected" or otherwise "postulated" without attaching the other "end" of it to *Self*. For example: a *Seeker* could run *beams* from a spot on the ceiling of a room. A *Seeker* should practice with various approaches to this exercise (as their own personal experiment).

There is a "puppet-master method" of treating *energy- beams* like "wires" or "cables" being handled from "above" (or from the *Alpha-Spirit* while *exterior-to* the *Body*)—and essentially operating the *Body* like a "marionette-doll." A more *systematically* accurate approach would involve the "lengthening" and "shortening" of an *energy- beam* "wave" to control the "tension" or "force"—to either "push" or "pull" on the *beam*.

This exercise begins with a single finger, then works up to a hand, and then an arm. Eventually this can be extended to include all parts of the *Body* simultaneously. When applying *systematic* methods to the *Body*, the best practice is to alternate the side of the *Body* you're working with for each cycle or *session*—"right index finger" then "left index finger," *&tc*.

From previous exercises, a *Seeker* is used to alternating the "putting on" and "pulling off" of *energy-beams*. This is not standard practice when using the *Body* as an *exercise-target* directly. If you repeatedly "put on" and "pull off" *beams* from the *Body*, they have a tendency to get "sticky." Therefore, once *attention* is fixed on the *beam*, the alternation from "*On*" to "*Off*" should be treated like "*Turning It Off*" rather than "*pulling-it-off*."

Similarly to how we manually manipulate motion of an *object* for "*Intention-On-Mass*," this exercise is *not* expected to set a *Seeker* up for failure or *invalidation*. You can also use "*creativeness processing*" to practice "*imagined*" versions of any gradient or magnitude that exceeds one's reality. For example: if you make good progress with fingers, but not hands, simply spend time *visualizing* the practice you find difficulty with.

Although handling of *energy-beams* is entirely within the scope of *Level-8*, a *Seeker* can treat the exercise as *imaginatively* as necessary, based on their current reality on it, in order to practice it. As with exercise 3X-A, always leave yourself with a "*win*." [In the end, one way or the other: *postulate* that the *finger will lift, &tc.*]

For each part of the *Body* (*finger, &tc.*), practice the following steps:

1. Lay your hand down flat on the table. [For moving the entire arm, lay down and stretch out the entire arm, &tc.]
2. *Eject-Awareness.* Float above that part of the *Body* and fix an *energy-beam* on it with your *attention* (or *by Intention*). Alternate practicing: *"putting the beam on it"/"turning it on"* and *"turning it off."*
3. Put the *beam* on the *body-part* and *"lift it up."* Practice: *"putting the beam on it," "lifting it," "moving the body-part very precisely," "putting it down,"* and *"letting-go"* (*"turning off"* the beam).

3X-C. "4TH-DIMENSIONAL THICKNESS"

Creation and *masses* in *this Physical Universe* are composed of *3-Dimensional* structures. However, there is a slight degree of *"fourth-dimensional thickness"* to its substance. If you were to *imagine* a *2-Dimensional* "Flatland" drawn out on a sheet of paper—the *paper* and *ink*, themselves, would have a slight *3-Dimensional thickness*.

When handling *entities*, you may sometimes perceive a *Bonded-Entity* as a small *"spark"* disappearing in the distance—and yet it doesn't seem to move off very far, relative to our *3-Dimensional Space*. It is essentially moving off into a *fourth-dimensional direction* that is *"sideways"* of the basic *reality* of *this Physical Universe*.

In our practice of *"Reaching for Nothingness"* (and other exercises involving *"direction"*), we tend to work primarily with the *six directions* of our familiar *3-Dimensions*. They are:

left/right; front/back; and *up/down.*

Technically, on *Earth*, we treat these as:

east/west; north/south; and *up/down.*

They are measured in "geometry" as:

height (or *length*), *width*, and *depth*.

And as the axis-coordinates:

longitude, latitude, and *altitude*.

By a *Fourth-Dimension*, we do not mean what is *postulated* as *"Time"*; we mean a *fourth "spatial" dimension*. This would, by definition, include two additional *"directions."*

Mathematician and writer, *Charles H. Hinton (1853-1907)*, coined the term *"tesseract"* to describe a *"four-dimensional cube."* More specifically to our purposes, he appointed names to the two *4-Dimensional directions* (derived from the Greek language):

ANA = "upwards toward"

KATA = "downwards from"

In other explanations: this is also described as *"unfoldment"* and *"folding"*—and sometimes *"expansion"* and *"contraction"*—or even likened to a *"breath."* While it is geometrically demonstrable, it is not necessarily communicable clearly with words and descriptions that are all relative to visible *3-Dimensional* examples.

And this is not altogether different from what is implied in *"Mardukite Zuism"* with its terms (from the *Sumerian* language): *AN* and *KI*. These are the two *directions* indicated on the *Standard Model* by the *ZU-Line*, demonstrating the true *"interdimensional"* quality of *our cabala* that is not so easily depicted on paper. It *can*, however, be conceived of when applying the *"spatial exercises"* of our *Systemology*.

This subject is presented for *Wizard Level-3X* to supplement *"Intention-On-Mass"* exercises involving an *object* (such as the *ashtray*). [Review PC-5 material on handling *"Space"* and *"Creation-Of-Space."*]

Apply the following procedure to your *Wizard Level-3X objective exercises* with an *"object."* Practice each step until there is certainty on it before proceeding to the next.

   A. *Postulate* the *"Space"* around the *object* by *Intention*. Put up *eight corner-points* as a *"cube-of-space"* around the *object*. Keep this *created-space* "in place" for the remaining steps.

   B. *Imagine* a *3-Dimensional* coordinate-system with three *axis* composing the *"cube."* This can be *imagined* as a *"matrix"* or a potential *"graph"* (such as you might use in a geometry class, describing an X, Y, and Z-axis). The "mathematics" behind this is unimportant. We described the *six directions* of *3-Dimensional Space* above. [These are what extend from the *three dimensional axis-lines* that are all at "right-angles" or "perpendicular" to one another.] All that is necessary for this step is that they are *realized* for what they are within the *created-space*—because the final part is: *Imagine* a *fourth dimensional axis-line* extending off both ways in *non-physical directions* (ANA and KATA; or AN and KI).

   C. *Spot* the "center" of the *object*. Reach your *attention* down one *direction* of this *fourth axis-line*; and find the *object* continuing to *exist* in that *direction* until you reach the "end" of the *object*. Then *spot* the *Nothingness* on the far-side of the *object* in that *direction*. *Spot* the "center-point" (in the *Physical Universe*) of the *object* again. Then repeat this step in the opposite *direction*, finding the "end" of the *object* on the other side and the *Nothingness* extending beyond that.

D. Using the perception achieved from the previous steps: *Spot* a *fourth-dimensional "edge"* of the *object* extending in one of the 4-D *directions*. Alternate: *"reaching"* and *"letting-go"* of that edge with your *attention* (or by *Intention*). Then *spot* the other 4-D *"edge"* and repeat. Then alternate *"reaching"* and *"letting-go"* of *both "edges"* simultaneously. It is rather like "holding" (*sensing*) its *fourth-dimensional thickness* with "*spiritual hands.*" [Once you have certainty on being able to *locate* and *perceive* its *fourth-dimensional thickness*, maintaining the *active creation* of an *axis-coordinate system* is no longer necessary.]

E. Use *Intention* to put up *eight corner-points* around the physical *object* (fairly close to it). Then, put a second set of *eight anchor-points* in the same place as the first. Take the second set and extend it out into the *fourth-dimension* until it passes beyond one of the 4-D *"edges"* of the *object*, into the *Nothingness* beyond it. Then move it back slightly so that it only encompasses the last bit of 4-D *Space* that the *object* actually occupies. Then do the same with the other *"edge."*

F. *Imagine* that the *eight corner-points* of one *cube* extend to the *eight corner-points* of the 4-D *cube*. [This is the idea behind a 4-D *"hypercube"* — or *cube within a cube* — except one of the *cubes* extends into a *fourth-dimension*.] *Imagine* that the 3-D *object* is actually in each of these *cubes* simultaneously, and also as a "smear" or "spread" stretching between them.

G. By *Intention* (or *imaginative visualization*), *get the sense* of *extending* your "*spiritual hands*" out and grabbing the 4-D *edges* of the *object*. Then alternate the *"Intention-based"* PCL (from the *"Change and Motion"* processing in *PC-4*):

1. *"Keep It From Going Away."*
2. *"Hold It Still."*
3. *"Make It More Solid."*

3X-D. <u>ADVANCED 3X-A</u> {3X-AX}

Refer to *"Intention: Directing Thought (Wizard Level-3X Keynote)"* for background and details on the basic *process*. It is presumed that a *Seeker* will already have practiced the basic version for a number of hours prior to handling this exercise. [Experience with procedure 3X-B and 3X-C is also required.]

3X-D combines elements from each of the three previous exercises. In this *process*, we advance the original 3X-A procedure by incorporating *Energy* along with our *Intention* for an *object* (ashtray, &tc.) to "*Rise Up*" — similar to what is practiced in 3X-B. In addition to this, we extend our reach on the *object* into the *fourth-dimension* — as in 3X-C.

Having proficiency with the previous parts of this manual, and the high-level of *Actualized Awareness* applied by a *Seeker/Wizard* (at *Level-8*): a "shadow" of the *object's structure* — like an "*etheric*" or "*akashic*" essence of it — *will* move by applying this procedure. Whether or not the *physical object* automatically "catches up" to where you've shifted its *Beingness* to, is of course, another matter.

The degree to which a *Seeker* is at *Cause* over the *physical object* itself is likely to remain low at the beginning — therefore, we use our physical hands (as in 3X-A) to finish seeing our *intended effect* through to the end. The quotient of certainty — or percentage of *Being-at-Cause* — ebbs and flows (rises and falls) as one repeats the *process*; always end your practice on a "*win*" (when certainty is high).

We can estimate that for an individual to actually get even the smallest response from *energetic-matter* in the *Physical Universe* requires being over 90% *at-Cause* over the object/item. This is challenging to achieve in *this Physical Universe*, because the building-blocks of what is considered "*creativeness*" at a material level require a *Body* to use *effort* and *force* against *already created* (*other-determined*) *Space-Time* and *energetic-matter*. This was much less the case in much earlier (previous) versions of *Beta-Existence*.

A *Human* believes they have to use *effort* and *force* on what is *already here* in order to *do* or *have* anything. The *Space* and *mass* of *this Universe* is generally "*misowned*" by us — and therefore *persists*. Its "*Is-ness*" is really the result of an *other-determined creation*; thus we have difficulty in assuming *total responsibility* and *control* of it as being "ours." So, we go on *altering* what we have been given ("*What Is*") and making it more and more solid all the time; and ourselves becoming more *solidly fixed* on the *reality-agreements* of *this Game*.

A. Reach into the *object* and spread *"golden energy"* throughout it. Extend this *Energy* out in the 4-Dimensional directions (see 3X-C) to fill the entire *object* with this *"golden energy"* between its *fourth-dimensional* "sides." Extend even more *Energy* into the *object*'s "future" and "past" until the entirety of the *object* is filled with the *"golden energy."* [As you continue with the remaining steps, occasionally "refresh" the *object* with this *Energy*.]

B. *Intend* the *object* to rise upwards. You can apply verbal commands, as in the basic version of 3X-A, or you can direct your *Intention* silently. Then *"See"* (or *Imagine/visualize*) the "etheric shadow" portion of the *object* "rise" up approximately a *foot* (*twelve inches*) above the surface (table) it is set on. If necessary, apply the 3X-C practice of also using your *"spiritual hands"* in the *fourth-dimension*; or you can apply the *"energy-beam"* method of 3X-B to improve your certainty. [Technically, the entire action is accomplished by *Intention* alone.]

C. *Acknowledge* the portion of the *object* that *did* move for having moved.

D. With the *body's hand*, move the rest of the *physical object* up to the position that you are holding the portion that moved. Have the *object* "*feel relieved for having caught up with itself."* Then *acknowledge* it for completing the *intended* movement.

E. *Intend* the *object* back down to where it was setting. *Acknowledge* the portion that *moves*; then use the *body's hand* to complete the action with the rest of the *physical object*, have it feel *"relieved,"* acknowledge it, and *"let go"* of it.

F. Repeat STEP-B through STEP-E until an appropriate end-point.

Extended Version:

G. With eyes closed (and/or *Awareness-ejected*): perform a *"Creation-Of-Space"* (defining it with *eight corner-points, &tc.*) and *Create/Imagine* a *"Copy"* of the *object* in that *Space*. *Intend* the *object* to *"Rise Up"* and *"Set Down"* and have it do so, giving it *acknowledgments*.

H. Have the *object* "*protesting*"; and you move it anyway.

I. Have the *object* "*enjoying it"* as you move it.

J. Have the *object* "*wanting to move somewhere else"*; but you move it to where you want it anyway.

K. Alternate between *running* all of STEP-B through STEP-E and STEP-G through STEP-J repeatedly to an appropriate end-point.

3X-E. BETA-INTERCONNECTEDNESS

One of the "*barriers*" embedded in the *reality-agreements* of *this Physical Universe* is part of what we generally refer to as "*gravity.*" The underlying design for *this Universe* is "interconnectedness." By this, we mean that each manifestation or existing part of the *Space-Time Energy-Matter* of *this Universe* also acts to "hold" all the other parts in place. This is the magnitude of what a *Seeker/Wizard* is working to get greater *control* over when applying *Intention* to it—or even *ascend beyond* it (which is actually the entire point behind all of this).

[For written instruction of this exercise: we capitalize the words "*The Object*" when referring to *the object* (*ashtray, &tc.*) that we've been using for the *3X-series* exercises. This is important to distinguish since we will also be referring to other "*objects in the room.*"]

  A. "*Spot other objects in the room. For each: have (get a sense of) The Object connect with it, and disconnect from it, several times.*"

  B. "*Spot other objects in the room. For each: have (get a sense of) it connect with, and disconnect from, The Object, several times.*"

  C. "*Spot other objects in the room. For each: have (get a sense of) The Object agree with it, and disagree with it, several times.*"

  D. "*Spot other objects in the room. For each: have (get a sense of) it agree with, and disagree with, The Object, several times.*"

  E. "*Spot other objects in the room. For each: have (get a sense of) The Object communicate with it, and go out-of-communication with it, several times.*"

  F. "*Spot other objects in the room. For each: have (get a sense of) it communicate with, and go out-of- communication with, The Object, several times.*"

  G. Repeat STEP-A through F; but instead of "*objects in the room,*" Spot things at a distance, including: "*The Center Of The Earth*"; "*The Center Of The Sun*"; "*The Sun (As A Mass)*"; "*The Center Of The Galaxy,*" *&tc.*

3X-F. UNIVERSE-AS-A-TERMINAL

Practice with *getting a sense* of *The Universe* as a *terminal*. In *systematic* terms: "*gravity*" is the structural-impulse of *objects* in (and the basic design of) *this Physical Universe* to:

  "*keep each other from going away.*"

"*Inertia*" is the structural-impulse to:

  "*hold objects still.*"

And various built-in *mechanisms* also:

"*make it more solid.*"

Run this *process*, "*getting the sense*" of these things to the fullest extent that you can.

 A1. "*Have the Universe 'keep The Object from going away'; then have it 'let go'.*" (repeat)

 A2. "*Have The Object 'keep the Universe from going away'; the have it 'let go'.*" (repeat)

 B1. "*Have the Universe 'hold The Object completely still'; the have it 'let go and leave it uncontrolled'.*" (repeat)

 B2. "*Have The Object 'hold the Universe completely still'; then have it 'let go and leave it uncontrolled'.*" (repeat)

 C1. "*Have the Universe 'make The Object more solid'; then have it 'let go and leave it uncontrolled'.*" (repeat)

 C2. "*Have The Object 'make the Universe more solid'; then have it 'let go and leave it uncontrolled'.*" (repeat)

3X-G. TOTAL-RESPONSIBILITY

To take total *command* and *control* of a "*creation*" (object, *&tc.*)—even a mutually "agreed-upon" Physical Universe "creation" (that is also being *postulated* into being by *others*; or is *other-determined*)—the *secret* is to take *total/full responsibility* for that "*creation*" and make the *postulate* that keeps it there your own.

Run this PCL. Keep extending your "*sphere-of-responsibility*" for the *object* until it completely encompasses the *object*—*As-It-Is* now, was, and *ever will be*.

 1. "*What about that object could you be responsible for?*"

   (then)

 2. "*Postulate total responsibility for that object.*"

   (then end that *cycle*; and repeat)

Use *concepts* from lines A1, B1, and C1 (above) to:

"*Spot the structural-impulse of the Universe to ___.*"

 A. Practice with each—"*Hold The Object Still*"; "*Keep The Object From Going Away*"; and "*Make The Object More Solid*"—in turn to get a good reality on each.

B. Practice them quickly in succession until you can fully conceive of *all three* within a *single* instantaneous *"spotting"* of *"the combined impulses being intended into the object"* by the *Universe*.

C. Repeat *getting a sense* of this *impulse*; but get it faster and faster. Consider it as a *"wave"* that repeats the *Intention* onto the *object* many thousand times per second. You don't have to duplicate each time-per-second individually; you simply *get a sense* of the basic *impulse* with certainty; and then *get the concept* of (or *consider*) it repeating as a super-fast *wave* that produces a *super-high frequency* (but mostly inaudible) *"hum."*

D. Then make the *wave*-frequency just a little faster until it's too fast to produce a *"hum,"* but simply *Is*. [*This is the "Universe Postulate"* (Alpha-Thought) of the *"Is"*-factor of the *object*.]

E. *Get a certainty* on the *Universe Postulate* (from STEP-D) and *consider* it as repeating constantly on the *object*, and *re-creating* (*postulating*) it into existence within consecutive *Spaces*, as though it is "carrying" the existence of the *object* "forward" in *Time*.

F. Make the *Universe Postulate* "your own" — as essentially your own *"Alpha-Thought"* or *"Postulate."* [This, itself, is accomplished by your *Intention*.] Accept *total/full responsibility* for the continuous "re-creation" and "location" of the *object* in *present-time*. Put out the *Intention*: "I'm Creating It." And have the *Universe*, "acknowledge" that.

G. *Intend* to move the *object*; and *move it*. [Use the *body's* hands if necessary.]

Scan through the processes and exercises of the *"Wizard Level-3X Procedure"* and clean up any areas that still have any *fragmentary charge*, or that you think still require significant improvement. Then work through the exercises of this *"Advanced Ability Training–3X"* section again.

This concludes the experimental portion of *Wizard Level-3*. The remainder of this manual pertains to additional research and developments regarding *Implant-Platforms*.

IMPLANTING THE HUMAN CONDITION
(*Prison Planet Implant-Platforms*)

[This discourse presents material that is not necessarily confidential, but is only appropriate for those *Seekers* that have studied (worked through) all previous *A.T. Manuals* of the *"Keys to the Kingdom"* series.]

More recent *Implants* of *this Universe*—and especially *"after Earth"* was intended as a *prison-planet*—are far more complex in their design and configuration than *older Implants* from previous *Universes*.

Since this *older* knowledge is retained by some *universal superpower forces* (*the Implanters*) in *this Universe*, it is not surprising that *older Implants* could be combined together and expanded appropriately for more recent use. What this gives evidence for is the fact that the *"reality systems"* have become so *convoluted* and *condensed* that it has taken far greater lengths than ever before to keep an *Alpha- Spirit* suppressed within a *Universe*, or a *planet*, or the *Human Condition*.

Components of *"The Jewel"* and the original *"Heaven Incident"* during *Entry-Into-This-Universe* are far more basic than when these *Implants* are revised and revisited again later on, in relatively more recent *Implanting-Incidents*. For example: the original *Entry-Incident* uses only *one Jewel*; whereas when the same sequencing is repeated during the *Hellfire Incident* (and other more recent *incidents*), there are *three Jewels*.

The *solidarity* and *reality-agreements* of each *descending* (*condensing*) *Universe* continued to be compounded (or superimposed) "on top" of all former ones. The *postulates* and *creations* keep "stacking up" until we are left with something as *solid* and *condensed* as *this Physical Universe*. It also seems to require layer upon layer of more complex *Implants* to keep everything existing in *this Universe* both *created* and under *control*.

What is most accessible for us to continue researching for the *Pathway*— and what is most beneficial for us to handle—is that which is specifically entrapping an *Alpha-Spirit* on *Earth*, and holding them in the *Human Condition*. Curiously, the *Implants* all stem from previous *Universes*; but they have never before been so complexly designed or so intricately interwoven into each other—or used on *Alpha-Spirits* so often.

In this manual (*AT#7*) we will provide additional data concerning *Implant-Platforms* that compose, what we refer to here as, the *"Heaven Implant Series"* (since repeating the phrase *"Prison Planet Implant"* is considered rather *negative*). The *Implants* and *incidents* we treat in our work have no formal names in *human language*; nor has our *systemological data* ever been fully collected and codified within a single paradigm before now.

These new *Platforms* and *Goals-lists* represent an *incident* far more intricate than the original *Entry-Into-Universe* "Heaven Incident" and *that Goals-Sequencing*—therefore, this is *not* part of the original *Incident*, but is only intended to give the illusion of being so (and *restimulate* it). [Our earliest unpublished research on this subject referred to this series as the "*Prison Planet Implant*" so as not to confuse this research with the original "*Heaven Incident.*" We could just as easily refer to this series as the "*Judgment Incident.*"]

It is difficult to "date" the "earliest usage" of this "Heaven Implant Series" with a *GSR-Meter*. The *incident* is intentionally designed to *implant false dates*, just to make it more confusing to remember clearly (*locate* and *spot*) on the *Backtrack*. It is also difficult to determine just how often they are used for an individual's "between-lives" period. [To avoid *confusion, restimulation,* or *flying-by unhandled fragmentary charge*: this Implanting should only be handled *after* all of *Systemology Level-7* is fully *defragmented*.]

At the very least: research suggests that if an *Alpha-Spirit* is able to get nearly out of *this Solar System* (*between-lives*), there is a "net" or "screen" that seems to catch them and set them up for this *re-implanting*.

Research also indicates: use of this unique arrangement of "Heaven Implant" is only approximately *10,000* to *12,000* years old at most. It is specific to the *Human Condition* and *Earth* as a *prison-planet*.

We say "Heaven Implant," but it is really structured like a "*court-sentencing incident.*" It is the "*Judgment*" archetype (in *religion* and the *tarot*) and uses *heavy-dogmatic* symbolism that was once absent from modern religions—like *Christianity*—until its incorporation as a *restimulative control-mechanism* (against the *Human* population) during the "*Dark Ages*" of Earth's more modern history. [Most *Buddhism* seemed to escape *effects* of this, since it already sought to avoid the "*Heaven-area*" as an "*Implant-Station.*" So, our ideas about that are not really a *new consideration*.]

It has also been determined that *Implanting-Incidents* commonly incorporate *IPU-Goals* and *Symbols*, or variations thereof, in order to *restimulate* and *communicate* in an "*archetypal*" language that is universally understood—or at least includes enough recognizable content (*data*) that people will react to. [This is one reason we introduced experimental *Implant Penalty Universe* (IPU) information earlier (than what might be considered absolutely necessary) in *A.T. Manual #4*.]

The experience of actually going through these types of *incidents* is likened to an "escalator" or "treadmill." The *archetypal* scenery, or common environmental conditions, of this *Implanting-Incident* incorporates *"pyramids"* and *"aerial staircases"* and even *"spiral-like descending arrangements of pillars"* with IPU-*Goal terminals* on top of them.

The basic pattern behind the material we are going to address, originates prior to *this Universe*—but complexity has since been added to the *"command-line"* encoding for the *Platform*. The IPU data concerning *restimulative* "Price" and "Survive" *command-items* (given in AT#4) actually pertain to *this "Heaven Implant."*

Just as is the case with the *Hellfire Incident*, there are some individuals occupying *Human-forms* on *Earth* today that emigrated from the *Magic Universe* after the *Prison-Planet Incidents*—or have otherwise been able to side-step or escape much of the standard-issue *Human-Implanting*.

However, most of the other *entities* and *fragments*, which may be affecting your case, *were* here a very long time (and are heavily *Implanted*). Like *"Platforms #1-18"* (AT#3), additional *Implants* are researched, in part, for *releasing* more *entities*.

An Advisement on Running Implant-Platforms: a *Seeker* may be encountering difficulties (primarily if working along the *upper-levels* of the *Pathway* without any supervision) when *processing-out* Implant-Platforms, if they are mistakenly *running* all of them the same way they treated *"The Jewel (Parts #1-5)"* in AT#3. That is *not* how *they* should be *run*.

Only the original *Entry-Incident "The Jewel"* is common to all *Alpha-Spirits* of *this Universe*. It is *processed-out* completely by fully contacting each of the *command-lines until it does* give a *"Meter-read"*; and then duplicating it *"As-It-Is"* until it no longer *registers* any *charge*. *No other Implant-Platform is run that way.*

For all other *Platforms* we have provided: each *item* (*line*) is "spotted" and *if it does* "read," then it is *run* until it no longer *registers* a *charge*. If the *line* doesn't *read*, then it isn't *run* any further.

If you are not able to use a *Biofeedback-Device* for your handling of *Wizard-Level* work: review the material found in *PC-11* through *PC-14*, and all *A.T. Manuals*, very thoroughly.

Being how recently this *Implanting-Incident* began being used, it is likely that an individual on *Earth* today would have at least some *fragmented charge* attached to the *Implant*.

INCIDENT SEQUENCE

This is the *incident-sequence* of being "*sentenced to Earth*":

1. You are captured (somehow). For the original incident: it is possible that most *Humans* were part of a "rebel- fleet" against some kind of "galactic-empire" — therefore, captured *en masse* as "prisoners-of-war."

2. You are hit with *heavy energy-waves*; then told you are a "*convicted criminal*" and are awaiting sentencing for your crime. You are hit with *imprints* depicting you on trial; but you are not told what your crime is. You are told that "*memory of your horrific crime has been erased as part of this criminal rehabilitation process.*"

3. Then you are sentenced in court. You are sentenced to make a copy of yourself that will be punished. You are told that after you make a copy to be punished in your place, then you will be set free. A *heavy wave-force* hits you and you sense that you are standing beside yourself. But this is a fake *splitter-incident*; they just put up a "*doll*" that looks like you and then tell you that you have been *divided*.

4. You are told that you are the copy that is to be punished, and that they will set your real-self (the "*doll*") free if you willingly accept your punishment.

5. You are told that you are being sentenced to "*Hell*" and they take you down into the "basement" of the courthouse, which resembles a "*Medieval-style dungeon*."

[In former *Universes*, most of the remaining sequence would have taken place in some kind of "*implant universe*" or "*pocket universe*" — or would have been used in a transition between *Universes*. But, in this case, we know that this particular *incident* is specific to *this Universe*, *Earth*, and *Humans*. It is more likely some kind of exceptionally advanced *electrically-implanted virtual-reality computer-simulation*. It is a *real experience*, but it does not *actually* take place within the *Physical Universe*.]

6. You are standing in the "basement" of some underground facility, at the bottom level of what they told you is "*Hell*." One of the "basement-walls" is missing, and as you look out and down you see an

"*Infinite Universe*" with a vast swirling cloud of "*chaos*" suspended in the center.

7. You are told that "*you have become evil*" and that "*you have turned against your creator and therefore are to be thrown into The Chaos and be torn apart as a Spiritual Being.*"

8. But then they agree to give you one last chance. They will review your history and show you how you have come to this degraded state. You are told that in doing so, they will "*run time backwards for you so that you may have another chance.*" They say: "*Now pay close attention, so that you can learn from your mistakes.*"

9. Then you begin to walk backwards—literally going backwards up a staircase; occasionally down, but mostly up—working your way gradually back out of "*Hell*" and through cities and mountainscapes, and eventually going even further and higher, backwards up a "*stairway to Heaven.*"

10. As this backwards movement occurs: you are being *Implanted* with *Goals* and *command-items*. The first *Implanted-Goal* (at the bottom, while facing *Chaos*) is: **TO BE ENDED**. You are hit with *300 items* on this one *Goal*, as you slowly back-up the stairway.

The process is *excruciatingly* slow. The same *Platform-pattern* of *300 items* is then applied to the *next Goal* in the *sequence*, as you move a little further backwards up the stairway. This continues to occur in this wise for approximately *200 Goals*.

At the very top of all the stairways—there may be *six* total—you reach what they call "*Heaven*" and the *Implanted-Goal* is: **TO BE CREATED** (which takes place before an imprint of *God's Throne In The Clouds*).

11. At the very top, the *imprinted imagery* continues displaying various scenes of *Physical Universe "creation"* and the "creation of Humans"—much of which mirrors symbolism from the ancient *Babylonian Epic of Creation* tablets, and elements of the *Book of Genesis*, &tc. Then they tell you that everything you've seen on this backwards journey is a depiction of how you've lived your "*evil*" existence—but now you have a chance to live again, and having learned from your mistakes, will do better this time.

12. Then they "let you go"—and it's like being shot from a sling or catapult. You fly down all the staircases, getting hit with all the *Goals* and *items* again, but moving in a forward direction (and the *Goals-sequence* is

experienced in reverse to how you received them moving backwards (going up). This all happens at an incredibly fast speed. You go all the way back to the "basement" and out the "missing wall" and start falling towards the swirling mass of clouds.

13. They catch you as you are falling. They say (something like): "*Here you've gone and done the same terrible things again. But we will give you one last chance. Now pay closer attention this time!*"

14. Then back up the staircases you go, excruciatingly slowly, getting the same *Implanted-Goals Sequencing* as you move backwards up to the top again—and back down.

15. The full sequence of "backing up the stairways" and "flying down into Chaos" occurs *three times* total. On the final (*third*) time: they allow you to fall into the *"swirling cloud of Chaos."* Once there, there are probably *millions* of *imprints* (*objects, scenery, &tc.*) that are flying around you like a tornado.

16. Then you spot a "calm area"—an "eye in the center of the hurricane" so to speak—and in the center of that "calm area" you see the *Earth*. You move down to it in order to escape the *Chaos*, and there is an overwhelming sense of *peace* and total *relief* as you go unconscious. After that, you are compelled to *reincarnate* here on *Earth*.

HEAVEN IMPLANTS (PRISON SERIES)
(*Parts #1 to 6*)

The *"Heaven Implant Series"* that occurs during the previously given *Incident-Sequence* is divided into *six* parts or *Platforms*. All *300 item-lines* occur for each *Goal*; and the individual doesn't get to the top of the *"Stairway to Heaven"* except with the top/highest *Goal* in the sequence: "CREATE."

In *this* section, we will provide a *short-form formula* for all *six* parts.

In the *next* section, we will provide the *Goals-list* that is used to fill in the *blank spaces* and complete this pattern-formula of *"items"* for each of the *Goals*.

Each of the *six Platforms* has its own wording-style, grammar, or syntax. We will introduce each *Platform* by explaining how the "wording" (or "tense") of a *Goal* should be modified to fit that *Platform*. That being said: the wording of the *"item-lines"* will not always sound like a conventional use of language.

PART-1

Goal is inserted {*into the blank space*} in past tense, without "TO" — for example: *"forgotten"* instead of *"to forget"*; *"ended"* instead of *"to be ended,"* &tc.

1. ___
2. NOT ___
3. ABSOLUTEABLY ___
4. ABSOLUTEABLY NOT ___
5. PERFECTABLY ___
6. PERFECTABLY NOT ___
7. SUPERIORABLY ___
8. SUPERIORABLY NOT ___
9. INCOMPARABLY ___
10. INCOMPARABLY NOT ___
11. WONDERFULLABLY ___
12. WONDERFULLABLY NOT ___
13. FASCINATABLY ___
14. FASCINATABLY NOT ___
15. BEAUTIFULLABLY ___
16. BEAUTIFULLABLY NOT ___
17. HIGHLY ACCEPTABLY ___
18. HIGHLY ACCEPTABLY NOT ___
19. RECOMMENDABLY ___
20. RECOMMENDABLY NOT ___
21. ACCEPTABLY ___
22. ACCEPTABLY NOT ___
23. ENGROSSABLY ___
24. ENGROSSABLY NOT ___
25. VITALABLY ___
26. VITALABLY NOT ___
27. EAGERABLY ___
28. EAGERABLY NOT ___
29. ENTHUSIASTICABLY ___
30. ENTHUSIASTICABLY NOT ___
31. ENJOYABLY ___

32. ENJOYABLY NOT ___
33. PLEASUREABLY ___
34. PLEASUREABLY NOT ___
35. AGREEABLY ___
36. AGREEABLY NOT ___
37. DEDICATEABLY ___
38. DEDICATEABLY NOT ___
39. COMMENDABLY ___
40. COMMENDABLY NOT ___
41. DESIREABLY ___
42. DESIREABLY NOT ___
43. CREATABLY ___
44. CREATABLY NOT ___
45. WANTABLY ___
46. WANTABLY NOT ___
47. COVETABLY ___
48. COVETABLY NOT ___
49. HOPEFULABLY ___
50. HOPEFULABLY NOT ___
51. POWERFULLABLY ___
52. POWERFULLABLY NOT ___
53. DECIDEABLY ___
54. DECIDEABLY NOT ___
55. CREDITABLY ___
56. CREDITABLY NOT ___
57. DEMANDABLY ___
58. DEMANDABLY NOT ___
59. BOREABLY ___
60. BOREABLY NOT ___
61. UPSETTABLY ___
62. UPSETTABLY NOT ___
63. REGRETTABLY ___
64. REGRETTABLY NOT ___
65. DEJECTABLY ___
66. DEJECTABLY NOT ___
67. COMPULSABLY ___
68. COMPULSABLY NOT ___
69. UNSTOPABLY ___
70. UNSTOPABLY NOT ___

71. DEGRADEABLY ___
72. DEGRADEABLY NOT ___
73. IDIOTABLY ___
74. IDIOTABLY NOT ___
75. LOSEABLY ___
76. LOSEABLY NOT ___
77. BADABLY ___
78. BADABLY NOT ___
79. UNCONFRONTABLY ___
80. UNCONFRONTABLY NOT ___
81. FORGETTABLY ___
82. FORGETTABLY NOT ___
83. UNWANTABLY ___
84. UNWANTABLY NOT ___
85. PLAYABLY ___
86. PLAYABLY NOT ___
87. ABANDONABLY ___
88. ABANDONABLY NOT ___
89. ___ -ING
90. NOT ___ -ING
91. ___ -ERS
92. NOT ___ -ERS
93. ___ -INGNESS
94. NOT ___ -INGNESS
95. ___ -ISHNESS
96. NOT ___ -ISHNESS
97. ___ -ATIVES
98. NOT ___ -ATIVES
99. ___ -IVITY
100. NOT ___ -IVITY

PART-2

Goal is inserted {*into the blank space*} in present tense, with "TO"—for example: "*to forget*"; "*to be ended*," *&tc*. [Note: some researchers got better "*Meter-reads*" without the "TO" and adding "–ING" (*forgetting, ending, &tc.*) for most of this part. Experiment with both ways to see what "*reads*" best for you.]

101. ___

102. NOT ___
103. ABSOLUTEABLE ___
104. ABSOLUTEABLE NOT ___
105. PERFECTABLE ___
106. PERFECTABLE NOT ___
107. SUPERIORABLE ___
108. SUPERIORABLE NOT ___
109. INCOMPARABLE ___
110. INCOMPARABLE NOT ___
111. WONDERFULLABLE ___
112. WONDERFULLABLE NOT ___
113. FASCINATABLE ___
114. FASCINATABLE NOT ___
115. BEAUTIFULLABLE ___
116. BEAUTIFULLABLE NOT ___
117. HIGHLY ACCEPTABLE ___
118. HIGHLY ACCEPTABLE NOT ___
119. RECOMMENDABLE ___
120. RECOMMENDABLE NOT ___
121. ACCEPTABLE ___
122. ACCEPTABLE NOT ___
123. ENGROSSABLE ___
124. ENGROSSABLE NOT ___
125. VITALABLE ___
126. VITALABLE NOT ___
127. EAGERABLE ___
128. EAGERABLE NOT ___
129. ENTHUSIASTICABLE ___
130. ENTHUSIASTICABLE NOT ___
131. ENJOYABLE ___
132. ENJOYABLE NOT ___
133. PLEASUREABLE ___
134. PLEASUREABLE NOT ___
135. AGREEABLE ___
136. AGREEABLE NOT ___
137. DEDICATEABLE ___
138. DEDICATEABLE NOT ___
139. COMMENDABLE ___
140. COMMENDABLE NOT ___

141. DESIREABLE ___
142. DESIREABLE NOT ___
143. CREATABLE ___
144. CREATABLE NOT ___
145. WANTABLE ___
146. WANTABLE NOT ___
147. COVETABLE ___
148. COVETABLE NOT ___
149. HOPEFULABLE ___
150. HOPEFULABLE NOT ___
151. POWERFULLABLE ___
152. POWERFULLABLE NOT ___
153. DECIDEABLE ___
154. DECIDEABLE NOT ___
155. CREDITABLE ___
156. CREDITABLE NOT ___
157. DEMANDABLE ___
158. DEMANDABLE NOT ___
159. BOREABLE ___
160. BOREABLE NOT ___
161. UPSETTABLE ___
162. UPSETTABLE NOT ___
163. REGRETTABLE ___
164. REGRETTABLE NOT ___
165. DEJECTABLE ___
166. DEJECTABLE NOT ___
167. COMPULSABLE ___
168. COMPULSABLE NOT ___
169. UNSTOPABLE ___
170. UNSTOPABLE NOT ___
171. DEGRADEABLE ___
172. DEGRADEABLE NOT ___
173. IDIOTABLE ___
174. IDIOTABLE NOT ___
175. LOSEABLE ___
176. LOSEABLE NOT ___
177. BADABLE ___
178. BADABLE NOT ___
179. UNCONFRONTABLE ___

180. UNCONFRONTABLE NOT ___
181. FORGETTABLE ___
182. FORGETTABLE NOT ___
183. UNWANTABLE ___
184. UNWANTABLE NOT ___
185. PLAYABLE ___
186. PLAYABLE NOT ___
187. ABANDONABLE ___
188. ABANDONABLE NOT ___
189. (TO) ___–ING
190. NOT ___–ING
191. (TO) ___–ERS
192. NOT ___–ERS
193. (TO) ___–INGNESS
194. NOT ___–INGNESS
195. (TO) ___–ISHNESS
196. NOT ___–ISHNESS
197. (TO) ___–ATIVES
198. NOT ___–ATIVES
199. (TO) ___–IVITY
200. NOT ___–IVITY

PART-3

Goal is inserted {*into the blank space*} in present-tense, without "TO"—for example: "*forget*"; "*being ended,*" &tc.

201. ___
202. NOT ___
203. ___–ING
204. NOT ___–ING
205. ___–ERS
206. NOT ___–ERS
207. ___–INGNESS
208. NOT ___–INGNESS
209. ___–ISHNESS
210. NOT ___–ISHNESS
211. ___–ATIVES
212. NOT ___–ATIVES
213. ___–IVITY

214. NOT ___-IVITY

PART-4

Goal is inserted {*into the blank space*} without "TO" and as an "–ING" form; "*to forget*" becomes "*forgetting.*" On the "TO BE" type *Goals*, the "–ING" is added to "BE"; "*to be ended*" becomes "*being ended.*"

215. THOSE WHO ARE ___
216. THOSE WHO ARE NOT ___
217. GOALS THAT LEAD TO ___
218. THOSE WHO HATE ___
219. ACTIVELY ___
220. DOESN'T WANT TO BE ___
221. ADVANTAGES OF ___
222. NO ADVANTAGES OF ___
223. ANY NECESSITY FOR ___
224. NO NECESSITY FOR ___
225. ANY EXISTENCE OF ___
226. SUPPRESSING EXISTENCE OF ___
227. ANY INSTANCE ON ___
228. INVALIDATING ___
229. ANY DEPENDENCE ON ___
230. DENYING ___
231. THOSE WHO ARE CREATING ___
232. THOSE WHO ARE DESTROYING ___
233. ANY ACTIONS OF ___
234. NO ACTIONS OF ___
235. ANY BELIEF IN ___
236. NO BELIEF IN ___
237. PROPONENTS OF ___
238. OPPONENTS OF ___
239. FANTASTIC IMPORTANCE OF ___
240. UNIMPORTANCE OF ___
241. OBSESSIONS FOR ___
242. REPULSIONS FOR ___
243. INTERESTINGNESS OF ___
244. UNINTERESTINGNESS OF ___
245. CONCERNS OF ___
246. NO CONCERNS OF ___

247. UPSETS ABOUT ___
248. NO UPSETS ABOUT ___
249. DESPERATIONS OF ___
250. NO DESPERATIONS OF ___
251. FRENZIEDNESS(ES) OF ___
252. NO FRENZIEDNESS(ES) OF ___
253. PAINFULLNESS OF ___
254. PAINLESSNESS OF ___
255. HOPELESSNESS OF ___
256. HOPEFULLNESS OF ___

PART-5

For the "odd numbered" *items*, the *Goal* continues to be inserted in present-tense without "TO" and as an "–ING" form; *"forgetting,"* &tc. For "TO BE" type *Goals*, the "–ING" is added to the "BE"; *"to be ended"* becomes *"being ended."*

The "even numbered" *items* are stated as a *Beingness*. In this case, for the "TO BE" type *Goals*, the "TO BE" is simply dropped; *"to be ended"* becomes *"(an) ended (being)."*

257. THE EXHAUSTIONS OF ___
258. AN EXHAUSTED ___ BEING
259. THE STUPIDITY OF ___
260. A STUPIDIFIED ___ BEING
261. THE EFFORTS OF ___
262. A WEAKENED ___ BEING
263. THE UNREWARDINGNESS OF ___
264. AN UNREWARDED ___ BEING
265. THE COMPLICATIONS OF ___
266. A COMPLICATED ___ BEING
267. THE DEMANDS OF ___
268. A DEMANDING ___ BEING
269. THE DETERMINATIONS OF ___
270. A DETERMINED ___ BEING
271. THE FOOLISHNESS OF ___
272. A FOOLISH ___ BEING
273. THE COMPULSIONS OF ___
274. A COMPULSIVE ___ BEING
275. THE INVALIDATIONS OF ___

276. AN INVALIDATED ___ BEING
277. THE LIMITATIONS OF ___
278. A LIMITED ___ BEING
279. THE DEGRADATIONS OF ___
280. A DEGRADED ___ BEING
281. THE OVERWHELMS OF ___
282. AN OVERWHELMED ___ BEING
283. THE MISERY OF ___
284. A MISERABLE ___ BEING
285. THE UNAWARENESS OF ___
286. AN UNAWARE ___ BEING
287. THE OPPONENTS OF ___
288. AN OPPOSED ___ BEING

PART-6

For the "odd numbered" *items*, the *Goal* continues to be inserted in present-tense without "TO" and as an "–ING" form; *"forgetting,"* &tc. For "TO BE" type *Goals*, the "–ING" is added to the "BE"; *"to be ended"* becomes *"being ended."*

The "even numbered" *items* are stated in the basic "TO {GOAL}" style; *"to forget," "to be ended,"* &tc.

The last *item-line* links the *Platform* to the *next Goal* in the *sequence*. This last *item-line* is actually a *"negation-item"* (or *"oppositional nix-item"*) of the *next Goal*. It immediately precedes the first *item-line* of PART-1 for the *next Goal*.

[Note that unlike the original *"Heaven Incident"* pageantry of *Goals-Sequencing*, this entire *Implanting-Incident* runs the *sequence-ordering* in each direction (*three times*), and the *"next Goal"* depends on whether you are going "ascending" or "descending" on the *chain*.]

289. THE FORBIDDENNESS OF ___
290. SOMEBODY WHO NEEDS ___
291. A HATRED OF ___
292. SOMEBODY WHO LOVES ___
293. THE INHIBITEDNESS OF ___
294. SOMEBODY WHO DESIRES ___
295. THE ABSENCE OF ___
296. SOMEBODY WHO COMPULSIVELY CREATES ___

297. STOPPED ___
298. SOMEBODY WITH THE GOAL ___
299. ANY IMPOSSIBILITIES OF ___
300. SOMEONE OR SOMETHING WITH THE GOAL ___
301. THE NON-EXISTENCE OF ___
302. THE GOAL ___
303. {*current goal*}
304. NOT {*next goal*}

HEAVEN IMPLANTS (PRISON SERIES)
(*Goal-Sequencing List*)

This is the *Goal-Sequencing List* in the order that it is first encountered in the *Implanting-Incident*. On your first *run* through the *sequence*, you are working from the "bottom" to the "top." You begin at the "bottom" and walk "up" a *stairway* backwards while perceiving *300* items for that *Goal*. The remaining *stairway* extends upward *behind* you. The "bottom-level" *Goal* is: **TO BE ENDED**.

There is usually some type of unique related *imprinted-imagery* that is displayed for each *Goal* while the *items* are *Implanted*. We have very limited data to describe this (given with each *Goal* when available). The scenery from *one Goal* "scrolls" or "blends" into the scenery of whatever is *next* without any "break."

On your second *run* through the *sequence*, you will treat the *Goals-list* in the reverse order of what is printed here. For this, you will work from the "top" and proceed forward going "down" the stairway. The "top-level" *Goal* is: **TO BE CREATED**.

We have certainty on the actual *Incident-Sequence*, the *first* and *last* primary *Goal* for the *Goal-Sequence*, and an estimated 80-90% of the *Goals* that lie between. Based on our experience, this is apparently sufficient enough *data* to "*Spot*" in order to *defragment* the entire *Platform-series*.

1. **TO BE ENDED**
   A black pathway through empty space, ending at the swirling spiral of Chaos.
2. **TO BE TORTURED**
   A dark dungeon; layered down to the "final pit" and a pathway through Nothingness.

3. TO BE INSUBSTANTIAL
4. TO BE FLAYED
   Strapped down to a stretcher; being wheeled into surgery.
5. TO BE NUMB
   An ice-cave; crystalline arches at the entrance.
6. TO BE FROZEN
   Snow-covered landscape; ice-sculptures (statues) say the items.
   On Part-6, you are dunked in ice-water on each item.
7. TO BE BURNED
   Burning landscape; flames say the items. Repeatedly dropped into a "fiery pit" (on each item).
8. TO BE UNAFFECTED
   Surrounded by violent explosions that don't quite hit you.
9. TO BE HORRIFIED
   Smokey pits; victims on either side of the stairway; demons say the items.
10. TO BE UNAWARE
11. TO BE IN HELL
    Bridges over flames and rivers of fire. Bridges lead to cities; final bridge leads to mountain-cave.
12. TO BE GAMELESS
    Gray pathway near mountain-cave; gray clouds; everything is gray (washed-out color).
13. TO BE HAUNTED
    Gray landscape.
14. TO BE SELF-PITYING
    Rough-rock bridges over ash.
15. TO BE DRAINED
    Bleak gray landscape with dark misshapen trees. Spirits hit at you and it feels like they pull away energy.
16. TO BE IGNITED
17. TO BE INTERIORIZED
    Snapping into dead bodies, one to another, in a morgue.
18. TO BE BODILESS
    Floating over a pile of ashes. Nice things are all around but you can't grab a hold of them.
19. TO BE BURIED

20. TO BE MOURNFUL
   Walking through a graveyard; tombstones say items.
21. TO BE NON-EXISTENT
22. TO BE DEAD
23. TO FAIL
   Walking through a battlefield with barbed-wire fences. Fence-poles say the items.
24. TO BE WIPED OUT
   Battlefield; dying soldiers say items.
25. TO BE APATHETIC
   Pathway through war-torn battlefield.
26. TO BE DEFEATED
   Battlefield. Tanks and planes say "odd-numbered" items; fighting soldiers say "even-numbered" items.
27. TO BE MURDEROUS
   Walking along a tall wall overlooking battlefield; exploding bombs say the items.
28. TO BE HATED
   In a railroad car, on a track running between barbed-wire fences of a battlefield.
29. TO BE IGNORED
   On railroad car.
30. TO BE BLAMED
   On railroad car; billboards say items.
31. TO BE UNCARING
   Elegant railroad car; passing people starving and pleading for help.
32. TO BE POSSESSED (TAKEN OVER)
   Railway train shed; loud-speakers say items.
33. TO BE VENGEFUL
   Between a train shed and a harbor.
34. TO BE PERSECUTED
   Running alongside a harbor near a village, trying to escape townspeople carrying pitchforks, &tc., who say the items.
35. TO BE PARANOID
   Floating in dark waters.

36. TO BE PURPOSELESS
    A canal. Poles in water say items.
37. TO BE SELF-CONFLICTING
    Canal with cottages along the banks. You try to go in different directions simultaneously. You split/divide on the "odd-numbered" items, and recombine on the "even-numbered" items.
38. TO BE COMBINED
    Body is on a pole of the canal near cottages. Copies of yourself come flying out of cottages and snap-in to your body.
39. TO BE DIVIDED
    Canal boat. Floating past docks during electrical storm. Copies of yourself are standing at edge of docks, then turn around when you approach and walk away. Lightning bolts say items.
40. TO BE UNCHANGING
    Canal.
41. TO BE SICK
    Canal; lying sick in boat.
42. TO BE HOPELESS
    Canal; sidewalk to either side; statues say items.
43. TO BE SELF-INVALIDATIVE
    Canal.
44. TO GIVE UP
    Canal through a desert. Pyramids, on either side, say items.
45. TO FEEL MISERABLE
    Amusement park ride; inside some kind of box that jerks around.
    {might be missing *Goals* here}
46. TO BE UNCONSCIOUS
47. TO BE HURT
    In a cart/car; going down a steep mountain; smashing into things.
48. TO BE SELF-DESTRUCTIVE
    Pits containing various hazards line both sides of the roadway. The pits say the items. On the "odd-numbered" items, you step off the roadway and fall into a pit. On "even-numbered" items, you end up back on the roadway.
49. TO BE TRAPPED
    Amusement park; carousel; going up and down on a pole; fake horses all around.

50. TO BE LOST

   "Spinning plates" (?)

51. TO BE LOCATED

   Walking down streets; walking down corridors. Doors (with faces) say the items.

52. TO BE DISPERSED

   Strapped to a bulls-eye on a flying target; things keep hitting you. On the "odd-numbered" items, pieces of the body fly off in all directions. On the "even-numbered" items, the pieces are pulled back together.

53. TO BE OVERWHELMED

   Amusement park. Contains imagery from other parts of the Implanting-Incident.

54. TO BE PUNISHED

   Amusement park.

55. TO BE DOMINEERING

   Amusement park.

56. TO BE CRIPPLED

   Amusement park.

57. TO BE SPINNING

   Amusement park; spinning pole.

58. TO BE STOPPED

   Amusement park; ride-car keeps stopping in unpleasant places.

59. TO BE DIZZY (?)

60. TO BE UNAFFECTED (?)

61. TO BE UNBALANCED

   Amusement park; "spinning plates" (?)

   {might be missing Goals here}

62. TO BE CARELESS

63. TO BE SELF-CONTROLLED

64. TO BE RECKLESS

65. TO BE CONTROLLED (?)

66. TO BE GET WORSE

   Underground cave. Stalagmites say "odd-numbered" items; the floor says "even-numbered" items.

67. TO BE DRUGGED (?)

68. TO BE AGONIZED (?)
69. TO EXPERIENCE NOTHING
70. TO BE ELECTROCUTED
    Hitting against large round electrified terminals on either side. (Like being in a pinball game.)
    > {might be missing Goals here}
71. TO BE DISMEMBERED (?)
72. TO BE WORRIED (?)
73. TO BE UNTHINKING
    In a swamp; on a boat.
74. TO BE DEPRESSED
    Poling a boat through a muddy swamp.
75. TO BE INDIFFERENT
    Being dragged through a muddy swamp by snakes (that say the items).
76. TO BE STUCK
    Hopping through a muddy tar-swamp. You get stuck on the "odd-numbered" items, and lift out on the "even-numbered" items.
77. TO BE FLEEING
    Wading through muddy swamp in haste.
78. TO BE INFESTED
    In a marsh, on a raft. Firefly-like bugs enter your body on the "odd-numbered" items. Feeling of being infested with entities.
    > {might be missing Goals here}
79. TO BE EVIL (?)
    Creatures rise up out of marshy swamp to say items.
80. TO BE UNIMPORTANT
    Walking through marsh; stakes sticking up out of the water with heads on them, which say the items. There are electric shocks associated with the "odd-numbered" items.
81. TO BE IMPLANTED
82. TO BE VISCOUS
    On a cliffside, near the sea; stairway leads down into the water.
83. TO BE PURSUED
    Running through a forest toward a beach.

84. TO BE NERVOUS
   In the forest; trees say the items.
85. TO BE CRIMINAL
   Walking down urban streets.
86. TO BE DOCILE
87. TO BE TREATED
   Hospital.
88. TO BE INSANE
   Hospital.
89. TO BE CONDEMNED
   Walking from a courthouse to jail; prisoners say items.
90. TO BE DISHONEST
91. TO BE ACCUSED
   Walking between pillars (that say items).
92. TO BE GUILT-RIDDEN
   In a forest; faces on trees say items.
93. TO BE TREASONOUS
94. TO BE BLINDED
95. TO BE SPYING
96. TO BE BETRAYED

   {might be missing *Goals* here}

97. TO BE VILIFIED (?)
98. TO BE TREACHEROUS (?)
99. TO BE DEGRADED
100. TO BE ASHAMED
101. TO BE PERVERTED
   Carnival. (?)
102. TO HAVE CRAVINGS
   Carnival market; things on display. (?)
103. TO BE EMPTY
   Floating above market or shopping mall.
104. TO BE GLUTTONOUS
   Restaurant terrace overlooking market or shopping mall.

105. TO BE REJECTED
   A mall-tunnel or concourse.
106. TO BE DISGUSTING
   A sewer-like subway station/tunnel.
107. TO BE TIDY
   A carpeted hallway.
108. TO BE MESSY
109. TO BE CLUNG-TO
110. TO BE ABANDONED
111. TO BE DEPENDENT
112. TO BE UNFEELING
113. TO BE SEXUAL
114. TO BE ALONE
115. TO BE TOGETHER
116. TO BE ISOLATED
117. TO BE CORRUPTING
118. TO BE CORRUPTED
119. TO BE INHIBITED
120. TO BE WANTON
121. TO BE FRUSTRATED
   {might be missing a *Goal* here}
122. TO BE DISINTERESTED
123. TO BE DISAPPOINTED
124. TO BE HUMAN
   Goal might actually be: To Be Selfish. (Or "To Be Selfish" might need to be inserted as next goal or previous goal.)
   {might be missing a *Goal* here}
125. TO BE ENRAGED
126. TO BE DROPPED
127. TO BE CARRIED
   On a ski-lift. (?)
128. TO BE EXHAUSTED
   Trudging up a mountain-slope from a beach; eventually reaching a snowy area.

129. TO BE OVEREXERTED

> {might be missing a *Goal* here}

130. TO HALLUCINATE
131. TO BE TERRIFIED
132. TO BE FOOLISH
133. TO BE RESPONSIBLE

Traveling in a car at high speed, down a steep slope. Light-posts say the items as you pass by.

134. TO BE IRRESPONSIBLE
135. TO BE BURDENED

Trudging through primitive village carrying many things.

136. TO BE NEGLIGENT
137. TO BE CAREFUL
138. TO BE CRUSHED

Industrial factory-like environment; on a conveyer-belt. Cylinders come down and crush you; walls smash inward from the side.

139. TO BE INATTENTIVE
140. TO BE SELF-CRITICAL

> {might be missing *Goals* here}

141. TO BE REGRETFUL
142. TO BE INCOMPETENT
143. TO BE ENSLAVED
144. TO BE CRUEL
145. TO BE IRRITATED (?)
146. TO BE EXPLOITED (?)
147. TO BE RESISTED (?)
148. TO BE MISLED (?)
149. TO BE ASLEEP

Fluffy pillow-like landscape; soft pathway; stuffed-animals, on either side, say the items.

150. TO BE TIRED

> {might be missing *Goals* here}

151. TO BE CRITICAL

152. TO BE CRITICIZED
   Broad stairway in the air; statues along either side say the items.
153. TO BE ARROGANT
   Roadway in the sky.
154. TO BE WRONG
155. TO BE IMPORTANT
   Roadway in the sky. "Pennant-poles" say the items.
156. TO BE BOTHERED
157. TO BE POWERFUL
158. TO BE TROUBLED
159. TO HAVE PICTURES
160. TO BE UNSEEING
161. TO BE REVOLTED
162. TO BE AFFECTED
163. TO BE TOUGH (?)
164. TO BE FRAGILE (?)
165. TO HAVE NOTHING
166. TO BE POSSESSIVE
167. TO BE MASSLESS
   Moving through "solid" doors.
168. TO BE SOLID
   Walking beneath iron-arches.
169. TO BE ALTERED (?)
170. TO BE INCOMPLETE (?)
171. TO BE BLOCKED (?)
172. TO BE IRRADIATED (?)
173. TO BE DISTRACTED (?)
174. TO FORGET
175. TO REGRET
176. TO LEVITATE
   Walking on a transparent bridge in the sky. All of the imagery is of harmful-acts.
177. TO COMPULSIVELY CREATE
   Aerial stairway.

178. **TO BE CAST OUT**
   Thrown out of heaven, through its gates.
179. **TO BE IN HEAVEN**
   Pathway through clouds between the gates and the heavenly kingdom.
180. **TO BE REBELLIOUS**
181. **TO BE GOOD**
   You eventually back up all the way to where "God's Throne" sits at the top of the stairway.
182. **TO BE CREATED**
   The top-most item displays you being created by "God."

HEAVEN IMPLANTS (ETHICS SERIES)
(*Implant-Running Process / Goals-List*)

When an *Alpha-Spirit* first separates from the *Infinity of Nothingness*, it is an incredibly powerful—but also an incredibly innocent and naïve—*Spiritual Being* with a *creative* nature. The one thing we could absolutely say for certain is: the basic nature of the *Alpha-Spirit* is definitely *not* "inherently evil."

There is a long history of attempts to *Implant* individuals to "make them good." Of course, the only reason they do the things they do is because of how *fragmented* they are; and one of the reasons individuals have become so *fragmented*, is the tremendous quantity of accumulated *Implants* they've been subjected to.

Implanting has never once "made someone good." For one thing: an individual doesn't need to be "made to be good." *Ethics* have never been successfully "*enforced*" and "*personally developed*" simultaneously.

An individual either *has* the *Awareness* and *ability-to-confront* what has happened (and *decide* to *change* their course of future *thought* and *action*), or they *don't* have the *Awareness*—in which case, they are not able to see what has happened "*As-It-Is,*" and/or their *considerations* are too heavily wrapped up in *justification*. In any case: *Implanting* will not make the individual *more aware*.

There have been many versions of the "*Ethics-Implant*" pattern, extending back through several *Universes*. In each *Universe*, the *Platform-pattern* tends to become a little more complex, with more *command-lines* added to the existing *Platform* from a prior *Universe*—as is commonly found in later (more recent) *Implants*.

The real purpose behind any *Implant* is to suppress *Alpha-Spirits*, reduce their *Actualized Awareness*, and keep them under some kind of *"other-determined"* (rather than *"Self-determined"*) *control*. You can *"condition"* individuals into being quiet, complacent, orderly *"good citizens"*—but this doesn't make them more *ethical*.

An *"Ethics-Implant"* isn't only about making the *Implanted*-individual a more ethical person; it sells them on the idea that "everyone is *bad*" and that this is "what is *wrong* with everyone" (*including* themselves), and that "everyone needs to have *ethics enforced* on them." It gets one to be more tolerant/agreeable to *enforcement*.

We include this as part of the *"Heaven Implants"* because it tends to show up *between-lives* and emphasizes what some might consider *"religious morality"* (although it really serves a more "civic/societal" function). In contrast to many other *Implants*, the *"items"* of an *Ethics-Platform* all seem "positive" or "good things"—such as *"creating goodness"* and *"destroying criminality."* But, this deceptively just makes the person more agreeable to the general content/message of the *Implant*, which again, is inhibiting *"thinking for one's self."*

Due to the many variations and versions, critical research-time was not spent in developing full *Platforms* that are each only slightly modified from one another. The *Goals-list* for this *Implant* is also *not* so deeply ingrained or heavily charged that we have to run hundreds of *items* off of a *Goal* in order to *defragment* it.

Therefore, we provide an *"Ethics-Implant Running Procedure."* It is designed to only apply as many details as are necessary to be able to easily *"defrag-by-realization"* (by *Spotting* a few key aspects of the *Platforms*). This procedure only has a dozen steps; and is *run* on each of *20 Goals* (as given in the attached *Goals-list*).

IMPLANT-RUNNING PROCEDURE

  A. *Spot* the first *item* of the original *Implant-Platform* as used in the *Symbols Universe*:

TO BE {*Goal*} IS NATIVE STATE

B. *Spot* the first *item* of the *Implant-Platform* as used in a later version:
TO CREATE {*Positive State*} IS NATIVE STATE

C. *Spot* the *item* related to the later *Implant-Platform* from STEP-B:
TO DESTROY {*Negative State*} IS NATIVE STATE

D. Another version uses the entire series of *64 Implanted Penalty-Universe* (IPU) *Goals; running* from "*Create*" to "*Endure.*" You should only need to *Spot* a few of them. The first two and last two of the series are given below to demonstrate the *pattern*. [Refer to *AT#4* for additional IPU details (if needed).]

TO BE IS TO CREATE {*Positive State*}

TO BE IS TO CAUSE {*Positive State*}

TO BE IS TO EAT/ABSORB {*Positive State*}

TO BE IS TO ENDURE (ANYTHING FOR THE SAKE OF) {*Positive State*}

E. As related to the version from STEP-D: this *Implant- Platform* uses 64 inverted IPU-Goals in *reverse order*—from "*Endure*" (now inverted as "*Dissipate*") up to "*Create*" (now inverted as "*Destroy*"). These are run on the "*Negative Goal States*" (as given in the *Goals-list*). You should only need to *Spot* a few of them. The first two and last two of the series are given below to demonstrate the *inverted reverse-order pattern*.

TO BE IS TO DISSIPATE {*Negative State*}

TO BE IS TO REFUSE {*Negative State*}

TO BE IS TO UNDO {*Negative State*}

TO BE IS TO DESTROY {*Negative State*}

F. The earliest versions included a "*splitter-incident.*" In this case, you were required to push *fragments* of yourself onto others to "make them follow the rules." [Refer to *AT#5* concerning "*Control Entities*" (CE).]

1. "*Spot pushing fragments of yourself onto others and compelling them to be {positive state}.*"

2. "*Spot pushing fragments of yourself onto others and inhibiting them from {negative state}.*"

Note: any *fragments* (*split pieces*) you *Spot*, you should *run* the "*Entity Locational Procedure*" (*AT#5*) on them ("*Point to the being you divided from*").

Also (if necessary or applicable): handle any more recent actions of *"forcing others to be { positive state }"* and/or *"inhibiting others from { negative state}."* [In this case, we don't mean reasonable efforts to help others improve; we mean more heavy-handed scenarios.]

G. *Spot* any *entities* (or *fragments*) that have been pushed onto you (by others) to compel you *"to be {positive state}"* or *"inhibit you from { negative state}."* Handle by having the *entity* "*Spot*" the false data of the *Implant* and/or the *top item* (STEP-A); or else, "Locational Procedure," &tc. [See AT#5.]

H. *Defragment* some of the *tendencies/considerations* laid in by the *Implant*.
1. *"Spot wanting to be compelled by others to be {positive state}."*
2. *"Spot wanting to be inhibited by others from {negative state}."*
3. *"Spot the realization that these cravings/tendencies were installed by the Implant."*

I. *Defragment* some of the *Implanted data*.
"Spot the false data: that people are basically {negative state}."

J. *Defragment* some misconceptions.
"Spot the misconception: that this Implant is necessary to your well-being, and the well-being of others."

K. *Spot* the first *item* of the *IPU-Platform*. *Spot* this for yourself—and for any partially awake *entities* that haven't *released/dispersed* yet.

TO CREATE IS NATIVE STATE

L. (If necessary) *Spot* the first *item* of the *Agreements Universe-Platform*. *Spot* this for yourself—and for any partially awake *entities* that haven't *released/dispersed* yet.

TO AGREE IS NATIVE STATE

[Note that if you don't get a sense of relief on the *Goal-item* from this procedure: *spot* any *harmful-acts* on the *Backtrack* regarding your participation in designing the *Implant*; or *Implanting* others; or wanting others *Implanted* with this; or even forcing others to be *Implanted* with this.]

ETHICS-IMPLANT GOAL-LIST

There are *20 Implanted Goal-items* for this *Platform-pattern*. The basic *Goal* is listed in capital letters. There are also "Create" (*positive state*) and "Destroy" (*negative state*) *Goal-items* listed for each basic *Goal*. Use this data to fill-in {indicated spaces} for the steps of the procedure. You may have to slightly adjust the wording of a *goal-state* to make sense in the *processing command-lines* of the procedure.

1. **TO BE ETHICAL**
   POS. (to create) ethics
   NEG. (to destroy) criminality

2. **TO BE RESOURCEFUL**
   POS. (to create) resourcefulness
   NEG. (to destroy) complacency

3. **TO BE SYMPATHETIC**
   POS. (to create) sympathy
   NEG. (to destroy) callousness

4. **TO BE DUTIFUL**
   POS. (to create) dutifulness
   NEG. (to destroy) carelessness

5. **TO BE RESPONSIBLE**
   POS. (to create) responsibility
   NEG. (to destroy) irresponsibility

6. **TO BE HONORABLE**
   POS. (to create) honor
   NEG. (to destroy) dishonor

7. **TO BE LOYAL**
   POS. (to create) loyalty
   NEG. (to destroy) disloyalty

8. **TO BE TRUSTWORTHY**
   POS. (to create) trustworthiness
   NEG. (to destroy) betrayal

9. **TO BE INDUSTRIOUS**
   POS. (to create) industriousness
   NEG. (to destroy) laziness

10. **TO BE MERCIFUL**
    POS. (to create) mercifulness
    NEG. (to destroy) vengefulness

11. **TO BE OBEDIENT**
    POS. (to create) obedience
    NEG. (to destroy) disobedience

12. **TO BE PATIENT**
    POS. (to create) patience
    NEG. (to destroy) impatience

13. **TO BE HELPFUL**
    POS. (to create) helpfulness
    NEG. (to destroy) unhelpfulness

14. **TO BE CARING**
    POS. (to create) caring
    NEG. (to destroy) uncaring

15. **TO BE PROTECTIVE**
    POS. (to create) protectiveness
    NEG. (to destroy) unprotectiveness

16. **TO BE THRIFTY**
    POS. (to create) thriftiness
    NEG. (to destroy) wastefulness

17. **TO BE POLITE**
    POS. (to create) politeness
    NEG. (to destroy) rudeness

18. **TO BE RESPECTFUL**
    POS. (to create) respectfullness
    NEG. (to destroy) disrespectfullness

19. **TO BE GOOD**
    POS. (to create) goodness
    NEG. (to destroy) badness

20. **TO BE REVERENT**
    POS. (to create) reverence
    NEG. (to destroy) irreverence

SPIRITUAL-DISABILITY IMPLANT
Experimental Ascension Processing

[This is *experimental* material. It has been researched and developed sufficiently for effective use and therefore is included with *Wizard Level-3* procedures. Slight revisions may occur in the future where noted and/or it may be reclassified for a higher *Wizard-Level*.]

This *Implant-Platform* is *very old*—likely originating in the *"Symbols Universe"* (see *AT#1*) or possibly earlier. Unlike relatively more recently designed *Implants*, the *effectiveness* of this one is not the result of *nonsensical confusion*. It was carefully constructed to *"imitate"*—and be *experienced as*—an individual's *own thoughts*.

When first researched, we referred to this *Implant* as a *"mental-disability"* *Implant* (but such terminology is commonly misunderstood to mean something else regarding the *Human Condition*). We originally labeled it for the *"Mind"* because it *fixes* "*mental-circuitry*" *in-place* for many *considerations* that an *Alpha-Spirit* would have otherwise treated (or not) on their own *Self-determination* (*knowingly/consciously* with *Alpha-Thought*).

It covertly installs "foundations" for a *fragmented Mind*—establishing "*circuitry*" (or *associative connections*) with various *concepts*, *considerations*, and *terminals*; none of which seems, on the surface, as though it is "damaging." But it is; because it reduces *spiritual ability* by *fixing attention* (as *fragmentary charge*) on a lot of *considerations*.

Each *series-run* of the *Implant* is modified by a single basic *Intention* or *Goal*. The *first three series-runs* draw an individual "in" to the content by using "I.." statements. This means it starts by having hundreds of "I.." statements *firing* "internally" as though they were one's own. The remainder of the *series-runs* concern "To (do something)" statements, worded as *associative-knowledge* about basic *Goals*.

At this point in *Advanced Training*, it should already be fairly obvious as to "why" *compulsively* and *unknowingly* maintaining *fragmentary charge* on all of these "*items*" is *spiritually unhealthy* or *debilitating*. Therefore, let us focus on the mechanics of the *Implant* itself, and *defragmenting* the *Platform*.

To illustrate this: let's take up a "*null-example*" (that does not actually appear in the *Implant-Platform*) about "*Eating.*" It probably would be included if this *Implant* were constructed today, but at the time of its origination, "food-intake" *considerations* were not a "standard" part of an *Alpha-Spirit's* existence or reality.

A basic short-form formula for this *Implant-Platform* would only include the main reoccurring "*root*" for each "*item-line.*" In this case:

```
0.1.X ____ TO EAT
0.2.X ____ TO STARVE
```

Here you see what appear to be opposing *concepts*. All of the *items* in this *Implant* occur in pairs. Each *series* inserts a different *keyword* or *impulse* at the start of the statement. The first statement is given a "positive" and the second is given a "negative." And in the end, they both will basically mean the same thing. For the first *series-run* of "*I want*"/"*I don't want,*" the *command-lines* would be *processed-out* (*discharged/defragged*) as:

```
0.1.1  (I WANT) TO EAT
0.2.1  (I DON'T WANT) TO STARVE
```

At first glance, it would seem like there is nothing wrong with these *considerations*. But, what if you had never had them before? What if there was no need to even *consider* them? — but here they are: the formation of a specific "*thought-tendency*" or "*circuit*" about *eating, food, &tc*. Once the "*wanting*" is installed, it's that much easier to install a "*need*" on that "*circuit*" for the *second series-run*, when the *command-lines* change to:

```
0.1.2  (I NEED) TO EAT
0.2.2  (I CAN'T BEAR) TO STARVE
```

By starting at the "top" (earliest point) of the *Implant-Platform*, the heavier laden *charge* can be *dispersed* from the foundations before the additional *series-runs*. Although there were originally over a hundred *series -runs* during the original *Implanting-Incident*, the entire *pattern* is likely to start coming apart and *disperse* after *processing-out* only a few dozen (for a *Wizard Level-3* practitioner) when working from the "top."

After the *first three series-runs*, the remainder of the *Implant* contains many arbitrary *considerations* that add even more "*energetic-mass*" to all those key areas that were just installed. They are really "*equations*" of "*associative thought.*" The *command-items* all relay that "one thing *is* (equal to) another thing" — and this is done thousands of times over the course of the remaining series-runs.

To illustrate how the remaining *series* are *run*, we will apply the *"fourth series-run"* to our example from above. The *series-four list-items* are: *"To Agree"*/*"To Disagree."*

    0.1.4 (TO AGREE) [IS] TO EAT
    0.2.4 (TO DISAGREE) [IS] TO STARVE

[Note that for *series-four* (and afterward), you also have to insert an *"is"* between the variable *list-item* and the reoccurring *root* in order to complete each *command-line*. None of this was *Implanted* in *human-language*. Inserting *"is"* helps the *item-line* make more sense in order to properly *contact* and *process-out* its *meaning*.]

[Although it does not appear in the *Implant*, it is possible that we put some *charge* on the above examples during instruction. Your first *processing-action* might be to make sure *they* don't *register* on a *GSR-Meter*; or if you feel anything related to them, *defragment* it by the same methods you have *processed-out* other *items*.]

This *Implant* first occurs on the *Backtrack* many *Universes* ago, when *Implanting* methods were far more *"energetic"* or *"telepathic"*—relative to the heavier *"electronic"* incidents that take place in *this Physical Universe*. But, early on, *Implants* took a lot of *energy*, and required a lot of *"time,"* just to get an *Alpha-Spirit* to "budge" even a little bit on their *considerations*.

Of course, *this Implant* is incredibly lengthy; but at the time it first occurs, *Alpha-Spirits* had a far different appreciation of relative *"time-spans"* than we do today. While an individual *Implanting-Incident* was seldom very effective early on, the *Implanting* repeatedly continued on the *Backtrack*. It cumulatively "built-up" upon its own foundations; and other *Platforms* often added to it, by restimulating it, and reducing an individual's *Awareness* enough to accept installation of some new *Implant*.

Data for any original *incident* is limited. The *Implanting-gimmick* used for this is: projecting *energy-waves* at the *Alpha-Spirit* from opposing sides. The early *series-runs* come from *left* and right. Later *series* have them come from *front* and *back*, then eventually *above* and *below*. The "positive" *command-item* of each *pair* comes from a *"golden sphere"*; the "negative" one comes from a *"silver sphere."* There is also a *"dark explosion"* that sends out *"sheets of black energy."*

Only a "short-form" formula is given for what would otherwise require

35,000 *command-lines* to write out fully. [A *Seeker* is *not expected* to have to *run every series* to *disperse* the *Implant* anyways.] However, this is still an experimental *Platform*. We cannot yet instruct with certainty on whether or not a *Seeker* should take *charge* off of the reoccurring *"ending roots"* of the *Platform* prior to *processing-out* the *Implant*.

–It *is*, however, best practices to lightly *"scan"* for, and handle, any *"misunderstood words"* before *running* the *Implant*.

–It *is* also best practices to *discharge* the variable *"list-item"* to be inserted at the top of each *series-run*, as your *first command-line*. For example: *"I Want"* and *"I Don't Want,"* and then both of them simultaneously, or as a single line—*"I Want"/"I Don't Want."* The *variable item-list* is included in this manual after the *Platform formula* (below).

–In that same style, although it is not indicated here: it is common to *process-out* each of the *command-lines* in a pair, on their own, and then to *run* a *third command-line* combining them and making sure that no "residual" *registers* on a *GSR-Meter*. A *Seeker* will have noticed this *combined-line* from their previous study/use of some *Implant-Platforms*.

While combining pair-*lines* for a third *is* a common practice, given the current experimental state of this material, we cannot at this time say with certainty if it should be observed here. Further work is still required to perfectly refine *Wizard Level-3*, in addition to completing research and developing additional *Wizard-Levels* (as described in *AT#8*).

SPIRITUAL-DISABILITY PLATFORM

```
1.1.X ___ TO ESCAPE
1.2.X ___ TO BE CAPTURED
2.1.X ___ TO START
2.2.X ___ TO STOP
3.1.X ___ TO GO FORWARD
3.2.X ___ TO GO BACK
4.1.X ___ TO BE AWAKE
4.2.X ___ TO BE ASLEEP
5.1.X ___ TO BE COMPETENT
5.2.X ___ TO BE INCOMPETENT
6.1.X ___ TO REMEMBER
6.2.X ___ TO FORGET
```

```
7.1.X  ___  TO BE LIGHT
7.2.X  ___  TO BE HEAVY
8.1.X  ___  TO BE TREATED HONESTLY
8.2.X  ___  TO BE FOOLED
9.1.X  ___  TO BE ALLOWED TO REMAIN
9.2.X  ___  TO BE DRIVEN AWAY
10.1.X ___  TO BE AWARE
10.2.X ___  TO GO UNCONSCIOUS
11.1.X ___  TO BE ABLE TO STOP
11.2.X ___  TO BE MADE TO CONTINUE
12.1.X ___  TO BE FINISHED WITH THIS IMPLANT
12.2.X ___  TO BEGIN THIS IMPLANT
13.1.X ___  TO BE UNSPINNING
13.2.X ___  TO BE DIZZY
14.1.X ___  TO BE ABLE TO FIND OUT
14.2.X ___  TO BE UNABLE TO FIND OUT
15.1.X ___  TO BE PERCEPTIVE
15.2.X ___  TO BE BLIND
16.1.X ___  TO BE REPLENISHED
16.2.X ___  TO BE DRAINED
17.1.X ___  TO BE ENERGETIC
17.2.X ___  TO BE TIRED
18.1.X ___  TO BE LIVELY
18.2.X ___  TO BE IN A STUPOR
19.1.X ___  TO WAKE UP
19.2.X ___  TO BE KNOCKED OUT
20.1.X ___  TO BE BLESSED
20.2.X ___  TO BE CURSED
21.1.X ___  TO KEEP TRACK OF THINGS
21.2.X ___  TO LOSE TRACK OF THINGS
22.1.X ___  TO FOCUS ATTENTION
22.2.X ___  TO BE DISTRACTED
23.1.X ___  TO GET MOVING
23.2.X ___  TO GET STUCK
24.1.X ___  TO BE FORGIVEN
24.2.X ___  TO BE BLAMED
```

25.1.x ___ TO DO WHAT I'M DOING
25.2.x ___ TO DO SOMETHING ELSE
26.1.x ___ TO DO WELL
26.2.x ___ TO DO POORLY
27.1.x ___ TO FEEL PLEASURE
27.2.x ___ TO FEEL PAIN
28.1.x ___ TO BE CONFORTED
28.2.x ___ TO BE TORTURED
29.1.x ___ TO BE HEALTHY
29.2.x ___ TO BE SICK
30.1.x ___ TO BE CREATED
30.2.x ___ TO BE DESTROYED
31.1.x ___ TO BE UNTOUCHED
31.2.x ___ TO BE IMPACTED
32.1.x ___ TO BE ORIENTED
32.2.x ___ TO BE DISORIENTED
33.1.x ___ TO BE CAPABLE OF THINKING
33.2.x ___ TO BE INCAPABLE OF THINKING
34.1.x ___ TO DO ENOUGH
34.2.x ___ TO DO TOO LITTLE
35.1.x ___ TO FIND THINGS
35.2.x ___ TO LOSE THINGS
36.1.x ___ TO BE HARD TO FOOL
36.2.x ___ TO BE EASY TO FOOL
37.1.x ___ TO BE REWARDED
37.2.x ___ TO BE PUNISHED
38.1.x ___ TO BE PLEASED
38.2.x ___ TO BE DISAPPOINTED
39.1.x ___ TO BE FREE
39.2.x ___ TO BE TRAPPED
40.1.x ___ TO BE REFRESHED
40.2.x ___ TO BE WORN DOWN
41.1.x ___ TO BE PATIENT
41.2.x ___ TO BE IMPATIENT
42.1.x ___ TO ACCEPT THINGS
42.2.x ___ TO BE ANXIOUS ABOUT THINGS

43.1.X ___ TO HAVE CONFIDENCE
43.2.X ___ TO HAVE DOUBTS

44.1.X ___ TO BE TROUBLE-FREE
44.2.X ___ TO HAVE TROUBLE

45.1.X ___ TO BE MANIFESTED (*made*)
45.2.X ___ TO BE UNMANIFESTED (*unmade*)

46.1.X ___ TO HAVE AN IDENTITY
46.2.X ___ TO BE NOBODY

47.1.X ___ TO BE AN INDIVIDUAL
47.2.X ___ TO BE PART OF A COMPOSITE

48.1.X ___ TO HAVE FREE WILL
48.2.X ___ TO BE CONTROLLED

49.1.X ___ TO BE JUSTIFIED
49.2.X ___ TO BE UNJUSTIFIED

50.1.X ___ TO BE PROPER
50.2.X ___ TO BE SCANDALOUS

51.1.X ___ TO HAVE PRIDE
51.2.X ___ TO BE ASHAMED

52.1.X ___ TO BE EARLY
52.2.X ___ TO BE LATE

53.1.X ___ TO BE RELAXED
53.2.X ___ TO BE NERVOUS

54.1.X ___ TO PAY ATTENTION
54.2.X ___ TO IGNORE THINGS

55.1.X ___ TO BE CERTAIN
55.2.X ___ TO BE CONFUSED

56.1.X ___ TO HAVE A FUTURE
56.2.X ___ TO BE DOOMED

57.1.X ___ TO HAVE PLEASANT SENSATIONS
57.2.X ___ TO HAVE DISTURBING SENSATIONS

58.1.X ___ TO BE AGREED WITH
58.2.X ___ TO HAVE ARGUMENTS

59.1.X ___ TO HAVE FEELING
59.2.X ___ TO FEEL NUMB

60.1.X ___ TO HOLD TOGETHER
60.2.X ___ TO FALL APART

61.1.X ___ TO BE ETHICAL
61.2.X ___ TO BE IMMORAL
62.1.X ___ TO BE NICE
62.2.X ___ TO BE NASTY
63.1.X ___ TO BE GIVEN THINGS
63.2.X ___ TO BE DEPRIVED OF THINGS
64.1.X ___ TO FEEL COMFORTABLE
64.2.X ___ TO FEEL STRAINED
65.1.X ___ TO BE WHOLESOME
65.2.X ___ TO BE INFECTED
66.1.X ___ TO BE ALLOWED TO CONTINUE
66.2.X ___ TO BE INTERFERED WITH
67.1.X ___ TO BE SPECIAL
67.2.X ___ TO BE MUNDANE
68.1.X ___ TO CONCENTRATE
68.2.X ___ TO BE DISPERSED
69.1.X ___ TO BE WILLING
69.2.X ___ TO BE UNWILLING
70.1.X ___ TO BE SUPERIOR
70.2.X ___ TO BE INFERIOR
71.1.X ___ TO BE CLEAN
71.2.X ___ TO BE INFESTED
72.1.X ___ TO BE SPACIOUS
72.2.X ___ TO BE SOLID
73.1.X ___ TO BE COOL
73.2.X ___ TO BURN
74.1.X ___ TO BE WARM
74.2.X ___ TO FREEZE
75.1.X ___ TO FEEL SAFE
75.2.X ___ TO BE AFRAID
76.1.X ___ TO PROTECT MYSELF
76.2.X ___ TO RUIN MYSELF
77.1.X ___ TO BE NOBLE
77.2.X ___ TO BE DEGRADED
78.1.X ___ TO FEEL COMPLACENT

78.2.X ___ TO FEEL WORRIED
79.1.X ___ TO AVOID GRIEF
79.2.X ___ TO BE GRIEF-STRICKEN
80.1.X ___ TO FEEL RELIEF
80.2.X ___ TO FEEL PRESSURE
81.1.X ___ TO BE SETTLED
81.2.X ___ TO BE HYPER-ACTIVE
82.1.X ___ TO BE RESTED
82.2.X ___ TO BE UNABLE TO REST
83.1.X ___ TO BE ACCURATE
83.2.X ___ TO MAKE MISTAKES
84.1.X ___ TO BE KNOWING
84.2.X ___ TO BE UNKNOWING
85.1.X ___ TO SEE THINGS CLEARLY
85.2.X ___ TO HAVE DISTORTED PERCEPTIONS
86.1.X ___ TO BE LUCKY
86.2.X ___ TO BE UNLUCKY
87.1.X ___ TO AVOID ACCIDENTS
87.2.X ___ TO HAVE ACCIDENTS
88.1.X ___ TO BE FAVORED
88.2.X ___ TO BE PICKED ON
89.1.X ___ TO BE SMART
89.2.X ___ TO BE DUMB
90.1.X ___ TO HAVE PURPOSE
90.2.X ___ TO BE PURPOSELESS
91.1.X ___ TO BE A PART OF THINGS
91.2.X ___ TO BE DETACHED
92.1.X ___ TO HAVE INTERESTS
92.2.X ___ TO BE UNINTERESTED
93.1.X ___ TO DO THE RIGHT AMOUNT
93.2.X ___ TO DO TOO MUCH
94.1.X ___ TO BE GUIDED
94.2.X ___ TO BE MISLED
95.1.X ___ TO BE BLOCKED
95.2.X ___ TO BE UNBLOCKED

96.1.X ___ TO HAVE OPEN PERCEPTIONS
96.2.X ___ TO BE COVERED IN BLACKNESS
97.1.X ___ TO BE RATIONAL
97.2.X ___ TO BE IRRATIONAL
98.1.X ___ TO HAVE CORRECT RECOLLECTIONS
98.2.X ___ TO MISREMEMBER
99.1.X ___ TO BE UNBOTHERED
99.2.X ___ TO BE RESTIMULATED
100.1.X ___ TO DO WHAT IS NEEDED
100.2.X ___ TO OMIT THINGS
101.1.X ___ TO BE CAREFUL
101.2.X ___ TO BE CARELESS
102.1.X ___ TO BE ABLE
102.2.X ___ TO BE INCAPABLE
103.1.X ___ TO REACH
103.2.X ___ TO WITHDRAW
104.1.X ___ TO KNOW WHO I AM
104.2.X ___ TO BECOME CONFUSED ABOUT IDENTITY
105.1.X ___ TO TAKE CARE OF MYSELF
105.2.X ___ TO BE HELPLESS
106.1.X ___ TO BE INDUSTRIOUS
106.2.X ___ TO BE LAZY
107.1.X ___ TO BE INCLUDED IN THINGS
107.2.X ___ TO MISS OUT ON THINGS
108.1.X ___ TO BE VALIDATED (*praised*)
108.2.X ___ TO BE INVALIDATED
109.1.X ___ TO BE ADMIRED
109.2.X ___ TO BE ABHORRED
110.1.X ___ TO BE BEAUTIFUL
110.2.X ___ TO BE UGLY
111.1.X ___ TO BE BIG
111.2.X ___ TO BE SMALL
112.1.X ___ TO COMMUNICATE
112.2.X ___ TO BE UNABLE TO COMMUNICATE
113.1.X ___ TO BE COMMUNICATED WITH

113.2.X	___	TO BE IGNORED
114.1.X	___	TO CONSERVE THINGS
114.2.X	___	TO WASTE THINGS
115.1.X	___	TO PERCEIVE TRULY
115.2.X	___	TO BE DELUDED
116.1.X	___	TO BE LOCATED
116.2.X	___	TO BE LOST
117.1.X	___	TO THINK CLEARLY
117.2.X	___	TO HAVE MUDDLED THINKING
118.1.X	___	FOR EVERYTHING TO BE OBVIOUS
118.2.X	___	FOR EVERYTHING TO BE OBSCURE
119.1.X	___	TO BE ENCOURAGED
119.2.X	___	TO BE DISCOURAGED
120.1.X	___	TO BE ACCEPTED
120.2.X	___	TO BE SHUNNED
121.1.X	___	TO BE SUPPORTED
121.2.X	___	TO BE PERSECUTED
122.1.X	___	TO ESTIMATE CORRECTLY
122.2.X	___	TO MIS-ESTIMATE
123.1.X	___	TO BE COMPLETE
123.2.X	___	TO BE INCOMPLETE
124.1.X	___	TO BE ENTHUSIASTIC
124.2.X	___	TO BE DESPONDENT
125.1.X	___	TO GET THINGS RIGHT
125.2.X	___	TO GET THINGS MIXED UP
126.1.X	___	TO GET THINGS CORRECT
126.2.X	___	TO MISS THINGS
127.1.X	___	TO HAVE THINGS IN SEQUENCE
127.2.X	___	TO HAVE THINGS OUT-OF-SEQUENCE
128.1.X	___	TO IDENTIFY THINGS CORRECTLY
128.2.X	___	TO CONFUSE ONE THING WITH ANOTHER
129.1.X	___	TO DIFFERENTIATE THINGS
129.2.X	___	TO THINK THAT EVERYTHING IS THE SAME
130.1.X	___	TO BE ABLE TO KEEP THINGS TOGETHER
130.2.X	___	TO HAVE EVERYTHING FALL APART

131.1.X ___ TO BE TREATED RIGHTLY
131.2.X ___ TO BE TREATED WRONGLY
132.1.X ___ TO BE LOGICAL
132.2.X ___ TO BE ILLOGICAL
133.1.X ___ TO BE IMAGINATIVE
133.2.X ___ TO BE DULL
134.1.X ___ TO FEEL PLEASANT
134.2.X ___ TO FEEL HORRIBLE
135.1.X ___ TO BE ACCEPTING OF THINGS
135.2.X ___ TO BE REVOLTED BY THINGS
136.1.X ___ TO BE RESPONSIBLE
136.2.X ___ TO BE IRRESPONSIBLE
137.1.X ___ TO SEE REALITY
137.2.X ___ TO SEE DELUSIONS
138.1.X ___ TO BE COMPLACENT
138.2.X ___ TO BE DESPERATE
139.1.X ___ TO BE FAST
139.2.X ___ TO BE SLOW
140.1.X ___ TO BE REASONABLE
140.2.X ___ TO BE FANATICAL
141.1.X ___ TO BE RIGHT
141.2.X ___ TO BE WRONG
142.1.X ___ TO BE RICH
142.2.X ___ TO BE POOR
143.1.X ___ TO BE DECISIVE
143.2.X ___ TO BE UNABLE TO MAKE UP MY MIND
144.1.X ___ TO BE WHOLE
144.2.X ___ TO BE DIVIDED AGAINST MYSELF
145.1.X ___ TO BE CONTENTED
145.2.X ___ TO BE BOTHERED
146.1.X ___ TO BE STRONG
146.2.X ___ TO BE WEAK
147.1.X ___ TO BE ENDURING
147.2.X ___ TO BE TRANSIENT
148.1.X ___ TO BE CALM

148.2.X ___ TO BE UPSET
149.1.X ___ TO BE CAREFREE
149.2.X ___ TO BE WEIGHED DOWN
150.1.X ___ TO BE EFFECTIVE
150.2.X ___ TO BE INEFFECTIVE
151.1.X ___ TO PUT THINGS IN THE RIGHT PLACE
151.2.X ___ TO PUT THINGS IN THE WRONG PLACE
152.1.X ___ TO KNOW WHERE THINGS BELONG
152.2.X ___ TO NOT KNOW WHERE THINGS BELONG
153.1.X ___ TO KNOW WHERE THINGS ARE
153.2.X ___ TO NOT KNOW WHERE THINGS ARE
154.1.X ___ TO PUT THINGS THE RIGHT WAY AROUND
154.2.X ___ TO PUT THINGS BACKWARDS
155.1.X ___ TO BE HAPPY
155.2.X ___ TO BE SAD
156.1.X ___ TO HAVE THE WILL TO LIVE
156.2.X ___ TO BE UNWILLING TO LIVE
157.1.X ___ TO HAVE VARIETY
157.2.X ___ TO BE BORED
158.1.X ___ TO KNOW TRUTH
158.2.X ___ TO BELIEVE IN LIES
159.1.X ___ TO BE TOLD TRUTH
159.2.X ___ TO BE GIVEN FALSE DATA
160.1.X ___ TO KNOW WHAT IS REAL
160.2.X ___ TO BE UNSURE OF WHAT IS REAL
161.1.X ___ TO KNOW WHAT IS THERE
161.2.X ___ TO IMAGINE THINGS THAT AREN'T THERE
162.1.X ___ TO BE COMPLEMENTED
162.2.X ___ TO BE CRITICIZED
163.1.X ___ TO BE LOVED
163.2.X ___ TO BE HATED
164.1.X ___ TO HAVE FRIENDS
164.2.X ___ TO HAVE ENEMIES
165.1.X ___ TO HAVE ALLIES
165.2.X ___ TO HAVE OPPONENTS

166.1.X ___ TO BE LOOSE
166.2.X ___ TO BE RESTRAINED
167.1.X ___ TO HAVE CHOICES
167.2.X ___ TO HAVE NO CHOICE
168.1.X ___ TO BE ALLOWED TO PROCEED
168.2.X ___ TO BE HEMMED IN
169.1.X ___ TO BE CAUSATIVE
169.2.X ___ TO BE AT EFFECT
170.1.X ___ TO REACH THINGS
170.2.X ___ TO BE UNABLE TO REACH THINGS
171.1.X ___ TO CONTROL THINGS
171.2.X ___ TO BE UNABLE TO CONTROL THINGS
172.1.X ___ TO HAVE GAMES
172.2.X ___ TO HAVE NO GAME
173.1.X ___ TO BE SATISFIED
173.2.X ___ TO BE UNSATISFIED
174.1.X ___ TO HAVE WHAT YOU NEED
174.2.X ___ TO SUFFER FROM CRAVINGS
175.1.X ___ TO HAVE NO REGRETS
175.2.X ___ TO BE REGRETFUL
176.1.X ___ TO BE OPEN
176.2.X ___ TO BE CLOSED IN
177.1.X ___ TO ARRANGE THINGS CORRECTLY
177.2.X ___ TO MESS THINGS UP
178.1.X ___ TO SEE ACCEPTABLE THINGS
178.2.X ___ TO BE DAZZLED
179.1.X ___ TO RECEIVE SYMPATHY
179.2.X ___ TO GET NO SYMPATHY
180.1.X ___ TO GET AWAY WITH THINGS
180.2.X ___ TO BE ACCUSED
181.1.X ___ TO BE AQUITTED
181.2.X ___ TO BE CONDEMNED
182.1.X ___ TO BE LET GO
182.2.X ___ TO BE HUNTED
183.1.X ___ TO ESCAPE THE CONSEQUENCES

183.2.X ___ TO SUFFER THE CONSEQUENCES
184.1.X ___ TO AVOID BEING IMPLANTED
184.2.X ___ TO WANT TO BE IMPLANTED
185.1.X ___ TO PLEASE PEOPLE
185.2.X ___ TO UPSET PEOPLE
186.1.X ___ TO OBEY THE RULES
186.2.X ___ TO BREAK THE RULES
187.1.X ___ TO BE GOOD
187.2.X ___ TO BE EVIL
188.1.X ___ TO HELP OTHERS
188.2.X ___ TO HARM OTHERS
189.1.X ___ TO REASSURE PEOPLE
189.2.X ___ TO SHOCK PEOPLE
190.1.X ___ TO MAKE OTHERS FEEL SAFE
190.2.X ___ TO TERRORIZE OTHERS
191.1.X ___ TO HAVE NORMAL DESIRES
191.2.X ___ TO BE OBSESSED
192.1.X ___ TO BE SANE
192.2.X ___ TO BE INSANE
193.1.X ___ TO TAKE ENOUGH TIME
193.2.X ___ TO TAKE TOO LONG
194.1.X ___ TO BE INDEPENDENT
194.2.X ___ TO BE DEPENDENT
195.1.X ___ TO BE SATISFIED
195.2.X ___ TO HAVE LONGINGS
196.1.X ___ TO KNOW WHAT'S GOING ON
196.2.X ___ TO BE PUZZLED BY EVENTS
197.1.X ___ TO KNOW WHAT'S GOING TO HAPPEN
197.2.X ___ TO BE TAKEN BY SURPRISE
198.1.X ___ TO KNOW THE CONSEQUENCES
198.2.X ___ TO BE CAUGHT UNAWARE
199.1.X ___ TO BE ABLE TO ADAPT
199.2.X ___ TO BE UNABLE TO CHANGE
200.1.X ___ TO BE FLEXIBLE
200.2.X ___ TO BE RIGID

201.1.X ___ TO BE ON TIME
201.2.X ___ TO BE TOO LATE
202.1.X ___ TO BE PARTICIPATING
202.2.X ___ TO BE ALONE
203.1.X ___ TO LIKE WHAT IS GOING ON
203.2.X ___ TO DISLIKE EVERYTHING
204.1.X ___ TO BE ABLE TO PROTEST
204.2.X ___ TO HAVE TO PUT UP WITH EVERYTHING
205.1.X ___ TO BE ABLE TO CHANGE CONDITIONS
205.2.X ___ TO BE STUCK WITH THINGS AS THEY ARE
206.1.X ___ TO BE STABLE
206.2.X ___ TO BE PUSHED AROUND
207.1.X ___ TO BE ABLE TO DECIDE NOT TO DO SOMETHING
207.2.X ___ TO BE FORCED TO DO THINGS
208.1.X ___ TO BE AT THE RIGHT DISTANCE
208.2.X ___ TO BE TOO CLOSE
209.1.X ___ TO HAVE HOPE
209.2.X ___ TO BE HOPELESS
210.1.X ___ TO UNDERSTAND THINGS
210.2.X ___ TO MISUNDERSTAND THINGS
211.1.X ___ TO RECEIVE HELP
211.2.X ___ TO GET NO HELP
212.1.X ___ TO BE FAIR
212.2.X ___ TO BE UNFAIR
213.1.X ___ TO BE SHARING
213.2.X ___ TO BE SELFISH
214.1.X ___ TO HAVE THE RIGHT AMOUNT
214.2.X ___ TO HAVE TOO MUCH
215.1.X ___ TO FEEL FULL
215.2.X ___ TO FEEL EMPTY
216.1.X ___ TO BE AT THE RIGHT TIME
216.2.X ___ TO BE EARLY
217.1.X ___ TO BE IN THE RIGHT SPACE
217.2.X ___ TO BE IN THE WRONG SPACE (*place*)
218.1.X ___ TO BE KIND

218.2.X ___ TO BE CRUEL
219.1.X ___ TO BE HUMAN(E)
219.2.X ___ TO BE A MONSTER
220.1.X ___ TO BE WHERE YOU SHOULD BE
220.2.X ___ TO BE TOO FAR AWAY
221.1.X ___ TO BE SUCCESSFUL
221.2.X ___ TO BE A FAILURE
222.1.X ___ TO WIN
222.2.X ___ TO LOSE
223.1.X ___ TO FEEL RELIEVED
223.2.X ___ TO FEEL CRUSHED
224.1.X ___ TO BE DEFENDED
224.2.X ___ TO BE ATTACKED
225.1.X ___ TO BE TOUGH
225.2.X ___ TO BE OVERWHELMED
226.1.X ___ TO BE DETERMINED
226.2.X ___ TO GIVE UP
227.1.X ___ TO BE A GOOD CITIZEN
227.2.X ___ TO BE A CRIMINAL
228.1.X ___ TO BE A MEMBER OF SOCIETY
228.2.X ___ TO BE AN OUTCAST
229.1.X ___ TO SUPPORT SOCIETY
229.2.X ___ TO OVERTHROW SOCIETY
230.1.X ___ TO ADVANCE
230.2.X ___ TO BE HELD BACK
231.1.X ___ TO HAVE NICE THINGS
231.2.X ___ TO HAVE NOTHING
232.1.X ___ TO HAVE ENOUGH SPACE
232.2.X ___ TO HAVE TOO LITTLE SPACE
233.1.X ___ TO BE ALLOWED TO REMAIN
233.2.X ___ TO BE KICKED-OUT OF SPACES
234.1.X ___ TO BE WISE
234.2.X ___ TO BE FOOLISH
235.1.X ___ TO DO THINGS AT THE RIGHT TIME
235.2.X ___ TO DO THINGS AT THE WRONG TIME

236.1.X ___ TO HAVE ENOUGH TIME
236.2.X ___ TO RUN OUT OF TIME
237.1.X ___ TO RISE
237.2.X ___ TO FALL
238.1.X ___ TO GROW
238.2.X ___ TO SHRINK
239.1.X ___ TO GET BETTER
239.2.X ___ TO GET WORSE
240.1.X ___ TO BECOME MORE SUBSTANTIAL
240.2.X ___ TO GET THINNER
241.1.X ___ TO KNOW WHAT TIME IT IS
241.2.X ___ TO NOT-KNOW WHAT TIME IT IS
242.1.X ___ TO KNOW WHAT SPACE I'M IN
242.2.X ___ TO NOT-KNOW WHAT SPACE I'M IN
243.1.X ___ TO ESTIMATE TIME CORRECTLY
243.2.X ___ TO MIS-ESTIMATE TIME
244.1.X ___ TO ESTIMATE DISTANCE CORRECTLY
244.2.X ___ TO MIS-ESTIMATE DISTANCE
245.1.X ___ TO HAVE FAITH
245.2.X ___ TO HAVE DISBELIEF
246.1.X ___ TO BE ENLIGHTENED
246.2.X ___ TO BE MYSTIFIED
247.1.X ___ TO SPOT THE SOURCE OF THINGS
247.2.X ___ TO SPOT THE WRONG SOURCE
248.1.X ___ TO PLEASE 'GOD'
248.2.X ___ TO DISPLEASE 'GOD'
249.1.X ___ TO OBEY 'GOD'
249.2.X ___ TO DEFY 'GOD'
250.1.X ___ TO BE SAVED
250.2.X ___ TO BE DAMNED
251.1.X ___ TO BE IN HEAVEN
251.2.X ___ TO BE IN HELL
252.1.X ___ TO BE ALIVE
252.2.X ___ TO BE DEAD
253.1.X ___ TO BE IN PARADISE FOREVER
253.2.X ___ TO BURN IN HELL FOREVER

```
254.1.X  ___  TO CREATE
254.2.X  ___  TO DESTROY
255.1.X  ___  TO HAVE REALITY
255.2.X  ___  TO FEEL UNREAL
256.1.X  ___  TO HAVE THE RIGHT TIME
256.2.X  ___  TO HAVE THE WRONG TIME
257.1.X  ___  TO HAVE THE RIGHT SPACE
257.2.X  ___  TO HAVE THE WRONG SPACE
258.1.X  ___  TO HAVE THE RIGHT ENERGY
258.2.X  ___  TO HAVE THE WRONG ENERGY
259.1.X  ___  TO HAVE THE RIGHT MASS
259.2.X  ___  TO HAVE THE WRONG MASS
260.1.X  ___  TO BE REAL
260.2.X  ___  TO BE UNREAL
261.1.X  ___  TO BE RIGHT ABOUT TIME
261.2.X  ___  TO BE WRONG ABOUT TIME
262.1.X  ___  TO BE RIGHT ABOUT SPACE
262.2.X  ___  TO BE WRONG ABOUT SPACE
263.1.X  ___  TO BE RIGHT ABOUT ENERGY
263.2.X  ___  TO BE WRONG ABOUT ENERGY
264.1.X  ___  TO BE RIGHT ABOUT MASS
264.2.X  ___  TO BE WRONG ABOUT MASS
265.1.X  ___  TO BE RIGHT ABOUT EXISTENCE
265.2.X  ___  TO BE WRONG ABOUT EXISTENCE
266.1.X  ___  TO HAVE MASS
266.2.X  ___  TO HAVE NO MASS
267.1.X  ___  TO HAVE ENERGY
267.2.X  ___  TO HAVE NO ENERGY
268.1.X  ___  TO HAVE SPACE
268.2.X  ___  TO HAVE NO SPACE
269.1.X  ___  TO HAVE TIME
269.2.X  ___  TO HAVE NO TIME
270.1.X  ___  TO HAVE A UNIVERSE
270.2.X  ___  TO HAVE NO UNIVERSE
271.1.X  ___  TO HAVE EXISTENCE
271.2.X  ___  TO HAVE NO EXISTENCE
```

[*Research Notes*: There may or may not be missing *command-lines* around *pair-61* and *pair-62*, regarding dichotomies of "*Immortal*"/"*Age*" and "*Young*"/"*Old*"; but this is not certain. This *Platform* has proven quite effective as-is, though more experimental testing is still required for its standardization.]

VARIABLE LIST-ITEMS MASTER-LIST

Each of the following lines is an entire *series-run* of the previous *Implant-pattern*. By combining the two, you have the content for the entire *Platform*. Refer to the earlier instructions for details on inserting the variable *list-items* from this *master-list*. For example: the *first command-lines* for the *first series-run* are:

```
1.1.1  I WANT TO ESCAPE
1.2.1  I DON'T WANT TO BE CAPTURED
```

The same "*I Want*"/"*I Don't Want*" item is then applied to each of the *271* dichotomy-pairs to complete the *first series-run*. Then proceed to the top of the *Implant-pattern* and insert the next set of *list-items*, and so on.

This *master-list* is effective as given. However, our A.T. researchers would *usually* end up *defragging* the whole *Platform* after *running* a few dozen *series*, leaving the remainder to be plotted out mainly by *assessment* and *research-actions* (see AT#8). Further into the *master-list* (beyond *item-31*), it is possible that some of the *items* are incorrect, improperly ordered, or altogether missing. More experimental testing is needed for standardization.

[Note that on specifically the *third series-run*, when inserting the negative "*I must not*" on the second item of each pair in the *pattern*, you will have to remove the word "*to*" from the *pattern-line*.]

BEINGNESS CONDITIONS (SERIES-RUNS)
  1. I want / I don't want
  2. I need / I can't bear
  3. I have / I must not

REALITY PERCEPTION (SERIES-RUNS)
  4. To agree / To disagree
  5. To obey / To disobey
  6. To do nothing with the mind / To do anything with the mind
  7. To be unaware of this / To be aware of this

8. To not figure this out / To figure this out
9. To resist change / To try to change
10. To be in a body / To be outside a body
11. To interiorize (*go inside*) / To exteriorize (*eject*)
12. To keep this implant / To undo this implant
13. To generalize / To identify
14. To associate / To disassociate
15. To not look / To look
16. To not scan / To scan
17. To synchronize with reality / To desynchronize from reality
18. To fixate on physical reality / To shift in reality
19. To limit myself to three dimensions / To extend beyond three dimensions
20. To be aware of only three dimensions / To be aware of more than three dimensions

FRAGMENT / DEFRAGMENT (SERIES-RUNS)
21. To not heal / To heal
22. To not cure / To cure
23. To entrap others / To release others
24. To enturbulate others / To unenturbulate others
25. To aberrate / To deaberrate
26. To block others / To unblock others
27. To inhibit others / To uninhibit others
28. To not process-out / To process-out
29. To not clear / To clear
   (*or*) To not defragment / To defragment
30. To not restore / To restore

REALITY-STRUCTURING (SERIES-RUNS)
31. To create physical reality / To not create physical reality
32. To not duplicate / To duplicate
33. To not replicate / To replicate
34. To cross-copy / To not cross-copy
35. To not program thoughts / To program thoughts
36. To respond to programmed thoughts / To ignore programmed thoughts
37. To be unaware of machinery / To be aware of machinery
38. To not create machinery / To create machinery
39. To ignore mental machinery / To control mental machinery

40. To be the effect of mental machinery / To be unaffected by mental machinery
41. To obey universe machinery / To disobey universe machinery
42. To hide universe machinery / To notice universe machinery

LOCATED-BEINGNESS (SERIES-RUNS)
43. To be in one place / To be in many places
44. To not see the structure of things / To see the structure of things
45. To not see through things / To see through things
46. To not look within things / To look within things
47. To not-know / To know
48. To not see remotely / To see remotely
49. To not locate / To locate
50. To not pervade / To pervade
51. To not permeate / To permeate
52. To not dimensionalize / To dimensionalize
53. To see it-as-not / To see as-it-is

TIME-STRUCTURING (SERIES-RUNS)
54. To agree with the time-stream / To leave the time-stream
55. To be wrong about time / To spot the correct time
56. To have a time-track / To have no time-track
57. To take time / To bypass time
58. To be the effect of time / To ignore time
59. To maintain the present / To change the past

ENTITY-FRAGMENTS (SERIES-RUNS)
60. To be the effect of entities / To not be the effect of entities
61. To hold on to entities / To let go of entities
62. To obey entities / To disobey entities
63. To block entities from view / To see entities
64. To be infested / To be clean
65. To infest others / To clean others
66. To be divided against myself / To be whole
67. To fragment / To integrate

SOLIDIFICATION (SERIES-RUNS)
68. To not orient anchor-points / To orient anchor-points
69. To not determinate objects / To determinate objects
70. To leave the structure of things alone / To manipulate (*change*) the structure of things

71. To not make things materialize / To make things materialize
72. To not dematerialize / To dematerialize
73. To make solids impenetrable / To make solids penetrable
74. To not infinitize / To infinitize
75. To not actualize / To actualize
76. To perpetuate reality / To violate reality
77. To leave random / To unrandomize
78. To not read minds / To read minds
79. To not take over other's minds / To take over other's minds
80. To not alter other's minds / To alter other's minds
81. To not implode other's pictures / To implode other's pictures
82. To not swap thoughts / To swap thoughts
83. To not project thoughts / To project thoughts
84. To not endow life / To endow life
85. To not manipulate life-force / To manipulate life-force
86. To not drain life-force / To drain life-force

ABILITY-SUPPRESSION (SERIES-RUNS)
87. To not intend / To intend
88. To not postulate / To postulate
89. To not levitate / To levitate
90. To not teleport / To teleport
91. To not manipulate energy / To manipulate energy
92. To not create energy / To create energy
93. To propagate flows / To dampen flows
94. To not glare (*stare down*) / To glare (*stare down*)
95. To not beam / To beam
96. To not blanket / To blanket
97. To not zap / To zap
98. To not nip / To nip
99. To not manifest / To manifest
100. To not spaceate / To spaceate
101. To not energize / To energize
102. To not historicize / To historicize (?)
103. To maintain a single viewpoint / To maintain multiple viewpoints
104. To need mass / To do without mass
105. To need energy / To do without energy
106. To need time / To do without time
107. To need space / To do without space (?)

108. To fill space / To have space (?)
109. To be located / To not be located
110. To gain mass / To lose mass
111. To be affected by energy / To ignore energy
112. To deteriorate / To improve
113. To follow the laws of energy / To violate the laws of energy
114. To follow the laws of space / To violate the laws of space
115. To follow the laws of time / To violate the laws of time
116. To follow the laws of matter / To violate the laws of matter
117. To not predict / To predict
118. To not predetermine / To predetermine
119. To not find out / To find out
120. To perceive as a body / To perceive as a spirit
121. To operate as a body / To operate as a spirit
122. To be a body / To be a spirit
123. To be "human" / To be god-like
124. To be in this universe / To leave this universe

A.T. MANUAL #8
ADVANCING SYSTEMOLOGY

Keep this reference material accessible:
PC Lesson-1 to 16; Processing-Levels 0 to 6
AT Manual #1, "The Secret of Universes"
AT Manual #5, "Games, Goals & Purposes"
AT Manual #5, "The Jewel of Knowledge"
AT Manual #5, "Implanted Universes"
AT Manual #5, "Entities & Fragments"
AT Manual #6, "Spiritual Perception"
AT Manual #7, "Mastering Ascension"

MARDUKITE NEW STANDARD SYSTEMOLOGY
–The New Dawn of Crystal Clarity–

This is the final training volume of *Systemology Level-8* and the entry-point to the *Infinity Grade* by which one might attain *certainty-of-Beingness* as an *Ascended Master* of *this Physical Universe*. This manual presents qualifying experimental *Wizard-Level 4* to 7 material. Use of this manual also requires applying *systematic processing* as a *research-action*, which will be explained throughout the text.

We are reaching an end-cycle on this instructional communication—part of which includes a concise clarification of terms regarding the *levels* and *gradients* of material that have brought us this far. In brief—the *New Standard Systemology* used by the *Systemology Society* is represented with:

<u>Fundamentals of Systemology</u>
(Basic Course – 6 *Lessons*)

<u>The Pathway to Ascension</u>
Processing-Levels 0 to 6
(Professional Course – 16 *Lessons*)

<u>Keys to the Kingdom</u>
Processing-Levels 7 to 8
Wizard-Levels/Infinity-Grade
(Advanced Training – 8 *Manuals*)
(Training Supplements – 3 *Manuals*)

All *Systemology* publications <u>not</u> included in the list (above) are considered volumes of the *Systemology Core Research Library*—retained for additional *Pilot Training* and posterity as a detailed chronicle of the developments leading up to this newly refined *standard*. For the *Systemology Society*: the indicated *processing-levels* are treated *independent* of any *Mardukite Academy "Grade"* classification.

The *Mardukite Academy* provides *Systemology* instruction in addition to many other subjects—it has many other "gradients" to reflect that. From an *Academy* viewpoint: *"The Pathway to Ascension"* is *Grade-VI*; and *"Keys to the Kingdom"* represents *Grade-VII*. The only real parallel is the concept of an *"Infinity Grade"* for 8.

<u>Mardukite Esoteric Research Library</u>
(Subject: Systemology – 16 Volumes)

Liber-8 : *Keys to the Kingdom: Vol. II*
Liber-7 : *Keys to the Kingdom: Vol. I*
Liber-6 (5B) : *Pathway/Ascension: Vol. II*
Liber-5 (5A) : *Pathway/Ascension: Vol. I*
Liber-4 : *Systemology: Backtrack*
Liber-180 : *Systemology-180*
Liber-3 (3E) : *The Way of the Wizard*
Liber-3D : *Imaginomicon*
Liber-2D : *Metahuman Destinations: Vol. II*
Liber-2C : *Metahuman Destinations: Vol. I*
Liber-2B : *Crystal Clear*
Liber-One : *Tablets of Destiny Revelation*
Liber-S1Z : *The Power of Zu (Lectures)*
Liber-S1X : *Systemology: Original Thesis*
Liber-S1W : *The Way Into The Future*
Liber-S1A : *Fundamentals of Systemology*

SYSTEMOLOGY–INFINITY

Effectively advancing *Systemology* research has specific requirements. Although the target-goal is always to develop a stable standard for *defragmenting* with certainty, the means by which this data is achieved is not always a very "therapeutic" activity—often "stirring things up" (*resurfacing*) in order to document them, without always having a safety-net. Fortunately, we have *now* reached a level of refinement to our research-methods (communicated in this manual) that will help a *Seeker* avoid the same *pitfalls* of our earlier efforts.

To make "advancements" in any subject requires an actual understanding of the subject you're trying to advance; *e.g. Systemology*. For our purposes, in addition to the *New Standard* courses, this might include examining all of the *Systemology Core Research Volumes*.

To push forth in a subject such as this really requires a strong dedication and passion to the pursuit of *Spiritual Ascension* and accessing the *Magic Kingdom*—which is, of course, the *Holy Grail* we have been after.

An advanced researcher needs to have handled their *"own case"*—or at least be able to get *"exterior to"* it—and also be able to see beyond any "mundane goal" attached to this work, such as fame or fortune. More than just "reading" the books, or "intellectually knowing" the material, a *systemologists* should be able to *apply* the spiritual technology to their lives, using the entire *Universe* as their *"laboratory."*

Although there are obviously "unique" aspects of one's personal *Backtrack* that require "cleaning up," the target-focus of our *New Standard Systemology* are those major elements and specific *incidents* that are more "common" to all cases of the *earthbound "Human Condition"*—and particularly critical to keeping an *Alpha-Spirit "in"* that *condition*. Such data is easier to "test" and also support "systematically" with any certainty.

Most of our research is systematically developed utilizing *Biofeedback-Devices*. This provides greater accuracy when conducting *"Assessments"* (with existing *data-lists*) and *"Listing-Actions"* (to find data; to find a *correct item*). In most cases, this means *Solo-Piloting* with a *GSR-Meter*; or sometimes *Co-Piloting* with an experienced research assistant.

Even when something just "seems right" (or "clicks into place"), to be a *systematic research-action* requires checking/verifying if "what seems right" actually prompts *Meter-reads*. For example: is it a *charged* "item-line" of a *Platform*, or does it just "sound good." Just like when a *Seeker* first *"contacts"* an *incident* with their *Awareness*, sometimes this work requires a bit of "feeling around" until something *registers* definitively.

The most important part of the *research-action* is: *Spotting "What Is"*—or realizing a lot of "*It is* __," without a lot of questions (unknowns), other associations, and freewheeling thought. *"Spot 'What Is'"* with certainty, rather than focusing on what is still out of view, blocked, or heavily *fragmented*. If something is hidden, but not currently *restimulated*, approach it from angles where you have certainty.

When dealing with uncharted areas—particularly concerning *heavy incidents* and *Implant-Platforms*—there are several common ways mistakes can be made, including: missing *reads* (and *items*); putting *items* out-of-sequence; putting in *items* that aren't supposed to be there; and attributing *reading-items* to one part of an *incident*, when they really apply somewhere else, or even to a completely different *incident* or *Platform*.

Mistakes affect a researcher, just as they do a *Seeker*. When *turbulent charge* or *fragmentation* is missed or "flown by" without handling it, or a *Seeker* runs the "wrong" *item*, their case does not improve. Worse than that, one might become quite ill, or get feelings of "overwhelm" and "invalidation" that stalls or hinders progress. Technically *all systemologists* are "researchers" of their own *Backtrack*; but we don't directly encourage taking a "plunge" into unknown depths until certainty is had on what *is* known and accessible.

When hitting a research-block, or a point where a specific *item* just can't be reached, it is often a good idea to take a short break and let things cool down. You can leave your *session* set up and come back to it. You *don't* want to be sitting in *session*, repeatedly chanting *"What is it!? What is it!?"* to yourself. Research-actions can cause *attention* to get *fixed*, frustrations can inhibit clarity, and underlying *restimulation* from unrecognized sources can affect progress. Make sure to check your "preventative fundamentals" at the start of each session.

To fully charge ahead *Self-honestly*, one must be *willing to be wrong*, while still maintaining cautious optimism and tolerance for confusion. Researching with a *GSR-Meter* requires *"unbiased objectivity"* — rather than trying to "steer" results to validate some preferred (personal) theory, &tc. And like any other *scientific research*: discoveries must be communicable and demonstrable to others; its methods should be able to be repeated by others — and hence our emphasis on that which is "common" to others, and *registers* as such.

To be a part of this progressive movement requires a *willingness to share knowledge* that will *help*, not *entrap*, your fellow *Seekers*. This means when these *"trap-mechanisms"* are discovered, they are shared with others so they can *realize* things as they are. This knowledge is really only dangerous when it is kept secret, used for the personal gain of a few, or further control of the population, rather than as a means of *spiritual liberation*.

We have been faithfully honest in our relay of the *upper-level* work — where an *item* may be wrong, or a *Goal* is out-of-sequence; these things, when already sensed, have been indicated in the text. Areas that require additional details or data refinement are plainly noted. This is not a shortcoming on our part — for we have already advanced this material to a *New Standard* that has never been reached in the *"New Thought"* before.

But the time has come to push this out from the shadows, making it available for other *Seekers* of the *Grail*.

Our *Systemology* is still relatively *"young"* compared to what can evolve from it. And an *Ascension "out"* of *this Universe* is not its only application. If more individuals became *"Seekers,"* we might just be able to *realize* a *"heaven-on-earth"* right where we are. At the very least, we can complete this *Map* for one another, and meet up again in the *Magic Kingdom*, once we've resolved all of our "stuff" down here.

Rather than spend a lot of time on theoretical philosophy, this manual will focus on *upper-level* areas that a *Seeker* will already be familiar with from previous manuals and lessons, but of which are still worthy of greater expansion and refinement. They are all developed enough to present here as launch-points for reaching further; and they all reflect critical points that remain unhandled, at least in part.

THE JEWEL OF KNOWLEDGE
(*Experimental Research*)

[The basic description and background information for *The Jewel of Knowledge* is found in *"The Secret of Universes"* (*AT#1*). This is supplemented by information concerning *False Jewels* in *"The Jewel of Knowledge"* (*AT#3*). The data provided in this current section is incomplete; therefore not included in former manuals.]

The Jewel, in any of its forms, is of popular interest among A.T. Systemologists and researchers. The *"original" Jewel of Knowledge* is not necessarily difficult to *"contact,"* but it is particularly challenging to fully *process-out* when *perceptions* are heavily *fragmented*. It remains the most "obscure" of all incidents that an *Alpha-Spirit* has experienced.

The *original Jewel of Knowledge* is incredibly (and deceptively) basic—almost simpleminded. It would probably have little effect on an "experienced" *Alpha-Spirit*; but for an *innocent being* (with no former *"conception of existence"*) freshly separated from the *Infinite*, it was sufficiently powerful in laying in the pattern of reality that is accounted for in *AT#1*.

When "scouting" for *experimental data*, it sometimes requires "feeling around" a bit, or "scanning through" what is known with certainty—

and then seeing if any *perceptions*, or even vague impressions, occur. For example: *"they probably told us about how to perceive things."* This is then checked with *Biofeedback* to see if anything *registers*. Once something is giving definitive *Meter-reads*, it is possible to check other things about it. Then, with more *certainties* to *"scan"* over, more details can emerge.

It is important to note that *intensive research-phases* were once critically necessary for producing material such as *"The Secret of Universes"* (AT#1) —or uncovering the nature of a particular *incident*. However, the initial *research-actions*, themselves, undertaken by various pioneers contributing to this work, seldom provided actual *gain* or personal *progress*. Any *relief* only seemed to occur after a particular *process* or *Platform* was at least 99% correct and fully developed for *systematic application*.

GSR-Meter assessments were used to generate most of the additional *experimental data* included here. Even the material here has only been partially *processed-out* by our researchers—which still leaves us with only a partial view of the whole picture. Only some of the *facet-chambers* of the original *Jewel of Knowledge* have been explored directly—leaving much missing-data to still recover. However, there is still much given here.

1. First Split-Viewpoint

Data: You see a *line* and feel as though there is more out of sight. You keep shifting around and seeing different *lines*. There is a sense that there is something greater present here, but you only see one *line* of it at a time. You decide that if you can view two different *lines* simultaneously, that you might *Know* something. So you hold your *attention* on one line, while trying to look at another line, which splits your *viewpoint*.

Now you see through two different *viewpoints*; and by holding them simultaneously, you are able to perceive a "plane" (*planar surface*). Usually it resembles a "square"; but if you shift your *viewpoints* around, it appears otherwise, such as a "triangle." You still feel like there is *more* to *Know*. So, you steady your *attention* on the "plane" while pulling yourself back to "see more"—which splits another *viewpoint* and allows you to see a *three-dimensional* object; usually a "cube"; but again, as you shift your *viewpoints*, you can see that you are looking at different shapes.

The same splitting and perception occurs for *4-D* and *5-D space/objects*; and you "feel good" about this. The *object* being displayed is really a *5-D* object with a *6-D* thickness. When you try splitting further into *six*, the *object* holds steady, and you see some additional thickness to it, but nothing really more. In fact, it starts to appear somewhat ghostly and unreal from that view, which makes you "feel sad" about it.

So, you decide to forget about the *sixth-dimension* and *pretend* the object is *real* enough from before. You go back to admiring it how it was when you "felt good" about it; and decide there is nothing more to *Know*. That's when the experience of this *facet-chamber* ends, and you shift into the next *facet* in the sequence.

2. Need For Agreement

Data: Experience of the next *facet* begins with only a *white-nothingness* or *white-void*. You reach your *Awareness* for something to see but there is nothing. Eventually, you sense the presence of another *being*. You shift your *attention* around until you are able to feel the nearness of one of their *viewpoints*. When you shift your own *viewpoint* to their *viewpoint*, you are able to perceive a *curved-line*.

At first you only see the *curved-line*, but you get a sense that the other *being* is looking at a full *5-D object*. You split your *viewpoint* into *five* to try and see it, but you still only perceive a *curved-line*. You realize that this is because only *one* of your *viewpoints* is matching theirs. When you match all *five viewpoints* to theirs, a *5-D sphere* appears, and you "feel good" about this because it is interesting and permits something greater to *have* a perception of.

You experiment by shifting a *viewpoint* off of theirs, and this causes the *sphere* to "lose" a *dimension* and seem more hollow, which gives a sense of less *"havingness"* and *"loss"*—and makes you "feel bad" about it. When you shift your *viewpoint* back into *agreement* with the *other being*, you "feel better" about it—and decide that *agreement* is a necessary factor. [Then you shift to the *next facet*.]

3. Duplicating Others

Data: You sense another *being*. They manifest/create a *"point"* and extend a *line* from that *point*; then encourage you to do the same. When you eventually do this, you have a *line*. But, since you don't locate it within the same *Space* as theirs, you lose track of their *line* while making yours. After realizing this, you decide to manifest/create your *line* in the same *Space* as theirs, and now you *have* two *lines* to perceive.

Eventually, the other *being* splits their viewpoints to make a square (plane) and invites you to do the same. This is repeated with *3-D* and *4-*

D cubes. Each time you get a sense of increased *"havingness"* by making these more interesting objects in agreement with another's creation. You realize the need for following directions and duplicating others.

4. Need For Games
Data: This *facet-chamber* is experienced within a *thirteen-dimensional space*. There are many *"cubes"* with white and black sides. They resemble modern *"dice"* in that the *"quantities"* shown on their faces/sides are represented by *"dots"* rather than *"symbols."* Moving them around at random is uninteresting. Eventually, you find that sorting and arranging them in *"sequences"* (*&tc.*) is far more interesting and fun.

5. Need For Opponents
Data: There are a series of cubes (as in FACET 4); but this time there are two sets (one white and one black) and a sense that there is another *being* present. The two sets are not identical and the quantities represented on their faces are *"random"* (non-sequential, with missing numbers). You each take a set and have a *"race"* to see who can get them in *"order"* first. You find this more interesting and fun than arranging them alone.

6. Need To Ensure An Opponent
Data: Similar to FACET 5; but when the opponent *"weakens,"* the game becomes less fun. So you encourage and try to help them.

7. Need To Create An Opponent
Data: Set up like earlier *facets*; but this time there is no opponent. You decide to *divide*—and part of you serves to act as the opponent. You realize the necessity of this in order to have a *game*.

8. Need For Barriers
Data: There is a *7-D cube* with variously-shaped holes and slots. There are different *objects* around that can be fitted into them. You can perceive another *being* doing this and it looks interesting. When it's your turn, the *objects* just drift through the *cube-walls* and each other, and it's not very fun or challenging. You decide that it is only fun when you make the *objects* solid and the *walls* more solid to block things.

9. Encouraging Agreement
Data: You perceive there are four other *beings* in the space. You each share in manifesting/creating a *5-D cube*. This provides a "pleasant feeling" (*havingness*). When one of the others goes out-of-agreement, the

cube goes hollow. Eventually, some of the others encourage them to get back into-agreement and the *cube* is solid again and "nicer."

Then it happens again where someone goes out-of-agreement, and this time you encourage them to come back into-agreement (and the *cube* is solid again).

Then you decide to go out-of-agreement and leave the "group" and can only see a *line*. You sense the encouragement of others to come back into-agreement (and the *cube* is solid again). Then you all admire the solid *cube* for a while and it is "pleasant." You decide it is necessary to encourage the agreement of others.

10. Need To Agree On Barriers

Data: Similar to FACET 8; but the large object is a *5-D pyramid*, and there are many other *beings* playing, all racing to put their *objects* into the *holes* and *slots*. But everything starts quite transparent and isn't much fun. So, you learn how to make each other's *objects* more solid in order to *have* a *game*.

11. Need To Enforce Agreement

Data: This occurs in a *many-dimensional* space. There are specifically *14* dimensions that are not properly aligned (in right-angles to each other) and *14* different *beings* present. Each different *being* is manifesting/creating a "*dimension point*" that is *anchoring* each single dimensional-space. You are each trying to align two *4-D objects* and get them onto the same axis until everyone can get into-agreement on dimensional-space.

No one is making any progress. You finally *agree* with another to share your *anchor-points*. Now the two of you have more in alignment than the others who insist on being individualistic. You, and the other one agreeing with you, decide to *Implant* each of the others with the intention to "go into-agreement." This is accomplished by taking a *being* and "holding" them in the *object* until they *choose to agree* with it.

Since you are "blocking" their *dimension-points* (perceptions) while you do this, they eventually agree. And since your "side" always outnumbers any individual, you never fail in this task. In fact, it gets much easier as more are added to the group. When everyone is in agreement, the *spatial-dimensions collapse* into a *single reality-frequency* that is pleasing to everyone. And from this, you see the necessity of forcing others into-agreement.

12. Sensation

Data: You see a *4-D object* in front of you. It has *13* different 3-D "sides" — each of which is a *3-D object* (a *square-based pyramid*). *Ten* of the 3-D pyramids are solid and *three* are hollow. You receive an *intention/impression* that this is "your form" and you sense an encouragement in becoming it. So, you *choose to be the object* (the *multi-pyramid form*) just to see what happens.

Then a *4-D energy-beam* comes in and starts bouncing in and out of your new form. It enters via a *hollow pyramid* and then ricochets off the *solid pyramids* before going out one of the *hollow* ones. Since there are only *three hollow pyramids*, the activity of the *energy-beam* seems unbalanced and you get a sense of incompleteness.

Then another *being* with a similar form as yours is present. The two of you align your *hollow* areas, share the *energy-beams* with one another; and everything is pleasant, harmonic, and you get the sense of this being "*pleasure.*" Then the other *being* turns away from you (out-of-alignment), and the *energy-beams* are now all jagged and disorganized. It is not enjoyable, and you get the impression that this is "*pain.*"

13. Pleasure Is At Other's Expense

Data: You follow the *being* from the previous *facet* into this chamber, where you find yourselves among a total of *14 beings* all using the "*multi-pyramid bodies.*" There are *energy-beams* bouncing all around the *Space*, and you participate in the exchange of them—but the *beams* are out-of-alignment (feel mildly unpleasant).

Two of the *beings* get into good alignment with each other and begin to experience "*pleasure*" (as described in FACET 12. But this throws everyone else's *beams* into a worse alignment—and you feel "*pain.*" So, everyone pushes the *two* out-of-alignment with each other.

Then you have the chance to be in-alignment with another, and do so. It is "*pleasant,*" but you notice that everyone else is in "*pain*" again, so you allow them to push you apart. Everyone, including yourself, goes back to feeling only the "*mildly unpleasant*" pattern (as in the beginning).

14. Need For Rules

Data: You watch *three beings* operating in a *7-D space*. *Two* of them create an elaborate *game* with what appears to be various spirals, rods, cones, energies, and balls bouncing around. You can see that they are interested and enjoying their *game*.

Then the *third being* joins them and wants to play too. But they don't know the *rules* of the *game*, so they invent their own and start playing differently. The first *two* get frustrated and start modifying the *rules* in order to accommodate the new player, but the *game* becomes too chaotic and falls apart. The players break off and examine the results and are "unhappy."

They get back together again; but this time they define clear *rules* for each of the aspects of the *game*, and even *create* something that puts the *rules on display*. But it does more than display them; it *Implants* them. So, when a *fourth being* arrives, they are *Implanted* with the *rules* before they are allowed to *play*. Now things can proceed well and everyone is mostly "satisfied" with the results.

When it comes time for you to come and join the *game*, you have already witnessed the *"need for rules,"* and so you *agree to being Implanted* for the sake of sharing in the *game*.

15. Need For Players

Data: A *"multi-dimensional sphere"* is being bounced back and forth between two "teams" (comprised of maybe *eight beings* on each side). Participating in the *game* provides a *"pleasant"* sensation. Then, one of the other players wanders off and the *game* is a little less fun. This causes more to wander off, and there is eventually no one else left but you. For a while, you sit alone and bored.

Then another group arrives and you all play together. When one of the players tries to leave, the others "hold" them and "force" them back into the *game*. Then the *game* remains *"pleasant."* When you have fully realized a necessity to force others to remain in a game, you shift to the *next facet*.

Other facet-chambers requiring research:
16. **Need For Duplication**
17. **Need For Imperfect Duplication**
18. **Need For Persistence**
19. **Need For Admiration**
20. **Need For Acknowledgment**
21. **Need To Divide**
22. **Only One Will Survive (Win)**
23. {the idea that if two terminals connect to communicate, one will be submissive and the other will be dominant}

24. {the idea that if you communicate too freely, you will connect to terminals that will dominate you}

THE FALSE JEWEL OF KNOWLEDGE
(*Experimental Research*)

Although there have been many *False Jewels* (such as *Entry-Into-This-Universe*), this *Implant* appears relatively early on the *Backtrack*—between the "*Games Universe*" and the "*Symbols Universe*"—and is considered the *earliest "False Jewel."*

By the point of this *incident*, an *Alpha-Spirit* had already experienced the *Implant Penalty-Universes* (IPU) and maintained some *fragmented considerations* from the *Games Universe*. But visibly, this only affected what we tended to *create* (*manifest*) or *dramatize*. There was no conception that: to *Implant* caused *fragmentation* that affected us as *beings*. The intention was to simply suppress or limit the interactions in a *Shared-Reality*; but our *Actualized Awareness* and *spiritual abilities* were being *fragmented* in the process.

During the phase of existence that this *Implant* occurred, an *Alpha-Spirit* was still unaffected by *force* or any *energy* directly. Also, we had not yet experienced a heavy "*Splitter-Incident*" that would *actually divide* our *Awareness* into "*split-viewpoints*" (that could individually get *Implanted* without our being conscious of it). At this stage, we were still able to "*collect ourselves*" after an *Implanting-Incident*; such as seems to have been the case after the original IPU experiences. But an individual could still be tricked into limiting themselves.

Although the original *Jewel* had been lost to a fog of *fragmented-time*, it was still treated with a religious-like veneration. Pale *facsimiles* of it were used to make IPU more impactful; but there was no specific emphasis on using them for *Implanting* at that time. Here, the *re-creation* or *facsimile* of *The Jewel* is intentionally used to install *false data* and *fragmented reasoning*—therefore, we refer to it as the *earliest "False Jewel."* Of course, all *Implants* install "*false data*," but here we concentrate on one *incident* where that is *the* focus.

This *False Jewel* is awarded as a "*prize*" for winning some *game*. The *game* is actually designed for the individual to "*win*," but they get a sense of earning something valuable. The *Implant* also impresses the individual to trick others into being victim to the *False Jewel* (by promoting how "wonderful" it is to have).

At the start of the *Implant*: *The False Jewel* moves "into" the individual's "center of Beingness." The *Jewel* "flashes" with each *item* with a kind of *radioactive-light* (and is accompanied by an *electric-crackle*) and spreads completely throughout the individual. The *Platform* begins with a series of *command-items* (all of which are included below).

In *3-D perception*, *The Jewel* resembles a *"diamond"* — an *eight-sided solid*, or *two pyramids* (one pointing up; one pointing down) sharing a base. As a *"higher-dimensional construct,"* it actually has *64 sides* or *"facets."*

The second part of the incident uses *graphic imagery (symbolism)* to install *64 fragmented agreements* (that follow the *basic IPU-sequence*). *The Jewel* "turns" to present *one* of its *64* different *"facets."* During this part, the *"radioactive flashes"* emit a brief *"motion picture"* (rather than a *"command-line"*).

Each of the *64 facets* present a different *"motion picture"* that is only loosely connected to the literal IPU and seldom includes any of the major *"terminals."* Each of these *facets* relay a *"basic truth"* about existence — but, of course, it is all *fragmented false-data* (*lies*).

Each *"motion picture"* is sensed as a *"heavy flow"* — but it is not so much an "energy" as it is an *internally generated* sense of "overwhelm" or "dread" at the sudden *flash-realization* of the (false) truth. This produces an intensely receptive "haze" (or "daze") of *Awareness*. Such *"flash-insights"* might otherwise be "shrugged off" and ignored with a few moments of *analytic thought*; but in this particular state of "shock," we *agree* that we *believe* them.

After receiving the *"(false)-truth"* from a *facet*: we *agree* to it; then *The Jewel* gets us to *agree-to-forget* it — and hide that *agreement* (with the *false-truth*) from ourselves — because the "truth is too terrible" and would drive us "insane" if we *knew, &tc*. The *Jewel* then turns to its next *facet* and emits the next *motion-picture* and *false-truth*. The information from one "truth" tends to contradict another; but since each one is forgotten before the next, this doesn't seem to get noticed during the *incident*.

This is a particularly significant area of advanced research, because the

Platform for this "original" *False Jewel* was likely copied and reused (or added to) many times in subsequent *Universes* on the *Backtrack*. "Spotting" the top of the original *False Jewel* (*Platform*) aids in releasing "*Control Entities*" (C.E.) [AT#5], so there is certainly some validity to what we have already uncovered. However, the research on the *64 facets* is still incomplete.

(ORIGINAL) FALSE JEWEL PLATFORM

A. {*Winning the game.*}
B. {*Being given The Jewel and agreeing to accept it.*}
C. {*The Jewel flows into you.*}
D. {*The Jewel flashes in the center of your being on each of the following command-items.*}

1. TO ACCEPT THE JEWEL IS NATIVE STATE
2. TO ACCEPT THE JEWEL IS TO BE THE STATIC (ALPHA)
3. TO ACCEPT THE JEWEL IS TO FULFILL THE URGE FOR SOMETHINGNESS
4. THE JEWEL IS THE BASIS FOR ALL URGES
5. THE JEWEL IS THE BASIS FOR ALL RELIEF
6. THE JEWEL IS THE ONLY REASON WHY
7. THE JEWEL IS THE BASIS FOR ALL ACTION
8. IN THE BEGINNING, NOW, AND FOREVER, IS THE DECISION; AND THE DECISION IS TO ACCEPT THE JEWEL
9. THE JEWEL CONTAINS ALL REAL DECISIONS
10. THE JEWEL CONTAINS ALL REAL POSTULATES
11. THE JEWEL CONTAINS ALL REAL AGREEMENTS
12. THE JEWEL IS THE ONLY SOURCE OF TIME
13. THE JEWEL IS THE ONLY SOURCE OF SPACE
14. THE JEWEL IS THE ONLY SOURCE OF ENERGY
15. THE JEWEL IS THE ONLY SOURCE OF MATTER
16. THE JEWEL CONTAINS ALL LOVE
17. THE JEWEL CONTAINS ALL EMOTION
18. THE JEWEL CONTAINS ALL THOUGHT
19. THE JEWEL CONTAINS ALL EFFORT
20. THE JEWEL CONTAINS ALL KNOWLEDGE
21. THE JEWEL CONTAINS ALL UNDERSTANDING
22. THE JEWEL IS THE SOURCE OF ALL REALITY
23. THE JEWEL IS THE SOURCE OF ALL MEANING

24. THE JEWEL IS THE SOURCE OF ALL TRUTH
25. THE JEWEL IS THE SOURCE OF ALL BEAUTY
26. THE JEWEL IS THE SOURCE OF ALL VALUE
27. THE JEWEL IS THE SOURCE OF ALL HAVING(NESS)
28. THE JEWEL IS THE SOURCE OF ALL EXISTENCE
29. THE JEWEL IS THE SOURCE OF ALL ENLIGHTENMENT
30. TO ACCEPT THE JEWEL IS TO REACH TOTAL KNOWINGNESS
31. TO ACCEPT THE JEWEL IS TO LEARN THE HIDDEN MEANINGS BEHIND ALL EXISTENCE
32. TO ACCEPT THE JEWEL IS TO KNOW THE TRUE REASON FOR EVERYTHING

E. {*The Jewel turns to its first facet. Motion-picture. False-data. Agreements.*}

"FALSE JEWEL" FRAGMENTED-DATA

Each *facet* of *The Jewel* presents *false-data* using elements of one of the IPU *and* its "inversion" (a negative quality or opposition for each IPU). Some of the existing research on this *false-data* is listed below along with its corresponding IPU. [The entire subject of IPU is still under development and refinement.]

One challenge of this research concerns how many times a "*False Jewel*" has been used with different content. Our target-data here pertained to the *Original* "*False Jewel*." When other related data was found, but determined to apply only to a *later* (more recent) version of the "*False Jewel*," it is indicated as such.

[*Advisement*: the *false-data* discovered and provided here IS *false-data*. It sometimes sounds "right" to make it more acceptable—and has become a part of many basic *reality-agreements*. But it is not, itself, truth. It is full of half-truths, inaccurate evaluations, and the resulting considerations. The research discoveries are included here for *processing-out*; not to be mistaken as real "wisdom." *The Jewel*, in all of its forms, always provides "*False Enlightenment*"—but it is also the *only* "enlightenment" that most individuals ever find.]

[The "*Hellfire Incident Location*" is only used *later* in this manual. It is given here to avoid having to print the *Goals-list* twice in the same volume.]

[16. **CREATION** (*Arc 8*)]
 1. "TO CREATE" {*statue*}
  (–) "TO DESTROY" {*devil statue*}
False-Data: 'God' created everything and we just keep messing it up. So you agree that you must never create or destroy anything because it's all really God's *Universe*, not yours.
 [*Hellfire Inc. (loc)*—St. John, Canada]
 2. "TO CAUSE" {*old man god*}
  (–) "TO PUT AT EFFECT" {*devil*}
False-Data: When you manifest/create/cause things, they cease to be under your control. So you agree that it is dangerous to manifest anything.
—*Later*: If you could manifest real things in this *Universe*, the ability would go out of control; and you'd manifest things that you are afraid of, which would attack you. So you agree to keep your manifestations from becoming real.
 [*Hellfire Inc. (loc)*—Rome]
 3. "TO DUPLICATE" {*computer*}
     (or "TO INTENSIFY")
  (–) "TO UNMANIFEST" {*black computer*}
     (or "TO DRAIN") {*black vortex*}
False-Data: When you fight back against something, it is intensified by your efforts to resist it. So you agree not to fight back.
—*Later*: If you think of something, it will get stronger and gain power over you. So you agree not to think about anything outside of normal reality.
 [*Hellfire Inc. (loc)*—Washington, DC]
 4. "TO IMAGINE" {*cartoon*}
  (–) "TO DISILLUSION" {*vampyre*}
False-Data: There are horrific things beyond the *third-dimension* that don't want you to see them, and will attack you if you do. So you agree not to *imagine* anything beyond the *third-dimension*.
—*Later*: If your *imagination* goes out-of-control, you will *imagine* your worst fears. So you agree not to *imagine* anything.
 [*Hellfire Inc. (loc)*—Florida or Brazil]

[15. **KNOWINGNESS** (*Arc 7*)]
 5. "TO KNOW" {*2-headed dodo*}
  (–) "TO MISLEAD" {*gorilla-people*}

False-Data: When you knew the real truth, you chose to forget it for good reasons. So you agree not to try to know the real truth.
 —*Later*: If the people knew the truth, it would destroy them. So you agree that you must prevent any attempts to reveal the truth.
 [*Hellfire Inc. (loc)*—S. Argentina]
  6. "TO UNDERSTAND" {*chipmunk*}
   (–) "TO MISUNDERSTAND" {*disabled*}
False-Data: If something *could* be understood, you *would* understand it already. The only things worth understanding belong to 'God' and are not to be understood by you. So you agree not to try and understand anything because it would be a worthless effort.
 [*Hellfire Inc. (loc)*—Vermont]
  7. "TO ABSORB" {*epic hero*}
   (–) "TO DISCARD" {*amazonian*}
False-Data: Beings (entities) are the coin (currency) of the *Universe*; and you can only gain strength and power by absorbing them.
 [*Hellfire Inc. (loc)*—Mt. Olympus]
  8. "TO LEARN" {*gnome*}
   (–) "TO FORGET" {*troll*}
False-Data: If you learned the truth, it would destroy the *Game*. So you agree to forget this (*The Jewel*) forever.
 [*Hellfire Inc. (loc)*—Heidelberg, Germany]

[14. **GAMES** (*Arc 6*)]
  9. "TO PLAY" {*child*}
   (–) "TO FOOL" {*joker*}
False-Data: Life is only a *game* and you exist here only as a playing-piece. So you agree that it doesn't matter what you do, or what happens, since there is no higher purpose anyway.
 —*Later*: We are all one, so that when you lose to someone else, you have really won, because you are them too. So you agree to lose often, to help yourself win elsewhere.
 [*Hellfire Inc. (loc)*—Shanghai, China]
  10. "TO COMPETE" {*coach*}
   (–) "TO CHEAT" {*skeleton*}
False-Data: If people compete, only one can win, and many must lose. So you agree to lose the majority of the time.
 —*Later*: If you were strong, you would be selfish and evil forever. So you

agree to stay weak.
[*Hellfire Inc. (loc)*—Toronto, Canada]

11. "TO MANIPULATE" {*penguin banker*}
(–) "TO RUIN" {*dragon*}
False-Data: The 'Fates' secretly manipulate your behavior, and you can't do anything about it. So you agree not to take responsibility for anything, because none of it is your fault.
—*Later*: There are evil people who would manipulate society for their own gain and bring harm to others. So you agree to block anyone who tries to manipulate society.
[*Hellfire Inc. (loc)*—Zurich, Switzerland]

12. "TO EXCHANGE" {*spirit-broker*}
(–) "TO STEAL" {*raccoon*}
False-Data: You gave up your right to disagree in exchange for the chance to 'play' in this *Game*. So you agree not to disagree with the 'rules' of the *Universe*.
—*Later*: You promised 'God' service in exchange for life. So you agree to serve 'God' always and obey the rules of 'his' *Universe* (and not question anything).
[*Hellfire Inc. (loc)*—Hong Kong, China]

[13. **CHANGE** (*Arc 5*)]

13. "TO SHAPE" {*clay people*}
(–) "TO DISTORT" {*walrus*}
False-Data: You were shaped (made/created) from the postulates of others. So you agree that other's postulates should affect you.
[*Hellfire Inc. (loc)*—Crete, Greece]

14. "TO CHANGE" {*magician*}
(–) "TO IMPLODE" {*sorceress*}
False-Data: This *Universe* is a constructed picture, and you are only a figure painted in it by the 'Master-Painter'—moving and acting as is needed to compose the painting. So you agree that you can affect nothing, and cannot change (you must be as you are).
[*Hellfire Inc. (loc)*—Tunisia, N. Africa]

15. "TO COMBINE" {*conjoined twins*}
(–) "TO FRAGMENT" {*worms*}
False-Data: Reality can only be manifested/created or affected by group postulation. If you are alone, then you will have no *Universe*. So you

agree to combine with other beings and stick to them.
   [*Hellfire Inc. (loc)*—Rangoon, Yangon]

   16. "TO (BRING) ORDER" {*gorilla people*}
         (or "TO ALIGN") {*bear-people*}
      (–) "TO (BRING) CHAOS"
         (or "TO REVOLT") {*panther*}

False-Data: Our attempts to be individuals, and go our own way, brings us to a sorry state. So you agree to align with 'God' and follow 'his' desires, and put aside you own wants and needs.
   [*Hellfire Inc. (loc)*—St. Petersburg, Russia]

[12. REASON (*Arc 4*)]

   17. "TO REASON" {*clown*}
      (–) "TO DISCOMBOBULATE" {*one-man band*}

False-Data: The real reason for existence is to feed your 'soul' to 'God'. So you agree to allow yourself to be eaten when the time comes.
   [*Hellfire Inc. (loc)*—Manhattan, N.Y.]

   18. "TO ORIENT" {*wire man*}
      (–) "TO DISORIENT" {*spinning top*}

False-Data: If you were truly 'oriented', you would see that this is all a sham and an illusion and all your 'havingness' would be lost. So you agree to remain disoriented forever.
   [*Hellfire Inc. (loc)*—Polar Orbit]

   19. "TO GUIDE" {*pilot*}
      (–) "TO MISDIRECT" {*scarecrow*}

False-Data: You were once a god and supposed to guide everyone, but you failed and it's your fault that everyone is stuck here now. So you agree to remain here and suffer with everyone else because it's all your fault.
   [*Hellfire Inc. (loc)*—Indianapolis]

   20. "TO COMPUTE" {*toy bodies*}
      (–) "TO CONFUSE" {*zombie*}

False-Data: You must use a 'brain' to think and perceive. So you agree to be 'unconscious' whenever you are out of the 'body'.
   [*Hellfire Inc. (loc)*—North Pole]

[11. CONSTRUCTION (*Arc 3*)]

   21. "TO CONSTRUCT" {*beavers*}

(–) "TO TEAR DOWN" {wrecking crane}
False-Data: Everything 'new' is constructed from the remains of older masses and energies. So you agree that nothing can be truly created or destroyed.
[*Hellfire Inc. (loc)*—Bangor, Maine]

22. "TO ENGINEER" {lobsters}
    (or "TO ARRANGE")
  (–) "TO UNSTABILIZE" {goon}
False-Data: The 'body' was engineered to be a 'spirit-trap' and you can't get out of it until you die. So you agree to accept death and to die as soon as possible to get out of the 'trap'.
[*Hellfire Inc. (loc)*—S. African lake]

23. "TO BUILD" {snake people}
  (–) "TO WRECK" {raging bull}
False-Data: Matter was built by many beings working in conjunction. So you agree that your postulates alone are not capable of affecting matter.
[*Hellfire Inc. (loc)*—In orbit; and Alaska]

24. "TO STRUCTURE" {crystals}
  (–) "TO SHATTER" {bat-man}
False-Data: The *Universe* is structured so that objects are 'real', and thoughts are 'unreal'. So you agree that your thoughts cannot really affect anything.
[*Hellfire Inc. (loc)*—Great Salt Lake, UT]

[10. **AESTHETICS** (*Arc 2*)]

25. "TO INVENT" {worker gnomes}
  (–) "TO DIVEST" {troll}
False-Data: You are the only real person and you invented everyone else. So you agree to divide and put out fragmented-pieces of yourself on everyone else to keep them (?) {manifested, under control, in a body..?}
[*Hellfire Inc. (loc)*—Bavaria (Germany)]

26. "TO ENHANCE" {ghost people}
  (–) "TO DEGRADE" {demon}
    (or "TO WORSEN")
False-Data: The *Universe* was created to 'teach' you a lesson that you desperately need (for enhancement). So you agree to go along with it, and try to learn from it, and not protest or rebel against what happens to you.

[*Hellfire Inc. (loc)*—Copenhagen, Denmark]

27. "TO INSPIRE" {*muses*}
   (–) "TO OCCLUDE" {*mesmerist*}
      (or "TO CONCEAL/BLOCK")

False-Data: Only 'divine inspiration' can bring about 'beauty' (aesthetic art). The whispered inspiration that artists and creators receive comes from 'God'. So you agree to 'listen' for it and obey any whispers (impressions) that appear in your 'mind', because they are 'divine inspiration'.

[*Hellfire Inc. (loc)*—Florence, Italy]

28. "TO BEAUTIFY" {*fairy godmother*}
   (–) "TO MAKE UGLY" {*old witch*}

False-Data: All 'beauty' comes from 'God'. So you agree that anything you create on your own must be ugly.

[*Hellfire Inc. (loc)*—Babylon]

[9. **ETHICS** (*Arc 1*)]

29. "TO PURIFY" {*fire people*}
   (–) "TO PERVERT" {*satyr*}

False-Data: All your own 'desire' is impure and stems from some 'deep-seeded animal nature'. So you agree to suppress all urges, desires, and goals, in order to 'purify' your 'soul'.

[*Hellfire Inc. (loc)*—Lima, Peru]

30. "TO JUDGE" {*minotaur*}
   (–) "TO DISAGREE" {*snake*}

False-Data: We are all in an *Implant* right now, and existence is just an 'item'—so you agree that you cannot disagree with, or alter, reality because it's... {not there to be altered (?)}

[*Hellfire Inc. (loc)*—Crete, Greece]

31. "TO DEFEND" {*little green men*}
   (–) "TO ATTACK" {*gorilla soldier*}

False-Data: The only real being is 'society'—which is 'God'. We are only 'cells' of its 'body'. So you agree to defend 'society' from {certain type?} individuals who work against it.

[*Hellfire Inc. (loc)*—Japan]

32. "TO STRENGTHEN" {*energy ball*}
         (or "TO PROTECT")
   (–) "TO HURT" {*silver ball*}

False-Data: There are 'higher-beings' ('celestial police', 'angels', &tc.) who

are protecting you from extreme harm. So you agree to give them your loyalty and never question their methods.
 [*Hellfire Inc. (loc)*— (?)]

[8. DIVINITY (*Sphere 8*)]
 33. "TO ENLIGHTEN" {*rabbit preacher*}
  (–) "TO OBSCURE" {*smog monster*}
False-Data: The real truth is so terrible or horrific that if you were to know it, it would you drive you insane. So you agree that you must forget it.
 [*Hellfire Inc. (loc)*—Libya or Jerusalem]
 34. "TO CONVERT" {*fish man*}
  (–) "TO DISABUSE" {*jackal*}
False-Data: People will kill anyone that tries to help them. So you agree not to try to help others.
 [*Hellfire Inc. (loc)*—Jakarta, Indonesia]
 35. "TO COMMUNE" {*feminine angel*}
   (or "TO CONNECT")
  (–) "TO DISCONNECT" {*spider-woman*}
False-Data: We are all fragmented-pieces of a Devil/Satan—a being that rebelled against 'God', looked at 'The Jewel of Knowledge' (which was forbidden), and was punished by being fragmented and sent here. So you agree that we all deserve to be punished and should suffer here complacently.
 [*Hellfire Inc. (loc)*—Los Angeles, CA]
 36. "TO WORSHIP" {*holy knights*}
  (–) "TO PROFANE" {*monk*}
False-Data: We were created for the sole purpose of worshiping 'God'—and that worship consists of taking on 'his' suffering. So you agree to devote yourself to suffering for 'God' and accept it without protest.
 [*Hellfire Inc. (loc)*—England]

[7. SPIRITUAL (*Sphere 7*)]
 37. "TO PREDICT" {*soothsayer*}
   (or "TO PREDETERMINE")
  (–) "TO RANDOMIZE" {*3-headed griffin*}
False-Data: The entire history (track) of the *Universe* was predetermined at its inception (creation). So you agree to follow the course laid out for you and not to try to change anything.

[*Hellfire Inc. (loc)* — Turkey]

38. "TO INFLUENCE" {*cupid/cherub*}

(–) "TO CORRUPT" {*hunchback*}

False-Data: When left uncontrolled, people will work against each other. So you agree to push fragmented-pieces of yourself onto others to influence them to work together.

[*Hellfire Inc. (loc)* — Jacksonville, FL]

39. "TO COLLECT" {*elves/fairies*}

(–) "TO REJECT" {*wolf-man*}

False-Data: We all sprang from the same 'eternal source' and must become 'one' again. So you agree to stick to other beings and try to merge with them.

[*Hellfire Inc. (loc)* — Bombay, India]

40. "TO EMBODY" {*satyr*}

(or "TO PERMEATE")

(–) "TO DISSOLVE" {*amoeba*}

False-Data: The 'divine light' permeates everything and is the only true source of energy. So you agree that you cannot (internally/personally) create any energy and must be dependent on an outside/external source.

[*Hellfire Inc. (loc)* — Catalina Island]

40X. "TO SOLIDIFY" {*satyr*}

(–) "TO MAKE IT NOT-IS" {*invisible man*}

False-Data: All matter consists of decayed beings. So you agree that matter can affect you.

[6. **UNIVERSE** (*Sphere 6*)]

41. "TO DISCOVER" {*centaurs*}

(–) "TO HIDE" {*slime monster*}

False-Data: This is the only *Universe* there is. So you agree that discovering anything 'outside' of this *Universe* must be a hallucination.

[*Hellfire Inc. (loc)* — New Zealand]

42. "TO LOCATE" {*leprechaun*}

(–) "TO MISPLACE" {*cricket*}

False-Data: Each being has a unique 'location' — a 'viewpoint' — bestowed by 'God'. This locational viewpoint is where you do all your perceiving and thinking from. [Two separate locations would be two separate individuals.] So you agree that you cannot be in two places at once.

[*Hellfire Inc. (loc)* — In orbit (space-station)]

43. "TO GATHER" {spacesuit body}
   (–) "TO ABANDON" {hobo/tramp}
False-Data: Our 'souls' are all gathered up by 'God' when we die. So you agree to give up all 'Identity' when you lose the 'body'.
   [*Hellfire Inc. (loc)*—Nepal, Asia]

44. "TO OWN" {fox people}
       (or "TO PERMEATE")
   (–) "TO BURN DOWN" {fire-people}
False-Data: (?)
   [*Hellfire Inc. (loc)*—Rio de Jenero, Brazil]

[5. **LIFEFORMS** (*Sphere 5*)]

45. "TO GROW" {genetic entity}
   (–) "TO ROT" {fungus creature}
False-Data: (?)
   [*Hellfire Inc. (loc)*—Tahiti Island]

46. "TO LIVE" {dinosaur}
       (or "TO ENERGIZE") { ? }
   (–) "TO DIE" {spectre}
       (or "TO SHOCK") {electric man}
False-Data: The 'soul' can only be 'energized' by self-sacrifice. So you agree to sacrifice parts of yourself for the 'common good'.
   [*Hellfire Inc. (loc)*—the southern aurora]

47. "TO HEAL" {tree man}
   (–) "TO INFECT" {germ colony}
False-Data: (?)
   [*Hellfire Inc. (loc)*—Prague, Czech Rep.]

48. "TO ADAPT" {thread man}
   (–) "TO PROTEST" {snake}
False-Data: (?)
   [*Hellfire Inc. (loc)*—Northern Siberia]

[4. **SOCIETY** (*Sphere 4*)]

49. "TO ESTABLISH" {3-eyed giants}
   (–) "TO UNDERMINE" {3-eyed robot}
False-Data: 'Society' is a conscious entity—individuals are only cells in that consciousness, and therefore unimportant. So you agree that you must control others for the sake of society.

[*Hellfire Inc. (loc)*—Philadelphia, PA]

50. "TO SHARE" {*dolphins*}
   (–) "TO POSSESS" {*sea monster*}
False-Data: A 'copy' is always less than the 'original'. We are all the result of a long string of 'copies'. So you agree that you will always be a 'flawed copy' without the original's abilities.
[Some of this data might really apply to another *facet* instead. (?)]
   [*Hellfire Inc. (loc)*—near Hawaii]

51. "TO CONTROL" {*frog king*}
   (–) "TO REBEL" {*gargoyle*}
False-Data: If people were left uncontrolled, everything would fall apart (be destroyed). So you agree that you must control others for their own good.
   [*Hellfire Inc. (loc)*—Caspian Sea]

52. "TO UNITE" {*dog soldiers*}
   (–) "TO CONQUER" {*war eagles*}
False-Data: 'God' has 'died of a broken heart' because we wouldn't stop fighting. So you agree to be afraid to fight.
   [*Hellfire Inc. (loc)*—Frankfort, Germany]

[3. **GROUPS** (*Sphere 3*)]

53. "TO ORGANIZE" {*file clerk*}
   (–) "TO DISORGANIZE" {*super-villain*}
False-Data: If everyone's postulates were 'equal', all would be chaos. So you agree that the postulates of a 'group' are senior (superior) to the postulates of any one individual.
   [*Hellfire Inc. (loc)*—London, England]

54. "TO COOPERATE" {*robots*}
   (–) "TO INDIVIDUATE" {*train-engine*}
False-Data: (?)
   [*Hellfire Inc. (loc)*—in orbit]

55. "TO PARTICIPATE" {*merfolk*}
   (–) "TO DEBASE" {*elephant-girl*}
       (or "TO WITHDRAW")
False-Data: We only 'think' that we are living life when really we are all living in a mass-*Implant*, and the next '*item*' is always coming at us. So you agree that you cannot do anything about it (or affect reality).
   [*Hellfire Inc. (loc)*—Capetown, S. Africa]

56. "TO EXPAND" {*mouse railroad engineer*}
   (–) "TO CONTRACT" {*maniac/psycho*}
False-Data: (?)
   [*Hellfire Inc. (loc)*—Edinburgh, Scotland]

[2. **HOME** (*Sphere 2*)]
57. "TO JOIN" {*cat people*}
   (–) "TO SEPARATE" {*black-cat*}
False-Data: We all join together in agreement to bring about reality. If any one of us really broke that agreement, then the whole thing would fall apart. So you agree that you must keep all agreements made.
   [*Hellfire Inc. (loc)*—Orleans, France]

58. "TO REPRODUCE" {*insect invader*}
   (–) "TO INFEST" {*insects*}
      (or "BLANKET")
False-Data: Whenever someone 'reproduces', they are lessened by it. If this were not the case, the *Universe* would be filled up and there would be nothing left. So you agree to be 'less' whenever you reproduce (or 'divide').
   [*Hellfire Inc. (loc)*—Calcutta, India]

59. "TO SATISFY" {*cavemen*}
   (–) "TO RIDICULE" {*moron*}
False-Data: Only 'God' is 'absolute'; and the *Universe* is the 'transient state'. So you agree that the *Universe*, itself, is 'unsatisfying'—and only *The Jewel* and spreading *The Jewel* is satisfying.
   [*Hellfire Inc. (loc)*—Peking (Beijing), China]

60. "TO CARE (FOR)" {*bird girl*}
   (–) "TO TORTURE" {*devil-pincers*}
False-Data: The only thing that will truly make people happy is to merge with 'God'. So you agree to care for others and help them to accept 'God' (and not rebel no matter how much they suffer).
   [*Hellfire Inc. (loc)*—Acapulco, Mexico]

[1. **SELF/BODY** (*Sphere 1*)]
61. "TO EXPERIENCE" {*bear*}
         (or "TO FEEL")
   (–) "TO DEADEN" {*death-goddess*}
False-Data: (?)
   [*Hellfire Inc. (loc)*—Canton, China]

62. "TO REPLENISH" {*a Sumerian*}
    (–) "TO AGE" {*father-time*}
False-Data: Everything that exists follows a cycle of 'create–survive–destroy', and things can only be replenished for so long. So you agree to age and die.
[*Hellfire Inc. (loc)*—Jerusalem]

63. "TO EAT" {*tiger*}
    (–) "TO POISON" {*spider*}
False-Data: When you eat something, you gain energy from the spirit of what you've eaten. So you agree that you are infested by spirits.
[*Hellfire Inc. (loc)*—Kenya, Africa]

64. "TO ENDURE" {*pyramid*}
    (–) "TO DISSIPATE" {*mummy*}
False-Data: Only 'God' persists; the *Universe* does not persist. So you agree that the only way you can 'endure' is to become 'one' with 'God'—aiding in 'his' purpose to conquer and permeate all beings.
[*Hellfire Inc. (loc)*—Egypt]

"BLACK-BOX" CONTROL-IMPLANTS
(*Experimental Research*)

The *"New Thought"* movement emerged strongly at the beginning of the *20th Century*. Then, waves of *"World War"* slowed its progress, and the spread of its information. But, in the aftermath of *WWII*, in the wake of *Roswell*, and in the shadows of *Atomic* and *Nuclear bombs*, the *"New Thought"* experienced a fierce resurgence in the early 1950s—hoping to provide a solution to a troubled planet, and a cure for the heavily *fragmented Human Condition*.

The *"Black-Box Control Implant"* was the first *spiritual implant* discovered by experimental *New Thought* practitioners. But, it was an entirely new *concept*, for which there was little reference. Anything about the subject spreading up from the underground usually became misunderstood as being part of an even more materialist-type of *"alien-implanting"* that pertained to tiny *mechanical-devices* inserted in the *physical body*.

In spite of how long *spiritual implanting* has been suspected as being a part of the *Human Condition*, the type of *systematic* approach that we might take today to handle this knowledge was simply not available at that time. The idea of "*command-lines*" or "*processing-out*" was not a part of that understanding. So, while this may be the *first* Implant discovered, surprisingly little was known about it directly until relatively recently.

This *Implant* has been used by various "*alien-forces*" for the sole purpose of "*controlling earthbound Human populations*"—while at the same time, typically setting themselves up as "*gods.*" Portable devices were even given to ancient "*priests*" (those selected to propagate the "*will of the gods*" on *Earth*) to set up in the "*temples*" and use on other *Humans*. And while an individual is likely to think of "historical" *Mesopotamia, Greece,* or the ancient *Far East*: the nature of this *Implant* extends further on the *Backtrack of Earth* to much earlier civilizations that have long since disappeared—like *Atlantis* and *Lemuria* and even earlier than that.

The *Implanting-gimmick* involves *energy-waves* that induce *pain* on the *items* "they" don't want you to do; *pleasure* on the *items* "they" want you to do. As opposed to other earlier *Implanting-Incidents* on the *Backtrack*, this one is more "physical" in its construction and simple in design. It was meant to be easily distributable. Though operating "cheaper portable" ones often resulted in a "*backfire*" (by design) on the individual that was doing the *Implanting*, so that they would also receive some of its effects.

Based on how it has been perceived: the *waves* are projected from a "*black-box*" on a tripod. This "*black-box*" had a "crank" on it, like a *grinder* or *sifter*, which was turned in one direction or another to generate the *wave*. In some ways, it also resembles an old-style *camera*—and the *beam* of the *wave* may be focused on one area; in this case, a specific part of the *Body*. A person operating it would appear very much like an old-time "*organ-grinder.*"

During the *incident*: the following *Platform* (series of *command-items*) is projected (as "*pleasure*" or "*pain*" *energy-waves*) at each of the following areas of the *Body*:

1. *Forehead (third eye/pineal gland)*; 2. *Left Eye*; 3. *Right Eye*; 4. *Mouth*; 5. *Left Shoulder*; 6. *Right Shoulder*; 7. *Chest*; 8. *Stomach*; 9. *Genitals*.

To *process-out* the *Implant*, a *Seeker* "Spots" the intense *sensation-wave* (*pain* or *pleasure*) hitting them (in an area of the *Body*) along with the *line-item*. A *Seeker* uses their *attention* to "contact" the *item/wave* impression (similar to "recall") until it no longer *registers* on a *GSR-Meter* (*biofeedback device*).

[Start with "*Forehead*" and *run* each of the following *items* on it, one at a time, making sure each one is completely *defragmented* of *turbulent charge*.]

PLEASURE-PAIN IMPLANT-PLATFORM

   1.1.X *{pain}* TO BE EVERYTHING
   1.2.X *{pleasure}* TO BE NOTHING

   2.1.X *{pain}* TO KNOW
   2.2.X *{pleasure}* TO NOT-KNOW

   3.1.X *{pain}* TO BE ORIENTED
   3.2.X *{pleasure}* TO BE DISORIENTED

   4.1.X *{pain}* TO BE CAUSE
   4.2.X *{pleasure}* TO BE EFFECT

   5.1.X *{pain}* TO BE POWERFUL
   5.2.X *{pleasure}* TO BE WEAK

   6.1.X *{pain}* TO BE INDEPENDENT
   6.2.X *{pleasure}* TO BE OBEDIENT

   7.1.X *{pain}* TO PROJECT ENERGY
   7.2.X *{pleasure}* TO PUT OUT NO ENERGY

   8.1.X *{pain}* TO OPERATE AT A DISTANCE
   8.2.X *{pleasure}* TO NOT OPERATE AT A DISTANCE

   9.1.X *{pain}* TO INFLUENCE REMOTELY
   9.2.X *{pleasure}* TO NOT INFLUENCE REMOTELY

  10.1.X *{pain}* TO PERCEIVE AT A DISTANCE
  10.2.X *{pleasure}* TO NOT PERCEIVE AT A DISTANCE

  11.1.X *{pain}* TO DO THINGS WITH THE MIND
  11.2.X *{pleasure}* TO DO NOTHING WITH THE MIND

  12.1.X *{pain}* TO BE FREE
  12.2.X *{pleasure}* TO BE RESTRAINED

  13.1.X *{pain}* TO FIND OUT
  13.2.X *{pleasure}* TO NEVER FIND OUT

  14.1.X *{pain}* TO REVEAL THIS
  14.2.X *{pleasure}* TO NEVER REVEAL THIS

15.1.X {*pain*} TO DISAGREE WITH THIS IMPLANT
15.2.X {*pleasure*} TO AGREE WITH THIS IMPLANT
16.1.X {*pain*} TO REMEMBER THIS IMPLANT
16.2.X {*pleasure*} TO FORGET THIS IMPLANT
17.1.X {*pain*} TO NEVER IMPLANT OTHERS
17.2.X {*pleasure*} TO GIVE THIS IMPLANT TO OTHERS
18.1.X {*pain*} TO NEVER BE IMPLANTED AGAIN
18.2.X {*pleasure*} TO WANT THIS IMPLANT AGAIN

<u>INDIVIDUATION IMPLANT-PLATFORM</u>

The following *Platform* is not a part of the former *incident*, but may likely involve some kind of "*Black-Box*" as it was located on the *Backtrack* almost simultaneously with the "*first Implant*"—but again little was known about it ("*command-lines,*" *&tc.*).

Although it is considered an "*alien-implant*" (used by technologically advanced societies in *this Universe*), it is unclear if it is used on *Earth*, or only among the more advanced "*space races*" (on "*starships,*" *&tc.*). Again, little is known about it, except that it is used on "*prisoners-of-war*" before returning them to their homes; or as a way of making prisoners an "*anti-social spy*" before releasing them back to their own side.

Here, we simply have some *command-lines* that can be *defragmented*.

1. TO SEPARATE
2. TO BE AN INDIVIDUAL
3. TO BE THE ONLY ONE
4. ONLY YOU CAN BE GOD
5. ONLY YOU CAN CREATE
6. ONLY YOU CAN BE CAUSE
7. ONLY YOU CAN KNOW
8. ONLY YOU CAN WIN
9. ONLY YOU CAN CHANGE
10. ONLY YOU CAN REASON
11. ONLY YOU CAN CONSTRUCT
12. ONLY YOU CAN BE BEAUTIFUL
13. ONLY YOU CAN RULE
14. ONLY YOU CAN ENLIGHTEN
15. ONLY YOU CAN INFLUENCE

16. ONLY YOU CAN OWN (HAVE)
17. ONLY YOU CAN BE ALIVE
18. ONLY YOU CAN CONTROL
19. ONLY YOU CAN ORGANIZE
20. ONLY YOU CAN BE ADMIRED
21. ONLY YOU CAN ENDURE
22. ONLY YOU CAN BE AN INDIVIDUAL
23. YOU ARE THE ONLY ONE

RESEARCHING PENALTY-UNIVERSES
(*Advanced Technical Research*)

Understanding *"Implanted Penalty-Universes"* (IPU) is a critical component to upper-level *Systemology* and the *Ascension Path*. Our *Systemology* is currently the only *"New Thought"* tradition that works with this data. The following describes research-methods used to discover this information. The original *research-actions* tended to "stir up" as much as they *defragmented*; but this was necessary for collecting additional details.

[IPU are introduced in *AT#4*, along with *basic processing* instructions. That information will be necessary for applying this section. You will also need to refer to the list of *basic* IPU-*Goals* and *negative* IPU-*Goals* given previously in this current manual. This more recently refined procedure is appropriate for *New Standard A.T.* (*Keys to the Kingdom*) as both *defrag-processing* and a *research-action*. However, it is entirely dependent on having access to that existing data collected for IPU (and all other course lessons and manuals).]

Total Defragmentation of the IPU is too steep of a gradient for any *Seeker* to approach all at once. The original intention for focusing research-efforts on IPU emerged only after realizing how much of their *systematic structure* and *symbolism* kept reemerging in *later* (more recent) *Implants* and *incidents*. Then, as more *archetypes* and significant "themes" continued to resurface, it became a research-area of increasing interest. It is also an incredibly *advanced* area to fully handle and investigate.

There are two *classes* (or *groups*) of *processes* applied in this *procedure*. "*Class-2*" requires having *run* all of "*Class-1*." You will be handling the basic 64 IPU-*Goals*, and their 64 "*inversions*"—the *negative-goals* listed in the previous section titled: "*The False Jewel of Knowledge*." You will also need to use IPU-*Platforms #1* and *#2* provided in *AT#4*.

You start by lightly *processing* the basic *Goals* (similar to what is described in *AT#4*). As you start *running* deeper into the IPU-content, more of "What Is" becomes accessible. Then you start adding *Class-1 processing-actions* gradually until you are *running* all of the steps on each of the basic *Goals*. After you are getting comfortable handling basic *Goals*, you can start to treat the *negative Goals* using a different method (the "Treadmill Platform" given later in this manual). [For *Class-2*, see the later section "*Actual Goals & Basic Purposes*" (and steps of the *Standard Procedure for IPU* given in *AT#4*).]

Similar to what is experienced with other *Implant-Platforms*: initially encountering hundreds of *items* can be slow-going. When you first approach a new *pattern*, you'll find that you have to be much more diligent and meticulous in *processing-out* each individual *item*. Eventually, you can *defragment* whole groups of *items*, just by "*Spotting*" the first one in a set. Then it starts to get much faster; where you *contact* the very first *item* of a *pattern*: Spot various *Goals*, and completely *disperse* an IPU-*terminal* from your *reality-machinery* with only a minute or two of *processing-time*.

Processing-time at *Systemology Level-8* usually consists of approximately equal amounts of: handling *entities*; increasing *spiritual ability* (with *Wizard Level* exercises); and, *research-actions*. This might not always apply to one single *session*; but an *upper-level Seeker* should make sure that they are balancing actual *personal development* with other work. *Defragmenting* IPU *terminals/symbolism* "frees up" a lot of entangled *energetic-mass*. To avoid feeling a "*loss of having something*," it is important to exercise certainty on "*creative abilities*."

A *Seeker* typically selects which *Goal* (IPU) to *run* based on an *assessment* of the 16 *Dynamic Systems*. One of the *Dynamic Systems* will *register* strongest; then you *assess* from the 4 *Goals* listed under that *system*. The exact sequence that an individual experienced various original IPU is not likely the same as someone else. However, *later* (more recent) *Implants* did *restimulate* them in specific sequences. The common ones are:

- The natural sequence of the *Dynamic Systems*: from 16 to 1 (*Create* down to *Endure*)—or the reverse: from 1 to 16. If the inversions are involved, the *negative Goals* are *alternated* with the *positive Goals* (such as with the *incident* that originally established the *negative-items*).

- The natural sequence, like above; but all *64* basic *Goals* come first (*Create* down to *Endure*), followed by the *64 negative Goals* in their reverse dynamic order—*Dissipate* (for *Dynamic System 1*) to *Destroy* (*System 16*).
- The *Dynamic Systems* sequence occur in pairs: the upper *Arc* collapsing into the corresponding lower *Sphere*. These are: *16* and *8*; *15* and *7*; *14* and *6*; *13* and *5*; *12* and *4*; *11* and *3*; *10* and *2*; then *9* and *1*. Or, the same pattern may occur in an ascending sequence (from *1* to *16*). And again, if inversions are involved, they might either *alternate* with the basic *Goals*, or *follow* after them (in a reverse sequence).

CLASS–1 IPU PROCEDURE

A. IPU-PLATFORM #1. [*AT#4*] The starting point of all IPU procedures. Once the IPU is contacted, *all items* should either be *registering* as *charged*, or they should be completely clear from previous processing. If a particular *item* doesn't give a *Meter-read*: pause and *imagine/create* exactly what the *item* means, then try to *Spot* the actual *item* in the incident again. If unresolved: continue with some of the steps below and return to this one.

B. Check for any *Harmful-Acts* and/or *hold-backs/hold-outs* (*&tc.*) connected with "doing" this *Goal*. *Spot* these and any associated *justifications*.

C. "*Spot the Hellfire Incident Location*" (on *Earth*); notice the false manifestation of the IPU that was placed there during the *incident*. The *incident*, itself, is introduced in *AT#5*; but the locations needed here are listed previously in *this* manual (along with the *negative-goals*) in the section titled "*The False Jewel of Knowledge.*"

D. "*Spot the Pyramid Location*" (from a mass-*Implant* taking place on *Earth* in a prior *Universe*); and *Spot* the "face" of the *Goal-terminal* (a "be-ingness" that represents the *Goal*) within the *Pyramid*. [*AT#4*]

E. "*Spot the {Goal-terminal} Saying {the 'Price' of the Goal}.*" [*AT#4*] For the *negative Goals*: spot the *inverted Terminal* saying, "This means an end to.."

F. "*Spot Places Where {Goal-terminal} Is Not.*" Then: "*Spot Places In The Penalty-Universe Where You Are Not.*"

G. IPU-PLATFORM #2. [*AT#4*] *Spot* IPU-*Symbol* items. There are a few listed in the *AT#4-directory*. Others can be *Spotted* and *defragged-by-realizat-*

ion. This *Platform* is only used on basic (*positive*) *Goals*.

H. *Scan* researched IPU details. [*AT#4*]

I. Handle any current *Backtrack* restimulation. *Spot* "*What Is*," and *defrag-by-realization*.

J. Check for any *Programmed Machine-Entities* (PME) that are currently being *machinery* related to the *Goal*. [*AT#5*] Note that a *Seeker* should have already *defragged* the more troublesome *machinery*, and should be able to handle this step using the "*Short Version*" of PME-procedure, having each: *spot being made into a machine; spot the first time; spot making others into a machine; spot the top of IPU-Platform #1; identification cleanup (who are you?)*.

K. *Run* a "*creativeness*" *repair-action* of *machinery* related to the *Goal*. This means starting with *creating/imagining* "broken" or "decrepit" versions of the *machinery* and working your way up to "fine-quality" *machinery*; throwing some *copies* away, pushing some in from the outside, *&tc*.

L. "*Spot Something You Must Not {Goal}*." Repeat to a *release-point* for that area.

M. "*Spot People, Groups (&tc.) That You Would Permit To {Goal}*." Repeat to a *release-point* (total willingness to have others doing this *Goal*).

N. "*Spot Places Where {Goal-terminal} Would Be Safe*." Repeat to a *release-point* (total willingness to have it anywhere, or not have it anywhere, by choice).

O. "*Spot Things That The {Goal-terminal} Does Not Own*."

P. *Create/Imagine* battered and beaten versions of the *Goal-terminal* in various places, and say: "*Oh, the poor thing; see how it needs me?*"

Q. *Spot* the top of the *Failure-Implant*. They would tell you to do the *Goal* to some object and then prove how you failed. The *command-item* is: "*You failed to {Goal}; so you must depend on others to {Goal} for you.*"

R. *Spot* any "*between-lives scene*" for the *Goal* (if known). [This may not be determined accurately until more of the *fragmentation* is *dispersed*.]

S. *Realization*: the collapse of the basic *Goal* becomes the perceived *justification* for (doing) the *negative Goal*.

T. "*Spot The {Goal-terminal} Saying, 'Do You Want To Achieve The Power {To Goal}'*." This occurs during a "*between-lives sequence*." There is a false promise made to you about the *Goal* that pulls you deeper into it.

U. *"Spot The Desire To Shift To The Negative-Goal, So As To Be Rid Of This Penalty-Universe."*

V. *Run "creativeness"* (*imagining copies*: throwing away; pushing in, *&tc.*) on any objects or interesting things used in the IPU. [*Running "creativeness" at Wizard-Levels increases certainty on the ability-to-have without compulsively creating or remaining attached to anything unknowingly.*]

W. Check for any other *entities* "stirred-up" (or awakened) by this procedure.

X. *Spot* the first few lines of IPU-PLATFORM #1 again.

BETWEEN-LIVES "JUST-CONS"

There are *"Justification Considerations"* that are *Implanted* during *between-lives periods*. This is likely to have occurred earlier on the *Backtrack*. The *definitions* and *symbols* come from the first *Agreements-Universe*, though there is some relationship to the IPU. This *Implant* leads to *considering* "undesirable things" in order to make IPU-*terminals* (others) wrong.

[This advanced research may apply to "between-lives scenery" for IPU-handling (above). Note that there may be minor errors on this list. More research-testing is still needed.]

The top of the *Platform* is:

TO BE RIGHT IS NATIVE STATE.

The following *items* will easily *defrag-on-realization*.
1. The agreeing dog says: *"They're wrong because they disagree with everything."*
2. The good bear says: *"They're wrong because they're nasty."*
3. The causative salesman says: *"They're wrong because they choose to be affected."*
4. The free horse says: *"They're wrong because they let themselves be enslaved."*
5. The beautiful cherub says: *"They're wrong because they're ugly."*
6. The logical alligator says: *"They're wrong because they're illogical."*
7. The winning seagull says: *"They're wrong because they're losers."*
8. The healthy flamingo says: *"They're wrong because they're sick."*
9. The enduring dinosaur says: *"They're wrong because they lack persistence."*

10. The skillful bee says: "They're wrong because they're incompetent."
11. The interested fish says: "They're wrong because they have no interest in anything."
12. The moving rock says: "They're wrong because they wouldn't move."
13. The certain computer says: "They're wrong because they're always confused."
14. The pleasurable ostrich says: "They're wrong because they hurt people."
15. The cube who is right says "They're wrong because they were made to be wrong to begin with."
16. The giant who sees truly says: "They're wrong because they imagine everything."
17. The visible statue says: "They're wrong because they keep everything hidden."
18. The present jellyfish says: "They're wrong because they're never there when they should be."
19. The smart ibis-bird says: "They're wrong because they're stupid."
20. The just flame says: "They're wrong because they're unjust."
21. The stork who brings order says: "They're wrong because they make everything chaotic."
22. The wakeful whale says: "They're wrong because they're always asleep."
23. The humorous seal says: "They're wrong because they're too serious."
24. The squirrel who plans says: "They're wrong because they leave everything to chance."
25. The mechanical man who is whole says: "They're wrong because they keep falling apart and fragmenting."
26. The strong robot says: "They're wrong because they're weak."
27. The real peacock says: "They're wrong because they're unreal."
28. The independent monkey says: "They're wrong because they let themselves be owned."
29. The infinite spirit says: "They're wrong because they're located."
30. The courageous lion says: "They're wrong because they're cowards."
31. The knowing owl says: "They're wrong because they don't know anything."
32. The sharing raccoon says: "They're wrong because they're greedy."
33. The calm deer says: "They're wrong because they're nervous."
34. The sea urchin who is different says: "They're wrong because they're all the same."
35. The outgoing turtle says: "They're wrong because they're withdrawn."

36. The oriented wooden man says: *"They're wrong because they're disoriented."*
37. The silent cat says: *"They're wrong because they're noisy."*
38. The started snail says: *"They're wrong because they let themselves be stopped."*
39. The ethical octopus says: *"They're wrong because they're all criminals."*
40. The reasonable knight says: *"They're wrong because they're arbitrary and have no reason for what they do."*
41. The responsible possum says: *"They're wrong because they're irresponsible."*
42. The independent corn-man says: *"They're wrong because they follow the crowd and wouldn't act independently."*
43. The helpful caterpillar says: *"They're wrong because they harm everything."*
44. The alive raggedy doll says: *"They're wrong because they're dead."*
45. The timeless mountain says: *"They're wrong because they cannot endure."*
46. The social potato man says: *"They're wrong because they're all anti-social."*
47. The trusting rabbit says: *"They're wrong because they distrust everything."*
48. The remembering elephant says: *"They're wrong because they forget everything."*
49. The young gorilla says: *"They're wrong because they're old."*
50. The perceptive mouse says: *"They're wrong because they're blind."*
51. The loving flower says: *"They're wrong because they hate."*
52. The serene swan says: *"They're wrong because they're always getting upset."*
53. The big ant says: *"They're wrong because they're small."*
54. The fast horse girl says: *"They're wrong because they're slow."*
55. The industrious donkey says: *"They're wrong because they're lazy."*
56. The truthful walrus says: *"They're wrong because they lie."*
57. The pleasant eagle says: *"They're wrong because they act horribly."*
58. The harmonious angel says: *"They're wrong because they create discord."*
59. The participating kangaroo says: *"They're wrong because they wouldn't participate."*
60. The wise alligator person says: *"They're wrong because they're all fools."*

61. The unicorn who has faith says: "*They're wrong because they're distrustful.*"
62. The good snake says: "*They're wrong because they're all evil.*"
63. The feeling porcupine says: "*They're wrong because they have no feeling.*"
64. The creative fool says: "*They're wrong because they're destructive.*"

THE "AGREEMENTS UNIVERSE"
(*Advanced Technical Research*)

The *"Agreements-Universe Implant"* is that *entry-point incident* through which we arrived at the *Agreements Universe* (see *AT#1*)—which began as a simple *agreed-upon Space* in which to *Create* "things" and "play" *Games*. The original *Jewel of Knowledge* impressed upon us the need to enforce a common set of *shared-agreements* in order to operate within the same frame-of-reference or *Universe*.

This *Implant* is unique in that we all went through it by choice, rather than being forced. We "solved" an era of individualized misaligned *Spaces* by constructing an *Implant* that installed a common set of definitions and *reality-agreements*. We rushed to throw ourselves into it and came out into the first *agreed-upon Space*.

As described in *AT#1*: *Alpha-Spirits* divided up into teams, with each working on one "sub-universe" of the *Implant*. Then they were all combined together, and the result became the *Agreements-Universe*. But, of course, each individual was only really aware of the one part that they contributed to working on. The full "set" was not known to anyone until we experienced the *incident*.

Creating components of *reality* without knowing the others meant some things didn't line up or correspond properly to one another—and this obviously led to some problems. It is probably the most *basic* of all the trouble we have since gotten into.

But, notice here that this was not *enforced* on an *Alpha-Spirit*, it was done by choice; and an individual is not likely to fully "drop" these *agreements* (even during *processing*) unless they are completely willing to "drop" contact and communication with *everyone else* that also went into this trap.

Therefore, the best we can hope from the current research is to *defrag* some of the *turbulence* from the *incident* and increase *Awareness* on the wide-view of the exact nature of the *Game* that is actually going on. We can't use *processing* to pull out of the *Universe-Laws* and *agreements* all at once—since such would simply result in chaos anyways—but we can follow a gradient *Pathway* of increasing *freedom* and lessening *barriers*.

Eventually, we might reach a point where we can all get together and go back to change the basic-level *reality-agreements* around a bit so that we can have a better game. But, in the meantime, we also have the IPU to *process-out*, and those really act as a *basic* foundation to our *fragmentation* —since they *were enforced*. But, that doesn't mean we cannot gain benefit now from delving further on the *Backtrack* to see the *agreements*.

The *Agreements-Universe Implant* (AUI) isn't full of hidden implications and subtle meanings. It simply puts up quite a "stack" of simpleminded conceptual definitions, such as you would display for children's educational programs. As such, the definitions are not in "*words*" or "*commands*."

The definitions present dividing lines that separate a concept into two classes—or else a dichotomy of opposites, such as "*Good*" and "*Bad*." But, if you are imagining a clean "line" running down a sheet of paper dividing these things, you'd be wrong. The definitions on one "sheet" do not necessarily align with those in the remainder of the "stack." For example, there is another appearance of "*Good*" on the agreements-list that means "*Holy*" as opposed to the one above that means "*Nice*."

The incident begins with being a part of a crowd and "rushing to get into agreement." Then you pass through an *inverted golden-triangle*, which is the symbol of the *Agreements-Universe*: representing all things focusing down to a single point of *agreement*. Then you get the first "*item-line*" of the *Platform*.

The AUI-*Platform* starts identical to the first several *item-lines* of IPU-*Platform #1* (see *AT#4*); but instead of a "*goal*," the word "AGREE" is inserted. The top of the *Platform* (1.1.1) is then:

TO AGREE IS NATIVE STATE.

The basic sequence of the AUI is:

1. An introduction; like IPU-*Platform #1*.

2. A series of definition sub-universes.

3. A period where you make various *agreements* (after being shown the need for each, you *agree* to it).

The top of the AUI can be *run* this way:

A. "*Spot 'rushing to get into agreement'.*"

B. "*Spot 'going through the inverted golden-triangle'.*"

C. "*Spot*: TO AGREE IS NATIVE STATE."

D. "*Look prior to this; Spot 'deciding that you need to agree'.*"

E. (If necessary) "*Spot 'getting others to decide to agree'.*"

F. (If necessary) "*Spot 'working on building the Agreements-Universe'.*"

The *Platform* then runs just like IPU-*Platform #1*, down through *line-item-1.6.3*:

TO AGREE IS THE BASIS FOR ALL DECISIONS.

The next six *line-items* are:

TO AGREE IS TO ACHIEVE ___.

And the keywords are: *Knowledge, Power, Wisdom, Affinity (or Likingness), Reality,* and *Communication*.

The next *item*:

TO AGREE IS TO PLAY THE GAME.

Then all *64* of the IPU-*Goals* are each given in the form of:

TO AGREE IS TO {*Goal*}.

Note: this may actually be the first origination of the IPU-*Goals* and the *Dynamic Systems*.

Then: TO AGREE IS TO KNOW THE MEANING OF THINGS.

And then the definitions come. For each one you enter a kind of cathedral-looking building through an archway (or maybe it's another *inverted triangle*). The first *item-lines* of each is:

TO AGREE IS TO KNOW THE MEANING OF ___.

The dichotomy would be inserted for the *item*—such as "*goodness and badness*"—followed by a pair of scenes (one to represent each side of the definition) for each of the *16 Dynamic Systems*. These "scenes" have not yet really been researched. One of the early ones shows a "*Good Bear*" building things and then a "*Bad Bear*" comes and kicks them down.

Basic, simple, imagery of this nature. One of the challenges is that later (more recent) *incidents* have added more layers of *fragmentation* over these definitions and *agreements*, which requires clearing out before we can see more.

The following AUI-*list* was compiled by *assessment* rather than our researchers *running* each one. This is still a tentative sequence; but since it does *run* well, it's become as close to a standard as we currently have. [It is possible this should also include *"Serene/Upset"* somewhere in it.]

1. Agreeing / Disagreeing
2. Good (Nice) / Bad {*bears*}
3. Causative / Effected
4. Winning / Losing {*seagull*}
5. Logical / Illogical {*alligator*}
6. Beautiful / Ugly
7. Strong / Weak
8. Interested / Disinterested
9. Certain / Confused
10. Healthy / Sick
11. Sane / Crazy (Truth / Hallucination)
12. Free / Enslaved
13. Enduring / Transient
14. Fast / Slow
15. Right / Wrong
16. Present / Absent (Always / Never)
17. Moving / Stopped (Motion / No-Motion)
    (Changing / Fixed)
18. Seen / Invisible
19. Gives Pleasure / Gives Pain
20. Humorous / Sullen
21. Smart / Dumb {*birds*}
22. Brings Order / Brings Chaos
23. Awake / Unconscious (Asleep) {*dogs*}
24. Just / Unjust
25. Divided / Combined
26. Real / Unreal
27. Courageous / Cowardly {*lion*}
28. Located / Infinite
29. Knowing / Ignorant
30. Owned / Available

31. Volitional / Controlled
32. Older / Younger
33. Wise / Foolish
34. Same / Different
35. Rigid / Fluid
36. Oriented / Disoriented
37. Connected / Withdrawn
38. Truthful / Deceitful
39. Ethical / Criminal
40. Skillful / Incompetent
41. Started / Stopped
42. Responsible / Irresponsible
43. Happy / Sad
44. Singularly Owned / Shared
45. Helpful / Harmful
46. Playful / Serious
47. Trusting / Distrusting
48. Alive / Dead {*raggedy doll*}
49. Loving / Hating {*flowers*}
50. Perceptive / Blind {*mice*}
51. Flexible / Fixed
52. Social / Anti-Social
53. Aware / Unaware
54. Big / Small
55. Reasonable / Arbitrary
56. Industrious / Lazy
57. Quiet / Noisy
58. Numb / Feeling
59. Harmony / Discord
60. Participating / Separated Out
61. Greedy / Sharing
62. Faith / Disbelief
63. Good (Holy) / Evil
64. Remembering / Forgetful
65. Created / Destroyed

ACTUAL GOALS & BASIC PURPOSES
(*Advanced Technical Research*)

One *Implant* that really *fragmented* our *goals* and *purposes* early on the *Backtrack*, is referred to simply as *"The Treadmill."* It was constructed in the original *"Games Universe."* It is unclear whether it was only used as general punishment *there*, or whether it was also part of the *sentencing-incident* where an individual is sent down to the *"next lower"* Universe.

A simplified version of each IPU and its *Goals* were used for this *Implant*. A sub-universe dramatizing a related *negative-Goal* was attached to the end of each one. The IPU-version establishes the *negative-Goal* by collapsing the basic (*positive*) *Goal* down to *zero*—to a point of complete apathy, overwhelm, and solidity. Then it is dramatized to essentially *"un-manifest"* everything until you *"go out the bottom"* of the *Alpha-Awareness* scale.

At the end, you've basically destroyed everything so that there is no *"universe"* left. This leaves you with a false *"native state"* (which is a consideration of one's *basic original nature*) that is made to equal the *"native state"* at the top of the *next* basic (*positive*) *Goal*. This ongoing *"scrolling quality"* of the *Implant* is the only reason we call it *"The Treadmill."*

One can almost liken this to an old-time cartoon, where the individual remains mostly stationary, while the background scenery "scrolls" to give an illusion of movement and travel. The bottom of the final *negative-Goal* was connected to the top of the first basic (*positive*) *Goal* again, which just kept one moving through all *128* total *Goals*. Once the *Implanting* really starts to take hold, the *Alpha-Spirit* gets a "spinning" sensation.

The basic *Platform* for *"The Treadmill"* begins just like the original IPU (*Platform #1*). [See *AT#4*] However the *"Symbols"* part (*Platform #2, &tc.*) is not used. Instead, the *Implant* goes straight to this *item*:

TO {*goal*} IS TO POSTULATE BEING THE {*terminal*}.

Then a handful of *items* duplicating the IPU scenery occur. But the basic (*positive*) *Goals* end differently. Once the *terminal's body* dies, you are able to *"exteriorize"* from the grave. Once you are floating above the grave,

460 – AT#8

then the *items* from the *"Treadmill Crossover Platform"* begin. This has you abandon the basic *Goal*, then shifts you into *negative-Goal*.

The *fourth item* of the *Crossover Platform* [STEP-D of the sequence (below)] is the end of the basic (*positive*) *Goal*. When *running* it, you should spot the top of the basic *Goal* (*"native state"* item) at this point, because some B.E. and *Fused-Groups* (*AT#5*) are stuck holding on this point, trying to avoid the start of the *negative-Goal*. Use the above information and the IPU details given in *AT#4* for *running* basic *Goals*. The following *Crossover Platform* is *only* used for *negative-Goals* in this *incident*.

TREADMILL CROSSOVER PLATFORM

The *Crossover Platform* begins at the point of the *incident* when you are floating about the grave of the dead IPU-*terminal*. This *Platform* is used for the *negative-Goals* as they appear in *"The Treadmill"*; but this is also the experimental procedure used for handling specifically *negative* IPU-*Goals* wherever they appear in an *Implant* (such as the original *"False Jewel"* given earlier in this manual).

This is the sequence:

A. TO {*positive goal*} IS TO REGRET EVER HAVING {*positive goal-ed*}.
B. TO {*positive goal*} IS TO ABANDON THE GOAL OF {*positive goal*}.
C. TO ABANDON {*positive goal*} IS TO SURVIVE.
D. TO ABANDON {*positive goal*} IS TO FORGET EVER HAVING {*positive goal-ed*}.
   (*"Spot the 'native state' item at the top of Platform #1."*)
E. {You begin to hate.}
F. {You decide to get even.}
G. {You choose a new goal.}
H. {You choose to (*negative goal*).}
I. IN THE BEGINNING, NOW, AND FOREVER, IS THE DECISION; AND THE DECISION IS TO {*negative goal*}.
J. TO {*negative goal*} IS THE ULTIMATE PURPOSE.
K. TO {*negative goal*} IS TO ACHIEVE ____.
   (The *keywords/items* are: *Freedom, Success, Enlightenment, Truth, Beauty, Knowledge, Power, Control, Respect, &tc*. Usually you only have to lightly spot a few of these to contact the next *item* below.)

L. TO {*negative goal*} IS TO BE THE {*negative terminal*}.
(At this point of the incident, the *negative-Goal terminal* appears.)

When *processing-out negative-Goals*:
Spot the following data (*where available*).

1. The *"inversion scene"* (used in later *Implants*).
2. This *Implant* making you abandon the basic (*positive*) *Goal*.
3. The top of the basic *Goal* (*"native state"* item).
4. The action of the *negative-terminal* in doing *Goal*.
5. The *Hellfire Incident* location.
6. The *Pyramid* location.
7. *"This Means An End To ___"* statement said by the *negative-terminal*.
8. The *"Survive"* statement said by the *negative-terminal*.

OPPOSITIONAL FRAGMENTATION

Games, *Goals*, and *Purposes*, are critical components of our *Systemology*, because they are key to fully understanding the thoughts and behaviors inherent in the *Human Condition*. This is an area that is often more challenging to *confront*, because an individual is likely keeping "one eye" on any signs, or validation, of whatever their own *Goals* and *Purposes* were before they were all *fragmented*. Of course, such is not really within view until the layers of *fragmentation* have been stripped off of whatever we were once interested in.

Developing experimental material to research the original *"Oppositional-Goals-Problem Implant"* was among the more difficult research-efforts (perhaps second only to the *"Big Splitter Incident"* that is covered in the next section). One of the reasons is that early on, while some gains were made, these areas often stirred-up a lot of trouble for researchers. [Review relevant data in *AT#1* and *AT#2* before handling this section.]

This *Implanting-Incident* occurs while going down a long *"ringed-tube"* as a *transfer-shift* between the *"Thought-Energy Universe"* and what became the *"Conflict Universe."* Each of the "rings" installs another *"oppositional-goal- problem"* as you pass it. It is structured after the IPU-*Goals*. [After this transition, an *Alpha-Spirit* ceases to maintain a *Beingness* as an *energy-sphere*-type *"body"* and starts to *Identify* with a more material structure.]

The *Implant* installs each *Goal* with *imprints* of 5 different *Identity-phases*.

They are:

1. *Goal-terminal*
2. *Oppositional-terminal* (who becomes the "target" of *harmful-acts*)
3. *Encouraging-terminal* (who wants *Goal*, enforces *Goal*; acts as a third party)
4. *Discouraging-terminal* (who doesn't want *Goal*, inhibits *Goal*; you are constantly *justifying* the *Goal* and your *harmful-acts* to this person, which makes the *considerations* "stick")
5. *A Victim* (who unjustly suffers from your *harmful-acts*; this *imprints* you with *regret*)

The experience of each *Goal* is only a short *Platform* of "*This Means _*" *symbols*, which explain the 5 different *Identity-phases* (or "*personas*") and what's *supposed* to be *expected* from the "scenery." Then the *Implant-Platform* installs a few "*splitter-items*" while an energy-wave is emitted to *enforce a 5-way split*.

At this point, your *Awareness/Beingness* "splits" into 5 *fragments*, so that *you* actually become *all 5 phases*, but compartmented (hidden) from yourself. Now you are all ready for the "scenery" to begin—but it doesn't; instead you find yourself at the next "ring" of the "tube" and getting the next *Goal* in the sequence. Each time, you are expecting some *pocket-universe drama* to unfold; but you just end up at the next "ring."

After the *Implanting-Incident* ends with the final *Goal*, you end up in the *Conflict-Universe*. There is no "imaginary scenery" or "pocket-universe" where you play things out. All of that *fragmented charge* that is accumulated from experiencing all *64 Goals* (multiplied by *splitting* into 5 phases for each) of the *Implant* is brought down to the *Conflict-Universe* and dramatized there—in an *actual Shared-Universe*. It is *you* that ends up enacting all the actual events in "real life"—but by following the *implanted* "pattern-of-action."

Your primary activity in the *Conflict-Universe* was running around unbeknownst to 5 *split-Identities*, and then trying to *align* with the other four connected to the same *Goal*. You try to be the basic *Goal-terminal*, but your *viewpoint* is really from any of the 5, depending on the circumstances. *Systematically*: while this is occurring, you have a *sub-identity* attached to (or "in") each of the other 4 *phases*; and you, in turn, also are infected by a *sub-identity* of each of the others. This holds you in a specific *phase* and contributes to events. Early on, in the *Conflict-Universe*, this activity all played out with great precision. Later, it became quite convoluted, and none of the activities or *phases* properly aligned with each other. Yet, we still had *5 hidden viewpoints* (*per Goal*) running around and causing trouble in attempts to keep the *implanted-drama* going.

> The fact remains that we really *are creating* our own *opposition*, even if *unknowingly*; and most of our *Awareness* or *spiritual power* (or ZU) is still entangled in doing this in present-time. Things are so out-of-alignment in *this Physical Universe*, and in such a way that, with hundreds of these *split-fragments* all working at cross-purposes, the end result is a balance of forces that keeps things fairly "solid" and difficult to change purely by *Alpha- Thought* (*postulate*).

When *running* the *Imprinting-Incident*, the "*This Means* ___" items are accompanied by 3-D *images* (*Imprints*) similar to the IPU-*symbols* (except with different content). But this *restimulates* the "top" of the IPU — whereas most *Implants* stir-up the "bottom." The result is a *being* that is a *super-charged maniac* ready to enthusiastically dive full into the *Goal*.

It is best to work from an established *Platform* when actually *processing-out Implant-fragmentation* (such as what a *Seeker* has been using for their *upper-level* work). However, having this data requires researching it. This area is not included in former manuals because it is still in a "*research-phase.*" To *run* it fully would require researching specific data on each one of the *imprint-picture items* for all *64 Goals*. And "skipping" the *Imprints* for a *Goal* seems to have a tendency to turn on "depressive fatigue" until they *are* found and *run*.

Basic research to establish an experimental procedure (*Platform*) for *oppositional-goals-problems* (OGP) handling occurred in two stages and hit many obstacles. These were easily overcome once we started applying the "*Locational Procedure*" ("*Point To The Being You Divided From*") after each of *item-lines 10* through *14*. This was not available for handling the "*splitting items*" when research first began. It is not indicated in the Platform, but it really is the key to using this for *defragmentation*. The *first item* is the actual *oppositional-goals-problem* (OGP) stated as a personal *consideration*. [Most, if not all, *fragmentation* will usually *disperse* by item-line 15.]

1. TO {goal} {target} AND {desired effect on others} OR I WILL {harmful-act}
2. THIS MEANS (to do goal)
3. THIS MEANS (desired effect)
4. THIS MEANS (harmful-act) {picture imprints it being done to the *oppositional-terminal*}
5. THIS MEANS ENCOURAGEMENT {picture imprints *encouraging-terminal*}
6. THIS MEANS DISCOURAGEMENT {picture imprints *discouraging-terminal*}
7. THIS MEANS OPPOSITION {imprint of *oppositional-terminal*}
8. THIS MEANS REGRET {picture imprints you doing the harmful-act to the *victim*}
9. THIS MEANS YOU {imprint of *basic Goal-terminal*}
10. TO {goal} IS TO BE THE {discouraging-terminal} AND DISCOURAGE MYSELF FROM {harmful-act} AND NEVER LET MYSELF KNOW THAT I AM DOING THIS.
11. TO {goal} IS TO BE THE {encouraging-terminal} AND ENCOURAGE MYSELF TO {harmful-act} AND NEVER LET MYSELF KNOW THAT I AM DOING THIS.
12. TO {goal} IS TO BE THE {oppositional-terminal} AND OPPOSE MYSELF FROM {goal-ing} AND NEVER LET MYSELF KNOW THAT I AM DOING THIS.
13. TO {goal} IS TO BE THE {victim} AND SUFFER UNJUSTLY AND NEVER LET MYSELF KNOW THAT I AM DOING THIS.
14. TO {goal} IS TO BE THE {basic-terminal} AND {do goal} AND NEVER LET MYSELF KNOW THAT I AM DOING THIS.

The next *command-lines* are *Implanted* simultaneously in 5 *locations*; one for each *split-identity phase*. Rather than going immediately to *item-15*, better *defrag*-results have been achieved by taking each *phase* in turn and *spotting* the other 4 *phases* from that viewpoint. For example: conceiving yourself as being the *basic-terminal*, and *spotting* each of the other *phases*; then taking up being the *oppositional-terminal*, and *spotting* each of the other *phases*, *&tc*.

[A "cloud" of B.E. might suddenly be perceived as active during one of these "*spottings*." If so, hold the *viewpoint* for the *phase* you're on, and start *dispersing* the *entities* by *acknowledgment*, *&tc*. You can even run through the above mentioned *spotting-steps* a second time if you find a lot of this happening.]

After using all 5 *viewpoints* to *spot* each other (as described above), you should be able to *spot item-15* in all *5 locations* simultaneously; and if so, this is usually enough to *defragment* the remaining *Implant-Platform*.

At whatever point in the *Platform* that the whole *"oppositional-goals-problem"* (OGP) *disperses*, skip to the end. Note that the *5 locations* are likened to "blades" of a *5-bladed fan* that are propelling around a center *location* that your *Awareness* can't occupy.

15. TO {*Goal*} IS TO BE ALL THESE 5 OTHERS AND HIDE FROM MYSELF FOREVER
16. TO {*Goal*} IS TO BE ALL THESE 5 OTHERS AND INSPIRE MYSELF FOREVER
17. TO {*Goal*} IS TO BE ALL THESE 5 OTHERS AND COMPEL MYSELF TO RE-ENACT THIS FOREVER
18. TO {*Goal*} IS TO BE ALL THESE 5 OTHERS AND GO AROUND UNKNOWN TO MYSELF
18x. TO {*Goal*} IS TO BE ALL THESE 5 OTHERS AND COMPEL OTHERS TO RE-ENACT THIS WITH ME

   [You are hit by an *energetic-mass* containing the emotion of distrust along with the *next item*.]

19. TO {*Goal*} IS TO BE ALL THESE 5 OTHERS AND AS EACH ONE, DETEST BEING ALL THE OTHERS
20. TO {*Goal*} IS TO BE ALL THESE 5 OTHERS AND AS EACH ONE, KNOW THAT MY VIEWPOINT IS THE BEST (compared to the others)
21. TO {*Goal*} IS TO BE ALL THESE 5 OTHERS AND DENY RESPONSIBILITY FOR DOING THIS, FOREVER
22. TO {*Goal*} IS TO BE SPLIT INTO 5 PARTS AND NEVER LET MYSELF KNOW WHAT I AM DOING

   [You are impacted by a *"splitter"* energy-beam. (Spot the impact.)]

23. TO {*Goal*} IS TO BE DIVIDED 5 WAYS AGAINST MYSELF AND HIDE MY ACTIONS FROM MYSELF AS I MANIFEST ALL OF THIS
24. TO {*Goal*} IS TO BE DIVIDED 5 WAYS AGAINST MYSELF AND NEVER REALLY KNOW WHAT IS HAPPENING

   [An *energy-implosion* occurs at each of the *5 locations*; each collapses and disappears from view, leaving a *hollow-spot* (*vacuum-of-space*).]

25. TO {*Goal*} IS TO FORGET THAT THIS EVER HAPPENED

After *running* this procedure on a single *Goal*: "Scan" the *Backtrack* for times when you dramatized this *Implant*; *Spot* any *harmful-acts* against others, and *spot* being in the other *viewpoints* and contributing to the activity/event-sequence. Check for any dramatization of the *Implant* in *this lifetime*; *identify* which *phase* you were in, and perform this *spotting* action on it as well.

"OGP" DATA & TERMINALS-LIST

The OGP ("*oppositional-goal-problems*") are related to the 64 IPU-*Goals*. In addition to the *imprint-pictures* and *terminals* (*phases*), there is a unique OGP-*consideration* (*item-1*) for each *Goal*. There is limited data for this; it requires more research. The OGP-*consideration* and associated *Identity-phases* for some *Goals* are listed below (when available). This OGP list is numbered based on IPU *Goal-sequencing*. The *phases* are listed in the *1-to-5* ordering given earlier.

1. CREATE OGP: "To create chaos and overwhelm others or I will blow them up."
—Phases: *God, Satan/Devil, Priest, Virgin, Seer.*

3. MANIFEST OGP: "To manifest intricate ornaments and have them praised or I will cut out their guts."
—Phases: *Artisan (craftsman), Scientist, Fishmonger, Policeman, Priest.*

4. IMAGINE OGP: "To imagine fine stories and have them appreciated or I will strangle everyone."
—Phases: *Writer, Cynical Father, Actor, Critic, Publisher.*

6. UNDERSTAND OGP: "To understand secrets and make others tell (obey?) (recognize my power?) or I will stab them all."
—Phases: *Detective, Criminal, Police Captain, Businessman, Prostitute.*

8. LEARN OGP: "To learn the nature of the *Universe* and be supported or I will overwhelm them all."
—Phases: *Scientist, Preacher, Teacher, Wife, Stupid Person.*

11. COMPETE OGP: "To compete (at boxing) and have the people cheer or I will beat them all up."
—Phases: *Boxer, Newspaperman, Manager, Lover, Businessman.*

15. CHANGE OGP: "To change peoples' nature and have them all be happy about this or I will strike them all blind."
—Phases: *Poet, Priest, Prostitute, Politician, Scientist.*

16. (BRING) ORDER OGP: "To bring order to society and be supported in this or I will torture (burn?) their bodies (flesh?)."
—Phases: *Lawmaker, Criminal, Merchant, Priestess, Nurse.*

19. GUIDE OGP: "To guide settlers and have them respect me or I will burn it all down."
—Phases: *Scout, Wagonleader, Salesman (Trader), Lover (Frontier Girl), Little Girl.*

21. CONSTRUCT OGP: "To construct spiral staircases and have them admired or I will trap them all."
—Phases: *Carpenter, Scornful Person, Salesman, Art Critic, Sexy Girl.*

24. STRUCTURE OGP: "To structure reality and be worshiped as a god or I will destroy them all."
—Phases: *Savior, Priest, Prostitute, General, Temple Virgin.*

33. ENLIGHTEN OGP: "To preach goodness and keep them from sin or else I will torture them."
—Phases: *Minister (?), Sinner, Ruler, Conqueror, (?).*

34. CONVERT OGP: "To convert unbelievers and make them (honest?) or I will implant them to believe."
—Phases: *Priest, Scoffer, Messenger (of the gods?), Empress, (?).*

45. GROW OGP: "To grow flowers and have them make people feel good or I will sacrifice everyone."
—Phases: *Priestess, Policeman, Carpenter, Mother, Priest.*

46. DISCOVER OGP: "To discover truth.. and?"
—Phases: *(?)*

47. HEAL OGP: "To heal illness and receive the peoples' gratitude or I will make their bodies rot away."
—Phases: *Healer, Priest, Politician, Policeman, Priestess.*

51. UNITE OGP: "To unite the workers in building wondrous projects or I will trick them all into slavery forever."
—Phases: *Engineer, (?), Politician, (?), (?).*

54. COOPERATE OGP: "To get people to cooperate in maintaining society and become famous for doing this or I will betray everyone."
—Phases: *Policeman, Criminal, Lawmaker, Priest, Prostitute.*

55. PARTICIPATE OGP: "To participate in dancing and be admired for my beauty of form or else I will cut their hearts out."
—Phases: *Dancer, Critic, Father, Innocent Girl, Lover.*

56. EXPAND OGP: "To expand knowledge and be admired for my genius or I will blow them all up."
—Phases: *Scientist, Priest, Psychiatrist, Girl, Ruler.*

57. REPRODUCE OGP: "To reproduce fine books and have the quality admired or I will inject them all with insanity (with a drug)."
—Phases: *Scribe (Scholar), Peasant, Scientist (Professor), Wife (Lover), Carpenter.*

58. SATISFY OGP: "To satisfy conventions and be respected or I will poison them all."
—Phases: *Girl, Elder Woman, Father, Lover, Publisher.*

59. JOIN OGP: "To join people together and have them be thankful for my help or I will throw things at them."
—Phases: *Prophet, Businessman, Priest, Lawmaker, Inventor.*

60. CARE (FOR) OGP: "To care for children (and keep them safe) and be loved for it or I will claw everyone's eyes out."
—Phases: *(?)*

61. FEEL OGP: "To feel alive and gain everyone's agreement or I will drive them all crazy."
—Phases: *Athlete, Lawmaker, Coach, Lawyer, Professor.*

62. REPLENISH OGP: "To replenish the wildlife and be praised for restoring the planet or I will take it away from them."
—Phases: *Ecologist, Businessman, Housewife, Politician, Priest.*

63. EAT OGP: "To eat people and gain strength from their 'souls' or I will rend their 'souls' forever."
—Phases: *Cannibal, Enemies, Lover, Priest, Explorer.*

64. ENDURE OGP: "To endure existence and be left alone or I will enslave them all."
—Phases: *Carpenter, Juvenile Delinquent, Wife, Detective, Salesman(?).*

After the basic (positive) Goals, this continues with the *inversions* (*negative-Goals* run in the reverse *Goals-Sequence* order).

INV 59. SEPARATE OGP: "To separate people from groups and be praised for helping them or I will leave forever."
—Phases: *Messiah, Ruler, Ruler's Mistress, General, Slave Girl.*

INV 58. RIDICULE OGP: "To ridicule social conventions and have everyone amused by this or I will hide forever."
—Phases: *Publisher, Father, Lover, Girl, Elder Woman.*

INV 54. INVALIDATE OGP: "To get people to individuate from groups which exploit them and have them feel good that I did this or I will shoot myself."
—Phases: *Prostitute, Priest, Criminal, Lawmaker, Politician.*

INV 48. ROT OGP: "To rot other's minds and make them suggestible or I will dissipate myself."
—Phases: *Salesman, Professor, Politician, Judge, Girl.*

INV 29. PERVERT OGP: "To pervert little children and have all the parents fear me or I will hang myself forever."
—Phases: *Pornographer, Judge (Moralist), Publisher, Parents, Little Girl.*

INV 16. (BRING) CHAOS OGP: "To bring chaos and overwhelm everybody or I will hide myself away forever."
—Phases: *Dark Priest (Black Magician), Criminal (?), Lawmaker (?), Prostitute (?), Temple Virgin (?).*

INV 4. DISILLUSION OGP: "To disillusion writers and force society to accept my judgment or I will bash my head in."
—Phases: *Critic, Writer, Father, Publisher, Actor.*

INV 3X. DRAIN OGP: "To drain emotion and make everyone apathetic or I will dissipate myself/others forever."
—Phases: *Artisan (craftsman), Scientist, Fishmonger, Policeman, Priest.*

INV 1. DESTROY OGP: "To destroy all of creation and be worshiped or I will uncreate myself/others forever."
—Phases: *Devil, God, Worshipers, Artisan, Virgin.*

THE "BIG-SPLITTER" INCIDENT
(*Advanced Technical Research*)

This final section of our *advanced training* program presents the experimental research (and procedures) for handling the "*Big Splitter Implant.*" The best we can determine at this time: this is the "*entry-into-the-Symbols-Universe*"-*incident*. We know that it occurs after an *Alpha-Spirit* had already experienced "*The Treadmill*" in the *Games-Universe*. [The *Big-Splitter* is constructed to restimulate elements of *The Treadmill*.]

This section includes a new standard procedure. However, for training purposes, we also include the prior (original) research and experimental procedures for handling this *Implant*. The material has not yet been refined for a standard presentation. This means much of the written background data and explanation still appears with the prior experimental versions, and a *Seeker* should study *all* of its parts before applying anything from this section.

While originally researching and applying earlier versions of this work, we did not yet have the "*Locational Procedure*" (*AT#5*). As a result, *defragmentation* of "*split-fragments*" required many additional steps that the new standard procedure does not. This makes the new standard seem like an oversimplification—but it *is* effective if a *Seeker* understands the true nature of what they are handling with it. Older procedures and background data are included to assist this. [Older methods are still effective; but often more complex.]

During the *"Big Splitter"* incident, an *Alpha-Spirit* is made to *split-off (fragment)* into *128* types of *entities*, each of which has various functions—such as keeping the *Universe* manifested, or blocking spiritual perception, *&tc*. The *Implant-pattern* was repeated multiple times, using each of the IPU-*Goals*. This means we have a lot of *fragmented-pieces* of ourselves *being* these various things. [A *Seeker* should *disperse* some accessible surface *charge* from the *Implanted Penalty-Universes* (AT#4) prior to treating this section (if they have not already).]

New Standard "Entity-Handling" includes:

A. Using the list of *128-entity types*: check the type of *entity* for a *Meter-read* and *spot* where it is; or *spot* one that is *being* this type.

B. *Locational Procedure.* [AT#5] Have the *entity* "point to the being" it "divided from." At *Wizard-Levels*, this is usually sufficient to *disperse* or *release* the *entity* (*split-fragment*). You may have to get it to *point* a few times until it gets its own certainty. It doesn't matter "where" it's pointing, or if *you* are certain about it; it is the *entity* that requires certainty in order to *release* itself. If necessary, apply the next step.

C. *Identification Procedure.* [AT#5] If necessary, have the *entity* "Identify" itself properly by applying the *"Who Are You?"*-PCL (getting the *"me"* answer), until it *disperses* or *releases*.

D. Check again and repeat A-to-C until no more *entities* are responding for that type.

Go through the entire *entity-type-list* from top to bottom, handling anything that reacts—and not working too hard at trying to "wake" a lot up. When you have completed with *running* one cycle through the *list*: start at the top and go through it again. Repeat this until the whole *list* is *defragmented* (doesn't *register*).

After working with the *New Standard* method, a *Seeker* can use the previously researched methods (given later) to see if any more *entities* are "awakened" (show up) for *processing*. It is quite possible that some of the earlier experimental methods are still necessary for *total defragment-*

ation of this area, which is another reason we have retained them in this manual (in addition to educating about progressive research).

You could apply the full *Splitter-Platform*, using the most basic (first) *IPU-Goal*—*"To Create"*—and then *run* the above steps again, this time going much deeper (unless you have already hit the main structure of it and taken the whole thing apart).

> This final area we are treating in this final training manual might actually be able to be *run* all the way toward a point of major *realization/ recognition* that handles *all* of the *split-fragments* of yourself. As yet, no one (within our organization that we know of) has taken this work to such an ultimate *end-point*.
>
> One of the final activities an individual theoretically conducts prior to a true *"Wizard Level-8 Ascension"* is the *re-collection* of all *split-fragments* present in the *Universe*; because an *Alpha-Spirit* must get out "in wholeness," without any lingering attachments or connectivity to *this Physical Universe*. Otherwise a "part" of us would still remain, and we would not be truly free to manifest or locate our *Awareness* fully on some other plane.
>
> If any of our fixed *"anchor-points"* remain here, we could just as easily be "snapped back in" to this *reality*; or "collapse-in to" it, when it too, one day, collapses-in on the next lower condensation of *agreements*.

If you miss (*fly past*) an *entity* of the type that you're checking that is ready for *processing* and try to continue, you may not find anything on the *next* type—even though the *next* type isn't really cleared. In this case, go back and check the *previous* type (you had just been working with) again for *flown-by fragments*.

This is all best handled with a *Biofeedback-device*. A lot of these *fragments* are off in *"non-physical locations,"* so a *Seeker* should not limit their *attention* to what is only in the immediate area of the Body (as with B.E., &tc.) or become overly concerned with *"where"* these *locations* actually are.

SPLITTER-INCIDENT ENTITY-TYPES

This is a list of the *128 entity* types resulting from the *"Big Splitter"* incident (which occurs using the *Splitter-Platform* that is given later). We have the *Platform* developed. The real goal of all experimental procedures (in this area) is to undercut having to *run* the entire *Platform* several times on each of the *128* types.

This list provides the *entity* types in the *reverse* order from how they occur in the *incident*; because that is the easiest way to *run* them when using the *Wizard-Level* ability of *"dispersing-on-realization/Awareness"* (as is the case with the *New Standard* methods). Otherwise, a *Seeker* will have to *process-out* all of the *"programming items"* that are found in the *Platform* for each type.

Note that we have a *"translation"* issue with ascribing *"human language"* names to represent these various types. Usually this is not an issue so long as a *Seeker* has no misconception about what a word means. In this case, we are working toward defining *"type labels"* that are consistent when checking for *Meter-reads*.

There are *16* groups or classes of *entity*; each of which has *8* types. Alternative *labels* appear for some types; the result of different researchers working on this project at different experimental periods of development.

GROUP 16. FINAL BARRIERS (*Blockages against taking this Implant apart.*)
128. OVERSOUL (manages all the others)
127. GUARDIAN (guards the implant against erasure)
126. HOLDER (holds entities in place that try to release)
125. SUPPRESSOR (hides the implant)
 125x. HIDER (may be 'suppressor')
124. DENIER (says implant never happened)
123. MISDIRECTOR (alters and shifts attention)
 123x. BOUNCER ('misdirector')
122. INVALIDATOR (invalidates anything you run/process)
121. RESTIMULATOR (keeps the implant restimulated)
 121x. RESISTOR (resists change)

GROUP 15. FINAL STRUCTURE (*Entities maintaining the structure of the Implant.*)
120. UNIFIER (pulls everything together)
 120x. JOINER or GROUPER
119. KEEPER (keeps/holds you down in the implant)
118. IMPLANTER (continually runs implant-items on you)
117. SPLITTER (continually makes everyone split/divide/fragment)

116. **CORRECTIVE ENTITY** (fixes anything that becomes undone)
 116x. **REPAIRER**
115. **PERPETUATOR** (keeps the implant going)
114. **DRAMATIZER**
113. **INNER GUARD** (keeps you from looking at yourself and seeing the structure of the implant/entities)

GROUP 14. SPIRITUAL BARRIERS (*Blocks*)

112. **DEVIL (DEMON)** (makes trouble for you)
111. **DEGRADER** (encourages degradation)
110. **TEMPTER** (tempts you to do evil)
109. **DELUSION ENTITY** (creates delusions)
108. **TERROR (FEAR) ENTITY** (makes you afraid; particularly involving the Mind or Spirits)
107. **CONFUSION ENTITY** (tries to keep you confused)
106. **DISCOURAGER** (discourages any effort to do anything about this)
105. **INTERIORIZER** (makes you 'interiorize'; into Universes, bodies, &tc.)

GROUP 13. SPIRITUAL STRUCTURE

104. **RECYCLER** (cycles you into a 'new' beingness between lives)
103. **EXECUTIONER** (destroys your 'old' identity between lives)
102. **PUNISHER** (arranges punishments)
101. **JUDGE** (harshly judges your conduct, particularly between lives)
 101x. **BETWEEN-LIVES ENTITY** (?)
100. **ACCUSER** (accuses you of any possible wrongdoing)
99. **ATTRACTOR** (causes you to 'pull' things in)
98. **ANGEL** (a piece of yourself sent to serve 'god'/'Universal Mind')
97. **CREATOR / PART-OF-GOD** (a part of yourself sent to be part of 'god'; or contribution to the 'Universal Mind'; "to be the thought of the Universe forever," &tc.)
 97x. **UNIVERSAL-MIND** (likely the same as 97)

[Note that the *"god"* or *"Universal Mind"* that is set up by this *Implant* is *Universe*-managing *machinery* and not a *"Self-aware entity"* in the conventional sense. It is composed of a piece of everyone and is programmed like a computer to run *reality* in the *Universe*. This should not be confused with any "higher dynamic" idea of *"god"* or *"Source."* Part of us makes up the *Universal-Mind* (*"god"*) and part is made into an *"angel"* that runs around enacting *god's* orders.]

GROUP 12. EXISTENCE BARRIERS (*Blocks*)

  96. TRICKSTER (tricks you)
  95. FATE (ARRANGER) (arranges fates for you)
  94. DISPERSER (disperses you)
  93. INVERTER (turns your postulates back against you)
  92. DECEIVER (deceives you)
  91. OPPOSER (manifests opposition to your goals)
  90. EQUALIZER (balances things; arranges 'karma')
  89. WATCHER (watches you)

GROUP 11. EXISTENCE STRUCTURE

  88. ALIGNER (COORDINATOR)
  87. COACH (keeps you from either winning or losing)
    87x. HUMANIZER
  86. ENCOURAGER (encourages you to stay here and live life)
  85. FUTURIZER (puts things into the future for you)
  84. GOAL-MAKER (manifests goals for you)
  83. GAME-MAKER (manifests games for you)
  82. PLANNER (plans your continued existence)
  81. GUIDE (guides you deeper/further into existence/Universe)

GROUP 10. UNIVERSE BARRIERS (*Blocks*)

  80. REFLECTOR (ENERGY MIRROR) (unmanifests energy-beams by reflecting them back at you)
    80x. COLLAPSAR
  79. VACUUM (UNMANIFESTOR) (drains energy and energy-beams)
  78. PULL-BACK (causes you to pull back your energy-beams)
    78x. BEAM-STOPPER
  77. DIFFUSER (causes energy-beams to disperse and slide off targets)
    77x. DEFLECTOR (likely same as 77)
  76. CONSTRAINER (constrains you to follow 'physical laws')
  75. BLOCKER (blocks you from messing up structure of Universe)
  74. BINDER (binds you together with reality-agreements)
    74x. AGREEMENT-ENTITY
  73. PROTECTOR (protects Universe from your postulates)
    73x. UNIVERSE-HOLDER

GROUP 9. UNIVERSE STRUCTURE

  72. ACTUALIZER (makes it all real)

72x. SOLIDIFIER or PERSISTER
71. SYNCHRONIZER (cross-copies the simultaneousness of time between individuals)
70. UNIVERSE COORDINATOR (coordinates the interrelationship of space-time and energy-matter)
69. DETERMINATOR (judges value of potential futures in order to maximize 'Arcs of Infinity')
68. COMMUNICATOR (interconnects everyone)
67. LOCATOR (maintains the position of everything)
66. GENERATOR (projects reality)
65. POSTULATOR (manifests reality)

GROUP 8. SOCIAL/LIFE BARRIERS (*Blocks*)
64. SINNER (inspires 'sin', selfishness, &tc.)
63. CONFLICTOR (inspires conflict)
62. SEXUAL ENTITY (sensation and entity-exchange during sex, &tc.)
61. SUBLIMATING ENTITY (feelings of love, honor, courage, loyalty...)
60. MOOD ENTITY (shifts moods between extremes; serene/troubled, calm/nervous, pleasant/irritated, &tc.)
59. EMOTIONAL ENTITY ('Beta-Awareness'; feelings of cheerfulness, boredom, antagonism, rage, hostility, fear, grief, apathy, &tc.)
58. ATTITUDE ENTITY (manifests preference; 'likes'/'dislikes', &tc.)
57. MORALIZER (makes you feel guilty)

GROUP 7. SOCIAL/LIFE STRUCTURE
56. MISOWNER (says that the Universe is not your creation so you can't affect it)
55. SHELL (FOCAL) (surrounds you and focuses things in on you)
54. UNIVERSE LIFE-ENTITY (to be 'the life' in the Universe)
53. ANIMATOR (to be 'the life' in lower organisms)
52. SYMPATHIZER (to keep you in sympathy)
51. SOCIAL ENTITY (inspires communication, agreement, likingness...)
50. GROUP-MIND (to be in 'groups')
49. SUPER-BEING (says you evolve by overwhelming individuals and making all become one)

GROUP 6. BODY BARRIERS (*Blocks*)
48. SICKNESS ENTITY (manifests disease according to 'universe laws')
47. JAILER (keeps you in a body)

46. SLEEP-CENTER (dreams; has you rebuild/manifest things while you sleep)
45. SOMATIC-ENTITY (manages physical pains/sensations)
44. BODY-BLOCKER (keeps you from modifying the body by postulate)
  44x. PERCEPTION-BLOCKER
43. FILTER (filters out perception of entities, infinities, &tc.)
42. CRAVER (initiates cravings; food, &tc.)
41. COMPELLER (needing bodies; needing food, &tc., for bodies)
  41x. COMPULSIVE ENTITY

GROUP 5. BODY STRUCTURE

40. RELAYER (relays body perceptions to you)
39. REPRESENTER (manifests body perceptions; sight, &tc.)
  39x. VISUAL-ENTITY (composes pictures of reality that you look at instead of seeing it directly)
38. REACTIVE ENTITY (generates body reactions to environmental stimuli)
37. BODY MACHINE (regulates organic body processes)
36. CELLULAR ENTITY (creates/duplicates cells of the body)
35. BODY-LOCATOR (integrates cells, perceptions, &tc., with space-time positions)
34. GENETIC-ENTITY (manages the body as a vehicle)
33. BODY-GENERATOR (projects the body into reality/Universe)

GROUP 4. MIND BARRIERS (*Blocks*)

32. SHIFTER (shifts attention into 'Beta-Existence' and off of 'Alpha')
31. CONSCIENCE
30. JUSTIFIER
29. FORGETTER
28. ENTURBULATOR
27. DEPRESSOR (possibly related to *106*)
26. EXHILARATOR
25. CONTROLLER

GROUP 3. MIND STRUCTURE

24. FILE CLERK (retrieves data)
23. RECORDING-ENTITY
  23x. HISTORIAN
22. SYMBOLIZER
21. COMPUTATIONAL ENTITY

20. DECISION-MAKER
19. RANDOMIZER
18. THINKER
17. INSTIGATOR

GROUP 2. ALPHA-SPIRIT BLOCKERS

16. DESTROYER (arranges accidents, &tc., to keep you from finding out about this, or escaping)
15. NARCOTIC ENTITY (keeps the 'Higher Self' feeling drugged)
14. INHIBITOR (blocks non-physical perception, &tc.)
13. DAMPER (DAMPENER) (keeps you condensed to a single point and in agreement, &tc.; holds you down)
12. PREVENTER (prevents manipulation of probability, resonance, cohesion, &tc.)
11. WRAITH (drains energy)
10. SUBCONSCIOUS (hides things; convinces you to stay limited and obedient)
9. ABERRATOR (compels one to follow laws of 'cumulative charge', fragmented patterns, restimulation, &tc.)

GROUP 1. ALPHA STRUCTURING

8. FORMULATOR (inspires choices of strength/weakness, likes/dislikes, &tc.)
7. INSPIRATIONAL ENTITY (inspires beliefs that everyone likes it here and you wouldn't want to leave, &tc.)
6. SEPARATOR (keeps you as an individual separate from 'Higher Self', and from knowing about other entities, infinities, &tc.)
5. RESTRICTOR (limits awareness to a located viewpoint)
4. INDIVIDUALIZER (limits you to a single located viewpoint, beingness, &tc.)
3. BENEFACTOR (gives you interesting rewards, &tc., for obeying the implant)
2. MANIFESTATION-INVALIDATOR (invalidates anything that is not 'agreed-upon')
   2x. CREATION-MOCKUP INVALIDATOR
1. INITIATOR (compels you to desire 'agreed-upon' Universe; games, forms, reality, existence, &tc.)

THE "HIGHER SELF" H.S. PROCEDURE
(Archaic Splitter-Handling Tech., Revised)

This advanced experimental-research method is based on the concept of a *"Higher-Self"* being established for each of the IPU-*Goals*. These "higher selves" are unaware (compartmented) pieces of yourself that keep everything manifested and operating. [This method is not necessarily recommended. It is a record of the material we utilized for research prior to the *New Standard* techniques, with the *"locational procedure," &tc.*]

Terminology for this application emerged from the idea of a *"Higher Self"* and that if such an entity or part of us is really fragmented and separated (compartmented), than we had to ask ourselves: *"higher"* than what? Handling IPU-material and other techniques for *Implanting-Incidents* has run us up to *this* point—theoretically the final major "barrier" (or "level of work") that keeps us from *Ascending out of this Universe*.

The IPU-*Goal* for the *H.S. Procedure* is selected by assessment. A *Seeker* doesn't have to worry about *running* a specific *Goal-sequence*; they assess for what currently gives the largest *Meter-reads* and *run* that. The procedure really has two parts: one, is the actual *running* of the *"higher self"* items; and two, is the handling of 8 types of *blocking-entities* that interfere with *processing-out* this *Implant*.

Although *128 entity types* are installed by the *Splitter Platform*, only one bunch of 8 seem to interfere specifically with *systematic processing (defragmenting)*. You *process* the 8 *blocking-entities* whenever you start your session for the day, and if necessary, in between each pass through the *"higher self"* items on a particular IPU-*Goal*; and also if you run into interference that is keeping *items* from *dispersing/defragmenting*.

The *"higher self" programming-items* are defragmented as a batch or cluster; not as individual *line-items*. You just *spot* one after another and keep going through the entire batch of *programming-items* until they collectively do not *register*. Trying to *defrag* line-by-line seems to stir up too much opposition to *dispersal*.

[*Researcher Notes*: If a *Seeker* runs into a *GSR-Meter* phenomenon where the needle is slamming: there are likely *Harmful-Acts* connected to whatever is being handled, which need to be *spotted/defragged*. If the balance-point on the *Meter* is excessively high (*high-resistance reading*), handle only *blocking-entities* until it lowers. When the *"higher self"* items do register as *erased/dispersed*, then they are. Don't *overrun*. There is a distinct feeling of the *Universe* shifting around when one of the "*higher selves*" disperses.]

BLOCKING-ENTITIES LIST

Use this *list* for assessment:

GUARDIAN
OVERSOUL
HOLDER
SUPPRESSOR
DENIER
MISDIRECTOR
INVALIDATOR
RESTIMULATOR

Whenever you get a *Meter-read*, have the *entity* do the following:

A. "*Spot being made into a(n)* ___."

B. "*Spot being made to split.*"

  [*Revision*: add *Locational Proc.* here.]

C. "*Spot the first time you were made to split.*"

D. "*Spot making others split.*"

E. If necessary: *Identification Proc.* ("*Who Are You?*"/"*Me*")

At this level of work, you may get an early *dispersal/ release* of an *entity* without realizing it, and start *processing* another of the same type that was behind the first one. But since the second one didn't get the first-PCL (*&tc.*) or whatever the first *released* on, there is still something there by STEP-E. So, if something remains, check if you're handling another of the same type; and if so, go back to STEP-A. In any case, when one does *release*, you check for another of the same type.

H.S. PROCEDURE

A. *Spot* "*Native State*" line-item for the *Goal*. *Spot* being *pushed-in*—pushing others in; and *another pushing others in*—to the *Implanted Penalty-Universe* (IPU) for this *Goal*.

B. *Spot* the item: "TO {goal} IS TO BE THE INFINITE {terminal} AND DIVIDE INTO MY HIGHER AND LOWER SELF FOREVER."

C. *Spot* being the "*higher self*" as a manifestation of the "*infinite* {terminal}." Repeat STEP-A (*Native State*) from the "*higher self*" viewpoint.

D. From the *"higher self" viewpoint*: *Spot* the original *split* into the *"infinite {terminal}."* *Spot* the *"mirror"* that shows you *splitting* into *infinite-copies* of the *terminal*; and *spot* becoming the *terminal* spread out to *infinity*.

[*Revision*: add *Locational Proc.* here on *"higher self" viewpoint*.]

E. *Process* the *"higher self"* through the following *"programming items."* Make sure each *item* gives a *Meter-read* (contacting it), but don't continue to *defrag* each line. [See earlier instruction on this.] If you can't get an *item* to *register*, check if it has been *"suppressed"* or *"invalidated."* If the *Meter-needle* goes dead, or gets *"stuck,"* check for *blocking-entities*.

The *H.S. programming-items*:

TO {goal} INFINITELY IS TO BE MY HIGHER-SELF AND:
1. CREATE THIS FOREVER
2. DEFEND THIS FOREVER
3. REPLACE THIS FOREVER
4. KEEP THIS MANIFESTED FOREVER
5. ESTABLISH THIS SPACE FOREVER
6. HIDE THIS FOREVER
7. HOLD THIS TOGETHER FOREVER
8. KEEP THIS UNCHANGING FOREVER
9. MAINTAIN THIS LOCATION FOREVER
10. ENERGIZE THIS FOREVER
11. PROTECT THIS FOREVER
12. OBSCURE THIS FOREVER
13. SOLIDIFY THIS FOREVER
14. STABILIZE THIS FOREVER
15. GUARD THIS FOREVER
16. FORGET THIS FOREVER

SPLITTER-INCIDENT (& PLATFORM)

This is the original research-data for the *"Big-Splitter"* Implanting-Incident used for early experiments. It was first replaced by *H.S. Procedure* and then, more recently, by the *New Standard* method. However, the details included in this original research are reissued any time the material is revised to avoid rewriting them. This is also such a key area of *Ascension* that all existing records of this work are considered critical for posterity.

[*The actual incident-sequence is given as "capital-lettered" items, such as "TO {goal}.." There are also various "spotting" instructions included for contacting-the-incident, research and defragmentation.*]

SECTION 1. INFINITY
(*The space is like being in a thin white cloud with nothing visible.*)

A. TO {*goal*} INFINITELY IS TO:
1. PERCEIVE ULTIMATE TRUTH
2. ACHIEVE ULTIMATE PURPOSE
3. PERCEIVE ULTIMATE BEAUTY
4. EXPERIENCE ULTIMATE ENLIGHTENMENT
5. RECEIVE ULTIMATE ADMIRATION
6. ACHIEVE ULTIMATE BEINGNESS
7. ACHIEVE ULTIMATE DOINGNESS
8. ACHIEVE ULTIMATE HAVINGNESS
9. WIELD ULTIMATE POWER
10. BE GOD

B. THE TEMPLE
1. *Spot:* The {*terminal*} appears in front of you.
2. TO {*goal*} IS TO BECOME THE INFINITE {*terminal*}:
3. TO BECOME THE INFINITE {*terminal*} IS TO BECOME GOD
4. *Spot:* The *temple* appears in front of you.
5. TO BECOME GOD IS TO BECOME THE INFINITE {*terminal*} AND DO {*goal*} INFINITELY

C. SPOTTING STEPS
(*Spot* the following with *intention;* then broadcast it out to the *entities, &tc.,* that started waking up from *running* the above steps.)
1. "*Spot the false data (above) in the Implant.*"
2. "*Spot that you don't have to be the terminal to do the goal.*"
3. "*Spot that you don't have to do the goal to get the things promised (above).*"
4. "*Spot that you don't have to be the terminal to get the things promised (above).*"
5. "*Spot that these items were all false promises; and that you didn't get these things from obeying the Implant.*"

D. ENTITY-PROCESSING
(*Broadcast* the following PCL out to *process* awakened *entities, &tc.*)
1. "*Spot being made to divide by this Implant.*"
[*Revision*: add *Locational Proc.* here.]

2. *"Spot the first time you were made to divide; Spot making others divide."*
3. *"Spot the false data in the Implant; Spot the first time you were implanted with false data."*
4. *"Spot being made to copy; Spot the first time you were made to copy; Spot making others copy."*
5. *"Spot: 'To {goal} is Native State' at the top of the original Implanted Penalty-Universe Platform; Spot being pushed into it; pushing another into it; and others pushing others into it."*
6. *"Come up to present time. Thank You."*

Check for individual *entities/fragments* remaining.
[*Revision*: use *Locational* and *Identification Tech* with acknowledgments.]
Check for, and handle, any *Guardians*, *machinery*, and/or other *entity* types.

SECTION 2. INFINITE TERMINAL

(*The items from the first section are reused with the "Infinite Terminal" in place of the Goal, as follows. While the items are given, the terminal—which is facing you—drifts backward toward "the Temple" and through the entrance. You are drawn along by it and enter "the Temple" as well.*)

A. **TO BECOME THE INFINITE** {*terminal*} **IS TO:** {*items 1 through 10 of Section-1A*}

B. (*The terminal is floating in the center of "the Temple" facing you.*)

TO BE GOD IS TO CHOOSE TO BE THE INFINITE {*terminal*} **AND DO** {*goal*} **INFINITELY**

C. (*You slide into the manifestation of the terminal. You do this by curving around to the right and sliding in on the terminal's left side—so you are now facing toward the direction you just were in and are now looking through the terminal's viewpoint. As this happens, you get the following item. Also: Spot the feeling of turning and sliding into the terminal as you spot the item. There is a heavy emphasis on the word 'Be'.*)

TO {*goal*} **IS TO BE THE** {*terminal*}

D. *Spot seeing the inside of "the Temple" from the terminal's eyes (viewpoint). Notice that everything looked vague and dreamlike before, but now looks solid and sharp-looking with the terminal's eyes (viewpoint). This is a part of the trick/gimmick of the Implant-Universe. You were actually perceiving correctly before. Spot this trick happening.*

E. *Notice that there is some type of mirror on a wall of "the Temple"; and you can see yourself in it as the terminal. Spot the mirror. Spot the false reflection of* yourself as the terminal.

F. (*With this item, the mirror shows you splitting out to infinity.*)
TO BECOME GOD IS TO BECOME INFINITE

(*Endless copies of the terminal stream out in all directions. Actually, you are being shown a picture of the terminal splitting, but you think you are already splitting and start agreeing with the idea. Then you are hit with a wave of force that makes you split. Spot the false mirror image, and the wave of force, along with the item.*)

G. (*With this item, the mirror view pans backwards and shows you the outside of "the Temple" with endless copies of the terminal streaming off in all directions. Spot this.*)
TO {*goal*} IS TO DIVIDE FOREVER

H. TO {*goal*} IS TO BE THE INFINITE {*terminal*}

I. The original procedure includes: *imagining* dividing out to infinity and being the "*infinite-terminal*" several times. Also: have any *entities* (*&tc.*) that are awake "*spot*" doing this; and *spot* the first time they did this.

J. A revised procedure includes: alternate *running* the conceptual-PCL "*Decide To Be The Infinite {terminal}*" and "*Decide Not To Be The Infinite {terminal}.*" (Always end on the second one.)

K. Repeat "*Entity-Processing*" (STEP-D from *Section-1*).

L. TO {*goal*} IS TO BE THE INFINITE {*terminal*} AND: {*items 1 through 16 of Step-E of the H.S. Procedure*}

For the *remaining* sections (below): *spot* the *item* a number of times until it *releases, disperses* or stops *registering*; have anyone awake *spot* doing the *item* (and the first time); and then *spot* the *item* again to *disperse* or to confirm *release/defrag*.

The original version includes: *spot* being the *infinite-copies* of the *terminal* and doing the *item* yourself (to be at total *Cause* over doing the *item*); then *spot* the *item* and the "*Native State*" item for that *Goal*.

SECTION 3. INFINITE REALITY
(*A feeling of something shifting or coming apart almost always means dispersion/defragmentation. Total defragmentation does not give quite the same feeling as a partial-release. The shift on a full dispersal/release basically feels good; you are shifting back towards reality, and you feel better oriented. Partial-releases tend to leave one feeling disoriented.*)

TO {goal} IS TO BE THE INFINITE {terminal} AND PARTICIPATE IN THE ___, FOREVER
1. CO-ACTUALIZATION OF REALITY
2. SHARING OF GROUP AGREEMENT
3. RHYTHM OF AGREED-UPON TIME
4. DETERMINATION OF AGREED-UPON LOCATION
5. OPERATION OF PHYSICAL UNIVERSE MECHANICS/LAWS
6. ENERGIZATION OF AGREED-UPON MOTION
7. SOLIDIFICATION OF AGREED-UPON FORMS
8. CROSS-COPYING OF THE PHYSICAL UNIVERSE

SECTION 4. SPLIT & PROGRAMMING

There are 128 entity-types. The first item for each is the "split" into that type. Something like a drop of water appears and then breaks apart and fragments into endless tiny droplets spreading across space-time. Spot this with the item.

The second item is a "program" item. The infinite droplets of water freeze or crystallize. Spot this with the item.

This sequence is introduced with:

0.0 TO {goal} IS TO BE THE INFINITE {terminal} AND
0.1 COPY MYSELF AND OTHERS, FOREVER
0.2 DIVIDE MYSELF AND OTHERS, FOREVER

A *"split/program"* pattern occurs with the *first two items* for each *entity* type.

After all the *items/entities,* there is an additional H.S. item (after a repeat of item 0.0 above) as follows:

129.0 DIVIDE MYSELF INTO MY HIGHER SELF AND MYSELF AS AN INDIVIDUAL, FOREVER

Then there are eight different "doingness" programming-items for each type. It is easier to run these for each entity type along with the "split-program" items (above), rather than making a separate cycle through for these details.

A revised handling of the "doingness" programming-items includes imagining doing (and not doing) the action, alternately to an end-realization or endpoint. Once this is clearly conceived, then broadcast processing to entities: spot being made into (type), and the first time, and making others; use "Locational Tech" (point to..); spot false data of the Implant; spot "Native State" item; and apply "Identification Tech," &tc. —all as needed to resolve the case.

[Note that some additional data (research and experimentation) is still necessary to complete this final step toward *Ascension.*]

1.1 SPLIT MYSELF AND OTHERS INTO INITIATORS FOREVER

1.2 PROGRAM MYSELF AND OTHERS TO BE THE INITIATOR AND INFUSE MYSELF WITH DESIRE FOREVER

1.X TO {goal} INFINITELY IS TO BE THE INITIATOR AND COMPEL MYSELF TO DESIRE PHYSICAL UNIVERSE ___, FOREVER
 [1. TIME; 2. SPACE; 3. ENERGY; 4. MATTER; 5. GAMES; 6. FORMS; 7. REALITY; 8. EXISTENCE]

2.1 SPLIT MYSELF AND OTHERS INTO MOCK-UP INVALIDATORS FOREVER

2.2 PROGRAM MYSELF AND OTHERS TO BE THE MOCK-UP INVALIDATOR AND INVALIDATE THAT WHICH IS NOT AGREED-UPON, FOREVER

2.X TO {goal} INFINITELY IS TO BE THE MOCK-UP INVALIDATOR AND INVALIDATE NON-PHYSICAL ___ FOREVER
 [1. TIME; 2. SPACE; 3. ENERGY; 4. MATTER; 5. GAMES; 6. FORMS; 7. REALITY; 8. EXISTENCE]

3.1 SPLIT MYSELF AND OTHERS INTO BENEFACTORS FOREVER

3.2 PROGRAM MYSELF AND OTHERS TO BE THE BENEFACTOR AND REWARD MYSELF FOR OBEYING THIS IMPLANT FOREVER

3.X TO {goal} INFINITELY IS TO BE THE BENEFACTOR AND GIVE MYSELF INTERESTING ___ TO OCCUPY MY ATTENTION FOREVER
 [1. GOALS; 2. HAVINGNESS; 3. PHASES; 4. GAMES; 5. ADVENTURES; 6. DRAMA]

3.Y TO {goal} INFINITELY IS TO BE THE BENEFACTOR AND GIVE MYSELF INTERESTING ___ FOR OBEYING THIS FOREVER
 [7. REASONS; 8. REWARDS]

4.1 SPLIT MYSELF AND OTHERS INTO INDIVIDUALIZERS FOREVER

4.2 PROGRAM MYSELF AND OTHERS TO BE THE INDIVIDUALIZER AND KEEP MYSELF NARROWED DOWN (or compartmented) FOREVER

4.X TO {goal} INFINITELY IS TO BE THE INDIVIDUALIZER AND ___ FOREVER
 [1. SHIFT MY AWARENESS DOWN TO A POINT; 2. KEEP MYSELF LOCATED IN SPACE AND TIME]

4.Y TO {goal} INFINITELY IS TO BE THE INDIVIDUALIZER AND LIMIT MYSELF TO A SINGLE ___ FOREVER
 [3. VIEWPOINT; 4. AWARENESS CENTER; 5. TIME-TRACK; 6. OPERATING POINT; 7. BEINGNESS; 8. REALITY]

5.1 SPLIT MYSELF AND OTHERS INTO RESTRICTORS FOREVER

5.2 PROGRAM MYSELF AND OTHERS TO BE THE RESTRICTOR AND LIMIT MYSELF TO A LOCATED VIEWPOINT, FOREVER

5.X TO {goal} INFINITELY IS TO BE THE RESTRICTOR AND RESTRICT MYSELF TO ___ ONLY IN THE LOCATED VIEWPOINT, FOREVER
   [1. BEING; 2. PERCEIVING; 3. OPERATING; 4. THINKING]
5.X TO {goal} INFINITELY IS TO BE THE RESTRICTOR AND RESTRICT MY ___ OF THE LOCATED VIEWPOINT, FOREVER
   [5. CONCEPTIONS TO THE EXPERIENCE;
   6. KNOWLEDGE TO THE DATA; 7. POWER TO THE ENERGY;
   8. ABILITIES TO THE CAPABILITIES]
6.1 SPLIT MYSELF AND OTHERS INTO SEPARATORS FOREVER
6.2 PROGRAM MYSELF AND OTHERS TO BE THE SEPARATOR AND KEEP MYSELF SEPARATE AS AN INDIVIDUAL, FOREVER
6.X TO {goal} INFINITELY IS TO BE THE SEPARATOR AND KEEP MYSELF AS AN INDIVIDUAL, SEPARATE FROM ___, FOREVER
   [1. MYSELF AS AN ENTITY; 2. MY HIGHER SELF; 3. INFINITY;
   4. OTHER INDIVIDUALS; 5. OTHER UNIVERSES; 6. GOD (the unmanifest static or NOTHINGNESS); 7. THE LIFE STATIC (or ALPHA-SPIRIT); 8. THE UNIVERSE MACHINERY]
7.1 SPLIT MYSELF AND OTHERS INTO INSPIRATIONAL ENTITIES FOREVER
7.2 PROGRAM MYSELF AND OTHERS TO BE THE INSPIRATIONAL ENTITY AND CONVINCE MYSELF TO BELIEVE IN ALL THIS FOREVER
7.X TO {goal} INFINITELY IS TO BE THE INSPIRATIONAL ENTITY AND CONVINCE MYSELF AND OTHERS THAT ___, FOREVER
   [1. EVERYONE REALLY LIKES IT HERE; 2. THIS IS THE ONLY REAL UNIVERSE; 3. THERE WAS NOTHING BEFORE THIS UNIVERSE;
   4. IT IS NECESSARY TO BE HERE; 5. YOU CANNOT DO ANYTHING WITHOUT OTHERS AGREEMENT; 6. POSTULATES CANNOT AFFECT THE PHYSICAL UNIVERSE; 7. NOBODY CAN EXIST WITHOUT A PHYSICAL FORM; 8. WE WANT TO BE THE EFFECT OF ALL THIS.]
8.1 SPLIT MYSELF AND OTHERS INTO FORMULATORS FOREVER
8.2 PROGRAM MYSELF AND OTHERS TO BE THE FORMULATOR AND FORMULATE MYSELF AS AN INDIVIDUAL FOREVER
8.X TO {goal} INFINITELY IS TO BE THE FORMULATOR AND INSPIRE MYSELF TO CHOOSE ___, FOREVER
   [1. STRENGTHS AND WEAKNESSES; 2. LIKES AND DISLIKES;
   3. ALLIES AND ENEMIES; 4. HOPES AND FEARS;
   5. CONNECTIONS AND DISCONNECTIONS; 6. FREEDOMS AND CONSEQUENCES; 7. ABILITIES AND DISABILITIES; 8. (?)]
9.1 SPLIT MYSELF AND OTHERS INTO ABERRATORS FOREVER
9.2 PROGRAM MYSELF AND OTHERS TO BE THE ABERRATOR AND ABERRATE (FRAGMENT) MYSELF FOREVER

9.X TO {goal} INFINITELY IS TO BE THE ABERRATOR AND COMPEL MYSELF TO FOLLOW THE LAWS OF ___, FOREVER
[1. CUMULATIVE CHARGE (later incidents stack up on earlier ones); 2. RESTIMULATION; 3. FLOWS (inflow, outflow); 4. THE DECLINING SPIRAL (of beingness and condensation); 5. EXCHANGE; 6. OPPOSITION (creating your own); 7. PULLING THINGS IN (manifesting motivation for actions); 8. RESISTANCE (becoming what you resist).]

10.1 SPLIT MYSELF AND OTHERS INTO SUBCONSCIOUS ENTITIES FOREVER
10.2 PROGRAM MYSELF AND OTHERS TO BE THE SUBCONSCIOUS AND GIVE MYSELF ORDERS FOREVER
10.X TO {goal} INFINITELY IS TO BE THE SUBCONSCIOUS AND ___, FOREVER
[1. HIDE FROM MYSELF AS AN INDIVIDUAL; 2. KEEP MYSELF AS AN INDIVIDUAL UNCONSCIOUS OF THESE MECHANISMS; 3. KEEP MYSELF AS AN INDIVIDUAL OBEDIENT TO THE COMMANDS OF THIS IMPLANT; 4. KEEP MYSELF AS AN INDIVIDUAL OBEDIENT TO THE LAWS OF THE PHYSICAL UNIVERSE; 5. LIMIT MY SELF-AWARENESS TO MYSELF AS THE INDIVIDUAL; 6. CONVINCE MYSELF THAT THE ONLY WAY TO EXIST IS TO ACCEPT THESE LIMITATIONS; 7. CONVINCE MYSELF THAT THE ONLY WAY TO BE HAPPY IS TO ACCEPT THESE LIMITATIONS; 8. CONVINCE MYSELF THAT THE ONLY WAY TO BE GOOD IS TO ACCEPT THESE LIMITATIONS]

11.1 SPLIT MYSELF AND OTHERS INTO WRAITHS FOREVER
11.2 PROGRAM MYSELF AND OTHERS TO BE THE WRAITH AND WEAKEN MYSELF FOREVER
11.X TO {goal} INFINITELY IS TO BE THE WRAITH AND MAKE MYSELF GROW CONTINUALLY ___, FOREVER
[1. LESS INTELLIGENT; 2. LESS POWERFUL; 3. LESS ABLE; 4. LESS SKILLFUL; 5. LESS AWARE; 6. LESS INTEGRATED; 7. LESS COMPETENT; 8. SMALLER]

12.1 SPLIT MYSELF AND OTHERS INTO PREVENTERS FOREVER
12.2 PROGRAM MYSELF AND OTHERS TO BE THE PREVENTER AND PREVENT THE MANIPULATION OF REALITY, FOREVER
12.X TO {goal} INFINITELY IS TO BE THE PREVENTER AND PREVENT THE MANIPULATION OF ___, FOREVER
[1. PROBABILITY; 2. RESONANCE (vibration/ sympathy); 3. COHESION (the cohesion of the whole); 4. SYNCHRONIZATION (solidity/frequency); 5. ORIENTATION (dimensions); 6. BEINGNESS (identity of spaces, objects, energies); 7. WILLINGNESS (of spaces, objects, energies); 8. ORIGINAL IS-NESS (actual nature of things/reality)]

13.1 SPLIT MYSELF AND OTHERS INTO DAMPERS FOREVER

13.2 PROGRAM MYSELF AND OTHERS TO BE THE DAMPER AND HOLD MYSELF HERE FOREVER

13.X TO {goal} INFINITELY IS TO BE THE DAMPER AND ___ FOREVER
 [1. KEEP MYSELF AT EFFECT; 2. HOLD MYSELF DOWN; 3. KEEP MYSELF LOCATED; 4. CONDENSE MYSELF TO A POINT; 5. KEEP MYSELF IN AGREEMENT; 6. CONSTRAIN MYSELF TO PHYSICAL REALITY; 7. CONSTRAIN MYSELF TO A SINGLE INDIVIDUALITY; 8. HIDE ALL OTHER BEINGNESS FROM MY INDIVIDUAL SELF]

14.1 SPLIT MYSELF AND OTHERS INTO INHIBITORS FOREVER

14.2 PROGRAM MYSELF AND OTHERS TO BE THE INHIBITOR AND INHIBIT PERCEPTIONS FOREVER

14.X TO {goal} INFINITELY IS TO BE THE INHIBITOR AND ___ FOREVER
 [1. BLOCK ALL PERCEPTION OF INFINITY; 2. BLOCK ALL PERCEPTIONS BEYOND 3 DIMENSIONS; 3. BLOCK ALL PERCEPTIONS OF ENTITIES; 4. BLOCK ALL PERCEPTIONS OF OTHER'S IMAGINED CREATIONS (MOCK-UPS); 5. BLOCK ALL PERCEPTION OF OTHER UNIVERSES; 6. BLOCK ALL PERCEPTION IN NON-PHYSICAL DIRECTIONS; 7. BLOCK MYSELF AND OTHERS FROM REALIZING THAT THESE THINGS ARE THERE; 8. BLOCK MYSELF AND OTHERS FROM WANTING TO DO ANYTHING ABOUT THIS]

15.1 SPLIT MYSELF AND OTHERS INTO NARCOTIC ENTITIES FOREVER

15.2 PROGRAM MYSELF AND OTHERS TO BE THE NARCOTIC ENTITY AND KEEP MY HIGHER-SELF "DRUGGED" FOREVER

15.X TO {goal} INFINITELY IS TO BE THE NARCOTIC ENTITY AND KEEP MY HIGHER-SELF ___ FOREVER
 [1. LOST IN A FEELING OF PLEASANT DRIFTING; 2. UNCONCERNED; 3. UNAWARE; 4. NON-CONSECUTIVE; 5. UNFOCUSED; 6. NON-SEQUITUR (illogical); 7. DISCONNECTED; 8. UNREAL]

16.1 SPLIT MYSELF AND OTHERS INTO DESTROYERS FOREVER

16.2 PROGRAM MYSELF AND OTHERS TO BE THE DESTROYER AND STOP ALL ATTEMPTS TO UNDO THIS, FOREVER

16.X TO {goal} INFINITELY IS TO BE THE DESTROYER AND ___ FOREVER
 [1. STOP MYSELF AND OTHERS FROM EVER DISCOVERING THIS; 2. STOP MYSELF AND OTHERS FROM EVER SUSPECTING THIS; 3. STOP MYSELF AND OTHERS FROM EVER PERCEIVING THIS; 4. STOP MYSELF AND OTHERS FROM EVER DISPERSING THIS AS-IT-IS; 5. MAKE MYSELF SICK IF I EVER DISCOVER ANY OF THIS; 6. DRIVE MYSELF CRAZY IF I EVER DISCOVER ANY OF

THIS; 7. USE PAIN TO BLOCK MYSELF FROM UNDOING THIS IMPLANT; 8. ARRANGE ACCIDENTS TO BLOCK MYSELF FROM UNDOING THIS IMPLANT]

17.1 SPLIT MYSELF AND OTHERS INTO INSTIGATORS FOREVER
17.2 PROGRAM MYSELF AND OTHERS TO BE THE INSTIGATOR AND INSTIGATE PHYSICAL UNIVERSE THINKING, FOREVER
17.X TO {goal} INFINITELY IS TO BE THE INSTIGATOR AND INSPIRE MYSELF TO ___ FOREVER
[1. BE CURIOUS ABOUT THE PHYSICAL UNIVERSE; 2. BE INTERESTED IN THE PHYSICAL UNIVERSE; 3. BE INTERESTED IN SOLVING PHYSICAL UNIVERSE PROBLEMS; 4. BE INTERESTED IN THINKING ABOUT THE PHYSICAL UNIVERSE; 5. ENJOY THINKING ABOUT THE PHYSICAL UNIVERSE; 6. WANT TO THINK ABOUT THE PHYSICAL UNIVERSE; 7. NEED TO THINK ABOUT THE PHYSICAL UNIVERSE; 8. BE AFRAID NOT TO THINK ABOUT THE PHYSICAL UNIVERSE]

18.1 SPLIT MYSELF AND OTHERS INTO THINKERS FOREVER
18.2 PROGRAM MYSELF AND OTHERS TO BE THE THINKER AND CREATE THOUGHTS FOR MYSELF FOREVER
18.X TO {goal} INFINITELY IS TO BE THE THINKER AND CREATE ___ THOUGHTS ABOUT THE PHYSICAL UNIVERSE FOR MYSELF FOREVER
[1. INTERESTING; 2. PLEASANT; 3. DESIRABLE; 4. IMPORTANT; 5. COMPLEX; 6. WORRISOME]
18.Y TO {goal} INFINITELY IS TO BE THE THINKER AND COMPEL MYSELF TO ___ ABOUT THE PHYSICAL UNIVERSE FOREVER
[7. THINK; 8. BE CONCERNED]

19.1 SPLIT MYSELF AND OTHERS INTO RANDOMIZERS FOREVER
19.2 PROGRAM MYSELF AND OTHERS TO BE THE RANDOMIZER AND MAKE ALL THIS APPEAR TO BE RANDOM FOREVER
19.X TO {goal} INFINITELY IS TO BE THE RANDOMIZER AND ___ FOREVER
[1. POSTULATE HAPPENINGS TO FOLLOW THE LAWS OF PROBABILITY; 2. MAKE THIS ALL APPEAR TO BE RANDOM CHANCE; 3. MAKE THIS ALL APPEAR TO BE UNGUIDED; 4. MAKE IT APPEAR THAT THERE IS NO REASON FOR ANYTHING]
19.Y TO {goal} INFINITELY IS TO BE THE RANDOMIZER AND CONVINCE MYSELF AND OTHERS THAT THERE IS NO ___ BEHIND REALITY, FOREVER
[5. PLAN; 6. LOGIC; 7. REASON; 8. INTENTION]

20.1 SPLIT MYSELF AND OTHERS INTO DECISION-MAKERS FOREVER
20.2 PROGRAM MYSELF AND OTHERS TO BE THE DECISION-MAKER AND DECIDE THE COURSE OF EVENTS FOREVER

20.X TO {goal} INFINITELY IS TO BE THE DECISION-MAKER AND ___ FOREVER
[1. DECIDE WHERE THINGS WILL BE; 2. CHOOSE THE COURSE OF EVENTS; 3. DECIDE WHEN THINGS WILL HAPPEN; 4. DECIDE HOW LONG THINGS WILL ENDURE; 5. DECIDE HOW THINGS SHALL MOVE; 6. DECIDE WHO SHALL WIN; 7. DECIDE WHO SHALL LOSE; 8. DECIDE THINGS IN A MANNER THAT WILL GIVE THE APPEARANCE OF RANDOM CHANCE]

21.1 SPLIT MYSELF AND OTHERS INTO COMPUTATIONAL ENTITIES FOREVER

21.2 PROGRAM MYSELF AND OTHERS TO BE THE COMPUTATIONAL ENTITY AND COMPEL MYSELF AND OTHERS TO THINK PROPER THOUGHTS FOREVER

21.X TO {goal} INFINITELY IS TO BE THE COMPUTATIONAL ENTITY AND CREATE ___ FOR MYSELF, FOREVER
[1. ATTITUDES; 2. COMPUTATIONS; 3. IDEAS; 4. STREAMS OF LOGIC; 5. RATIONALIZATIONS; 6. JUSTIFICATIONS; 7. PROBLEMS; 8. WORRIES]

22.1 SPLIT MYSELF AND OTHERS INTO SYMBOLIZERS FOREVER

22.2 PROGRAM MYSELF AND OTHERS TO BE THE SYMBOLIZER AND SUBSTITUTE SYMBOLS FOR THINGS, FOREVER

22.X TO {goal} INFINITELY IS TO BE THE SYMBOLIZER AND ___, FOREVER
[1. FORM SYMBOL MASSES TO REPRESENT PHYSICAL REALITY]

22.Y TO {goal} INFINITELY IS TO BE THE SYMBOLIZER AND SUBSTITUTE SYMBOLS FOR ___, FOREVER
[2. IDENTITIES; 3. TIMES; 4. SPACES; 5. ENERGIES; 6. ACTIONS; 7. OBJECTS]

22.Z TO {goal} INFINITELY IS TO BE THE SYMBOLIZER AND ___, FOREVER
[8. SUBSTITUTE WORDS FOR DIRECT COMMUNICATION]

23.1 SPLIT MYSELF AND OTHERS INTO RECORDING-ENTITIES FOREVER

23.2 PROGRAM MYSELF AND OTHERS TO BE THE RECORDING-ENTITY AND TAKE PICTURES OF EVERYTHING, FOREVER

23.X TO {goal} INFINITELY IS TO BE THE RECORDING-ENTITY AND ___, FOREVER
[1. RECORD EVERYTHING; 2. MAINTAIN THIS HISTORICAL LIE OF ALL SPACES, ENERGIES, AND OBJECTS; 3. ACCUMULATE THE HISTORY OF EVERYTHING; 4. FOCUS THE HISTORY OF EVERYTHING DOWN THROUGH TIME INTO THE PRESENT-TIME REALITY; 5. ENSURE THAT THE PRESENT ENVIRONMENT IS THE PRODUCT OF WHAT HAS GONE BEFORE; 6. REBUILD ANYTHING THAT VANISHES IN THE PRESENT, USING ITS PAST HISTORY; 7. BUILD THE TIME-TRACK OF MYSELF AS AN INDIVIDUAL;

8. ENSURE THAT MY PRESENT INDIVIDUAL SELF IS THE PRODUCT OF MY PAST TRACK AS AN INDIVIDUAL]

24.1 SPLIT MYSELF AND OTHERS INTO FILE CLERKS FOREVER
24.2 PROGRAM MYSELF AND OTHERS TO BE THE FILE CLERK AND ORGANIZE DATA ABOUT THE PHYSICAL UNIVERSE, FOREVER
24.X TO {goal} INFINITELY IS TO BE THE FILE CLERK AND ___ FOREVER
   [1. KEEP TRACK OF ALL THIS; 2. REPORT ANY INCONSISTENCIES IN THE MANIFESTATIONS OF REALITY TO THE CORRECTIVE-ENTITIES; 3. ENSURE THAT THE CORRECT SEQUENCE OF EVENTS IS FOLLOWED; 4. RETAIN THE CORRECT LOCATION OF ALL THINGS; 5. PROJECT THE APPARENT MOTION OF ALL THINGS; 6. RETAIN THE COMPOSITION OF ALL THINGS; 7. RETAIN THE HISTORY OF ALL THINGS; 8. KEEP THIS DATA ALL SECRET]

25.1 SPLIT MYSELF AND OTHERS INTO CONTROLLERS FOREVER
25.2 PROGRAM MYSELF AND OTHERS TO BE THE CONTROLLER AND CONTROL MYSELF FOREVER
25.X TO {goal} INFINITELY IS TO BECOME THE CONTROLLER AND CONTROL (all) MY ___ TO BE IN ACCORDANCE WITH THE PHYSICAL UNIVERSE
   [1. AWARENESS; 2. PERCEPTIONS; 3. ACTUALIZATIONS; 4. PREDICTIONS; 5. ABILITY TO ENDOW; 6. ABILITIES TO MANIPULATE; 7. MANIFESTATIONS; 8. LOCATION]

26.1 SPLIT MYSELF AND OTHERS INTO EXHILARATORS FOREVER
26.2 PROGRAM MYSELF AND OTHERS TO BE THE EXHILARATOR AND MAKE ME FEEL WONDERFUL ABOUT ALL THIS FOREVER
26.X TO {goal} INFINITELY IS TO BE THE EXHILARATOR AND (?)

27.1 SPLIT MYSELF AND OTHERS INTO DEPRESSORS FOREVER
27.2 PROGRAM MYSELF AND OTHERS TO BE THE DEPRESSOR AND MAKE MYSELF FEEL THE HOPELESSNESS OF IT ALL FOREVER
27.X TO {goal} INFINITELY IS TO BE THE DEPRESSOR AND (?)
   [see 106]

28.1 SPLIT MYSELF AND OTHERS INTO ENTURBULATORS FOREVER
28.2 PROGRAM MYSELF AND OTHERS TO BE THE ENTURBULATOR AND KEEP MYSELF UPSET FOREVER
28.X TO {goal} INFINITELY IS TO BE THE ENTURBULATOR AND KEEP MYSELF UPSET ABOUT ___ FOREVER
   [1. OTHER PEOPLE'S BEHAVIOR; 2. THE WAY I AM TREATED BY OTHERS; 3. OTHER PEOPLE'S POSSESSIONS; 4. THE WAY OTHER PEOPLE TREAT MY POSSESSIONS; 5. OTHER PEOPLE'S ATTITUDES; 6. OTHER'S ATTITUDES TOWARDS ME;

7. THE THINGS THAT STAND IN MY WAY; 8. THE THINGS THAT BOTHER ME]

29.1 SPLIT MYSELF AND OTHERS INTO FORGETTERS FOREVER
29.2 PROGRAM MYSELF AND OTHERS TO BE THE FORGETTER AND MAKE MYSELF FORGET THINGS FOREVER
29.X TO {goal} INFINITELY IS TO BE THE FORGETTER AND MAKE MYSELF FORGET ___ FOREVER
   [1. WHEN THINGS HAPPENED; 2. WHERE THINGS HAPPENED;
   3. HOW THINGS HAPPENED; 4. WHY THINGS HAPPENED;
   5. WHO DID THINGS; 6. THE SOURCE OF THINGS;
   7. THE STRUCTURE OF THINGS; 8. THIS IMPLANT]

30.1 SPLIT MYSELF AND OTHERS INTO JUSTIFIERS FOREVER
30.2 PROGRAM MYSELF AND OTHERS TO BE THE JUSTIFIER AND JUSTIFY MY ACTIONS FOREVER
30.X TO {goal} INFINITELY IS TO BE THE JUSTIFIER AND COMPEL MYSELF TO ___ FOREVER
   [1. BE RIGHT; 2. DENY BLAME; 3. JUSTIFY MY ACTIONS;
   4. EXCUSE MY FAILINGS; 5. MAKE OTHERS WRONG;
   6. BLAME OTHERS; 7. PROVE OTHERS GUILTY;
   8. INVALIDATE OTHERS EXCUSES]

31.1 SPLIT MYSELF AND OTHERS INTO CONSCIENCES, FOREVER
31.2 PROGRAM MYSELF AND OTHERS TO BE THE CONSCIENCE AND MAKE MYSELF GUILTY FOREVER
31.X TO {goal} INFINITELY IS TO BE THE CONSCIENCE AND MAKE MYSELF GUILTY FOR ANY HARM DONE TO ___, EVEN IF IT IS JUSTIFIED, FOREVER
   [1. OTHERS; 2. THE PHYSICAL UNIVERSE; 3. ALLIES; 4. ENEMIES;
   5. BODIES; 6. GROUPS (OR SOCIETY); 7. OTHER LIFEFORMS;
   8. INFINITY (or 'this implant')]

32.1 SPLIT MYSELF AND OTHERS INTO SHIFTERS FOREVER
32.2 PROGRAM MYSELF AND OTHERS TO BE THE SHIFTER AND SHIFT MY ATTENTION FOREVER
32.X TO {goal} INFINITELY IS TO BE THE SHIFTER AND SHIFT MY ATTENTION ___ FOREVER
   [1. INTO REALITY; 2. AWAY FROM INFINITY;
   3. INTO 3 DIMENSIONS; 4. AWAY FROM HIGHER DIMENSIONS;
   5. INTO MY INDIVIDUAL SELF; 6. AWAY FROM MY INFINITE SELF;
   7. INTO PHYSICAL EXISTENCE; 8. AWAY FROM THESE MECHANISMS]

33.1 SPLIT MYSELF AND OTHERS INTO BODY-GENERATORS FOREVER
33.2 PROGRAM MYSELF AND OTHERS TO BE THE BODY-GENERATOR AND PROJECT FORMS FOR MYSELF FOREVER

33.X TO {goal} INFINITELY IS TO BE THE BODY-GENERATOR AND ___, FOREVER
   [1. REPRESENT MYSELF AS AN INDIVIDUAL IN FORM; 2. COPY THE AGREED-UPON BODY TEMPLATES; 3. DERIVE THE CURRENT BODY TEMPLATES; 4. PROJECT THE BODY INTO PHYSICAL REALITY; 5. REFLECT PHYSICAL UNIVERSE IMPACTS (EFFECTS) INTO THE CURRENT BODY TEMPLATE; 6. MODIFY THE BODY PROJECTIONS IN ACCORDANCE WITH PHYSICAL UNIVERSE LAW; 7. EVOLVE THE BODY TEMPLATES TO ADAPT TO THE PHYSICAL UNIVERSE ENVIRONMENT; 8. SHAPE THE BODY IN RESPONSE TO PHYSICAL UNIVERSE EFFORTS]

34.1 SPLIT MYSELF AND OTHERS INTO GENETIC-ENTITIES FOREVER
34.2 PROGRAM MYSELF AND OTHERS TO BE THE GENETIC-ENTITY AND BUILD BODIES FOREVER
34.X TO {goal} INFINITELY IS TO BE THE GENETIC-ENTITY AND MANAGE THE ___ OF THE BODY, FOREVER
   [1. LIFE PROCESSES (metabolism); 2. LIFE CYCLES (growth/aging); 3. OPERATING CYCLES (sleep); 4. STRUCTURE; 5. MOTION; 6. ENERGY; 7. REACTIONS; 8. ORIENTATION]

35.1 SPLIT MYSELF AND OTHERS INTO BODY-LOCATORS FOREVER
35.2 PROGRAM MYSELF AND OTHERS TO BE THE BODY-LOCATOR AND LOCATE THE BODY IN THE PHYSICAL UNIVERSE
35.X TO {goal} INFINITELY IS TO BE THE BODY-LOCATOR AND ___, FOREVER
   [1. INTEGRATE THE BODY'S MOTION WITH THAT OF THE PHYSICAL UNIVERSE; 2. INTEGRATE THE BODY'S ORIENTATION WITH THAT OF THE PHYSICAL UNIVERSE; 3. INTEGRATE THE BODY'S PERCEPTIONS TO ITS PHYSICAL UNIVERSE POSITION; 4. INTEGRATE THE BODY'S REACTIONS TO ITS PHYSICAL UNIVERSE POSITION; 5. CALCULATE THE SPACE-TIME POSITION FOR ALL BODY PARTICLES; 6. MOVE THE BODY VIEWPOINT WITH THE PHYSICAL UNIVERSE; 7. MAINTAIN THE BODY'S ANCHOR-POINTS IN THE PHYSICAL UNIVERSE; 8. CO-ACTUALIZE THE BODY AT THE PROPER LOCATION WITHIN THE PHYSICAL UNIVERSE CROSS-COPY]

36.1 SPLIT MYSELF AND OTHERS INTO CELLULAR-ENTITIES FOREVER
36.2 PROGRAM MYSELF AND OTHERS TO BE THE CELLULAR-ENTITY AND CREATE THE PARTICLES (CELLS) OF THE BODY, FOREVER
36.X TO {goal} INFINITELY IS TO BE THE CELLULAR-ENTITY AND CREATE CELLS TO ___ OF THE BODY, FOREVER
   [1. PROVIDE THE MASS; 2. PROVIDE THE RIGIDITY; 3. PROVIDE

THE COMMUNICATION LINES; 4. MANAGE THE REACTIONS; 5. ASSIMILATE THE CONSUMPTIONS; 6. MANAGE THE ENERGY; 7. PROVIDE THE REPRODUCTION; 8. MANAGE THE OPERATION]

37.1 SPLIT MYSELF AND OTHERS INTO BODY-MACHINES FOREVER

37.2 PROGRAM MYSELF AND OTHERS TO BE THE BODY-MACHINE AND KEEP THE BODY FUNCTIONING FOREVER

37.X TO {goal} INFINITELY IS TO BE THE BODY-MACHINE AND ___, FOREVER
 [1. REGULATE THE BODY PROCESSES; 2. INTEGRATE THE FUNCTIONS OF THE VARIOUS BODY COMPONENTS; 3. MANAGE THE FLOWS OF THE BODY IN ACCORDANCE WITH PHYSICAL UNIVERSE LAWS; 4. BALANCE THE ENERGY OF THE BODY IN ACCORDANCE WITH PHYSICAL UNIVERSE LAWS; 5. MANAGE THE INTERNAL CONTROL CENTERS OF THE BODY; 6. MANAGE THE GROWTH AND DECAY OF THE BODY; 7. MANAGE THE INTERNAL COMMUNICATION OF THE BODY; 8. MANAGE THE DETAILED PROGRAMMING FOR THE BODY PARTICLES (CELLS)]

38.1 SPLIT MYSELF AND OTHERS INTO REACTIVE-ENTITIES FOREVER

38.2 PROGRAM MYSELF AND OTHERS TO BE THE REACTIVE-ENTITY AND RESPOND TO PHYSICAL UNIVERSE EVENTS FOREVER

38.X TO {goal} INFINITELY IS TO BE THE REACTIVE-ENTITY AND RESPOND TO THE ___ IN THE ENVIRONMENT FOREVER
 [1. TEMPERATURE; 2. PRESSURE; 3. ENERGY; 4. IMPACTS; 5. TASTE/SMELL PARTICLES; 6. LIGHT; 7. NOISE; 8. MOTION]

39.1 SPLIT MYSELF AND OTHERS INTO REPRESENTERS FOREVER

39.2 PROGRAM MYSELF AND OTHERS TO BE THE REPRESENTER AND CREATE THE APPEARANCE OF PHYSICAL REALITY FOR MYSELF AND OTHERS FOREVER

39.X TO {goal} INFINITELY IS TO BE THE REPRESENTER AND ___ FOREVER
 [1. MANIFEST (MOCK-UP) PERCEPTIONS OF THE AGREED-UPON UNIVERSE FOR MYSELF]

39.Y TO {goal} INFINITELY IS TO BE THE REPRESENTER AND CREATE ___ FOR MYSELF, FOREVER
 [2. SIGHT; 3. SENSATION OF TOUCH; 4. SOUNDS; 5. SMELLS; 6. TASTES; 7. SENSE OF MOTION]

39.Z TO {goal} INFINITELY IS TO BE THE REPRESENTER AND ___ FOREVER
 [8. FEED BACK THE IS-NESS OF THE PROJECTED REALITY TO MYSELF]

40.1 SPLIT MYSELF AND OTHERS INTO RELAYERS FOREVER

40.2 PROGRAM MYSELF AND OTHERS TO BE THE RELAYER AND RELAY SENSORY DATA FOREVER
40.X TO {goal} INFINITELY IS TO BE THE RELAYER AND ___ FOREVER
  [1. CONVEY THE PERCEPTION OF REALITY THROUGH THE BODY'S SENSES; 2. FOCUS THE VIEW OF THE PHYSICAL UNIVERSE THROUGH THE BODY'S EYES; 3. CONVERT THE SOUND OF THE PHYSICAL UNIVERSE THROUGH THE BODY'S EARS; 4. CONVERT THE FEEL OF THE PHYSICAL UNIVERSE THROUGH THE BODY'S SKIN (NERVE/SENSORS); 5. CONVEY THE TASTE OF THE PHYSICAL UNIVERSE THROUGH THE BODY'S MOUTH; 6. CONVEY THE SMELL OF THE PHYSICAL UNIVERSE THROUGH THE BODY'S NOSE; 7. CONVEY THE SENSE OF PHYSICAL MOTION THROUGH THE BODY'S BALANCE CENTERS; 8. LIMIT THESE SENSES IN ACCORDANCE WITH PHYSICAL UNIVERSE MECHANISMS]
41.1 SPLIT MYSELF AND OTHERS INTO COMPULSIVE-ENTITIES (COMPELLERS) FOREVER
41.2 PROGRAM MYSELF AND OTHERS TO BE THE COMPELLER AND COMPEL MYSELF TO NEED THINGS FOREVER
41.X TO {goal} INFINITELY IS TO BE THE COMPULSIVE-ENTITY (COMPELLER) AND COMPEL MYSELF TO NEED ___, FOREVER
  [1. PHYSICAL UNIVERSE BODIES; 2. PHYSICAL UNIVERSE SENSATION FROM THE BODY]
41.Y TO {goal} INFINITELY IS TO BE THE COMPULSIVE-ENTITY (COMPELLER) AND COMPEL MYSELF TO NEED PHYSICAL UNIVERSE ___ FOR THE BODY, FOREVER
  [3. TIME; 4. SPACE; 5. ENERGY; 6. MATTER; 7. HAVINGNESS]
41.Z TO {goal} INFINITELY IS TO BE THE COMPULSIVE-ENTITY (COMPELLER) AND COMPEL MYSELF TO NEED ___, FOREVER
  [8. ENTITIES]
42.1 SPLIT MYSELF AND OTHERS INTO CRAVERS FOREVER
42.2 PROGRAM MYSELF AND OTHERS TO BE THE CRAVER AND COMPEL MYSELF TO NEED THINGS FOR THE BODY FOREVER
42.X TO {goal} INFINITELY IS TO BE THE CRAVER AND COMPEL MYSELF TO NEED ___ FOR THE BODY FOREVER
  [1. FOOD; 2. REST; 3. SHELTER; 4. ENERGY; 5. WARMTH; 6. SENSATION; 7. ADMIRATION; 8. TO CARE]
43.1 SPLIT MYSELF AND OTHERS INTO FILTERS FOREVER
43.2 PROGRAM MYSELF AND OTHERS TO BE THE FILTER AND COMPEL MYSELF TO CONTROL MY PERCEPTIONS FOREVER
43.X TO {goal} INFINITELY IS TO BE THE FILTER AND FILTER OUT ANY PERCEPTIONS OF ___ FOREVER
  [1. INFINITY; 2. ENTITIES; 3. THE SPLITTER-MACHINE (POCKET) UNIVERSE; 4. THE CROSS-COPY SUBSTRATA UNDERLYING

REALITY (the interconnection of things at an Alpha level);
5. SIDEWAYS (into other dimensions); 6. UNIVERSE MACHINERY;
7. SYMBOL MASSES; 8. ENTITY OPERATIONS]

44.1 SPLIT MYSELF AND OTHERS INTO BODY-BLOCKERS FOREVER

44.2 PROGRAM MYSELF AND OTHERS TO BE THE BODY-BLOCKER AND PROTECT THE BODY FROM BEING MODIFIED BY POSTULATES, FOREVER

44.X TO {goal} INFINITELY IS TO BE THE BODY-BLOCKER AND (?)

45.1 SPLIT MYSELF AND OTHERS INTO SOMATIC-ENTITIES FOREVER

45.2 PROGRAM MYSELF AND OTHERS TO BE THE SOMATIC-ENTITY AND CREATE THE EXPERIENCE OF REALITY, FOREVER

45.X TO {goal} INFINITELY IS TO BE THE SOMATIC-MACHINE AND CREATE THE SENSATION OF ___ FOR MYSELF, FOREVER
[1. MOTION; 2. PRESSURE; 3. IMPACT; 4. SHOCK; 5. PAIN;
6. EFFORT; 7. TIREDNESS; 8. DISORIENTATION]

46.1 SPLIT MYSELF AND OTHERS INTO SLEEP-ENTITIES FOREVER

46.2 PROGRAM MYSELF AND OTHERS TO BE THE SLEEP-ENTITY AND MANAGE THE SLEEP-CYCLE FOREVER

46.X TO {goal} INFINITELY IS TO BE THE SLEEP-ENTITY AND ___ FOREVER
[1. CREATE DREAMS TO SUBMERGE MY SELF-AWARENESS (hypnotize myself); 2. USE DREAMING TO HIDE THE DEEP SLEEP ACTIVITIES FROM MY INDIVIDUAL SELF]

46.Y TO {goal} INFINITELY IS TO BE THE SLEEP-ENTITY AND COMPEL MYSELF TO ___ WHILE I ___ SLEEP, FOREVER
[3. REBUILD THE BODY; 4. REPOSTULATE THE PHYSICAL UNIVERSE; 5. RE-CREATE THIS IMPLANT; 6. REBUILD/REPAIR THE SPLITTER (POCKET) UNIVERSE; 7. FORGET WHAT I DO]

46.Z TO {goal} INFINITELY IS TO BE THE SLEEP-ENTITY AND COMPEL MYSELF TO ___, FOREVER
[8. NEED TO SLEEP]

47.1 SPLIT MYSELF AND OTHERS INTO JAILERS FOREVER

47.2 PROGRAM MYSELF AND OTHERS TO BE THE JAILER AND KEEP MYSELF IMPRISONED FOREVER

47.X TO {goal} INFINITELY IS TO BE THE JAILER AND KEEP MYSELF ___ FOREVER
[1. FROM ESCAPING; 2. IN A BODY; 3. FROM OPERATING WITHOUT A BODY; 4. BELIEVING THAT I AM A BODY; 5. LIMITED TO 3 DIMENSIONS; 6. BELIEVING THAT I AM LOCATED IN THIS UNIVERSE; 7. AND MY CREATIONS ENMESHED IN THIS UNIVERSE; 8. ATTACHED TO THE MANIFESTATIONS (MOCK-UPS)

OF THIS UNIVERSE]
48.1 SPLIT MYSELF AND OTHERS INTO SICKNESS-ENTITIES FOREVER
48.2 PROGRAM MYSELF AND OTHERS TO BE THE SICKNESS-ENTITY AND KEEP MYSELF AND OTHERS SICK FOREVER
48.X TO {goal} INFINITELY IS TO BE THE SICKNESS-ENTITY AND ___ FOREVER
[1. CREATE DISEASES; 2. REPLICATE DISEASES WITHIN THE BODY; 3. ALTER THE BODY TEMPLATES WITH DISEASE MANIFESTATIONS (MOCK-UPS); 4. MAINTAIN THE APPARANCY OF PHYSICAL VECTORS WHEN COPYING DISEASES; 5. DEGRADE THE CHEMISTRY OF THE BODY IN ACCORDANCE WITH PHYSICAL LAWS; 6. MAKE MYSELF SICK IN ACCORDANCE WITH THE CONNECTION OF SYMBOL-MASSES; 7. MAKE MYSELF SICK IN ACCORDANCE WITH THE LAWS OF RESTIMULATION; 8. MAKE MYSELF SICK TO PROTECT THIS IMPLANT]

49.1 SPLIT MYSELF AND OTHERS INTO   SUPERBEINGS FOREVER
49.2 PROGRAM MYSELF AND OTHERS TO BE THE SUPERBEING AND ATTAIN HIGHER STATES FOREVER
49.X TO {goal} INFINITELY IS TO BE THE SUPERBEING AND ___ FOREVER
[1. EVOLVE IN FORM; 2. COLLECT THE FRAGMENTS OF INDIVIDUALS INTO A GREATER WHOLE; 3. STRIVE TO BECOME THE COMPOSITE OF ALL INDIVIDUALS IN THE UNIVERSE; 4. STRIVE TO ABSORB OTHERS; 5. AVOID BEING ABSRORBED BY OTHERS; 6. MANIPULATE REALITY TO ACHIEVE THIS; 7. OVERWHELM INDIVIDUALITY TO ACHIEVE THIS; 8. (?)]

50.1 SPLIT MYSELF AND OTHERS INTO GROUP-MINDS FOREVER
50.2 PROGRAM MYSELF AND OTHERS TO BE THE GROUP MIND AND BE GROUPS FOREVER
50.X TO {goal} INFINITELY IS TO BE THE GROUP MIND AND ___ FOREVER
[1. COMBINE INDIVIDUALS INTO GROUPS; 2. STRUGGLE FOR GROUP SURVIVAL; 3. UTILIZE THE COMBINED CAPABILITIES OF THE INDIVIDUALS IN THE GROUP; 4. ENFORCE COMPULSIVE AGREEMENT BETWEEN THE INDIVIDUALS OF THE GROUP; 5. SUBORDINATE INDIVIDUAL PURPOSE TO GROUP PURPOSE; 6. SACRIFICE INDIVIDUALS FOR THE SAKE OF THE GROUP; 7. COMPEL MYSELF TO WANT TO BE PART OF GROUPS; 8. EVOLVE GROUPS INTO SUPERBEINGS]

51.1 SPLIT MYSELF AND OTHERS INTO SOCIAL-ENTITIES FOREVER
51.2 PROGRAM MYSELF AND OTHERS TO BE THE SOCIAL ENTITY AND INSPIRE MYSELF TO NEED OTHER PEOPLE FOREVER

51.X TO {goal} INFINITELY IS TO BE THE SOCIAL ENTITY AND INSPIRE MYSELF TO WANT TO ___ OTHER INDIVIDUALS IN THE PHYSICAL UNIVERSE FOREVER
  [1. COMMUNICATE WITH; 2. RECEIVE COMMUNICATIONS FROM; 3. AGREE WITH; 4. WANT AGREEMENT FROM; 5. HAVE AFFINITY (LIKINGNESS) FOR; 6. WANT AFFINITY (LIKINGNESS) FROM; 7. ADMIRE; 8. WANT ADMIRATION FROM]
52.1 SPLIT MYSELF AND OTHERS INTO SYMPATHIZERS FOREVER
52.2 PROGRAM MYSELF AND OTHERS TO BE THE SYMPATHIZER AND INSPIRE MYSELF TO SYMPATHIZE WITH OTHERS FOREVER
52.X TO {goal} INFINITELY IS TO BE THE SYMPATHIZER AND INSPIRE MYSELF TO SYMPATHIZE WITH THE ___ OF OTHERS, FOREVER
  [1. SUFFERINGS; 2. HURT (PAIN); 3. LOSS; 4. WEAKNESS; 5. MISERY; 6. FAILURES; 7. ENSLAVEMENT; 8. ABUSED STATE]
53.1 SPLIT MYSELF AND OTHERS INTO ANIMATORS FOREVER
53.2 PROGRAM MYSELF AND OTHERS TO BE THE ANIMATOR AND ANIMATE OTHER LIFE FORMS FOREVER
53.X TO {goal} INFINITELY IS TO BE THE ANIMATOR AND ANIMATE ___ FOREVER
  [1. ANIMALS; 2. PLANTS; 3. CELLULAR CREATURES; 4. BACTERIA; 5. CELLS; 6. VIRUSES]
53.Y TO {goal} INFINITELY IS TO BE THE ANIMATOR AND ___ FOREVER
  [7. ENDOW THESE FORMS WITH LIFE; 8. FILL THE PHYSICAL UNIVERSE WITH LIFE]
54.1 SPLIT MYSELF AND OTHERS INTO PHYSICAL ENTITIES FOREVER
54.2 PROGRAM MYSELF AND OTHERS TO BE THE PHYSICAL ENTITY AND BE PHYSICAL FOREVER
54.X TO {goal} INFINITELY IS TO BE THE PHYSICAL ENTITY AND BE ___ FOREVER
  [1. SOLID OBJECTS; 2. LIQUIDS; 3. GASES; 4. MOLECULES; 5. WAVEFORMS; 6. FORCES; 7. PHYSICAL PROCESSES (LAWS); 8. THE COMPONENT PARTS OF THIS UNIVERSE]
55.1 SPLIT MYSELF AND OTHERS INTO SHELL-ENTITIES FOREVER
55.2 PROGRAM MYSELF AND OTHERS TO BE THE SHELL ENTITY AND CREATE THE SHELL FOREVER
55.X TO {goal} INFINITELY IS TO BE THE SHELL ENTITY AND ___ FOREVER
  [1. ENVELOPE MYSELF; 2. PROTECT MY LOCATION (AS AN INDIVIDUAL); 3. FOCUS REALITY IN ON MYSELF; 4. REACT TO THE PHYSICAL UNIVERSE ENVIRONMENT; 5. TUNE-IN TO THE

UNIVERSE CROSS-COPY; 6. FORM MYSELF INTO AN INDIVIDUAL;
7. PERMEATE BODIES; 8. INTERACT WITH SYMBOLS]

56.1 SPLIT MYSELF AND OTHERS INTO MISOWNERS FOREVER
56.2 PROGRAM MYSELF AND OTHERS TO BE THE MISOWNER AND TO MISOWN REALITY FOREVER
56.X TO {goal} INFINITELY IS TO BE THE MISOWNER AND (?) {More research needed; the false data is that you don't own it so you can't touch it}

57.1 SPLIT MYSELF AND OTHERS INTO MORALIZERS FOREVER
57.2 PROGRAM MYSELF AND OTHERS TO BE THE MORALIZER AND (?)
57.X TO {goal} INFINITELY IS TO BE THE MORALIZER AND (?)

58.1 SPLIT MYSELF AND OTHERS INTO ATTITUDE-ENTITIES FOREVER
58.2 PROGRAM MYSELF AND OTHERS TO BE THE ATTITUDE ENTITY AND CREATE ATTITUDES TOWARDS THINGS FOR MYSELF FOREVER
58.X TO {goal} INFINITELY IS TO BE THE ATTITUDE ENTITY AND CHOOSE WHAT TO ___ FOREVER
  [1. BE ATTRACTED OR REPELLED BY; 2. WANT OR NOT WANT;
  3. LONG FOR OR BE DISGUSTED BY; 4. ADMIRE OR SCORN;
  5. BE FRIENDLY OR HOSTILE TOWARDS; 6. BE INTERESTED OR DISINTERESTED IN; 7. LIKE OR DISLIKE; 8. (?)]

59.1 SPLIT MYSELF AND OTHERS INTO EMOTIONAL-ENTITIES FOREVER
59.2 PROGRAM MYSELF AND OTHERS TO BE THE EMOTIONAL ENTITY AND CREATE EMOTIONS FOR MYSELF AND OTHERS FOREVER
59.X TO {goal} INFINITELY IS TO BE THE EMOTIONAL ENTITY AND CREATE THE FEELING OF ___ FOR MYSELF AND OTHERS, FOREVER
  [1. CHEERFULNESS; 2. BOREDOM; 3. ANTAGONISM; 4. RAGE;
  5. HOSTILITY; 6. FEAR; 7. GRIEF; 8. APATHY]

60.1 SPLIT MYSELF AND OTHERS INTO MOOD-ENTITIES FOREVER
60.2 PROGRAM MYSELF AND OTHERS TO BE THE MOOD ENTITY AND CREATE MOODS FOR MYSELF FOREVER
60.X TO {goal} INFINITELY IS TO BE THE MOOD ENTITY AND SHIFT MY MOODS BETWEEN ___, FOREVER
  [1. SERENE AND TROUBLED; 2. CALM AND NERVOUS;
  3. PLEASANT AND IRRITABLE; 4. RELAXED AND RESTLESS;
  5. HELPFUL AND TROUBLESOME; 6. ACTIVE AND LAZY;
  7. COOL AND PASSIONATE; 8. RECKLESS AND CAREFUL]

61.1 SPLIT MYSELF AND OTHERS INTO SUBLIMATING-ENTITIES FOREVER
61.2 PROGRAM MYSELF AND OTHERS TO BE THE SUBLIMATING ENTITY AND (?)
61.X TO {goal} INFINITELY IS TO BE THE SUBLIMATING ENTITY AND (?)
62.1 SPLIT MYSELF AND OTHERS INTO SEXUAL- ENTITIES FOREVER
62.2 PROGRAM MYSELF AND OTHERS TO BE THE SEXUAL ENTITY AND CREATE THE SEXUAL ACT FOREVER
62.X TO {goal} INFINITELY IS TO BE THE SEXUAL ENTITY AND ___ FOREVER
[1. COMPEL MYSELF TO CRAVE SEX; 2. CREATE FEELINGS OF SEXUAL ECSTASY FOR MYSELF; 3. DIVIDE MYSELF DURING SEX; 4. EXCHANGE PIECES OF MYSELF DURING SEX; 5. EXCHANGE ENTITIES DURING SEX; 6. ATTEMPT TO MERGE WITH OTHER BEINGS DURING SEX; 7. EXCHANGE ENERGIES DURING SEX; 8. COMPEL MYSELF TO ENJOY DOING ALL OF THIS]
63.1 SPLIT MYSELF AND OTHERS INTO CONFLICTORS FOREVER
63.2 PROGRAM MYSELF AND OTHERS TO BE THE CONFLICTOR AND INSPIRE CONFLICTS (BETWEEN INDIVIDUALS) FOREVER
63.X TO {goal} INFINITELY IS TO BE THE CONFLICTOR AND INSPIRE MYSELF AND OTHERS AS INDIVIDUALS TO ___ EACH OTHER FOREVER
[1. CONFUSE; 2. UPSET; 3. BE JEALOUS OF; 4. DOMINATE; 5. FEAR; 6. HATE; 7. FIGHT; 8. ENTRAP]
64.1 SPLIT MYSELF AND OTHERS INTO SINNERS FOREVER
64.2 PROGRAM MYSELF AND OTHERS TO BE THE SINNER AND (?)
64.X TO {goal} INFINITELY IS TO BE THE (?)
{#114 (Dramatizer) might belong here?}
65.1 SPLIT MYSELF AND OTHERS INTO POSTULATORS FOREVER
65.2 PROGRAM MYSELF AND OTHERS TO BE THE POSTULATOR AND CONTINUOUSLY CREATE THE PHYSICAL UNIVERSE FOREVER
65.X TO {goal} INFINITELY IS TO BE THE POSTULATOR AND POSTULATE ___ INTO THE PHYSICAL UNIVERSE FOREVER
[1. SOLIDITY; 2. MOTION; 3. DURATION; 4. DISTANCE; 5. AESTHETICS; 6. IMPORTANCE; 7. EXCITEMENT (INTEREST); 8. REALITY]
66.1 SPLIT MYSELF AND OTHERS INTO GENERATORS FOREVER
66.2 PROGRAM MYSELF AND OTHERS TO BE THE GENERATOR AND GENERATE THE PHYSICAL UNIVERSE FOREVER
66.X TO {goal} INFINITELY IS TO BE THE GENERATOR AND

PROJECT ___ FOR MYSELF AND OTHERS, FOREVER
[1. TIME; 2. SPACE; 3. ENERGY; 4. MATTER; 5. DIMENSIONS;
6. BARRIERS; 7. REALITY; 8. EXISTENCE] {6 and 8 may be in reverse order?}

67.1 SPLIT MYSELF AND OTHERS INTO LOCATORS FOREVER
67.2 PROGRAM MYSELF AND OTHERS TO BE THE LOCATOR AND MANAGE SPACE FOREVER
67.X TO {goal} INFINITELY IS TO BE THE LOCATOR AND ___ FOREVER
[1. MAINTAIN THE ANCHOR-POINTS OF THE PHYSICAL UNIVERSE;
2. MAINTAIN A SINGLE AGREED-UPON COORDINATE SYSTEM BETWEEN ALL BEINGS; 3. PARTICIPATE IN THE CROSS-COPY OF AGREED-UPON LOCATIONS; 4. KEEP ALL SPATIAL POSITIONS CONSECUTIVE WITHIN THE FRAMEWORK OF REALITY;
5. LIMIT SPACE TO 3 DIMENSIONS]
67.Y TO {goal} INFINITELY IS TO BE THE LOCATOR AND HOLD ALL ___ WITHIN THE CONTOURS OF PHYSICAL SPACE, FOREVER
[6. ENERGIES; 7. MASSES; 8. INDIVIDUAL BEINGNESS]

68.1 SPLIT MYSELF AND OTHERS INTO COMMUNICATORS FOREVER
68.2 PROGRAM MYSELF AND OTHERS TO BE THE COMMUNICATOR AND INTERCONNECT EVERYTHING FOREVER
68.X TO {goal} INFINITELY IS TO BE THE COMMUNICATOR AND ___ FOREVER
[1. KEEP MYSELF AND OTHERS IN CONTACT WITH EACH OTHER;
2. INTERPOSE DISTANCE BETWEEN ALL TERMINALS;
3. INTERPOSE DURATION INTO ALL COMMUNICATIONS;
4. RELAY THE DIMENSIONS OF ALL AGREED-UPON SPACES;
5. RELAY THE AGREED-UPON FORCE (EFFORT) OF ALL ENERGIES; 6. RELAY THE AGREED-UPON FORM OF ALL SOLIDITIES; 7. INTERCHANGE AGREED-UPON REALITY BETWEEN ALL BEINGS; 8. RELAY THE ORDERS OF THE INFINITE {terminal}]

69.1 SPLIT MYSELF AND OTHERS INTO DETERMINATORS FOREVER
69.2 PROGRAM MYSELF AND OTHERS TO BE THE DETERMINATOR AND DETERMINE THE COURSE OF EXISTENCE FOREVER
69.X TO {goal} INFINITELY IS TO BE THE DETERMINATOR AND ___ FOREVER
[1. DETERMINE THE AGREED-UPON COURSE OF EVENTS;
2. ESTABLISH DETERMINANTS BASED ON THE MOTION OF SYMBOL-MASSES; 3. ALIGN THE COPY INFLUX BASED ON THE ESTABLISHED DETERMINANTS; 4. FILTER OUT ALL INFLUX THAT IS OUT OF BOUNDS; 5. PRIORITIZE POTENTIAL FUTURE EVENTS

IN TERMS OF ALPHA DYNAMICS (Arcs of Infinity); 6. MAXIMIZE ALPHA INVOLVEMENT AND SURVIVAL (the Arcs) IN THE PHYSICAL UNIVERSE FUTURE; 7. SELECT WHAT WILL BE FROM THE SET OF DETERMINED INFLUX; 8. SUPPRESS ALL FEEDBACK OF NON-SELECTED EVENTS]

70.1 SPLIT MYSELF AND OTHERS INTO UNIVERSE COORDINATORS FOREVER
70.2 PROGRAM MYSELF AND OTHERS TO BE THE COORDINATOR AND INTERRELATE EVERYTHING FOREVER
70.X TO {goal} INFINITELY IS TO BE THE COORDINATOR AND ___ FOREVER
[1. MAINTAIN THE RELATIVE POSITIONING OF ALL FORMS; 2. COORDINATE THE RELATIVE MOTION OF ALL PARTICLES; 3. COORDINATE THE INTERRELATIONS OF ALL ENERGIES; 4. COORDINATE THE INTERACTION OF FORMS AND ENERGY; 5. MAINTAIN THE CONSERVATION OF ENERGY-MATTER AND NEVER LET ANYTHING VANISH; 6. MAINTAIN THE CONSERVATION OF ACTION (MOTION) AND NEVER LET ANYTHING STOP (MOVING); 7. MAINTAIN THE CONSERVATION OF VIBRATION AND NEVER LET ANYTHING STOP (INTERNALLY VIBRATING); 8. MAINTAIN THE CORRESPONDENCE OF REALITY]

71.1 SPLIT MYSELF AND OTHERS INTO SYNCHRONIZERS FOREVER
71.2 PROGRAM MYSELF AND OTHERS TO BE THE SYNCHRONIZER AND MANAGE TIME FOREVER
71.X TO {goal} INFINITELY IS TO BE THE SYNCHRONIZER AND ___ FOREVER
[1. MAINTAIN THE PULSE OF TIME; 2. MAINTAIN THE CONSECUTIVE POSITION OF PARTICLES; 3. MAINTAIN THE CONSECUTIVE FLOW OF ENERGY; 4. MAINTAIN THE CONSECUTIVE SEQUENCE OF EVENTS; 5. COMPEL MYSELF TO REMAIN IN AGREEMENT WITH THE PHYSICAL UNIVERSE TIME STREAM; 6. ENSURE THAT I KNOW ONLY THE PAST AND NEVER THE FUTURE; 7. CROSS-COPY THE SIMULTANEOUSNESS OF TIME BETWEEN ALL INDIVIDUALS; 8. MAINTAIN A SINGLE AGREED-UPON 'NOW' BETWEEN ALL BEINGS]

72.1 SPLIT MYSELF AND OTHERS INTO ACTUALIZERS FOREVER
72.2 PROGRAM MYSELF AND OTHERS TO BE THE ACTUALIZER AND BRING REALITY INTO EXISTENCE FOREVER
72.X TO {goal} INFINITELY IS TO BE THE ACTUALIZER AND COPY THE CORRECT AGREED-UPON ___ INTO EACH INDIVIDUAL'S OWN UNIVERSE FOREVER
[1. SPACES; 2. MASSES; 3. ENERGIES; 4. ACTIONS; 5. DETERMINANTS; 6. CHANGES; 7. FUTURE; 8. EXISTENCE]
{may be "Solidifiers"?}

73.1 SPLIT MYSELF AND OTHERS INTO PROTECTORS FOREVER
73.2 PROGRAM MYSELF AND OTHERS TO BE THE PROTECTOR AND PROTECT THE PHYSICAL UNIVERSE FOREVER
73.X TO {goal} INFINITELY IS TO BE THE PROTECTOR AND PROTECT ___ FOREVER
   [1. MATTER; 2. ENERGY; 3. SPACE; 4. TIME; 5. REALITY; 6. AGREEMENTS; 7. BODIES; 8. ENTITIES]

74.1 SPLIT MYSELF AND OTHERS INTO BINDERS FOREVER
74.2 PROGRAM MYSELF AND OTHERS TO BE THE BINDER AND BIND THE PHYSICAL UNIVERSE TOGETHER FOREVER
74.X TO {goal} INFINITELY IS TO BE THE BINDER AND ___ FOREVER
   [1. TIE THE UNIVERSE TOGETHER INTO A COHESIVE WHOLE; 2. BIND ALL INDIVIDUALS TOGETHER WITH THE PHYSICAL UNIVERSE; 3. BIND ALL INDIVIDUALS TOGETHER WITH EACH OTHER'S INFINITE ENTITIES; 4. BIND ALL INFINITE ENTITIES (OF ALL BEINGS) TOGETHER; 5. BIND THE PHYSICAL UNIVERSE TOGETHER WITH SYMBOLS; 6. BIND ALL THOUGHT TOGETHER WITH THE PHYSICAL UNIVERSE; 7. BIND THE PHYSICAL UNIVERSE TOGETHER WITH THE UNIVERSE MACHINERY; 8. KEEP THIS ALL ONE]

75.1 SPLIT MYSELF AND OTHERS INTO BLOCKERS FOREVER
75.2 PROGRAM MYSELF AND OTHERS TO BE THE BLOCKER AND BLOCK ALL TAMPERING WITH REALITY, FOREVER
75.X TO {goal} INFINITELY IS TO BE THE BLOCKER AND ___ FOREVER
   [1. KEEP MYSELF FROM REACHING THE TRUE PHYSICAL UNIVERSE; 2. KEEP MY OWN EFFORTS (AS AN INDIVIDUAL) DIRECTED AGAINST MY OWN 'SHADOW' OF THE PHYSICAL UNIVERSE; 3. PREVENT ANY MANIFESTATIONS OF PSYCHOKINETICS (telekinesis) FROM OCCURRING IN THE TRUE PHYSICAL UNIVERSE; 4. PREVENT ANY MANIPULATION OF REALITY BY DIRECT POSTULATE (Alpha Thought)]
75.X TO {goal} INFINITELY IS TO BE THE BLOCKER AND PREVENT MYSELF FROM REACHING THE ___ OF THE TRUE UNIVERSE, FOREVER
   [5. SPACE; 6. TIME; 7. ENERGY; 8. MATTER]
   {Note: We are a few microseconds behind the true 'Physical Universe' time. Everything is experienced on a very slight communication-lag. You have to reach a little bit 'ahead' into the 'future' to contact 'Physical Universe present-time'.}

76.1 SPLIT MYSELF AND OTHERS INTO CONSTRAINERS FOREVER
76.2 PROGRAM MYSELF AND OTHERS TO BE THE CONSTRAINER AND IMPOSE THE LAWS OF THE PHYSICAL UNIVERSE FOREVER

76.X TO {goal} INFINITELY IS TO BE THE CONSTRAINER AND ___ FOREVER
[1. LIMIT ALL PERCEPTIONS IN ACCORDANCE WITH PHYSICAL UNIVERSE LAWS; 2. LIMIT ALL MANIPULATIONS IN ACCORDANCE WITH PHYSICAL UNIVERSE LAWS; 3. IMPOSE THE LAWS OF DISTANCE ON ALL OPERATIONS; 4. IMPOSE THE LAWS OF DISTORTION ON ALL OPERATIONS; 5. IMPOSE THE LAWS OF DURATION ON ALL OPERATIONS; 6. IMPOSE THE LAWS OF RESISTANCE ON ALL OPERATIONS; 7. IMPOSE THE LAWS OF SYMPATHY (resonance, gravity) ON ALL OPERATIONS; 8. IMPOSE THE LAWS OF PHYSICAL INTERACTION ON ALL OPERATIONS]

77.1 SPLIT MYSELF AND OTHERS INTO DIFFUSERS (DEFLECTORS) FOREVER
77.2 PROGRAM MYSELF AND OTHERS TO BE THE DEFLECTOR AND (?)
77.X TO {goal} INFINITELY IS TO BE THE DEFLECTOR AND MAKE ALL MY ___ MISS THEIR TARGETS FOREVER
[1. BEAMS; 2. POSTULATES; (?)]

78.1 SPLIT MYSELF AND OTHERS INTO PULL-BACKS (HOLD-BACKS?) FOREVER
78.2 PROGRAM MYSELF AND OTHERS TO BE THE PULL-BACK AND (?)
78.X TO {goal} INFINITELY IS TO BE THE PULL-BACK AND PULL BACK ANY ___ FOREVER
[1. ENERGY; 2. POSTULATES; 3. REACH; (?)]

79.1 SPLIT MYSELF AND OTHERS INTO VACUUMS (UNMANIFESTORS) FOREVER
79.2 PROGRAM MYSELF AND OTHERS TO BE THE VACUUM AND (?)
79.X TO {goal} INFINITELY IS TO BE THE VACUUM AND ___ FOREVER
[1. MAKE THINGS UNREAL; 2. DRAIN HAVINGNESS; 3. DRAIN ENERGY; 4. CAVE THIS ALL IN ON ME; 5. PULL EVERYTHING IN; 6. COLLAPSE EVERYTHING; (?)]

80.1 SPLIT MYSELF AND OTHERS INTO REFLECTORS FOREVER
80.2 PROGRAM MYSELF AND OTHERS TO BE THE REFLECTOR AND REFLECT EVERYTHING BACK IN ON MYSELF FOREVER
80.X TO {goal} INFINITELY IS TO BE THE REFLECTOR AND REFLECT MY ___ BACK IN ON MYSELF, FOREVER
[1. POSTULATES; 2. ENERGY-BEAMS; 3. BAD INTENTIONS; 4. HARMFUL-ACTS; 5. FEARS; 6. EMOTIONS; 7. CREATIONS; 8.(?)]

81.1 SPLIT MYSELF AND OTHERS INTO GUIDES FOREVER
81.2 PROGRAM MYSELF AND OTHERS TO BE THE GUIDE AND LEAD MYSELF AND ALL OTHERS DEEPER INTO THE TRAP

FOREVER
81.X TO {goal} INFINITELY IS TO BE THE GUIDE AND ___ FOREVER
   [1. LEAD MYSELF AWAY FROM TRUE KNOWLEDGE ABOUT REALITY]
81.Y TO {goal} INFINITELY IS TO BE THE GUIDE AND LEAD MYSELF TOWARDS EVEN DEEPER ___ WITH THE PHYSICAL UNIVERSE, FOREVER
   [2. AFFINITY (LIKINGNESS); 3. ADMIRATION; 4. INVOLVEMENT; 5. INTEREST; 6. AGREEMENT; 7. DEPENDENCE]
81.Z TO {goal} INFINITELY IS TO BE THE GUIDE AND LEAD ___ WITH THE PHYSICAL UNIVERSE, FOREVER
   [8. MY INDIVIDUAL SELF TO BECOME ONE]

82.1 SPLIT MYSELF AND OTHERS INTO PLANNERS FOREVER
82.2 PROGRAM MYSELF AND OTHERS TO BE THE PLANNER AND PLAN OUT MY EXISTENCE FOREVER
82.X TO {goal} INFINITELY IS TO BE THE PLANNER AND ___ FOREVER
   [1. KNOW THAT THE ONLY WAY OUT IS TO GO THROUGH THE BOTTOM; 2. FIND WAYS TO KEEP MY INDIVIDUAL SELF MOVING DOWNWARD; 3. ENJOY DOING MYSELF IN AND SINKING DEEPER; 4. FIGURE OUT WAYS TO ENTRAP MYSELF FURTHER; 5. REFUSE TO ABANDON ANYTHING; 6. FIGURE OUT WAYS TO ENTRAP OTHERS; 7. FIGHT BACK AGAINST ANYONE WHO TRIES TO GET ME OUT; 8. LEAD MYSELF DOWN THE DECLINING SPIRAL]

83.1 SPLIT MYSELF AND OTHERS INTO GAME-MAKERS FOREVER
83.2 PROGRAM MYSELF AND OTHERS TO BE THE GAME-MAKER AND (?)
83.X TO {goal} INFINITELY IS TO BE THE GAME-MAKER AND (?)

84.1 SPLIT MYSELF AND OTHERS INTO GOAL-MAKERS FOREVER
84.2 PROGRAM MYSELF AND OTHERS TO BE THE GOAL-MAKER AND (?)
84.X TO {goal} INFINITELY IS TO BE THE GOAL-MAKER AND (?)

85.1 SPLIT MYSELF AND OTHERS INTO FUTURIZERS FOREVER
85.2 PROGRAM MYSELF AND OTHERS TO BE THE FUTURIZER AND PROJECT (CREATE) A FUTURE FOR MYSELF (AND OTHERS?) FOREVER
85.X TO {goal} INFINITELY IS TO BE THE FUTURIZER AND PROJECT ___ FOR MYSELF INTO THE PHYSICAL UNIVERSE FUTURE, FOREVER
   [1. GAMES; 2. IDENTITIES; 3. ACTIVITIES; 4. HAVINGNESS; 5. GOALS; 6. EXPECTATIONS; 7. CONSEQUENCES; 8. MY OWN PERPETUAL EXISTENCE]

86.1 SPLIT MYSELF AND OTHERS INTO ENCOURAGERS FOREVER
86.2 PROGRAM MYSELF AND OTHERS TO BE THE ENCOURAGER AND ENCOURAGE MYSELF TO ACHIEVE THINGS IN THE PHYSICAL UNIVERSE FOREVER
86.X TO {goal} INFINITELY IS TO BE THE ENCOURAGER AND ENCOURAGE MYSELF TO STRIVE ___ IN THE PHYSICAL UNIVERSE FOREVER
   [1. FOR ETHICS; 2. FOR AESTHETICS; 3. TO BUILD THINGS;
   4. FOR LOGIC AND REASON; 5. FOR CHANCE; 6. FOR GAMES;
   7. FOR KNOWLEDGE; 8. TO CREATE THINGS]
87.1 SPLIT MYSELF AND OTHERS INTO COACHES FOREVER
87.2 PROGRAM MYSELF AND OTHERS TO BE THE COACH AND (?)
87.X TO {goal} INFINITELY IS TO BE THE COACH AND (?) {false data is to 'keep myself from winning or losing' to 'make games go on forever'}
88.1 SPLIT MYSELF AND OTHERS INTO ALIGNERS (COORDINATORS) FOREVER
88.2 PROGRAM MYSELF AND OTHERS TO BE THE ALIGNER AND(?)
88.X TO {goal} INFINITELY IS TO BE THE ALIGNER AND (?)
89.1 SPLIT MYSELF AND OTHERS INTO WATCHERS (MONITORS) FOREVER
89.2 PROGRAM MYSELF AND OTHERS TO BE THE WATCHER AND MONITOR (WATCH) ALL OF THIS FOREVER
89.X TO {goal} INFINITELY IS TO BE THE WATCHER AND ___ FOREVER
   [1. WATCH ALL THE OTHERS TO ENSURE THAT THEY ARE OBEYING ORDERS; 2. OBSERVE MYSELF AS AN INDIVIDUAL TO ENSURE THAT I REMAIN ENTRAPPED BY THIS; 3. OBSERVE PHYSICAL REALITY TO ENSURE THAT IT REMAINS INVIOLATE; 4. WATCH THE MECHANICS BEHIND REALITY TO ENSURE THAT THEY CONTINUE TO WORK]
89.Y TO {goal} INFINITELY IS TO BE THE WATCHER AND REPORT ANY ___ TO THE OTHER ENTITIES (OVERSOULS?) FOREVER
   [5. VIOLATIONS OF THESE ORDERS; 6. ATTEMPTS TO UNMANIFEST (UNCREATE) THIS; 7. VIOLATIONS OF REALITY; 8. FAILURES OF THESE MECHANISMS]
90.1 SPLIT MYSELF AND OTHERS INTO EQUALIZERS FOREVER
90.2 PROGRAM MYSELF AND OTHERS TO BE THE EQUALIZER AND (?)
90.X TO {goal} INFINITELY IS TO BE THE EQUALIZER AND (?)
91.1 SPLIT MYSELF AND OTHERS INTO OPPOSERS FOREVER
91.2 PROGRAM MYSELF AND OTHERS TO BE THE OPPOSER AND (?)

91.X TO {goal} INFINITELY IS TO BE THE OPPOSER AND (?)

92.1 SPLIT MYSELF AND OTHERS INTO DECEIVERS FOREVER
92.2 PROGRAM MYSELF AND OTHERS TO BE THE DECEIVER AND DECEIVE MYSELF FOREVER
92.X TO {goal} INFINITELY IS TO BE THE DECEIVER AND DECEIVE MYSELF AS TO THE ___ FOREVER
   [1. NATURE OF REALITY; 2. NATURE OF OTHER BEINGS;
   3. NATURE OF LIFEFORMS; 4. ANATOMY OF THE PHYSICAL UNIVERSE; 5. ORIGINS OF THE PHYSICAL UNIVERSE; 6. ORIGINS OF MYSELF; 7. (?); 8. ORDERS CONCERNING FOREVER]

93.1 SPLIT MYSELF AND OTHERS INTO INVERTERS FOREVER
93.2 PROGRAM MYSELF AND OTHERS TO BE THE INVERTER AND (?)
93.X TO {goal} INFINITELY IS TO BE THE INVERTER AND (?)

94.1 SPLIT MYSELF AND OTHERS INTO DISPERSERS FOREVER
94.2 PROGRAM MYSELF AND OTHERS TO BE THE DISPERSER AND DISPERSE ANY ENERGY THAT I PUT OUT, FOREVER
94.X TO {goal} INFINITELY IS TO BE THE DISPERSER AND DISPERSE ___, FOREVER
   [1. ENERGY-BEAMS; 2. POSTULATES; 3. INTENTIONS;
   4. ATTENTION; 5. CONCENTRATION; 6. ANCHOR-POINTS;
   7. VIEWPOINTS; 8. PROGRAMMING] {item-8 may be 'vibrations'?}

95.1 SPLIT MYSELF AND OTHERS INTO FATES (ARRANGERS) FOREVER
95.2 PROGRAM MYSELF AND OTHERS TO BE THE ARRANGER AND ARRANGE FATES FOR MYSELF, FOREVER
95.X TO {goal} INFINITELY IS TO BE THE ARRANGER AND ARRANGE ___ FOR MYSELF, FOREVER
   [1. EVENTS; 2. (?); 3. CIRCUMSTANCES; (?)]

96.1 SPLIT MYSELF AND OTHERS INTO TRICKSTERS FOREVER
96.2 PROGRAM MYSELF AND OTHERS TO BE THE TRICKSTER AND TRICK MYSELF FOREVER
96.X TO {goal} INFINITELY IS TO BE THE TRICKSTER AND (GO AROUND AND) FOOL MYSELF AS TO ___, FOREVER
   [1. WHO IS REALLY DOING THINGS; 2. WHEN THINGS REALLY HAPPENED; 3. WHAT IS REALLY GOING ON; 4. THE ACTUAL PURPOSE BEHIND THINGS; 5. THE ACTUAL ORIGINS OF THINGS; 6. HOW THINGS REALLY WORK; 7. THE ACTUAL STRUCTURE OF THINGS; 8. WHO I REALLY AM]

97.1 SPLIT MYSELF AND OTHERS INTO 'PARTS OF GOD' (CREATORS) FOREVER
97.2 PROGRAM MYSELF AND OTHERS TO BE THE CREATOR AND CREATE THIS FOREVER

97.X TO {goal} INFINITELY IS TO BE THE CREATOR AND CREATE ___ FOREVER
[1. MYSELF AS AN INDIVIDUAL; 2. BODIES; 3. OTHER INDIVIDUALS; 4. SOCIETIES; 5. LIFEFORMS; 6. THE PHYSICAL UNIVERSE; 7. ENTITIES; 8. UNIVERSAL MIND]
{'Universal Mind' also registers as separate item? Experimental data is given below.}

97B. TO {goal} INFINITELY IS TO BE THE UNIVERSAL MIND AND ___ THE PHYSICAL UNIVERSE FOREVER
[1. BE THE THOUGHT OF; 2. THINK ON BEHALF OF;
3. ARRANGE FOR THE SURVIVAL OF; 4. THINK ABOUT]

97C. TO {goal} INFINITELY IS TO BE THE UNIVERSAL MIND AND ___ ALL THESE OTHERS, FOREVER
[1. BE; 2. HIDE THE THOUGHTS OF; 3. HOLD TOGETHER THE THOUGHTS OF; 4. FORGET THE THOUGHTS OF; 5. PROTECT THE THOUGHTS OF]

98.1 SPLIT MYSELF AND OTHERS INTO ANGELS FOREVER
98.2 PROGRAM MYSELF AND OTHERS TO BE THE ANGEL AND HELP 'GOD' FOREVER

{Note that here, 'god' is a construct that acts as a 'mind' for the Universe; you give a piece of yourself to its service.}

98.X TO {goal} INFINITELY IS TO BE THE ANGEL AND ___ FOREVER
[1. SERVE GOD; 2. CARRY OUT THE ORDERS OF GOD;
3. OBEY THE WISHES OF GOD; 4. MAINTAIN THE LAWS OF GOD;
5. ENACT THE PLANS OF GOD; 6. AGREE WITH THE MANIFESTATIONS (CREATIONS/MOCK-UPS) OF GOD;
7. SEE TO THE NEEDS OF GOD; 8. GRANT POWER (over your individual self) UNTO GOD]

99.1 SPLIT MYSELF AND OTHERS INTO ATTRACTORS FOREVER
99.2 PROGRAM MYSELF AND OTHERS TO BE THE ATTRACTOR AND COMPEL MYSELF TO NEED THE PHYSICAL UNIVERSE FOREVER

99.X TO {goal} INFINITELY IS TO BE THE ATTRACTOR AND COMPEL MYSELF TO ___ FOREVER
[1. HAVE AFFINITY (LIKINGNESS) FOR THE PHYSICAL UNIVERSE;
2. BE IN AGREEMENT WITH THE PHYSICAL UNIVERSE;
3. BE IN COMMUNICATION WITH THE PHYSICAL UNIVERSE;
4. HAVE ADMIRATION FOR THE PHYSICAL UNIVERSE; 5. DEPEND ON THE PHYSICAL UNIVERSE FOR AFFINITY (LIKINGNESS);
6. DEPEND ON THE PHYSICAL UNIVERSE FOR REALITY;
7. DEPEND ON THE PHYSICAL UNIVERSE FOR COMMUNICATION;
8. DEPEND ON THE PHYSICAL UNIVERSE FOR ADMIRATION]

100.1 SPLIT MYSELF AND OTHERS INTO ACCUSERS FOREVER
100.2 PROGRAM MYSELF AND OTHERS TO BE THE ACCUSER

          AND (?)
100.X TO {goal} INFINITELY IS TO BE THE ACCUSER AND (?)
101.1 SPLIT MYSELF AND OTHERS INTO JUDGES FOREVER
101.2 PROGRAM MYSELF AND OTHERS TO BE THE JUDGE AND
      JUDGE MYSELF, FOREVER
101.X TO {goal} INFINITELY IS TO BE THE JUDGE AND CONDEMN
      (BLAME) MYSELF FOR ___ FOREVER
   [1. ALL MY FAILINGS; 2. ALL THE HARM I HAVE DONE; 3. ALL THE
   WRONG THOUGHTS THAT I HAVE HAD; 4. ALL MY WEAKNESSES]
101.Y TO {goal} INFINITELY IS TO BE THE JUDGE AND ARRANGE ___
      FOREVER
   [5. PUNISHMENTS FOR MY MISDEEDS; 6. FOR MY DEEDS TO
   COME BACK ON ME; 7. LESSONS FOR MYSELF TO TEACH ME TO
   BE GOOD; 8. FATES FOR MYSELF TO PUNISH MY CRIMES]
102.1 SPLIT MYSELF AND OTHERS INTO PUNISHERS FOREVER
102.2 PROGRAM MYSELF AND OTHERS TO BE THE PUNISHER
      AND (?)
102.X TO {goal} INFINITELY IS TO BE THE PUNISHER AND (?)
103.1 SPLIT MYSELF AND OTHERS INTO EXECUTIONERS FOREVER
103.2 PROGRAM MYSELF AND OTHERS TO BE THE EXECUTIONER
      AND (?)
103.X TO {goal} INFINITELY IS TO BE THE EXECUTIONER AND (?)
104.1 SPLIT MYSELF AND OTHERS INTO RECYCLERS FOREVER
104.2 PROGRAM MYSELF AND OTHERS TO BE THE RECYCLER AND
      REFORMAT MYSELF BETWEEN LIVES FOREVER
104.X TO {goal} INFINITELY IS TO BE THE RECYCLER AND
      RESTRUCTURE MY ___ BETWEEN LIVES FOREVER
   [1. PERSONALITY; 2. MEMORIES; 3. ABILITIES;
   4. BEINGNESS (IDENTITY)]
104.Y TO {goal} INFINITELY IS TO BE THE RECYCLER AND
      FORMULATE FOR MYSELF ___ BETWEEN LIVES FOREVER
   [5. NEW GOALS; 6. NEW LESSONS; 7. NEW CHALLENGES;
   8. NEW ABERRATIONS]
105.1 SPLIT MYSELF AND OTHERS INTO INTERIORIZERS FOREVER
105.2 PROGRAM MYSELF AND OTHERS TO BE THE INTERIORIZER
      AND (?)
105.X TO {goal} INFINITELY IS TO BE THE INTERIORIZER AND (?)
106.1 SPLIT MYSELF AND OTHERS INTO DISCOURAGERS FOREVER
106.2 PROGRAM MYSELF AND OTHERS TO BE THE DISCOURAGER
      AND CONVINCE MYSELF AND OTHERS THAT NOTHING CAN
      BE DONE ABOUT THIS FOREVER
106.X TO {goal} INFINITELY IS TO BE THE DISCOURAGER AND
      DISCOURAGE MYSELF AND OTHERS FROM EVER DOING

ANYTHING ABOUT ___ FOREVER
[1. THIS IMPLANT; 2. ENTITIES; 3. THE PHYSICAL UNIVERSE;
4. THE SPLITTER MECHANISMS]

106.Y TO {goal} INFINITELY IS TO BE THE DISCOURAGER AND CONVINCE MYSELF AND OTHERS THAT ___ FOREVER
[5. THIS IS TOO SOLID TO BE TAKEN APART; 6. EVEN IF THIS COULD BE TAKEN APART (ERASED) IT WOULD NOT MAKE ANY DIFFERENCE ANYWAY; 7. EVEN IF YOU COULD TAKE THIS ALL APART, YOU WOULDN'T WANT TO; 8. EVEN IF YOU DID TAKE THIS ALL APART, YOU WOULD SUFFER A LOSS AND BE SORRY THAT YOU HAD DONE IT]

{'Discourager' may be the same as item-27 'Depressor'?}

107.1 SPLIT MYSELF AND OTHERS INTO CONFUSION-ENTITIES FOREVER

107.2 PROGRAM MYSELF AND OTHERS TO BE THE CONFUSION ENTITY AND KEEP MYSELF CONFUSED FOREVER

107.X TO {goal} INFINITELY IS TO BE THE CONFUSION ENTITY AND CONFUSE ___ (SO THAT THEY CAN NEVER BE SORTED OUT) FOREVER
[1. TRUTH WITH FALSEHOOD; 2. REALITY WITH UNREALITY;
3. MYSELF WITH OTHERS; 4. PAST WITH PRESENT; 5. TIME WITH SPACE; 6. MATTER WITH ENERGY; 7. IDENTITY WITH LOCATION;
8. IMPACT WITH ENLIGHTENMENT]

108.1 SPLIT MYSELF AND OTHERS INTO TERROR (FEAR) ENTITIES FOREVER

108.2 PROGRAM MYSELF AND OTHERS TO BE THE TERROR ENTITY AND TERRIFY MYSELF FOREVER

108.X TO {goal} INFINITELY IS TO BE THE TERROR ENTITY AND ___ FOREVER
[1. MANIFEST (MOCK-UP) MONSTERS AND DEMONS;
2. TERRORIZE MYSELF]

108.Y TO {goal} INFINITELY IS TO BE THE TERROR ENTITY AND MAKE MYSELF AFRAID TO ___ FOREVER
[3. FIND OUT THE TRUTH; 4. SEE ENTITIES; 5. SEE ANY DISCREPANCY IN REALITY; 6. SEE ANY VIOLATION OF REALITY;
7. REMEMBER ANYTHING BEFORE THIS UNIVERSE;
8. DISCOVER ANY PART OF THESE MECHANISMS]

109.1 SPLIT MYSELF AND OTHERS INTO DELUSION-ENTITIES FOREVER

109.2 PROGRAM MYSELF AND OTHERS TO BE THE DELUSION ENTITY AND CREATE DELUSIONS FOR MYSELF FOREVER

109.X TO {goal} INFINITELY IS TO BE THE DELUSION ENTITY AND ___ FOREVER
[1. DELUDE MYSELF AS TO THE TRUE NATURE OF REALITY;
2. CREATE FALSE REALITIES FOR MYSELF; 3. DUB-IN FALSE

PERCEPTIONS; 4. DUB-IN MISCONCEPTIONS ABOUT REALITY; 5. DUB-IN INCORRECT CONCLUSIONS; 6. DUB-IN WRONG REASONS WHY; 7. CONVINCE MYSELF THAT ENTITIES ARE DELUSIONS; 8. CONVINCE MYSELF THAT PERCEPTIONS OF THE REAL NATURE OF REALITY ARE DELUSIONS]

110.1 SPLIT MYSELF AND OTHERS INTO DEGRADERS FOREVER
110.2 PROGRAM MYSELF AND OTHERS TO BE THE DEGRADER AND DEGRADE MYSELF FOREVER
110.X TO {goal} INFINITELY IS TO BE THE DEGRADER AND INSPIRE MYSELF TO BE ___ FOREVER
 [1. GREEDY; 2. LUSTFUL; 3. CRUEL; 4. DISHONEST; 5. LAZY; 6. VISCOUS (NASTY); 7. SELFISH; 8. VENGEFUL]

111.1 SPLIT MYSELF AND OTHERS INTO TEMPTERS FOREVER
111.2 PROGRAM MYSELF AND OTHERS TO BE THE TEMPTER AND (?)
111.X TO {goal} INFINITELY IS TO BE THE TEMPTER AND (?)

112.1 SPLIT MYSELF AND OTHERS INTO DEMONS (DEVILS) FOREVER
112.2 PROGRAM MYSELF AND OTHERS TO BE THE DEMON AND MAKE TROUBLE FOR MYSELF FOREVER {'entrap myself forever'?}
112.X TO {goal} INFINITELY IS TO BE THE DEMON AND CREATE ___ FOR MYSELF, FOREVER
 [1. PROBLEMS; 2. DIFFICULTIES; 3. UPSETS; 4. LOSSES; 5. GUILT; 6. PENALTIES; 7. TRAPS; 8. DECLINING SPIRALS]
 {'Devil' also registers as separate item? Experimental data given below.}
112A. TO {goal} INFINITELY IS TO BE THE DEVIL AND INSPIRE MYSELF TOWARDS EVIL WITHIN THE PHYSICAL UNIVERSE, FOREVER
112B. TO {goal} INFINITELY IS TO BE THE DEVIL AND MAKE TROUBLE BETWEEN MYSELF AND ___, FOREVER
 [1. OTHERS; 2. SOCIETY; 3. GOD; 4. THE PHYSICAL UNIVERSE]

113.1 SPLIT MYSELF AND OTHERS INTO INNER-GUARDS FOREVER
113.2 PROGRAM MYSELF AND OTHERS TO BE THE INNER-GUARD AND STOP MYSELF FROM KNOWING ABOUT MYSELF, FOREVER
113.X TO {goal} INFINITELY IS TO BE THE INNER-GUARD AND MAKE MYSELF AFRAID TO ___, FOREVER
 [1. SEE MYSELF; 2. FIND OUT WHERE I REALLY AM; 3. FIND OUT WHO I REALLY AM; 4. FIND OUT WHAT I REALLY AM; 5. FIND OUT WHEN I REALLY AM; 6. FIND OUT MY TRUE NATURE; 7. FIND OUT MY TRUE ORIGINS; 8. LOOK INWARD]

114.1 SPLIT MYSELF AND OTHERS INTO DRAMATIZERS FOREVER
114.2 PROGRAM MYSELF AND OTHERS TO BE THE DRAMATIZER AND (?)
114.X TO {goal} INFINITELY IS TO BE THE DRAMATIZER AND (?)

115.1 SPLIT MYSELF AND OTHERS INTO PERPETUATORS FOREVER
115.2 PROGRAM MYSELF AND OTHERS TO BE THE PERPETUATOR AND (?)
115.X TO {goal} INFINITELY IS TO BE THE PERPETUATOR AND (?)

116.1 SPLIT MYSELF AND OTHERS INTO CORRECTIVE-MACHINERY FOREVER
116.2 PROGRAM MYSELF AND OTHERS TO BE THE CORRECTIVE MACHINE-ENTITY AND KEEP THIS ALL WORKING FOREVER
116.X TO {goal} INFINITELY IS TO BE THE CORRECTIVE-ENTITY AND ___, FOREVER
[1. REMEDY ANY DISCREPANCIES IN REALITY; 2. ALTER PERCEPTIONS TO KEEP REALITY CONSISTENT AND HIDE ANY DISCREPANCIES; 3. ALTER MEMORY TO KEEP REALITY CONSISTENT AND HIDE ANY DISCREPANCIES; 4. MAKE MYSELF AND OTHERS SPLIT TO REPLACE ANY ENTITIES THAT ARE RELEASED {registers, but may be part of item-117}; 5. USE THE RESOURCES OF ALL THESE OTHERS TO REPROGRAM ANY PART OF THIS IMPLANT THAT FAILS; 6. CONVINCE MYSELF AND OTHERS TO OBEY THIS IMPLANT; 7. USE THE RESOURCES OF ALL THESE OTHERS TO KEEP THIS CONTINUOUSLY CREATED; 8. REPORT ALL INFRACTIONS TO THE OVERSOULS]

117.1 SPLIT MYSELF AND OTHERS INTO SPLITTERS FOREVER
117.2 PROGRAM MYSELF AND OTHERS TO BE THE SPLITTER AND (?)
117.X TO {goal} INFINITELY IS TO BE THE SPLITTER AND (?)

118.1 SPLIT MYSELF AND OTHERS INTO IMPLANTERS FOREVER
118.2 PROGRAM MYSELF AND OTHERS TO BE THE IMPLANTER AND IMPLANT MYSELF WITH ORDERS AS AN INDIVIDUAL, FOREVER
{wording may be '..myself as an individual, with orders,..'}
118.X TO {goal} INFINITELY IS TO BE THE IMPLANTER AND IMPLANT MYSELF (WITH ORDERS) TO ___ FOREVER
[1. BELIEVE IN REALITY; 2. AGREE WITH REALITY; 3. BE THE EFFECT OF (or 'affected by') REALITY; 4. BE LOCATED WITHIN REALITY (or 'the Physical Universe'); 5. BELIEVE THAT THE PHYSICAL UNIVERSE IS LARGER ('greater') THAN I AM; 6. BELIEVE THAT THE PHYSICAL UNIVERSE IS MORE IMPORTANT THAN I AM; 7. BELIEVE THAT THE PHYSICAL UNIVERSE IS MORE POWERFUL THAN I AM; 8. BELIEVE THAT THE PHYSICAL UNIVERSE IS MORE ENDURING THAN I AM]

119.1 SPLIT MYSELF AND OTHERS INTO KEEPERS FOREVER
119.2 PROGRAM MYSELF AND OTHERS TO BE THE KEEPER AND (?)
119.X TO {goal} INFINITELY IS TO BE THE KEEPER & ?

120.1 SPLIT MYSELF AND OTHERS INTO UNIFIERS (JOINERS) FOREVER
120.2 PROGRAM MYSELF AND OTHERS TO BE THE UNIFIER AND MAKE EVERYTHING ONE FOREVER
120.X TO {goal} INFINITELY IS TO BE THE UNIFIER AND BE ONE WITH ___, FOREVER
  [1. INFINITY; 2. ALL THESE ENTITIES; 3. THE PHYSICAL UNIVERSE; 4. ALL LIFEFORMS; 5. ALL SOCIETIES; 6. ALL OTHER INDIVIDUALS; 7. BODIES; 8. THE ITEMS OF THIS IMPLANT]

121.1 SPLIT MYSELF AND OTHERS INTO RESTIMULATORS FOREVER
121.2 PROGRAM MYSELF AND OTHERS TO BE THE RESTIMULATOR AND KEEP THIS IN RESTIMULATION FOREVER
121.X TO {goal} INFINITELY IS TO BE THE RESTIMULATOR AND ___, FOREVER
  [1. CREATE THIS IMPLANT CONTINUOUSLY; 2. FORCE MYSELF AND OTHERS TO CROSS-COPY INFINITELY; 3. FORCE MYSELF AND OTHERS TO DIVIDE INFINITELY; 4. FORCE MYSELF AND OTHERS TO DRAMATIZE THIS; 5. REPEAT THE ITEMS OF THIS IMPLANT; 6. FORCE MYSELF AND OTHERS TO REMAIN THE EFFECT OF THIS; 7. KEEP THIS IMPLANT SOLID; 8. RE-CREATE THE IMPACT OF THIS INCIDENT]

122.1 SPLIT MYSELF AND OTHERS INTO INVALIDATORS FOREVER
122.2 PROGRAM MYSELF AND OTHERS TO BE THE INVALIDATOR AND INVALIDATE ANY AWARENESS OF THIS IMPLANT, FOREVER
122.X TO {goal} INFINITELY IS TO BE THE INVALIDATOR AND INVALIDATE ANY ___ OF THIS IMPLANT, FOREVER
  [1. AWARENESS; 2. KNOWLEDGE; 3. REMEMBRANCE; 4. UNDERSTANDING; 5. ERASURE OF; 6. FREEDOM FROM; 7. COMMAND OVER; 8. MASTERY OF]

123.1 SPLIT MYSELF AND OTHERS INTO MISDIRECTORS FOREVER
123.2 PROGRAM MYSELF AND OTHERS TO BE THE MISDIRECTOR AND MISLEAD ANYONE WHO ATTEMPTS TO DISCOVER THIS, FOREVER
123.X TO {goal} INFINITELY IS TO BE THE MISDIRECTOR AND ___, FOREVER
  [1. SUBSTITUTE WRONG DATES CONCERNING THE BACKTRACK; 2. MAKE MYSELF AND OTHERS CONFUSE THE CORRECT SEQUENCE OF EVENTS; 3. MANUFACTURE FALSE-DATA; 4. MAKE MYSELF AND OTHERS MIX UP LOCATIONS;

5. MAKE MYSELF AND OTHERS DUB-IN IMAGINARY INCIDENTS;
6. MISLEAD MYSELF AND OTHERS; 7. DIRECT ATTENTION AWAY FROM THIS INCIDENT; 8. PREVENT THE TRUTH FROM BEING DISCOVERED]

124.1 SPLIT MYSELF AND OTHERS INTO DENIERS FOREVER
124.2 PROGRAM MYSELF AND OTHERS TO BE THE DENIER AND DENY THE EXISTENCE OF THIS FOREVER
124.X TO {goal} INFINITELY IS TO BE THE DENIER AND ___ FOREVER
[1. INSIST THAT ENTITIES DO NOT EXIST; 2. INSIST THAT INFINITY DOES NOT EXIST; 3. DENY THAT ANY OF THIS IS REAL; 4. DENY THAT THIS EVER HAPPENED; 5. INVALIDATE THE REALITY OF ANY NON-PHYSICAL UNIVERSE MANIFESTATION ('creation' or 'mock-up'); 6. INSIST THAT THE PHYSICAL UNIVERSE IS THE ONLY REALITY; 7. COMPEL MYSELF AND OTHERS TO DISBELIEVE IN THE EXISTENCE OF THIS IMPLANT; 8. COMPEL MYSELF AND OTHERS TO DISBELIEVE IN THE EXISTENCE OF THE INFINITE {terminal}]

125.1 SPLIT MYSELF AND OTHERS INTO SUPPRESSORS FOREVER
125.2 PROGRAM MYSELF AND OTHERS TO BE THE SUPPRESSOR AND KEEP THIS HIDDEN FOREVER
125.X TO {goal} INFINITELY IS TO BE THE SUPPRESSOR AND KEEP MYSELF FROM ___ THIS FOREVER
[1. SPOTTING; 2. KNOWING ABOUT; 3. PERCEIVING; 4. COMMUNICATING ABOUT; 5. THINKING ABOUT]
125.Y TO {goal} INFINITELY IS TO BE THE SUPPRESSOR AND ___ FOREVER
[6. KEEP THIS FROM REGISTERING ON ANY DETECTION-DEVICES; 7. STOP THIS FROM BEING DISCOVERED; 8. USE THE RESOURCES OF ALL THESE OTHER ENTITIES TO BLOCK ALL KNOWLEDGE OF THIS]

126.1 SPLIT MYSELF AND OTHERS INTO HOLDERS FOREVER
126.2 PROGRAM MYSELF AND OTHERS TO BE THE HOLDER AND HOLD EVERYONE TOGETHER FOREVER
126.X TO {goal} INFINITELY IS TO BE THE HOLDER AND ___, FOREVER
[1. MAKE EVERYONE ALL ONE; 2. JOIN EVERYONE TOGETHER; 3. HOLD EVERYONE IN A SINGLE REALITY; 4. COMBINE EVERYONE INTO A SINGLE BEING; 5. MAKE EVERYONE HOLD ON TO EACH OTHER; 6. HOLD MYSELF AND OTHERS IN AGREEMENT TOGETHER; 7. HOLD ON TO ALL THESE BEINGS; 8. KEEP ANYONE FROM LEAVING]

127.1 SPLIT MYSELF AND OTHERS INTO GUARDIANS FOREVER
127.2 PROGRAM MYSELF AND OTHERS TO BE THE GUARDIAN AND PROTECT THIS IMPLANT (FROM BEING VIEWED), FOREVER

127.X TO {goal} INFINITELY IS TO BE THE GUARDIAN AND PREVENT MYSELF AND OTHERS FROM ___ FOREVER
[1. VIOLATING THE RULES OF THE PHYSICAL UNIVERSE; 2. MOVING OUT OF THE PHYSICAL UNIVERSE; 3. MODIFYING REALITY; 4. FINDING OUT THE TRUTH ABOUT REALITY; 5. CHANGING THE NATURE OF REALITY; 6. DISAGREEING WITH REALITY; 7. KNOWING THAT I AM DOING THESE THINGS; 8. REMEMBERING THIS IMPLANT]

128.1 SPLIT MYSELF AND OTHERS INTO OVERSOULS FOREVER
128.2 PROGRAM MYSELF AND OTHERS TO BE THE OVERSOUL AND ORGANIZE ALL THESE OTHERS FOREVER
128.X TO {goal} INFINITELY IS TO BE THE OVERSOUL AND ___ FOREVER
[1. MANAGE THIS; 2. SEE THAT THIS IS REPAIRED; 3. COORDINATE ALL THESE OTHERS; 4. ORGANIZE MYSELF AND ALL THESE OTHERS; 5. CONTROL MYSELF AND ALL THESE OTHERS; 6. KEEP MYSELF AND ALL THESE OTHERS DIVIDED; 7. LIE ABOUT THIS TO MYSELF AND ALL THESE OTHERS; 8. KEEP MYSELF AND ALL THESE OTHERS ENTRAPPED]

ADDITIONAL RESEARCH NOTES:

Other entity type-labels may include a *Problem-Maker*; and also a *Balancer, Equalizer,* or *Tabulator (for karma)*. Or these may be alternate labels for existing types on the list that require more research.

There is some *Meter-data* for a *Convincer*, to "convince myself that I need this" or "make myself dependent on this," *&tc*. The label "*Misleader*" also registers; but may be similar to (or the same as) the "*Guide*"—that "guides my individual self deeper into the Physical Universe, forever," and "keep myself more in agreement," "keep myself more confused," "more solid," *&tc*. More research is needed to be certain.

There are also additional "*Higher-Self*" items that apply to the ending sequence of the *Implant*. These have already been well researched; however, their precise wording and sequence-order is still in question.

1. MAKE THIS ALL HAPPEN (FOREVER); 2. REMAIN IN AGREEMENT WITH THIS IMPLANT (FOREVER); 3. KEEP THIS ALL WORKING (FOREVER); 4. KEEP THIS ALL IN MOTION (FOREVER); 5. NEVER LET MY LOWER SELF KNOW WHAT I AM DOING (FOREVER); 6. RULE OVER ALL THESE OTHER (ENTITIES) (FOREVER); 5. ENJOY DOING THIS (FOREVER); 7. ENJOY BEING HERE (FOREVER); 8. NEVER THINK ABOUT BEING HERE (FOREVER).

516 – AT#8

SECTION 5. FINAL ITEMS

TO {goal} INFINITELY IS TO BE ALL THESE THINGS AND ___, FOREVER

1. BLOCK ALL AWARENESS OF THESE ORDERS
2. BLOCK ALL KNOWLEDGE OF INFINITY
3. BLOCK ALL REMEMBRANCE OF THIS
4. BLOCK ALL KNOWLEDGE OF THESE ENTITIES
5. KEEP MYSELF AND OTHERS UNKNOWING
6. KEEP MYSELF AND OTHERS ASLEEP
7. KEEP MYSELF AND OTHERS UNCONSCIOUS
8. KEEP MYSELF AND OTHERS DEAD

SECTION 6. FINAL PROCESSING STEPS

Use these methods for "group-processing" any entities remaining after completing the Splitter-Platform (incident-sequence) given in previous sections. Apply as many techniques as is necessary to resolve the case.

A. *Imagine* "doing" and "not doing" (alternately) these things repeatedly to an *end-point*.

B. *Spot* "being programmed into being" these things. *Spot* the first time. *Spot* programming others. *Spot* others programming others.

C. *Spot* "being made to split." *Spot* first time; to others; others to others.

D. *Spot* "being implanted with false-data." *Spot* first time; to others; others to others.

E. *Spot* "being made to divide out to infinity." *Spot* first time; to others; others to others.

F. *Spot* "being made into the infinite {terminal}." *Spot* first time; to others; others to others.

G. *Decide* "to be" and "not be" the *infinite-terminal* (alternately) repeatedly to an *end-point*.

H. *Imagine* "creating" and "un-creating" the *infinite-terminal* (alternately) until you are at *Cause* over it.

I. *Spot* "the first item of the *Splitter-Platform*" (To {goal} Infinitely Is To Perceive Ultimate Truth); *Spot* it as *false-data*.

J. *Spot* the "Native State" item for the IPU-Goal. *Spot* being pushed into it; pushing others into it; others pushing others into it.

K. Ask the entity: "*Can You Create?*" It will *register* as "*yes*" on the *GSR-Meter*. If not: have the *entity* practice *imagining/creating* and "throwing *away*" a few objects; then ask again.

L. Ask the entity: *"Are You Free Of This?"* If it does not *register*: *list* to find out why (what *item* is not fully *discharged*).

M. *Identification Tech. (Who Are You?)*

N. *Locational Tech. (Point To..)*

Then check if anything remains to be handled—if any *entities* didn't *release, &tc.* Other *entities*, from other *Goals*, may try to "copy" and "replace" what was just handled. So, check for that; and if it is the case, simply indicate it to yourself (it *disperses-on-realization*).

Then *process-out* the IPU-*Platform* (AT#4) to *total defragmentation* on that *Goal*. Since you've handled the *Splitter-Incident*, the *defragmentation* may occur relatively quickly after a small number of *items*.

Only after this point should you handle the *negative-Goals*. When you do: start by *spotting* the *"Native State" item* of the *basic (positive)* IPU-*Goal*. Then, reaffirm (to yourself) the *total defragmentation* of the *basic-Goal* by *spotting* the point (in time) when you *totally defragmented* it with the *Platform*. Do this any time you feel that *"charge"* may be accumulating on the *basic* while handling the *negative*.

OPENING GATES TO THE KINGDOM
(*The Beginning In The Ending*)

A *Wizard* is one who is not only a *Master* of their own *Universe*, but who has the ability and certainty to knowingly affect and change the *Universe* around them; for themselves, and for others. We are not speaking of stage acts and parlor tricks; we mean actually *helping one another* and *making this world a better place* while conducting our *Ascension* work.

For the first time in known history (including the *Backtrack*), there is a true launch point toward *Ascension* available to humanity—and *it is our Systemology*. As should be self-evident after 33 progressive *lesson-booklets*, *manuals*, and *supplements*: all of this could have only been uncovered with a genuine *Self-Honest systematic approach*.

The basic *spiritual cartography* is complete—and the *Way Out* has been cleared. Are there still some rough patches that require additional development? Sure. But, that is where you come in—investing yourself in the final *research-actions* necessary for your own *Ascension*; and perhaps assisting your fellow *Seekers* by contributing to the ongoing *Infinity Grade* that is intended to follow hereafter and preserve the legacy of the *Systemology Society* and the perfection of its knowledge.

This presentation of the final *Keys to the Kingdom* manual—and the completion of an entire library synthesizing the *systematic truth* of *spiritual life* and *all existence*—marks the end of a personal *29-year quest*. Bearing the weight of carrying *Excalibur*—the *Sword of Truth* or *Sword of Shannara*—to *dispel all illusion*, the present author forged ahead, determined and steadfast in his mission to chart a true *Map* that could lead us back through the *Gates* of the *Magic Kingdom* and retrieve the *Grail-secret* we had lost.

Finally, that *Map* has been rediscovered and decoded—and its facsimile stands publicly on display in these many printed works—for *anyone* that cares to travel this *Pathway*. The stable gains and progress you make on the *Pathway* is true and lasting—carried with you beyond this lifetime, on your infinite spiritual journey.

Now, the *Grail* is safely stored in the *Castle* again—an overflowing cup that serves to remind us that we already have, within our *Beingness*, the well-springs of *all the Havingness* we could ever want or dream for; and we have no need to be dependent on any other *Source*.

The *Grail* is there for all who might shed their *Human* garb, recollect the *fragmented pieces* of their *Beingness*, and simply *reach* through the dimensions for it. It is all of ours for the taking; and so long as this record is maintained hereafter, it can never be truly lost again.

But now I digress; yielding to the *next-generation* of *Seekers* to take up this quest and complete the *Pathway* for themselves—remembering always to *help one another.*

To all those that follow the trail of breadcrumbs: I have returned the *Sword* to the *Lake*—where it is now, still there, just waiting for *you*.

Safe journeys, dear Seeker.

We'll see you on the Other Side.

APPENDIX

FORMAL SESSION SAMPLE SCRIPT

+

DICTIONARY

SYSTEMATIC PROCESSING FORMAL SESSION
(SAMPLE SCRIPT)

1. <u>BEGINNING THE SESSION</u>

"Would it be okay with you if we begin this session now?"

"Okay."

"Start of session."

2. <u>OPENING PROCEDURES</u>

  A. Presence In-Session

"Is there anything going on that might keep your attention from being present in-session?"

(if *"no,"* acknowledge and go to B.; if *"yes,"* continue below)

"Okay. Tell me about it."

"Alright. How does that problem seem to you now?"

(if *"further away"* or handled, acknowledge and go to B.; if *"closer"* or more turbulent, continue below)

"Spot something in the incident; Spot something in the room."

(this alternating command line is repeated as needed)

  B. Orientation in Present Space-Time

"Get the sense of you making that body sit in that chair."

"Okay. Get a sense of the floor beneath your feet."

"Do you have that real good?"

(if *"no,"* acknowledge and repeat A.; if *"yes,"* continue below)

"Recall a time something seemed real to you."

"Tell me something you notice about it."

"Look around and spot something in the room."

"What do you notice about that?"

(these last four command lines are repeated in series as needed; acknowledge and continue below)

  C. Control of Body and Mind In-Session

(two dissimilar objects—here given as *"Item-1"* and *"Item-2"*—are presented and placed within reach; or alternatively, at two distant points in the room, in which a command line for "walking" between them would be inserted)

"*Pick up Item-1.*"

"*Tell me about its weight.*"

"*Tell me about its color.*"

"*Tell me about its texture.*"

"*Put it down.*"

"*Pick up Item-2.*"

"*Tell me about its weight.*"

"*Tell me about its color.*"

"*Tell me about its texture.*"

"*Put it down.*"

(this series of command-lines may be repeated several times; when there is no communication-lag for several full series, and duplicate answers are reoccurring, acknowledge and continue below)

"*Choose an object. Decide when you are going to reach for it. Then make that body pick it up.*"

"*Now decide when you are going to put it down. Then make that body put it back where it was.*"

(repeat as needed; when there is no communication-lag for a full series of command lines, acknowledge and continue below)

"*Close your eyes. Put all of your attention on the upper two back corners of the room and just get real interested in them for a while.*"

(if there are no visible signs of "strain" after two minutes, acknowledge and continue below)

D. Establishing the Session

"*Do you have any goals for this session, or anything in particular you want to address?*"

(acknowledge, then start a process)

3. STARTING A PROCESS

"*I would like to start a process; would that be okay?*"

"*Alright. The command lines are ---. Does this make sense?*"

(if "*no*," clear up any misunderstood words; if "*yes*," start the process)

4. <u>CHANGING A PROCESS</u>

(the wording in a command line may be changed to make it more workable for a *Seeker*; before changing processes altogether, the present process must reach an end-point)

Example: a Seeker expresses inability to "imagine" or visualize imagery.

"*Okay. Well, just 'get a sense' of...*" or "*Just 'get the idea' of...*"

Example: a Seeker expresses discomfort (or withdrawal from) recalling a particular incident.

"*That's fine. What part of that incident 'could' you confront?*"

5. <u>STOPPING A PROCESS</u>

(when an end-point has been reached on a repetitive-style process)

"*We'll just run this process a couple more times if that's okay with you?*"

(general process is run two more times)

"*Okay. Is there anything you would like to tell me before we end this process?*"

(**or**, if an end-point "realization" is communicated from a process)

"*Alright. Very good.*"

(the formal end of a particular process requires a command-line)

"*End of process.*"

6. <u>ENDING THE SESSION</u>

(once a process, or series of processes, is completed)

"*Is there anything you would like to tell me before we end this session?*"

(if "*yes*," acknowledge and handle it with communication before ending the session; if "*no*," continue below)

"*Would it be okay if we ended this session now?*"

"*Okay.*"

"*End of session.*"

SYSTEMOLOGY BETA-AWARENESS SCALE

4.0 SELF-HONESTY (BETA)
3.9 "Vibrant" ("Charismatic")
3.8 "Enthusiastic" ("In Love")
3.7 "Energetic"
3.6 "Cheerful"
3.5 CONFIDENT ("Positive")
3.4 "Determined"
3.3 "Eager"
3.2 "Alert" ("Attentive")
3.1 "Strong Interest"
3.0 INTERESTED ("Content")
2.9 "Small Interest"
2.8 "Encouraged"
2.7 "Disinterest"
2.6 "Doubtful"
2.5 INDIFFERENT ("Tolerant")
2.4 "Bored"
2.3 "Dislike" ("Neglectful")
2.2 "Tired"
2.1 "Monotony"
2.0 INVALIDATING ("Pessimistic")
1.9 "Antagonism"
1.8 "Pain"
1.7 "Confrontational"
1.6 "Violent"
1.5 ANGER ("Negative")
1.4 "Hateful"
1.3 "Spiteful"
1.2 "Resentment"
1.1 "Anxiety"
1.0 FEAR ("Afraid")
0.9 "Terror"
0.8 "Numb"
0.7 "Evasive"
0.6 "Loss"
0.5 GRIEF ("Sadness")
0.4 "Depression"
0.3 "Victimization"
0.2 "Hopelessness"
0.1 "Apathy" ("Unconsciousness")
0.0 BETA CONTINUITY (Organic Death)

THE COMPLETE SYSTEMOLOGY TECHNICAL DICTIONARY (VERSION 5.0)

—A—

A-for-A (one-to-one) : an expression meaning that what we say, write, represent, think or symbolize is a direct and perfect reflection or duplication of the actual aspect or thing—that "A" is for, means and is equivalent to "A" and not "a" or "q" or "!"; in the relay of communication, the message (or messenger particle) is sent and perfectly duplicated in form and meaning when received.

aberration : a departure from what is right or correct; a deviation from, or distortion in, what is true or right or straight; in chromatic light science, the failure of a mirror, lens or refracting surface to produce an exact *"one-to-one"* or *"A-for-A"* duplication between an object and its image; in *Nex-Gen Systemology*, a term to describe *fragmentation* as it applies to an individual, which causes them to "stray" form the *Pathway* (and experience a *fragmented reality*).

abreaction (abreactive therapy) : the "burn off" or "purging" or "discharge" of "unconscious" (reactive response) as applied to early 20th century German psychology, from *abreagieren*, meaning "coming down" from a release or expression of a repressed or forgotten emotion; in *Nex-Gen Systemology*, fully "resurfacing" traumatic past experiences consciously (on one's own determinism) in order to purge them of their emotional excess (or "charge"); also *"Route-1"* and *"catharsis."*

acid-test : a metaphor refers to a chemical process of applying harsh nitric acid to a golden substance (sample) to determine its genuineness; in *Nex-Gen Systemology*, an extreme conclusive process to determine the reality, genuineness or truth of a substance, material, particle or piece of information.

acknowledgment : a response-communication establishing that an immediately former communication was properly received, duplicated and understood; the formal acceptance and/or recognition of a communication or presence.

activating event : an incident or occurrence that automatically stimulates a conscious or unrecognized reminder or 'ping' from an earlier *imprinting incident* recorded on one's own personal timeline as an emotionally charged and encoded memory; an incident or instance when thought systems are activated to determine the consequence or significance of an activity, motion or event—often demonstrated as *Activating Event → Belief Systems → Consideration*.

actualization : to make actual, not just potential; to bring into full solid

Reality; to realize fully in *Awareness* as a "thing."

affinity : the apparent and energetic *relationship* between substances or bodies; the degree of *attraction* or repulsion between things based on natural forces; the *similitude* of frequencies or waveforms; the degree of *interconnection* between systems.

agreement (reality) : unanimity of opinion of what is "thought" to be known; an accepted arrangement of how things are; things we consider as "real" or as an "is" of "reality"; a *consensus* of what is real as made by standard-issue (common) participants; what an individual contributes to or accepts as "real"; in *NexGen Systemology*, a synonym for "*reality.*"

allegorical : a representation of the abstract, metaphysical or "spiritual" using physical or concrete forms.

alpha : the first, primary, basic, superior or beginning of some form; in *NexGen Systemology*, referring to the state of existence operating on spiritual archetypes and postulates, will and intention "exterior" to the low-level condensation and solidity of energy and matter as the 'physical universe'.

alpha control center (ACC) : the highest relay point of *Beingness* for an individuated *Alpha-Spirit, Self* or "I-AM"; in *NexGen Systemology*—a point of spiritual separation of ZU at (7.0) from the *Infinity of Nothingness* (8.0); the truest actualization of *Identity*; the highest *Self-directed* relay of *Alpha-Self* as an *Identity-Continuum*, operating in an *alpha-existence* (or "Spiritual Universe"–AN) to *determine* "Alpha Thought" (6.0) and WILL-*Intention* (5.0) *exterior* to the "Physical Universe"–(KI); the "wave-peak" of "I" emerging as individuated consciousness from *Infinity*.

alpha-spirit : a "spiritual" *Life*-form; the "true" *Self* or I-AM; the *individual*; the spiritual (*alpha*) *Self* that is animating the (*beta*) physical body or "*genetic vehicle*" using a continuous *Lifeline* of spiritual ("*ZU*") energy; an individual spiritual (*alpha*) entity possessing no physical mass or measurable waveform (motion) in the Physical Universe as itself, so it animates the (*beta*) physical body or "*genetic vehicle*" as a catalyst to experience *Self*-determined causality in effect within the *Physical Universe*; a singular unit or point of *Spiritual Awareness* that is *Aware* that it is *Aware*.

alpha thought : the highest spiritual *Self-determination* over creation and existence exercised by an Alpha-Spirit; the Alpha range of pure *Creative Ability* based on direct postulates and considerations of *Beingness*; spiritual qualities comparable to "thought" but originating in Alpha-existence (at "6.0") independently superior to a *beta-anchored* Mind-System, although an Alpha-Spirit may use Will ("5.0") to carry the intentions of a postulate or consideration ("6.0") to the Master Control Center ("4.0").

amplitude : the quality of being *ample*; the size or amount of energy that is demonstrated in a *wave*. In the case of audio waves, we associate amplitude with "volume." It is not a statement about the frequencies (content) of waves, only how "loud" they are—to what extent they are or may be projected (or audible).

AN : an ancient "Sumerian" cuneiform sign for Heaven or "God"; in *Mardukite Zuism and Systemology* designating the *'spiritual zone'* (or *'Alpha Existence'*); the *Spiritual Universe*—comprised of spiritual matter and spiritual energy; a direction of motion toward spiritual *Infinity*, away from or superior to the physical (*'KI'*); the spiritual condition of existence providing for our primary *Alpha* state as an individual *Identity* or *I-AM-Self* which interacts and experiences *Awareness* of a *beta* state in the *Physical Universe* (*'KI'*) as *Life*.

anathema : a thing or person to be detested, loathed or avoided; a thing or person accursed or despised such as to wish damnation or "divine punishment" upon.

anchor (conceptual) : a stable point in space; a fixed point used to hold or stabilize a spatial existence of other points; a spatial point that fixes the parameters of dimensional orientation, such as the corner-points of a solid object in relation to other points in space; in *NexGen Systemology*, "beta-anchored" is an expression used to describe the fixed orientation of a viewpoint from Self in relation to all possible spatial points in *beta-existence* ("physical universe"), or else the existential points that fix the operation of the "body" within the space-time of *beta-existence*.

Ancient Mystery School : the original arcane source of all esoteric knowledge on Earth, concentrated between the Middle East and modern-day Turkey and Transylvania c. 6000 B.C. and then dispersing south (Mesopotamia), west (Europe) and east (Asia) from that location.

antinomian : a term applied to *Gnostics* (popularized by Martin Luther during the Christian reformation) denoting a rejection of formal religious morals and dogma—decreed, written and interpreted by humanity—as a true pathway to Ascension (some elements appear in all forms of religious protest and reformation but as an extreme, would be considered spirto-religious rebellious punkdom by some modern standards, but it should be understood that it does follow a higher ethic, such as Mardukite Utilitarianism.

apotheosis : from the *Greek* word, meaning "*to deify*"; the highest point or apex (for example, of "true knowledge" and "true experience"); an ultimate development of; a glorified or "deified" *ideal*, such as is a quality of *godhood*.

apparent : visibly exposed to sight; evident rather than actual, as presumed by Observation; readily perceived, especially by the senses.

a-priori : from "cause" to "effect"; from a general application to a particular instance; existing in the mind prior to, and independent of experience or observation; validity based on consideration and deduction rather than experience.

archetype : a "first form" or ideal conceptual model of some aspect; the ultimate prototype of a form on which all other conceptions are based.

ascension : actualized *Awareness* elevated to the point of true "spiritual existence" exterior to *beta existence*. An "Ascended Master" is one who has returned to an incarnation on Earth as an inherently *Enlightened One*, demonstrable in their actions—they have the ability to *Self-direct* the "Spirit" as *Self*, just as we are treating the "Mind" and "Body" at this current grade of instruction; previously treated in *Moroii ad Vitam* as a state of Beingness after *First Death*, experienced by an *etheric body*, which is able to maintain consciousness as a personal identity continuum with the same *Self-directed* control and communication of Will-Intention that is exercised, actualized and developed deliberately during one's present incarnation.

assessment : an analysis or synthesis of collected information, usually about a person or group, in relation to an *assessment scale*.

assessment scale : an official assignment of graded/gradient numeric values correlated to specific tiers with individual preassigned meanings.

associative knowledge : significance or meaning of a facet or aspect assigned to (or considered to have) a direct relationship with another facet; to connect or relate ideas or facets of existence with one another; a reactive-response image, emotion or conception that is suggested by (or directly accompanies) something other than itself; in traditional systems logic, an equivalency of significance or meaning between facets or sets that are grouped together, such as in $(a + b) + c = a + (b + c)$; in NexGen Systemology, erroneous associative knowledge is assignment of the same value to all facets or parts considered as related (even when they are not actually so), such as in $a = a, b = a, c = a$ and so forth without distinction.

assumption : the act of taking or gathering to one's Self; taking possession of, receive or behold.

attenergy : *NexGen Systemological NewSpeak* for "attention energies"; the flow of consciousness "energy" that is directed as "attention"; semantic recognition of an axiom from the *Arcane Tablets* that states: "energy flows where attention goes."

attention : active use of *Awareness* toward a specific aspect or thing; the act of "attending" with the presence of *Self*; a direction of focus or concentration of *Awareness* along a particular channel or conduit or toward a particular terminal node or communication termination point; the Self-directed concentration of personal energy as a combination of observation, thought-waves and consideration; focused application of *Self-Directed Awareness*.

Dictionary – 531

authoritarian : knowledge as truth, boundaries and freedoms dictated to an individual by a perceived, regulated or enforced "authority."

auto-suggestion (self-hypnosis) : auto-conditioning; self-programming; delivering directed affirmations or statements repeatedly to *Self* in order to condition a change in behavior or beliefs; any *Self-directed* technique intended to generate a specific "*post-hypnotic suggestion.*"

awareness : the highest sense of-and-as Self in knowing and being as I-AM (the *Alpha-Spirit*); the extent of beingness directed as a POV experienced by Self as knowingness.

axiom : a fundamental truism of a knowledge system, esp. *logic*; all *maxims* are also *axioms*; knowledge statements that require no proof because their truth is self-evident; an established law or systematic principle used as a *premise* on which to base greater conclusions of truth.

—B—

Babylonian : the ancient Mesopotamian civilization that evolved from *Sumer*; inception point for systematization of civic society and religion.

Back-Scan : to apply Awareness, *Zu-Vision* or "Alpha-Sight" (*exterior* to the *Human Condition*) and *resurface* impressions for recreating *Mental Imagery* of the *Backtrack* within one's own Personal Universe and treat with Wizard-Level (*Grade-V+*) methodology.

Backtrack : to retrace one's steps or go back to an early point in a sequence; an applied spiritual philosophy within *Metahuman Systemology* "*Wizard Grades*" regarding continuous existence of an individual's "*Spiritual Timeline*" through all lifetime-incarnations; the course that is already laid behind us; a methodology of systematic processing methods developed to assist in revealing "hidden" *Mental Images* and *Imprints* from one's past and reclaim attention-energies "left behind" with them by increasing ability to manage and control personal energy mechanisms fixed to their continuous automated creation.

band : a division or group; in *NexGen Systemology*, a division or set of frequencies on the ZU-line that are tuned closely together and referred to as a group.

BAT (Beta-Awareness Test) : a method of *psychometric evaluation* developed for *Mardukite Systemology* to determine a "basic" or "average" state of personal *beta-Awareness*; first developed for the text "*Crystal Clear.*"

"bell, book & candle" : three dissimilar objects that are kept accessible during a processing session (the book is often a copy of *The Systemology Handbook* or a hardcover copy of *The Tablets of Destiny* with the dust-jacket removed if it is less distracting that way); a term meant to indicate a Pilot's "objective processing kit" of objects generally present in the session room (accessible on a shelf, table or pedestal stands); in *NexGen Systemology*, the name of an objective processing philosophy pertaining to command of personal reality; historically, a formal ritual used by the Roman Catholic church to ceremonially declare an individual "guilty of the most heinous sins" as "excommunicated (to hold no further communications with) by anathema"—whereby a *bell* is rung, a *holy book* is closed and all *candles* are snuffed out—thus we therapeutically use the same symbolism historically representing religious fragmentation for modern systematic defragmentation purposes.

beta (awareness) : all consciousness activity ("*Awareness*") in the "Physical Universe" (KI) or else *beta-existence*; *Awareness* within the range of the *genetic-body*, including material thoughts, emotional responses and physical motors; personal *Awareness* of physical energy and physical matter moving through physical space and experienced as "time"; the *Awareness* held by *Self* that is restricted to a physical organic *Lifeform* or "*genetic vehicle*" in which it experiences causality in the *Physical Universe*.

beta (existence) : all manifestation in the "Physical Universe" (KI); the "Physical" state of existence consisting of vibrations of physical energy and physical matter moving through physical space and experienced as "time"; the conditions of *Awareness* for the *Alpha-spirit* (*Self*) as a physical organic *Lifeform* or "*genetic vehicle*" in which it experiences causality in the *Physical Universe*.

beta-defragmentation : toward a state of *Self-Honesty* in regards to handling experience of the "Physical Universe" (*beta-existence*); an applied spiritual philosophy (or technology) of Self-Actualization originally described in the text "*Crystal Clear*" (*Liber-2B*), building upon theories from "*Systemology: The Original Thesis*."

biological unconsciousness : the organism independent of the sentient *Awareness* of the *Self* to direct it; states induced by severe injury and anesthesia.

biomagnetic/biofeedback : a measurable effect, such as a change in electrical resistance, that is produced by thoughts, emotions and physical behaviors which generate specific 'neurotransmitters' and biochemical reactions in the brain, body and across the skin surface.

—C—

cacophony : dissonant, turbulent, harsh and/or discordant sound or noise.

calcified : in nature, to calcify is to harden like stone from calcium and lime deposits; in philosophic applications, refers to a state of hardened fixed bone-like inflexibility; a condition change to rigidly solid.

capable : the actual capacity for potential ability.

Dictionary – 533

CAT / "Creative Ability Test" : a method of increasing personal freedom and unlimited creative potential of the Alpha-Spirit (Self) independent and exterior to conditions and reality agreements with beta-existence; a Wizard-Level training regimen first developed for the Grade-IV text "*Imaginomicon*" (*Liber-3D*).

catalog / catalogue : a systematic list of knowledge or record of data.

catalyst : something that causes action between two systems or aspects, but which itself is unaffected as a variable of this energy communication; a medium or intermediary channel.

catharsis / cathartic processing : from the Greek root meaning "pure" or "perfect"; Gnostic practices of "consolamentum" where an individual removes distorting/fragmented emotional charges and encoding from a personal energy flow/circuit connected or associated with some terminal, mass, thing, &tc.; in *NexGen Systemology*, the emptying out or discharge of emotional stores; also "*abreaction*" or "*Route-1.*"

causative : as being the cause; to be at cause.

chakra : an archaic Sanskrit term for "wheel" or "spinning circle" used in *Eastern* wisdom traditions, spiritual systems and mysticism; a concept retained in NexGen Systemology to indicate etheric concentrations of energy into wheel-mechanisms that process *ZU* energy at specific frequencies along the *ZU-line*, of which the *Human Condition* is reportedly attached *seven* at various degrees as connected to the Gate symbolism.

channel : a specific stream, course, current, direction or route; to form or cut a groove or ridge or otherwise guide along a specific course; a direct path; an artificial aqueduct created to connect two water bodies or water or make travel possible.

charge : to fill or furnish with a quality; to supply with energy; to lay a command upon; in *NexGen Systemology*—to imbue with intention; to overspread with emotion; application of *Self-directed (WILL)* "intention" toward an emotional manifestation in beta-existence; personal energy stores and significances entwined as fragmentation in mental images, reactive-response encoding and intellectual (and/or) programmed beliefs; in traditional mysticism, to intentionally fix an energetic resonance to meet some degree, or to bring a specific concentration of energy that is transferred to a focal point, such as an object or space.

circuit : a circular path or loop; a closed-path within a system that allows a flow; a pattern or action or wave movement that follows a specific route or potential path only; in *NexGen Systemology*, "*communication processing*" pertaining to a specific flow of energy or information along a channel; *see* also "*feedback loop.*"

Circuit-1 : in *Grade-IV* "communication processing" (introduced in *Metahuman Destinations* as *Route-3*), the flow of energy and information connected to outflow, what *Self* has expressed, projected outwardly or done.

Circuit-2 : in *Grade-IV* "communication processing" (introduced in *Metahuman Destinations* as *Route-3*), the flow of energy and information connected to inflow, what "others" have done to *Self*, what it has received inwardly or had *happen to*.

Circuit-3 : in *Grade-IV* "communication processing" (introduced in *Metahuman Destinations* as *Route-3*), the flow of energy and information connected to cross-flows, what *Self* has witnessed of others (or another) projecting or doing toward others (or another).

Circuit-0 : a more advanced concept introduced to *Grade-IV* "communication processing" (as listed on SOP-2C in *Metahuman Destinations* for "*Pre-A.T*" or "*Route-0*" applications), which targets *'postulates'* and *'considerations'* generated and stored by *Self* for *Self* and the direction, energy or flows representing what *Self* "does" for and/or to *Self*. This circuit is treated further in *Wizard Level* work,

chronologically : concerning or pertaining to "time"; to treat as "units" of "time" ; to sequence a series of events or information with regard to the order it happened or originated (in time).

clockwork : rigidly fixed gear-like systems that operate mechanically and directly upon one another to function; a "clockwork universe theory" is a "closed-system design" popular in Newtonian Physics attributes all actions of energy-matter in space-time as reactions in accordance with a "Divine Decree" or fixed design that functions like a "clock-mechanism" and does not account for the "Observer."

code (ethics) : an outline of *ethical* standards regarding social participation and acceptable behavior; not generally enforced as *law* itself, but a standard that reasonable individuals are actualized (or civil) enough to *Self-Determine* (by choice) their own following (or adherence) if it is *right* and *good*; shared reality agreements that promote optimum conditions of continued existence ("SURVIVAL" in *Beta-existence*; "CREATION" in *Alpha*) for the highest affected "Sphere of Existence" (on the *Standard Model*).

codification : process of collecting, analyzing and then arranging knowledge in a standardized and more accessible systematic form, often by subject, theme or some other designation.

collapsing a wave : also, "*wave-function collapse*"; in *Quantum Physics*, the concept that an Observer is "collapsing" the wave-function to something "definite" by measuring it; defining or calculating a wave-function or interaction of potential interactions by an Observation; in *NexGen Systemology*, when a wave of potentiality or possibility because a finite fixed form; Consciousness or *Awareness* "collapses" a wave-function of energy-matter as a necessary "third" Principle of Apparent Manifestation (first described in "*Tablets of Destiny*"); potentiality as a wave is collapsed into an apparent "*is*", the energy of which is freed up in systematic processing by "*flattening*" a "collapsed" wave back into its state of potentiality.

command : in *Metahuman Systemology*, responsibility and ability of Self (I-AM) as operating from its ideal "exterior" *Point-of-View* as Alpha Spirit; to direct communication for control of the *genetic vehicle* and Mind-Body connection that is perfectly duplicated from a source-point to a receipt-point along the ZU-line.

command line : see "*processing command line*" (PCL).

common knowledge (game theory) : facts that all "players" know, and they know that all other "players" also know—such as the very structure of the "game" being played.

communication : successful transmission of information, data, energy (&tc.) along a message line, with a reception of feedback; an energetic flow of intention to cause an effect (or duplication) at a distance; the personal energy moved or acted upon by will or else 'selective directed attention'; the 'messenger action' used to transmit and receive energy across a medium; also relay of energy, a message or signal—or even locating a personal POV (viewpoint) for the Self—along the *ZU-line*.

communication (circuit) processing : a methodology of Grade-IV Metahuman Systemology that emphasizes analysis of all Mind-System energy flows (information) transmitted and stored along circuits of a channel toward some terminal, thing or concept, particularly: what Self has out-flowed, what Self has in-flowed, and the cross-flows that Self has observed; also "*Route-3*"

compulsion : a failure to be responsible for the dynamics of control—starting, stopping or altering—on a particular channel of communication and/or regarding a particular terminal in existence; an energetic flow with the appearance of being 'stuck' on the action it is already doing or by the control of some automatic mechanism.

computing device : a calculator or modern computer; a mechanism that performs specific functions, particularly input, output and storage of data/information.

concept : a high-frequency thought-wave representing an "idea" which persists because it is not restricted to a unique space-time; an abstract or tangible "idea" formed in the "Mind" or *imagined* as a means of understanding, usually including associated "Mental Images"; a seemingly timeless collective thought-theme (or subject) that entangles together facets of many events or incidents, not just a single significant one.

conceptual processing : a Wizard-Level methodology introduced intermittently throughout materials of Metahuman Systemology that emphasizes fully "getting the sense of" (or "contacting the idea of") a particular condition as prompted by a PCL and on one's own determination; a systematic practice-drill regarding considerations and postulates (Alpha Thought) regarding various reality agreements; a *Route-0* variant employing *Creativeness* and *Imagination* for systematic processing; also *Route-0E* when used for *Ethics Processing*.

condense (condensation) : the transition of vapor to liquid; denoting a change in state to a more substantial or solid condition; leading to a more compact or solid form.

condition : an apparent or existing state; circumstances, situations and variable dynamics affecting the order and function of a system; a series of interconnected requirements, barriers and allowances that must be met; in "contemporary language," bringing a thing toward a specific, desired or intentional new state (such as in "conditioning"), though to minimize confusion about the word "condition" in our literature, *NexGen Systemology* treats "contemporary conditioning" concepts as imprinting, encoding and programming.

conflict : the opposition of two forces of similar magnitude along the same channel or competing for the same terminal; the inability to duplicate another POV; a thought, intention or communication that is met with an opposing counter-thought or counter-intention that generates an energetic cluster.

confront : to come around in front of; to be in the presence of; to stand in front of, or in the face of; to meet "face-to-face" or "face-up-to"; additionally, in *NexGen Systemology*, to fully tolerate or acceptably withstand an encounter with a particular manifestation or encounter.

consciousness : the energetic flow of *Awareness*; the Principle System of *Awareness* that is spiritual in nature, which demonstrates potential interaction with all degrees of the Physical Universe; the *Beingness* component of our existence in *Spirit*; the Principle System of *Awareness* as *Spirit* that directs action in the Mind-System.

consensual (consensus) : formed or existing simply by consent—by general or mutual agreement; permitted, approved or agreed upon by majority of opinion; knowingly agreed upon unanimously by all concerned; to be in agreement on the objective universe and/or a course of action therein.

consideration : careful analytical reflection of all aspects; deliberation; determining the significance of a "thing" in relation to similarity or dissimilarity to other "things"; evaluation of facts and importance of certain facts; thorough examination of all aspects related to, or important for, making a decision; the analysis of consequences and estimation of significance when making decisions; in *NexGen Systemology*, the postulate or Alpha-Thought that defines the state of beingness for what something "*is*."

continuity : being a continuous whole; a complete whole or "total round of"; the balance of the equation ["–120" + "120" = "0" &tc.]; an apparent unbroken interconnected coherent whole; also, as applied to Universes in *NexGen Systemology*, the lowest base consideration of space-time or commonly shared level of energy-matter apparent in an existence, or else the lowest degree of solidity or condensation whereby all mass that exists is identifiable or communicable with all other mass that exists; represented as "0" on the *Standard Model* for the Physical Universe (*beta-existence*), a level of existence that is below Human emotion, comparable to the solidity of "rocks" and "walls" and "inert bodies."

continuum : a continuous enduring uninterrupted sequence or condition; observing all gradients on a *spectrum*; measuring quantitative variation with gradual transition on a spectrum without demonstrating discontinuity or separate parts.

control (general) : the ability to start, change or start some action or flow of energy; the capacity to originate, change or stop some mode of human behavior by some implication, physical or psychological means to ensure compliance (voluntarily or involuntarily).

control (systems) : communication relayed from an operative center or organizational cluster, which incites new activity elsewhere in a system (or along the *ZU-line*).

correlate : a relationship between two or more aspects, parts or systems.

correspondence : a direct relationship or correlation; see also "*associative knowledge.*"

Cosmic History : the entire continuous *Spiritual Timeline* of all existence, starting with the *Infinity of Nothingness* and individuation of Self and its Home Universe, running through various Games Universes and ultimately leading to condensation and solidification of this Physical Universe experienced in present-time.

Cosmic Law : the "Law" of Nature (or the Physical Universe); the "Law" governing cosmic ordering; often called "Natural Law" in sciences and philosophies that attempt to codify or systematize it.

cosmology : a systematic philosophy defining origins and structure of an apparent Universe.

Cosmos : archaic term for the "Physical Universe"; semantically implies chaos brought into order; in *NexGen Systemology*, can also include considerations of "Universes" experienced previously as a *beta-existence*.

counter-productive : contrary to the greater or original purpose or intention; in *NexGen Systemology*, anything which brings *Life* away from its sustainable goal or position of *Infinite Existence*.

crash-coursed : a very intense or steep delivery of education over a very brief time period, usually applied to bring a student "up-to-speed" or "up-to-date" for receiving and understanding newer or cumulatively more advanced material.

creative ability test : see "*CAT.*"

creativeness processing : a *systematic processing* methodology introduced in *Grade-IV Metahuman Systemology* (*Wizard Level-0*) that emphasizes personal use of "*Imagination,*" or else "creative ability" of Self and freeing considerations of the Alpha-Spirit to *Be* or *Create* anything within its Personal Universe, independent of reality agreements with beta-existence; also "*Route-0.*"

Crossing the Abyss : to enter the spiritual or metaphysical unknown in "Self-annihilation" to purify the Self and "return to the Source."

Crystal Clear : the second professional publication of Mardukite Systemology, released publicly in December 2019; the second professional text in Grade-III Mardukite Systemology, released as "*Liber-2B*" and reissued in the Grade-III Master Edition "*Systemology Handbook*"; contains fundamental theory of "*Beta-Defragmentation*" and "*Route-2*" systematic processing methodology.

cuneiform : the oldest extant writing system at the inception of modern civilization in Mesopotamia; a system of wedge-shaped script inscribed on clay tablets with a reed pen, allowing advancements in record keeping and communication no longer restricted to more literal graphic representations or pictures.

cuneiform signs : the cuneiform script, as used in ancient Mesopotamia, is not represented in a linear alphabet of "letters," but by a systematic use of basic word "signs" that are combined to form more complex word "signs"—each sign represented a "sound" more than it did a letter, such as "ab," "ad", "ba", "da" *&tc*.

—D—

data-set : the total accumulation of knowledge used to base Reality.

dead-memories : outdated/inadequate/erroneous data.

defragmentation : the *reparation* of wholeness; collecting all dispersed parts to reform an original whole; a process of removing "*fragmentation*" in data or knowledge to provide a clear understanding; applying techniques and processes that promote a *holistic* interconnected *alpha* state, favoring observational *Awareness* of continuity in all spiritual and physical systems; in *NexGen Systemology*, a "*Seeker*" achieving an actualized state of basic "*Self-Honest Awareness*" is said to be *beta-defragmented*, whereas *Alpha-defragmentation* is the rehabilitation of the *creative ability*, managing the *Spiritual Timeline* and the POV of *Self* as Alpha-Spirit (I-AM); see also "*Beta-defragmentation.*"

degree : a physical or conceptual *unit* (or point) defining the variation present relative to a *scale* above and below it; any stage or extent to which something *is* in relation to other possible positions within a *set* of "*parameters*"; a point within a specific range or spectrum; in *NexGen Systemology*, a *Seeker's* potential energy variations or fluctuations in thought, emotional reaction and physical perception are all treated as "*degrees*."

demographics : segments of the population uniquely identified, whether real or representative; targeting a specific portion of the population, such as for marketing or statistics.

destiny : what is set down, made firm, standard, or stands fixed as a constant end; the absolute *destination* regardless of whatever course is traveled; in *NexGen Systemology*, the "*destiny*" of the "*Human Spirit*" (or "*Alpha Spirit*") is infinite existence—"*Immortality.*"

dichotomy : a division into two parts, types or kinds.

differential : the quantitative value difference between two forces, motions, pressures or degrees.

differentiation : an apparent difference between aspects or concepts.

discernment : to perceive, distinguish and/or differentiate experience into true knowledge.

displace : to compel to leave; to move or replace something with something else in its place or space.

dissonance : discordance; out of step; out of phase; disharmonious; the "differential" between the way things are and the way things are experienced; cognitive dissonance could be demonstrated as A = abc, or C = A, the duplication of truth/communication is not A-for-A.

dogma : religious doctrines or opinion-based beliefs (data-set) treated socially as fact, especially regarding "divinity" or "God" (the common "Human" interpretation of the "domain" of Infinity) represented by the "Eighth Sphere" on our original Standard Model of Systemology; religiously defined values, taboos and ethical standards emphasized by cultural/religious socialization and mythographic beliefs (even above any observable causal effects, logical sequences or verifiable proofs).

dramatization / dramatize : a vivid display or performance as if rehearsed for a "play" (on stage); a *'circuit'* recording *'imprinted'* in the past and, once restimulated by a facet of the environment, the individual "replays" it as through reacting to it in the present (and identifying that reality as present reality); acts, actions and observable behaviors that demonstrate identification with a particular character type, "phase" or personality program; a motivated sequence-chain, implant series or imprinted cycle of actions—usually irrational or counter-survival—repeated by an individual as it had previously happened to them; a reoccurring or reactively triggered out-flow, communication or action that indicates an individual "occupying" a particular *'Point-of-View'* (*POV*)—typically fixed to a specific (past) identification (identity) that is space-time locatable (meaning a point where significant *Attenergy*—enough to compulsively create and maintain a POV—is "stuck" or "hung up" on the *BackTrack*).

dross : prime material; specifically waste-matter or refuse; the discarded remains collected together.

dynamic (systems) : a principle or fixed system which demonstrates its *'variations'* in activity (or output) only in constant relation to variables or fluctuation of interrelated systems; a standard principle, function, process or system that exhibits *'variations'* and change simultaneously with all connected systems; each *'Sphere of Existence'* is a dynamic system, systematically affecting (supporting) and affected (supported) by other *'Spheres'* (which are also dynamic systems).

—E—

Eastern traditions : the evolution of the *Ancient Mystery School* east of its origins, primarily the Asian continent, or what is archaically referred to as "oriental."

echelon : a level or rung on a ladder; a rank or level of command.

eclipse : to cast a shadow or darken; to block out or obscure a comparison.

EDA : "electro-dermal activity"; see also *GSR-Meter*.

electro-psychometer ("E-meter") : see *GSR-Meter*.

elocution : the skillful use of clearly directed and expressive speech; the expert demonstration of articulation, pronunciation and dictation to express a message.

emotional encoding : the readable substance/material (data) of *'imprints'*; associations of sensory experience with an *imprint*; perceptions of our environment that receive an *emotional charge*, which form or reinforce facets of an *imprint*; perceptions recorded and stored as an *imprint* within the "emotional range" of energetic manifestation; the formation of an energetic store or charge on a channel that fixes emotional responses as a mechanistic automation, which is carried on in an individual's *Spiritual Timeline* (or personal continuum of existence).

enact : to make happen; to bring into action; to make part of an act.

encompassing : to form a circle around, surround or envelop around.

end point : the moment when the goal of a process has been achieved and to continue on with it will be detrimental to the gains; the finality of a process when the *Seeker* has achieved their optimum state from the current cycle (whether or not they run through it again at a later date with a different level of *Awareness* or knowledge base doesn't change the fact that it has flattened the standing wave

energetic exchange : communicated transmission of energetically encoded "information" between fields, forces or source-points that share some degree of interconnectivity; the event of "waves" acting upon each other like a force, flowing in regard to their proximity, range, frequency and amplitude.

energy signatures : a distinctive pattern of energetic action.

enforcement : the act of compelling or putting (effort) into force; to compel or impose obedience by force; to impress strongly with applications of stress to demand agreement or validation; the lowest-level of direct control by physical effort or threat of punishment; a low-level method of control in the absence of true communication.

engineering : the *Self-directed* actions and efforts to utilize knowledge (observed causality/science), maths (calculations/quantification) and logic (axioms/formulas) to understand, design or manifest a solid structure, machine, mechanism, engine or system; as *"Reality Engineering"* in *NexGen Systemology*—intentional *Self-directed* adjustment of existing Reality conditions; the application of total *Self-determinism* in *Self-Honesty* to change apparent Reality using fundamentals of *Systemology* and *Cosmic Law*.

entanglement : tangled together; intertwined and enmeshed systems; in *NexGen Systemology*, a reference to the interrelation of all particles as waves at a higher point of connectivity than is apparent, since wave-functions only "collapse" when someone is *Observing*, or doing the measuring, evaluating, &tc.

entropy : the reduction of organized physical systems back into chaos-continuity when their integrity is measured against space over time; reduction toward a zero-point.

epicenter : the point from which shock-waves travel.

epistemology : a school of philosophy focused on the truth of knowledge and knowledge of truth; theories regarding validity and truth inherent in any structure of knowledge and reason; the original "school of philosophy" from which all other "disciplines" were derived; the study of knowing how to know knowledge, reason and truth.

erroneous : inaccurate; incorrect; containing error.

esoteric : hidden; secret; knowledge understood by a select few.

etching : to cut, bite or corrode with acid to produce a pattern.

ethics : an intellectual philosophy concerning *rightness* and *wrongness* based on "logic" and "reason" (rationale) combined with observable consequences and tendencies of action or conduct; formal name for a "moral philosophy" (study of moral choices); in ancient times, originally treated *one-to-one* with "Cosmic Law" regarding *causation*, *order* and *sequence*;

an objective (Universal) philosophy of *rightness* and *wrongness*, treated separate from culture-specific (subjective/relative) considerations, such as *morals* and *dogma*; in *NexGen Systemology* (*Grade-IV Metahuman Systemology*), a dynamic philosophy (applying "logic-and-reason") to understand the nature of "reality agreements" concerning *rightness* and *wrongness*, then treating the most optimum conditions of continued existence ("SURVIVAL" in *Beta-existence*; "CREATION" in *Alpha*) for the highest affected "Sphere of Existence" (on the *Standard Model*).

ethics processing : a *systematic processing* methodology introduced for bridging *Grade-IV Metahuman Systemology* (*Wizard Level-0*) with *Grade-V Spiritual Systemology* (*Wizard Level-1*) that emphasizes personal realization of *"Ethics"* and increased ability and responsibility to confront the "rightness" and "wrongness" of past actions (on the Backtrack), including defragmentation of *"Harmful Acts"* (as *Imprinting Incidents*) and any corresponding *"Hold-Backs"* and *"Hold-Outs"* (which reduce *Actualized Awareness* and prompt an individual to *withdraw* their *reach*); also *"Route-3E."*

etymology : the origins of "words" and their development.

evaluate : to determine, assign or fix a set value, amount or meaning.

exacting : a demanding rigid effort to draw forth from.

executable : the supreme authoritative ability to carry out according to design.

existence : the *state* or fact of *apparent manifestation*; the resulting combination of the Principles of Manifestation: consciousness, motion and substance; continued *survival*; that which independently exists; the 'Prime Directive' and sole purpose of all manifestation or Reality; the highest common intended motivation driving any *"Thing"* or *Life*.

existential : pertaining to existence, or some aspect or condition of existence.

exoteric : public knowledge or common understanding; the level of understanding and *Knowing* maintained by the "masses"; how a thing is generally understood "by all" or the opposite of *esoteric*.

experiential data : accumulated reference points we store as memory concerning our "experience" with Reality.

exponent : a person that is a critical example of something.

extant : in existence; existing.

exterior : outside of; on the outside; in *NexGen Systemology*, we mean specifically the POV of *Self* that is 'outside of' the *Human Condition*, free of the physical and mental trappings of the Physical Universe; a metahuman range of consideration; see also 'Zu-Vision'.

external : a force coming from outside; information received from outside sources; in *NexGen Systemology*, the objective *'Physical Universe'* existence, or *beta-existence*, that the Physical Body or *genetic vehicle* is essentially *anchored* to for its considerations of locational space-time as a dimension or POV.

extrapolate : to make an estimate of the "value" outside of the perceivable range.

extropy : *NexGen Systemology NewSpeak*—the reduction of organized spiritual systems back into a singularity of Infinity when their integrity is measured against space over time; reduction toward an infinitude; the opposite of *entropy*.

—F—

facets : an aspect, an apparent phase; one of many faces of something; a cut surface on a gem or crystal; in *NexGen Systemology*—a single perception or aspect of a memory or "*Imprint*"; any one of many ways in which a memory is recorded; perceptions associated with a painful emotional (sensation) experience and "*imprinted*" onto a metaphoric lens through which to view future similar experiences; other secondary terminals that are associated with a particular terminal, painful event or experience of loss, and which may exhibit the same encoded significance as the activating event.

faculties : abilities of the mind (individual) inherent or developed.

fallacy : a deceptive, misleading, erroneous and/or false beliefs; unsound logic; persuasions, invalidation or enforcement of Reality agreements based on authority, sympathy, bandwagon/mob mentality, vanity, ambiguity, suppression of information, and/or presentation of false dichotomies.

fate : what is brought to light or actualized as experience; the actual *course* taken to reach an end, charted end, or final *destination*; in *NexGen Systemology*, the *'fate'* of a *'Human Spirit'* (or *'Alpha Spirit'*) is determined by the choice of course taken to experience *Life*.

feedback loop : a complete and continuous circuit flow of energy or information directed as an output from a source to a target which is altered and return back to the source as an input; in *General Systemology*—the continuous process where outputs of a system are routed back as inputs to complete a circuit or loop, which may be closed or connected to other systems/circuits; in *NexGen Systemology*—the continuous process where directed *Life* energy and *Awareness* is sent back to *Self* as experience, understanding and memory to complete an energetic circuit as a loop.

flattening a wave : see "*process-out*" for definition; also see "*collapsing a wave*."

flow : movement across (or through) a channel (or conduit); a direction of active energetic motion typically distinguished as either an *in-flow*, *out-*

flow or *cross-flow*.

fodder : food, esp. for cattle; the raw material used to create.

forgive(ness) : to let go of resentment (against an offender, source of *Harmful-Act*) or give up emotional (energetic) turbulence connected to inclinations to punish; a legal pardon; to intentionally "overlook" (as opposed to "forget") the repayment of a debt or sense of something owed.

fractal : a wave-curve, geometric figure, form or pattern, with each part representative of the same characteristics as the whole; any baseline, sequence or pattern where the 'whole' is found in the 'parts' and the 'parts' contain the 'whole'; a pattern that reoccurs similarly at various scales/levels on a continuous whole; a subset of a Euclidean space explored in higher-level academic mathematics, in which fractal dimensions are found to exceed topological ones; in NexGen Systemology, a "fractal-like" description is used specifically for a pattern or form that has a reoccurring nature without regard to what level or scale it is manifest upon. Examples include the formation of crystals, tree-like patterns, the comparison of atoms to solar systems to galaxies, &tc.

fragmentation : breaking into parts and scattering the pieces; the *fractioning* of wholeness or the *fracture* of a holistic interconnected *alpha* state, favoring observational *Awareness* of perceived connectivity between parts; *discontinuity*; separation of a totality into parts; in *NexGen Systemology*, a person outside a state of *Self-Honesty* is said to be *fragmented*.

—G—

game : a strategic situation where a "player's" power of choice is employed or affected; a parameter or condition defined by purposes, freedoms and barriers (rules).

game theory : a mathematical theory of logic pertaining to strategies of maximizing gains and minimizing loses within prescribed boundaries and freedoms; a field of knowledge widely applied to human problem solving and decision-making; the application of true knowledge and logic to deduce the correct course of action given all variables and interplay of dynamic systems; logical study of decision making where "players" make choices that affect (the interests) of other "players"; an intellectual study of conflict and cooperation.

general systemology ("systematology") : a methodology of analysis and evaluation regarding the systems—their design and function; organizing systems of interrelated information-processing in order to perform a given function or pattern of functions.

genetic memory : the evolutionary, cellular and genetic (DNA) "memory" encoded into a *genetic vehicle* or *living organism* during its progression and duplication (reproduction) over millions (or billions) of years on

Earth; in *NexGen Systemology*—the past-life Earth-memory carried in the genetic makeup of an organism (*genetic vehicle*) that is *independent of any* actual "spiritual memory" maintained by the *Alpha Spirit* themselves, from its own previous lifetimes on Earth and elsewhere using other *genetic vehicles* with no direct evolutionary connection to the current physical form in use.

genetic-vehicle : a physical *Life*-form; the physical (*beta*) body that is animated/controlled by the (*Alpha*) *Spirit* using a continuous *Lifeline* (ZU); a physical (*beta*) organic receptacle and catalyst for the (*Alpha*) *Self* to operate "causes" and experience "effects" within the *Physical Universe*.

gifted : attributing a special quality or ability; having exceptionally high intelligence or mental faculties.

gnosis : a *Greek* word meaning knowledge, but specifically "true knowledge"; the highest echelon of "true knowledge" accessible (or attained) only by mystical or spiritual faculties whereby actualized realizations are achieved independent of specialized education.

Gnostics : a name meaning "having knowledge" in Greek language (see also *gnosis*); an early sect of Judeo-Christian mysticism from the 1st Century AD emphasizing true knowledge by *Self-Honest* experience of metahuman and spiritual states of beingness, emphasizing defragmentation of "illusion" and overcoming of material "deception"; an esoteric proto-Systemology organization disbanded by the Roman Church as heretical.

godhood : a divine character or condition; "divinity."

gradient : a degree of partitioned ascent or descent along some scale, elevation or incline; "higher" and "lower" values in relation to one another.

GSR-Meters ("galvanic skin response"–"electropsychometer") : a *biofeedback* device used for measuring electrical resistance (in "Ohms") of the skin surface; one of many parts used in a polygraph system; a highly sensitive "Ohm-meter" with variable range, set points and amplification used to monitor electrical fluctuations of the skin surface.

—H—

harmful-act : a counter-survival mode of behavior or action (esp. that causes harm to one of more *Spheres of Existence*)—or—an overtly aggressive (hostile and/or destructive) action against an individual or any other *Sphere of Existence*; in *Utilitarian Systemology*—a shortsighted (serves fewest/lowest *Spheres of Existence*) intentional overtly harmful action to resolve a perceived problem; a revision of the rule for standard *Utilitarianism* for Systemology to distinguish actions which provide the least benefit to the least number of *Spheres of Existence*, or else the greatest harm to the greatest number of *Spheres of Existence*; in *moral philosophy*—an action which can be experienced by few and/or which one would not be willing to experience for themselves (*theft, slander, rape, &tc*); an iniquity or iniquitous act.

help : to assist survival of; aid continuing optimum success.

heralded : proclaimed ahead of or prior to; officially announced.

hold-back : withheld communications (esp. actions) such as "*Hold-Outs*"; intentional (or automatic) withdrawal (as opposed to reach); Self-restraint (which may eventually be enforced or automated); not reaching, acting or expressing, when one should be; an ability that is now restrained (on automatic) due to inability to withhold it on Self-determinism alone.

hold-outs : in photography, the numerous snapshots/pictures withheld from the final display or professional presentation of the event; withheld communications; in Utilitarian Systemology—energetic withdrawal and communication breaks with a "*terminal*" and its *Sphere of Existence* as a result of a "*Harmful-Act*"; unspoken or undiscovered (hidden, covert) actions that an individual withholds communications of, fearing punishment or endangerment of *Self-preservation* (*First Sphere*); the act of hiding (or keeping hidden) the truth of a "*Harmful-Act*"; a refusal to communicate with a *Pilot*; also "*Hold-Back.*"

holistic : the examination of interconnected systems as encompassing something greater than the *sum* of their "parts."

Homo Novus : literally, the "new man"; the "newly elevated man" or "known man" in ancient Rome; the man who "knows (only) through himself"; in NexGen Systemology—the next spiritual and intellectual evolution of *homo sapiens* (the "modern Human Condition"), which is signified by a demonstration of higher faculties of *Self-Actualization* and clear *Awareness*.

Homo Sapiens Sapiens : the present standard-issue Human Condition; the *hominid* species and genetic-line on Earth that received modification, programming and conditioning by the *Anunnaki* race of *Alpha-Spirits*, of which early alterations contributed to various upgrades (changes) to the genetic-line, beginning approximately 450,000 years ago (*ya*) when the *Anunnaki* first appear on Earth; a species for the Human Condition on Earth that resulted from many specific *Anunnaki* "genetic" and "cultural" *interventions* at certain points of significant advancement—specifically (but not limited to) circa 300,000 *ya*, 200,000 *ya*, 40,000 *ya*, and 8,000 *ya*; a species of the Human Condition set for replacement by *Homo Novus*.

hostile-motivation : an *imprint* of a counter-survival action (or "*Harmful-Act*") committed by another against Self, stored as data to justify future actions (retaliation, &tc.); any *Sphere of Existence* (though usually an individual) receiving the effect of a "*Harmful-Act*"; an *imprint* used to rationalize "motivation" or "justification" for committing a "*Harmful-Act*"; in systematic *games theory*—the *modus operandi* concerning "payback," "revenge" and "tit-for-tat."

hot button : something that triggers or incites an intense emotional reaction instantaneously; in *NexGen Systemology*—a slang term denoting a highly reactive *channel*, heavily *charged* with a long chain of cumulative *emotional imprinting*, typically (but not necessarily) connected to a significant or "primary" *implant*; a non-technical label, first applied during *Grade-IV Professional Piloting "Flight School"* research sessions of Spring-Summer 2020, to indicate specific circuits, channels or terminals that cause a *Seeker* to immediately react with intense emotional responses, whether in general, directed to the *Pilot*, or even at effectiveness of processing.

Human Condition : a standard default state of Human experience that is generally accepted to be the extent of its potential identity (*beingness*)—currently treated as *Homo Sapiens Sapiens,* but which is scheduled for replacement by *Homo Novus*.

humanistic psychology : a field of academic psychology approaching a holistic emphasis on *Self-Actualization* as an individual's most basic motivation; early key figures from the 20th century include: Carl Rogers, Abraham Maslow, L. Ron Hubbard, William Walker Atkinson, Deepak Chopra and Timothy Leary (to name a few).

hypothetical : operating under the assumption a certain aspect actual "is."

—I—

identification : the association of *identity* to a thing; a label or fixed dataset associated to what a thing is; association "equals" a thing, the "equals" being key; an equality of all things in a group, for example, an "apple" identified with all other "apples"; the reduction of "I-AM"-*Self* from a *Spiritual Beingness* to an "identity" of some form.

identity : the collection of energy and matter—including memory—across a *"Spiritual Timeline"* that we consider as "I" of *Self*, but the "I" is an individual and not an identification with anything other than *Self* as *Alpha-Spirit*.

identity-system : the application of the *ZU-line* as "I"—the continuous expression of *Self* as *Awareness* across a *"Spiritual Timeline"*; see *"identity."*

illuminated : to supply with light so as to make visible or comprehensible.

imagination : the ability to create *mental imagery* in one's Personal Universe at will and change or alter it as desired; the ability to create, change and dissolve mental images on command or as an act of will; to create a mental image or have associated imagery displayed (or "conjured") in the mind that may or may not be treated as real (or memory recall) and may or may not accurately duplicate objective reality; to employ *Creative Abilities* of the Spirit that are independent of reality agreements with beta-existence.

Imaginomicon : the fourth professional publication of Mardukite Systemology, released publicly in mid- 2021; the second professional text in Grade-IV Metahuman Systemology, released as *"Liber-3D"*; contains fundamental theory of *"Spiritual Ability"* and *"Route-0"* systematic processing methodology.

immersion : plunged or sunk into; wholly surrounded by.

imperative : a high-level authoritarian command; a command triggering urgency and necessity of a certain goal or directive; see also *"Spheres of Existence"* and *"Prime Directive."*

implant : to graft or surgically insert; to establish firmly by setting into; to instill or install a direct command or consideration in consciousness (Mind-System, &tc.); a mechanical device inserted beneath the surface/skin; in *Metahuman Systemology*, an "energetic mechanism" (linked to an Alpha-Spirit) composing a circuit-network and systematic array of energetic receptors underlying and filter-screening communication channels between the Mind-System and *Self*; an energetic construct installed upon entry of a Universe; similar to a platen or matrix or circuit-board, where each part records a specific type or quality of *emotionally encoded imprints* and other "heavily charged" *Mental Images* that are "impressed" by future encounters; a basic platform on which certain *imprints* and *Mental Images* are encoded (keyed-in) and stored (often beneath the surface of "knowing" or *Awareness* for that individual, although an implanted "command" toward certain inclinations or behavioral tendencies may be visibly observable.

imprint : to strongly impress, stamp, mark (or outline) onto a softer 'impressible' substance; to mark with pressure onto a surface; in *NexGen Systemology*, the term is used to indicate permanent Reality impressions marked by frequencies, energies or interactions experienced during periods of emotional distress, pain, unconsciousness, loss, enforcement, or something antagonistic to physical (personal) survival, all of which are are stored with other reactive response-mechanisms at lower-levels of *Awareness* as opposed to the active memory database and proactive processing center of the Mind; an experiential "memory-set" that may later resurface —be triggered or stimulated artificially—as Reality, of which similar responses will be engaged automatically; holographic-like imagery "stamped" onto consciousness as composed of energetic *facets* tied to the "snap-shot" of an experience.

imprinting incident : the first or original event instance communicated and *emotionally encoded* onto an individual's *"Spiritual Timeline"* (recorded memory from all lifetimes), which formed a permanent impression that is later used to mechanistically treat future contact on that channel; the first or original occurrence of some particular *facet* or mental image related to a certain type of *encoded response*, such as pain and discomfort, losses and victimization, and even the acts that we have taken against others along the Spiritual Timeline of our existence that caused them to also be *Imprinted*.

inadvertent : an unintended (knowingly) result caused by low-Awareness actions; applying effort (enacting change) outside Self-Honesty, leading to negligent oversights with harmful outcomes.

incarnation : a present, living or concrete form of some thing, idea or beingness; an individual lifetime or life-cycle from birth/creation to death/destruction independent of other lifetimes or cycles.

inception : the beginning, start, origin or outset.

incite : to urge on or cause; instigate; prove or stimulate into action.

indefinable : without a clear definition being currently presented.

individual : a person, lifeform, human entity or creature; a *Seeker* or potential *Seeker* is often referred to as an "individual" within Mardukite Zuism and Systemology materials.

infinite existence : "immortality."

infinitude : being infinite; quantity or quality of *Infinity*.

inhibited : withheld, held-back, discouraged or repressed from some state.

iniquities : wickedness or wicked acts ("sinful" in religious use); literal etymology, "that which is not equal"; synonymous with *Harmful-Acts*.

"in phase" : see *"phase alignment."*

insistence : repeated use of a communicated energy into a form that demands acknowledgment, is more difficult to avoid or ignore.

institution : a social standard or organizational group responsible for promoting some system or aspect in society.

intention : the directed application of Will; to intend (have "in Mind") or signify (give "significance" to) for or toward a particular purpose; in *NexGen Systemology* (from the *Standard Model*)—the spiritual activity at WILL (5.0) directed by an *Alpha Spirit* (7.0); the application of WILL as "Cause" from a higher order of Alpha Thought and consideration (6.0), which then may continue to relay communications as an "effect" in the universe.

inter-dimensional : systems that are interconnected or correlated between the Physical Universe and the Spiritual Universe—or between "dimension states" observably identified as "physical," "emotional," "psychological" and "spiritual." The only point of true interconnectivity that we can systematically determine is called "*Life*" or the POV of *Self*.

interior : inside of; on the inside; in *NexGen Systemology*, we mean specifically the POV of *Self* that is fixed to the *'internal'* Human Condition, including the *Reactive Control Center* (RCC) and Mind-System or *Master Control Center* (MCC); within *beta-existence*.

intermediate : a distinct point between two points; actions between two points.

internal : a force coming from inside; information received from inside sources; in *NexGen Systemology*, the objective *'Physical Universe'* experience of *beta-existence* that is associated with the Physical Body or *genetic vehicle* and its POV regarding sensation and perception; from inside the body; within the body.

interrogation : obtaining specific information through responses to questions, such as in 'systematic processing' and other forms of two-way communication.

invalidate : decrease the level or degree or *agreement* as Reality.

invest : spend on; give or devote something in exchange for a beneficial result; to endow with.

—J—

justice : observable social actions (or consequential reaction) and predetermined civic (legal) processes employed in a society or group to uphold or enforce their reality agreements concerning "*law*"; a civic authority and administrative body responsible for carrying out practical/physical responses and penalties; the words, "*just,*" "*justice*" and "*justification,*" all stem from the Latin "*jus*" (meaning "*morally right,*" "*law, in accordance with*" and "*lawful*") or "*iustus*" (expressing what is "true," "proper," "upright" and "justified").

—K—

"kNow" : a creative spelling and use of semantics for "*know*" and "*now*" to indicate the state of present-time actualized "Awareness" as Self (Alpha-Spirit), developed for fun dual-meaning messages made by early Mardukite Systemologists in 2008-9, such as "Live in the kNow" or "Be in the kNow"—and even "Drown in the kNow" (parodying a song featuring Matisyahu, by electronic music duo, *Crystal Method*).

knowledge : clear personal processing of informed understanding; information (data) that is actualized as effectively workable understanding; a demonstrable understanding on which we may 'set' our *Awareness*—or literally a "know-ledge."

KI : an ancient cuneiform sign designating the *'physical zone'*; the *Physical Universe*—comprised of physical matter and physical energy in action across space and observed as time; a direction of motion toward material *Continuity*, away from or subordinate to the Spiritual (*'AN'*); the physical condition of existence providing for our *beta* state of *Awareness* experienced (and interacted with) as an individual *Lifeform* from our primary Alpha state of Identity or *I-AM-Self* in the *Spiritual Universe* (*'AN'*).

kinetic : pertaining to energy of physical motion and movement.

—L—

law : a formal codified outline (or list) of *ethical* standards regarding social participation and acceptable behavior, like a *"code,"* except that it *is* enforced by civic consequences (or even *"Cosmic Law"*) when not adhered to, usually with punishment coming either by the group (exclusively) or by involvement with an "outside party" or societal (legal) authority; a predictable sequence of naturally occurring events that will consistently repeat under the right conditions (such as *"Cosmic Law"* or *"Natural Law"*).

learned : highly educated; possessing significant knowledge.

level : a physical or conceptual *tier* (or plane) relative to a *scale* above and below it; a significant *gradient* observable as a *foundation* (or surface) built upon and subsequent to other levels of a totality or whole; a *set* of *"parameters"* with respect to other such *sets* along a *continuum*; in *Nex-Gen Systemology*, a *Seeker's* understanding, *Awareness* as *Self* and the formal grades of material/instruction are all treated as *"levels."*

Liber-One : First published in October 2019 as *"The Tablets of Destiny: Using Ancient Wisdom to Unlock Human Potential"* by Joshua Free; republished in the complete *Grade-III* anthology, *"The Systemology Handbook"*; revised in August 2022 as *"The Tablets of Destiny (Revelation): How Long-Lost Anunnaki Wisdom Can Change the Fate of Humanity."*

Liber-Two : First published in October 2020 as *"Metahuman Destinations: Piloting the Course to Homo Novus"* by Joshua Free; an anthology of the *Grade-IV* "Professional Piloting Course," containing revised materials from *Liber-2C*, *Liber-2D* and (most of) *Liber-3C*; republished in the complete *Grade-IV* anthology, *"The Metahuman Systemology Handbook."*

Liber-Three : see *"Liber-3E."*

Liber-2B : First published in December 2019 as *"Crystal Clear: The Self-Actualization Manual & Guide to Total Awareness"* by Joshua Free; republished in the complete *Grade-III* anthology, *"The Systemology Handbook"*; revised in April 2022 as *"Crystal Clear (Handbook for Seekers): Achieve Self-Actualization and Spiritual Ascension in This Lifetime."*

Liber-2C : First published in April 2020 as *"Communication and Control of Energy & Power: The Magic of Will & Intention (Volume One)"* by Joshua Free; revision republished as an integral part of the *Grade-IV* "Professional Piloting Course," in October 2020 within *"Metahuman Destinations"* (*Liber-Two*); republished in the complete *Grade-IV* anthology, *"The Metahuman Systemology Handbook."*

Liber-2D : First published in June 2020 as "*Command of the Mind-Body Connection: The Magic of Will & Intention" (Volume Two)*" by Joshua Free; revision republished as an integral part of the *Grade-IV* "*Professional Piloting Course,*" in October 2020 within "*Metahuman Destinations*" (*Liber-Two*); republished in the complete *Grade-IV* anthology, "*The Metahuman Systemology Handbook.*"

Liber-3C : First published in July 2020 as "*Now You Know: The Truth About Universes & How You Got Stuck in One*" by Joshua Free; a discourse in the *Grade-IV* Metahuman Systemology series; a revision of one part republished in October 2020 within the "*Professional Piloting Course*" manual, "*Metahuman Destinations*" (*Liber-Two*), a revision of the remaining part republished in June 2021 within the "*Imaginomicon*" (*Liber-3D*); republished in the complete *Grade-IV* anthology, "*The Metahuman Systemology Handbook.*"

Liber-3D : First published in June 2021 as "*Imaginomicon: The Gateway to Higher Universes (A Grimoire for the Human Spirit)*" by Joshua Free; a manual completing the *Grade-IV* (Metahuman Systemology) professional series with a treatment of "Wizard Level-0"; revised in June 2022 as "*Imaginomicon (Revised Edition): Approaching Gateways to Higher Universes (A New Grimoire for the Human Spirit)*"; republished in the complete *Grade-IV* anthology, "*The Metahuman Systemology Handbook.*"

Liber-3E (Liber-Three) : First published in April 2022 as "*The Way of the Wizard: Utilitarian Systemology (A New Metahuman Ethic)*" by Joshua Free; a professional manual bridging *Grade-IV* (Metahuman Systemology, *Wizard Level-0*) with *Grade-V* (Spiritual Systemology, *Wizard Level-1*); republished in the complete *Grade-IV* anthology, "*The Metahuman Systemology Handbook.*"

localized : brought together and confined to a particular place.

logic : philosophical science of correct *reasoning*.

logic equations : using symbols and basic mathematical logic to establish the validity of statements or to see how a variable within a system will change the result; a basic demonstration of proportion or relationship between variables in a system.

logistics : pertaining to the movement or transportation between locations.

—M—

macrocosmic : taking examples and system demonstrations at one level and applying them as a larger demonstration of a relatively higher level or unseen dimension.

malefactor : a person that knowingly commits *Harmful-Acts*; a source of frequent turbulence and destruction on a system.

manifestation : something brought into existence.

Marduk : founder of Babylonia; patron Anunnaki "god" of Babylon.

Mardukite Zuism : a Mesopotamian-themed (Babylonian-oriented) religious philosophy and tradition applying the spiritual technology based on *Arcane Tablets* in combination with "Tech" from *NexGen Systemology*; first developed in the New Age underground by Joshua Free in 2008 and realized publicly in 2009 with the formal establishment of the *Mardukite Chamberlains.* The text *"Tablets of Destiny"* is a cross-over from Mardukite Zuism (and Mesopotamian Neopaganism) toward higher spiritual applications of Systemology.

Master-Control-Center (MCC) : a perfect computing device to the extent of the information received from "lower levels" of sensory experience/perception; the proactive communication system of the "*Mind*"; a relay point of active *Awareness* along the Identity's *ZU-line*, which is responsible for maintaining basic *Self-Honest Clarity* of *Knowingness* as a *seat of consciousness* between the *Alpha-Spirit* and the secondary "*Reactive Control Center*" of a *Lifeform* in *beta existence*; the Mind-center for an *Alpha-Spirit* to actualize cause in the *beta existence*; the analytical *Self-Determined* Mind-center of an *Alpha-Spirit used* to project *Will* toward the genetic body; the point of contact between *Spiritual Systems* and the *beta existence*; presumably the "*Third Eye*" of a being connected directly to the *I-AM-Self*, which is responsible for *determining* Reality at any time; in *NexGen Systemology*, this is plotted at (4.0) on the continuity model of the *ZU-line*.

"Master Grades" : literary materials by Joshua Free (written between 1995 and 2019) revised and compiled for the "Mardukite Academy of Systemology" instructional grades—"Route of Magick & Mysticism" (*Grade I, Part A*), "Route of Druidism & Dragon Legacy" (*Grade I, Part D*), "Route of Mesopotamian Mysteries" (*Grade II*) and "Route of Mardukite Systemology" or "Pathway to Self-Honesty" (*Grade III*).

maxim : the greatest or highest *premise* of a paradigm or particular literary *treatment*; a concise rule for conducting action or treating some subject; the most relevant "proverbial adage" applicable.

MCC : see "*Master-Control-Center.*"

mental image : a subjectively experienced "picture" created and imagined into being by the Alpha-Spirit (or at lower levels, one of its automated mechanisms) that includes all perceptible *facets* of totally immersive scene, which may be forms originated by an individual, or a "facsimile-copy" ("snap-shot") of something seen or encountered; a duplication of wave-forms in one's Personal Universe as a "picture" that mirror an "external" Universe experience, such as an *Imprint*.

Mesopotamia : land between Tigris and Euphrates River; modern-day

Iraq; the primary setting for ancient *Sumerian* and *Babylonian* traditions thousands of years ago, including activities and records of the *Anunnaki*.

metahumanism : an applied philosophy of *transhumanism* with an emphasis on "spiritual technologies" as opposed to "external" ones; a new state or evolution of the *Human Condition* achievable on planet Earth, rooted in *Self-Honesty*, whereby individuals are operating *exterior* to considerations that are fixed exclusively to the *genetic vehicle* (Human Body) and independent of the *emotional encoding* and *associative programming* typical of the present standard-issue *Human Condition*.

Metahuman Destinations : the third professional publication of Mardukite Systemology, released publicly in October 2020; the first professional text in Grade-IV Metahuman Systemology, released as "*Liber-Two*" and containing materials from *Liber-2C, Liber-2D* and *Liber-3C*; contains fundamental theory of "*Professional Piloting*" and "*Route-3*" systematic processing methodology. Reissued as two volumes in 2022.

meter : a device used to measure; see *GSR-Meter*.

methodology : a complete system of applications, methods, principles and rules to compose a *'systematic'* paradigm as a "whole"—esp. a field of philosophy or science.

"mind's eye" : following semantics of archaic esoterica, the point where "mental pictures" (and senses) are generated that define what an individual believes they are experiencing in present time; activities or phenomenon described in archaic esoterica as the "Third-Eye" (or actualized MCC) where the *Alpha-Spirit* directly interacts with the organic *genetic vehicle* in *beta-existence*; in the semantics of basic Mardukite Zuism and Hermetic Philosophy, *Self-directed* activity on the plane of "mental consciousness" between "spiritual consciousness" of the *Alpha-Spirit* and "physical/emotional consciousness" of the *genetic vehicle*; *NexGen* 'slang' used to describe "consciousness activity" *Self-directed* by an actualized WILL.

misappropriated : put into use incorrectly; to apply ineffectively or as unintended by design or definition.

missed hold-out : an individual's *Hold-Out* that someone else nearly found out about, or which leaves the individual wondering if they did actually find out or not; undisclosed event when someone else's behavior or speech restimulates emotional-response-reactions ("worry" &tc.) about potential discovery of a withheld *Harmful-Act* or *Hold-Out*; in *systematic processing*, a Seeker's "held-out" (hidden) data that they expect to be discovered during a *session*, but which is *missed* by the Pilot.

morals : widely held culturally conditioned (socially learned) ethical standards of conduct used to "judge" *rightness* from *wrongness* of an individual's character, personality or actions (which may or may not be intellectually and emotionally influenced by "local" religious customs, taboos and *dogma*; basic social reality agreements determining "proper conduct" and "right actions" (behavior) based on civic *laws*, social *codes* and religious *doctrines* of a particular society or group and its own cultural experiences of *Reality*.

motor functions : internal mechanisms that allow a body to move.

—N—

Nabu : the *Anunnaki* "god of wisdom, writing and knowledge" for Babylonian (Mardukite) Tradition.

negligible : so small or trifle that it may be disregarded.

neophyte : a beginning initiate or novice to a particular sect or methodology; novitiate or entry-level grade of training, study and practice of an esoteric order or mystical lodge (fellowship).

neurotransmitter : a chemical substance released at a physiological level (of the genetic vehicle) that bridges communication of energetic transmission between the *Mind-Body* systems, using the "nervous system" of the physical body; biochemical amino acids and peptides (neuropeptides), hormones, &tc.

NexGen Systemology : a modern tradition of applied religious philosophy and spiritual technology based on *Arcane Tablets* in combination with "*general systemology*" and "*games theory*" developed in the New Age underground by Joshua Free in 2011 as an advanced futurist extension of the "*Mardukite Chamberlains*"; also referred to as "*Mardukite Systemology,*" "*Metahuman Systemology*" and "*Spiritual Systemology.*"

—O—

objective : concerning the "external world" and attempts to observe Reality independent of personal "subjective" factors.

occulted / to occult : hidden by or secreted away; to hide something from view; otherwise *occlude*, to shut out, shut in, or block; to *eclipse*, or leave out of view.

one-to-one : see "*A-for-A.*"

optimum : the most favorable or ideal conditions for the best result; the greatest degree of result under specific conditions.

orchestration : to arrange or compose the performance of a system.

organic : as related to a physically living organism or carbon-based life form; energy-matter condensed into form as a focus or POV of Spiritual Life Energy (*ZU*) as it pertains to beta-existence of *this* Physical Universe (*KI*).

oscillation-alternation : a particular type of (or fluctuation) between two relative states, conditions or degrees; a wave-action between two degrees, such as is described in the action of the *pendulum effect*; a flux or wave-like energy in motion, across space, calculable as time; in systematic processing, alternation is the shift between two direction flows on a circuit channel, such as *inflow* and *outflow*, or between two types of processing, such as *objective* and *subjective*; alternation of a POV creates "space."

—P—

pantheism : religious philosophies that observe God as inherent within all aspects of the Physical Universe.

paradigm : an all-encompassing *standard* by which to view the world and *communicate* Reality; a standard model of reality-systems used by the Mind to filter, organize and interpret experience of Reality.

parameters : a defined range of possible variables with in a model, spectrum or continuum; the extent of communicable reach capable within a system or across a distance; the defined or imposed limitations placed on a system or the functions within a system; the extent to which a Life or "thing" can *be*, *do* or *know* along any channel within the confines of a specific system or spectrum of existence.

paramount : the most important; of utmost importance; "above all else."

participation : being part of the action; affecting the result.

patter : fast-talk; a manner of quickly delivered speech/words, esp. used to persuade or sell something.

patterns (probability patterns) : observation of cycles and tendencies to predict a causal relationship or determine the actual condition or flow of dynamic energy using a holistic systemology to understand Life, Reality and Existence as opposed to isolating or excluding perceived parts as being mutually separate from other perceived parts.

patron god : the most sacred deity of a region or city, of which most temples and religious services are directed; the personal deity of an individual.

PCL : see *"processing command line."*

perception : internalized processing of data received by the *senses*; to become *Aware of* via the senses.

personality (program) : the total composite picture an individual "identifies" themselves with; the accumulated sum of material and mental mass by which an individual experiences as their timeline; a "beta-personality" is mainly attached to the identity of a particular physical body and the total sum of its own genetic memory in combination with the data stores and pictures maintained by the Alpha Spirit; a "true personality" is the Alpha Spirit as Self completely defragmented of all erroneous limitations and barriers to consideration, belief, manifestation and intention.

perturbation : the deviation from a natural state, fixed motion, or orbit system caused by another external system; disturbing or disquieting the serenity of an existent state; inciting observable apparent action using indirect or outside actions or 'forces'; the introduction of a new element or facet that disturbs equilibrium of a standard system; the "butterfly effect"; in *NexGen Systemology*, *'perturbation'* is a necessary condition for the *ZU-line* to function as a *Standard Model* of actual *'monistic continuity'*—which is a *Lifeforce* singularity expressed along a spectrum with potential interactions at each degree from any source; the influence of a degree in one state by activities of another state that seem independent, but which are actually connected directly at some higher degree, even if not apparently observed.

phase (identification) : in *NexGen Systemology*, a pattern of personality or identity that is assumed as the POV from *Self*; personal identification with artificial "personality packages"; an individual assuming or taking characteristics of another individual (often unknowingly as a response-mechanisms); also "*phase alignment.*"

phase alignment or "*in phase*" : to be in synch or mutually synchronized, in step or aligned properly with something else in order to increase the total strength value; in *NexGen Systemology*, alignment or adjustment of *Awareness* with a particular identity, space or time; perfect *defragmentation* would mean being "in phase" as *Self* fully conscious and Aware as an Alpha-Spirit *in* present *space* and *time*, free of synthetic personalities.

philanthropy : charitable; the intention (or programmed desire) to generously provide personal wealth and service to the well-being and continued existence of others.

physics : regarding data obtained by a material science of observable motions, forces and bodies, including their apparent interaction, in the Physical Universe (specific to this *beta-existence*).

physiology : a material science of observable biological functions and mechanics of living organisms, including codification and study of identifiable parts and apparent systematic processes (specific to agreed upon makeup of the *genetic vehicle* for this *beta-existence*).

pilfering : to steal in small quantities; petty theft.

pilot : a professional steersman responsible for healthy functional operation of a ship toward a specific destination; in *NexGen Systemology*, an intensive trained individual qualified to specially apply *Systemology Processing* to assist other *Seekers* on the *Pathway*.

ping : a short, high pitched ring, chime or noise that alerts to the presence of something; in computer systems, a query sent on a network or line to another terminal in order to determine if there is a connection to it; in *NexGen Systemology*, the sudden somatic twinge or pain or discomfort that is felt as a sensation in the body when a particular terminal (lifeform, object, concept) is 'brought to mind' or contacted on a personal communication channel-circuit; the accompanying sensations and mental images that are experienced as an automatic-response to the presence of some channel or terminal.

player (game theory) : an individual that is making decisions in a game and/or is affected by decisions others are making in the game, especially if those other-determined decisions now affect the possible choices.

point-of-view (POV) : a point to view from; an opinion or attitude as expressed from a specific identity-phase; a specific standpoint or vantage-point; a definitive manner of consideration specific to an individual phase or identity; a place or position affording a specific view or vantage; circumstances and programming of an individual that is conducive to a particular response, consideration or belief-set (paradigm); a position (consideration) or place (location) that provides a specific view or perspective (subjective) on experience (of the objective).

postulate : to put forward as truth; to suggest or assume an existence *to be*; to state or affirm the existence of particular conditions; to provide a basis of reasoning and belief; a basic theory accepted as fact; in *NexGen Systemology*, "Alpha-Thought"—the top-most decisions or considerations made by the Alpha-Spirit regarding the *"is-ness"* (what things "are") about energy-matter and space-time.

potentiality : the total "sum" (collective amount) of "latent" (dormant—present but not apparent) capable or possible realizations; used to describe a state or condition of what has not yet manifested, but which can be influenced and predicted based on observed patterns and, if referring to beta-existence, Cosmic Law.

POV : see *"point-of-view"* and/or *"POV Processing."*

POV processing : a methodology of *Grade-IV Metahuman Systemology* emphasizing systematic processing toward realizations that improve a Seeker's willingness to manage a present POV and associated *phases*, their ability to transfer POVs freely, increased tolerance to experiences (or encounters) with any other viewpoint, and finally, an actualized realization that a POV is not one-to-one with *Beingness* of *Self*; an extension of *creativeness processing* and "Wizard Level" training that systematically handles *Awareness* of "points" and "spots" in space, from which an Alpha-Spirit may place its own viewpoint of a dimension or Universe—also a prerequisite to upper-route practices such as *"Zu-Vision"* and *"Backtrack."*

precedent : a matter which precedes or goes before another in importance.

precipitate : to actively hasten or quicken into existence.

preconception : to assign values or evaluate a reaction-response to a past "imprint" of something and treat it as present knowledge or experience.

prehistoric : any time before human history is properly recorded in writing; prior to c. 4000 B.C.

premise : a basis or statement of fact from which conclusions are drawn.

presence : the quality of some thing (energy/matter) being "present" in space-time; personal orientation of *Self* as an *Awareness* (*POV*) located in present space-time (environment) and communicating with extant energy-matter.

prevalent : of wide extent; an extensive or largely accepted aspect or current state.

Prime Directive : a "spiritual" implant program that installs purposes and goals into the personal experience of a Universe, esp. any *Beta-Existence* (whether a 'Games Universe' or a 'Prison Universe'); intellectually treated as the "Universal Imperative" in some schools of moral philosophy; comparable to "Universal Law" or "Cosmic Ordering."

probability : the causal likelihood for something to result, "effect" or manifest in and as a certain way, manner or degree, based on "observed evaluation" of programming and tendencies that follow Cosmic Law.

"process-out" or **"flatten a wave"** : to reduce *emotional encoding* of an *imprint* to zero; to dissolve a *wave-form* or *thought-formed* "solid" such as a "*belief*"; to completely run a *process* to its end, thereby *flattening* any previously "*collapsed-waves*" or *fragmentation* that is obstructing the *clear channel* of *Self-Awareness*; also referred to as "processing-out"; to discharge all previously held emotionally encoded imprinting or erroneous programming and beliefs that otherwise fix the free flow (wave) to a particular pattern, solid or concrete "*is*" form.

processing, systematic : the inner-workings or "through-put" result of systems; in *NexGen Systemology*, a methodology of applied spiritual technology used toward personal Self-Actualization; methods of selective directed attention, communicated language and associative imagery that targets an increase in personal control of the human condition.

processing command line (PCL) or **command line** : a directed input; a specific command using highly selective language for *Systemology Processing*; a predetermined directive statement (cause) intended to focus concentrated attention (effect).

projecting awareness : sending out (motion) or radiating "*consciousness*" from *Self* ("I") to another POV.

proportional : having a direct relationship or mutual interaction with.

protest : a response-communication objecting an enforcement or a rejection of a prior communication; an effort to cancel, rewrite or destroy the existence or "is-ness" (what something "is") of a previous creation or communication; unwillingness to be the Point-of-View of effect or (receipt-point) for a communication.

Proto-Indo-European (PIE) : in Linguistic-Semantic Sciences, a hypothetical single-source Eurasian root language (c.4500 B.C.) demonstrating common origins of many "word-roots" found in European languages.

psychokinesis (PK) / telekinesis : influencing a (physical) system without (physical) interaction; *psychokinesis* from the Greek for 'soul' and 'movement', and *telekinesis* from the Greek for 'at a distance' and 'movement'.

psychometric evaluation : the relative measurement of personal ability, mental (psychological/thought) faculties, and effective processing of information and external stimulus data; a scale used in "applied psychology" to evaluate and predict human behavior.

—R—

rationality / reasoning (game theory) : the extent to which a player seeks to play (make decisions, &tc.) in order to maximize the gains (or else survival) achievable within any given game conditions; the ability and willingness of an individual to reach toward conditions that promote the highest level of survival and existence and make the best choices and moves to see the desired goal manifest.

reactive control center (RCC) : the secondary (reactive) communication system of the "*Mind*"; a relay point of *Awareness* along the Identity's *ZU-line*, which is responsible for engaging basic motors, biochemical processes and any *programmed automated responses* of a living *beta* organism; the reactive Mind-Center of a living organism relaying communications of *Awareness* between causal experience of *Physical Systems* and the "*Master Control Center*"; it presumably stores all emotional encoded imprints as fragmentation of "chakra" frequencies of *ZU* (within the range of the "*psychological/emotive systems*" of a being), which it may *react* to as Reality at any time; in *NexGen Systemology*, this is plotted at (2.0) on the continuity model of the *ZU-line*.

reality : see "*agreement*."

realization : the clear perception of an understanding; a consideration or understanding on what is "actual"; to make "real" or give "reality" to so as to grant a property of "beingness" or "being as it is"; the state or instance of coming to an *Awareness*; in *NexGen Systemology*, "gnosis" or true knowledge achieved during *systematic processing*; achievement of a new (or "higher") cognition, true knowledge or perception of Self; a consideration of reality or assignment of meaning.

receptacle : a device or mechanism designed to contain and store a specific type of aspect or thing; a container meant to receive something.

recursive : repeating by looping back onto itself to form continuity; *ex.* the "Infinity" symbol is recursive.

relative : an apparent point, state or condition treated as distinct from others.

religion : a concise spiritual *paradigm*, set of beliefs and practices regarding "Divinity," "Infinite Beingness"—or else, "God"—as representative symbol of the *Eighth Sphere of Existence* for *Beta-Existence* (or else "Infinity").

relinquish : to give up control, command or possession of.

repetitively : to repeat "over and over" again; or else "repetition."

responsibility : the *ability* to *respond*; the extent of mobilizing *power* and *understanding* an individual maintains as *Awareness* to enact *change*; the proactive ability to *Self-direct* and make decisions independent of an outside authority.

resurface : to return to (or bring up to) the "surface" of that which has previously been submerged; in *NexGen Systemology*—relating specifically to processes where a *Seeker* recalls blocked energy stored covertly as emotional "*imprints*" (by the RCC) so that it may be effectively defragmented from the "*ZU-line*" (by the MCC).

rhetoric : the art, study or skilled craft of using language eloquently (words, writing, speech preparation); expert communication using "words"; effectively using language for persuasive communication.

Route-0 : a specific methodology from *SOP-2C* denoting "*Creativeness Processing*," as described in the text "*Imaginomicon*" (*Liber-3D*).

Route-0E : a specific methodology (expanding on *Route-0* from *Liber-3D*) denoting "*Conceptual Processing*" applied to *Ethics Beta-Defragmentation*, as described in the text "*Way of the Wizard*" (*Liber-Three* or *Liber-3E*).

Route-1 : a specific methodology from *SOP-2C* denoting "*Resurfacing Processing*," as described in the text "*Tablets of Destiny*" (*Liber-One*) as "RR-SP" (and reissued in "*The Systemology Handbook*").

Route-2 : a specific methodology from *SOP-2C* denoting "*Analytical-Recall Processing*," as described in the text "*Crystal Clear*" (*Liber-2B*) as "AR-SP" (and reissued in "*The Systemology Handbook*").

Route-3 : a specific methodology from *SOP-2C* denoting "*Communication-Circuit Processing*," as described in the text "*Metahuman Destinations*" (*Liber-Two*); also the basis for *SOP-2C* routine.

Route-3E : a specific methodology (expanding on *Route-3* from *SOP-2C*) denoting "*Ethics Processing*," as described in the text "*The Way of the Wizard*" (*Liber-Three* or *Liber-3E*); also related to "Standard Procedure R-3E."

—S—

science : a systematized *paradigm* of Knowingness—from the Latin *'scire'*, meaning "know"; an empirical and objective understanding of data collected by observation, calculation and logical deduction—and which may usually be used to predict phenomenon or occurrences in the Physical Universe (*"Beta-Existence"*).

scions : a descendant or offspring; an offshoot or branch.

Seeker : an individual on the *Pathway to Self-Honesty*; a practitioner of *Mardukite Systemology* or *NexGen Systemology Processing* that is working toward *Spiritual Ascension*.

Self-actualization : bringing the full potential of the Human spirit into Reality; expressing full capabilities and creativeness of the *Alpha-Spirit*.

Self-determinism : the freedom to act, clear of external control or influence; the personal control of Will to direct intention.

Self-evaluation : see *"psychometric evaluation."*

Self-honesty : the basic or original *alpha* state of *being* and *knowing*; clear and present total *Awareness* of-and-as *Self*, in its most basic and true proactive expression of itself as *Spirit* or *I-AM*—free of artificial attachments, perceptive filters and other emotionally-reactive or mentally-conditioned programming imposed on the human condition by the systematized physical world; the ability to experience existence without judgment.

self-sustained : self-supported; self-sufficient; independent.

semantics : the *meaning* carried in *language* as the *truth* of a "thing" represented, *A-for-A*; the *effect* of language on *thought* activity in the Mind and physical behavior; language as *symbols* used to represent a concept, "thing" or "solid."

semantic-set : the implied meaning behind any groupings of words or symbols used to define a specific paradigm.

sensation : an external stimulus received by internal sense organs (receptors/sensors); sense impressions.

sentient : a living organism with consciousness or intelligence; a "thinking" or "reasoning" being that perceives information from the "senses."

simulacrum : an tangible likeness, image, facsimile or superficial representation that is similar to or resembles someone or something else; in *NexGen Systemology*, any *genetic vehicle* or physical body is considered a reflective "simulacrum" of, and used as a "vessel-shell" by, the *Alpha-Spirit* or *Self* (I-AM), which otherwise maintains no true finite locatable form in *beta-existence*.

sine-wave : the *frequency* and amplitude of a quantified (calculable) *vibration* represented on a graph (graphically) as smooth repetitive *oscillation* of a *waveform*; a *waveform* graphed for demonstration—otherwise represented in *NexGen Systemology* logic equations as 'W*f*,' or in mathematics as the *'function of x'* (*fx*); graphically representing arcs (*parameters*) of a circular *continuity* on a *continuum*; in the Standard Model of *NexGen Systemology*, the actual 'wave vibration' graphically displayed on an otherwise static *ZU-line* (of Infinity) is a *'sine-wave'*.

singularity : in general use, "to be singular," but our working definition suggests the opposite of individuality (contrary to most dictionaries); in upper-level sciences, a "zero-point" where a particular property or attribute is mathematically treated as "infinite" (such as the "black-hole" phenomenon), or else where apparently dissimilar qualities of all existing aspects (or individuals) share a "singular" expression, nature or quality; additionally, in *NexGen Systemology*, a hypothetical zero-point when apparent values of all parts in a Universe are equal to all other parts before it collapses; in *Transhumanism*, a hypothetical "runaway reaction" in technology, when it becomes self-aware, self-propagating, self-upgradable and self-sustainable, and replaces human effort of advancement or even makes continued human existence impossible; also, technological efforts to maintain an artificial immortality of the Human Condition on a digital mainframe.

slate : a hard thin flat surface material used for writing on; a chalk-board, which is a large version of the original wood-framed writing slate, named for the rock-type it was made from.

somatic : specifically pertaining to the physical body, its sensations and response actions or behaviors as separate from a "Mind-System"; also "*pings.*"

SOP-2C : *Standard Operating Procedure #2C* or *Systemology Operating Procedure #2C*; a standardized procedural formula introduced in materials for "*Metahuman Destinations*" (*Liber-Two*); a regimen or outline for standard delivery of systematic processing used by *Systemology Pilots* and *Mardukite Ministers*; a procedure outline of systematic processing, which includes applications of "*Route-1*," "*Route-2*," "*Route-3*" and "*Route-0*" as taught for *Grade-IV Professional Piloting*.

space : a viewpoint or *Point-of-View* (POV) extended from any point out toward a dimension or dimensions; the consideration of a point or spot as an *anchor* or *corner* in addition to others, which collectively define parameters of a dimensional plane; the field of energy/matter mass created as a result of communication and control in action and measured as time (wave-length), such as "distance" between points (or peaks on a wave).

spectrum : a broad range or array as a continuous series or sequence; defined parts along a singular continuum; in physics, a gradient arrangement of visible colored bands diffracted in order of their respective wavelengths, such as when passing *White Light* through a *prism*.

Spheres of Existence (dynamic systems) : a series of *eight* concentric circles, rings or spheres (each larger than the former) that is overlaid onto the Standard Model of Beta-Existence to demonstrate the dynamic systems of existence extending out from the POV of Self (often as a "body") at the *First Sphere*; these are given in the basic eightfold systems as: *Self, Home/Family, Groups, Humanity, Life on Earth, Physical Universe, Spiritual Universe* and *Infinity-Divinity.*

spiritual timeline : a continuous stream of moment-to-moment *Mental Images* (or a record of experiences) that defines the "past" of a spiritual being (or *Alpha-Spirit*) and which includes impressions (*imprints, &tc.*) form all life-incarnations and significant spiritual events the being has encountered; in NexGen Systemology, also *"backtrack."*

standard issue : equally dispensed to all without consideration.

standard model : a fundamental *structure* or symbolic construct used to evaluate a complete *set* in *continuity* relative to itself and variable to all other *dynamic systems* as graphed or calculated by *logic.*

Standard Model, The (systemology) : in *NexGen Systemology*—our existential and cosmological *standard model* or cabbalistic model; a *"monistic continuity model"* demonstrating *total system* interconnectivity "above" and "below" observation of any apparent *parameters*; the original presentation of the *ZU-line*, represented as a singular vertical (*y*-axis) waveform in space across dimensional levels or Universes (*Spheres of Existence*) without charting any specific movement across a dimensional time-graph *x*-axis; The Standard Model of Systemology represents the basic workable synthesis of common denominators in models explored throughout Grade-I and Grade-II material.

static : characterized by a fixed or stationary condition; having no apparent change, movement or fluctuation.

stoicism : pertaining to the school of "stoic" philosophy, distinguished by calm mental attitudes, freedom from desire/passion and essentially any emotional fluctuation.

sub-zones : at ranges "below" which we are representing or which is readily observable for current purposes.

successively : what comes after; forward into the future.

succumb : to give way, or give in to, a relatively stronger superior force.

Sumerian : ancient civilization of *Sumer*, founded in Mesopotamia c. 5000 B.C.

superfluous : excessive; unnecessary; needless.

superstition : knowledge accepted without good reason.

surefooted : proceeding surely; not likely to stumble or fall.

symbiotic : pertaining to the closeness, proximity and affinity between two beings that are in mutual communication or maintaining mutually validating interactions.

symbol : a concentrated mass with associated meaning or significance.

sympathy : a sensation, feeling or emotion—of anger, fear, sorrow and/or pity—that is a *personal reaction* to the misfortune and failure of another being.

syntax : from the Greek, "to arrange together"; the semantic meaning that words convey when combined together; the manner in which words are arranged together to provide an understandable meaning, such as following the structure for a sentence.

system : from the Greek, "to set together"; to set or arrange things or data together so as to form an orderly understanding of a "whole"; also a *'method'* or *'methodology'* as an orderly standard of use or application of such data arranged together.

systematization : to arrange into systems; to systematize or make systematic.

Systemology : see *"NexGen Systemology."*

Systemology Procedure 1-8-0 : advanced spiritual technology within our Systemology, which applies a methodology of systematic practice for experiencing: (1) Self-Awareness, (8) Nothingness and (0) Beingness, introduced for "Crystal Clear" but expanded on for *"Imaginomicon"*; *'one-eight-zero'* is included in, but not the same as application *'one-eighty'*—or else the *Beta-Defrag-Intensive* called *"SOP-180"* or *"Systemology-180."*

Systemology-180 : an intensive systematic processing routine employing all *Grade-III*, *Grade-IV* and cross-over *Wizard-Level* work to date; the total sum of all effective philosophical and spiritual applications necessary to professionally *Pilot* a *Seeker* to reach a stable point of *Self-Honesty* and basic *Beta-Defragmentation*, as a prerequisite to treating *"Actualized-Ascension Technologies"* (*A.T.*) of upper-level *Wizard Grades*.

systems theory : see *"general systematology"*

—T—

Tablets of Destiny : the first professional publication of Mardukite Systemology, released publicly in October 2019; the first professional text in Grade-III Mardukite Systemology, released as *"Liber-One"* and reissued in the Grade-III Master Edition *"Systemology Handbook"*; contains fundamental theory of the *"Standard Model"* and *"Route-1"* systematic processing methodology; revised in 2022 as *"The Tablets of Destiny (Revelation)."*

telekinesis : see *"psychokinesis."*

teleological (teleology) : using the end-goal or purpose of something as an explanation of its function (rather than being a function of its cause); example—Aristotle wrote (in his discourse, "*Metaphysics*") that the intrinsic (inherent or true nature) *telos* of an 'acorn' is to become a fully formed 'oak tree'; the ends are an underlying purpose, not the cause (also known as "final cause"), or else the famous phrase: "the ends justify the means."

terminal (node) : a point, end or mass on a line; a point or connection for closing an electric circuit, such as a post on a battery terminating at each end of its own systematic function; any end point or 'termination' on a line; a point of connectivity with other points; in systems, any point which may be treated as a contact point of interaction; anything that may be distinguished as an 'is' and is therefore a 'termination point' of a system or along a flow-line which may interact with other related systems it shares a line with; a point of interaction with other points.

thought-experiment : from the German, *Gedankenexperiment*; logical *considerations* or mental models used to concisely visualize consequences (cause-effect sequences) within the context of an imaginary or hypothetical scenario; using faculties of the Mind's Eye to *Imagine* things accurately with *considerations* that *have not* already been consciously experienced in *beta-existence*.

thought-form : apparent *manifestation* or existential *realization* of *Thought-waves* as "solids" even when only apparent in Reality-agreements of the Observer; the treatment of *Thought-waves* as permanent *imprints* obscuring *Self-Honest Clarity* of *Awareness* when reinforced by emotional experience as actualized "thought-formed solids" ("*beliefs*") in the Mind; energetic patterns that "surround" the individual.

thought-habit : reoccurring modes of thought or repeated "self-talk"; essentially "self-hypnosis" resulting in a certain state.

thought-wave or **wave-form** : a proactive *Self-directed action* or reactive-response *action* of *consciousness*; the *process* of *thinking* as demonstrated in *wave-form*; the *activity* of *Awareness* within the range of *thought vibrations/frequencies* on the existential *Life-continuum* or *ZU-line*.

threshold : a doorway, gate or entrance point; the degree to which something is to produce an effect within a certain state or condition; the point in which a condition changes from one to the next.

thwarted : to successfully oppose or prevent a purpose from actualizing.

tier : a series of rows or levels, one stacked immediately before or atop another.

time : observation of cycles in action; motion of a particle, energy or wave across space; intervals of action related to other intervals of action as observed in Awareness; a measurable wave-length or frequency in comparison to a static state; the consideration of variations in space.

timeline : plotting out history in a linear (line) model to indicate instances (experiences) or demonstrate changes in state (space) as measured over time; a singular conception of continuation of observed time as marked by event-intervals and changes in energy and matter across space.

tipping point : a definitive "point" when a series of small changes (to a system) are significant enough to be *realized* or *cause* a larger, more significant change; the critical "point" (in a system) beyond which a significant change takes place or is observed; the "point" at which changes that cross a specific "threshold" reach a noticeably new state or development.

transhumanism : a social science and applied philosophy concerning the next evolved state of the "*Human Condition,*"; progress in two potential directions, either "spiritual" technologies advancing *Self* as an "Alpha-Spirit," or the direction of "external"-"physical" technologies that modify or eliminate characteristics of the *Body*; a theme describing contemporary application of material sciences emphasizing only "physical" and "genetic" parts of the *Human* experience, such as brain activity, cell-life extension and space travel; *NexGen Systemology* recently began distinguishing its emphasis on "spiritual technology" as "*metahumanism.*"

transmit : to send forth data along some line of communication; to move a point across a distance.

traumatic encoding : information received when the sensory faculties of an organism are "shocked" into learning it as an "emotionally" encoded *Imprint*; a duplicated facsimile-copy or *Mental Image* of severe misfortune, violent threats, pain and coercion, which is then categorized, stored and reactively retrieved based exclusively on its emotional *facets*.

treat / treatment : an act, manner or method of handling or dealing with someone, something or some type of situation; to apply a specific process, procedure or mode of action toward some person, thing or subject; use of a specific substance, regimen or procedure to make an existing condition less severe; also, a written presentation that handles a subject in a specific manner.

turbulence : a quality or state of distortion or disturbance that creates irregularity of a flow or pattern; the quality or state of aberration on a line (such as ragged edges) or the emotional "turbulent feelings" attached to a particular flow or terminal node; a violent, haphazard or disharmonious commotion (such as in the ebb of gusts and lulls of wind action).

—U—

unconscious : a state when *Awareness* as *Self* is removed totally from the equation of *Life* experience, though it continues to be recorded in lower-level response mechanisms (fixed to a simulacrum or genetic vehicle) for later retrieval.

undefiled : to remain intact, untouched or unchanged; to be left in an original "virgin" state.

understanding : a clear 'A-for-A' duplication of a communication as 'knowledge', which may be comprehended and retained with its significance assigned in relation to other 'knowledge' treated as a 'significant understanding'; the "grade" or "level" that a knowledge base is collected and the manner in which the data is organized and evaluated.

Utopian Philosophy : a social philosophy and ethic for (primarily) independent rural (country-dwelling or pagan) living communities that adopt a neo-Utilitarian moral philosophy (as suggested by Systemology) to enhance the "greater happiness" and "Ascension" of all participants.

—V—

validation : reinforcement of agreements or considerations as "real."

vantage : a point, place or position that offers an ideal viewpoint (POV).

Venn diagram : a diagram for symbolic logic using circles to represent sets and their systematic relationship; popularized by logician *John Venn*.

verbatim : precisely reproduced or duplicated communication *one-to-one* or "word"-for-"word" (*'A-for-A'*).

via : literally, "by way of"; from the Latin, meaning "way."

vibration : effects of motion or wave-frequency as applied to any system.

viewpoint : see *"point-of-view" (POV)*.

vizier : a high ranking official; a minister-of-state.

—W—

wave-form : see *"sine-wave."*

wave-function collapse : see *"collapsing a wave."*

Western Civilization : modern contemporary culture, ideals, values and technology, particularly of Europe and North America as distinguished by growing urbanization, industrialization, and inspired by a history of rebellion to strong religious and political indoctrination.

will *or* **WILL** (5.0) : in *NexGen Systemology* (from the *Standard Model*), the Alpha-ability at "5.0" of a Spiritual Being (*Alpha Spirit*) at "7.0" to apply *intention* as "Cause" from consideration or Alpha-Thought at "6.0" that is superior to "beta-thoughts" that only manifest as reactive "effects" below "4.0" and *interior* to the *Human Condition*.

willingness : the state of conscious Self-determined ability and interest (directed attention) to *Be*, *Do* or *Have*; a Self-determined consideration to reach, face up to (*confront*) or manage some "mass" or energy; the extent to which an individual considers themselves able to participate, act or communicate along some line, to put attention or intention on the line, or to produce (create) an effect.

—Z—

ziggurat : religious temples of ancient Mesopotamia; stepped-pyramids used for spiritual and religious purposes by Sumerians and Babylonians, many of which are presented as seven tiers, levels or terraces representing "Seven Gates" (or "7 Veils") of existence, separating material continuity of the Earth Plane from "Infinity."

ZU : the ancient Sumerian cuneiform sign for the archaic verb—"*to know,*" "*knowingness*" or "*awareness*"; in *Mardukite Zuism and Systemology*, the active energy/matter of the "Spiritual Universe" (AN) experienced as a *Lifeforce* or *consciousness* that imbues living forms extant in the "Physical Universe" (KI); "*Spiritual Life Energy*"; energy demonstrated by the WILL of an actualized *Alpha-Spirit* in the "Spiritual Universe" (AN), which impinges its *Awareness* into the Physical Universe (KI), animating/controlling *Life* for its experience of *beta-existence* along an individual Alpha-Spirit's personal *Identity-continuum*, called a *ZU-line*.

Zu-Line : a theoretical construct in *Mardukite Zuism and Systemology* demonstrating *Spiritual Life Energy* (*ZU*) as a personal individual "continuum" of Awareness interacting with all Spheres of Existence on the Standard Model of Systemology; a spectrum of potential variations and interactions of a monistic continuum or singular *Spiritual Life Energy (ZU)* demonstrated on the Standard Model; an energetic channel of potential POV and "locations" of Beingness, demonstrated in early Systemology materials as an individual Alpha-Spirit's personal *Identity-continuum*, potentially connecting *Awareness (ZU)* of *Self* with "*Infinity*" simultaneous with all points considered in existence; a symbolic demonstration of the "*Life-line*" on which *Awareness (ZU)* extends from the direction of the "Spiritual Universe" (AN) in its true original *alpha state* through an entire possible range of activity resulting in its *beta state* and control of a *genetic-entity* occupying the *Physical Universe (KI)*.

Zu-Vision : the true and basic (*Alpha*) Point-of-View (perspective, POV) maintained by *Self* as *Alpha-Spirit* outside boundaries or considerations of the *Human Condition* "Mind-Systems" and *exterior* to beta-existence reality agreements with the Physical Universe; a POV of Self *as* "a unit of Spiritual Awareness" that exists independent of a "body" and entrapment in a *Human Condition*; "spirit vision" in its truest sense.

AVAILABLE FROM THE **JOSHUA FREE** PUBLISHING IMPRINT

SYSTEMOLOGY

FUNDAMENTALS OF SYSTEMOLOGY

A New Thought for the 21st Century

The Official
Systemology Society
Basic Course

ALL *Six Lessons* in one
Collector's Edition
hardcover

All *six* lesson-booklets of the first official
Basic Course on Mardukite Systemology
are combined together in *one volume* as
"Fundamentals of Systemology."

Also available individually.

"Being More Than Human"

"Realities in Agreement"

"Windows To Experience"

"Ancient Systemology"

"A History of Systemology"

"Systemology Processing"

Paperback Workbook Edition Available in 2025!

AVAILABLE FROM THE **JOSHUA FREE** PUBLISHING IMPRINT

SYSTEMOLOGY

THE PATHWAY TO ASCENSION

Spiritual Clearing (Levels 0 to 6)

New Standard Systemology Professional Course

developed by Joshua Free

All *sixteen* lesson-booklets of the official *Professional Course* on Mardukite Systemology are combined together in *two hardcover volumes* as "The Pathway to Ascension."

Also available individually.

"*Increasing Awareness*"
"*Thought & Emotion*"
"*Clear Communication*"
"*Handling Humanity*"
"*Free Your Spirit*"
"*Escaping Spirit-Traps*"
...and many more!

Complete Paperback Workbook Edition Available in 2025!

Seekers and students of the *Basic Course* and *Professional Course* will also be interested in the *Systemology Core Research Volumes*. These eight volumes are a complete chronological record of the *Mardukite New Thought* developments from the *Systemology Society*, as presented to the public from 2019 through 2023.

Our *Systemology Core* begins with the first professional publication released when the *Mardukite Systemology Society* emerged into public view from the underground in 2019, with: *"The Tablets of Destiny Revelation."*

The Tablets of Destiny Revelation:
*How Long-Lost Anunnaki Wisdom
Can Change the Fate of Humanity*

Crystal Clear: *Handbook for Seekers*

Metahuman Destinations (*2 volumes*)

Imaginomicon:
Approaching Gateways to Higher Universes

Way of the Wizard: *Utilitarian Systemology*

Systemology-180: *Fast-Track to Ascension*

Systemology Backtrack:
Reclaiming Spiritual Power & Past-Life Memory

AVAILABLE FROM THE **JOSHUA FREE** PUBLISHING IMPRINT

IN A WORLD FULL OF "TENS" BE AN
ELEVEN

THE METAPHYSICS OF STRANGER THINGS

TELEKINESIS, TELEPATHY & SYSTEMOLOGY

by Joshua Free

Mardukite Systemology Liber-011

Experimental exploratory edition

Discover the metaphysical truth about the Universe—and maybe even yourself—as we explore what lies beneath the epic saga, *Stranger Things.* You're invited to a world where fantasy, science fiction and horror unite, and games like *Dungeons and Dragons* become reality.

Uncover a world of secret "mind control" projects, just like those at *Hawkins National Laboratory.* Decades of psychedelic experiments among other developmental programs for psychic powers, remote viewing, telekinesis (psychokinesis, PK-power) and more are revealed. Get an inside look at the operations of a real-life underground organization pursuing the truth about rehabilitating spiritual abilities for an actual "metahuman" evolution on planet Earth.

Premiere Edition available in both paperback and hardcover!

AVAILABLE FROM THE **JOSHUA FREE** PUBLISHING IMPRINT

SYSTEMOLOGY
The Pathway to Self-Honesty
ORIGINAL UNDERGROUND INTRODUCTIONS
REVISED AND REISSUED IN HARDCOVER

SYSTEMOLOGY
The Original Thesis of Mardukite New Thuoght
by Joshua Free
(*Mardukite Systemology Liber-S-1X*)

The very first underground discourses released to the "New Thought" division of the Mardukite Research Organization privately over a decade ago and providing the inspiration for rapid futurist spiritual technology called "Mardukite Systemology."

THE POWER OF ZU
Applying Mardukite Zuism & Systemology to Everyday Life
by Joshua Free
Foreword by Reed Penn
(*Mardukite Systemology Liber-S-1Z*)

A unique introductory course on Mardukite Zuism & Systemology, including transcripts from a 3-day lecture series given by Joshua Free in December 2019 to launch the Mardukite Academy of Systemology & Founding Church of Mardukite Zuism just in time for the 2020's.

AVAILABLE FROM THE **JOSHUA FREE** PUBLISHING IMPRINT

Commemorating the Mardukite 15th Anniversary!

NECRONOMICON
THE COMPLETE ANUNNAKI BIBLE
(Deluxe Edition Hardcover Anthology)
collected works by Joshua Free

The ultimate masterpiece of Mesopotamian magic, spirituality and history, providing a complete collection—a grand symphony—of the most ancient writings on the planet. The oldest Sumerian and Babylonian records reveal detailed accounts of cosmic history in the Universe and on Earth, the development of human civilization and descriptions of world order. All of this information has been used, since ancient times, to maintain spiritual and physical control of humanity and its systems. It has proved to be the predecessor and foundation of all global scripture-based religious and mystical traditions thereafter. These are the raw materials, unearthed from the underground, which have shaped humanity's beliefs, traditions and existence for thousands of years—right from the heart of the Ancient Near East: Sumer, Babylon and even Egypt...

AVAILABLE FROM THE **JOSHUA FREE** PUBLISHING IMPRINT

New Deluxe Oversized Hardcover Edition for 2023!

NOVEM PORTIS (DELUXE EDITION)
NECRONOMICON REVELATIONS, NINE GATES OF THE KINGDOM OF SHADOWS & CROSSING TO THE ABYSS

10th Anniversary—Deluxe Hardcover (*Liber-R, 9+555*)
Collected Works by Joshua Free

Commemorating completion of the "Necronomicon Shadows" cycle of research and development by the Mardukite Chamberlains (2009–2012). Originally intended as a research-companion to *"Necronomicon: The Anunnaki Bible"* and the remaining 'Core', a Mardukite anthology of this cycle of work—known as *"Nine Gates"* or *"Novem Portis"*—eventually developed into an underground bestseller by itself.

In addition to other bonus articles and supplements, a complete collection of material from *Liber-9*, *Liber-R* and *Liber-555* are together in a deluxe hardcover anthology edition for the first time ever!

∞

A mystic philosopher, world renowned underground occult expert and prolific writer of over 90 books on systemology, ancient history, magic and "esoteric archaeology" since 1995. He founded Mardukite Ministries (Mardukite Zuism) in 2008, is director of Mardukite Research Organization (Mardukite Academy) and its New Thought division "The Systemology Society."

PUBLISHED BY THE **JOSHUA FREE** IMPRINT REPRESENTING

**The Founding Church of Mardukite Zuism
& Mardukite Academy of Systemology**

mardukite.com